W9-DDO-930

St. Louis Community College

Library

5801 Wilson Avenue
St. Louis, Missouri 63110

Foodservice Organizations

A MANAGERIAL
AND SYSTEMS APPROACH

MARIAN C. SPEARS
ALLENE G. VADEN

Foodservice Organizations

A MANAGERIAL AND SYSTEMS APPROACH

Macmillan Publishing Company
New York

Collier Macmillan Publishers
London

Macmillan Publishing Company
866 Third Avenue, New York, New York 10022

Collier Macmillan Canada, Inc.

Library of Congress Cataloging in Publication Data
Spears, Marian C.
  Foodservice organizations.

  Includes bibliographies and indexes.
  1. Food service management.   I. Vaden, Allene G.
II. Title.

TX911.3.M27S69   1985   647'.95'068   85-9269
ISBN 0-02-414250-6

Printed in the United States of America

Printing 2 3 4 5 6   Year 6 7 8 9 0

ISBN 0-02-414250-6

Dedicated to Sholto, Dick, Val, and Erich
for their continuing support and encouragement

ABOUT THE AUTHORS

Marian C. Spears, Ph.D., R.D., Professor and Head of the Department of Dietetics, Restaurant and Institutional Management at Kansas State University, is a native of Ohio. She holds Bachelor's and Master's degrees from Western Reserve University and a Ph.D. from the University of Missouri, Columbia. During her 17 years of professional practice before entering academe, she worked as a manager of a commercial foodservice, Chief Dietitian of a nationally known children's home, Chief Dietetian of a private hospital, and Associate Director of Dietetics at Barnes Hospital, St. Louis, MO. Her academic experience began as Assistant Professor of Home Economics at the University of Arkansas, Fayetteville in 1959. During her years in Arkansas, she maintained an extensive consulting practice in the design and operation of hospital foodservice facilities. In 1971 she became Associate Professor and Director of Education, Food Systems Management, at the University of Missouri, Columbia.

Dr. Spears' professional memberships are in The American Dietetic Association, the American Home Economics Association, the American School Food Service Association, the Foodservice Systems Management Education Council, the National Restaurant Association, and the Academy of Management. In addition, she has held numerous elective and appointive offices in local, state, and national dietetic associations. She has authored and coauthored more than 20 publications in refereed journals. Her honors include membership in Sigma Xi, Phi Kappa Phi, Gamma Sigma Delta, and Omicron Nu. She is also a biographee in *Who's Who in America* and *Who's Who in American Men and Women of Science.*

Allene G. Vaden, Ph.D., R.D., is the dean of the School of Home Economics and Professor of Institutional Management, University of Southern Mississippi, Hattiesburg, MS. Prior to assuming this position in August, 1984, Dr. Vaden was on the faculty at Kansas State University for 11 years, most recently as Professor of Dietetics and Institutional Management and Scientist, Kansas Agricultural Experiment Station. She served on the faculty of Texas Tech University before moving to Kansas.

Her Ph.D. is from Kansas State University, M.S. from Texas Tech University, and B.S. from The University of Texas at Austin. She has held management positions in hospital and college foodservice and in club management in Texas and Louisiana.

Dr. Vaden has published more than 60 papers in professional journals and has conducted extensive research related to foodservice management and dietetics. She serves as editor of the *School Food Service Research Review* and recently co-edited a volume published by the American School Food Service Association entitled *Nutrition and the School Age Child.*

Dr. Vaden is active in a number of professional societies, including The American Dietetic Association (ADA), the American Society of Hospital Food Service Administrators, the Academy of Management, the American School Food Service Association, the American Society for Public Administrators, the National Restaurant Association, and the Society for Nutrition Education. In 1982, Dr. Vaden was recognized as Kansas Distinguished Dietitian. She is listed in *Who's Who in American Women* and holds membership in several honor societies: Sigma Xi, Phi Kappa Phi, Omicron Nu, Gamma Sigma Delta, Phi Upsilon Omicron, Phi Delta Kappa, and Delta Kappa Gamma. In October 1985, Dr. Vaden was installed as Speaker of the House of Delegates, ADA's policy making body. She has served on the board of directors for ADA and several other groups and as a consultant on long-range planning.

PREFACE

Foodservice Organizations: A Managerial and Systems Approach was designed and written as a text for use in educating managers for the increasingly complex foodservice industry. The intent, also, was to produce an up-to-date resource book for practitioners in all segments of the industry.

The book is designed for use over an academic year, in two or three courses. Its primary target audience is upper-division students in undergraduate courses in foodservice management, both in dietetic and restaurant management programs. The book could also be used in two-year associate degree programs, although some portions are beyond the level of expected competencies for graduates of those programs. For example, the sections on forecasting, decision making techniques, and financial analysis might be a resource for faculty but would not be assigned in courses in junior or community colleges.

Foodservice Organizations would also be useful in many first-level graduate courses, especially for those students whose baccalaureate degrees are not in dietetics or foodservice management. However, we would presume that at the graduate level this book would be supplemented by assignments from other references and periodical literature.

Coverage of various segments of the industry is balanced, with both commercial and institutional operations emphasized throughout the book. Many examples are included to elucidate application of theory to practice. Numerous figures and operational forms illustrate concepts, and each chapter has an extensive, up-to-date reference list.

Quality assurance, systems theory, value analysis, "make or buy" decisions, materials management, inventory control tools, forecasting models, ingredient control, sanitation standards and audits, quality circles, energy management, and productivity analysis and improvement are among topics included that are *not* covered in most other texts or are included only in limited detail. In addition, management topics discussed in more depth include decision making techniques, communication, job enrichment, human resource planning, labor-management relations, emerging concepts in organizational leadership, financial analysis tools, budgeting, and computer-assisted management. The book has been field-tested at Purdue and at Kansas State University. At both institutions, hotel and restaurant and dietetic students described it as easy to read, understandable, and interesting.

In developing the text, numerous references in foodservice management, food science, industrial engineering, finance, accounting, marketing, and management were consulted. To assist in identifying level of concepts, we used widely accepted junior-senior texts from the business administration literature as models.

A foodservice systems model provides the organizing framework unifying the book, and management concepts are a common thread throughout. The book includes 22 chapters divided into 6 sections. The following is an example of the way in which the book might be used in several foodservice management courses:

Course	Chapters
Quantity Food Production	1–4, 6, 8, 10–12, 16
Foodservice Systems	2–5, 7–9, 14–16
Organization and Management	2–4, 13, 17–22

Chapters are integrated and interrelated; however, they are each written as an independent unit and can be utilized in various sequences to meet the needs of varying course designs.

The initial chapters in Section I provide an overview of the field; Section II includes models related to designing foodservice systems and presents the menu as the primary control. Sections III, IV, and V include indepth discussions of the subsystems of a foodservice system—procurement, production, distribution and service, and maintenance. The final section is comprised of six chapters that discuss management of foodservice operations, including chapters on organization structure, communication and decision making, leadership, personnel management, financial management, and computers in foodservice systems.

Appreciation is expressed to Judy Jensen, at Kansas State University (KSU), who competently typed and retyped the entire manuscript, both cheerfully and patiently. Janet Helm and Sharon Hearne, graduate research assistants, provided much assistance in proofreading, preparing reference lists, locating resource material, and editing. Mary Hamil, graphic artist at Kansas State University, did an excellent job in preparing most of the line drawings and illustrations. In the final stages of development, Patricia L. Simonis, Della Rieley, Linda Yarrow, Janet Beary, and Robin Zingheim at Kansas State University and Carol Davidson and Regina Partlow at the University of Southern Mississippi were extremely helpful. Frances Jensen and Nedra Sylvis also provided technical assistance.

Milt Santee, W. Milt Santee and Associates, foodservice equipment and layout consultants, in Kansas City, Missouri, assisted by identifying appropriate equipment and suppliers for illustrations and examples in several chapters. Appreciation also is extended to professional colleagues in the Kansas State University Residence Halls; University of Kansas Medical Center, College of Health Sciences and Hospital; Indiana University Medical Center; and New England Deaconess Hospital, who provided selected forms, examples, and data used in various chapters.

The reviewers deserve mention for their helpful suggestions that assisted in strengthening the book: the faculty in hotel, restaurant, and institutional management at Iowa State University; Dr. Lynne Baltzer, Iowa State University; Prof. Martha Barclay, Macomb, IL; Marsha Bronson, R.D., Sacramento, CA; Prof. Bert Connell, Loma Linda University; Prof. Lea L. Ebro, Oklahoma State University; Prof. Karen Fiedler, Case Western Reserve University; Helen Guley, Ph.D, R.D., Syracuse University; Prof. Mahmood A. Khan, University of Illinois; Prof. Marcia

Pfeiffer, St. Louis Community College at Florissant Valley; Prof. Kathryn Price, Middle Tennessee State University; and Ruby P. Puckett, Shands Hospital, University of Florida, Gainesville. Recognition should also be given to the faculty and students at Kansas State University and to Dr. Stephen Hiemstra at Purdue University, who assisted with field-testing the book.

Writing an extensive textbook such as this is truly a "labor of love." Our intent in this undertaking was to develop a comprehensive resource that would integrate current theory with practice and application.

Marian C. Spears
Allene G. Vaden

March 1985

Note: Transparency masters of all text illustrations are available to adoptus, to receive a set, contact your local Wiley representative or write to:

Nutrition Editor
John Wiley & Sons
605 Third Avenue
New York, NY 10158

SUMMARY CONTENTS

CONTENTS

I. Introduction

II. Designing the Foodservice System

III. Procurement

IV. Production

V. *Distribution, Service, and Maintenance*

VI. *Management of Foodservice Systems*

Appendixes

I

Introduction

1

The Foodservice Industry

This introductory chapter is an overview of the size, scope, and current status of the foodservice industry in preparation for in-depth discussions of the organization and management of the foodservice operation and its technical components. A review of the size, types of establishments, and key societal trends affecting the industry and an examination of the characteristics of its various facets should assist in gaining an understanding of the complexity and challenges inherent in foodservice management.

SCOPE AND STATUS OF THE INDUSTRY

The foodservice industry is large and complex, it currently accounts for 37 percent of all consumer expenditures for food, up from 33 percent in 1970. Foodservice industry sales equaled nearly 5 percent of the Gross National Product (GNP) in the United States with sales of $133 billion in 1982. In the decade between 1970 and 1980, foodservice sales more than doubled from $42.7 billion to $114.7 billion. The average person eats away from home 3.5 times a week and over 77 million customer transactions occur each day in commercial foodservice estab-

3

lishments alone. Seventy-eight percent of all families report regularly eating at foodservice establishments. In addition, considerable numbers of people are served in institutional and military establishments daily (NRA, 1982).

In 1985, commercial food and drink sales are projected to be approximately $153 billion; institutional sales an additional $24 billion, and military sales approximately $904 million. Foodservice units equal 559,000 and food and beverage purchases should total over $72 billion.

Finally, the foodservice industry is the largest retail employer in the nation. The industry employs more than eight million persons, with wages and benefits totaling about $42 billion, and is a major employer of women and teenagers. Sixty-six percent of the total number of employees in the industry are women, and 24 percent are teens.

TYPES OF ESTABLISHMENTS

The National Restaurant Association (NRA) divides the industry into three major groups (NRA News, 1982b). Group 1, commercial feeding, includes eating and drinking places, food contractors, foodservice in lodging establishments (hotels, motels, and motor hotels), and other miscellaneous commercial foodservice retailers. This latter category includes drug and proprietary store restaurants, grocery store restaurants and carryout services, movie and other recreational centers, and mobile and vending caterers. Group 1 comprises those establishments that are open to the public and operated for profit and that operate facilities and/or supply meal service on a regular basis for others.

Group 2, the institutional feeding group, includes business, educational, government, or institutional organizations that operate their own foodservices. Food is provided as an auxiliary service to complement other activities. While some establishments operate at a profit, this is not the aim of the foodservice activity. Rather, they serve food principally as a convenience for other employees, students, and patients. Military feeding, group 3, includes officer and NCO (Non-Commissioned Officers) clubs and foodservice military exchanges, as well as foodservice to troops.

As shown in Table 1.1, eating and drinking places account for almost 70 percent of the total foodservice industry sales, reaching an estimated $112 billion in 1984 (NRA News, 1984). The next two largest categories were food contractors and restaurants in lodging places, totalling about $20 billion in 1984. Miscellaneous types of foodservice establishments accounted for the remainder of the estimated $142 billion of estimated sales in the commercial group in 1984. In the institutional feeding group, hospitals and other healthcare facilities were responsible for more than half of the sales. Elementary and secondary schools and colleges and universities represent the second largest segment in this group. Excluded from this group in the NRA data are correctional institutions. The military feeding group data are limited to installations in the continental United States.

Table 1.1. _Food and drink sales in the foodservice industry, projected to 1985_

Group	Estimated food and drink sales			
	1980	1982	1984	1985[1]
	← billions →			
GROUP I: COMMERCIAL FEEDING				
Eating places				
Restaurants, lunchrooms	$ 36.0	$ 46.3	$ 54.9	$ 59.3
Limited menu restaurants (refreshment places)	27.4	35.1	43.0	47.1
Commercial cafeterias	2.2	2.4	2.8	3.0
Social caterers	.8	.8	.9	.9
Ice cream, frozen custard stands	1.3	1.5	1.8	2.0
Total eating places	$ 67.7	$ 86.1	$103.4	$112.3
Bars and taverns	8.0	7.9	8.9	9.5
Total eating and drinking places	$ 75.7	$ 94.0	$112.3	$121.8
Food contractors				
Manufacturing and industrial plants	$ 2.1	$ 2.3	$ 2.6	$ 2.8
Commercial and office buildings	.6	.7	.8	.9
Hospitals and nursing homes	.8	1.0	1.2	1.3
Colleges and universities	1.1	1.4	1.7	1.8
Primary and secondary schools	.6	.7	.7	.8
In-transit feeding (airlines)	.5	.5	.7	.7
Recreation and sports centers	1.0	1.1	1.2	1.3
Total food contractors	$ 6.7	$ 7.7	$ 8.9	$ 9.6
Lodging places				
Hotel restaurants	$ 4.4	$ 6.0	$ 7.0	$ 7.6
Motor hotel restaurants	.8	1.0	1.2	1.3
Motel restaurants	1.4	1.6	2.0	2.1
Total lodging places	$ 6.6	$ 8.6	$ 10.2	$ 11.0
Other				
Retail hosts	$ 3.3	$ 4.0	$ 4.6	$ 5.0
Recreation and sports	1.4	1.7	1.9	2.0
Mobile caterers	.5	.5	.6	.6
Vending and nonstore retailers	2.5	2.7	3.1	3.3
TOTAL Group I	$ 96.7	$119.2	$131.4	$153.3
GROUP II: INSTITUTIONAL FEEDING				
Employee feeding	$ 1.6	$ 1.7	$ 2.0	$ 2.0
Public and parochial elementary and secondary schools	2.3	2.5	2.5	2.6
Colleges and universities	2.3	2.8	3.3	3.6
Transportation	.6	.7	.8	.9
Hospitals	6.7	7.6	8.5	9.0
Nursing homes, homes for aged, blind, orphans, mentally and physically handicapped	2.4	2.7	3.0	3.2
Clubs, sporting and recreational camps	1.1	1.4	1.6	1.7
Community centers	.4	.3	.3	.4
TOTAL Group II	$ 17.4	$ 19.7	$ 22.0	$ 23.4

Table 1.1. *(cont.)*

Group	Estimated food and drink sales			
	1980	*1982*	*1984*	*1985*[1]
	←——————————— *billions* ———————————→			
GROUP III—MILITARY FEEDING				
Officers and NCO clubs ("Open Mess")	$ .4	$ .5	$ .6	$ .6
Foodservice—military exchanges	.2	.2	.3	.3
TOTAL Group III	$ .6	$ .7	$ .9	$ .9
GRAND TOTAL	$114.7	$139.6	$154.3	$177.6

Source: Adapted from *NRA News,* the magazine of the National Restaurant Association.
[1]Projected.

SOCIETAL TRENDS AFFECTING THE INDUSTRY

Long term demographic and social trends continue to have a significant effect on the foodservice industry. Major trends that have had beneficial effects are increasing numbers of working women, more affluent two-income households, smaller families, more single-person households, greater numbers of people in the 24 to 44 age group, a better-educated population, growing importance of convenience as a factor in decision making, and increasing desire for leisure activities. In addition, a recent NRA consumer survey (NRA News, 1982c) indicated that the public's desire for meals away from home is far from satisfied. A further indication was that if all persons were able to eat out as often as they would like, restaurant customers would increase by one-third.

Negative influences on the industry include double-digit unemployment, high interest rates, and a pessimistic consumer view of economic conditions. Unemployment and inflation are major consumer concerns. Many Americans have apparently foregone restaurant visits as a result of being without jobs or fearing unemployment, or they have tended to opt for low and moderately priced establishments.

Structural changes in the economy cloud the employment picture in the United States. Heavy manufacturing industries have laid off substantial numbers of workers during the last several years. The jobs that are being and will continue to be created are in the nonmanufacturing sector, which are often lower-paying jobs.

Real disposable income (adjusted for inflation) is expected to increase slightly. Moderating inflation and a lessening of cost increases for necessities such as housing, energy, and transportation may lead to increased consumer expenditures on eating out. The extent to which consumers will spend or save their income, however, will be affected by higher social security taxes and increases in state and local taxes.

■■■ Consumer Price Index (all items)
■■■ Food away from home (restaurants)
IIIII Food at home (grocery)

R&I estimate.
Source: Bureau of Labor Statistics.

Figure 1.1. *Index of food prices.* **Source: Restaurants and Institutions Magazine,** *Cahners Publishing Co., Mar. 15, 1982, p. 42.*

Another major trend that has had an effect on the industry is the increased scrutiny of corporate expense account spending. Business travel has been cut, fewer people are attending out-of-town meetings, and corporations are trimming their management and clerical staffs and limiting pay raises.

An important indicator of future foodservice sales is the comparative rate of price increases for food away from home and food at home. Another important indicator to the industry is the Consumer Price Index. As shown in Figure 1.1, the food at home index shifted in favor of the supermarkets in 1981.

The commercial segment of the industry has been particularly affected by tight economic conditions. In 1980, the largest number of business failures was reported among eating and drinking places since 1967 (NRA News, 1982a). An inability to cope with the recession, double-digit inflation, and declining customer counts contributed to the rapid rise of failures. The failure rate of eating and drinking places was 26 per 10,000 in 1980, up from 17 per 10,000 in 1979. According to Dun & Bradstreet, eating and drinking places ranked thirteenth among retail concern failures. For comparative purposes, the highest failure rate was 58 per 10,000 for infants' and children's wear stores and the lowest, 9 per 10,000 for women's accessories stores. According to Dun & Bradstreet, lack of managerial expertise is the underlying factor in nine out of ten business failures during either an economic expansion or recession.

In the institutional feeding group, the elementary and secondary schools have been affected by budget cuts in federal child feeding programs. Cost containment pressures have had a major impact across the institutional feeding group, particularly in healthcare institutions. Changes in price support programs for farm commodities have had effects throughout the industry with respect to food prices.

Changing demographics of the U.S. population have a major impact on all

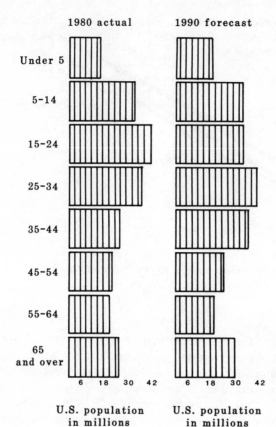

1980 actual   1990 forecast

Under 5

5-14

15-24

25-34

35-44

45-54

55-64

65
and over

6   18   30   42   6   18   30   42

U.S. population   U.S. population
in millions   in millions

Figure 1.2. *Population profile by age.* **Source: Restaurant Hospitality Magazine,** *copyright* © *Sept. 1982, p. 52.*

segments of the foodservice industry. Figure 1.2 shows the population profile by age for 1980 and the forecast for 1990, which illustrates the changing age groupings in the population. In the mid-1980s, the baby boom generation is beginning to mature, which represents the major change in the population. The increased numbers of elderly Americans or those 65 and over is affecting the healthcare industry in particular.

The changing profile of the age distribution in the population has implications not only from the clientele/customer perspective but also from the standpoint of the labor force for the industry. If government predictions are correct, by 1990 the foodservice industry will face an employment problem of unprecedented magnitude. Census Bureau data indicate that 15- to 24-year-olds as a segment of the population will decline from 42.5 million in 1980 to 34.9 million by 1990, an 18 percent decline. This trend is of particular concern to the industry because this age group has been a prime source for foodservice workers. On the flip side, data from the U.S. Bureau of Labor Statistics indicate that employment opportunities in foodservice will increase from 5.6 million full time employees in 1978 to an estimated 7.8 million in 1990, or a 39.5 percent gain (Table 1.2).

Table 1.2. *Employment in selected foodservice occupations, projected to 1995*

Occupation	1982		1995 (projected)		% change
Bakers, bread and pastry	36,000		46,000		28
Bartenders	84,000		505,000		32
Butchers and meat cutters	191,000		179,000		−6
Professional cooks	1,211,000		1,613,000		33
cooks, institutional	423,000		536,000		27
cooks, short order/					
fast food	437,000		578,000		32
cook, restaurant	351,000		500,000		42
Food prep and service/fast food	809,000		1,106,000		37
Host/hostesses	113,000		154,000		36
Kitchen helpers	850,000		1,155,000		36
Pantry, sandwich, coffee makers	84,000		112,000		34
Waiters/Waitresses	1,665,000		2,227,000		34
Waiters' assistants	302,000		388,000		29
Restaurant, cafeteria, and					
bar managers	574,000		711,000		24
Other	559,000		734,000		31
Total	6,778,000		8,931,000		32

Source: Monthly Labor Review, November 1983.

Indications are that foodservice will employ more immigrants to fulfill labor needs. Traditionally, foodservice has been a more important employer of immigrants than any other industry except the garment and agricultural industries. This population segment may become the primary labor pool for foodservices in the future. Increased numbers of Hispanic and Asian immigrants, in particular, are anticipated in the decade ahead.

Increased labor force participation by women and seniors is also predicted to meet future employment needs in the industry. As the population gets older and inflation continues to erode the value of pension funds, the elderly are anticipated to work longer and take second jobs after retirement. On the whole, workers will be older, more stable, more concerned with job security, and will probably demand better pay, benefits, working conditions, and opportunities. The predictions are that the era of cheap, plentiful labor is fast coming to a close.

Life-style changes will also have notable effects throughout the industry. Among these changes are increases in dual-career marriages, single parents, working single women, childless couples, and older parents. Young dual-career couples in their twenties and early thirties and the young singles of the past decade will be progressing in the age income profile. Their purchasing power will rise, they will be growing older, and their tastes will probably be more sophisticated. The two-income family will be especially powerful economically. Predictions are that these couples will have fewer children, later in life, and will value convenience and status.

Another important trend with long-range strategy implications is the resurgence of a home and family orientation. An outgrowth has been increased demand for eaten-but-not-prepared-at-home foods or retailing food for home consumption. "Gourmet take-out," currently in an embryonic stage, is predicted to grow and flourish in the 1980s.

Industry prognosticators predict that the successful foodservice operators will have targeted segments of the population and focused on specific consumer wants. Marketing research and targeted advertising strategies will be requisite for survival in the industry.

Changing food habits of the population also have tremendous implications for all segments of the foodservice industry. A major influence on eating habit changes is the increased health consciousness of the population. Concern about weight, fitness, and wellness has been translated into a desire for menu items lower in fat, sugar, calories, and salt. Increased fiber content of the diet is also being demanded by many consumers. These health concerns have been translated into increased use of chicken, fish, fruits, vegetables, and whole grain bread and cereals.

Consumers have begun to realize that the food they eat away from home is important to their overall diet. Industry leaders in the commercial segment contend that restaurateurs have an opportunity to increase business and enhance the industry's image by identifying and satisfying the needs of today's nutrition-conscious customers. Greater acceptance of ethnic foods and of foods traditional to particular regions of the United States and altered meal patterns are other food habit trends with implications for the industry, including the institutional and military segments as well.

CHARACTERISTICS OF VARIOUS SEGMENTS OF THE INDUSTRY

Healthcare

The healthcare segment of the industry includes foodservices in hospitals, nursing homes and other long-term care facilities, and facilities for the mentally and physically handicapped. In 1980, the American Hospital Association (AHA) reported 6,965 hospitals operating in the United States with a total of 1,365,000 beds (AHA, 1981). A second major segment of the healthcare industry includes the various types of nursing homes and extended care facilities. As of 1980, more than 25,000 nursing homes and related facilities were in operation. Hospitals include voluntary, state, local, federal, and proprietary institutions; nursing homes and other long-term care facilities include those that are nonprofit and those that are operated for profit. Foodservice in healthcare institutions is either operated by the facility or provided by a food contractor. Food and drink sales in the healthcare feeding category will total approximately $13.5 billion in 1985.

Increasing costs, the aging population, and competition are major challenges

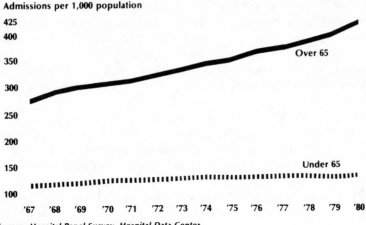

Admissions per 1,000 population

Source: Hospital Panel Survey, Hospital Data Center.
Developed by: American Hospital Assn.,
The Hospital Research and Educational Trust.

Figure 1.3. *Hospital admission rates 1967–1980.* Source: Restaurants and Institutions Magazine, *Cahners Publishing Co., Mar. 15, 1982, p. 178.*

facing the healthcare industry in the 1980s. Despite efforts to contain costs, operating expenses of hospitals and nursing homes and other long-term care facilities have continued to race ahead of the general inflation rate. As a result, federal legislation now calls for prospective payment systems, referred to as the DRG system (diagnosis related groups). The DRGs establish a standard cost for reimbursing hospitals for care of patients with various health problems, rather than providing reimbursement for actual costs. Private insurors are tending to follow suit in an attempt to control healthcare costs.

The upward shift in the age structure of the American population is one of the most pressing trends affecting healthcare. By the year 2000, 11.7 percent of the population will be over 65, compared to 8.1 percent in 1950, 9.8 percent in 1970, and 11 percent in 1980. The growth in the over-65 population accounted for an admission increase of more than 40 percent between 1967 and 1980, although total hospital admissions have increased steadily for the last 13 years for both the under-65 and over-65 age groups (Figure 1.3). Older patients tend to have complicated regimens and require modified diets more frequently than younger patients.

The healthcare industry is taking on characteristics of many commercial businesses as it has learned to deal with competition. Foodservice departments in hospitals are concerned with increasing productivity to become more efficient. Community involvement is another way healthcare operations are becoming more competitive; providing community services is being viewed as a way of increasing revenues.

Ambulatory care in healthcare operations is on the rise. Increased demand for nutrition counseling in outpatient areas and demand for outpatient foodservices are two major implications of this trend. Also, feeding facilities for employees and the public are being seen as areas for potential increased revenues. Increasing costs and competition have led to hospitals joining multihospital systems, which are two or more systems owned, leased, or managed by a single entity. According to AHA, 256 multihospital systems controlled 32 percent of all hospitals in 1981, an increase of 580 percent from 1940 to 1980. Shared staff, centralized management, and shared services are among the benefits of these systems.

Foodservice in nursing homes and other extended care facilities offers special challenges because of the long-term stay of most residents. Provision of day care and a continuum of services are significant current trends. Residents may come for a single day, part of a day, or on a regular basis for care while other family members are working or otherwise not available to provide care. Also, full-time residents may be provided housing only, meals on an "as desired" or contract basis, and various levels of nursing care dependent on their capabilities.

The increased demand for nursing home services over the past several decades has been due to population growth, longer life span, health insurance benefits, and a mobile society with families being separated geographically. The Medicare and Medicaid legislation in the 1960s had a major impact on the industry because of the greater benefits available and the establishment of minimum standards for all phases of nursing home operations, including dietetic services.

A current trend is to provide services to permit the older citizen to live as independently as possible. Meals-on-wheels (programs designed to transport food to people unable to leave their homes) and congregate meal programs (group feeding sites) are two examples of services being provided.

The growing and changing population of American retirees has changed traditional assumptions about old age. Nursing home beds for the invalid elderly represent a fraction of the services today's Americans age 65 and older need. Many of today's elderly are what gerontologists are now calling the "young old": active, competent, and living in a period between complete independence of working life and the illnesses of the "old old." In condominium complexes and retirement villages across the country, innovative foodservice programs are evolving for this "young old" market.

Life-care communities are an expanding share of the retirement-community market. Many of these facilities are hybrids of country clubs, college residence halls, and hospitals, providing facilities for independent living and health centers for residents who need nursing care. To enter a life-care, or continuing-care community, an individual or couple generally pays an entrance fee and subsequent monthly fees for a lifetime service contract. The fees cover most living expenses, including meals and most medical expenses. These centers enable adults to continue living independently and have social activities rather than becoming isolated and dependent on family and friends.

College and University

Projected foodservice sales in the college and university market totaled approximately $5.4 billion in 1985, with food contractors accounting for about one-third of this total. Many changes are anticipated in this market. The academic year 1983–1984 may mark the last gain in enrollment in higher education institutions. College costs, reduced student aid, and fewer college-age persons in the population will result in fewer students. To offset these trends, however, colleges and universities are developing innovative ways to attract nontraditional students, particularly older students and employed individuals, which has led to increased numbers of part-time students.

Over the last decade, major changes have occurred in college and university foodservices. Cash operations, à la carte programs, nontraditional board plans, and greater variety of menus are among the innovations that have been developed. On some campuses, students may eat at various foodservice units rather than being required to eat regularly at only one. Cash sales have become increasingly important in many collegiate foodservice operations. Increased numbers of off-campus students are participating in board plans because of economic concerns.

Junior and community colleges have gained new strength as enrollments rise with an influx of students who cannot afford away-from-home educations or private colleges. This trend has led to an increased demand for a wider variety of foodservices on these campuses, particularly fast food and vending. Another trend in community colleges is the greatly increased demand by commuting students for lunch-only service.

A diversity of foodservices is available on many campuses. These may include residence hall dining rooms that provide meals for students living within a unit, a central facility for students from several living units, and student union buildings that provide foodservice and other types of services for students, including recreational and meeting facilities and bookstores. Union foodservices often provide cafeterias, snack bars, vending services, and fast service units, and sometimes provide table service dining rooms, banquet facilities, and catering services for university functions and perhaps community affairs.

Formal seated service was characteristic of college and university foodservice in the 1800s and early 1900s. After World War II, college enrollments expanded greatly and class schedules no longer included specific meal periods. As a result, seated table service became impractical and was replaced by cafeteria service, which is the dominant approach today.

Increased size of operations and centralization of various functions has also been a key trend. For example, purchasing, storage, prepreparation, and some or most production may be centralized. Food, other products, and possibly partly or totally prepared foods are then transported to various service centers. Vegetable prepreparation and baking are functions frequently performed at a central commissary facility. Shared services among two or more small colleges is another trend that has emerged over the last decade; for example, several small colleges may band together to increase their purchasing power.

Some of the trends in personal food habits discussed previously in this chapter are having a major impact on college and university foodservice as well. Weight and health consciousness is causing students to demand salad bars, vegetarian meals, and other low-calorie alternatives. To create student interest, greater emphasis is being placed on special events or "monotony breakers" in residence hall foodservice operations. In addition, nutrition education and provisions for special dietary needs of students are being considered essential services in college and university foodservices.

Schools

Service of lunch at school in the United States dates to the mid-1800s, when various charitable and civic groups in large cities banded together to initiate programs because of concern for the health of school children. The poor nutritional status of many young men, which led to rejection for military service in World Wars I and II, raised concerns about the health of the nation's youth—this gave impetus to the development of the school lunch program. The earliest federal legislation provided loans for communities to pay labor costs of school lunch programs. Subsequent legislation was designed to utilize surplus farm commodities in schools; as a result, the school lunch became increasingly common in elementary and secondary schools.

These developments led to the passage of the National School Lunch Act in 1946. The dual purposes of the Act were "to safeguard the health and well-being of the Nation's children, and to encourage the domestic consumption of nutritious agricultural products." Federal regulations promulgated from the Act specified the meal pattern and provided for joint administration of the program through a federal–state–local school district relationship. Statistics show that approximately 91,200 elementary and secondary schools in the United States operated under this program in 1981, a decline from the peak number of 94,500 schools operating programs in 1979. These schools served some 23.5 million children daily in 1983–84, about 50 percent of whom received free or reduced price meals (Hiemstra, 1984).

Legislation enacted in 1980 and 1981 had a dramatic impact on school lunch participation. Reduced federal reimbursements caused school lunch operators to increase prices of lunches approximately 29 percent, which led to a paid-meal participation drop of 14 percent. Tightened eligibility criteria have led to declines in free and reduced price meal categories as well; and overall participation was down 11 percent during the 1981–82 school year compared to the 1980–81 year.

Legislation is being proposed at the national level to transfer responsibility for school feeding to the states, which could have a major impact in years ahead. In 1980, similar legislation was enacted in England, which has led to major changes in the program in that country in both the participation and the nutritional quality of the meals served (Ball, 1982).

The goal of the National School Lunch Program is to provide one-third of a child's daily nutrient requirements. The meal pattern defined in federal regulations for the program specifies minimum servings of various types of foods to be included. The pattern, previously referred to as Type A, has been revised a number of times since the National School Lunch Act was enacted in 1946. Currently, schools are required to offer a complete meal to each student, but students may choose only what they wish to eat. This option is commonly referred to as "offer versus serve." National concern about plate waste in the program led to adoption of this provision. Changes in the Recommended Dietary Allowances (RDAs) and food guidance information have influenced changes in the meal pattern through the years. Student and parent involvement in the program in an advisory capacity is also included in the federal regulations.

The Child Nutrition Act of 1966 initiated the School Breakfast Program on an experimental basis. Subsequent legislation has made the program available to all schools. Participation in the program was approximately 3.4 million daily in 1983–84, down somewhat because of legislative changes mentioned above. Students who receive free breakfast account for about 85 percent of the participation in the breakfast program. Since the program was initiated, it has been targeted to schools serving children from low-income families.

The Child Care Food Program is another child-feeding program that makes available federal funds for meals in day care centers for children. Meals served under this program totaled 41.6 million during September 1982. Current legislation permits service of two meals and one supplement per child daily and includes provisions for free and reduced price meals. The Child Care Program is also controlled by federal regulations that specify minimum nutritional requirements. Children in residential child care institutions are covered under the National School Lunch Program.

The Summer Foodservice and Special Milk Programs are also part of the federal Child Nutrition Programs. The scope of both of these programs was decreased in 1981–82 because of federal limitations. During the summer of 1982, almost 70 million meals were served under the summer program, most of which were lunches, although breakfast, supper, and supplements were also included. The Special Milk Program, previously available for any school, is currently limited to schools with no other federally subsidized foodservice program.

As indicated above, one of the initial purposes of the National School Lunch Program was utilization of surplus farm commodities, which have continued to be provided to schools through the years totaling $841 million in the 1983–84 school year. Schools receive approximately 21.8 cents worth of commodities for each lunch served, including bonus commodities from surplus foods purchased by the U.S. Department of Agriculture, paid for by other than Child Nutrition Program funds (Hiemstra, 1983). Planning for the storage and use of commodities is a unique managerial aspect in administration of school foodservice programs.

Although a part of the philosophy and intent of the School Lunch Program since its beginning, the educational component of school foodservice programs has been emphasized to a greater extent during the last decade than in the early years of the program. Legislation in 1970 established nutrition education as a part of the school foodservice program, and establishment of the Nutrition Education and Training Program (NETP) in 1977 led to expansion of these efforts. After the initial three-year period, federal funding for this program was cut drastically; however, many significant programs for nutrition training of students, teachers, and employees were initiated using NETP funds.

Although limited federal monies are currently available, many school districts have initiated innovative nutrition education programs integrated with the school lunch program. Encouraging students to eat school lunch has been a part of these efforts, and school foodservice directors have implemented wider choices in menus, complete meal salad bars, and nutritious snack type meals to achieve this objective. Studies have repeatedly shown that students who eat school lunch eat a more nutritious meal than those who eat lunch from other sources.

The type of organization and management of a school foodservice program varies from the simple, one cook-manager operation found in a small independent school to a complex, centrally managed unit in a large city school system. In addition to centralized management, some school systems have established centralized food preparation centers. Items prepared in these centers may be distributed in bulk or preplated, either hot or refrigerated, for service to students in schools with satellite service centers.

Changes in program regulations in the early 1970s permitted schools to negotiate with food contractors to provide meals. Although the vast majority of schools continue to operate their own programs, this change represented a major departure from previous regulations. In 1981, contractors accounted for only about 10 percent of the total food and drink sales in schools.

Employee Feeding

Employee feeding is projected to total $5.5 billion in 1985. Food contractors account for approximately two-thirds of this volume by providing services in industrial plants and in commercial and office buildings. The institutional component of employee feeding includes foodservices operated by industrial and commercial organizations, primarily as a service to employees, and also, foodservices on sea-going ships and inland waterway vessels. Sales in commercial and office buildings have tended to increase in recent years because white collar employment has risen; also, the relatively low cost of meals at these locations together with the higher cost of gasoline have influenced employees to remain at their workplaces for lunch. Declines in blue collar and manufacturing employment have had negative effects on food sales at industrial plants. Interestingly, increased use of inland waterway vessels for shipment of goods has led to increased sales in this segment of employee feeding.

Employee feeding operations, particularly the food contractors, are emphasizing marketing strategies to increase sales. For example, on-site bakeries may offer cookies and cakes for take-home sales, game cards redeemable for free drinks or meals are being distributed to encourage sales, and much wider choices of meals as well as à la carte items are being provided. Employee feeding includes a variety of operations from the top-rate executive dining rooms, to vending operations, to coffee carts for work breaks. Corporation executives are tending to use facilities in their organizations to a greater degree for conducting business with clients rather than taking them out for meals. As in other segments of the foodservice industry, the current emphasis is on quality and meeting the needs of the customer.

Commercial

Tremendous diversity is the primary characteristic of the commercial segment of the foodservice industry. As indicated earlier, this segment includes eating and drinking places, food contractors, foodservice and lodging places, and various other types of foodservices operated for profit. This last category includes operations such as restaurants in variety and drug stores, grocery store delis, foodservices in recreational and sports centers, and others.

Full service restaurants account for about 35 percent of the foodservice market, with a total of 167,500 units in 1982. The competition to capture consumers' disposable dollars has led to increased use of promotions, menu revision, and provision of entertainment in various forms—from musicians to magicians to video games. Upscaling of the menu, decor, and service are characterizing the 1980s among full service operations. Catering is being expanded with many operations offering creative, customized catering services. A major trend among chain restaurants is to individualize units to different locales.

The full service segment includes the following types of operations: fine dining establishments, family restaurants, coffee shops, cafeterias, theme/specialty restaurants, and membership clubs. The more expensive restaurants are often the most vulnerable in inflationary times as customers will tend to frequent lower- and moderately-priced restaurants instead. As a result, a great deal of experimentation is evident among fine dining restaurants in an attempt to maintain competitive positions.

The chain operations are particularly strong in the theme and specialty area. While the independents have the advantage of menu and market flexibility, chains have the advantage of sophisticated systems and buying power.

Commercial cafeterias are expected to face a favorable climate in the decade ahead and are beginning to attract a broader range of the market. The typical customer of yesteryear was the middle-aged and older adult. Now the typical customer is described as "everybody"—young families, business executives, homemakers, shoppers, students, and retirees. The wide variety of menu items is a primary "calling card" of commercial cafeterias.

Recent data indicate that Americans are joining private clubs at a growing rate. Despite the current consumer trend to cut spending on nonessential items, country club membership has been stable and city club membership has grown. Total revenues, however, have increased in both segments of the private club industry. Apparently, the affluent club customer is one of the last to be affected by economic declines. These customers perceive the private club with athletic facilities, social amenities, and service as a relatively inexpensive way to entertain and vacation. Keeping members content with quality products, services, and management is important to successful club operations.

The fast food segment represents more than 20 percent of the total foodservice market. Sandwich shops, seafood chains, pizza parlors, and operations featuring chicken or tacos and other Mexican foods account for the majority of the market. The market is highly competitive both within and without the fast food sector. Coffee shops and cafeterias, with their heavily discounted specials and price-oriented advertising, are major competitors of the fast foods.

The fast food segment of the industry should continue to remain relatively strong, not only because of the fast service provided but also because customers will continue to trade down as they look for a good price/value relationship. To remain competitive, the fast food industry has responded by expanding menus, putting more emphasis on take-out, upgrading facilities, and increasing advertising. Some chains have attempted to draw customers at new meal periods; for example, breakfast items have been added and service hours lengthened. Many fast food operations have learned that menu expansion is not a panacea, however. Broader menus may mean slower service and customers switching from old standbys to new items; as a result, larger menus do not necessarily translate into incremental sales volume and may even reduce profit.

Chains and franchisers dominate the fast food market, with some organizations being comprised of units that they totally operate. Others may have a combination of self-owned and franchised operations, and others may be almost completely franchised. Because of the widespread geographic area in which units are operated, managerial control offers a particular challenge in the fast food industry. Maintaining control of franchise operations can also present a particular challenge, since the businesses are owned by local operators with a less direct relationship with the company.

Foodservice in lodging places represents an approximate $11 billion market, with hotel restaurants accounting for almost 70 percent of this total. Nearly half of all meals consumed in hotel restaurants are business-related occasions, indicating that the business traveler is the primary customer target for this segment of the industry. Hotel foodservice operations may run the entire gamut from snack bars, to coffee shops, to fine restaurants, to a wide variety of room service and catering operations. Foodservice represents an essential and increasingly more important profit center for lodging places. Hotels are beginning to recognize the importance of good foodservice in the customer's overall assessment of the quality of services offered. Inflation, high interest rates, air travel cuts, and fewer vacationers are pressures facing the lodging segment of the industry. The drop in vacation travel has affected the motel restaurant segment more than hotels.

Tourist travel is down and spendable income has been reduced; however, amusement parks and sports and other recreational centers remain popular. Interestingly, the amusement parks are attracting a larger segment of the adult market rather than depending so heavily on the teenage market. Also, the trend is for people to spend more time in one park to get full value for their dollar investment. For example, at one California park average time has lengthened from four to five hours to five to six hours. As a result, theme parks are focusing resources on increasing per capita spending by offering more rides, shows, food selections, and big-name entertainment. Catering is becoming a more important source of revenue at these theme parks as well.

Professional sporting events have had tremendous growth over the past decade and attendance continues to be on the upswing, except at racetracks. Foodservice sales have increased at sporting events and menu offerings have been expanded. In addition, many sports complexes have fine upscale restaurants in addition to fast food operations. Food contractors provide foodservices for a major segment of the recreation market.

The retail portion of the commercial market includes foodservice operations in other types of retail outlets, such as department stores, supermarkets, and discount houses. Take-out food is becoming a greatly expanding part of the market. The fastest growing subsegment of this market is that of convenience stores. The quick-stop food markets have greatly expanded sales of fast foods. Many supermarkets have expanded in-store operations to include breakfast sales, enabling customers to eat and then do their grocery shopping. Supermarkets are also gaining an increased share of the foodservice market with delicatessen sales. Take-out foods are becoming a major source of revenue for department stores as well. In many of these stores, offering a unique concept in their restaurants is being recognized as important.

Greater emphasis on a family- and home-centered life style, mentioned earlier, means that foodservice must appeal to more people who want to spend more time at home. This challenge is not impossible, since people who want to stay at home do not necessarily want to cook there. For example, the working mother is a prime customer for take-out foods. The gourmet food shop and home delivery are two approaches being used for capturing this market. While customers appear to want to eat at home in increasing numbers, the desire for TV dinners has not increased. Instead, customers often are looking for freshness and quality in foods prepared for at-home consumption.

The retail market can be segmented into three basic levels. At the first level, the discount store provides for the price-need purchase in which price is the essential lure: in other words, adequate product for the best possible price. Fast foods are typical in this market. In the middle, the customer is looking for higher quality items, but price is still important. At the top, price is no longer an object—personal fulfillment is. The carriage shop, specialty boutique, and fine department store with specialty cuisines cater to this market. The challenge in the retail foodservice is to produce high quality products to be held and transported.

In the 1980s, the whole world is becoming a marketplace for the restaurant industry. Expansion into foreign territories by U.S. foodservice companies is spurred by high population density and low market penetration in those areas. In addition, investors from abroad are testing their concepts on the American audience.

Regardless of the home-based location of the corporation, building a market abroad presents a variety of problems; these include fluctuating exchange rates, differing government regulations, and language barriers. Growth in the overseas market is presenting a challenge for American chains because of the stiff competition and uncertain economy in the United States. Teenagers and young families worldwide are becoming attracted to American foodservice concepts in markets from western Europe to the Far East. Hamburgers, fried chicken, doughnuts, and milkshakes are typical American fare gaining acceptance in international markets. Corporations with experience in the international market indicate, however, that consumer research is essential because products successful in America may not have appeal in other countries. As an indication of growth in the overseas market, the number of U.S. restaurant franchises grew from 2,147 in 1973 to 3,943 in 1980, according to the U.S. Department of Commerce (Rest. Bus., 1982a).

Transportation

Since the 1970s, inflation and deregulation have been challenges facing the airline segment of the transportation industry. Price wars and competition from regional carriers have caused major airlines to stress operational efficiency to remain profitable. Food contractors provide a major portion of in-transit airline feeding, adapting menus and food items to menu specifications of the various carriers. Real foodservice dollars in the transportation segment (i.e., adjusted for inflation) are expected to decline somewhat in the years ahead as major carriers curtail routes, meal flights become snack flights, hot service becomes cold, and regional carriers that serve less food gain market share.

Transportation feeding also includes foodservice on passenger/cargo liners and railroads. Sales in these segments of the market have declined and efficiency and productivity are becoming more important; for example, Amtrak is now offering dining service resembling airline service with improved portion control and reduced labor costs.

SUMMARY

The foodservice industry can be divided into three major groups—commercial, institutional, and military—and is large and complex, accounting for 37 percent of all consumer expenditures for food. In fact, the average person eats away from home about 3.5 times a week.

A number of social trends, such as increasing numbers of working women, growing importance of convenience in many aspects of living, and increasing desire for leisure activities, have led to increased eating away from home. Inflation and unemployment are among negative influences, causing many consumers to opt for lower price establishments. Industry forecasters predict that the successful foodservice operators will need to target segments of the population and focus on specific consumer wants. Changing food habits are also affecting the industry, particularly the increased concern for health and wellness influencing consumers to select items lower in fat, calories, sugar, and salt.

Increasing costs, an aging population, and competition are major challenges facing the healthcare segment of the industry. Foodservice departments in hospitals are becoming more concerned with such issues as productivity and increased revenues.

Diversity characterizes the college and university foodservice market. Declining enrollments and a greater proportion of older and part-time students are having a great effect on college and university foodservice.

School foodservice programs are designed to provide for the nutritional needs of school-age children. Elementary and secondary schools serve almost a quarter of a million children daily, about 50 percent of whom receive free or reduced-price meals. In addition, school breakfast, child care, and summer foodservice are other aspects of the federal child nutrition programs.

Employee feeding is a fairly large segment of the foodservice industry, with food contractors accounting for approximately two-thirds of the market. Employee feeding covers a broad range of operations from the coffee cart for work breaks to the top-rate executive dining room.

The tremendous diversity is the primary characteristic of the commercial segment of the market. Full service restaurants account for about 35 percent of the foodservice industry sales and range from upscale dining to family restaurants to theme and specialty restaurants. Chain operations are especially strong in the theme and specialty area. The fast food segment represents more than 20 percent of the industry with sandwich shops, seafood chains, pizza parlors, and operations featuring chicken or Mexican food accounting for the majority of the market.

The business traveler is the dominant customer for foodservice operations in lodging places. Hotels and motels are becoming increasingly aware that foodservice operations can be an important profit center.

The take-out market is becoming an expanding part of the foodservice industry, primarily because of greater emphasis on family- and home-centered life styles. The working mother is a prime customer for take-out foods because she often wants to eat at home but not cook at home.

The transportation segment of the industry is facing the challenges of inflation and deregulation. Price wars and competition from regional carriers have caused major airlines to be very cost-conscious, which affects inflight foodservice in particular.

REFERENCES

American Hospital Association: *AHA Guide, American Hospital Association Guide to the Health Care Field.* 1981 ed. Chicago: Am. Hosp. Assoc., 1981.

Ball, T. A.: School lunch in England in the early 1980s—An appraisal. *School Food Serv. Res. Rev.* 6:79, 1982.

Contract foodservice 1982–83. Reaching out: A break from convention. *Food Mgmt.* 17:48 (Nov.), 1982.

18th Annual "400" report, Part 1: Business and finance. *Restaurants & Institutions* 91:33 (Jul. 1), 1982.

Fifth annual state of the industry report. *Restaurant Hospitality* 66:37 (Sept.), 1982.

Food and Nutrition Service: *Food Program Update for September 1982.* Food and Nutr. Serv., USDA, Dec. 1982.

Foodservice trends, NRA forecast '82. *NRA News* 1:9 (Dec.), 1981.

Foodservice trends, eating and drinking place failures grew in 1980. *NRA News* 2:22 (Jan.), 1982a.

Foodservice trends, the foodservice industry, 1980 in review. *NRA News* 2:23 (Jun./Jul.), 1982b.

Foodservice trends, NRA forecast, What's brewing in 1983? *NRA News* 2:9 (Dec.), 1982c.

Foodservice trends, current and projected employment trends in the foodservice industry. *NRA News* 5:36 (Jan.), 1985.

Hiemstra, S. J.: Impact of the Omnibus Budget Reconciliation Act of 1981. *School Food Serv. Res. Rev.* 6:73, 1982.

Hiemstra, S. J.: National School Lunch Program trends. *School Food Serv. Res. Rev.* 7:6, 1983.

Hiemstra, S. J.: Program data & analysis: Summary of trends. *School Food Serv. Res. Rev.* 8:144, 1984.

Interpreting the international market. *Restaurant Bus.* 81:211 (Nov.), 1982.

Liesse, J.: Growth chains. *Restaurants & Institutions* 91:77 (Nov. 15), 1982.

National Restaurant Association: *Foodservice Industry Pocket Factbook.* Washington, DC: Natl. Rest. Assoc., 1982.

Riggs, S.: Aging well. A heyday ahead for retirement dining. *Restaurants & Institutions* 90:27 (Feb. 1), 1982.

Schuster, K., and Bendt, D.: The economy and you: The pinch begins. *Food Mgmt.* 17:32 (Feb.), 1982. Schuster, K.: College and university foodservice 1982–83, and how will they be fed? *Food Mgmt.* 17:38 (Jun.), 1982.

Seventh annual report. *Restaurants & Institutions* 90:33 (Mar. 15), 1982.

Silvestri, G. T., Lukasiewicz, J. M., and M. E. Einstein: Occupational employment projections through 1995. Monthly Labor Rev. 106:37 (Nov.), 1983.

Special report: Hotel foodservice. *Restaurant Hospitality* 66:41 (Oct.), 1982.

The 1985 NRA forecast: Foodservice sales to equal $178 billion. *NRA News* 4:13 (Dec.), 1984.

The regulatory climate overseas. *Restaurant Bus.* 81:229 (Nov. 1), 1982a.

20th annual "400" report. Part I: Business and finance. *Restaurant & Institutions* 94:89 (Aug. 1), 1984.

Wallace, J.: Foodservice goes retail. *Restaurants & Institutions* 91:57 (Oct. 1), 1982.

2

Systems Approach to Foodservice Operations

The systems approach to organizations and their management provides the basic framework for this book. This chapter examines the systems approach, describes characteristics of the organization as a system, and discusses applications of systems concepts to foodservice organizations.

The term "system" has been in vogue for some time in discussing and analyzing almost everything from families to philosophy to education to engineering. It has been applied to a broad spectrum of our physical, biological, and social world (Kast and Rosenzweig, 1979). In the universe, there are galactic systems, geophysical systems, and molecular systems. In biology, the organism is described as a system of mutually dependent parts, each of which includes many subsystems. The human body is a complex organism including a skeletal system, a digestive system, a circulatory system, and a nervous system, among others. Daily we come into contact with transportation systems, economic systems, data processing systems, and communication systems. The systems approach to organizations and management facilitates analysis and synthesis in today's complex and dynamic environment.

THE SYSTEMS APPROACH

Systems theory provides a basis for understanding and integrating knowledge from a variety of widely specialized fields, as well as a macro-view from which we may look at all types of systems. Systems may be viewed as closed or open. Physical and mechanical systems can be considered as closed in relation to their environment, whereas biological and social systems are in constant interaction with their environment and are thus open systems. According to Kast and Rosenzweig (1979), traditional theory assumes the organization to be a closed system, whereas a more modern view considers it an open system in interaction with its environment.

Managers of foodservice organizations are seeking approaches to deal with the complexities of foodservice organizations and to meet the continually changing technological, economic, political, and sociological demands of today's world. Drucker (1980) describes the current economic and social scene as turbulent and contends that an organization has to be managed well both to withstand sudden blows and to avail itself of sudden, unexpected opportunities.

One approach has been the application of systems concepts or the systems approach to facilitate problem solving and decision making for managers. The systems approach focuses on the totality of the organization, not on its processes or parts. The impact of both the internal and external environment on the organization and on the managing process are considered. Powers (1978) describes the service organization as an energetic system reactivated by an exchange through its environment, contending that without the energetic return the system dissipates.

With the advent of the computer age in the late 1950s and early 1960s, the usefulness of the systems approach to managing organizations became evident. Application of the systems approach in the foodservice industry occurred in about the mid-1960s, when authorities in the field began discussing foodservice operations as systems and the importance of the systems approach to designing foodservice operations and implementing change.

In the late 1960s and early 1970s, a number of models of foodservice systems were published in the trade and professional literature of the field. Livingston (1968) used the systems approach to design a foodservice systems model utilizing convenience foods, and Gue (1969) formulated a conceptual model of the hospital dietetics department as a system. Konnersman (1969) focused on the hospital dietetics department as a logistical system and emphasized the input-output flows of the system. Also in 1969, Freshwater developed a descriptive model of a foodservice system and contended that visualizing organizations from a systems concept enabled managers, suppliers, and others to evaluate current practices and the impact of proposed changes in terms of overall effects on the operation. David (1972), in describing a systems model of a foodservice organization developed at the University of Wisconsin-Madison, emphasized that the systems approach is an organized, practical application of common sense techniques to the design and analysis of an operation.

Prior to the 1960s, analytical fact-finding approaches were the focus for examining organizations; however, the need for synthesis and integration became obvious. The systems era has been described as an age of synthesis. Managers must be capable of coordinating complex organizations; the challenge facing managers is that of integration and synthesis of specialized activity. The systems

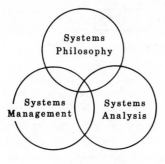

Figure 2.1. *The systems approach.* **Adapted from The Theory and Management of Systems, 3rd ed., R. A. Johnson, P. E. Kast, and J. E. Rosenzweig, copyright © 1973 3rd ed. by McGraw-Hill Book Co., New York, p. 18. Reprinted by permission.**

concept focuses on interactions and interrelationships of components and subsystems of the organization.

A system is defined as a collection of interrelated parts or subsystems unified by design to obtain one or more objectives. Luchsinger and Dock (1982) listed fundamental implications of the term "system."

- A system is designed to accomplish an objective.
- The elements of a system have an established arrangement.
- Interrelationships exist between the elements.
- Organization objectives are more important than the objectives of the elements or subsystems.

The systems approach to management is simply keeping the organization's objectives in mind throughout the performance of all activities. It requires a communication network and coordination among all parts of the organization. Essentially then, management is a process whereby unrelated resources are integrated into a total system for objective accomplishment.

According to Johnson, Kast, and Rosenzweig (1973), the systems approach encompasses three fundamental concepts: systems philosophy, systems analysis, and systems management (Figure 2.1). The systems philosophy is a way of thinking about an event in terms of wholes, including parts or subsystems, with emphasis on their interrelationships. Systems analysis is a method used in problem solving or decision making. Systems management involves the application of the systems theory to managing organizational systems or subsystems. Thus, the systems approach is (1) a way of thinking, (2) a method of analysis, and (3) a managerial style.

THE ORGANIZATION AS A SYSTEM

As indicated above, organizations are described as open systems because they are in continual interaction with the environment. They can also be described as people-machine systems, or systems in which people interact with machines to achieve desired objectives. In the production aspect of a system, machines are

Figure 2.2. *The organization as an open system*

ordinarily introduced to replace functions previously performed by workers or to assist workers in performing a task more effectively. Automated systems are becoming more important with the role of people being that of initiating, monitoring, or terminating the system. These systems relieve people from routine or heavy physical tasks, thus permitting them to perform more creative or innovative kinds of work.

Davis (1980) discusses new designs for organizations and emphasizes the importance of optimizing technical and social systems of the organization. He contends that engineers traditionally have designed technical systems with machine-tool components optimized on the basis of economic criteria; social criteria were seen as being satisfied by designing "people-proof" technical systems. Joint optimization seeks to combine the technical and social systems by integrating the adaptive problem solving capabilities of people with the productive capacity of technical systems.

The basic open systems model of an organization is shown in Figure 2.2. A system has a specific function, major parts, and unique characteristics. The function can be described as the aim, purpose, or primary objective of the system. It determines the major parts of a system: the input, transformation, and output, as shown in the model.

The inputs are resources that are changed in the transformation process to produce the outputs of the system. The transformation is the collective change of inputs into outputs. The output is the result from transforming the inputs and represents the achievement of the system's function. For example, a primary output in a foodservice system would be production of food of a desired quantity and quality to meet clientele needs.

The inputs of a system may be defined as any operational, physical, or human resources required to accomplish the objectives of the system. Operational resources refer to such items as time, money, and information. Physical resources include equipment, materials, and facilities. Human resources are the skills, knowledge, and energies of people required for the system to function.

The transformation element involves any action or activity which is utilized in changing inputs into outputs; for example, the activities involved in procurement and production of food. As stated above, output is the result from transforming the input. In addition to the production of quality food, other outputs of a foodservice system may be various types of services as well. Also, from a managerial perspective, achieving financial accountability is a necessary outcome.

The expanded systems model of the organization includes three additional parts: control, feedback, and memory. The expanded model is shown in Figure 2.3.

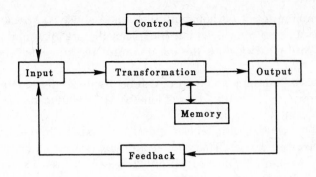

Figure 2.3. *Expanded model of an organizational system*

The control element provides guidance for the system, both internal and external. Internal controls include the objectives and other types of plans of the organization, while the external controls are the local, state, and federal laws and regulations. The various contracts into which an organization may enter are other types of controls.

The control element performs three functions in a system. It ensures that resources are used effectively and efficiently in accomplishing the organization's objectives. In addition, it ensures that the organization is functioning within legal and regulatory constraints. Finally, it provides the standards to be used in evaluation of the system's operations.

The menu is one of the most important internal controls of a foodservice system. The menu specifies the inputs, the transformation processes to be used in the production of food, and the output. Also, the food and labor costs are determined in large measure by the menu. For example, the decision to open a fried chicken franchise unit not only determines the overall objective of the operation but also the menu items to be offered, the type of advertising that will be used in promoting the business, and even the type of equipment to be purchased for preparation of the chicken and other items.

The laws and regulations governing sanitary practices in a foodservice operation are good examples of external controls. In addition, many other types of legal requirements govern the foodservice system, such as minimum wage legislation, safety requirements, and regulations affecting the food supply. Segments of the industry are affected by legislation directed specifically to operations in those sectors. For example, in the first chapter, we discussed some of the legislation and regulations affecting the school foodservice system.

Labor and purchasing contracts are two additional examples of system controls. In addition, many organizations are entering into contracts for provision of various types of services, such as security services and laundry services. One large segment of the foodservice industry is involved with contracting for foodservices in various types of organizations. The food contractors, as a group, provide foodservices for almost every type of organization where foodservices can be found. As we discussed in the first chapter, many healthcare institutions, colleges and schools, employee feeding operations, retail establishments, and recreational facilities have entered into contracts with these foodservice companies. In all of these operations, the contract negotiated between the organization in question and the food contractor provides the basic control for how the foodservice is managed.

The processes of planning and control will be discussed in more depth in the next chapter; however, from this discussion the interrelationship of organizational plans and controls should be obvious.

Feedback, the second additional element of the expanded model of a system, includes those processes by which a system continually receives information from its internal and external environment. If utilized, feedback assists the system to adjust to needed changes. For instance, a foodservice manager should evaluate acceptance of a new food item by clientele comments, plate waste, cost, and frequency of selection of the new item to determine future use on the menu. Organizations without effective feedback mechanisms become relatively closed systems and may deteriorate or perhaps go out of business if the organization is a commercial concern.

The third additional element shown in Figure 2.3 is that of memory. The memory element includes all the stored information and provides the historical records of the system's operations. Analysis of past records can assist the manager in making future plans and in avoiding past mistakes. The rapid advances in computer technology and data processing are revolutionizing the memory capability of all types of systems. Rather than relying on filing cabinets for storage of information, managers increasingly are relying on discs and magnetic tape for maintaining files and records of all aspects of operations.

CHARACTERISTICS OF SYSTEMS

A system has a number of unique characteristics: interrelatedness and interdependency of parts, dynamic equilibrium, equifinality, permeable boundaries, interface of systems and subsystems, and hierarchy of the system. In addition, linking processes are important for the effective functioning of a system.

The interdependence or reciprocal relationship among the parts or components of a system can be exemplified by a kaleidoscope. Each part mutually affects the performance of the other parts of a system. This characteristic emphasizes the importance of viewing the organization as a whole and not just the parts in isolation. Changes in one part of a system have implications or ripple effects throughout the system just as a turn of the kaleidoscope changes the entire design. For example, in a foodservice system a decision to purchase a new piece of automated equipment will have many effects. Employee skills, schedules, type of food purchased, and menu planning are among the aspects of the system that will be affected.

Interdependency also means that parts of an organization provide satisfaction for needs and means of attainment for other parts of the organization, although the nature and amount of these needs may vary between differing parts. This characteristic can be compared to a cobweb, which displays an interrelated relationship; a disturbance anywhere means that the disturbance may be transmitted to other parts of the cobweb. In the same way, decisions made in one part of an organization may affect other parts as well.

The interdependency implies an interactive or transactional relationship of some type between parts of the system. Parts of systems do not operate in a vacuum but continually relate with other units. For example, a purchasing department must interact with the production unit and the advertising department must interact with the sales department for the organization to function as an effective system. The result of effective interaction is integration, which leads to a synergistic effect, meaning that the units or parts of an organization acting in concert can produce more impact than the sum of their impacts when operating separately. Integration also means that parts of the system share objectives of the entire organization, having recognized their condition of interdependency and interaction with other parts of the organization.

Dynamic equilibrium, or steady state, is the continuous response and adaptation of a system to its internal and external environment. The environment includes all the conditions, circumstances, and influences surrounding and affecting the system. To remain viable, an organization must be responsive to social, political, and economic pressures. A foodservice director must continually evaluate cost and availability of food, labor, and supplies and advances in new technology and make changes to adapt to these new conditions in order to maintain a viable foodservice organization. The feedback processes discussed in the previous section of this chapter are important in maintaining dynamic equilibrium.

The term equifinality is applied to the organization as a system, meaning that a same or similar output can be achieved by using different inputs or by varying the transformation processes. In other words, various alternatives may be used to attain similar results, or in the vernacular, "There is more than one way to skin a cat." In a foodservice organization, a decision to change from conventional foods to convenience foods will affect the inputs and the transformation processes; however, a similar output, meals for a given clientele, will be achieved from these different inputs and processes.

Permeability of boundaries is another characteristic of an open system that allows the system to be penetrated or affected by the changing external environment. Boundaries define the limits of a system, but permeability allows the system to interact with the environment. For example, a hospital constantly interrelates with the community, other healthcare institutions, and government agencies, all of which are part of the external environment. An organization can be described as having three different levels or layers. The model shown in Figure 2.4 was adapted from that proposed initially by Parsons (1960) and modified by Petit (1967) and Kast and Rosenzweig (1979) as a way of conceptualizing the organization as a system.

The internal level or the technical or production level is where the goods and services of the organization are produced. The next level, the organizational level, provides coordination and services for the technical operations and has responsi-

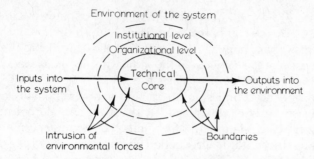

Environment of the system
Institutional level
Organizational level
Technical Core
Inputs into the system
Outputs into the environment
Intrusion of environmental forces
Boundaries

Figure 2.4. *Levels of the organization.* **Adapted from T. A. Petit, "A Behavioral Theory of Management." Academy of Management Journal, Vol. 10, Dec. 1967, p. 346.**

bility for relating the technical and institutional levels. The institutional level is the policy making level of the organization, which has primary responsibility for interaction with the environment and strategic long-range planning. While all three levels have permeable boundaries and environmental interaction, the degree of permeability increases from the technical to the institutional level.

The concept of boundaries among levels of a system, between subsystems, or between systems is a rather nebulous one. Above, we defined boundaries as the limits of a system. Boundaries are also described as the demarcation lines or regions for system activity. In other words, the boundaries set the "domain" of the organization's activities. For example, the activities of the production unit provide the boundaries for that subsystem. All the activities involved in the planning and preparation of food for service are functions of the production subsystem, whereas the service subsystem has a separate defined activity, that of service of food to the clientele of the foodservice system. While these two subsystems are interrelated and interdependent, each has a separate realm of activity.

The area of interrelationship between two subsystems or two systems is often referred to as their interface. The example above illustrates the interface between the production and service subsystems of a foodservice organization. The overall organizational system has many interfaces with other systems, for example, suppliers of materials, governmental agencies, community organizations, and unions.

Where two moving parts come together, a point of friction often occurs. Similarly, the interface between two subsystems within an organization is likely to be characterized by tension. In his landmark study of the restaurant industry, Whyte (1948) identified the service pantry as a point of maximum tension between waitresses and cooks. The dirty dish window in the dishroom and the service bar are other examples of interfaces in foodservice organizations. In a hospital, patient tray service, in which dietetic services come in direct contact with nursing, is a classical example of an area of interface in which conflict frequently occurs. An age-old argument in many hospitals has been "who shall roll up the patient's bed at meal time?" These interface areas often require special attention by managers.

Another characteristic of a system is the hierarchy. A system is composed of subsystems of lower order; the system is also part of a larger suprasystem. In fact, the ultimate system is the universe. For purposes of analysis, however, we generally define the largest unit with which we are working as the system and the units thereof become subsystems. A subsystem is an interrelated and interdependent part of the whole system but is in itself a system as well. No system is totally independent; it is always related to other entities.

In analyzing a hospital, we may view it as the system and the dietetic services department, the nursing department, radiology, and other departments may be viewed as subsystems. By the same token, a college or university may be viewed as the system and the academic units and student services as two of the subsystems. The foodservice department would then be viewed as a component of the student services division. We may, however, wish to analyze the foodservice departments in a hospital and college in more detail and thus view them as systems; the units within the foodservice would then become the subsystems.

Linking processes are needed to coordinate the activities of the system toward the accomplishment of the system's goals. These processes are decision making, communication, and balance. Decision making is defined as the selection by management of a course of action from a variety of alternatives. Communication is the vehicle whereby decisions and other information are transmitted. Communication includes all the oral, written, and electronic data processing forms used for various messages throughout the system. Balance refers to management's ability to maintain organization stability in the face of shifting technological, economical, political, and social conditions.

A FOODSERVICE SYSTEMS MODEL

In this part of the chapter, we will examine a foodservice systems model as a way of reinforcing understanding of the systems approach and applications of systems theory and concepts to a foodservice organization. This model will be referred to in subsequent chapters, which focus on functional subsystems and other aspects of managing foodservice operations.

A foodservice systems model is shown in Figure 2.5. An examination of the model will indicate that it is based on the open systems model of an organization presented earlier, which includes input, transformation, and output. The additional components of control, feedback, and memory are integral parts of the foodservice systems model. The arrows made with the heavy lines in the diagrammatic model represent the flow of materials, energy, and information throughout the system. The perforations in the heavy arrows from output to input on the periphery of the model represent the permeability of the boundaries of the foodservice system and reflect the environmental interaction inherent in the effectiveness of the system. The arrows with the fine lines on the model also represent environmental interactions, both internal and external to the system.

Inputs of the foodservice system are the physical and human resources that are transformed to produce the outputs of the system. Traditionally, these re-

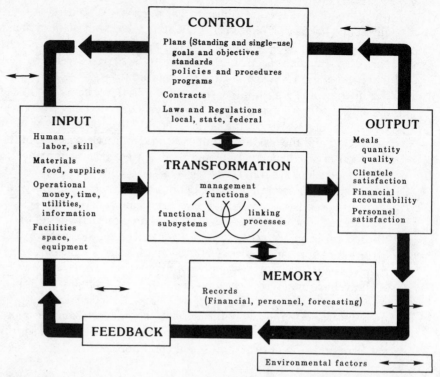

Figure 2.5. *A foodservice systems model.* **From A Model for Evaluating the Foodservice System, A. G. Vaden, copyright © 1980 by Kansas State University, Manhattan, Kansas. Reprinted by permission.**

sources have been referred to as men, machines, and money. We have expanded this traditional definition somewhat by defining four types of resources.

- *Human.* Labor and skill.
- *Materials.* Food and supplies.
- *Operational.* Money, time, utilities, and information.
- *Facilities.* Space and equipment.

The input requirements are dependent upon and specified by the objectives and plans of the organization. For example, the decision to open a full scale restaurant serving fine cuisine rather than a fast food operation with carry-out service would have a major impact on the type and skill of the staff, the food and supplies that are needed to produce the menu items, the capital investment, and the type of foodservice facility and layout.

In Chapter 5, we will discuss various types of foodservice systems; conventional, commissary, and others. The type of foodservice system selected will have a major influence on the input requirements of the foodservice. The decision to operate a conventional foodservice in which most foods are prepared from basic

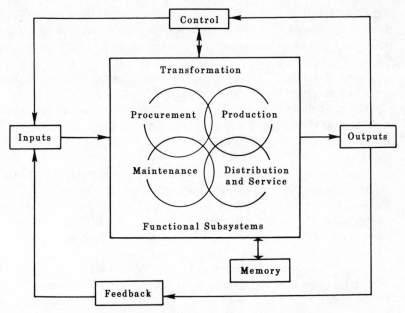

Figure 2.6. *Functional subsystems of a foodservice system*

ingredients will result in a very different specification of inputs than would be true for a system using primarily convenience foods.

Transformation has been defined as the collective change of inputs into outputs. In the foodservice systems model (Figure 2.5), the transformation element is depicted to include the functional subsystems of the foodservice operation, managerial functions, and linking processes. These are all interrelated and interdependent parts of the transformation element that function in a synergistic way to produce the outputs of the system.

The subsystems of a foodservice system (Figure 2.6) may be classified according to their purpose or function and may include procurement, pre-processing, production, distribution, service, and maintenance. Dependent on the type of the foodservice system, the subsystems that comprise the system may vary. For example, pre-processing would not be needed in a total convenience food system.

The type of system would determine the characteristics and activities of the subsystems. In the example given above, the full service restaurant with fine cuisine would have a much more sophisticated and elaborate production unit than would be needed in the fast food restaurant. The distribution and service subsystems in hospital foodservice represent very complex and difficult subsystems to control. The challenge is delivering the appropriate food at the right temperature and of a high quality to patients in many diverse locations. The catering division of a student union foodservice offers a wide variety of services not provided in the snack bar operation in the same facility. The food contractor providing meals for several airlines faces the complexities of different menus and schedules, varying numbers of passengers, and such other problems as delayed and canceled flights. Designing subsystems to meet the unique characteristics of these various types of foodservice organizations requires a systems approach in which the overall objectives of the organization are considered, as well as the interrelationships among the parts of the system.

The management functions are an integral component of the transformation element that provide for the coordination of the subsystems toward the accomplishment of the system's objectives. Although managerial concepts will be discussed in depth in Chapters 3 and 4 and also in Section VI, management functions are introduced here to illustrate the role of management in the foodservice system.

In this text, management functions are defined as planning, organizing, staffing, leading, and controlling. The manager performs these functions in the process of coordinating the system. Thus, management can be defined as the coordination of human and material resources toward accomplishment of objectives and the primary force within organizations that coordinates the activities of the subsystems.

The linking processes were discussed in an earlier part of this chapter and were defined as decision making, communication, and balance. Decision making is the selection of a course of action, and communication is a vehicle whereby decisions and other information are transmitted throughout the system. Balance refers to managerial adaptations to changing economical, political, social, and technological conditions. These processes are critical to the effective coordination of activities of the system.

Outputs are the products and services that result from transforming the inputs of the system and express how the objectives are achieved. The primary output in the foodservice system is meals; various types of services may be other primary outputs of the system, dependent on the type of foodservice operation. In addition, clientele and personnel satisfaction are desired outcomes.

Clientele satisfaction is closely linked to the types and quality of food and services provided and also to clientele expectations. For example, a college student may be very satisfied with a hamburger-spaghetti casserole on the luncheon menu of a college residence hall but would be very dissatisfied if that same item were served at a special function of a social fraternity at a country club, even though in both instances the product may be of a high quality. The student's expectations in these two situations are quite different.

Traditionally, textbooks in this field have stated that the objective of the foodservice is to produce the highest possible quality food. We prefer, however, to define the objective as production of food to satisfy the expectations, desires, and needs of the customers, clients, or patients of a particular foodservice. At the corner variety store lunch counter, the customer may accept a rather mediocre grilled cheese sandwich and tomato soup fresh out of the can; however, that evening at a private club, the expectations of the cuisine will be quite different. An important point to remember is that customers' desires, needs, and expectations must be taken into account in planning, producing, and evaluating the food served in any foodservice system.

Defining personnel satisfaction as an output of the system might be viewed by some as surprising. We contend, however, that managers must be concerned about assisting employees in achieving personal objectives at work and coordinating personal and organizational objectives. The effectiveness of any system, in large measure, is related to the quality of work done by the people staffing the organization.

Financial accountability is an output required to maintain a viable system. The term financial accountability rather than profit was used so the model could be applied either to a for-profit or non-profit foodservice organization. A foodservice manager must control costs in relation to revenues regardless of the type of operation. In the profit making organization, a specific profit objective is generally defined as a percent of income. In a non-profit organization, the financial objective may be to break even; in other words, costs must equal revenues. In others, however, a certain percentage of revenue in excess of expenses must be generated to provide funds for renovations, replacement costs, or expansion of operations.

The control element encompasses the goals and objectives, policies, procedures, standards, and programs of the foodservice organization. All of these plans are the internal controls of the system. These plans may be either standing or single-use. Standing plans are those which are used repeatedly over a period of time and are updated or reviewed periodically for changes. Single-use plans are those which are designed to be used only one time for a specific purpose or function.

A cycle menu is an example of a standing plan. For example, a hospital may have a two-week menu cycle that is repeated throughout a three-month seasonal period. Various types of organizational policies are also examples of standing plans.

The menu and other plans for a special catered function are examples of single-use plans. The National School Lunch Week menu, which changes annually, is a single-use plan that may be used by the foodservice department in a school district. A particular single-use plan may provide the basis for a subsequent plan of a similar type; however, a particular single-use plan is not intended to be used in its exact form on a second occasion.

Contracts and the various local, state, and federal laws and regulations are other components of the control element. Examples were provided in an earlier part of this chapter of various types of contractual and legal controls on the foodservice system. Depending on the type, contracts are either internal or external controls; legal requirements are externally imposed controls on the foodservice system. The foodservice operation must adhere to various contractual and legal obligations in order to avoid litigation. For example, in constructing a foodservice facility, the local and state building and fire codes must be adhered to in both the design and construction phases. Among other provisions, the sanitary practices codes specify the type of milk and the manner in which it must be served in a foodservice establishment. These are a few additional examples illustrating both internal and external controls of a system. Controls are the standards for evaluating the system and provide the basis for the managerial process of controlling.

The feedback element provides information essential to the continuing effectiveness of the system. Feedback provides information for evaluation and control of the system. As stated earlier, a system continually receives information from its internal operations and external environment which, if utilized, assists the system in adapting to changing conditions. Effective use of feedback is critical to maintaining viability of the system. Clientele comments, plate waste, patronage, profit or loss, and employee performance and morale are but a few examples of types of feedback that a foodservice manager must evaluate and utilize on a regular basis.

The memory element stores and updates information for use in the foodservice system. Inventory and financial records, forecasting and personnel records, and copies of menus with data on numbers and types of persons served are among the records that should be maintained in a foodservice system. Review of past records provides information to management for analyzing trends and making adjustments in the system.

QUALITY ASSURANCE IN THE FOODSERVICE SYSTEM

Assuring and improving quality is the theme of all industries in the 1980s, including the foodservice industry. Concern about declining quality of goods and services produced in the United States has led to a revival of managerial emphasis on quality standards and quality control in all types of organizations.

According to Thorner and Manning (1983), quality control and quality assurance are interchangeable terms, although quality assurance (QA) is gaining acceptance as the term applied to the process of defining quality standards and managing operations to ensure that quality goods and services are produced. Quality controls are essential at each step of an operation, from the development of procurement specifications through distribution and service to the clientele of the foodservice operation. Effective quality controls can mean the difference between substantial financial losses and profits. Clientele satisfaction, employee productivity, and financial accountability all depend on quality control throughout the foodservice system.

Figure 2.7 presents the foodservice system model with emphasis on quality assurance as a component of the control element. The organizational goals and objectives provide the beginning point for a quality assurance program. In the healthcare organization, for example, quality patient care is the overall goal to which each of the subsystems in the hospital system contribute.

The goals and objectives provide the basis for defining quality standards, which in turn are used for developing specific performance measures or criteria. The key to a quality assurance program is continuous monitoring to determine if quality standards are being maintained in all aspects of operations to ensure that

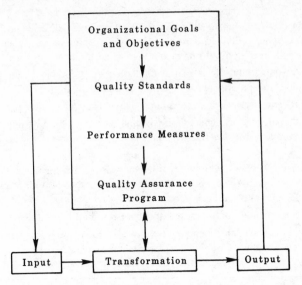

Figure 2.7. *Quality assurance in the foodservice system*

quality goods and services are produced. Feedback mechanisms are critical to provide information on the quality of both processes and products. The essence of quality assurance is determining the need for changes in inputs and/or transformation processes, and ensuring that necessary changes are made.

Among the first to give impetus to the establishment of formalized quality assurance programs was the healthcare segment of the foodservice industry. In 1979, the Joint Commission on Accreditation of Hospitals (JCAH) published the original quality assurance standard for hospitals. All JCAH standards, however, are designed to focus on the essential elements of quality care (JCAH, 1984). The major quality assurance standard for hospitals is as follows:

Standard I
There is an ongoing quality assurance program designed to objectively and systematically monitor and evaluate the quality and appropriateness of patient care, pursue opportunities to improve patient care, and resolve identified problems.

Standards are defined for dietetic services in the JCAH accreditation standards for hospitals, which are revised periodically, most recently in 1984. Currently, hospital dietetic services must demonstrate compliance with seven standards (Figure 2.8). The principle underlying these standards is that "dietetic services shall meet the nutritional needs of patients" (JCAH, 1984). In the latest edition of the accreditation standards manual, the requirements for quality assurance activities in dietetic services were revised to be consistent with the overall quality assurance standard for hospitals. In the revision, the monitoring and evaluation of patient care services in the dietetic department are emphasized as an ongoing systematic process through which opportunities to improve care are identified and important problems in patient care services are resolved.

Standard I.   The dietetic department/service shall be organized, directed and staffed, and integrated with other units and departments of the hospital in a manner designed to assure the provision of optimal nutritional care and quality foodservice.

Standard II.   Personnel shall be prepared for their responsibilities in the provision of dietetic services through appropriate training and education programs.

Standard III.   Dietetic services shall be guided by written policies and procedures.

Standard IV.   The dietetic department/service shall be designed and equipped to facilitate the safe, sanitary, and timely provision of foodservice to meet the nutritional needs of patients.

Standard V.   Dietetic services shall be provided to patients in accordance with a written order by the responsible practitioner, and appropriate dietetic information shall be recorded in the patient's medical record.

Standard VI.   Appropriate quality control mechanisms shall be established.

Standard VII.   As part of the hospital's quality assurance program, the quality and appropriateness of patient care services provided by the dietetic department/service are monitored and evaluated, and identified problems are resolved.

Figure 2.8.   *Accreditation standards for hospital dietetic services.* **Source: AMH/ 85–Accreditation Manual for Hospitals, 1984 edition. Copyright © 1985. Chicago: Joint Commission on Accreditation of Hospitals, 1984, pp. 9–16.**

Increased emphasis on quality control and quality assurance is evident in other segments of the foodservice industry as well. In 1982, the National Association of College and University Foodservices (NACUFS) published a professional standards manual, which defined standards and criteria to be used for self-monitoring or for a voluntary peer review program. Standards have been defined for all components of college and university foodservice operations.

Snyder (1981, 1983) described a quality assurance management system designed for use in the foodservice industry in Minnesota. The program is cosponsored by the Minnesota Department of Health and the Minnesota Restaurant Association and has as its objective the improvement of quality of foodservice operations in that state. In that program, quality assurance is defined as the management process by which customer expectations are met without error every time. Snyder indicated that the quality assurance program requires a participative management system in which employees are committed to, and involved in, maintaining quality standards.

The lodging segment of the industry is also beginning to place emphasis on quality assurance in hotel and motel operations. As described by Glover et al. (1984), the American Hotel and Motel Association's program is a formal framework for eliminating "slapdash" operations and replacing them with a consistent systematic approach to hotel management. The basic principle underlying the quality assurance program is that hotel operators should decide what services they want to offer their guests and see to it that high quality services are delivered.

Throughout this book, controls in all aspects of the system are emphasized. The critical importance of defining quality standards and monitoring operations to ensure adherence to these standards is stressed repeatedly. Achieving the goal of producing an acceptable quality product, served in an acceptable manner to the consumer, requires continuous diligence and surveillance. The foodservice manager is primarily responsible for ensuring the effectiveness of the quality assurance program.

SUMMARY

The systems approach has practical applications for foodservice organizations in meeting the challenges and demands of today's world. A system has been defined as an organized, integrated, or coordinated whole, composed of interrelated and interdependent parts. Characteristics of the system include dynamic equilibrium, equifinality, and permeability. Processes that link the system are communication, decision making, and balance. The systems approach to management encompasses a managerial philosophy, a method of analysis, and a managerial style. A foodservice systems model provides a logical method for viewing the organization in its totality, examining the interrelationships among the elements and subsystems of the foodservice system, and analyzing the system in relation to a continually changing environment.

Quality assurance in the foodservice system must be a high priority of management. The essence of quality assurance is the definition of quality standards and management of operations to ensure that quality goods and services are produced. Quality controls are essential throughout the foodservice system, from the development of procurement specifications to service to the clientele.

Formalized quality assurance programs are required in all aspects of a hospital's operation, including dietetic services. Standards for dietetic services include a requirement for an ongoing quality assurance program. Increased emphasis on quality assurance is evident in other segments of the foodservice industry as well, as managers are becoming increasingly aware that customers expect, and are entitled to, quality food and services.

REFERENCES

Adamow, C. L.: Self-assessment: A quality assurance tool. *J. Am. Dietet. A.* 81:62, 1982.

Allington, J. K., Matthews, M. E., and Johnson, N. E.: Methods for evaluating quality meals and implications for school food service. *School Food Serv. Res. Rev.* 5:68, 1981.

Bennett, A. C.: A picture of the hospital system. *Hosp. Topics* 51:25 (Apr.), 1973.

Bogle, M. L.: Implementing a quality assurance program. In Rose, J. C., ed.: *Handbook for Health Care Food Service Management.* Rockville, MD: Aspen Systems Corp., 1984.

Brown, W. B.: Systems, boundaries and information flow. *Acad. Mgmt. J.* 9:318 (Dec.), 1966.

Cleland, D. I., and King, W. R.: *Management: A Systems Approach.* New York: McGraw-Hill Book Co., 1972.

David, B. D.: A model for decision making. *Hospitals* 46:46 (Aug. 1), 1972.

Davis, L. E.: Individuals in the organization. *Calif. Mgmt. Rev.* 22:5 (Spring), 1980.

Drucker, P. F.: *Managing in Turbulent Times.* New York: Harper & Row, 1980.

Freshwater, J. F.: Future of foodservice systems. *Cornell Hotel Rest. Admin. Q.* 10:28 (Nov.), 1969.

Glover, W. G., Morrison, R. S., and Briggs, A. C.: Making quality count: Boca Raton's approach to Quality Assurance. *Cornell H.R.A. Quart.* 24:39 (May), 1984.

Gue, R. L.: An introduction to the systems approach in the dietary department. *Hospitals* 43:100 (Sept. 1), 1969.

Johnson, R. A., Kast, R. E., and Rosenzweig, J. E.: *The Theory and Management of Systems.* 2nd ed. New York: McGraw-Hill Book Co., 1973.

Joint Commission on Accreditation of Hospitals: *AMH/85—Accreditation Manual for Hospitals.* Chicago: Joint Commission on Accreditation of Hospitals, 1984.

Kast, R. E., and Rosenzweig, J. E.: *Organization and Management, A Systems and Contingency Approach.* 3rd ed. New York: McGraw-Hill Book Co., 1979.

Keiser, J.: Putting it all together . . . systems and the American hospital. *Food Mgmt.* 12:66 (Nov.), 1977.

King, D. C.: What the supervisor should know about . . . systems theory. Part 1. *Supervisory Mgmt.* 22:37 (Nov.), 1977.

King, D. C.: What the supervisor should know about . . . systems theory. Part 2. *Supervisory Mgmt.* 22:31 (Dec.), 1977.

Konnersman, P. M.: The dietary department as a logistics system. *Hospitals* 43:102 (Sept. 1), 1969.

Livingston, G. E.: Design of a food service system. *Food Technol.* 22:35 (Jan.), 1968.

Luchsinger, V. P., and Dock, V. T.: *Systems Approach: A Primer.* 2nd ed. Dubuque, IA: Kendall/Hunt Publishing Co., 1982.

Minor, L. J.: *Nutritional Standards.* Vol. 1. Westport, CT: AVI Publishing Co., 1983.

Minor, L. J.: *Sanitation, Safety, and Environmental Standards.* Vol. 2. Westport, CT: AVI Publishing Co., 1983.

National Association of College and University Food Services: *National Association of College and University Food Services Professional Standards Manual.* East Lansing, MI: Michigan State University, 1982.

Osterhaus, L. B.: Systems concepts for hospitals. *Hosp. Admin.* 14:57 (Summer), 1969.

Parsons, T.: *Structure and Process in Modern Societies.* New York: The Free Press, 1960.

Petit, T. A.: A behavioral theory of management. *Acad. Mgmt. J.* 10:346 (Dec.), 1967.

Powers, T. F.: A systems perspective for hospitality management. *Cornell Hotel Rest. Admin. Q.* 19:70 (May), 1978.

Richards, M. D. and Greenlaw, P. S.: *Management Decisions and Behavior.* Homewood, IL: Richard D. Irwin, 1972.

Schiller, R., and Bartlett, B.: Auditing dietetic services. Part III. *Hospitals* 53:118 (May 16), 1979.

Scott, W. G., and Mitchell, T. R.: *Organization Theory.* Rev. ed. Homewood, IL: Richard D. Irwin, 1972.

Scott, W. G.: Organization theory: An overview and an appraisal. *Acad. Mgmt. J.* 4:7 (Apr.), 1961.

Smalley, H. E.: The systems approach. *Hospitals* 46:50 (Feb. 1), 1972.

Snyder, O. P.: A model food service quality assurance system. *Food Technol.* 35:71 (Feb.), 1981.

Snyder, O. P.: A management system for foodservice quality assurance. *Food Technol.* 37:61 (Jun.), 1983.

Thorner, M. E., and Manning, P. B.: *Quality Control in Foodservice.* Rev. ed. Westport, CT: AVI Publishing Co., 1983.

Unklesbay, N.: Monitoring for quality control in alternative foodservice systems. *J. Am. Dietet. A.* 71:123, 1977.

Whyte, W. F.: *Human Relations in the Restaurant Industry.* New York: McGraw-Hill Book Co., 1948.

3

Managing Foodservice Systems

Management is a way of thinking as well as a method and a process. In the preface, we indicated that this book would approach the operational aspects of a foodservice system from the managerial perspective. In the discussion of the foodservice system in Chapter 2, the importance of management functions in coordination of the system was emphasized. In this chapter and the next, management concepts are introduced and reviewed to provide the necessary background for understanding the applications of these concepts to the various technical aspects of the foodservice system.

THE MANAGEMENT PROCESS

In the previous chapter, we defined management as a process whereby unrelated resources are integrated into a total system for accomplishment of objectives. Management was also described as the primary force within organizations that coordinates the activities of the subsystems, involving the functions of planning, organizing, staffing, leading, and controlling.

Management has also been explained as the process of "getting things done through other people." All of these definitions or descriptions, either directly or by implication, underscore the importance of managerial activity being directed toward achieving the goals and objectives of the organization.

Kast and Rosenzweig (1979) identify four basic elements of the management process.

- Toward objectives.
- Through people.
- Via techniques.
- In an organization.

Managers get things done by working with people and physical resources to accomplish the objectives of the system. They coordinate and integrate the activities of others. Managers facilitate conversion of diverse resources of people, machines, material, money, time, and space into a useful operation.

Managing Organizations

Although this book focuses on managing foodservice organizations, management concepts have broad applications because much of an individual's activity takes place within an organizational context. We are all members of a family, which is the basic unit of our society and the first organization in which most of us interact as members. We have spent a great deal of time in educational institutions. Also, everyone has been a member of many informal groups. Informal groups or organizations develop spontaneously when several people with common interests agree either implicitly or explicitly to pursue a common objective, which could be a shopping trip, a fishing trip, a picnic, or any other objective. Work organizations account for a large part of our time and other types of formal organizations provide activities that encompass much of our leisure time. Professional organizations, social clubs, and churches are examples of other organizations to which we belong.

The tendency to develop cooperative and interdependent relationships is a basic human characteristic. All organizations, ranging on a continuum from informal, ad hoc groups to formal, highly structured organizations, require managing (Figure 3.1). Organization is structured and integrated activity, or in other words people working together in interdependent relationships. The organization is where resources come together; the manager is responsible for coor-

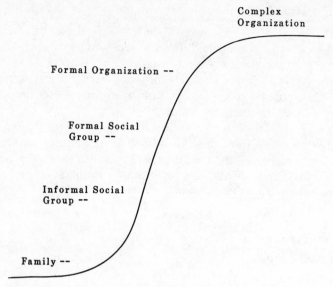

Figure 3.1. *Continuum of organizations*

dinating these resources in a sensible way. Managers are responsible for acquiring, organizing, and combining resources to accomplish goals. Although management is a process that applies to virtually every aspect of life—we plan activities, schedule our time, budget our money—in the context of this book, management will be viewed as a body of knowledge and a discipline practiced in various types of public and private work organizations.

Managerial Effectiveness

Management has also been described as the art of bringing ends and means together, or the art of purposeful action (American Institute of Management, 1959). Essentially then, it is a process that involves selection of a goal, the initiation of planned actions to reach it, and a continuous review of both the effectiveness of the actions and the efficacy of the goal. Above, we indicated that management concerns coordination of human and material resources; however, it is also concerned with morals, ethics, and ideals. The ends are determined by values and preferences and the means must be socially and morally acceptable. Management deals with problems of prediction; in other words, its chosen means operate under conditions unknown when plans are made. Some degree of uncertainty prevails in almost every situation faced by an organization and its managers.

Management can be described as having four dimensions: task, personnel, community, and institution. The task dimension is concerned with the performance aspect of the organization, with accomplishing objectives, and with producing goods and services, whereas the personnel dimension is directed toward the welfare of the people who comprise the organization. The community dimension encompasses management's social responsibility or concern for the public good, while the institution dimension is oriented toward responsibility for the good of the overall organization.

In the current rapidly changing times or, using Drucker's terminology (1980), today's turbulent times, an important role of managers is serving as change agents in an organization. In fact, much of the managerial task is concerned with determining how much of the future can be introduced today. As we discussed in the previous chapter, managers must continuously evaluate the changing social, economic, political, and technological conditions to assess applicability to their organizations.

Authority, responsibility, and accountability are concepts important to the process of management. Authority is delegated from the top level to lower levels of management and is the right of a manager to direct others and take actions because of his or her position in the organization. Responsibility is the obligation to perform an assigned activity or to see that someone else performs it. Since responsibility is an obligation a person accepts, it cannot be delegated or passed to another; in other words, the obligation remains with the person who accepted the responsibility. Accountability goes one step further than responsibility and is concerned with responsibility for achieving results, not only with an obligation to perform. In the systems context, management was described as a process for accomplishment of objectives, implying, therefore, that accountability is an integral aspect of the managerial role.

Managers must show results in today's inflationary era, in which scarce resources are increasingly a concern. Efficient and effective use of these resources to yield desired results is requisite to maintaining a viable organization. In contemporary jargon, efficiency is described as "doing things right" while effectiveness is defined as "doing the right things."

Managerial efficiency—that is, the ability to get things done correctly—is an "input-output" concept. An efficient manager is one who achieves outputs by using minimum inputs or resources to produce them. Managers who are able to reduce the cost of the resources they use to attain their goals are acting efficiently. Effectiveness, on the other hand, is the ability to choose appropriate objectives; therefore, an effective manager is one who selects the right things to accomplish.

The foodservice manager who plans a menu featuring chicken and dumplings when the customer would prefer fried chicken and french fries may be performing efficiently but not effectively. No amount of efficiency can compensate for lack of effectiveness. Drucker (1964), one of the first management authorities to discuss efficiency and effectiveness in relation to managerial performance, has stated that the question is not how to do things right but how to find the right things to do and to concentrate resources and efforts on them. Thus, effectiveness is at the heart of accountability.

Ineffective Management

In many organizations, including foodservice organizations, many examples of ineffective management can be seen. Some examples of ineffective managers follow.

- *The commandant.* The autocrat, the "I'm the boss and don't you ever forget it" type.
- *The nice guy, but.* The likeable manager who won't make a decision.
- *The mobile manager.* The manager who is going many ways simultaneously, who starts much and finishes little.
- *The petty bureaucrat.* The manager who "goes by the books," is very inflexible and rule oriented.
- *The free wheeler.* The manager who always has a deal going.
- *The panic button boss.* The crisis manager, the manager who is "out of one kettle of hot water and into another."
- *The empire builder.* The manager concerned with building power in his or her own unit and "to heck" with the organization.
- *The climber.* The opportunist, the person concerned with personal opportunities rather than organizational objectives.
- *The ostrich.* The manager who hopes the problem will go away and "buries his or her head in the sand."
- *The buck passer.* The "it's all your fault" manager.

These and other types of dysfunctional managerial behaviors contribute to ineffective performance. The goal of this chapter is to assist the reader in understanding effective managerial practices.

TYPES OF MANAGERS

The term manager has been used up to this point to refer to anyone who is responsible for people and other organizational resources. An organization, however, has different types of managers with diverse tasks and responsibilities. Managers can be classified by level in the organization and also by the nature of their organizational responsibilities.

Managerial Levels

In most organizations, there are three managerial levels (Figure 3.2): first line, middle, and top. The first line or first level managers are generally responsible for supervising operating employees and do not supervise other managers. In the foodservice organization, these first line or first level managers are usually referred to as foodservice supervisors, whereas in manufacturing organizations the term frequently used is foreman. Their functional responsibilities may be indicated as part of the title for foodservice supervisors. For example, in a college residence hall foodservice, first line supervisors may include a production supervisor, a service supervisor, and a sanitation supervisor.

In Chapter 2, we presented a model (Figure 2.4) of an organization that

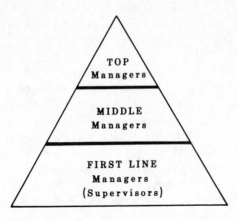

Figure 3.2. *Managerial levels in an organization*

depicted the three levels as technical, organizational, and institutional. The first line supervisors function at the technical core and are responsible for day-to-day operational activities.

Middle management may refer to more than one level in an organization, depending on the complexity of the organization. The primary responsibility of middle managers is to coordinate the activities that implement policies of the organization and to facilitate activities at the technical level. Middle managers direct the activities of other managers and sometimes those of operating employees. These middle managers are also responsible for facilitating communications between the lower and upper levels of the organization. Middle managers function at the organizational level in the model presented previously.

To continue with the example of the college residence hall foodservice, one or more middle managers may be responsible for coordinating each of the various units that make up the residence hall foodservice department. On a university campus there may be three foodservice centers, each of which would have a unit manager and an assistant unit manager. Within each of the units, the functional supervisors, or first level managers mentioned above, would report to the unit managers, who in turn would report to the campus foodservice director.

Top management is responsible for the overall management of the organization. It establishes operating policies and guides the organization's interactions with its environment. Referring back to the organizational model in Chapter 2, these managers operate at the institutional level of the organization.

In the example we have been developing thus far of the college residence hall foodservice, the campus foodservice director would be considered a top level manager. If we applied this analysis to the overall organization, however, the university president would be the top manager and the foodservice director would be considered a middle manager.

You may recall that in Chapter 2 we discussed application of systems concepts to the organization and indicated that the unit of analysis could be the overall organization, such as a university or a hospital, or one of its subunits, the foodservice department, if we wish to analyze it in detail, viewing it as a system and the units within it as the subsystems. The concept of organizational levels can be applied in much the same way. Our concern might be the overall organization or it may be a particular division within the organization. The concept of levels of management would vary depending on whether we are looking at the overall organization or a division or department, as in the example above of a university.

Top managers of the overall organization are the chief executive officers and are generally referred to as the president. In commercial organizations or in universities, for example, the chief executive officer is called president. In hospitals, the term frequently used is administrator; however, the titles of president or chief executive officer are becoming the accepted titles. Other top level managers who serve directly under the president or administrator are often referred to as vice presidents or assistant administrators.

The term most frequently used for the top level foodservice administrator in college foodservice is foodservice director, whereas, in a hospital, the administrator in charge of the dietetics department may be referred to as director of dietetics, director of nutrition and dietetics, or chief dietitian. The title foodservice director is the one most commonly used in the school foodservice.

The lower level managers in foodservice organizations are often employees who work up through the ranks of the organization and may not have formal training in foodservice management. In the institutional segment of the industry, however, many first line supervisors have completed a training program for dietary managers, which is a program offered at vocational technical schools, as a one-year program at a junior or community college, or by correspondence. Increasingly, in healthcare organizations, dietetic technicians are being employed as first level supervisors because of the complexity of the job. Generally, a technician is a person who has completed a two-year associate degree program. Middle and upper level managers are professionally trained in most instances, particularly in institutional foodservices. This is not as true in the commercial segment of the industry; however, more and more the large foodservice companies are recruiting persons with college degrees.

Functional and General Managers

Earlier in this chapter, we discussed types of managers by their level in the organization; managers can also be classified according to the range of organizational activities for which they are responsible. In this second classification, managers can be considered either as general or functional managers.

The functional manager is responsible for only one area of organizational activity, such as procurement, production, service, or sanitation. The people responsible to a functional manager will be engaged in a closely related set of activities.

A general manager, on the other hand, is responsible for all the activities of that unit. Referring back to the college residence hall foodservice discussed above, the unit manager would be an example of a general manager.

A small organization may have only one general manager, but a larger, more complex organization may have several. In our university residence hall organization example, the unit managers and assistant unit managers at the three foodservice centers and the campus foodservice director would all be considered general managers. Depending on the size of the units, two or more functional managers may be responsible for various areas of activity within each of the units.

ROLES OF MANAGERS

Mintzberg (1980) describes the manager's job in terms of various roles, which he refers to as organized sets of behaviors identified with a position. He defines a manager as being that person in charge of an organization or one of its units who is vested with formal authority over the organization or unit. From formal authority comes status, which leads to various interpersonal relationships, access to information, and authority to make decisions and develop strategies for an organization or unit thereof.

Mintzberg depicts the manager's job as being comprised of ten roles, shown in Figure 3.3. As shown in the figure, the formal authority of a manager gives rise to three interpersonal roles, three informational roles, and four decisional roles.

Interpersonal Roles

The interpersonal roles are figurehead, leader, and liaison. The figurehead role has been described by some authorities on management as the representational responsibility or function of management. By virtue of a manager's role as head of an organization or unit, duties of a ceremonial nature must be performed. These ceremonial duties may involve written communication or an appearance at an important function. For example, a manager's ceremonial tasks may include

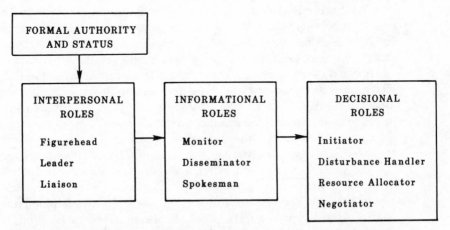

Figure 3.3. *Managerial roles.* **Adapted from *H. Mintzberg, "The Manager's Job: Folklore and Fact." Harvard Business Review, Vol. 53, Jul./Aug. 1975, p. 55.**

greeting a group of touring dignitaries or signing certificates for a group of employees who have completed a training program.

As the manager in charge of an organization or unit, the manager is responsible for the work of the staff. Actions related to this responsibility constitute the leader role. These responsibilities range from hiring and training employees to creating an environment that will motivate the staff. Mintzberg contends the influence of the manager is most clearly seen in the leader role. While formal authority vests the manager with great potential power, leadership determines, in large measure, how much of it he or she will realize. A manager must encourage employees and assist them in reconciling their needs with the goals of the organization.

The manager must also play the interpersonal role of liaison by dealing with people other than subordinates or superiors. These contacts are both internal and external to the organization. Managers must relate effectively to peers in other departments of the organization and to suppliers, clients, and others outside of it. Depending on a manager's level in the organization, the responsibility for liaison relationships will vary. In Mintzberg's research, the company chief executives he studied averaged 44 percent of their contact time with people outside their organizations. The liaison role is important in building a manager's information system.

Informational Roles

Mintzberg suggests that communication may be the most important aspect of a manager's job. A manager needs information to make sound decisions, and others in a manager's unit or organization depend on information they receive from and transmit through the manager. The informational roles of a manager are those of monitor, disseminator, and spokesman.

As monitor, the manager is constantly searching for information to use to become more effective. The manager queries liaison contacts and subordinates and must be alert to unsolicited information that may result from the network of contacts he or she has developed. The manager collects this information in many forms and must be alert to implications for the organization.

In the disseminator role, the manager transmits information to subordinates who otherwise would probably have no access to this information. An important aspect of the disseminator role is decisions about which staff members need what pieces of information. The manager must also take the responsibility and invest the time to disseminate information that will assist staff members to be well informed and have information, thus assisting them in being more effective.

The spokesman role of the manager is closely akin to the figurehead role. In the spokesman role, the manager sends information to people outside the organization or unit. The administrator of a hospital, for example, must keep the hospital board apprised of the problems and needs of the hospital; similarly, the director of dietetics must keep the administrator well informed about the problems of the dietetics department. The spokesman role may also include providing information to legislators, suppliers, and community groups, among others. For example, the school foodservice director should provide information to a variety of groups, such as parents, the school board, and students.

Decisional Roles

The manager plays the major role in the decision making system of the organization. Because of the formal authority vested in a manager, he or she can commit the unit to new courses of action and determine a unit's strategy. As Mintzberg indicates, the informational roles provide the manager the basic inputs for decision making. The manager has information on which to make a set of decisions for the unit. The decisional roles include those of initiator, disturbance handler, resource allocator, and negotiator.

As initiator, the manager seeks to improve the unit and adapt it to changing conditions in the environment. In the monitor role, the manager is constantly searching for new ideas that may have implications for the overall organization. The initiator role may involve a decision to change the menu, to build a new unit, or to change the decor. As an initiator, the manager implements change in the organization. Earlier in this chapter, we described the manager as a change agent and emphasized the importance of change to keep an organization vital.

In the role of disturbance handler, the manager responds to situations that are beyond his or her control. In this role, the manager must act because the pressures of the situation are too severe to be ignored—a strike looms, a supplier fails to provide goods or services, and the like. While a good manager attempts to avoid crisis situations, no organization is so well run or so systematized that every contingency in the uncertain environment can be avoided. Disturbances may arise because poor managers ignore situations until they reach crisis proportions, but good managers are also confronted with occasional crises with which they must deal.

As resource allocator, the manager decides how and to whom the resources of the organization will be distributed. In authorizing the important decisions of a unit, the manager must keep in mind its overall needs but must also consider priorities from the standpoint of the overall system. These decisions, then, will often involve compromise.

The final decisional role is that of negotiator. Managers have the responsibility to serve as negotiators in the organization because only they have the information and authority that negotiations require. Negotiations may involve working out complex contracts with suppliers or less formal negotiations within the organization. For example, the chief dietitian in a hospital may negotiate with nursing service about provision of space for clinical dietitians in the patient areas.

MANAGEMENT SKILLS

Katz (1974) has identified three basic types of skills—technical, human, and conceptual—which he says are needed by all managers. The relative importance of these three skills varies, however, with the level of managerial responsibility. Katz describes a skill as an ability that can be developed and that is manifested in performance. He describes the manager as one who directs the activities of others and who undertakes the responsibility for achieving certain objectives through these efforts. Technical, human, and conceptual skills are interrelated but are examined separately in the paragraphs below to assist the reader in understanding them.

Technical Skill

Technical skill involves an understanding of, and proficiency in, a specific kind of activity, particularly one involving methods or techniques. Technical skill requires specialized knowledge, analytical ability, and expertise in use of tools and techniques. The manager needs enough technical skill to understand and supervise activities in his or her area of responsibilities. The foodservice manager must understand quantity food production, operation of institutional equipment, and so forth. Technical expertise is important so that managers know the right questions to ask subordinates and have the ability to evaluate operations, train employees, and respond in crisis situations.

Human Skill

Human skill is the manager's ability to work effectively as a group member and to build cooperative efforts within the group he or she leads. Human skill, thus, is primarily concerned with working with people and involves understanding human behavior. Effective communication is an important aspect of this skill. Human skill is vital to everything a manager does and must be consistently demonstrated in a manager's actions. It must become an integral part of his or her behavior, because everything a manager says or does has an effect on staff. The importance of human skills is apparent. As Katz indicates, human skill cannot be a "sometime thing." Skillfulness in working with others must be a natural, continuous activity that involves being sensitive to the needs and motivation of others in the organization.

Katz describes two aspects of human skill: leadership within the manager's own unit and skill in intergroup relationships. This description of human skills is similar to Mintzberg's interpersonal roles of leader and liaison. Both of these authors emphasize the importance of a manager being effective in working with staff within his or her organizational unit and in working effectively with people outside the unit. The campus foodservice director described previously in this chapter must work effectively with the three unit managers within the foodservice department and also relate effectively to the housing director, the head of maintenance, and the campus purchasing director, among others.

Conceptual Skill

Conceptual skill is the ability to see the organization as a whole and to recognize how the various functions of the organization depend on one another and how changes in one part affect other parts. Conceptual skill also involves the ability to understand the organization within the environmental context; in other words, the relationships of the organization within the community, to other similar organizations, and to suppliers and others. It also includes understanding the potential impact of political, social, and economic forces on the organization. From this description, conceptual skill is obviously, in large measure, a systems approach to managing an organization. A manager needs conceptual skill to recognize how the various forces in a given situation are interrelated so the actions he or she takes will be in the best interest of the overall organization.

Katz describes conceptual skill as a "general management point of view" that involves thinking in terms of relative priorities among conflicting objectives, probabilities of occurrence, and relationships among elements of an organization. Development of conceptual ability depends to some extent on a manager's degree of experience.

Management Levels and Managerial Skills

Although all three skills are important at every managerial level, the technical, human, and conceptual skills used by managers vary at different levels of responsibility (Figure 3.4). Technical skill is most important at the lower levels of management and becomes less important as we move up the organization. The production supervisor, for example, is called upon to use technical skills frequently in supervising employees in day-to-day operations. These technical skills are important in evaluating products, in training employees, and in problem solving.

The middle manager uses technical skills in performing the tasks of evaluating operations and selecting employees who have appropriate skills to perform the various jobs in the organization. Also, in crisis situations, the middle manager's technical skills may be called into action. Top level managers, although not involved in day-to-day operations for the most part, need understanding of technical operations to enable them to be effective in strategic long-range planning.

Human skill, the ability to work effectively with others, is essential at every

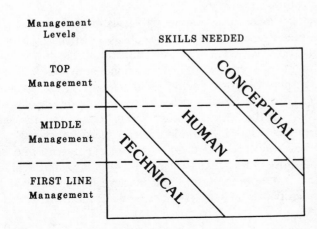

Figure 3.4. *Skill mix at various organizational levels.* **Adapted from Hersey, P., and Blanchard, K.: Management of Organizational Behavior: Utilizing Human Resources. 4th ed. Englewood Cliffs, NJ: Prentice-Hall, 1982.**

level of management, as reflected in the diagram (Figure 3.4). The first line manager, who is responsible for daily supervision of operating employees, must be effective in guiding and leading these individuals to accomplish the day-to-day activities for which they are responsible. These employees must be motivated to produce quality products, to serve customers or patients cheerfully, to wash dishes properly, and so forth. The morale and satisfaction of these operational employees is important to their effective performance.

Middle managers, because of their pivotal role in the organization, must be particularly effective in human skills. These managers must work effectively in leading their own groups and must also be effective in relating to other parts of the organization and to their superiors. At the top level of the organization, the manager must be particularly effective in working with people outside the organization.

The importance of <u>conceptual skill</u> increases as we move up the ranks of the organization. The higher a manager is in the hierarchy, the greater the involvement in broad, long-range decisions affecting large parts of the organization. At the top level of an organization, conceptual skill becomes the most important skill of all for successful administrators. If conceptual skills of top administrators are weak, the success of the whole organization may be jeopardized.

SUMMARY

Management is the process whereby unrelated resources are integrated into a system for the accomplishment of an organization's objectives. It is also the primary force within organizations responsible for coordinating subsystems' activities. Managers must continually evaluate changing social, economic, political, and technological conditions to assess applicability to their organizations. Authority, responsibility, and accountability are concepts important to the process of management. Also, efficiency and effectiveness are both important in the managerial task, meaning that managers must not only do the right things but must do the right things right.

In most organizations, three managerial levels exist: first line, middle, and top. Level in the organization influences the role and responsibility of managers. Managers can also be classified as general or functional. The functional manager has responsibility for only one area of organizational activities, whereas the general manager is responsible for all activities in a foodservice organization.

The manager's job can also be viewed as being made up of various roles. These roles evolve from the formal authority and status of the manager and can be classified as interpersonal, informational, and decisional.

Managerial skills have been defined as technical, human, and conceptual. The relative importance of these skills varies with level of managerial responsibility. Technical skills are more important at lower levels, whereas conceptual skills are the primary emphasis in top level positions. Human skills, however, are important at all managerial levels, since the essence of management is getting work done through other people.

REFERENCES

Adizes, I.: Mismanagement styles. *Calif. Mgmt. Rev.* 19:5 (Winter), 1976.

Am. Institute Mgmt.: *What is management?* New York: Am. Mgmt. Assoc. 1959.

Brush, D. H.: Technical knowledge or managerial skills? Recruiting graduates who have both. *Personnel J.* 58:771, 1979.

Burack, E. H., and Mathys, N. J.: *Introduction to Management: A Career Perspective.* New York: John Wiley & Sons, 1983.

Connor, P. E.: *Dimensions in Management.* 3rd ed. Boston: Houghton Mifflin Co., 1982.

Drucker, P. F.: *Managing for Results.* New York: Harper & Row, 1964.

Drucker, P. F.: *Managing in Turbulent Times.* New York: Harper & Row, 1980.

Haimann, T., Scott, W. G., and Connor, P. E.: *Management.* 4th ed. Boston: Houghton Mifflin Co., 1982.

Hersey, P., and Blanchard, K. H.: *Management of Organizational Behavior: Utilizing Human Resources.* 4th ed. Englewood Cliffs, NJ: Prentice-Hall, 1982.

Hoover, L. W.: Enhancing managerial effectiveness in dietetics. *J. Am. Dietet. A.* 82:58, 1983.

Kast, F. E., and Rosenzweig, J. E.: *Organization and Management, A Systems and Contingency Approach.* 3rd ed. New York: McGraw-Hill Book Co., 1979.

Katz, R. L.: Skills of an effective administrator. *Harvard Bus. Rev.* 52:90 (Sept./Oct.), 1974.

Koontz, H.: The management theory jungle revisited. *Acad. Mgmt. Rev.* 5:175, 1980.

Koontz, H., O'Donnell, C., and Weihrich, H.: *Management.* 7th ed. New York: McGraw-Hill Book Co., 1980.

Mintzberg, H.: The manager's job: Folklore and fact. *Harvard Bus. Rev.* 53:49 (Jul./Aug.), 1975.

Mintzberg, H.: *The Nature of Managerial Work.* Englewood Cliffs, NJ: Prentice-Hall, 1980.

Scanlon, B., and Keys, B.: *Management and Organizational Behavior.* 2nd ed. New York: John Wiley & Sons, 1983.

Stone, J. A.: *Management.* 2nd ed. Englewood Cliffs, NJ: Prentice-Hall, 1982.

4

Management Functions

The five management functions are planning, organizing, staffing, leading, and controlling. Management performs these functions in the process of coordinating the activities of the subsystems of the organization. Now that insights have been provided into the manager's many roles and responsibilities, the activities or functions of managers will be examined in greater detail in this chapter.

The interrelationship of the management functions is depicted in Figure 4.1, and the integral nature of the linking processes in performing these functions is illustrated. Although in practice managers find themselves performing several management functions simultaneously, these functions will be discussed separately. The two-way arrows in the diagram are used to illustrate the interdependency among the functions. For example, managerial plans provide the basis for control, and staff selected in the staffing function become the employees who must be led in achieving organizational objectives.

PLANNING

Definition of Planning

Plans, which are the result of the managerial process of planning, establish the organizational objectives and set up the procedures for reaching them. Plans

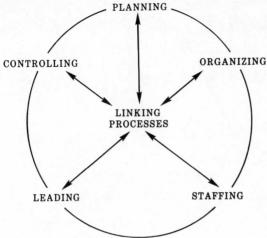

Figure 4.1. *Management functions*

provide the basis for obtaining and committing resources to reach objectives and for selecting members of the organization to carry on activities consistent with the objectives. Plans also provide the standards for monitoring performance of the organization and taking corrective action if deemed necessary.

Planning is defined as determining in advance what should happen and must be a continuing function of managers. Planning goes on while a manager organizes, staffs, leads, and controls and is the foundation of these other functions. Until activities are planned, managers cannot organize their implementation, or determine the number and types of workers needed and how to encourage productive performance. Without plans, managers do not have a basis for controlling activities. Planning, thus, is the basis, either directly or indirectly, of the other managerial functions.

The hierarchy of plans is shown in Figure 4.2. The initial plans established are the goals and objectives of the organization, which provide the basis for objectives of the organization's various units. Once the objectives are determined, more specific plans can be established for achieving them in a more systematic manner, with policies, procedures, standards, and methods. Policies are the guidelines for action in an organization, whereas procedures and methods define steps for implementation.

Dimensions of Planning

In Chapter 2, we identified plans as internal controls of the system and the two types of plans as standing and single-use. This distinction of standing versus single-use plans illustrates the planning dimensions of repetitiveness. Planning can be thought of as a continuum of repetitiveness—planning for novel, one-time projects as against development of policies and procedures for activities occurring repeatedly in organizations. Another relevant dimension of planning is the time

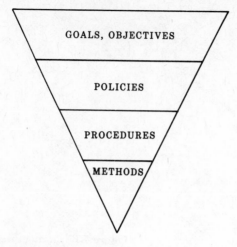

Figure 4.2. *Hierarchy of plans*

span. Planning may be considered in relation to day-to-day activities or in terms of long-term goals and objectives. Similarly, the scope of planning may vary from broad, comprehensive plans to specific, functionally oriented activities. Planning should also be considered from the standpoint of organizational level involved and the dimension of flexibility required. Some plans may be highly fixed and others may be more flexible, capable of adaptation to a variety of changing conditions.

Standing vs. Single-Use Plans

Figure 4.3 shows the relationships of standing and single-use plans to objectives. As illustrated in the diagram, organizational objectives provide the basis for developing standing plans and single-use plans. Standing plans are those that are used over and over again, whereas single-use or single-purpose plans are designed

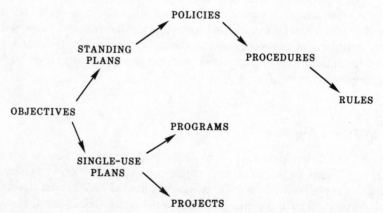

Figure 4.3. *Relationship of objectives and standing and single-use plans*

Policies	*Procedures*
• Guide decision making throughout the organization	• Specific guides to action
• Delimit an area within which a decision can be made	• Series of steps to complete a task arranged in predetermined best order
• Based on goals and objectives of the organization	• Step-by-step ordering of actions to be performed by workers
• Give direction for action	
• Established by governing body and/or top level management	

Figure 4.4. *Characteristics of policies and procedures*

to attain specific objectives. A single-use plan in a foodservice organization might be a major program for the design, development, and construction of a central food processing facility on a university campus or a plan for a "monotony breaker" in a college residence hall foodservice or a New Year's Eve celebration at a country club.

Plans for repetitive action—the policies, procedures and rules—are important to any established organization. Standing plans are a primary cohesive force connecting the various subsystems of an organization. They become the "habit patterns" of the organization.

Policies, Procedures, Methods, and Rules. Policies are the broadest of the standing plans and are general guides to organizational behavior. Organizations should have a wide variety of policies covering the most important functions. Frequently these policies are formalized and available in policy and procedure manuals. Characteristics of policies and procedures are listed in Figure 4.4.

Procedures and methods establish more definite steps for the performance of certain activities and are developed particularly for use at the technical level of the system. While procedures show a sequence of activities or chronological order, methods—which are even more detailed—relate to only one step, explaining exactly how that step should be performed.

Rules are another type of standing plan which specify action, stating what must or must not be done. Rules pertain whenever or wherever they are in effect; a no-smoking rule is an example. Requirements to wear a specific kind of uniform and hairnet in the production area of a foodservice operation are other examples of rules. A policy and one of its implementing procedures for a hospital department of dietetics are shown in Figure 4.5.

Types of Policies. Policies may be classified as originated, appealed, implied, and externally imposed. Originated policies are those developed by top management for the express purpose of guiding subordinates in the organization. They flow from the objective of the organization.

Policy

All diet orders, as prescribed by the physician, are given to the dietetics department in writing by the nursing department.

    Purpose: To ensure understanding and accuracy of diet orders, written orders are required.

Procedure

1 The diet order sheets are prepared by the night nursing shift and sent to the dietetics department by 6:30 a.m.

2 The day nursing shift sends changes or additions by 11:00 a.m. each day, and the evening shift sends changes by 4:00 p.m.

3 The appropriate forms are used by nursing service for ordering diets:

    a Dietary Changes Form. Used for transfers, holds, isolation, new admissions, diet changes, no trays, special requests, and dismissals

    b Modified Diet Order Form. Used for ordering modified diets as prescribed by the physician; these must be signed by the registered nurse on the unit and sent to the dietetics department as soon as possible after the order is made

4 Orders for new diets or changes that occur during meal time may be given by phone to the dietetics department followed by a written form from nursing.

Figure 4.5. *An example of a policy and procedure from a hospital*

In practice, many policies stem from appeal of exceptional cases up the managerial hierarchy. As appeals are taken upward and decisions are made, policies become established by the precedents of these managerial actions. Appealed policies are sometimes incomplete and uncoordinated and establish unintended precedents. Not uncommonly, organizations may have policies developed for a particular situation that are no longer needed yet continue to be operational.

Implied policies are those that develop from actions that people see and believe to constitute policy. Implied policies may develop because stated policies are not put into practice or do not exist. Externally imposed policies are those developed in response to government regulations or other external sources of influence. For example, labor unions may impose a policy on managers in the area of employee relations through the collective bargaining process.

Advantage and Disadvantage of Standing Plans. An advantage of the standing plan is that it creates a uniformity of operations throughout the system. Once established, understood, and accepted, the standing plan provides similarity of action in meeting certain situations; on the negative side, however, standing plans may create resistance to change.

Management by exception is an important concept in relation to standing plans. While the standing plans serve as guidelines for decision making, upper levels of management must become involved when situations occur that appear to be exceptions to policy or when existing policies do not cover the situation in question.

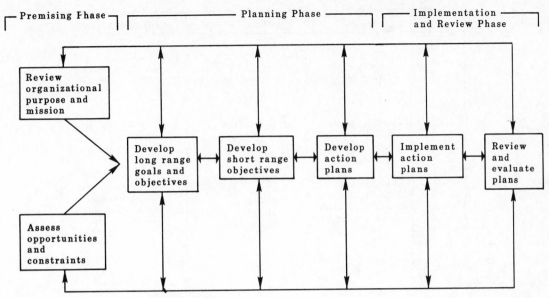

Figure 4.6. *A long-range planning model*

Time Span

The time span for planning refers to short-range versus long-range planning. Long-range or strategic planning is concerned with decisions regarding the broad technological aspects of the organization, the allocation of resources over an extended period of time, and the long-run integration of the organization with its environment. In recent years, long-range planning has received more emphasis in all types of organizations. Long-range planning in most organizations encompasses a five-year planning cycle; however, a longer range view may be important for some aspects of planning such as a major building program. Long-range planning begins with an assessment of the current environment and projections about changes and also involves reviewing and refining or developing a mission statement. As shown in Figure 4.6, this assessment phase provides the information for developing long-range plans, which in turn provide the basis for developing short-range objectives or intermediate plans and then specific action plans.

Scope

Another useful dimension in thinking about planning is that of scope. Scope refers to the continuum of plans, from broad and comprehensive to detailed and specific. The dimension of scope applies to all types of plans of an organization—goals and objectives, standing plans, and single-use plans. In Figure 4.7, examples are given of broad and more detailed plans within each of these three categories.

The objectives of the organization are the broadest type of goals; however, an organization also has more specific goals, such as performance standards. A performance standard for a foodservice organization might be the number of

	GOALS	STANDING PLANS	SINGLE-USE PLANS
(Broad)	Objectives (Missions)	Policies	General Programs
SCOPE	Budgets and Deadlines	Organization Structure	Projects
(Detail)	Performance Standards for Expense, Quality, Quantity, etc.	Standard Procedures, Standard Methods, Specifications, etc.	Personnel Assignments, Detailed Schedules, Methods, etc.

Figure 4.7. *Scope of plans*

meals per labor hour, a specified percentage of revenue dollar for food cost, or the number of customers a waitress might serve during a luncheon period.

A policy is a broad type of standing plan, whereas procedures and methods in an organization are much more specific. Programs are broad single-use plans, whereas projects are more specific ones.

An organization will have only a few broad plans but many very specific plans, as depicted in Figure 4.8. A school foodservice division in a school district, for example, may have only two broad goals, one concerned with provision of nutritious meals within federal and state guidelines and budgetary constraints, and another concerned with nutrition education. Many policies would be needed, however, to achieve these goals and assure uniformity of operations throughout the various schools in the district. An even greater number of procedures would be needed to give school foodservice employees specific instructions on implementation of the various policies.

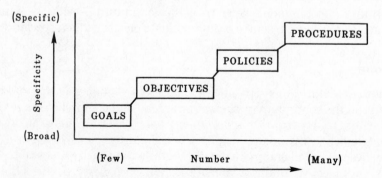

Figure 4.8. *Relationship of number and specificity of plans*

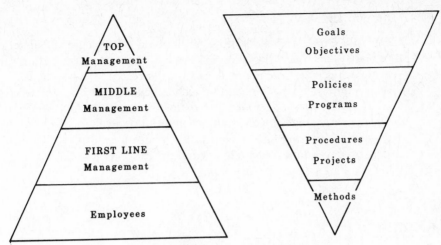

Figure 4.9. *Planning responsibilities by level of management*

Level of Management

A relationship exists between the scope of plans and the level of management involved in the planning effort (Figure 4.9). Generally, top managers who function at the institutional level of the organization are responsible for broad comprehensive planning. Middle managers, at the organizational or coordinative level, are responsible for medium-range plans, and managers at the technical or operational level are responsible for developing specific short-range plans.

This differentiation of planning responsibility in relation to managerial levels in the organization helps explain the skill mix used by managers that was discussed in Chapter 3. In the discussion of the three managerial skills—technical, human, and conceptual—the importance of conceptual skills at the top levels of the organization and, conversely, the importance of technical skills at the lower level were emphasized. The responsibility of these managers for broad versus specific operational plans should make these concepts more clear. Since long-range plans are broad and futuristically oriented, upper levels of managers must have conceptual ability, enabling them to view the overall organization in relation to its environment. By the same token, the first line manager must be well versed on technical operations because of the responsibility for planning day-to-day production and service activities.

To apply these concepts to a foodservice organization, the top management of a large national fast food company is concerned with such issues as identifying sites for new locations, assessing the impact of adding new menu items on costs, revenues, and profits, and projecting capital required for expansion. The manager of one of the units, however, would be concerned with scheduling employees, predicting the impact of bad weather on customer traffic, and ordering a sufficient supply of french fries for the next day's operations. As managers move up in the organization, they must develop skills in longer range planning.

Flexibility

One of the major considerations in planning is the degree of rigidity or flexibility of plans. This dimension presents a dilemma for managers. Long-range planning involves decision making which commits resources over the long run. On the other hand, the rapidly changing technology, competitive and market situations, and political pressures make forecasting extremely difficult. More thorough planning at early stages involves risk of inflexibility in the face of inevitable changes. Organizations may have to compromise on the rigidity versus flexibility dimension by developing relatively fixed short-range operations plans and the more flexible long-range strategic plans.

ORGANIZING

Organizing involves the establishment of a structure of roles by determining and enumerating the activities required to achieve the goals of the organization and each part of it. Organizing also involves grouping activities, delegating authority to carry out activities, and providing for coordination of relationships, both horizontally and vertically. An overview of the organizing function is included in this chapter; in Section VI, organization charts, departmentalization, job descriptions, and related concepts will be discussed in depth in Chapter 17.

The outcome of the organizing process is the development of the formal organization depicted by the organization chart. An example of an organization chart for a university residence hall foodservice department is shown in Figure 4.10. Once managers have established objectives and developed plans or pro-

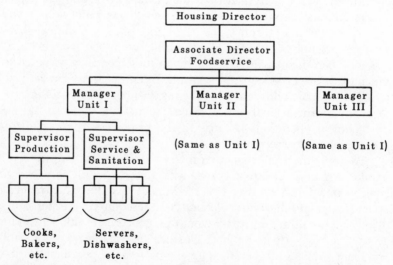

Figure 4.10. *Organization chart for a university residence hall foodservice department*

grams to reach them, they must design an organization to carry out these plans successfully.

Different objectives will require different kinds of organizations. For example, an organization for a fast food operation will be far different from one for an upscale gourmet restaurant. By the same token, the organization of a 50-bed nursing home foodservice department will differ markedly from a 500-bed teaching hospital. Managers must have the ability to determine what type of organization will be needed to accomplish a given set of objectives. The process of organizing is determining the way in which work is to be arranged and allocated among organization members so that the organization's goals can be achieved effectively.

Concepts of Organizing

Organizing is a dynamic process based on two concepts, span of management and authority. Span of management, sometimes referred to as span of control, is concerned with the number of people any one person can supervise effectively. Because that number is limited, organizations must be departmentalized by areas of activity, with someone in charge of each area. Authority is the basis through which we command work.

Span of Management

Managers cannot supervise unlimited numbers of workers. The determination of the appropriate number is a difficult problem. A number of factors come into play in determining the proper span.

- *Organizational policies.* Clear complete policies can reduce the time managers must spend making decisions. The more comprehensive the policies, the larger the span of management can be.

- *Availability of staff experts.* Managers can have increased span if staff experts are available to provide advice and services.

- *Competence of staff.* Well-trained competent workers can perform their jobs without close supervision, thus freeing managers to increase their span of management.

- *Objective standards.* In organizations in which objective standards have been established, workers have a basis with which to gauge their own progress, thus freeing managers to concentrate on exceptions. As a result, larger spans are possible.

- *Nature of the work.* Less complicated work tends to require less supervision than more complicated work. Generally, the simpler and more uniform the work, the larger the possible span.

Authority

Authority was defined in the last chapter as the right of a manager to direct others and to take action because of the position he or she holds in the organization. This authority is delegated down the hierarchy of the organization in those areas so designated by upper management. A sound organizing effort, therefore, includes defining job activities and scopes of authority for each position in the organization.

As we indicated previously, responsibility is a concept closely related to authority, and refers to obligation to perform an assigned activity. If a person accepts a job, he or she agrees to carry out its duties or see that someone else carries them out. Since responsibility is an obligation a person accepts, it cannot be delegated or passed to a subordinate; that is, the obligation remains with the person who accepted the job. Authority, however, must be delegated to enable individuals to carry out their responsibilities or obligations. Without proper authority, first line and middle managers may find completion of delegated job activities difficult.

Delegation is the process of assigning job activities to specific individuals within the organization. Through this process, authority and responsibility are transferred to lower level personnel within an organization. In a sense, delegation is the essence of management, since management has been defined as getting work done through other people.

Failure to delegate is a weakness common to many managers. Managers often do not delegate as much as they should because of the time and effort required to communicate clearly to others what they want done and to ensure that the task is proceeding as directed. All too frequently, managers believe that "it is easier to do it yourself" or "if you want a job done right, do it yourself."

Effective delegation, however, has many advantages. It is one of the most important means managers have of developing the potential of their subordinates; also, as subordinates are able to take on additional responsibility, managers are freed to do more planning and other conceptual level tasks. For effective delegation to occur, three elements are important.

- *Specific tasks must be assigned clearly.* Communicating the nature of a task is critical to ensure that a subordinate has a clear understanding.

- *Sufficient authority must be granted.* The subordinate must be given the power to accomplish the assigned duties. This authority must be understood by the subordinate and also by others whose cooperation is required by the subordinate to complete the task.

- *Responsibility is created.* A sense of accountability must be conveyed to the subordinate to assure commitment to completion of the assigned task.

Line and Staff

Organizing is the division of labor. Within organizations, labor can be divided both horizontally through departmentalization and vertically through the delegation of authority. In designing organizations, line and staff relationships are created. Generally, line personnel are those responsible for production of goods and services of an organization and staff are considered advisory.

With the growing complexity and size of organizations, the staff role has become particularly important. Staff personnel may function to extend the effectiveness of the line personnel, as does the administrative assistant to the president of an organization. Other staff personnel provide advice and service throughout an organization. Personnel and quality control are two examples. The personnel manager in an organization relieves the line manager of such functions as recruiting and screening for new employees. Quality control is responsible for developing standards for products and analyzing production problems. Staff may also provide advice or services to only a segment of an organization. For example, a dietetic consultant in a nursing home provides advice and counsel primarily to the dietetic services department.

The distinction between line and staff is not as clear as it might appear in the foregoing paragraphs. In many organizations, managers have both line and staff responsibilities. In a small foodservice operation, staff to perform such functions as personnel and quality control would probably not be available; thus, the manager would perform these functions in addition to being responsible for production of goods and services. And in larger organizations, middle managers may be advisers to various other units or departments in the organization. For example, the director of dietetics may serve on a quality assurance task force for the entire hospital.

STAFFING

The most important resources of an organization are its human resources—the people who provide the organization with their work, talent, drive, and commitment. Among the most critical tasks of a manager is staffing: the recruitment, selection, training, and development of people who will be most effective in helping the organization meet its goals. Competent people at all levels are required to ensure that appropriate goals are being pursued and that activities proceed in such a way that these goals are achieved.

In the organizing process, the various job positions in the organization are defined. The staffing process then involves a series of steps designed to supply the right people in the right positions at the right time. This process is performed on a continuing basis, since organizational personnel change over time because of resignation, retirement, and other reasons.

In many organizations, staffing is carried out primarily by a personnel department. The responsibility for staffing, however, lies with line managers. Every line manager, even one not involved in recruiting and selecting personnel, is responsible for training and development and other aspects of staffing.

Staffing is made up of several steps (Figure 4.11): human resource planning; recruitment and selection; orientation, training, and development; performance appraisal; and compensation. Closely linked to these steps are a variety of staffing functions concerned with maintenance of the work force. These functions include

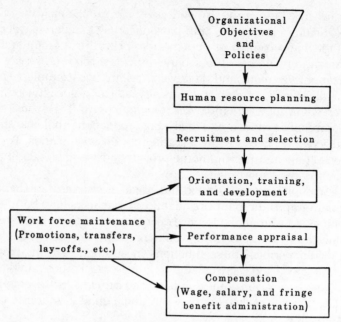

Figure 4.11. *Steps in the staffing process*

promotions, demotions, transfers, lay-offs, and dismissal. Human resource planning is designed to ensure that these staffing needs of the organization are continuously met, a process involving forecasting staffing needs and analyzing labor market conditions.

Recruitment and selection are concerned with developing a pool of job applicants and evaluating and choosing among them. As we will discuss in Section VI, these processes have become increasingly complex because of legislative mandates concerning recruitment and selection. For example, legislation dictates that nondiscriminatory practices must be followed in organizations.

Orientation, training, and development are processes designed first to assist newcomers to the organization in becoming informed about their responsibilities and the organization's policies and goals, and then to increase the ability of individuals to contribute to the organization. Training is designed to improve job skills, and development programs to prepare employees to assume new responsibilities.

Performance appraisal is concerned with comparison of an individual's job performance with the established standards for the job position. It also involves determination of rewards for high performance and corrective action to bring low performance in line with standards. Rewards may include bonuses, pay increments, or more challenging work assignments. Additional training is often called for with low performers.

Compensation encompasses all of those activities concerned with administration of the wage and salary program, including fringe benefits. Administration of fringe benefits includes insurance programs, leave time, retirement programs, and so forth.

LEADING

The leading function of management involves directing and channeling human effort for the accomplishment of objectives. Leading is the human resource function particularly concerned with individual and group behavior. All managing involves interaction with people and thus demands an understanding of how we affect and are affected by others. When a manager leads, he or she uses that understanding to get things done through members of the organization.

Management and leadership are often thought of as synonymous terms. Although effective managers generally will be effective leaders also, managing is more than leading. Leading, however, is certainly one of the most critical functions of management and success in management is closely related to success in leading. Leading also has been described as the interpersonal aspect of managing.

Leading is primarily concerned with creating an environment in which members of the organization are motivated to contribute to achieving goals of the organization. It has many dimensions, including such things as morale, employee satisfaction, and productivity, and communication. As we stated in Chapter 2 while discussing personnel satisfaction as an output of the system, managers must be concerned with assisting employees in achieving personal objectives at work and with coordinating personal and organizational objectives. The system's effectiveness is related closely to the quality of the staff's work.

The traditional view of the organization centered on the chain of command, negative sanctions, and economic incentives to motivate workers. In the late 1920s, the famous Hawthorne studies conducted by Western Electric and Harvard University researchers revealed that such things as social and psychological conditions, informal group pressure, participation in decision making, and recognition were factors influencing worker performance (Roethlisberger and Dickson, 1956). Since that time, the behavioral sciences have added new dimensions to understanding of motivation and behavior in the workplace. Today, leading is viewed as being concerned with interpersonal and intergroup relationships and the role of the manager is influencing these relationships to create cooperation and enlist commitment to organizational goals. The better-educated work force of today has been a significant force in managers' changing to more participative approaches in organizations.

While discussing the organizing function earlier, we described the formal authority of managers as flowing from the top of the organization. Acceptance authority is another aspect of authority that is related to the leading function. It is created by the degree to which members of the organization are willing to follow the leader.

The power of a manager is related closely to power that comes from formal position in the organization. Personal power, however, is a second dimension of a leader's power and is related to his or her expertise and personality. Chapter 19 will discuss these and other aspects of leadership in more detail, including factors affecting leadership style.

CONTROLLING

Controlling is the process concerned with ensuring that plans are being followed. It involves comparing what we set out to do with what we did and then taking corrective action, if necessary. Controlling must be a continuous process that affects and is affected by each of the other managerial functions. For example, the goals, objectives, and policies established in the planning process become control standards. When comparing performance to these standards, the need for new goals, objectives, and policies may become obvious. Effective organizing, staffing, and leading result in more effective control. By the same token, more effective control also leads to better organizing, staffing, and leading. Within this inter-relatedness and interdependency of the managerial functions, controlling relates most closely to planning.

The standards created in the planning process define the measurement of what we expect to happen. These standards are the criteria managers use to control performance; in turn, the feedback from the controlling process is the information managers use to evaluate and adjust plans (Figure 4.12). The controlling function of management involves three steps, as depicted in Figure 4.13.

- Measuring current performance and comparing it against established standards.
- Analyzing deviations between performance and standards and determining whether or not the deviations are within acceptable limits.
- Taking action to correct unacceptable deviations.

Taking corrective action is a process that cuts across both the leading and controlling functions, since many deviations from expected standards are related to workers' performance. For example, portion yield lower than expected from a particular recipe might be caused by a foodservice worker's failure to use the appropriate portioning tool, such as using a disher that is too large. Throughout Chapters 7 through 16, on the functional subsystems of a foodservice, appropriate controls within each of these subsystems will be discussed.

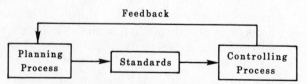

Feedback

Planning Process → Standards → Controlling Process

Figure 4.12. *The planning-controlling cycle*

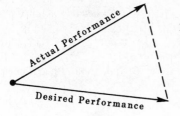

Deviation,
measured and
corrected by
controlling

Figure 4.13. *The controlling function of management*

SUMMARY

In summary, the five management functions are planning, organizing, staffing, leading, and controlling, performed by managers as they coordinate subsystems and facilitate transformation of resources into desired outputs. All of these managerial functions must be performed effectively for managers to achieve organizational goals and objectives.

REFERENCES

Boettinger, H. M.: Is management really an act? *Harvard Bus. Rev.* 53:54 (Jan./Feb.), 1975.

Boone, L. E., and Kurtz, D. L.: *Principles of Management.* New York: Random House, 1981.

Burack, E. H., and Mathys, N. J.: *Introduction to Management: A Career Perspective.* New York: John Wiley & Sons, 1983.

Carlisle, H. M.: *Management: Concepts, Methods, and Applications.* 2nd ed. Chicago: Science Research Associates, 1982.

Flippo, E. B., and Munsinger, G. M.: *Management.* 5th ed. Boston: Allyn and Bacon, 1982.

Fottler, M. D.: Is management really generic? *Acad. Mgmt. Rev.* 6:1, 1981.

Gannon, M. J.: *Management: An Integrated Framework.* 2nd ed. Boston: Little, Brown & Co., 1982.

Haimann, T., Scott, W. G., and Connor, P. E.: *Management.* 4th ed. Boston: Houghton Mifflin Co., 1982.

Hayes, J. L.: Making a professional manager. *Mgmt. Rev.* 69:2 (Nov.), 1980.

Hellreigel, D., and Slocum, J. W.: *Management.* 3rd ed. Reading, MA: Addison-Wesley Publishing Co., 1982.

Hersey, P., and Blanchard, K. H.: *Management of Organizational Behavior: Utilizing Human Resources.* 4th ed. Englewood Cliffs, NJ: Prentice-Hall, 1982.

Koontz, H., O'Donnell, C., and Weihrich, H.: *Management.* 7th ed. New York: McGraw-Hill Book Co., 1980.

Logan, H. H.: Line and staff: An obsolete concept? *Personnel* 43:26 (Jan./Feb.), 1966.

Moore, F. G.: *The Management of Organizations.* New York: John Wiley & Sons, 1982.

Owens, J.: The uses of leadership theory. *Michigan Bus. Rev.* 25:13 (Jan.), 1973.

Roethlisberger, F. J., and Dickson, W. J.: *Management and the Worker.* Cambridge, MA: Harvard University Press, 1956.

Rue, L. W., and Byars, L. L.: *Management Theory and Application.* 3rd ed. Homewood, IL: Richard D. Irwin, 1983.

Scanlon, B., and Keys, B.: *Management and Organizational Behavior.* 2nd ed. New York: John Wiley & Sons, 1983.

Shetty, Y. K.: Is there a best way to organize a business enterprise? *S.A.M. Advanced Mgmt. J.* 38:47 (Apr.), 1973.

Sisk, H. L., and Williams, J. C.: *Management & Organization.* 4th ed. Cincinnati: South-Western Publishing Co., 1981.

Skinner, W., and Sasser, W. E.: Managers with impact: Versatile and inconsistent. *Harvard Bus. Rev.* 55:140 (Nov./Dec.), 1977.

Stoner, J. A.: *Management.* 2nd ed. Englewood Cliffs, NJ: Prentice-Hall, 1982.

Szilagyi, A. D.: *Management and Performance.* Santa Monica, CA: Goodyear Publishing Co., 1981.

Tannenbaum, R., and Schmidt, W. H.: How to choose a leadership pattern. *Harvard Bus. Rev.* 51:162 (May/Jun.), 1973.

Zalenik, A.: Managers and leaders: Are they different? *Harvard Bus. Rev.* 55:67 (May/Jun.), 1977.

II

Designing the Foodservice System

5

Types of Foodservice Systems

CONVENTIONAL
COMMISSARY
READY PREPARED
ASSEMBLY/SERVE
SUMMARY
REFERENCES

New production/service systems for foodservice organizations have developed in recent years. Characterized by a separation of production and service of food in time and/or place, these new systems have been primarily aimed at increasing productivity, decreasing cost, or strengthening control of operations. Because foodservice managers assume primary responsibility for food safety and quality regardless of the type of system, complex managerial decisions are required to develop and implement appropriate foodservice systems that serve quality food at minimal cost. The physical, chemical, and microbiological changes occurring in food throughout all stages of procurement, production, and service must be monitored and controlled to ensure the quality and safety of the finished products.

Spiraling labor costs and technological innovation in both food and equipment have led to implementation of these new types of systems. Faced with these costs and a lack of available highly skilled employees, foodservice managers have been receptive to using the new forms of food with built-in convenience or labor-saving features. These foods, in their various forms and stages of preparation, have appeared on the market in increasing numbers each year. Many require specialized equipment for final production, delivery, and service. Four major types of foodservice systems have been identified—the conventional or traditionally used system, and three newer systems, commissary, ready prepared, and assembly/serve (Unklesbay et al., 1977). A series of conceptual diagrams for foodservice operations, developed by a regional research group to illustrate food product flow within these various types of foodservice systems, will be presented and discussed in this chapter.

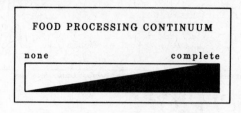

Figure 5.1. *Degree of processing of food used in various types of foodservice systems*

A major distinguishing characteristic of the four systems is the degree of processing of the foods, which may vary from little or no processing prior to purchase of the foods to completely prepared foods ready for service. This food processing continuum, illustrated in Figure 5.1, deals with the procurement subsystem and the process of bringing into the system one of the most important inputs, food. This diagram illustrates the interrelationship between the inputs of the system and the transformation processes. It also emphasizes the critical role procurement plays and indicates how the types of food used in the system affect the nature and characteristics of the entire system.

In many foodservices, a combination of foods with varying degrees of processing is utilized. At the far left of this diagrammatic continuum, food items receive little or no processing prior to purchase by the foodservice operation; at the far right, however, the food products have undergone complete processing and are ready for service. Fresh apples, sugar, flour, and shortening for use in baking an apple pie are examples of foods with little or no processing, whereas a frozen baked pie is an example at the other end of the food processing continuum.

In Chapter 2, we presented a foodservice systems model to be used for analyzing overall foodservice operations. The parts of the model were identified as input, transformation, and output, with the additional components of control, feedback, and memory. We indicated that the type of foodservice system selected has a major influence on input requirements and transformation processes. In this chapter, four major types of systems are examined in depth, with emphasis on food procurement and production throughout the various systems. The diagrams in this chapter will focus primarily on the transformation processes in a foodservice system.

CONVENTIONAL

The conventional foodservice system is the type most establishments have traditionally used. Foods are purchased for an individual operation in various stages of preparation, but all production is completed and foods are served on the same premises. Following production, foods are held hot or chilled, as appropriate for the menu item, and served as soon as possible.

In previous years, conventional foodservice systems often included a butcher shop, bake shop, and vegetable preparation unit. Currently, many conventional

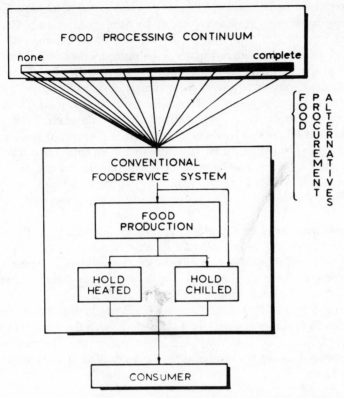

Figure 5.2. *Food flow in conventional foodservice systems*

foodservice operations use preportioned meats, baked goods, and canned and frozen vegetables rather than purchasing all types of foods raw and completing processing on premises.

Although alternative systems have evolved, the conventional system continues to be the dominant type of foodservice in the United States. Because of increasing labor costs, managers of conventional foodservices have gradually made changes in ingredients and menu items purchased in an attempt to reduce the labor needed for meal production. Food procured for conventional systems vary from those with no processing, to those with a limited amount of processing, to those processed completely.

Figure 5.2 illustrates the food product flow for a conventional foodservice system. Foods with varying degrees of processing are brought into the system and prepared for service in the food production subsystem. As shown by the arrows, some foods are merely purchased and held chilled before service, such as milk or butter patties, whereas other menu items are produced in the system from raw foods and held either heated or chilled until time of service.

Following receipt and appropriate storage of food items and ingredients, menu items should be prepared as near to service time as possible. Considerable labor is required before and during foodservice periods. Otherwise, food subjected to hot-holding conditions is affected by temperature, humidity, and length of holding time, all of which can adversely affect its nutritional and sensory quality and must be considered when scheduling food production.

Foods prepared in the conventional system may be distributed for service directly to an adjacent or nearby serving area, such as a cafeteria, dining room, or lunch counter. In hospitals or other healthcare facilities, food may be served on trays, using a centralized or decentralized service approach. In centralized service, the individual patient trays are assembled and set up at some central point in or close to the production area. Trays are then distributed by carts or conveyors to patient floors, where they are delivered to patient rooms. In decentralized service, food is distributed in bulk quantities to another area in the facility where trays are assembled. In some facilities, a combination of these two approaches is used.

The systems model in Chapter 2 is directly applicable to the conventional foodservice system. Foods are brought directly into the system and menu items are produced using conventional methods, then served without extensive holding. In discussions of the other three types of foodservice systems, we will point out modifications of the basic model.

Traditionally, a skilled labor force for food production has been utilized in conventional foodservice systems for long periods each day. According to Unklesbay et al. (1977), with constantly rising labor costs within the foodservice industry, the current trend in conventional foodservices is to procure more extensively processed foods.

COMMISSARY

Technological innovations and the design of sophisticated foodservice equipment have led to the evolution and development of commissary foodservice systems. Unklesbay et al. (1977) have described these commissary systems as characterized by a centralized food procurement and production facility, with distribution of prepared menu items to several remote areas for final preparation and service. The centralized production facilities are often referred to as central commissaries or food factories, and the service units as satellite service centers. The economies-of-scale concept has guided the design of these systems. The potential for economies from large-scale purchasing and production in a central facility has been used to justify design and construction of these complex operations with expensive automated equipment for production of foods from unprocessed states.

In commissary foodservice systems, the foods purchased have received little or no processing, as indicated in the continuum at the top of the diagram in Figure 5.3. These foods are generally purchased in large quantities and held after delivery at the facility under appropriate environmental conditions in frozen, refrigerated, or dry storage. Most menu items in commissary systems are pro-

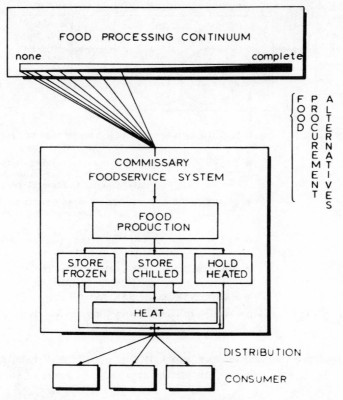

Figure 5.3. *Food flow in commissary foodservice systems*

cessed completely in the central facility. Because of the large quantities produced, the equipment for preprocessing and production is often different from the equipment used in conventional systems. These large central production centers may be designed using equipment frequently seen in food industry operations, such as canneries or frozen food processing plants. Because of the large-scale production quantities, recipes and food production techniques require major modification. For example, the degree of doneness is less for most menu items because of the additional heating or thermalization needed at the satellite service centers to bring the foods to an acceptable serving temperature.

As Figure 5.3 also shows, foods are held after production, either frozen, chilled, or heated, for distribution to the service centers. These menu items may be stored in bulk or in individual portions. The type of storage used may depend on the time lag necessary between production and service. In many instances, however, the type of storage for prepared menu items may be the concept guiding the design of the system. For example, a decision to use frozen storage for menu items may be made before proceeding with the design. Many menu items that have been held frozen or chilled require an additional thermal process to heat

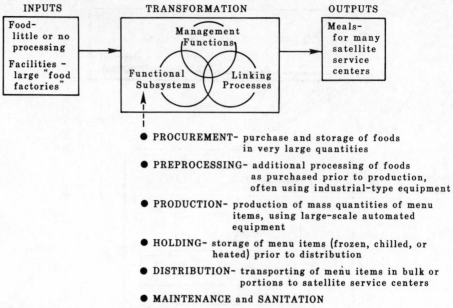

INPUTS   TRANSFORMATION   OUTPUTS

Food-
little or no
processing

Facilities –
large "food
factories"

Management
Functions

Functional
Subsystems

Linking
Processes

Meals–
for many
satellite
service
centers

- PROCUREMENT– purchase and storage of foods
  in very large quantities
- PREPROCESSING– additional processing of foods
  as purchased prior to production,
  often using industrial-type equipment
- PRODUCTION– production of mass quantities of menu
  items, using large-scale automated
  equipment
- HOLDING– storage of menu items (frozen, chilled, or
  heated) prior to distribution
- DISTRIBUTION– transporting of menu items in bulk or
  portions to satellite service centers
- MAINTENANCE and SANITATION

Figure 5.4. *Unique characteristics of commissary foodservice systems*

them to desirable service temperatures. Highly specialized distribution equipment may be needed, depending on the type and location of satellite service centers.

In Figure 5.4, a modification of the foodservice systems model in Chapter 2 illustrates unique characteristics of commissary foodservice systems. As indicated, the major modifications affecting inputs to the system are the type of food and facilities used. In the transformation element, the nature of the functional subsystems is vastly different from the conventional system, mainly because of the larger scale production capacity, the storage necessary for prepared menu items, and the distribution capabilities required for transporting prepared menu items to a wide array of satellite service centers.

The packaging and storage of prepared menu items present challenges for control in commissary systems. A variety of packaging materials and approaches is used in systems now in operation, varying from individual pouches or serving dishes, specially designed for frozen or chilled holding, to disposable or reusable metal pans adapted to various types of distribution and transportation equipment. Preserving the microbiological, sensory, and nutritional quality of foods during holding and thermalization at point of service can present problems. Specialized equipment is required for the packaging, storing, and distributing of products prepared in central commissaries. In large food factories, a food technologist or microbiologist is frequently on staff, responsible for monitoring quality control.

In foodservice organizations with many serving units, centralized production and other activities with commissary-type systems have been tried in an attempt to curtail labor and other costs. The commissary foodservice principles have been adopted in systems where service areas are remote from, yet accessible to, the production center. Reducing duplication of production, labor, and equipment that occurs if production centers are located at each foodservice site has been the objective. Space requirements at the service centers can also be minimized because of the limited production equipment required. The high capital cost for construction of these large central production units and also the high cost for transportation equipment and the increasing expenses for distribution are current concerns in evaluating the effectiveness of these systems.

Commissary systems are adaptable particularly for foodservice operations with service in unique places. One of the best examples can be found in airline foodservice, where the commissary system has been applied for many years. Menu items for airlines are produced in ground level facilities according to specifications of the various airlines, portioned into individual meals for passengers, and distributed in various containers and carts for holding on site in the production facility and on the planes until service. Commissary systems are, in large measure, an outgrowth of airline foodservice applied to other types of operations.

Commissary systems have long been applied in school foodservice, although many systems have combined conventional and commissary approaches. In recent years, centralized production facilities located away from schools have been constructed, usually in urban districts with a large number of schools. Often the larger secondary schools have their own conventional systems, so the central production facility only produces meals for the smaller elementary schools in the district. A more common system, however, uses the larger secondary school kitchens as the commissary for producing meals that are transported for service in bulk or portions to the smaller elementary schools. In this instance, the secondary school operation is both a commissary and a conventional system, because secondary students are also served in an adjacent cafeteria. These secondary school operations are often referred to as base kitchens.

In commercial foodservice in large, multi-unit operations, systems combining characteristics of commissary and conventional systems are found. For example, some menu items may be prepared in a central commissary and then shipped to a variety of operations, often great distances from the commissary. In the individual units, a combination of menu items are served, including both those procured from the central commissary and others prepared on site.

READY PREPARED

Ready prepared foodservice systems have been developed in response to increased labor costs and to a critical shortage of skilled food production personnel. In ready prepared systems, menu items are produced and held frozen or chilled for service. A key difference between ready prepared and conventional systems is that menu items are not produced for immediate service in ready systems. Many

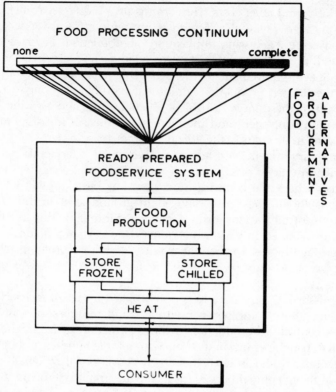

Figure 5.5. *Food flow in ready prepared foodservice systems*

of the production, packaging, and storage techniques are similar to those used in commissary systems; however, the scale of production is not as large because the ready prepared system is designed for a single operation. Generally, ready prepared systems have been adopted because completely prepared foods are not available in the market to meet the needs of an organization. In the healthcare industry, in particular, prepared foods are often not available to meet the specialized needs of patients with varying health problems.

In Figure 5.5, the food product flow in ready prepared foodservice systems is shown. As indicated at the top of the diagram, foods from the entire spectrum of the food processing continuum are used. Foods brought into the system that are completely processed are merely stored either frozen or chilled, as appropriate to the food item. Foods procured with little or no processing are used to produce menu items that are stored either frozen or chilled. A distinct feature of these systems is that prepared menu items are readily available at any time for final assembly and/or heating for service.

Menu items such as entrees and hot vegetables require two phases of heat processing in ready prepared food service systems, the first occurring during the quantity production of menu items. The second occurs after storage, in bringing items to the appropriate temperature for service to the consumer.

Cook-chill and cook-freeze are two variations of ready prepared systems. In cook-chill foodservice operations, most menu items are maintained in the chilled state for various periods of time. In cook-freeze systems, menu items are stored in the frozen state for periods generally ranging from two weeks up to three months.

As indicated in the diagram (Figure 5.5), procured foods are placed in appropriate storage conditions, then produced for holding in one of the two forms discussed above. Careful production scheduling is needed along with accurate forecasting to maintain quality of foods and avoid prolonged holding beyond the planned time. In cook-chill systems, prepared menu items are portioned for service several hours or as much as a day in advance of the serving period. In both cook-chill or cook-freeze approaches, final heating occurs just before service, usually in facilities near the serving areas. For example, hospitals have facilities on patient floors called galleys, where specialized heating equipment is used to finish the preparation of menu items immediately before service. Microwave ovens are the most commonly used heating equipment. Often, minor preparation, such as preparing toast for a breakfast menu, may occur in these galleys. In the initial preparation, menu items should be slightly undercooked to avoid overcooking and loss of sensory quality in the final heating for service.

In cook-freeze systems, special recipe formulations are needed for many menu items because of the changes that occur in freezing. Development of off-flavors may be a problem with some food items. Some of these changes may be controlled by substituting more stable ingredients, by exercising greater control of storage time, temperature, and packaging, or by adding stabilizers.

The challenge in the ready prepared systems using either cook-chill or cook-freeze approaches is retention of foods' nutrient content, microbial safety, and sensory quality. Prolonged holding should be avoided, and careful control in the final heating stage prior to service is important. In addition to microwave ovens for this final heating process, immersion techniques and convection ovens have also been proven to be effective. Convection ovens, in which the air is circulated during the heating process, are effective for heating foods held in bulk because appropriate temperatures are reached more rapidly than in conventional ovens. Immersion techniques, which involve immersing pouches of food in boiling water or in steamers, are used for reheating moist food items, such as entree items in sauces.

The foodservice systems model that we are using as a framework for this book has direct application to the ready prepared system. In the transformation process, however, special attention must be focused on the production and holding of prepared menu items. As indicated above, special systems for heating menu items for service to consumers are required.

Ready prepared foodservice systems have been adopted in many operations to reduce labor expenditures and use labor more effectively. Peak demands for labor are removed because production is designed to meet future rather than immediate needs. Production personnel can be scheduled for regular working hours rather than during the early morning and late evening shifts that are required in conventional systems. The heating and service of menu items does not require highly skilled employees and thus, reductions in labor costs are often possible. Food procurement in volume may decrease food costs in these systems.

ASSEMBLY/SERVE

The development of assembly/serve systems—also referred to as convenience food systems or systems using minimal cooking concepts—came about primarily because of the availability of foods that are ready to serve or that require little or no processing in the foodservice operation prior to service. Another factor has been the chronic shortage of skilled personnel in food production and the increasing cost of labor.

The primary objective of assembly/serve systems is to provide food ready for service while minimizing the amount of labor resources employed within the foodservice operation. The flow of food products in the assembly/serve foodservice system is illustrated in Figure 5.6. As the diagram shows, food products are brought into the system with a maximum degree of processing. Only storage, assembly, heating, and service functions are commonly performed in these systems; little if any preprocessing is done and production is very limited.

The three market forms of foods used predominantly in these systems are bulk, preportioned, and preplated frozen foods. The bulk form requires portioning before or after heating within the foodservice operation, whereas the preportioned market form requires only assembly and heating. The preplated products

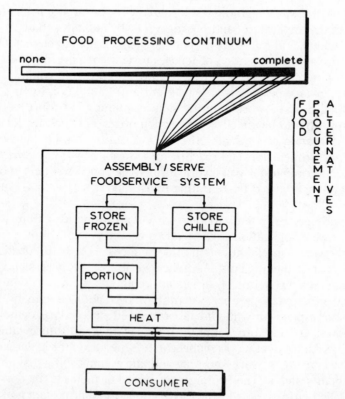

Figure 5.6. *Food flow in assembly/serve foodservice systems*

require only heating for distribution and service, and thus are the most easily handled of the three forms.

In many assembly/serve operations, a combination of foods is used, some requiring a limited degree of processing in the foodservice operation and others requiring none. Often partially prepared foods are purchased to be combined with other ingredients before heating or chilling. In many operations, completely processed foods may be enhanced in the assembly/serve system as a way of individualizing menu items; for example, a sauce may be added to an entree. Glew (1972), however, contends that the use of completely processed foods is probably more cost effective than using total convenience foods along with those requiring more preparation in the foodservice system.

Following procurement in assembly/serve systems, food items are held in dry, refrigerated, or frozen storage. When menu items are heated in either bulk or preportioned form, quality control is a particular concern. Foods must be thawed under appropriate conditions if thawing is required prior to heating. The thawing and heating processes must not be scheduled too long in advance of service because of the potential loss of microbial, nutritional, and sensory quality of the food. For this reason, specialized systems for heating frozen foods to appropriate serving temperatures have been developed, in which convection and microwave ovens are frequently used.

The assembly/serve approach to foodservice systems gained some degree of acceptance because it appeared to offer an easy solution to labor and production problems. However, a readily available supply of highly processed, high quality food products is a prerequisite for a successful assembly/serve operation. As indicated in the discussion of ready prepared systems, the availability of food products is sometimes a problem, particularly in healthcare institutions. Although foods for special modified dietary needs have been developed in recent years, these foods are not always readily available, particularly in rural and small communities. Therefore, if a convenience food system is used for patients or nursing home residents without special dietary needs, food production may be needed to prepare items for those on modified diets.

Another common complaint about the assembly/serve systems is the lack of individuality. Comments are frequently heard about the "sameness" of the ready prepared foods available in the market place. As we discussed in the section on conventional food systems, a trend toward use of foods with some degree of processing is evident. This trend appears to be more predominant than total adoption of assembly/serve systems. In some instances, however, an assembly/serve system meets the needs of particular operations in which space is very limited for production facilities or labor is not available.

SUMMARY

In designing foodservice systems, many factors have to be considered. What are the objectives of the operation? Who are the clientele to be served? What types of foods and other services will be provided? What is the availability of foods in the market place? What are the dynamics of the labor market in a particular geographic area? If a foodservice operation is part of a larger organization, what are the constraints in the existing facilities that must be considered? What are the initial and operating costs for the various systems? These are only a few of the questions that must be asked during the planning phase of systems design. Because of the tremendous investment involved, all factors must be considered carefully in making the basic decisions about the type of system selected: conventional, commissary, ready prepared, or assembly/serve.

REFERENCES

Byrd, R. C., and Morrow, J. T.: Convenience versus conventional operation. *Hospitals* 45:90 (Mar. 16), 1971.

Dorney, D. C., Millross, J., and Glew, G.: Packaging, storage and transport. *Hospitals* 48:81 (Jul. 16), 1974.

Farevaag, L., and Matthews, M. E.: Evaluating ready-service food. *Hospitals* 47:108 (Oct. 16), 1973.

Franzese, R.: Survey examines hospitals' use of convenience foods. *Hospitals* 55:109 (Jan. 16), 1981.

Glew, G.: Influence of convenience foods on hospital catering. *Royal Soc. Health J.* 92:227, 1972.

Goldberg, C. M., and Kohlligian, M.: Conventional, convenience or ready food service? *Hospitals* 48:80 (Apr. 16), 1974.

Harper, J. M., Jansen, G. R., Shigetomi, C. T., and Fallis, L. K.: Pilot study to evaluate food delivery systems used in school lunch programs. I. Menu item acceptability. *School Food Serv. Res. Rev.* 1:20, 1977.

Jansen, G. R., Harper, J. M., Kylen, A., Shigetomi, C. T., and Fallis, L. K.: Pilot study to evaluate food delivery systems used in school lunch programs. II. Nutritional value. *School Food Serv. Res. Rev.* 1:24, 1977.

Klein, B. P., Matthews, M. E., and Setser, C. S.: *Foodservice Systems: Time and Temperature Effects on Food Quality.* North Central Regional Research Publ. No. 293, Illinois Bulletin 779. Urbana-Champaign: Agric. Exper. Sta., College of Agric., Univ. of Ill., 1984.

Lough, J. B., Harper, J. M., Jansen, G. R., Shigetomi, C. T., and Anderson, J.: Pilot study to evaluate food delivery systems used in school lunch programs. III. Physical facilities. *School Food Serv. Res. Rev.* 2:18, 1978.

Lough, J. B., Harper, J. M., Jansen, G. R., Shigetomi, C. T., and Anderson, J.: Pilot study to evaluate food delivery systems used in school lunch programs. IV. Meal costs. *School Food Serv. Res. Rev.* 2:23, 1978.

Matthews, M. E.: Quality of food in cook/chill foodservice systems: A review. *School Food Serv. Res. Rev.* 1:15, 1977.

Merrick, M., and Sutton, P. J.: The minimal cooking concept. *Hospitals* 46:92 (Jun. 1), 1972.

National Academy of Sciences: *Hospital Patient Feeding Systems.* Washington, DC: Natl. Acad. Press, 1982.

Pinkert, M. S., ed.: *The Ready Foods System for Health Care Facilities.* Boston: Cahners Books, 1973.

Prusa, K. J., Bowers, J. A., Craig, J., and Greig, S.: Ascorbic acid, thiamin, and vitamin B_6 contents of selected items in different school food service approaches. *School Food Serv. Res. Rev.* 5:94, 1981.

Reed, R. M.: Food service: Conventional system may be best. *Hospitals* 47:161 (Jul. 16), 1973.

Reid, V.: Convenience foods decision: Yes. *Hospitals* 47:81 (Jan. 10), 1973.

Reni, M. J., Cremer, M. L., and Chipley, J. R.: Sensory and microbiological qualities of beef loaf in four commissary food service treatments. *J. Am. Dietet. A.* 78:483, 1981.

Rinke, W. J.: Three major systems reviewed and evaluated. *Hospitals* 50:73 (Feb. 16), 1976.

Unklesbay, N.: Monitoring for quality control in alternate foodservice systems. *J. Am. Dietet. A.* 71:423, 1977.

Unklesbay, N., Maxcy, R. B., Knickrehm, M., Stevenson, K., Cremer, M., and Matthews, M. E.: *Foodservice Systems: Product Flow and Microbial Quality and Safety of Foods.* North Central Regional Research Bull. No. 245. Missouri Agricultural Experiment Station, Columbia: 1977.

Williamson, B. J.: Tomorrow's system—the food factory—today. *J. Am. Dietet. A.* 66:499, 1975.

Zolber, K.: Research on assembly serve system. *Hospitals* 45:83 (Jan. 16), 1971.

6

The Menu: The Primary Control of the System

The menu serves as the primary control of the foodservice system and is the core around which most other aspects of the system revolve (Figure 6.1). It controls the procurement and production subsystems and provides the framework for the budget. In a new operation, it determines the equipment and layout. To the production worker, the menu provides a brief description of the work to be done, and to the service worker, it provides the foods to be offered to the clientele. The hospital, the fast food operation, the school foodservice, and the gourmet restaurant have widely varying menus because their objectives and clientele are different. The menu expresses the character of a foodservice operation and is largely responsible for its reputation, good or bad.

The term menu refers both to the list of items offered for service and to the card or form on which the list is printed for the customer, patient, student, or other clientele. In some types of operations, the menu may be posted on a menu board or conveyed verbally by service personnel. Because of its central importance

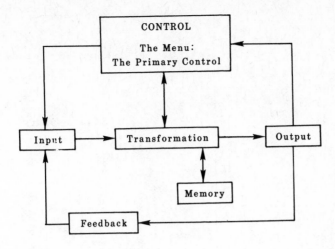

Figure 6.1. *The menu: the primary control of the foodservice system*

to the foodservice system, the menu must be a carefully planned document. A wide range of factors should be considered in constructing menus, such as food preferences of clientele, nutritional qualities of foods, operational demands for producing menu items, and cost of food and labor. These and other factors must be considered simultaneously in planning menus that will have clientele acceptance and meet the managerial and financial demands of running a successful operation. Because of the critical role the menu plays in controlling the foodservice operation, managers should understand and be competent in all aspects of the menu planning process.

TYPES OF MENUS

Many different kinds and styles of menus are used in foodservice operations; however, they can all be classified into three basic groups: static or fixed, cycle, and single-use. They can be further classified within these types as no choice, limited choice, or choice. Each of these terms will be defined and discussed in the paragraphs that follow.

A static menu is one in which the same menu items are offered day after day. Traditionally, the static menu has been characteristic of many commercial foodservice operations. In some institutional foodservices, however, the static or "restaurant-type" menu is being used. For example, a number of hospitals have adopted a static menu in which the same foods are offered day after day, generally with many choices. An example of a restaurant-type hospital menu is shown in Figure 6.2.

In the commercial foodservice industry, the entire concept for an operation is frequently built around the menu, including the decor, the advertising campaign, and the market segment identified as the target audience. The menu in Figure 6.3, for example, is from a small regional chain in the South that features fried

NOON MEAL CHOICES

Choose one Entree from either the Chilled or Hot Entrees.
Items indicated with (*) are prepared without salt.

BROTHS
Beef Broth
Chicken Broth

SOUPS
Chicken Noodle
Cream of Tomato
Cream of Mushroom

*GREEN PEPPER stuffed with Ground Beef and Onion in a Tomato Sauce on a bed of Rice.

SAN FRANCISCO STREETCAR—slices of Ham and Turkey on Raisin Bread covered with a light Cheese Sauce and garnished with a Hot Spiced Peach.

*HAMBURGER on BUN with Tomato and Lettuce.

ITALIAN SPAGHETTI with Meat Sauce accompanied by crisp Broccoli Spears.

*ROAST BEEF GROUND with mashed Potatoes and Green Beans.

*ROAST BEEF RIBEYE accompanied by Peas with Pearl Onions and Carrots.

*ROAST TURKEY GROUND with mashed Potatoes and Carrots.

SWISS STEAK braised in a zesty Tomato Sauce accompanied by a Baked Potato and Leaf Spinach.

FILET OF FISH baked in a Lemon Sauce and served with June Green Peas and Cauliflower.

STRAINED FOOD COMBINATION including Meat, Vegetable and Fruit.

SALMON LOAF served with a Vegetable Medley.

*MASHED POTATOES
Brown Gravy or Cream Gravy.

BARBEQUED HAM on a Round Bun served with Green Beans.

*BAKED BREAST OF CHICKEN with scalloped Potatoes and Mixed Greens.

ROAST BREAST OF TURKEY topped with a mild Cheese Sauce and served with Corn and Broccoli Spears.

ZUCCHINI QUICHE with a Hot Spiced Peach.

HOT DOG on BUN with crunchy Carrot sticks.

MACARONI WITH CHEDDAR CHEESE accompanied by Bacon-seasoned Green Beans.

SALADS
Fancy Mixed Fruit Salad
Assorted Crisp Garden Relishes
Tossed Green Salad and Dressing of your choice
Fresh Spinach Salad with Tangy Dressing
Gelatin Salad (See Noon and Evening Choices)

DESSERTS
Cherry Pie
Carrot Cake with Cream Cheese Icing
Peanut Butter Cookies

Fresh Fruit Choices
Monday . . . . Apples
Tuesday . . . . Fruit in Season
Wednesday . . . . Oranges
Thursday . . . . Bananas
Friday . . . . Apples
Saturday . . . . Fruit in Season
Sunday . . . . Oranges

EVENING CHOICES

Choose one Entree from either the Chilled or Hot Entrees.
Items indicated with (*) are prepared without salt.

BROTHS
Beef Broth
Chicken Broth

SOUPS
Vegetable Beef
Cream of Potato
Cream of Pea

SCALLOPED VEGETABLE CREPE with Sour Cream Celery Sauce.

HOT DOG on BUN with crunchy Carrot sticks.

*ROAST BEEF GROUND with mashed Potatoes and Green Beans.

*ROAST TURKEY GROUND with mashed Potatoes and Carrots.

STRAINED FOOD COMBINATION including Meat, Vegetable and Fruit.

*MASHED POTATOES
Brown Gravy or Cream Gravy.

*HAMBURGER on BUN with Tomato and Lettuce.

ROAST RIBEYE OF BEEF au jus served with Mashed Potatoes and seasoned Green Beans.

SAVORY BEEF STEAK smothered in a Mushroom Sauce plus au Gratin Potatoes and Paprika Cauliflower.

TACO—all the "fixins" for two Mexican Tacos—Meat Sauce, a salad of Tomatoes, Lettuce and Cheese, two Tortilla Shells and Taco Sauce.

*BREADED FILET OF FISH baked, served with Peas and Mushrooms on Rice.

*TUNA NOODLE CASSEROLE with Egg Noodles and Mushrooms accompanied by Carrots.

HAM CASSEROLE, a tasty combination of Ham chunks, Cheese and Egg Noodles accompanied by Leaf Spinach.

HUNGARIAN PORK, tender Roast Pork on Noodles with Sour Cream, Onion and Mushroom Sauce and Carrots on the side.

*CHICKEN in ORANGE SAUCE, chicken in tangy sauce with fluffy Rice and Broccoli Spears with unsalted margarine.

FRIED BREAST OF CHICKEN served with Mashed Potatoes and a special Broccoli Casserole.

*ROAST TURKEY BREAST served with mashed Sweet Potatoes and Green Beans.

SALADS
Combination Fruit Cup
Creamy Coleslaw
Tossed Green Salad and Dressing of your choice
Gelatin Salad
(See Noon and Evening Choices)

DESSERTS
Apple Pie
Banana Cake with Butter Cream Icing
Oatmeal Raisin Cookies

Fresh Fruit Choices
Monday . . . . . . Oranges   Friday . . . . . Oranges
Tuesday . . . . . Bananas   Saturday . . . . Bananas
Wednesday . . . Apples   Sunday . . . . . Apples
Thursday . . . Fruit in Season

NOON OR EVENING CHOICES

Chilled Entrees

CHEDDAR CHEESE SANDWICH—a traditional favorite on Whole Wheat Bread served with Fruit Cocktail in Gelatin.

*CHEF'S SALAD PLATE—crisp Greens topped with unsalted turkey and beef strips, tomato and Hard-Cooked Egg Half with your choice of Dressing.

DELUXE CLUB SANDWICH—Chicken, Ham and Cheese on Whole Wheat and White Bread with Potato Chips and Pickles.

COTTAGE CHEESE FRUIT PLATE—with a slice of Pineapple in its own juice and an unsweetened Peach half.

*TUNA PLATE—unsalted flaked Tuna on Lettuce with Melba Toast and Pineapple Rings in their own juice.

CREATE YOUR OWN SANDWICHES or order INDIVIDUALLY

MEATS AND CHEESES
1 oz. Served on Lettuce Leaf
Bologna Slice
Turkey Slice
Ham Slice
*Roast Beef Slice
American Cheese
Cottage Cheese
Peanut Butter
Hard-Cooked Egg

BREADS
Banana Nut Bread
Cinnamon Roll
Dinner Roll
White Bread
Whole Wheat Bread
Saltine Crackers
Graham Crackers

SALAD AND SANDWICH ACCENTS
Salad Dressing
French Dressing
1000 Island Dressing
Italian Dressing
Lemon Juice
Vinegar
Tartar Sauce
Pickle Relish
Mustard
Catsup

SPREADS
Margarine
Polyunsaturated Margarine
Butter
Honey
Jelly

GELATIN SALADS
Monday . . . . . Jellied Grapefruit & Cream Cheese
Tuesday . . . . . Arabian Peach
Wednesday . . . Pineapple Coconut
Thursday . . . . Cranberry
Friday . . . . . . Jellied Applesauce & Cream Cheese
Saturday . . . . Bing Cherry
Sunday . . . . . Jellied Fruit Cocktail

CONDIMENTS
Lemon Wedge
Non Dairy Creamer
Coffee Creamer
Sugar
Sugar Substitute
Salt
Pepper

CHILLED FRUITS AND DESSERTS
Applesauce
Peach Half
Pear Half
Apricot Halves
Gelatin Jewels
Orange Sherbet
Lime Sherbet
Vanilla Ice Cream
Chocolate Ice Cream
Baked Custard
Vanilla Pudding
Chocolate Pudding

BEVERAGES
Orange Juice
Pineapple Juice
Apple Juice
Prune Juice
Tomato Juice
2% Milk
Skim Milk
Buttermilk
Chocolate Milk
Hot Chocolate
Coffee
Decaffeinated Coffee
Hot Tea
Iced Tea
Vanilla Milkshake

Figure 6.2. Example of a restaurant style hospital menu from the University of Kansas Medical Center, College of Health Sciences and Hospital, Kansas City, Kansas.

Figure 6.3. *Example of a static, limited choice menu for a regional chain restaurant (permission granted by Cock of the Walk Restaurants, Natchez, MS)*

catfish. The menu is static, with a few limited choices of à la carte items, the decor rustic and service consistent with the menu concept. On a larger scale, one national hamburger chain identified the six- to twelve-year-old as their primary market and designed their menu, marketing strategies, and facilities around capturing it. Market research indicated that these potential customers wanted a hamburger with the condiments they preferred rather than a product with standard garnishes.

In many national franchises and chains, the same basic menu is offered nationwide, thus permitting cost control, advertising campaigns, planned purchasing, and production control not possible in operations offering more varied menus. Customers frequenting these operations know what to expect and are familiar with the menu choices provided. As a way of appealing to regional markets, addition of local favorites to the menu may be permitted.

In the institutional segment of the foodservice industry, short term hospitals and short order foodservices on university campuses are the main types of operations that have adopted static menus. Because of the short length of the average patient stay, some hospitals have found that a static menu, which offers the same choices day after day, has led to the advantages identified above. Short order foodservices on university campuses are modeled after fast food commercial establishments. Industrial feeding operations may include fast food static-type menus. In many commercial foodservices, a static menu may be offered with daily specials added to the offerings to provide variety and seasonal features.

A cycle menu is a series of menus offering different items from day to day on a weekly, biweekly, or some other basis, after which the cycle is repeated. In many institutional operations, seasonal cycle menus are common; that is, a three-week menu for winter, spring, summer, and fall may be repeated during each of these seasons. Cycle menus are typically used in healthcare institutions, schools, and industrial feeding operations. They offer the advantage of variety with some degree of control over purchasing, production, and cost. In addition, menu planners are not constantly being required to plan menus. Even though a cycle menu may be served over and over, however, menu planners must be alert to customer acceptance, changing costs of menu items, and new products in the market place, and revise menus accordingly.

Some foodservice operations may combine static and cycle menus, offering a few items day after day and others on a rotating basis. For example, a commercial cafeteria may serve fried chicken and roast beef every day and different specialty items each day of the week, such as Mexican food on Tuesday, Italian food on Wednesday, and so on. As a result, clientele can enjoy the greater variety but can count on certain basic mainstays.

The last of the three basic menu types, the single-use menu, is planned for service on a particular day and is not used in the exact form a second time. This type of menu is used most frequently in institutional foodservice in which the same clientele is served over a long period of time. Many college and university foodservices utilize a single-use menu approach or a modification of a cycle menu. For example, a cycle of entrees may be used with different combinations of side dishes, planned on a single-use basis.

Categorizing menus by choice, the no choice menu is often referred to as a non-selective menu and may be either cycle or single-use. This type of menu is used by many institutional operations as well as by most airline foodservices. A no choice menu is characteristic of many catered events. If clientele preferences are considered carefully, a no choice menu may still result in customer satisfaction while permitting more accurate forecasting and a greater degree of control. Non-selective menus are suitable in institutions serving clientele who may not care to make decisions or in operations required to serve meals in limited time periods, such as school foodservice. Menu choices are being encouraged in school lunch programs, however, as a way of increasing student acceptance.

A limited choice cycle or single-use menu may provide selections for some menu items but offer no choice for others. For example, a choice of entrees may be offered with no choices in vegetable, salad, or dessert. In some limited choice menus, only a small number of selections may be offered, such as two entrees and two salads. Sometimes the choices may be offered only in easily prepared items, such as beverages, salads, or desserts. A choice of fruit, gelatin dessert, baked custard, or ice cream, for example, may be the dessert choices on a hospital menu—all of which are readily available items.

Day 6, Week I, Summer Cycle

GENERAL MENU

Morning	Noon	Night
____ Freshly Squeezed Orange Juice	____ Chilled Tomato Juice with Crackers	____ Williamsburg Fruit Punch
____ Grapefruit Juice	____ Celery Broth	____ Chicken Consomme
____ Breakfast Prunes	____ Beef Stew with Vegetables	____ Turkey Pot Pie
____ Raisins	____ Browned Beef Hash with Beef Cubes	____ Braised Pork Chop with Gravy
____ Hot Pettijohn Cereal	____ Wiener in Long Bun with Mustard	____ Mashed Potatoes
____ Rice Krispies		____ Buttered Broccoli Spear
____ Puffed Rice	____ Buttered Green Beans	____ Buttered Beet Slices
____ Scrambled Eggs	____ Golden Corn Kernels	____ Tossed Salad Greens
____ Poached Egg		____ Zesty French Salad Dressing or
____ Fried Egg Sunny Side Up	____ Fresh Spinach Salad with Egg Slices and Bacon Mayonnaise Salad Dressing	____ Blue Cheese Salad Dressing
____ Fried Egg Over Light		
____ Fried Egg Hard		____ Herb Bread with Butter
____ Soft Cooked Egg in Shell	____ Petite Fruit Salad	____ White Bread or Toast with Butter
____ Hard Cooked Egg in Shell		
____ Broiled Bacon Strip	____ Luncheon Roll with Butter	____ Applesauce
____ Helen Corbitt's Coffee Cake	____ White Bread or Toast with Butter	____ Creme Brulee
____ Whole Wheat Toast with Butter	____ Royal Anne Cherries	
____ White Toast/Bread with Butter	____ Cocoa–Butterscotch Chip Cookie	

Figure 6.4. *An example of a choice menu from the four-week menu cycle of the Indiana University Medical Center (used by permission)*

A wide variety of <u>choice menus</u> are used in foodservice operations and may be static, cycle, or single-use. Choices may be many or few within each of the types of menu items. In some instances, the choice may be between several different complete menus or within menu items. Figure 6.4, for example, shows a menu from week 1, day 6, in a four-week cycle menu from the Indiana University Medical Center. Choices are offered in each of the major menu item categories.

In cafeterias and full service restaurants, offering many different choices has been characteristic. In institutional foodservice, however, no choice or limited choice menus have been characteristic historically. More recently, a greater variety of menu choices has become a common pattern in institutions, primarily as a way of increasing clientele satisfaction. Also, choice menus offer a way of serving less popular items with more popular menu offerings as a way of considering a wider range of food preferences and increasing variety. For example, liver can be included as an entree choice for those patrons who are "liver lovers," whereas a menu planner would be reluctant to offer liver as the only choice of a no choice menu.

The à la carte menu is actually not a separate menu type but a method of pricing a menu. In this method, menu items are priced separately, offered separately, and selected separately by the diner. This approach is typical of many types of commercial foodservices, ranging from the upscale gourmet restaurant to the fast food operation. Cafeterias, both commercial and institutional, generally offer à la carte pricing of menu items as well. A modified à la carte approach is used in many commercial foodservices, in which certain parts of the meal are grouped together and offered at one price, with other menu items priced separately. For example, the meat, potato or substitute, and salad may be offered for one price, with soup, vegetables, dessert, and beverages priced separately.

MENU STRUCTURE

Today's typical American meal pattern is a quick breakfast, a light lunch, and a heavy dinner in the evening, particularly for those living alone or in dual-career families. The types of foods eaten at different meals vary widely and traditional menu patterns have changed greatly through the years; however, each type of meal evokes a perception of specific food items. For example, breakfast conjures up an image of eggs, bacon, and toast in many people's minds with perhaps juice, cereal, milk, or coffee. The three-meal-a-day pattern, however, is atypical for many people, and eating throughout the day and night has brought about much diversification in the foodservice industry. Breakfast may be eaten at midmorning or as a late supper at night, and persons working night shifts may prefer food other than the traditional breakfast fare in the morning. Brunch is a popular meal for many, particularly on weekends when schedules may be less hectic. Whatever the meal of the day may be, it is the primary factor influencing menu planning.

Breakfast and Brunch

The American breakfast has remained fairly traditional: fruit or juice, cereal, eggs, breakfast meat, bread, and milk or coffee. Most breakfast menus, regardless of the type of foodservice establishment, include these items. According to the 1982 Restaurant and Institutions menu census, the top three listings on foodservice breakfast menus were scrambled eggs, toast, and bacon. For a "grab it and run" breakfast, sweet rolls and beverage are another common combination, particularly in hotel, industrial, and university foodservice operations. Interestingly, in the late 1970s and early 1980s, growth in breakfast sales has outpaced that for other meals in the commercial foodservice market.

Cereals are commonly included on menus in schools, colleges and universities, healthcare institutions, full service restaurants, hotels, and commercial cafeteria operations. Cooked cereals are most common on healthcare menus. In the South, however, grits are served on breakfast menus in all types of foodservices. As indicated above, scrambled is the most popular method of preparation for eggs; fried or poached eggs are also available in many types of operations. Omelets have gained in popularity in recent years, not only for breakfast but for other meals as well. More elaborate egg dishes, such as Eggs Benedict and Eggs Florentine, may be offered particularly in upscale restaurants. In the Southwest, Huevos Rancheros, or tortillas topped with egg and chili sauce, are commonly available.

As an alternative to an egg dish, pancakes, waffles, or french toast are available on many menus, particularly on full service restaurant, college or university foodservice, and healthcare menus. Pancakes and waffles have also become popular for service throughout the day and night; a number of commercial chain and franchise operations specialize in these menu items.

In many types of foodservice operations, brunch is often served on weekends or for catered events. Since brunch is a hybrid of breakfast and lunch, menus are varied and may include both breakfast and lunch food items. Commercial operations have turned Saturday and Sunday pre-lunch hours into profitable brunch business, and institutional foodservices, particularly retirement centers and college and university foodservices, may serve brunch in lieu of both breakfast and lunch on weekends. For example, Houlihan's Old Place in Kansas City serves a special brunch every Sunday. Its brunch menu, shown in Figure 6.5, is a static choice menu with à la carte pricing.

The basic brunch menu pattern generally begins with fruit and juice; entree offerings usually include egg dishes, breakfast meats in addition to such typical lunch and dinner entrees as roast beef, fried chicken, or Shrimp Newburg. A variety of hot breads are frequently included, with vegetables, salads, and an array of cheeses also offered as well. Menu selections will vary depending on type of service, however; the menu for a buffet will generally include a much wider array of selections than that planned for a sit-down brunch. The hours of service will also influence the menu pattern. Morning brunches tend to reflect breakfast items, but those served into the early afternoon hours may be more similar to lunch. A champagne brunch has become an extremely popular meal, especially in upscale restaurants or urban hotels.

Lunch

Lunch menus are far less traditional than those at other meals and may vary from a complete meal, similar to that served at dinner, to as simple a meal as soup and sandwich. The menu pattern is highly dependent on the type of operation. In healthcare institutions, lunch menus typically include an entree, potato or substitute, vegetable, salad, bread, dessert, and beverage, particularly for patient service. In other types of institutional foodservice, lunch menus are commonly composed of soups, a variety of cold or hot sandwiches, casseroles, or main dish salads, with small salads, desserts, and beverages as accompaniments. Sandwich selections are commonly served with french fries, potato or corn chips, and perhaps relishes. In many types of foodservice operations, the salad bar is extremely popular, especially at lunch. Menu selections may be limited to greens with a variety of vegetable toppings and dressings, or may include a wide array of

Houlihan's for Sunday Brunch

Make a special trip to Houlihan's Emporium Table. It's a brunch lovers'
delight, brimming with your Sunday morning favorites...fresh, warm
and delicious! Enjoy the Emporium Table alone, or as a perfect
compliment to your Houlihan's brunch entree.

Eye Opening Beverages

SCREWDRIVER Fresh-squeezed orange juice and vodka.

MIMOSA Champagne and fresh-squeezed orange juice.

BLOODY MARY All-time favorite!

BELLINI Champagne and peach nectar with a sliced peach garnish.

SALTY DOG Fresh-squeezed grapefruit juice and vodka with a salted rim.

IRISH COFFEE Famous Buena Vista® recipe.

CAPPUCCINO HOULIHAN With six kinds of liquors, whipped cream and chocolate shavings.

Starters

Fresh-squeezed ORANGE Juice 1.00

Fresh-squeezed GRAPEFRUIT Juice ... 1.00

CAPPUCCINO Espresso, steamed milk, whipped cream and cinnamon....1.75

BLOODY MARY Minus the vodka 1.00

TOMATO JUICE On the rocks .... .80

Bourbon Street Breakfast

Start with our freshly-squeezed orange or grapefruit juice

Followed by EGGS BENEDICT, hash browns, a strawberry crepe
and a cup of steaming cappuccino ... 7.95

Breakfast Houlihan®

Start with our freshly-squeezed orange or grapefruit juice

Followed by toasted English muffin halves, topped with grilled tomato slices,
poached eggs, mornay sauce and
crisp bacon strips. Served with hash browns ... 6.95

Brioche *French* Toast Thick slices of French Brioche, batter-dipped and pan-fried in butter. Served with Canadian bacon or link sausage.
Your choice of style...
With strawberry filling and topped with strawberries in sauce 5.95
Plain with maple syrup 5.25

Eggs Benedict Toasted English muffin halves topped with Canadian bacon, poached eggs and hollandaise sauce........................... 5.95

Huevos California Spicy omelette with peppers, tomatoes, onions and ham. Wrapped in a soft flour tortilla spread with guacamole and topped with mild salsa and sour cream. Served with toasted English muffin 6.45

Steak & Eggs Broiled strip sirloin and eggs, any style, with hash browns and toasted English muffin 6.95

Joe's Omelette Tomatoes, scallions, bell peppers, mushrooms and melted Old English cheese. Served with hash browns and toasted English muffin 5.95

Crabmeat Omelette Loaded with Alaskan crab. Flavored with chives and topped with hollandaise sauce. Served with hash browns and toasted English muffin 6.95

Goldenrod Omelette Ham, bacon, mushrooms, fresh broccoli and melted Swiss cheese. Served with hash browns and English muffin 5.95

Figure 6.5. *An example of a static choice menu for Sunday brunch from Houlihan's Old Place of Kansas City, Gilbert Robinson Co., Inc.*

SCHOOL LUNCH PATTERNS FOR VARIOUS AGE/GRADE GROUPS

U.S. Department of Agriculture, National School Lunch Program

USDA recommends, but does not require, that you adjust portions by age/grade group to better meet the food and nutritional needs of children according to their ages. If you adjust portions, Groups I-IV are minimum requirements for the age/grade groups specified. If you do not adjust portions, the Group IV portions in the shaded column are the portions to serve all children.

COMPONENTS	MINIMUM QUANTITIES				RECOMMENDED QUANTITIES[1]	SPECIFIC REQUIREMENTS
	Preschool		Grades K-3	Grades 4-12[1]	Grades 7-12	
	ages 1-2 (Group I)	ages 3-4 (Group II)	ages 5-8 (Group III)	age 9 & over (Group IV)	age 12 & over (Group V)	
MEAT OR MEAT ALTERNATE — A serving of one of the following or a combination to give an equivalent quantity:						• Must be served in the main dish or the main dish and one other menu item. • Textured vegetable protein products, cheese alternate products, and enriched macaroni with fortified protein may be used to meet part of the meat/meat alternate requirement. Fact sheets on each of these alternate foods give detailed instructions for use. NOTE: The amount you must serve of a single meat alternate may seem too large for the particular age group you are serving. To make the quantity of that meat alternate more reasonable, use a smaller amount to meet part of the requirement and supplement with another meat or meat alternate to meet the full requirement.
Lean meat, poultry, or fish (edible portion as served)	1 oz	1½ oz	1½ oz	2 oz	3 oz	
Cheese	1 oz	1½ oz	1½ oz	2 oz	3 oz	
Large egg(s)	1	1½	1½	2	3	
Cooked dry beans or peas	½ cup	¾ cup	¾ cup	1 cup	1½ cup	
Peanut butter	2 Tbsp	3 Tbsp	3 Tbsp	4 Tbsp	6 Tbsp	
VEGETABLE AND/OR FRUIT — Two or more servings of vegetable or fruit or both to total	½ cup	½ cup	½ cup	¾ cup	¾ cup	• No more than one-half of the total requirement may be met with full-strength fruit or vegetable juice. • Cooked dry beans or peas may be used as a meat alternate or as a vegetable but not as both in the same meal.
BREAD OR BREAD ALTERNATE — Servings of bread or bread alternate. A serving is • 1 slice of whole-grain or enriched bread • A whole-grain or enriched biscuit, roll, muffin, etc. • ½ cup of cooked whole-grain or enriched rice, macaroni, noodles, whole-grain or enriched pasta products, or other cereal grains such as bulgur or corn grits • A combination of any of the above	5 per week	8 per week	8 per week	8 per week	10 per week	• At least ½ serving of bread or an equivalent quantity of bread alternate for Group I, and 1 serving for Groups II-V, must be served daily. • Enriched macaroni with fortified protein may be used as a meat alternate or as a bread alternate but not as both in the same meal. NOTE: Food Buying Guide for School Food Service, PA-1257 (1980) provides the information for the minimum weight of a serving.
MILK — A serving of fluid milk	¾ cup (6 fl oz)	¾ cup (6 fl oz)	½ pint (8 fl oz)	½ pint (8 fl oz)	½ pint (8 fl oz)	At least one of the following forms of milk must be offered: • Unflavored lowfat milk • Unflavored skim milk • Unflavored buttermilk NOTE: This requirement does not prohibit offering other milks, such as whole milk or flavored milk, along with one or more of the above.

[1] Group IV is shaded because it is the one meal pattern which will satisfy all requirements if no portion size adjustments are made.

[2] Group V specifies recommended, not required, quantities for students 12 years and older. These students may request smaller portions, but not smaller than those specified in Group IV.

May 1990

Figure 6.6. *National School Lunch menu patterns*

other salads, such as potato salad, macaroni salad, and gelatin with vegetables or fruits. A choice of soups to accompany the salad bar may be offered.

The menu pattern for the National School Lunch Program is defined in federal regulations that specify type and amount of food according to the age and grade level of children served by the program. The menu pattern is shown in Figure 6.6. To qualify for reimbursement, schools must follow the defined menu pattern and offer the complete menu to all children. Current regulations, however, specify that students may decline menu items if they desire.

Dinner

Dinner in the evening is the main meal of the day in the United States; the traditional menu includes an entree of meat, fish, or poultry, potato or substitute, vegetable, and salad. For lighter or late evening meals, menus may be similar to those served at breakfast, brunch, or lunch.

An appetizer may be served before the main course which may be soup, seafood cocktail, fruit cup, or fruit or tomato juice. The first course menu offerings may be much more exotic in upscale restaurants such as caviar with lemon wedges, oysters on the half shell with cocktail sauce, and escargots in garlic butter. In fine restaurants featuring Italian food, small portions of pasta may be a first course in addition to the traditional antipasto.

Desserts are commonly included as a menu component in institutions. With the emphasis on weight control, fruit or other lower calorie dessert choices are frequently offered. In almost all commercial foodservices, however, desserts are offered as a separate menu item. Selections may be very limited or may include an array of fruits, baked desserts, ice creams, or specialty items, such as flaming desserts.

FACTORS AFFECTING MENU PLANNING

Many factors must be considered in planning menus, regardless of the type of foodservice operation. These factors can be clustered into those that are clientele-related and those that are management-related.

Clientele Considerations

Clientele considerations include sociocultural factors and nutritional needs. To enhance the client acceptability of a menu, esthetic factors also must be considered in menu planning.

Sociocultural Factors

Foods: Habits and Preferences. Consideration of food habits and preferences must be a priority in planning menus for a given clientele. Cultural food patterns, regional food preferences, and age of clientele are related considerations. Too often, menu planners are influenced by their own likes and dislikes of foods and food combinations rather than those of the clientele.

Eckstein (1978) defined <u>food habits</u> as the practices and associated attitudes that predetermine what, when, why, and how a person will eat. Individual food habits are determined by the interaction of environmental, physical, and psychological factors with previous food experiences; age, sex, culture, race, religion, economic and social status, and geographic area of residence are contributing factors. Regional and cultural food habits and patterns still exist in the United States, but the mobility of the population and the sophistication of the food marketing and distribution system have led to less obvious differences.

<u>Food preferences</u> express degree of liking for a food item (Peryam and Pilgrim, 1957). They are primarily determined by food habits, since people usually prefer foods they customarily consume.

Menu planners should be aware of changing food habits and food patterns. To evaluate changes in the American diet, per capita food use data have been employed. In a recent report, Welsh and Marston (1982) presented data on food consumption from the U.S. food supply over the last 70 years. Collected by the Economic Research Service of the U.S. Department of Agriculture, these data are shown in Table 6.1 by several major food groups for the years 1909–13, 1947–49, and 1980. This comparison shows on the whole increased use through 1949 in major food groups except grain products; however, the preliminary data for 1980 shows a decrease in most food groups except meats, fish, and poultry, fats and oils, and sugar and sweeteners. These changes may be attributed to the increased use of poultry and the emphasis on the dietary implications of saturated fats. For example, use of low-fat milk has increased and whole milk has decreased as the consumer apparently has been concerned about fat content of the diet.

<u>Restaurants & Institutions</u> conducts a periodic survey to determine popular menu offerings in the foodservice industry. The fifteen menu items offered most frequently, according to the 1983 census in industrial, commercial, and noncommercial foodservice operations for breakfast, lunch, and dinner and for the dessert course, are listed in Table 6.2. The contrast in types of menu offerings among the various segments of the industry are interesting and reflect current menu patterns in foodservice.

Assessing Menu Item Popularity. Analysis of food habits and preferences should be conducted to provide data for menu planning. Formal and informal methods may be used to examine clientele reactions to various menu items. Highly sophisticated market research studies are conducted by the large national multi-unit foodservice corporations prior to a major menu change or even introduction of a new menu item. As we discussed in Chapter 1, these companies are approaching addition of new menu items more cautiously than in the past in the recognition that these items may not generate additional sales but only be substitutions for present menu items.

Small-scale surveys, formal and informal interviews with clientele, customer comment cards, observations of plate waste, and tallying of menu selections are

Table 6.1. *Food content of the U.S. food supply, per capita per year*

Food group†	Years		
	1909–13	*1947–49*	*1980‡*
	←———lbs., retail wt.———→		
meat, poultry, and fish			
beef	54	52	78
pork	62	64	69
poultry	18	22	62
fish	13	13	17
total	172	176	245
eggs	37	47	35
dairy products			
whole milk	265	299	171
lowfat milk	61	36	106
cheese	5	10	22
total#	381	507	469
fats and oils			
butter	18	11	4
total	41	46	61
fruits			
citrus	17	66	77
non-citrus	159	142	119
total, fresh	168	164	107
total, processed	8	44	39
total	176	208	197
vegetables			
tomatoes	43	48	55
dark green, deep yellow	14	31	24
other	146	157	141
total, fresh	186	184	143
total, processed	17	52	77
total	203	236	219
potatoes			
white, fresh	182	110	51
white, processed¶	0	‖	62
sweet, fresh	23	12	4
sweet, processed¶	0	‖	1
total	205	123	118
dry beans, peas, nuts, soy products	16	17	18
grain products			
wheat flour	213	137	119
corn flour and meal	50	13	8
total	291	171	154
sugar and sweeteners			
refined cane/beet sugar	77	95	88
other sugar and sirup	14	19	54
total	91	114	143

Table 6.1. *(cont.)*

Food group†	Years		
	1909–13	*1947–49*	*1980‡*
	←————*lbs., retail wt.*————→		
miscellaneous**			
coffee	8	15	9
total	10	19	12

Source: Susan O. Welsh and Ruth M. Marston: Review of Trends in Food Use in the United States, 1909 to 1980. Reprinted from JOURNAL OF THE AMERICAN DIETETIC ASSOCIATION, Vol. 81:120, 1982.

†Totals include some foods not listed in this table; components may not add to a total due to rounding.

‡Preliminary data.

#Calcium equivalent pounds of whole milk (total calcium divided by the calcium per pound of whole milk).

¶Fresh equivalent weight.

‖Less than 0.5 lb.

**Includes coffee, tea, and chocolate liquor equivalent of cocoa and chocolate products.

various methods used to collect the data on food preferences and menu item popularity that can provide guidance to the menu planner. Offering a wide variety of menu items without regard for clientele preferences may be costly. Too often, menu planners are concerned with offering "variety for variety's sake." As we stated earlier in the chapter, however, offering menu selections is a method of satisfying the varying food preferences of the clientele. Pairing popular and less popular items is one way of providing foods liked by a small segment of the target population while also considering the preferences of the majority.

Food preference surveys usually employ a hedonic scale in which foods are rated by an individual on a continuum from "like extremely" to "dislike extremely" (Peryam and Pilgrim, 1957). Some of the classic work on food preference measurement was done by the U.S. Army Quartermaster Corps (1960). In those studies, a nine-point hedonic scale was used to measure preferences as predictors of army food acceptability. In other studies, two-, three-, and five-point scales have been used.

For measurement of food preferences among children, facial hedonic scales have been widely used, sometimes called the "smiley face" rating scale (Lachance, 1976; Comstock et al., 1981). An example of a facial hedonic scale is shown in Figure 6.7. Wells (1965) found that the facial method is easier to use with children than are words or numbers because it allows good communication and understanding regardless of age, intelligence, education, or even the ability to speak English.

Frequency of acceptance of foods is another method used for studying food habits and preferences. Knickrehm et al. (1969) studied frequency of acceptance of menu items by asking college students to indicate how often they would be willing to eat the food. They found that vegetables were acceptable less frequently than other types of menu items. Schultz (1965) developed an approach called the

Table 6.2. Most frequently offered menu items in industrial, commercial and noncommercial foodservice operations (1983 Menu Census)

	Breakfast			Lunch			Dinner			Dessert course		
	Industry	Commercial	Non-commercial	Industry	Commercial	Non-commercial	Industry	Commercial	Non-commercial	Industry	Commercial	Non-commercial
1.	Orange juice	Scrambled eggs	Orange juice	Hamburger	Hamburger	Green beans	French fries	French fries	Ice cream	Apple pie	Apple pie	Canned peaches
2.	Scrambled eggs	Orange juice	Cold cereal	French fries	French fries	Spaghetti	Baked potato	Steak	Green beans	Ice cream	Ice cream	Canned pears
3.	Toast	Bacon	Apple juice	Cheeseburger	Cheeseburger	Hamburger	Steak	Fried shrimp	Peas	Cheesecake	Cheesecake	Fresh fruit
4.	Bacon	Fried eggs	Toast	Ham and cheese	Ham and cheese	Peas	Coleslaw	Hamburger	Carrots	Cherry pie	Topped ice cream	Canned pineapple
5.	Pancakes	Pancakes	Scrambled eggs	Coleslaw	Coleslaw	French fries	Ice cream	Ice cream	Broccoli	Chocolate cake	Cherry pie	Gelatin
6.	Grapefruit juice	Hot chocolate	Bananas	Grilled cheese	Grilled cheese	Mashed potatoes	Hamburger	Cheeseburger	Mashed potatoes	Pumpkin pie	Pumpkin pie	Fruit cocktail
7.	Cold cereal	Ham	Grapefruit juice	Green beans	Ham sandwich	Canned peaches	Chicken soup	Coleslaw	Cottage cheese	Canned peaches	Sundaes	Cookies
8.	Hot chocolate	Toast	Pancakes	Apple pie	Chicken soup	Hot dog	Green beans	Chicken soup	Mixed vegetables	Gelatin	Pecan pie	Chocolate pudding
9.	Fried eggs	Omelet	Bacon	Chicken soup	Apple pie	Macaroni and cheese	Cheeseburger	Fried chicken	Coleslaw	Chocolate pudding	Carrot cake	Apple pie
10.	Tomato juice	Tomato juice	Doughnuts	Mashed potatoes	Bacon, lettuce, tomato sandwich	Coleslaw	Fried chicken	Cheesecake	Steak	Fresh fruit	Pie à la mode	Chocolate cake
11.	French toast	French toast	Cooked cereal	Fried chicken	Roast beef sandwich		Tossed greens	Green beans	Roast beef	Fruit cocktail	Blueberry pie	Brownies
12.	Danish	Grapefruit juice	Danish	Spaghetti	Ice cream	Canned pears	Cheesecake	Onion rings	White rice	Canned pears	Chocolate cake	Yellow cake
13.	Ham	Potatoes	French toast	Chili	Vegetable soup	Carrots	Roast beef	Tossed greens	Spaghetti	Carrot cake	Chocolate pie	Ice cream
14.	Cooked cereal	Poached eggs	Oranges	Vegetable soup	Roast beef	Fresh fruit	Broccoli	Bean soup	Baked ham	Topped ice cream	Sherbet/ices	Cobbler
15.	Poached eggs	Danish	Tomato juice	Ham sandwich	Chef salad	Applesauce / Mixed vegetables	Carrots	French onion soup	Spinach	Brownies	Coconut cream pie	White cake

Source: Restaurants & Institutions, a Cahners Publication.

Did you like what you ate?

Check (✓) the face that shows how you <u>felt</u> about
the food served today in the lunchroom.

FOOD

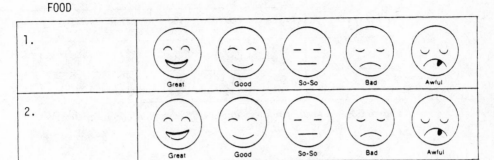

Figure 6.7. *A facial hedonic scale used for measuring children's food preferences*

Food Action Rating Scale for measuring preferences in which foods are rated on a
nine-point scale of "eat every opportunity" to "eat if forced."

Johnson and Vaden (1979) used a <u>decision making approach</u> to measure
intentions to select menu items from a list of choices. They found that college
students were more likely to report food selection accurately for entree items they
preferred when coupled with entrees less preferred. When two well-liked items
were offered together, however, intentions were a less accurate predictor of actual choices.

Sensory evaluation has been used to measure reactions to food in which
individuals are asked to rate foods on various dimensions such as flavor, temperature, texture, or appearance. In Figure 6.8, a sensory evaluation score card used to
evaluate elementary students' reactions to menu items is shown.

<u>Circle</u> the words that <u>best</u> describe how you feel about the food today.

FOOD

1.	TASTES	Circle one: Great Good So-So Bad Awful
	LOOKS	Circle one: Great Good So-So Bad Awful
	TEMPERATURE	Circle one: Just right O.K. Too cool
	AMOUNT	Circle one: Too much Right amount Not enough
2.	TASTES	Circle one: Great Good So-So Bad Awful
	LOOKS	Circle one: Great Good So-So Bad Awful
	TEMPERATURE	Circle one: Just right O.K. Too cool
	AMOUNT	Circle one: Too much Right amount Not enough

Figure 6.8. *An example of a sensory evaluation score card for menu items*

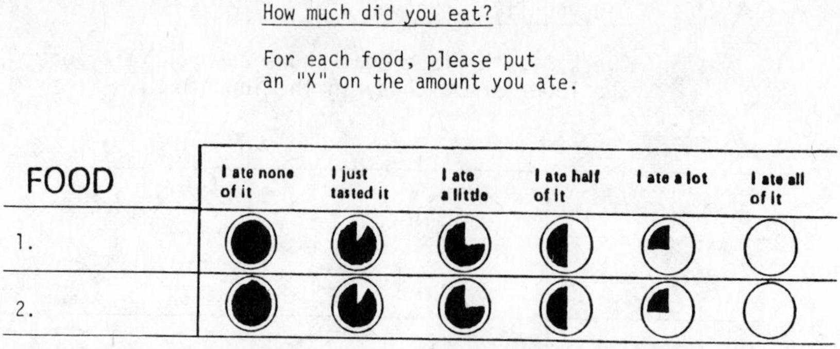

How much did you eat?

For each food, please put
an "X" on the amount you ate.

Figure 6.9. *A scale for measuring self-reported consumption*

Plate waste studies have been another important method for measuring food acceptability. Weighed plate waste has been the method used in many studies, particularly in the school lunch program. This method has been used to examine waste of menu items on an individual or group basis or to measure total waste for a meal.

Observational methods have been used in which trained observers estimate the amount of plate waste. Four- to six-point scales are used to estimate plate waste visually. Results of several studies have indicated that the visual estimation of plate waste is an accurate and simple method for assessing food acceptability. Self-reported consumption is another technique for measuring plate waste in which individuals are asked to estimate their plate waste using a scale similar to one used in the trained observer technique. An example of this type of scale is shown in Figure 6.9.

However they are analyzed, the menu planner must be cognizant of the food habits and preferences of the target clientele in order to plan menus that are acceptable and will generate participation, sales, and overall customer satisfaction. Age, cultural, and regional food patterns are important to consider as well as changing food patterns over time.

Nutritional Considerations

Nutritional needs of the consumer should be considered in menu planning for all types of foodservice operations, but they are a special concern in serving a captive clientele. For example, in healthcare facilities, college and university foodservice, and other types of institutions, most of the nutritional needs of the clientele must be provided by the foodservice. Because of the increasing public awareness of the importance of nutrition to health and wellness, commercial foodservice operators are also being requested to consider nutritional quality in menu selections.

For recommendations, menu planners may turn to the "Dietary Guidelines for Americans," issued in 1980 by the USDA and the U.S. Department of Health and Human Services. These guidelines (Figure 6.10) recommend including a variety of foods in the diet; limiting fat, sugar, and sodium intake; and increasing

Nutrition and Your Health

Dietary Guidelines for Americans

 Eat a Variety of Foods

 Maintain Ideal Weight

 Avoid Too Much Fat, Saturated Fat, and Cholesterol

 Eat Foods with Adequate Starch and Fiber

 Avoid Too Much Sugar

 Avoid Too Much Sodium

 If You Drink Alcohol, Do So in Moderation

Figure 6.10. *Dietary guidelines for Americans.* **Source: Nutrition and Your Health,** *USDA and USHHS, February, 1980.*

fiber consumption. In operations providing three meals a day, menus should fulfill the recommended dietary allowances (RDA) defined by the National Research Council (1980), which specify nutrient needs for various age groups by sex.

For some types of feeding programs, specific nutritional guidelines have been made mandatory. For example, the nutritional goal of the National School Lunch Program is to provide one-third of the RDAs. According to the Food and Nutrition Service, USDA (1980), *Menu Planning Guide for School Food Service*, each daily lunch is not expected to provide one-third of the RDAs for all nutrients; the average over a period of time, however, in which a wide variety of foods is served, should meet the goal. The menu pattern, specified by USDA to meet this goal, was shown earlier in this chapter (Figure 6.6).

Esthetic Factors

Flavor, texture, color, shape, and method of preparation are other factors to consider in planning menus. A balance should be maintained among flavors, such as tart and sweet, mild and highly seasoned, light and heavy. Foods of the same or similar flavor should generally not be repeated in a menu. In addition to the basic tastes of sweet, sour, salty, and bitter, menu planners need to consider strong and mild flavors and spicy or highly seasoned food in selecting combinations. A variety of flavors within a meal is more enjoyable than duplications, although exceptions are made to this rule. For instance, tomato in a tossed salad is an acceptable accompaniment to meat sauce and spaghetti; and a Mexican-style meal always includes several highly spiced menu items. Certain combinations have become traditional such as turkey and cranberries and roast beef and horseradish sauce. The flavors are complementary and customers tend to expect these combinations to be served together.

Texture refers to the structure of foods and is detected by the feel of foods in the mouth. Crisp, soft, grainy, smooth, hard, and chewy are among the descriptors of food texture. A variety of textures within a meal is more pleasing than a sameness of textures. A crisp salad served with soup on a luncheon menu is a more pleasing texture combination than a gelatin fruit salad or a peach and cottage cheese salad with soup. Consistency of foods is the degree of firmness, density, or viscosity. Runny, gelatinous, and firm are characteristics of consistency, as are thin, medium, and thick when referring to sauces. Considering the consistency of various menu items is also important in menu planning.

Color on the plate, tray, or cafeteria counter gives eye appeal and helps to merchandise the food. Whether it is introduced in a meal by a garnish or by one of the main dishes, the color of foods should always be considered in selecting menu items. The orange-red of tomatoes and the purple-red of beets, for example, is an unappealing combination, and a menu with several white foods is a dull combination. Contrast in colors, such as a green vegetable rather than cauliflower with a fish or poultry entree, makes a menu more appealing.

The shape of food can also be used to create interest in a menu through the variety of forms in which foods can be presented. Modern dicing and cutting machines provide an easy method for serving different forms and sizes of some foods. Carrots, for example, may be cut into strips, sliced, cubed, or shredded to give interest to a menu.

Combinations of foods using different methods of preparation can add variety to the menu. Foods prepared in the same manner generally should not be served in the same meal, barring some common exceptions such as fish and chips, both of which are fried. As an example of an unappealing combination, two menu items served in sauces would not be pleasing. Other ways to introduce variety—and texture—are to serve both cold and hot foods, or both raw and cooked foods. Today, some foods, previously served only in a cooked form, are now served raw, such as the cauliflower, broccoli, and mushrooms on salad bars.

Managerial Considerations

The type of foodservice system is a primary factor in all managerial considerations relating to menu planning. In conventional systems, menus may be limited by the amount of time available for food preparation and by the availability of food and labor. In the commissary and ready prepared systems, the holding characteristics of menu items are the key considerations. Not all food items are suitable for holding by cook-chill or cook-freeze methods, and extensive process modification is needed for some. The method of transporting foods and the manner in which foods are transported, in bulk or in individual serving portions, are also considerations in commissary or ready prepared systems. Service period deadlines, however, do not present the production limitations they do for the conventional system. In assembly/serve systems, the menu planner may have to deal with the constraint of limited availability of prepared foods in the market place.

As previously stated, the menu serves as the primary control of the foodservice system; therefore, the menu should be viewed as a managerial tool for controlling cost and production. In designing it, a number of management-related factors must be considered: food cost, production capability, type of service, and availability of foods.

Food Cost

In today's inflationary economy, foodservice managers must be cost-conscious in all areas of operations. Since the menu is a major determinant of the cost of goods sold in a foodservice operation, the manager and menu planner must be particularly aware of menu item cost, both raw food cost and portion cost of prepared food. With the rapid rise in food cost over the last few years, the menu planner must also be alert to changing food prices. This knowledge alone, however, is not enough; Bobeng (1982) stated that total cost of menu items, that is, both the raw food cost and labor cost, must be considered. She indicated that items with lower food cost may have a higher labor cost and vice versa.

Balancing menus in relation to cost is an important aspect of menu planning. For example, combining a high-cost item on a menu with a lower cost item that is more popular would control cost. On the other hand, if expensive items are served all on one day, lower cost items may need to be included on subsequent days.

In commercial operations, the selling price of a menu item must be taken into account. Their general objective is to maintain a stated percentage of food cost in relation to selling price. For example, a 33 percent raw food cost in relation to sales revenue has been a "rule of thumb" for many commercial operations. This objective does not necessarily apply to each menu item but to the overall sales mix. Some menu items, such as beverages, may have a much lower food cost in relation to sales while other items, especially entrees, may be higher. "What the traffic will bear," or in other words, what the customer is willing to pay, must be considered in selecting menu items.

In most institutional foodservices, a daily allowance per client is provided in the budget. This is true in most healthcare institutions, college and university foodservices, military feeding, and prisons. In school foodservice, the amount of federal and state reimbursements provide the basis for determining the budget available for food.

Production Capability

To produce a given menu, several resources must be considered, a primary one being labor. The number of labor hours, as well as the number and skill of personnel at a given time, determine the menu that can be produced. Some menu items may be produced or their preparation completed during slack periods to ease the production load during peak service periods; however, the effect on food quality of this production in advance of service may limit the amount that can be done. Employees' days off may need to be considered in menu planning because relief personnel may not match their skill or efficiency in meeting production requirements. Planning less complicated menu items or using convenience items may be alternatives.

Production capability is also affected by the layout of the food production facility and the availability of large and small equipment. The menu should be planned to balance the use of ovens, steam equipment, fryers, grills, and other equipment. Refrigeration and freezer capacity must also be considered. Many novice menu planners have been guilty of planning menus that overtax the oven capacity in a foodservice facility. In a hospital foodservice, for example, a menu with meat loaf, baked potato, and baked dessert may present a real production problem.

Inclusion of several food items requiring a great deal of last minute preparation may create production difficulties. However, because of the large number of items requiring preparation at the time of service in fast food operations, equipment for production and short term holding has been designed specifically to meet these production demands. Even so, employee shifts must still be scheduled carefully to ensure fast service to customers during peak service periods.

Type of Service

Type of service is a major influence on the food items that can be included on a menu. A restaurant with table service will have a different menu than a self-service operation or a cafeteria. A buffet service may serve items difficult to manage in a table or tray service operation.

Food items with longer holding capability should be selected for menus in healthcare facilities with patient tray service, because any last-minute preparation may present a problem. As we discussed in Chapter 5, however, galley kitchens may be available in some foodservice systems for last-minute preparation of menu items that do not hold well, such as toast and coffee.

Equipment for holding and serving will affect the menu selections that can be offered. Hot foods may be held in heated equipment, either fixed or portable. Required temperatures are relatively low and humidification is necessary for some foods. Cold foods may be held in refrigerated units or iced counters. Central commissaries and satellite units require insulated transport units for both hot and cold foods. The availability of sufficient china, flatware, and glassware is another problem. Certain menu items may require special serving equipment, such as chafing pans for flaming desserts or small forks and iced bowls for seafood cocktail appetizers. According to Bobeng (1982), this impact of menu items and combinations on the dishroom capability is often overlooked.

Some menu items deteriorate in temperature, color, or texture during the time between food production and service. Items that present a particular problem in a given type of system should be eliminated or prepared according to a new recipe. For example, a grilled cheese sandwich may be a well-liked food item among school children, but it does not lend itself to a menu for a satellite service center unless a grill is available for last-minute grilling prior to service.

Availability of Foods

The availability of foods from the market exerts great influence on the selection of menu items. Although most foods are now available in fresh and frozen forms throughout the country because of the sophistication of the marketing-distribution system, fresh foods produced locally are often of better quality and less expensive during the growing season than those shipped from distant markets. Taking advantage of foods abundantly available during various seasons of the year not only reduces costs but also enhances the acceptability of menu items.

Some operations may need to consider frequency of delivery from various food distributors in planning their menus. Distance from major markets may present special challenges in ensuring availability of foods for service, and may even necessitate menu changes if foods are not available when needed.

MENU PLANNING PROCEDURES

General Considerations

Thus far in this chapter, we have referred to the menu planner. In many foodservice systems, however, menu planning is often the responsibility of a team rather than an individual. This is particularly true in large operations, where the viewpoints of managerial personnel in production and those in service are important in menu planning. In addition, personnel responsible for procurement have valuable input on availability of food, cost, and new products in the market. In a healthcare institution, the clinical dietitian should be involved in the menu planning team to ensure that patient needs and patient acceptability are given appropriate consideration.

In the 1960s, with funding from the U.S. Public Health Service, Balintfy (1964) conducted some experimental work with menu planning by computer. Although additional experimentation has since been carried out, computer assisted menu planning is not widely used today because of the difficulty in quantifying the many variables involved in menu planning, such as flavor, color, and texture. Instead, the computer is more often used for analyzing menus for cost and nutrient composition.

Menu planning should proceed from the premise that the primary purpose of any foodservice organization is to plan, prepare, and serve acceptable food at a cost consistent with the objectives of the operation. Certain decisions must be made in advance and policies and procedures established for planning menus in a systematic manner. The design of the menu pattern, the number of days to be planned at one time, the number of choices to be offered, the format for writing and presentation of menus to the clientele, and the frequency with which revisions will be made if static or cycle menus are used are among the decisions that must be made. This planning must be done sufficiently in advance of actual production to allow delivery of food and supplies and to permit labor to be scheduled. Many operations also need time for printing or other reproduction of menus.

The design of the menu pattern, or the outline of food items to be served each meal, is the initial decision to be made. As we stated when discussing menu structure, the meal of the day is the key influence on the menu pattern, although it may vary from commercial to institutional operations. Menus for either type of operation, however, should be designed to inform the clientele of what items are available and, in many instances, their cost. Simple, clear, and graphic descriptions of menu items should be used, and confusing or overstated terms avoided. A pitfall with many menu planners is the use of interesting names to "jazz up" a menu when these flowery terms are often only confusing to the patron. For example, "Sunshine Salad" is less than descriptive, and might best be accompanied by a phrase explaining that it is a lemon gelatin salad with pineapple and shredded carrots.

Truth in menu legislation in a number of states has had an impact on names of menu offerings. In general, these laws require that a menu reflect the actual foods that will be served. For example, fresh fish should be fresh, not frozen. Gisslen (1983) outlined several types of menu labeling problems.

1 *Point of origin.* Generally accepted names or names that indicate type rather than origin can be used: for example, Swiss cheese or Swedish meatballs. But Maine lobsters must be from Maine and Idaho potatoes from Idaho.

2 *Grade or quality.* If the name of a U.S. food grade is used, that grade must be the food product served, such as U.S. Choice meat.

3 *Fresh.* If a menu item is called fresh, it must be fresh—not frozen, canned or dried.

4 *Imported.* An item labeled "imported" must come from outside the United States.

5 *Homemade.* The term "homemade" means the item was made on the premises. Adding a few fresh vegetables to canned soup does not make it homemade.

6 *Size or portion.* If a portion size is indicated on the menu, the portion served must be that size, within allowable tolerances; for example, a 12-ounce steak must weigh at least 12 ounces before cooking.

Keeping various types of records can assist not only in menu planning but also in the production and purchase of foods. Data on past acceptance of items, weather, day of the week, season, and special events that may have influenced patronage are essential for menu planning. Other resources should include files of standardized recipes with portion size and cost, market quotations, lists of suggestions from clientele, lists of food items classified by category (vegetables, entrees, desserts, etc.), trade publications, and cookbooks. A list of resources is included in Appendix A.

Menu Planning Process

Merchandising is the primary consideration in planning menus for commercial operations. Because of the varied types of commercial foodservice operations, the menu takes many forms. The static choice menu is the predominant type used in commercial foodservice, regardless of whether the operation is an upscale restaurant, fast food operation, or coffee shop. Menus are revised rather infrequently. Either all meals served are included on one menu or separate printed menus are available for each meal. Clip-ons may be used for daily specials. Usually the entrees and main dishes are planned first, followed by the vegetables, potatoes or substitutes, or salads that may be offered with the entree. Appetizers, soups, and desserts are then added.

With the exception of school foodservice, most institutional menus use the three-meal-a-day plan. A few institutions use a four- or five-meal plan built around brunch and an early dinner with some light nutritious snack meals at other times of the day.

Cycle menus are used widely in institutional foodservice with the length of the cycle varying from one to three weeks or longer. Also, cycles may change according to the season of the year to take advantage of plentiful foods on the market and to satisfy clientele expectations. The average length of patient stay is an important consideration in determining the length of the menu cycle in healthcare institutions. One- or two-week cycles have been used successfully in hospitals with a four- or five-day patient stay. In major medical centers, which provide care for patients with complex medical problems, a longer patient stay is characteristic; therefore, a three- or four-week cycle menu may be used. The general or regular menu provides the basis for planning menus for the various types of modified diets in hospitals. In institutions serving the same clientele over a long period of time, a single-use menu or a partial cycle menu may be used, as we discussed earlier in this chapter.

The recording of the menus on a form designed for that purpose and suited to the needs of a particular foodservice is recommended (see Figures 6.11 and 6.12). The menu pattern is often printed on the form as a ready guide.

A step-by-step procedure is outlined below for planning institutional menus with a three-meal-a-day menu pattern. Note that the entree is the main item around which the meal is planned and must therefore be selected before any of the complementary foods.

1 Plan the dinner meats or other entrees for the entire cycle. If a single-use menu is used, then the entrees for at least one week should be planned. Since they are the most expensive foods on the menu, cost can be controlled to a great extent through careful planning at this point. A balance between high- and low-price items will average out the cost over the week or period covered by the cycle.

Lunch Pattern	MONDAY	PORTION SIZE		TUESDAY	PORTION SIZE	
		Group	Group		Group	Group
Meat and Meat Alternate						
Vegetable and Fruit						
Bread and Bread Alternate						
Milk						
Other Foods						

	WEDNESDAY			THURSDAY		
Meat and Meat Alternate						
Vegetable and Fruit						
Bread and Bread Alternate						
Milk						
Other Foods						

	FRIDAY					
Meat and Meat Alternate						
Vegetable and Fruit						
Bread and Bread Alternate						
Milk						
Other Foods						

Week beginning _____

Figure 6.11. *Menu planning worksheet*

112

If the menu pattern provides entree choices, the selection should include a choice of a roast or portion cuts of meat, chicken or other fowl, a fish item, a meat alternate, and a meat extender, such as meat loaf or stew. In selecting these choices, duplication of types of meats is to be avoided; that is, fresh pork roast, pork chops, and baked ham would not appear as choices. A check of the menus of the preceding and succeeding days will prevent a similar repetition.

2   Select the luncheon entrees or main dishes. Note the dinner meats planned and avoid ʋ ing the same kind (pork, beef, lamb, and poultry). Give variety in method ʃ preparation. Here again, a cost balance can be attained by serving a less ʝpensive item one meal of the day when a more expensive food has been planned for the other meal. Soups, sandwiches, main dish salads, and casseroles are commonly served as luncheon entrees.

3   Decide on the vegetables appropriate to serve with the dinner meats. Usually, if the meat is one that will have drippings or juices for gravy, a plain potato, mashed, steamed, or baked, is best in order to use the gravy available. Scalloped, creamed, or au gratin potatoes are most appropriate with meats having no gravy. Rice or pasta are common substitutes for potatoes.

Variations in vegetables are obtained by serving them raw or cooked, peeled or unpeeled, or cut into different shapes and sizes. They may also be baked, buttered, creamed, and scalloped, or prepared with various sauces and seasonings.

4   Select salads, accompaniments, and appetizers next. Work back and forth between the lunch and dinner meals to avoid repetition, to introduce texture and color contrast into the meal, and to provide interesting flavor combinations.

5   Finally, plan desserts for both lunch and dinner. They may be selected from the following main groups: fruits, puddings, ice creams, sherbets, gelatins, cakes, pies, and cookies.

6   After the luncheon and dinner menus have been planned, add breakfast and other meals.

7   Review the entire day as a unit and evaluate if clientele and managerial considerations have been met. Check the menu for duplication and repetition from day to day. The use of a checklist aids in making certain that all factors of good menu planning have been met. An example of a menu evaluation checklist developed by the USDA for use in the school lunch program is shown in Figure 6.13.

MENU EVALUATION

Menu evaluation is an important process and not to be omitted from menu planning. It should be done prior to service, when the initial planning for a cycle

Week of January 30 through February 5, 1983

Unforeseeable Circumstances May Cause Menu Items to Change.
Ice, Milk, and Margarine Are Served in Dining Halls.

Date	*Breakfast*		*Entree*	*Potato or Substitute*	*Vegetable or Soup*	*Salad*	*Bread*	*Dessert*
Jan. 30 Sun.	Orange or V-8 Juice, Hot Chocolate, Baked Ham, Scrambled Eggs, Rum Raisin Buns, Assorted Cold Cereal, Toast, Jelly, Beverage	LUNCH	Roast Turkey, Shrimp Jambalaya	Bread Dressing w/ Gravy	Seasoned Peas, Cranberry Cocktail	Shredded Lettuce Salad, Jellied Waldorf Salad, Fruit Juice Gelatin	Hot Rolls	Strawberry Chiffon Pie, Ice Cream, Chilled Peaches
		DINNER						
Jan. 31	Orange or Grapefruit Juice, Hot Chocolate, Farina, Hard or Soft Cooked Egg, Pancakes w/ Syrup, Assorted Cold Cereal, Toast, Jelly, Beverage	LUNCH	Veal Cutlet on Bun w/ Potato Chips, Beef Noodle Casserole		Vegetable Soup, Whole Kernel Corn	Salad Bar		Honey Drop Cookies, Fudgesicle, Fresh Fruit
Mon.		DINNER	Grilled Pork Chop, Fruit Plate, Salisbury Steak	Potato Wedges	Seasoned Apple Slices, Parsley Seasoned Carrots	Tossed Salad, Orange Sherbet Gelatin	Hot Rolls	Banana Cake w/ Cream Cheese Frosting, Chilled Pear Half
Feb. 1	Orange or Pineapple Juice, Hot Chocolate, Malt-O-Meal, Sausage Links, Fried Egg, Walnut Kuchen, Assorted Cold Cereal, Toast, Jelly, Beverage	LUNCH	Chili, Egg Salad Plate		Seasoned Asparagus Cuts, Fruit Punch	Salad Bar		Almond Cookies, Chocolate Pudding, Fresh Fruit
Tues.		DINNER	WOMEN'S BASKETBALL—NEBRASKA, Steak a la Minute, Baked Fish	Baked Potato Bar	Beets in Orange Sauce, Seasoned Cut Green Beans	Tossed Spring Salad, Cole Slaw	Sesame Seed Rolls	Cherry Cobbler, Chilled Purple Plums
Feb. 2	Orange or Assorted Juices, Hot Chocolate, Oatmeal, Bacon, K-State Omelet, Butter Crumb Coffee Cake, Assorted Cold Cereal, Toast, Jelly, Beverage	LUNCH	Grilled Cheese Sandwich w/ Dill Pickle Spear, Beef Chop Suey		Cream of Tomato Soup, Seasoned Leaf Spinach	Salad Bar		Peanut Butter Cookies, Raspberry Apple Dessert, Fresh Fruit
Wed.		DINNER	Meat Turnover, Meat Loaf	Franconia Potatoes	Broccoli Spears, Black-Eyed Peas	Garden Salad, Grape Fruit Cup	Hofman Rolls	Ground Hog's Dessert

Feb. 3		Orange or Tomato Juice / Hot Chocolate / Ralston / Poached Egg / French Toast w/ Syrup / Hot Applesauce / Assorted Cold Cereal / Toast, Jelly, Beverage				
	LUNCH	Thinly Sliced Corned Beef on Rye / Beef, Tomato, & Macaroni Casserole	Pepper Pot Soup / French Fried Okra	Salad Bar		Dream Bar / Sherbet / Fresh Fruit
Thur.	**DINNER**	Roast Pork Loin / Beef Stroganoff	Seasoned Noodles	Seasoned Zucchini Squash / Wax Beans w/ Pimento	Tossed Salad / Jellied Cherry Salad	French Bread / Peach Pie / Chilled Blueberries
Feb. 4		Orange Juice or Apricot Nectar / Hot Chocolate / Rice & Raisins / Scrambled Eggs / Bishop's Bread / Fruit Cup / Assorted Cold Cereal / Toast, Jelly, Beverage				
	LUNCH	Turkey Sunflower Salad Plate / Beef French Dip	Seasoned Mixed Vegetables / Seasoned Brussel Sprouts	Salad Bar		Jumbo Golden Oatmeal Cookie / Refresho Bar / Fresh Fruit
Fri.	**DINNER**	Chicken Fried Steak / Hot Tuna Fish on a Bun	O'Brien Potatoes / Carrot Coins / Seasoned Peas	Tossed Salad / Banana Log	Whole Wheat Rolls	Rainbow Cake w/ Creamed Frosting / Hot Tangy Rhubarb
Feb. 5		Orange or Grape Juice / Hot Chocolate / Pettijohns / Fried Egg / Creamed Sausage on Biscuit / Granola / Assorted Cold Cereal / Toast, Jelly, Beverage				
	LUNCH	Grilled Quarter Pound Hot Dog w/ Sauerkraut / Banana Split Salad Bowl	Beef Noodle Soup / Fordhook Lima Beans	Salad Bar		Coconut Cream Pudding / Popsicle / Fresh Fruit
Sat.	**DINNER**	Super Tostada	Tator Tots / Refried Beans / Braised Celery	Chilled Applesauce / Cottage Cheese w/ Olive Garnish	Hot Rolls	Chocolate Brownie / Royal Ann Cherries

Figure 6.12. *Menu form and sample menus from Kansas State University Residence Hall Foodservice (used by permission)*

Menu Evaluation

After you have planned the menu items and serving sizes for the various age/grade groups, use the checklist below.

Requirements

	Yes	No
• Have you included all components of the meal?	—	—
• Have you planned serving sizes sufficient to provide all students the required quantity of:		
Meat or meat alternate?	—	—
Two or more vegetables and/or fruits?	—	—
Whole-grain or enriched bread or bread alternate?	—	—
Fluid milk?	—	—

Recommendations

	Yes	No
• Have you included an unflavored form of fluid lowfat milk, skim milk, or buttermilk?	—	—
• Have you included a vitamin A vegetable or fruit at least twice a week?	—	—
• Have you included a vitamin C vegetable or fruit at least 2 or 3 times a week?	—	—
• Have you included several foods for iron each day?	—	—
• Have you kept concentrated sweets and sugars to a minimum?	—	—
• Have you kept calories from fat to a moderate level?	—	—
• Have you kept foods high in salt to a minimum?	—	—
• If you have not planned choices, have you avoided serving any one meat alternate or form of meat more than 3 times per week?	—	—

Good Menu Planning Practices

	Yes	No
• Do your lunches include a good balance of:		

	Yes	No
Color—in the foods themselves and in garnishes?	—	—
Texture—soft and crisp or firm textured foods?	—	—
—starchy and other type foods?	—	—
Shape—different sized pieces and shapes of foods?	—	—
Flavor—bland and tart or mild and strong flavored foods?	—	—
Temperature—hot and cold foods?	—	—
• Have you included whole-grain bread and cereal products?	—	—
• Have you included fresh fruits and vegetables?	—	—
• Are most of the foods and food combinations ones your students have learned to eat?	—	—
• Have you considered students' cultural, ethnic, and religious food practices?	—	—
• Have you included a popular food in a lunch which includes a "new" or less popular food?	—	—
• Do you have a plan to introduce new foods?	—	—
• Have you planned festive foods for holidays, birthdays, and school activities?	—	—
• Have you included different kinds or forms of foods (fresh, canned, frozen, dried)?	—	—
• Have you included seasonal foods?	—	—
• Have you included less familiar foods or new methods of preparation occasionally?	—	—

Good Management Practices

	Yes	No
• Have you planned lunches so that some preparation can be done ahead?	—	—
• Have you balanced the workload among employees from day to day?	—	—
• Is oven, surface-cooking, or steam-		

	Yes	No			Yes	No
cooking space adequate for items planned for each lunch?	—	—	•	Have you taken advantage of USDA-donated foods?	—	—
• Are proper-sized cooking and serving utensils available?	—	—	•	Have you used foods in inventory to the extent possible?	—	—
• Can you easily serve foods planned for each meal?	—	—	•	Do high and low-cost foods and meals balance?	—	—
• Will foods "fit" on dishes or compartment trays?	—	—				

Figure 6.13. *Menu evaluation checklist for evaluating school lunch menus.* **Source: Food and Nutrition Service, USDA:** *Menu Planning Guide for School Food Service.* **Washington, DC: U.S. Govt. Prtg. Ofc., 1980.**

	Mon.	*Tues.*	*Wed.*	*Sun.*
Color Contrast attractive combinations garnishes used				
Flavor Contrast something: bland, tart, sweet combinations acceptable				
Texture Contrast something: crisp, firm, soft				
Form, Shape, Size Vary something: flat, round, long, chopped				
Preparation Type Not too many: starchy foods, sauces, mixtures, crunchy, chewy, some type fruit, veg.				
Repetition Do not repeat: same food in same meal food on same day of week				
Temperature Both hot and cold foods				

Figure 6.14. *Form for evaluating esthetic appeal of menus*

menu or set of menus has been completed, as noted in step 7 in the planning procedure outlined above. But menu evaluation is also an on-going process and should be done during production and service of each meal and after other major menu planning sessions, with needed revisions noted on a regular basis. All of the clientele and managerial considerations discussed earlier in this chapter provide the criteria for evaluating menus.

Food acceptability can be assessed using the various methods described previously, such as plate waste studies, data on menu selections, formal and informal clientele surveys, and observations in the service areas. In institutional foodservices, nutritional evaluation of menus is particularly important. A method as simple as checking if various food groups are represented on the menu may be used. Today, though, computer assisted nutrient analysis is often used, especially in hospital foodservices, to determine nutritional adequacy of menus. The esthetic factors may be evaluated using a form similar to that in Figure 6.14.

Menu cost should be estimated to determine if cost constraints were adequately considered in planning menus. Adjustments may be necessary if costs exceed the per person allowance. In a commercial operation, such estimation is important for adjusting menu selling prices at periodic intervals.

Another aspect in the preliminary assessment of menus is a review of the production demand on foodservice equipment and the estimate of labor requirements for producing the menu items. Again, adjustments may be needed if too many oven-prepared items are included, or too many items require extensive food preparation.

Production and service supervisors should make notations on a regular basis on problems that may occur in producing and serving the menus. Also, difficulties in procurement of various food items should be noted by the person responsible for purchasing.

SUMMARY

The menu is the primary control of the foodservice system; it controls the procurement and production subsystems and is a major determinant in cost control. To the clientele, the menu provides information on food selections available. To the foodservice manager responsible for purchasing, it outlines the foods required for production. To production personnel, the menu describes the work to be done and to the service personnel, the menu lists the items to be offered to the clientele. Many factors must be considered in constructing menus, such as the food habits and preferences of clientele, the nutritional quality of foods, and the operational demands for producing items.

Many kinds and styles of menus are used in foodservice operations. The static or fixed menu, which is widely used in commercial operations, offers the same menu items day after day, whereas a cycle menu is a series of menus offering different items from day to day for a certain period of time and then the cycle is repeated. The single-use menu is planned for a particular day and is never repeated in the same form. Menu choice may vary from no choice to limited choice to many choices on a static, cycle, or single-use menu. The à la carte menu is a method of pricing menu items and is used primarily in commercial operations.

Systematic procedures should be followed in planning menus. Evaluation of menus should be an on-going process, and foodservice managers should be continually alert to the need for menu changes. Both formal and informal evaluation techniques should be used for assessing menu item acceptability and for monitoring operational and service problems with menus.

REFERENCES

Annual growth chains report. *Restaurants & Institutions* 91:77 (Nov. 15), 1982.

Axler, B. H.: *Foodservice: A Managerial Approach.* Ch. 6. The menu planning system. Lexington, MA: D.C. Heath & Co., 1979.

Balintfy, J. L.: Menu planning by computer. *Assoc. Computing Machinery Communic.* 7:255, 1964.

Balintfy, J. L., Jarrett, K., Paige, F., and Sinha, P.: Comparison of Type A constrained and RDA constrained school lunch planning computer models. *School Food Serv. Res. Rev.* 4:54, 1980.

Balintfy, J. L., Rumpf, D. L., and Sinha, P.: The effect of preference—maximized menus on the consumption of school lunches. *School Food Serv. Res. Rev.* 4:48, 1980.

Bell, A. C., Stewart, A. M., Radford, A. J., and Cairney, P. T.: A method for describing food beliefs which may predict personal food choice. *J. Nutr. Educ.* 13:22, 1981.

Birch, L. L.: Dimensions of preschool children's food preference. *J. Nutr. Educ.* 11:77, 1979.

Birch, L. L.: The relationship between children's food preferences and those of their parents. *J. Nutr. Educ.* 12:14, 1980.

Bobeng, B.: A food service manager's perceptions of meal quality. In *Hospital Patient Feeding Systems.* Washington, DC: National Academy Press, 1982.

Breakfast menu workbook. *Restaurants & Institutions* 90:39 (Jun. 15), 1982.

Burt, J. V., and Hertzler, A. A.: Parental influence on the child's food preference. *J. Nutr. Educ.* 10:127, 1978.

Carlisle, J. C., and Boss, M. A.: Food preferences and connotative meaning of food of Alabama teenagers. *School Food Serv. Res. Rev.* 4:19, 1980.

Comstock, E. M., St. Pierre, R. G., and Mackiernan, Y. D.: Measuring individual plate waste in school lunches. *J. Am. Dietet. A.* 79:290, 1981.

Cronin, J. F., Krebs-Smith, S. M., Wyse, B. W., and Light, L.: Characterizing food usage by demographic variables. *J. Am. Dietet. A.* 81:661, 1982.

Dinner menu workbook. *Restaurants & Institutions* 90:35 (Jan. 15), 1982.

Dwyer, J.: Nutritional requirements of adolescence. *Nutr. Rev.* 39:56, 1981.

Eckstein, E. F.: *Menu Planning*, 2nd ed. Westport, CT: AVI Publishing Co., 1978.

Einstein, M. A., and Hornstein, I.: Food preferences of college students and nutritional implications. *J. Food Sci.* 35:429, 1970.

18th Annual "400" issue, Part II: Food and facilities. Food Concepts. *Restaurants & Institutions* 91:39 (Jul. 15), 1982.

Fairbrook, P.: *College and University Food Service Manual.* Ch. 9. Residence hall food service. Stockton, CA: Colman Publishers, 1979.

Feitelson, M., and Fiedler, K.: Kosher dietary laws and children's food preferences: Guide to a camp menu plan. *J. Am. Dietet. A.* 81:453, 1982.

Food and Nutrition Board: *Recommended Dietary Allowances.* 9th ed. Washington, DC: National Academy of Sciences, 1980.

Food and Nutrition Service, USDA: *Menu Planning Guide for School Food Service.* Washington, DC: U.S. Govt. Prtg. Ofc., 1980.

Foodservice trends: Beverage consumption continues to increase. *NRA News* 2:13 (Feb.), 1982.

Foodservice trends: Children and teens: Where they eat and what they eat. *NRA News* 2:30 (Nov.), 1982.

Foodservice trends: Consumer awareness of diet and health importance to restaurateurs. *NRA News* 1:17 (Oct.), 1981.

Frey, A. L., Harper, J. M., Jansen, G. R., Crews, R. H., Shigetomi, C. T., and Lough, J. B.: Comparison of Type A and nutrient standard menus for school lunch. I. Development of the Nutrient Standard Method (NSM). *J. Am. Dietet. A.* 66:242, 1975.

Gargano, T., and Vaden, A. G.: High school students intended and actual entree selections. *School Food Serv. Res. Rev.* 2:86, 1978.

Garrett, P. W., and Vaden, A. G.: Influence of student-selected menus on participation, plate waste, and student attitudes. *School Food Serv. Res. Rev.* 2:28, 1978.

Gisslen, W.: *Professional Cooking.* New York: John Wiley & Sons, 1983.

Green, E. M., and Appledorf, H.: Proximate and mineral content of restaurant steak meals. *J. Am. Dietet. A.* 82:142, 1983.

Harper, J. M., Jansen, G. R., Shigetomi, C. T., and Frey, A. L.: Menu planning in the nutrition program for the elderly: Modified nutrient standard method menu. *J. Am. Dietet. A.* 68:529, 1976.

Harper, J. M., Shigetomi, C. T., Mackin, S. D., Iyer, P. A., and Jansen, G. R.: Alternate lunch patterns in high schools. I. Labor requirements and meal costs. *J. Am. Dietet. A.* 77:152, 1980.

Head, M. K., Giesbrecht, F. G., and Johnson, G. N.: Food acceptability research: Comparative utility of three types of data from school children. *J. Food Sci.* 52:246, 1977.

Head, M. K., Giesbrecht, F. G., Johnson, G. N., Weeks, R. J.: Acceptability of school-served foods. I. Entrees, II. Fruits and vegetables, III. Breads and desserts. *School Food Serv. Res. Rev.* 6:87, 1982.

Hoover, L. W., Waller, A. L., Rastkar, A., and Johnson, V. A.: Development of on-line real-time menu management system. *J. Am. Dietet. A.* 80:46, 1982.

Howe, S. M., and Vaden, A. G.: Factors differentiating participants and nonparticipants of the National School Lunch Program. I. Nutrient intake of high school students. *J. Am. Dietet. A.* 76:451, 1980.

Jansen, G. R., and Harper, J. M. Consumption and plate waste of menu items served in the National School Lunch Program. *J. Am. Dietet. A.* 73:395, 1978.

Johnson, K. E., and Vaden, A. G.: Accuracy of college students' intended entree selections for forecasting production demand. *J. Food Sci.* 44:257, 1979.

Keiser, J., and Kallio, E.: *Controlling and Analyzing Costs in Food Service Operations.* New York: John Wiley & Sons, 1974.

Khan, M. A., and Lipke, L. K.: Snacking and its contribution to food and nutrient intake of college students. *J. Am. Dietet. A.* 81:583, 1982.

Knickrehm, M. E., Cotner, C. G., and Kendrick, J. G.: Acceptance of menu items by college students. *J. Am. Dietet. Assoc.* 55:117, 1969.

Kohrs, M. B., O'Haulon, P., and Eklund, D.: Title VII—Nutrition Program for the Elderly. I. Contribution to one day's dietary intake. *J. Am. Dietet. A.* 72:487, 1978.

Kotschevar, L. H.: *Foodservice for the Extended Care Facility.* Ch. 5. Menu planning. Boston: Cahners Books, 1973.

Kotschevar, L. H.: *Management by Menu*. Chicago: National Institute of the Foodservice Industry, 1975.

Kotschevar, L. H., and Terrell, M.: *Foodservice Planning: Layout and Equipment*. New York: John Wiley & Sons, 1985.

Kreck, L. A.: *Menus: Analysis and Planning*. Boston: Cahners Books, 1975.

Krondl, M., Lau, D., Yurkiw, M. A., and Coleman, P. H.: Food use and perceived food meanings of the elderly. *J. Am. Dietet. A.* 80:523, 1982.

Lachance, P. A.: Simple research techniques for school foodservice. Part I: Acceptance testing. *School Food Serv. J.* 30:54 (Sept.), 1976.

Leung, C., Koehler, H., and Hard, M. M.: Mineral contents of selected pre-prepared foods sampled in a hospital food service line. *J. Am. Dietet. A.* 80:530, 1982.

Lilly, H. D., Davis, D. W., Wilkening, V. L., and Shank, F. R.: Findings of the report on food consumption and nutrition education in the National School Lunch Program. *School Food Serv. Res. Rev.* 4:7, 1980.

Lunch menu workbook. *Restaurants & Institutions* 90:33 (Apr. 15), 1982.

Lyman, B.: Menu item preferences and emotions. *School Food Serv. Res. Rev.* 6:32, 1982.

Mahaffey, M. J., Mennes, M. E., and Miller, B. B.: *Food Service Manual for Health Care Institutions*. Ch. 7. Menu planning. Chicago: Am. Hosp. Assoc., 1981.

McConnell, P. E., and Shaw, J. B.: Developing school lunch menus using food preferences and frequency of preference. *School Food Serv. Res. Rev.* 4:125, 1980.

Meiselman, H. L., and Waterman, D.: Food preferences of enlisted personnel in the armed forces. *J. Am. Dietet. A.* 73:621, 1978.

Menu census. *Restaurants & Institutions* 90:31 (Apr. 1), 1982.

Menu census. *Restaurants & Institutions* 92:37 (Mar. 1), 1983.

Mizer, D. A., and Porter, M.: *Food Preparation for the Professional*. Ch. 20. Planning and presenting the meal. San Francisco: Canfield Press, 1978.

Morales, R., Spears, M. C., and Vaden, A. G.: Menu planning competencies in administrative dietetic practice. I. The methodology, II. Practitioners' ratings of competencies. *J. Am. Dietet. A.* 74:642, 1979.

National Association of College and University Food Services: *National Association of College and University Food Services Professional Standards Manual*. East Lansing, MI: NACUFS, 1982.

National Research Council: *Recommended Dietary Allowances*. 9th ed. Washington, DC: National Academy of Sciences, 1980.

Nelson, M. B., and King, P. C.: Snack and beverage preferences of university students. *J. Am. Dietet. A.* 81:65, 1982.

Peryam, D. R., and Pilgrim, F. J.: Hedonic scale method of measuring food preference. *Food Technol.* 11:9, 1957.

Peryam, D. R., Polemis, B. W., Kamen, J. M., Eindhoven, J., and Pilgrim, F. J.: *Food Preferences of Men in the U.S. Armed Forces*. Chicago: Institute for the Armed Forces, 1960.

Peterkin, B. B., Patterson, P. C., Blum, A. J., and Kerr, R. L.: Changes in dietary patterns: One approach to meeting standards. *J. Am. Dietet. A.* 78:453, 1981.

Price, D. Z.: Developing a food preference instrument. *School Food Serv. Res. Rev.* 4:101, 1980.

Price, D. Z.: Food preferences of eight- to twelve-year-old Washington children. *School Food Serv. Res. Rev.* 2:82, 1978.

Rose, J. C.: Cost containment with good will. *Food Mgmt.* 17:23 (Jul.), 1982.

Schultz, H. G.: A food action rating scale for measuring food acceptance. *J. Food Sci.* 30:365, 1965.

Seaberg, A. G.: *Menu Design, Merchandising and Marketing*. Boston: Cahners Books, 1973.

Semps, C. T., Johnson, N. E., Elmer, P. J., Allington, J. K., and Matthews, M. E.: A dietary survey of 14 Wisconsin nursing homes. *J. Am. Dietet. A.* 81:35, 1982.

17th Annual "400" issue, Report II: Food and facilities. Food concepts. *Restaurants & Institutions* 89:34 (Jul. 15), 1981.

Shriwise, M. A., and Vaden, A. G.: Implications of college students' food habits for foodservice operations. *NACUFS J.* 2:1, 1980.

Splaver, B. R.: *Successful Catering.* Ch. 15. Menus. Boston: Cahners Books, 1975.

Stephenson, S.: Sell that side dish. *Food Mgmt.* 17:64 (Nov.), 1982.

Stokes, J. F.: *Cost Effective Quality Food Service.* Ch. 2. Making cents out of cycle menus. Rockville, MD: Aspen Systems Corp., 1979.

Stokes, J. W.: *How to Manage a Restaurant.* Ch. 4. Planning the menu. Dubuque, IA: Wm. C. Brown Co., 1982.

Stults, V. J., Morgan, K. J., and Zabik, M. E.: Children's and teenagers' beverage consumption patterns. *School Food Serv. Res. Rev.* 6:20, 1982.

Truswell, A. S., and Darnton-Hill, I.: Food habits of adolescents. *Nutr. Rev.* 39:73, 1981.

U.S. Department of Agriculture and U.S. Department of Health, Education, and Welfare: *Nutrition and Your Health: Dietary Guidelines for Americans.* Washington, DC: Office of Government and Public Affairs, USDA, 1980.

VanEgmond-Pannell, D.: *School Foodservice,* 2nd ed. Westport, CT: AVI Publishing Co., 1981.

Wells, W. D.: Communicating with children. *J. Advertising Res.* 5:2 (Feb.), 1965.

Welsh, S. P., and Marston, R. M.: Review of trends in food use in the United States, 1909 to 1980. *J. Am. Dietet. A.* 81:120, 1982.

Wenzel, G. L., and Editors of CBI: *Wenzel's Menu Maker.* 2nd ed. Boston: CBI Publishing Co., 1979.

West, B. B., Shugart, G. S., and Wilson, M. F.: *Food for Fifty.* Part 3. Menu planning. New York: John Wiley & Sons, 1979.

Wheeler, M. L., and Wheeler, L. A.: Nutrient menu planning for clinical research centers. *J. Am. Dietet. A.* 67:347, 1975.

Wiley, C. J., and Vaden, A. G.: Actual and intended entree selections of college women from residence hall menus. *NACUFS J.* 2:10, 1980.

Williams, S., Henneman, A., and Fox, H.: Contribution of foodservice programs in preschool centers to children's nutritional needs. *J. Am. Dietet. A.* 71:610, 1977.

III
Procurement

7

Purchasing

PROCUREMENT

The goal of any foodservice system is to serve quality meals that satisfy the clientele. Before this goal can be met, however, the necessary materials must be procured, pre-processed, and produced as menu items. The first step in this process, procurement, is the managerial function of acquiring material for production. These materials include detergents and paper supplies, but the chief resource, and the one we will concentrate on, is food.

According to the foodservice systems model presented in Chapter 2, procurement is the first functional subsystem of the transformation element, as highlighted in Figure 7.1. Several important functions exist within this subsystem: purchasing will be discussed in this chapter, and receiving, storage, and inventory control in the next. Furthermore, each of these functions also requires many distinctive procedures. For example, within the purview of purchasing, procedures must be developed for forecasting, selecting products, writing specifications, choosing a purchasing method, selecting and evaluating vendors, and completing purchasing records.

In common with the other subsystems of the transformation element, the management of the procurement subsystem involves planning, organizing, staffing, leading, and controlling. Figure 7.2, developed from a survey of purchasing managers and their superiors in multi-unit commercial foodservice organizations (Loecker et al., 1983), sets these functions forth in more detail. The man-

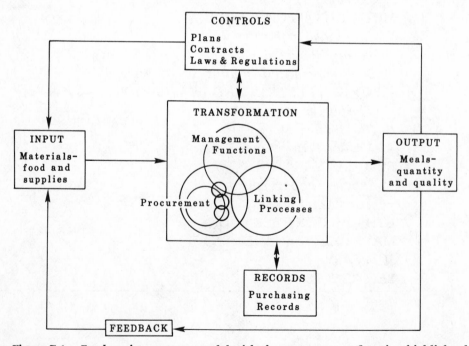

Figure 7.1. *Foodservice systems model with the procurement function highlighted*

agers whose jobs were examined in the study had primary responsibility for the procurement functional subsystem. In many foodservice organizations, however, procurement responsibilities are only a component of a foodservice manager's job, along with a number of other responsibilities in the operation. Whichever the arrangement may be, all of the tasks listed must be performed, whether by a single individual or by members of the management team. And because procurement in foodservice systems is considered an important profit generator, as in other industries, those responsible for the procurement function should be members of the top management team and involved in high-level decision making.

Other vital factors in the transformation element of the foodservice system are the linking processes discussed in Chapter 2: decision making, communication, and balance. Although procurement is considered separately in this chapter and the next, like all other subsystems it is interrelated and interdependent with all elements of the foodservice system.

PURCHASING AND THE MARKET

Purchasing is a procedure concerned with the acquisition of goods; it is often described as obtaining the right product, in the right amount, at the right time, and at the right price. To do this, the food buyer for institutional and commercial foodservices must know the market and the products, in addition to having general business astuteness. He or she can also rely on sales representatives, however, to give advice on purchasing decisions and to relay valuable information about available food items and new products.

The Market

The market is the medium through which a change in ownership moves commodities from producer to consumer. Markets may be described by:

- The type of food being purchased, e.g., meat, frozen food, produce, or processed foods and staple items;
- The marketing agent, e.g., a processor, wholesaler, or broker; or
- The location of the market, e.g., primary, secondary, or local, depending on geographical location.

Knowledge of the food market involves finding sources of supply and determining which food items can be obtained from which vendor. It also involves understanding the flow of supplies through the marketing channel and the effect of market regulations on this flow.

Marketing Channel

Exchange of ownership of a product occurs in the marketing channel, sometimes identified as the channel of distribution, as shown in Figure 7.3. The supplier,

Purchasing/Procurement

- Obtain the best value at the lowest price consistent with established quality standards and delivery schedules.
- Forecast market conditions, availability of materials, and economic conditions.
- Develop specifications for materials and services in cooperation with personnel responsible for production, including "make or buy" decisions.
- Authorize rejection of materials which fail to meet specifications.
- Maintain files or vendors' stock lists, catalogues, price sheets, and discounts.
- Negotiate contracts for food, supplies, and services.
- Determine whether open market or contract is preferable for purchasing various materials and services.
- Coordinate review of purchase contracts by legal counsel and/or other appropriate personnel.
- Determine the cost of deliveries and the best method of transportation.
- Issue purchasing orders for needed materials and services.
- Monitor purchase orders to determine if deliveries are correct.
- Handle communication concerning overshipment, shortages, price changes, etc.

Vendor/Supplier Relations

- Establish a system for vendor selection and rating.
- Select suppliers and negotiate reasonable terms.
- Compare suppliers' product quality, services, dependability, and cost.
- Act as a liaison between suppliers and other departments in your organization in solving problems.
- Oversee distribution of bids and receipt of quotations.
- Create goodwill for your organization through cordial trade relations.
- Work with sales representatives to identify new products, materials, processes, etc.
- Investigate suppliers' facilities, when appropriate.

Inventory/Warehouse Management

- Determine necessary stock levels to provide adequate food and supplies and minimize capital investment.
- Minimize operating costs for storage of food and supplies.
- Monitor records of inventory, materials on-order, and potential demands for food and supplies.

Personnel Management

- Determine staffing needs, develop job descriptions, and select qualified personnel for purchasing and storage functions.
- Train and manage purchasing and storeroom personnel.
- Promote good relations between purchasing and other personnel in the organization.

General Management

- Establish priorities for meeting objectives.
- Serve on policy making team of the organization.
- Monitor flow of materials through the system; i.e., from selection to production to service.
- Develop and monitor budget for operations within scope of responsibility.
- Support a program of data processing.
- Promote energy conservation in all operations within scope of responsibility.

Figure 7.2. *Procurement Manager: Commercial foodservice model job description.* **Source:** *Loecker, K. A., Spears, M. C., and Vaden, A. G.: Purchasing managers in commercial foodservice organizations: Clarifying the role.* **The Professional, Vol. I, No. 2.**

generally the farmer, supplies raw food products to manufacturers or processors, who process and sell them to middlemen, who in turn sell them to the consumer. For example, the rancher raises cattle for sale to a meat packing plant, which processes, portions, and sells it to a wholesaler, who stores it temporarily in specially manufactured cartons before selling it to the consumer. Similar sequences are followed for canned or frozen fruits and vegetables.

In today's economy, the cost of taking goods through the marketing channel often equals or even exceeds the initial cost of the product at the point of origin. Value is added to the product at each step in the marketing channel.

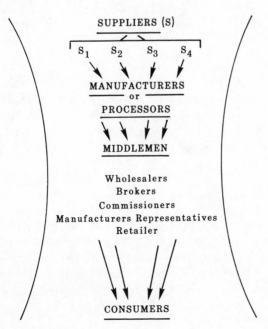

Figure 7.3. *The marketing channel*

Occasionally, the wholesale price of a food item may be more than the "bargain special" at the local supermarket. For example, a large chain-affiliated supermarket may bypass many middlemen by purchasing a carload of coffee directly from the processor. The supermarket price then could be much less than the institutional purchaser would pay to the wholesaler. Such price differentials are part of institutional purchasers' concerns but are usually beyond their control, as they are often either seasonal bargains or price inducements for supermarket customers.

Some small manufacturing or processing plants will sell products directly to the consumer, but the large size of most plants today precludes this type of selling. Instead, those who do not have their own sales forces must rely on agent middlemen both to promote their products with the potential buyer and to distribute them. Wholesalers are middlemen who purchase from various plants, provide storage, and resell the products to retailers. They generally carry large lines of stock, permitting the buyer to purchase everything from frozen and canned products, flour and sugar, china and glassware, paper goods, and cleaning supplies, to small kitchen equipment. This type of wholesale operation is commonly known as "one-stop shopping." Some wholesalers, however, deal with only one item, such as meat, produce, dairy products, or detergents.

Other prime examples of middlemen in the food industry are brokers, commissioners, and manufacturer's representatives. Brokers are in business for themselves but do not take title to the goods being sold. They regularly call on foodservice managers and promote items produced by one or more companies. Commissioners are similar to brokers except they take title to the merchandise, usually highly perishable produce. They generally are experienced in the business, know the market and the quality necessary to satisfy customers' needs, and are able to rush deliveries. Like brokers, manufacturer's representatives do not take title, bill, or set prices. They carry fewer and more specialized lines and, because they represent a minimum number of manufacturers, have greater product expertise than brokers.

Retailers are the final middlemen in the marketing channel and are the ones who sell products to the ultimate buyer, the consumer. In a commercial foodservice, the foodservice manager would be considered a retailer. Unless the operation is multi-unit, he or she will buy more often from the wholesaler than from the broker, commissioner, or manufacturer's representative because of the convenience of "one-stop shopping."

Market Regulation

The food industry is the most controlled industry in the United States today, covered as it is by comprehensive and complex federal regulations. Although many federal agencies promulgate regulations that directly affect the food industry, the U.S. Department of Agriculture and the U.S. Department of Health and Human Services are responsible for the bulk of the legislation. The present system of food regulation enforcement developed by them through the years has been influenced by many historic events.

Some of the need for the large amount of legislation can be attributed to the gradual change in the American lifestyle that occurred between 1900 and 1950. During that time, the majority of the population came to live in cities and towns, rather than on farms, and was therefore no longer self-sufficient. Furthermore, more and more consumers began to purchase prepared foods rather than ingredients. Legislation was also promoted by the growth of an understanding of the relationship between food-related diseases and health. For example, when the meat industry changed from local distribution of products to national distribution, and the United States started to export meat, Europe required documentation that meat products were being produced under sanitary conditions. Also, the Bureau of Chemistry in the U.S. Department of Agriculture began to develop methodologies to detect adulterants in foods.

Food, Drug and Cosmetic Act. The Federal Food, Drug and Cosmetic Act was passed in 1938, and is enforced by the Food and Drug Administration (FDA), an agency presently in the U.S. Department of Health and Human Services. The purposes of this act are to ensure that foods are pure and wholesome, safe to eat, and produced under sanitary conditions, and also that their packaging and labeling are truthful.

The act provides three mandatory standards for products being shipped across state lines: standards of identity, standards of minimum quality, and standards of fill of container. Standards of identity establish what a given food product contains. Certain ingredients must be present in a specific percentage before the standard name may be used. For example, the consumer is assured that any product labeled mayonnaise, regardless of its manufacturer, contains 65 percent by weight of vegetable oil, as well as vinegar or lemon juice and egg yolk. Standards of quality, or minimum regulatory standards for tenderness, color, and freedom from defects, have been set for a number of canned fruits and vegetables to supplement standards of identity. If a food does not meet the FDA quality standards, it must be labeled "Below Standard in Quality" and can bear an explanation such as "Good Food–Not High Grade," "Excessively Broken," or "Excessive Peel." Standards of fill of container tell the packer how full a container must be to avoid the charge of deception. In Figure 7.4, foods for which one or all three standards have been identified are classified by food groups.

The major amendments to the Federal Food, Drug and Cosmetic Act are the Food Additive (1958) and Color Additive (1960) Amendments, both of which provide for safeguarding the consumer against adulteration and misbranding of foods. Food is considered adulterated if it contains substances that are injurious to health, if it is prepared or held under unsanitary conditions, if any part is filthy or decomposed, or if it contains portions of diseased animals. Food is also considered to be adulterated if damage or inferiority is concealed, if its label or container is misleading, or if a valuable substance is omitted.

A food is considered misbranded if the label does not include adequate or mandatory information or gives misleading information. The objective of the Fair Packaging and Labeling Act of 1967 is to ensure that the consumer can obtain accurate information from a food's label as to its quantity or content, thus

Part no.	Food group
Part 131	Milk and cream
Part 133	Cheese and related cheese products (processed cheese, cheese spreads)
Part 135	Frozen desserts
Part 136	Bakery products
Part 137	Cereal flours and related products
Part 139	Macaroni and noodle products
Part 145	Canned fruits
Part 146	Canned fruit juices
Part 150	Fruit butters, jellies, preserves and related products
Part 152	Fruit pies
Part 155	Canned vegetables
Part 156	Vegetable juices
Part 158	Frozen vegetables
Part 160	Egg and egg products
Part 161	Fish and shellfish
Part 163	Cocoa products
Part 164	Tree nuts and peanut products
Part 165	Nonalcoholic beverages
Part 166	Margarine
Part 168	Sweeteners
Part 169	Food dressings and flavorings

Figure 7.4. *Definition and standards of identity, quality and/or fill of container of food groups established under the Federal Food, Drug and Cosmetic Act and published in the Federal Code of Regulations Title 21*

permitting value comparison. Specific kinds of information required on the label for each food are:

- Name and address of the manufacturer, distributor, or packer (including zip code);
- Name of the food;
- Net contents in terms of weight, measure or count; and
- A statement of ingredients listed by common or usual name in order of decreasing predominance by weight.

Nutritional information is mandatory on labels only for foods for which a nutritional claim is made or that have added vitamins, minerals, or protein. Nutrition labeling information for other foods is voluntary. Today, because of the emphasis on nutrition and health, many food processors supply nutrient composition data to the consumer upon request.

The Public Health Service Act. Under the Public Health Service Act, the FDA advises state and local governments on sanitation standards for prevention of infectious diseases. The most widely adopted standards deal with production,

Product		Grades		
Vegetable	US Fancy or US Grade A	US Standard US Grade C	Substandard	
Meat	US Prime	US Choice	US Good	US Standard
Eggs	US Grade AA	US Grade A	US Grade B	
Dairy (Dry Whole Milk)	US Premium	US Extra	US Standard	

Figure 7.5. *Summary of the major grades by food categories*

processing, and distribution of "Grade A" milk. In contrast to USDA quality grade standards for food, the Public Health Service standard for Grade A milk is largely a standard of wholesomeness. The Grade A designation on fresh milk means that it has met state or local requirements that equal or exceed federal requirements.

United States Department of Agriculture. The USDA has an important role in the food regulatory process having been authorized to promulgate food regulations by the Agricultural Marketing Act, the Federal Meat Inspection Act, the Poultry Product Inspection Act, and the Egg Products Inspection Act. One of its most important functions, authorized by the Agricultural Marketing Act, is the grading, inspection, and certification of all agricultural products. Quality, and U.S. grades are levels of quality and U.S. grade standards, which are voluntary, define the requirements that must be met by a product to obtain a particular grade.

The USDA has established grade standards for several categories of food: fruits, vegetables, eggs, dairy products, poultry, and meat products. The varying terminology in standard grades has led to much consumer confusion; many believe a uniform grade terminology is needed. Some of the grades in use today are shown in Figure 7.5.

The USDA also has the responsibility for enforcing the Federal Meat Inspection Act, the Poultry Products Inspection Act, and the Egg Products Inspection Act. Under them, it promulgates <u>mandatory</u> regulations to assure wholesomeness of these products. The major requirements of the three acts will illustrate how this objective is met. The Meat Inspection Act, for example, contains provisions for the detection and destruction of diseased and unfit meat, regulation of sanitation practices in meat plants, requirement of stamping inspected meat, prevention of the addition of harmful substances in meat products, and elimination of false or deceptive labeling. The Meat Inspection Act was amended by the Wholesome Meat Act of 1967, which requires inspection of all meat if it is moved within or between states. In addition, the amendment provides for inspection of foreign plants exporting meats to the United States.

The Poultry Products Inspection Act was amended in 1968 and designated as the Wholesome Poultry Products Act. Under it, inspectors are required to check on cleanliness of plants and maintenance of equipment; the inspection procedures are similar to those required for meat. Labels on poultry and poultry parts must also be approved. Under the Egg Products Inspection Act (1970), plants that break and further process shell eggs into liquid, frozen, or dried egg products are similarly inspected. In all three acts, monetary and technical assistance is provided to aid plants in meeting federal requirements.

The USDA Agricultural Marketing Service, in cooperation with state agencies, offers official grading or inspection for quality of manufactured dairy products, poultry and eggs, fresh and processed fruits and vegetables, and meat and meat products. Grading is based on U.S. grade standards developed by the USDA for these products. The food acceptance service, developed by the USDA to make institutional food buying easier, is included in the grading and inspection programs. This service provides impartial evaluation and certification that food purchases meet contract specifications. Any healthcare organization, commercial foodservice, governmental agency, educational institution, or public or private groups buying food in large quantities may use the service on request. Suppliers often use the acceptance service to ensure that they meet contract specifications.

If purchases are to be certified by the USDA acceptance service, contracts with suppliers should include this provision. The supplier is then responsible for obtaining certification, which, like all grading services, is provided for a fee. Contract specifications for the products can either be based on USDA grade standards or tailored to meet the buyer's needs. They may include factors such as USDA quality grades, condition, type of refrigeration, cut, trim, size, packaging, weight, shape, and color.

To provide acceptance service, an official grader employed by the Agricultural Marketing Service or a cooperating state agency examines the product at the manufacturing, processing, or packing plant or at the supplier's warehouse. If the product meets contract specifications, the grader stamps it with an official stamp. The grader also issues certificates indicating that the products comply with the contract specifications. A specimen certificate is shown in Figure 7.6.

This method of procurement assures purchasers that they are getting what they order. Moreover, it usually results in overall higher quality food and eliminates controversies between the buyer and the seller over compliance of the products. These products, when produced and graded under the U.S. Department of Commerce (USDC) inspection program, may be identified with the USDC "Federal Inspection" mark or the U.S. grade shield. This grade labeling, however, is not required by federal law, even though the inspection and grading carry official weight.

FORECASTING

Forecasting is the art and science of estimating future events, combining intuitive interpretation of data and use of mathematical models; as such, it provides the data base for decision making and planning. What to purchase and prepare is dictated by the menu, but when and how much to purchase and prepare must be

UNITED STATES DEPARTMENT OF AGRICULTURE
AGRICULTURAL MARKETING SERVICE

CERTIFICATE OF QUALITY AND CONDITION
(PROCESSED FOODS)

Please refer to this certificate by number and inspection office.

W- 090655

is certificate is receivable in all courts of the United States as prima facie evidence of the truth of the statements ..rein contained. It does not excuse failure to comply with any applicable Federal or State laws. *WARNING: Any person who knowingly falsely make, issue, alter, forge, or counterfeit this certificate, or participate in any such actions, is subject to a fine of not more than $1,000 or imprisonment for not more than one year, or both (7 U.S.C. 1622 (h)).*
The conduct of all services and the licensing of all personnel under the regulations governing such services shall be accomplished without discrimination as to race, color, religion, sex, or national origin.

DATE

May 10, 1983

APPLICANT	ADDRESS
PISCIOTTA F&V COMPANY, INC.	KANSAS CITY, MISSOURI 64142
RECEIVER OR BUYER	ADDRESS
STATE OF KANSAS	TOPEKA, KANSAS
SOURCE OF SAMPLES	PRODUCT INSPECTED
OFFICIALLY DRAWN	CANNED PEARS

CODE MARKS ON CONTAINERS

2D17
Only: D.

PRINCIPAL LABEL MARKS "HIFDA HALVES BARTLETT PEARS In Light Syrup Net Weight 6 lb. 9 oz. 2.98kg
Distributed by NATIONAL INSTITUTIONAL FOOD DISTRIBUTOR ASSOCIATES, INC., ATLANTA, GEORGIA 30325 SAN FRANCISCO, CALIF. 94126"

Net Weight — MEETS label declaration
Vacuum Readings — 9 to 13 inches
Drained Weight — MEETS recommended drained weight
Count — 35 and 36
Style — Halves
Brix — Light Sirup
Condition of Containers — MEETS applicable U. S. Standards for Condition of Food Containers

OFFICIALLY SAMPLED
MAY 3 '83
U.S. DEPARTMENT OF AGRICULTURE
FAYETTEVILLE, ARK.

GRADE:

U. S. GRADE A or U. S. FANCY
Average Score - 93 Points
MEETS requirements for the State of Kansas for item number 5161.

REMARKS:

This certificate covers 75 cases, packed 6/No. 10 cans per case. Product packed in beaded-bodied cans with enamel-lined ends. Lot located in Applicant's Wichita, Kansas warehouse. Cases stamped with USDA "OFFICIALLY SAMPLED" Stamp as shown above. Written statement from packer indicates product of latest season's pack.

Pursuant to the regulations issued by the Secretary of Agriculture under the Agricultural Marketing Act of 1946, as amended (7 U.S.C. 1621-1622), governing the inspection and certification of the product designated herein. I certify that the quality and condition of the product as shown by samples inspected on the above date were as shown, subject to any restrictions specified above.

ADDRESS OF INSPECTION OFFICE	SIGNATURE OF INSPECTOR
35 E. Mountain, Rm 209 Fayetteville, AR 72701	J. P. Christensen

FORM FV-146 (12-81)   (Formerly FVQ Form 146 (1/78), which may be used.)

COPY

Figure 7.6. *Sample USDA certificate of quality*

determined by accurately predicting the future needs of a particular foodservice. Reasonably accurate forecasts enable managers to determine the amount of risk associated with alternative actions and, thus, influence the decision process and permit effective planning.

Forecasting in Foodservice

Forecasting in a foodservice involves estimating not only the meals to be served at some future date but also the quantity of food to be produced and the amount of raw food needed for production on that date. Among the many factors that may affect the accuracy of forecasts are the availability of resources, including money, personnel, and raw materials; changes in technology; changes in society and government; and economic outlook.

Commercial foodservices are most influenced in their planning by market share, business cycles, population trends, and government regulation. General business conditions have a direct bearing on their planning for growth and expansion, as well as on current operations. Expansion cannot always be supported by the general business climate; in fact, a decrease in size may be a reasonable alternative.

Institutional foodservices—including healthcare, schools, and colleges and universities—are subject to many of the same conditions affecting commercial foodservices. Of special concern for them, though, are population trends and government regulations. The population trends induced by variations in birth rates and the preponderance of older citizens constitute important elements in forecasting future operations. Similar, but less direct effects are realized in commercial foodservices.

In all foodservices, forecasting and planning are affected to some degree by federal, state, and local regulations. Market regulations, discussed previously in this chapter, are a good example.

Elements in Foodservice Forecasting

The time is long past when a small foodservice operation may run to the "community grocer" or when a large operation may make an emergency appeal to a wholesaler when a shortage occurs. Today, life in business is too complex for such hand-to-mouth existence, and forecasting is an absolute essential. The acid test of forecasting is the ability of the organization to satisfy demand. This is particularly relevant for holiday and travel related services, such as airline and hotel foodservices. The demand for services may vary not only with the month of the year, however, but also with the day of the week and the hour of the day. Consequently, a forecasting model may need to focus on small time intervals that could be important for production scheduling of employees and other fundamental operating decisions.

Even after these are taken into account, forecasting demand in foodservice can still be very difficult because of the intangibles affecting consumers' perceptions, such as convenience and a pleasant dining atmosphere. For example, in a

---

SHADY GROVE BOY SCOUT CAMP

Date: July 4, Monday   *Weather:* 90°F; humid and sunny

Meal: Lunch   *Special Notes:* Serve on lawn in tent area

MENU

Barbequed Hot Dogs on Buns (2 per serving)

Mustard   Relish   Chopped Onions

Baked Beans (⅔ cup portion)

Carrot and Celery Sticks (4 sticks/person)

Ice-cold Watermelon (8/melon)

Chocolate Chip Cookies (2 each)

Lemonade (4 gal.)

Number served: 50 scouts and counselors

Figure 7.7. *Example of a historical record*

fast food restaurant, should demand be measured only by the amount of food sold, or should consideration be given to lost customers who leave because of long waiting lines or the attitude of customers toward the service in general? A proper forecasting model requires all data that accurately measure the volume of demand for the service offered.

Historical Records

Well-kept historical records constitute the base for most forecasting processes. This is especially true of foodservices in which records of the past have been used to determine food production quantities long before sophisticated forecasting procedures were available. In fact, such historical records are the root of most of these procedures. They must, however, be accurate and complete, or they cannot be extended into the future with any reliability.

Effective production records, in addition to listing food items, must be identified by date and day of the week, meal or hour of service, special event or holiday, and even weather conditions if applicable. An example of a record is shown in Figure 7.7.

Although the production unit records reveal the vital information on food items served to the consumers, it is by no means the only organizational unit that should keep records. Only by cross-referencing the records of sales with those of production can a reliable historical base for forecasting be formalized. In foodservices where meals are sold, as in restaurants, hospital employee and guest cafeterias, and schools, records of sales will yield customer count patterns that can be useful for the forecasting task. These data can be related to the percentage of customer consumption of a given menu item or the daily variations induced by weather or special events.

These historical records of the production unit provide the fundamental base for forecasting, but for effective purchasing, additional records are necessary for comparative analysis with the records from production. Beyond the relation to the production records essential for forecasting, records kept by purchasing managers are essential for performance of their function; these records include vendors used, performance of vendors, correlation with production, and price considerations.

Forecasting Models

Criteria for a Model

Numerous forecasting models have been developed during the past three decades, but, as one might expect, the trend has been toward sophisticated models using computer-based information systems. According to Fitzsimmons and Sullivan (1982), the factors deserving consideration when selecting a forecasting model are

- Cost.
- Required accuracy.
- Relevancy of past data.
- Forecasting lead time.
- Underlying pattern of behavior.

Cost of Model. The cost of a forecasting model involves the expenses of both development and operation. The developmental costs arise from constructing the model, validating the forecast stability, and, in the case of large operations, writing a computer program. In some cases, educating managers in the use of the model is another cost element. Operational costs include the cost of making a forecast after the model is developed, which is affected by the amount of data and computation time needed. Quite naturally, the more elaborate models require huge amounts of data and can be very expensive.

Accuracy of Model. The quality of a forecasting model must be judged primarily by the accuracy of its predictions of future occurrences. A quite expensive model that yields very accurate forecasts might not be as good a choice in some cases as a cheaper and less sophisticated model that is not extremely accurate. This is a decision a foodservice manager must make.

Relevancy of Past Data. In most forecasting models, the general assumption is that past behavioral patterns and relationships will continue in the future. If a clear relationship between the past and the future does not exist, the past data will not be relevant in developing forecasts. In these cases, subjective approaches, such as those that rely heavily upon the opinions of knowledgeable persons, may be more appropriate.

Forecasting Lead Time. The forecasting lead time pertains to the length of time into the future that the forecasts are made. Usually, these times are categorized as short-, medium-, or long-term. The choice of a lead time depends on the items being forecast: a short-term lead will be chosen for perishable produce, a medium- or long-term lead for canned goods.

Pattern of Behavior. As stated above, many forecasting models depend upon the assumption that behavioral patterns observed in the past will continue into the future and, even more basic, that actual occurrences follow some known pattern. These patterns, however, may be affected by random influences, which are unpredictable factors responsible for forecasting errors. Not all forecasting models work equally well for all patterns of data, and, therefore, the appropriate model must be selected for a particular situation.

Types of Models

Forecasting techniques have been categorized in numerous ways, but the three most common model classifications are time series, causal, and subjective. A model in one of the classifications may include some features of the others.

Time Series Model. The frequently used time series model involves the presumption that actual occurrences follow an identifiable pattern *over time*. Although time series data have a regular relationship to time, deviations in the data make forecasting difficult. To reduce the influence of these deviations, several methods have been developed for smoothing the data curve.

The most common and easiest of these to apply is the moving average method. In this method, the forecast is computed as the average of a selected number of observations. The averaging process is continued as additional observations are made by dropping the earliest and adding the most recent to yield the same number of observations for the moving average. This averaging process smooths out randomness in the data and leaves a comparatively constant pattern, which is the forecast. The moving average method must be adjusted for trends and seasonality.

Exponential smoothing methods are popular because they are readily available in standard computer software packages and require relatively little data storage and computation. These methods are specific averaging techniques, distinguished by the way each of the past demands is weighted in calculating an average. The pattern of weights is exponential in form. Data for the most recent period are weighted most heavily and the weights on successively older periods decline exponentially; that is, the weights decrease in magnitude by higher and higher factors the longer ago the data were recorded.

Fitzsimmons and Sullivan (1982) summarize exponential smoothing as a popular technique for short-term demand forecasting for the following reasons:

- all past data are considered in the smoothing process;
- more recent data are given more weight than older data;
- the technique requires only a few pieces of data to update a forecast;

- the model can be easily programmed and is expensive to use; and
- the rate at which the model responds to changes in the underlying pattern of data can be adjusted mathematically.

Causal Model. Causal models are based on the presumption that an identifiable relationship exists between the item being forecast and other factors. These other factors might include selling price, number of employees, and virtually anything else that might influence the item being forecast. As with time series models, the assumption is that relationships identified from past data will continue in the future. Causal models may vary in complexity from the simplest ones relating only one factor, such as selling price, to items being forecast, to the more complex ones utilizing a system of mathematical equations that includes many factors.

The cost of developing and using causal models is generally high, and consequently they are not used frequently for short-term forecasting. They are, however, popular for medium- and long-term forecasts.

The most commonly adopted causal models use regression analysis. Following standard statistical terminology, the items being forecast are called dependent variables and the factors determining the value of the dependent variables are called the independent variables. Regression models require a history of data for the dependent and independent variables so that they can be plotted over time. Once this is done, the regression process involves finding an equation for a line that minimizes the deviations of the dependent variable from it.

The values of the coefficients in this linear equation can be calculated by using regression equations found in most elementary statistics books; computer programs for regression analysis are also readily available. These methods may be applied when a plot of the data suggests that the underlying pattern is a straight line. Linear regression is not applied widely in individual item forecasting but is often useful in representing economic relationships.

Econometric models are also regression models but include a system of simultaneous equations that relate to one another and whose coefficients are determined by regression techniques. Econometric models tend to be sophisticated and expensive; they are more applicable to food processing plants and are seldom used in foodservices.

Subjective Model. A subjective forecasting model is generally used when relevant data are scarce or where patterns and relationships between data do not tend to persist over time. In these cases, little relationship exists between the past and the long-term future, so forecasters must rely on the assembly of opinions and any other information that might relate to the item being forecast, both frequently qualitative in nature.

One of the subjective forecasting models is the Delphi method. This method involves a panel of experts who individually complete questionnaires on a chosen topic, then return them to the investigator. The results of the first questionnaire are summarized and returned to the panel. This process of successively revising questionnaires is continued until some degree of agreement is reached. The Delphi method can be time-consuming and expensive and is not particularly suitable for foodservice forecasting.

Other qualitative forecasting techniques include market research, panel consensus, visionary forecast, and historical analogy. Market research is a systematic and formal procedure for developing and testing hypotheses about real markets. Panel consensus is based on the assumption that a group of experts can produce a better forecast than one person. This differs from the Delphi method by requiring free communication between the panel members. A visionary forecast is characterized by subjective guesswork and imagination; in general, the methods are not scientific. The historical analogy involves comparative analysis of the introduction and growth of new items with similar new product history.

PRODUCT SELECTION

Purchasing for a foodservice operation is a highly specialized job function. The purchaser must know not only the products to be procured but also the market, buying procedures, market trends, and how the materials are produced, processed, and moved to market. In addition, he or she must be able to forecast, plan, organize, control, and perform other management level functions.

The primary function of the purchaser is to procure the required products at the minimum cost for the desired use. The accomplishment of this function frequently involves some research by the purchaser to aid in decision making. For this reason, applied research techniques applicable to foodservice have been adapted from industry, most recently value analysis and make-or-buy decisions.

Value Analysis

In the most liberal sense, value analysis is virtually any organized technique applicable to cost reduction. In the most critical sense, however, value analysis is the methodical investigation of all components of an existing product or service with the goal of discovering and eliminating unnecessary costs without interfering with the effectiveness of the product or service (Miles, 1972). This definition of value analysis, related primarily to industry, contains broad implications for foodservice as well. For example, a value analysis of a menu item may reveal that some quality features may be eliminated without detracting from final product utility. When food products are being evaluated, the quality should depend on the form in which the product will be used. An example is the use of canned whole fruits or vegetables rather than the lower cost pieces when the recipe calls for chopped ingredients. Not only would this change reduce product cost but also would reduce labor time required for chopping.

Value Analysis in Foodservice

In the most meaningful sense, value is the result of the relationship between the price paid for a particular item and its utility in the function it fulfills. The resulting value depends on what is being measured and who is doing the measuring. For example, a food specification being judged by the foodservice manager may be seen in a different light by the purchasing manager. Economies in food-service, effected through the value analysis technique, generally take the form of some alternative action, such as change in specifications or change in source of supply. Value analysis has often been referred to as a new approach to the "best buy" problem in purchasing. The probability of changes in the factors evaluated makes periodic reevaluation desirable.

Although value analysis has often been used in the development of new products in industry, its effectiveness is not confined to such development; it is used much more frequently in evaluating existing product specifications and so finds ready application in foodservice. Take, for example, a major university residence hall foodservice, where value analysis was applied to a lasagne entree after students complained that its flavor was not like that of the product they were served in a local Italian restaurant. An associated problem was the foodservice director's concern that the product was extremely labor-intensive. In conference with the director, the foodservice manager decided to compare lasagne made by the current, standardized recipe calling for American cheese with that made by the identical recipe, but with Mozzarella cheese. For the secondary problem of labor intensity, one well-known brand of frozen lasagne was evaluated.

Reporting on the Value Analysis

An example of a brief value analysis report prepared for the foodservice director, based on our lasagne example, is shown in Figure 7.8. This example illustrates a primary requirement for reporting to management—brevity. Complete data on the methodology and the test procedure should be prepared for filing as a reference and only excerpted for the report to administration. The value analysis results for quality and cost and the recommendations are the aspects of the report that are of major interest to the foodservice director. This portion of the report should be concise and quite definite.

This particular example illustrates a good approach to a problem with a secondary problem. Quite properly, the evaluator gave a recommendation on the primary problem, that of clientele dissatisfaction, and suggested that a separate analysis should be made for several brands of frozen lasagne to examine the secondary problem of labor intensity of the on-site product preparation.

Make-or-Buy Decisions

The procedure of deciding whether to purchase from oneself (make) or purchase from vendors (buy) is a continuing process, and reviews of previous make-or-buy decisions should be conducted periodically. A foodservice has a choice of three basic decisions for production of a menu item. It may:

- produce the item completely, starting with the basic raw ingredients,
- purchase some of the ingredients and assemble them, or
- purchase the item completely from a wholesaler.

VALUE ANALYSIS
Report to Administration

Product Evaluated: Lasagne

Evaluator: Mary Smith

Date: November 2, 1984

Statement of Problem

- Students criticize flavor of lasagne prepared in Residence Hall foodservice.
- Management is concerned about labor intensity of the product.

Products Evaluated

- Residence Hall recipe with American cheese
- Residence Hall recipe with Mozzarella cheese
- Frozen prepared commercial brand

Methodology

- *Preparation of product*
  Two one-half size counter pans of the Residence Hall recipe were prepared at the same time from identical ingredients and the same recipe except one contained American cheese and one Mozzarella cheese. The frozen product was heated according to manufacturer's directions.

- *Test procedure*
  The three products, each identified by a three digit number, were cut into sample size portions and displayed side by side. Each product was rated on flavor, texture, and appearance by a taste panel consisting of 16 students, 6 foodservice employees, and 4 staff.

Value Analysis Results

- *Cost Evaluation*

Cost items	Residence Hall recipe (American cheese)	Residence Hall recipe (Mozzarella cheese)	Commercial frozen
	← cost per portion →		
Food	$ .6216	$ .6256	$ 1.165
Labor	.0676	.0676	---
Total	$ .6892	$ .6932	$ 1.165

- *Quality Evaluation*
  The lasagne prepared from the Residence Hall recipe with Mozzarella cheese ranked highest in flavor. Both Residence Hall products ranked similar in texture and appearance. The frozen commercial product ranked lowest in all three quality criteria.

Recommendation

- The recommendation based on taste panel evaluations is that the Residence Hall lasagne recipe with Mozzarella cheese be used. Also, the made-on-premise product is much less expensive than the purchased frozen. If a decision to serve a frozen prepared product is made because of labor intensity, other brands should be evaluated.

Figure 7.8. *Example of a value analysis report prepared for the Kansas State University Residence Hall Foodservices*

Few foodservice managers consider the first alternative, either because of the expense or the time and labor required. With the lasagne in the value analysis example, above, the second two alternatives were compared (Figure 7.8). A product prepared on-site from a recipe using many purchased items, such as lasagne noodles, canned tomatoes, and cheese, which were assembled for baking in the foodservice kitchen, was compared to a commercial frozen product. Based on cost and quality criteria, the alternative of making the lasagne on the premises, rather than that of purchasing a frozen product, was recommended.

Make-or-Buy Investigations

The initial make-or-buy investigation can originate in a variety of ways (Zenz, 1981b).

- Vendors may propose the alternative and request permission to submit quotations on a product they can produce.
- Vendors may perform unsatisfactorily, creating emergencies because of delivery problems or poor quality.
- Unreasonable vendor price increases can trigger an investigation.
- A new product may be added or an existing one substantially modified.
- A value analysis study of an existing product may necessitate the make-or-buy evaluation.
- Reduced sales and idle equipment or manpower may prompt the manager to consider making items previously purchased from outside vendors.

Make-or-Buy Decisions in Foodservice

The decision factors in foodservice are quality, quantity, service, and cost. The serving of *quality* food is a prime consideration in all types of foodservices, whether menu items are made in the operation or purchased as completely prepared or convenience food from the processor. Quality standards have become well established among most processors of ready-to-serve foods, although variations are evident.

In the lasagne example (Figure 7.8), the noodles in the convenience product were tender but firm enough to hold their shape, and the product held its shape when plated as specified in the standard. The top was covered with meat sauce and cheese and no juices were on the plate. The problem was the flavor of the product, which was not acceptable to the students. The standard was that the flavor should be a blend of cheese, meat, and pasta, with evidence of Italian seasoning, but that it should not be overpowering. The taste panel indicated that the frozen product had a strong tomato flavor and was too highly seasoned; however, the made-on-premises product with the Mozzarella cheese did satisfy the flavor standard.

Quantity enters into the decision process when the ability to produce in the desired amount is considered. The quantity needed may be too large for a satisfactory "make" decision or too small for the processor to consider. As a result of past make-or-buy decisions, many foodservices have closed bake shops and many have not included a bake shop in new facilities because bakery products that are acceptable for the operations are commercially available. As was noted in the discussion of value analysis, decisions are often reversible, but not when the production equipment is not present.

Service includes a wide variety of intangible factors influencing the satisfaction of the purchaser. Two important factors in the decision process are unreliable delivery and unpredictable service. Foodservices must operate on a rigid time schedule; a late delivery of a menu item cannot be tolerated. The dependability of a supplier in all circumstances must be assured. Clues to suppliers' reliability may be their record of labor relations and reputation in the industry, including the opinions of other customers. The geographic proximity of a supplier should also be considered.

When quality, quantity, and service factors are equal, a make-or-buy decision will be made by a comparison of the cost from the vendor with the cost of making the product. The cost from the vendor is known, but the cost of making must be estimated. In this process, the cost of raw food is easily determined, but the costs of labor, energy, equipment depreciation, and overhead may be difficult to calculate.

Set policies for reaching make-or-buy decisions should be avoided, because these and other purchasing decisions are influenced by a number of interrelated factors that are highly changeable. The critical factor on one occasion may be noncritical on the next. The purchaser must strike a fine balance among all factors and make a decision on the basis of what is best for the foodservice operation.

SPECIFICATIONS

Quality has become the watchword in foodservices. In addition to the assurance of quality in product selection, just discussed, other critical elements in producing quality food and foodservice are the development of and strict adherence to rigorous purchasing specifications. Although people are often surprised when reminded of it, the root of the word specification is "specific," which means that some condition or status must be met, definitely and without equivocation. Thus the primary safeguard of foodservice quality is the adherence to specifications.

A specification has been defined in many different ways, but it is essentially a statement, readily understood by both buyers and sellers, of the required qualities of the product, including the allowable limits of tolerance. In the simplest terms, a specification or "spec" may be described as a list of detailed characteristics desired in a product for a specific use.

Types of Specifications

The three types of specifications applicable to foodservices are: technical, approved brand, and performance. One of these types is selected on the basis of the product being purchased, whether food, supplies, or equipment.

Technical specifications are applicable to products for which quality may be measured objectively and impartially by testing instruments. These are particularly applicable to graded food items for which a nationally recognized standard exists. Other examples are equipment parts and metals in fabricated equipment, such as stainless steel and aluminum, which are subject to a thickness requirement that can be measured by gauges. Technical specifications can also be written for detergents and cleaning compounds that can be chemically analyzed.

Approved brand specifications indicate quality by designating a product of known desirable characteristics, such as a manufacturer's specifications for a dishmachine or even a processor's production formula for a canned food product. Paper and plastic disposable items could also be specified by brand name.

In performance specifications, quality is measured by the effective functioning of large or small equipment, disposable paper and plastic items, or detergents. For example, a specification for an insulated beverage carafe for room service in a hotel might include the minimum time requirement for maintaining a desired temperature for coffee.

Of the three types of specifications, the technical is used most often for food products purchased by schools, college and university foodservices, large healthcare facilities, and multi-unit commercial operations. The brand name specification is often used in smaller foodservices, in which a cook or supervisor might have the responsibility for purchasing in addition to operational responsibilities. A specification for a particular product might also be a combination spec, including both technical and performance criteria.

Developing Specifications

A written specification describing the food to be purchased must be developed to ensure the best quality food products. A specification can be simple or very complex, depending on the type used; the brand name type is the simplest, and the technical the most complex.

The criteria for writing a good specification are that it be:

- Clear, simple, and sufficiently specific so that both buyer and seller can readily identify all provisions required.
- Identifiable with products or grades currently on the market.
- Capable of being checked by label statements, USDA grades, weight determination, etc.
- Fair to seller and protective to the buyer.
- Capable of being met by several bidders to enable competition.

All specifications should include the following information:

- Name of product (trade or brand) or standard.
- Federal grade, brand, or other quality designation.
- Size of container (weight, can size, etc.).
- Count per container or approximate number per pound (number of pieces per container if applicable).
- Unit on which price will be based.

Any other information that helps to describe the condition of the product should be included, as appropriate:

- Canned goods: type or style, pack, syrup density, size, specific gravity.
- Meats and meat products: age, exact cutting instructions, weight range, composition, condition upon receipt of product, fat content, cut of meat to be used, market class.
- Fresh fruits and vegetables: variety, weight, degree of ripeness or maturity, geographical origin.
- Frozen foods: temperature during delivery and upon receipt, variety, sugar ratio.
- Dairy products: temperature during delivery and upon receipt, milk fat content, milk solids, bacteria content.

Were it not for the availability of nationally accepted grades and other criteria promulgated by the USDA and other organizations, writing a specification would be an almost insurmountable task for the buyer as well as difficult for the seller to interpret. Purchasers can now write very definite specifications by citing a known standard, which is in itself a rigorous specification. These referenced standards constitute a common technical language for buyers and sellers. For reasons of brevity, we have elected to confine further exposition of reference specifications primarily to meat products because meat is generally the major item of cost in foodservice. A list of key reference material on specifications is included in Appendix B.

Reference Materials for Specifications

The USDA has published a greater volume of specification material pertaining to foodservice than any other agency. As mentioned earlier in this chapter when discussing market regulations, the USDA has established grading standards for fruits, vegetables, eggs, poultry, and dairy and meat products.

USDA Institutional Meat Purchase Specifications, commonly referred to as IMPS, simplify specification writing for large-volume users of meat. The use of these specifications is related to the Meat Acceptance Service of the USDA, a part of the total service of federal inspection and grading.

An extremely valuable feature of IMPS is the numbering system for the identification of carcass cuts and of various cuts or types of meat products. In addition to the benefits of the numbering system, IMPS information on ordering includes quality grades and yield grades in the USDA system as well as weight ranges, portion cut tolerances, fat limitations, and refrigeration requirements for beef, pork, veal, and lamb.

One of the most useful guides for writers of meat purchase specifications is the *Meat Buyers Guide*, published by the National Association of Meat Purveyors. This organization, commonly referred to as NAMP, coordinated the publication of the guide with the USDA. The numbering system and the general purchasing information are identical with IMPS. The advantage of the NAMP Meat Buyers Guide is the arrangement of the text material and the excellent colored illustrations of each numbered item. Most wholesalers of meat products have membership in NAMP, so the guide provides an excellent adjunct to communication between purchaser and seller. Also included in the NAMP *Meat Buyers Guide* is a description of the USDA identification marks for Quality Grades, Yield Grades, and Federal Inspection stamps for beef.

Grades and Inspection. The USDA Quality Grades for beef are: U.S. PRIME, U.S. CHOICE, U.S. GOOD, U.S. STANDARD, U.S. COMMERCIAL, U.S. UTILITY, U.S. CANNER, and U.S. CUTTER. These grades pertain to the eating qualities of beef, namely tenderness, juiciness, and flavor. The USDA conducts a voluntary meat grading service to identify beef and when this service is used, a USDA Quality Stamp will appear on the carcass (Figure 7.9). Quality grades for other food products are included in the references in Appendix B.

Yield grades for beef provide a nationwide uniform method of identifying "cutability" differences among beef carcasses. Specifically, these grades are based on percentage yields of boneless, closely trimmed retail cuts. The Yield Grade

Stamp indicating
federal inspection

Stamp indicating
federal grade

Stamp denoting
yield grade
for a beef carcass

Figure 7.9. *USDA meat stamps*

Quality grades	Yield grades[a]				
	1	2	3	4	5
U.S. Prime			X	X	X
U.S. Choice		X	X	X	
U.S. Good		X	X		
U.S. Standard	X	X	X		
U.S. Commercial		X	X	X	X
U.S. Utility		X	X	X	
U.S. Cutter		X	X		
U.S. Canner		X	X		

USDA Grades

[a] The yield grades reflect differences in yields of boneless, closely trimmed, retail cuts. As such, they also reflect differences in the overall fatness of carcasses and cuts. Yield Grade 1 represents the highest yield of retail cuts and the least amount of fat trim. Yield Grade 5 represents the lowest yield of retail cuts and the highest amount of fat trim.

Figure 7.10. *Yield grades for beef carcasses.* **Source: *Institutional meat purchase specifications for fresh beef. Washington, DC: USDA Agricultural Marketing Service, Livestock Division, January, 1975.***

stamp is shown in Figure 7.9. Because of the trimming done by the purveying industry, however, Yield Grade stamps will rarely appear on cuts purchased by the foodservice industry. Yield grades are applicable to all quality grades; in Figure 7.10 those yield grades indicated by an "X" are in the largest supply.

The mark of Federal Inspection is a round stamp (Figure 7.9) identifying the slaughter house of origin for carcasses and the meat fabricating house for further cuts. This stamp indicates that all processing was done under government supervision and that the product is totally wholesome.

Packer's Brands. Many food producers use their own brand names and define their own quality standards. The grading system closely follows the USDA grades and standards, but with more flexibility than is allowed in the USDA system. For example, one brand or label may mean the highest quality while another is used to indicate a lower quality. Canners, packers, and distributors usually put their top ranking label on the highest quality products. For example, a meat packer might choose as its highest ranking label the word "select," which has the connotation of high quality, and so label the meat that would qualify at the top of the USDA Good range. The purchaser is assured of good value in choosing such a packer brand because the top of the Good range is near the low end of the Choice range and considerably lower in cost.

The same situation occurs with canned products. Many packers of canned and frozen fruits and vegetables choose their own quality labels rather than those established by USDA. The purchaser must realize that the word "Fancy" as a brand name does not mean that the product meets the requirements of the U.S. Fancy grade. Since not all canned fruits and vegetables are graded by the USDA, the careful purchaser will open cans of different brands for comparison before placing major orders. This process is commonly called "can cutting" and constitutes the only means of acquiring first-hand information about drained weight, appearance, texture, flavor, or any scoring factors of particular interest to the buyer. Following selection of a product by this or some other process, the purchaser of larger volume quantities might utilize the USDA Agricultural Marketing Service for inspection at the cannery. This service is provided for a fee and was discussed in the Market Regulation section of this chapter.

Specimen Specifications

The specimen specifications shown in Figure 7.11 are for the steak menu item in three distinct types of restaurants, each with a menu appropriate to its type. The first specification is for a first class hotel or restaurant, the second for a family style restaurant, and the third for a budget steakhouse. Note that, in each case, the NAMP Meat Buyers Guide numbers were used to define the meat product. The NAMP identifications define these steaks as follows:

- *NAMP #180.*   Strip loin, short cut, boneless
- *NAMP #1179.*   Strip loin steaks, bone-in, short cut
- *NAMP #1177.*   Strip loin steaks, bone-in, intermediate

The NAMP #180 is a whole loin and will be portion cut on the premises by the hotel chef, as indicated on the specification by the 10- to 12-pound weight for the loin.

In these three specifications, the term "strip steaks" has noticeably different meanings and further distinctions are necessary. The first class restaurant has specified USDA Prime, yield grade two. The family style restaurant calls for USDA low Choice and the budget steak house uses USDA Commercial (cows only, no bulls). In each case, the specifications also include trim factor, weight range, method of tenderization, packaging, special considerations, and state of refrigeration. The meat grades selected in each case, along with the additional specifications, reflect the judgment of the management on the desires and spending habits of the diners.

METHODS OF PURCHASING

The purchaser who has forecast a need for specific products and written specifications for them must then decide how to make the purchase. Whatever method is chosen, it will belong to one of two general categories of procedures, identified as either informal or formal, both applicable to independent and organizational buying.

Specification item	First-class hotel or restaurant	Family style restaurant	Budget steakhouse
Menu item	New York strip steak, 12-oz. boneless	New York strip steak, 12-oz. with bone	charbroiled strip loin
Product	strip loin	bone-in strip steak	bone-in strip steak
National meat buyers' guide number (NAMP#)	180	1179	1177
Grade	USDA Prime, yield grade two	USDA low Choice (note that this specifies where on the grade)	USDA Commercial (cows only, no bulls)
Trim factor	not to exceed ¼ inch fat with smooth trim	¼ inch to ½ inch fat cover, maximum two-inch tail	maximum ¾ inch fat, maximum three-inch tail
Weight range	10 to 12 pounds	12-oz. portion ± half ounce	14 oz. portion ± one oz., minimum ¾ inch thick
Method of tenderization	dry age 14 to 21 days	age whole strips seven to nine days prior to cutting; jackard before cutting	pin whole strip before cutting; individually dip portion steaks in liquid tenderizer
Packaging	wrapped in sanitary paper and tied	individual 12 portions per box, six boxes per case; show date of cutting	multivac, 24 portions per box
Special considerations	eye must be between 2½ and 3½ inches in diameter	¾ inch thick steaks with vein on both sides are not acceptable	
State of refrigeration	fresh only, ship chilled at temperature between 33 and 40°F	frozen—0°F or less	frozen—0°F or less

Figure 7.11. *Specifications for steak menu items in three types of restaurants.* **Source: Adapted from Mutkoski, S. A., and Schurer, M. L.: Meat and Fish Management.** *North Scituate, MA:* **Breton Publishers, 1981.**

Informal Purchasing

Informal purchasing, in which price quotations are given and orders made by telephone or personally with a salesperson, is often used when time is an important factor. It is usually done under the following circumstances:

• The amount of the purchase is so small that the time required for formal purchasing practices cannot be justified.

- An item can be obtained only from one or two sources of supply.
- A need is urgent and immediate delivery is required.
- The stability of market (and prices) is uncertain.
- The size of the operation may be too small to justify more formal procedures.

If possible, at least two prices for each item should be obtained, since informal quotations have little legal protection. Any prices quoted by telephone should be recorded by the buyer and then checked on the invoice at the time of delivery. Because of the lack of formal records, federal, state, or local laws often determine conditions under which informal purchasing can be used for tax-supported institutions.

Formal Purchasing

Competitive bidding is generally required when buying for an institution under federal, state, or local jurisdiction. For private institutions and commercial foodservices, however, competitive bidding is optional. With high-use items, competitive bidding usually culminates in a formal contract between the purchaser and the vendor.

Understanding the legal implications of contract buying is important for both the purchaser and the vendor. These legal considerations apply equally to buying for a single independent unit, a department within an organization, several departments of an organization, or a group of organizations.

Bid Buying

Bid buying is characterized by an availability of a sufficient number of vendors willing to compete over price quotes on the purchaser's item specifications. Purchasers using bid buying generally take one of two approaches, either the fixed bid or the daily bid, prior to initiating a bidding procedure.

Fixed Bid. The fixed bid is generally used for large quantities over a reasonably long period, particularly for nonperishable items. Vendors tend to avoid committing themselves to long periods of time, however, because of probable fluctuations in the price of the supply. The fixed bid plan consists of selecting a group of vendors and supplying them with specifications and bidding forms for submission to the buyer. Quite logically, vendors must agree informally to participate in the bidding procedure and to accept contract terms. Figure 7.12 is an example of a bid form.

Daily Bid. The daily bid is often used for items such as fresh produce, for which the purchased amount would be only enough to last for a few days. This method has sometimes been referred to as daily quotation buying. The daily bid plan also begins with a selected list of amenable vendors. The bids are usually made by

BID REQUEST

Bids will be received until _____ July 1, 1984 _____

Issued by: Community Hospital	*Address:* 100 North Street Sunnyvale, OK

Date issued: June 1, 1984	*Date to be delivered:* Weekly as ordered between 8/1/84–12/31/84

Increases in quantity up to 20 percent will be binding at the discretion of the buyer. All items are to be officially certified by the U.S. Department of Agriculture for acceptance no earlier than two days before delivery; costs of such service to be borne by the supplier.

Item No.	Description	Quantity	Unit	Unit price	Amount
1	Tomatoes, whole or in pieces, U.S. Grade B, #10 cans, 6/cs.	100	cs.		
2	Sweet Potatoes, vacuum pack, U.S. Grade B, #3 vacuum cans (enamel lined), 24/cs.	50	cs.		
3	Asparagus, all green, cuts and tips, U.S. Grade A, #10 cans, 6/cs.	50	cs.		
4	Corn, Cream Style, golden, U.S. Grade A, #10 cans (enamel lined), 6/cs.	60	cs.		
5	Blueberries, light sirup, U.S. Grade B, #10 cans (enamel lined), 6/cs.	20	cs.		

Vendor _____

Figure 7.12. *Example of a bid request form*

telephone with written confirmation subsequent to acceptance of a bid. Bids quoted by telephone are recorded by the buyer on a quotation record form similar to that in Figure 7.13.

For a single item bid on by several vendors, the purchaser will order from the lowest bidder. When a list of items such as fresh produce is put out for competitive bids on each item, vendors may refuse to bid on this basis because of small orders and the disproportionate cost of transportation. This quite reasonable reaction by vendors can lead the buyer into "one-stop shopping," meaning that the purchase is made from the vendor with the lowest sum of quotes on an entire list of items. The buyer who uses one-stop shopping recognizes the problems of vendors and accepts some penalty in item prices for the advantages of placing one order, receiving one delivery, and paying only one bill.

Bidding Procedure. Purchasing managers for federal, state, and local institutions must allow bidding by all qualified vendors, but purchasing agents for private institutions and commercial foodservices may select the companies they wish to submit bids. A bid request form is used to solicit bids from prospective suppliers, on which the item specification and the date for closing the bids also are indicated. Bids are usually required to be submitted in an unmarked, sealed envelope.

Bids are generally opened at a specified time, after which a tabulation of the bids is prepared. Government purchasing policies usually require that this be done publicly, with the award to be made to the lowest bidder. No such requirement is dictated to industry; however, if purchasers have selected qualified suppliers from whom bids are requested, and the bids are responsive to the specifications, the lowest bid should be the one accepted.

The Contract

Purchasing practices and the buyer/vendor relationship are usually predicated upon good faith, not dependent on legal considerations. The purchase/sale interchange, however, is a legal and binding commitment. The major legal areas involved concern the laws of agency and those of contracts. The legal considerations afford protection and in many cases require monetary recompense for nonperformance, but this is only used as a last resort. Purchasing personnel, therefore, should have a knowledge of basic principles of pertinent law to avoid litigation.

The Law of Agency. Every purchasing transaction is governed by at least one law, and in most purchases, many laws are involved. Without a basic understanding of how these laws affect the purchasing function, purchasing agents may involve their organizations and themselves in costly legal disputes. The law of agency should be understood by everyone involved in purchasing because it defines the scope of the purchasing agent's authority to act for the organization, in addition to the obligation each owes the other and the extent to which each may be held liable for the other's actions.

COMMUNITY HOSPITAL

QUOTATION RECORD FORM

Date: ___Wed., 7/27/84___

Delivery Date: ___7/29/84___

Circle accepted price quotation.

Item	Specifications	Amount needed	Amount on hand	Amount to order	Price quotations			
					Vendor L and M		Vendor Jones	
					per unit	total	per unit	total
					$	$	$	$
Tomatoes	U.S.#1, 20# lug, 5 × 6	4 lugs	1	3	6.50	19.50	6.75	20.25
Lettuce	U.S.#1, Untrimmed Iceberg, 40% hard head, 24 heads, 1 crate	4	1	3	7.25	21.75	6.95	20.85
Potatoes	U.S.#1, Long Russet Bakers 100 count (50# box)	6	2	4	7.00	28.00	7.25	28.75
Onions	U.S.#1, Yellow, med. size, 50# sack	1	0	1	6.75	6.75	6.50	6.50
Avocado	U.S.#1, 25–28# lug	1	0	1	15.00	15.00	15.00	15.00
Watermelon	U.S.#1, Red flesh	400#	0	400#	.075/#	30.00	.05/#	20.00
						$121.00		($111.35)

Figure 7.13. *Example of a form for telephone bids*

Some terms need to be defined before the law can be understood. An agent is an individual who has been authorized to act on behalf of another party known as the principal. The business relationship between the agent and principal is the agency. Agents have the power to commit their principals in a purchase contract with suppliers. The manner in which a purchasing agent is granted authority varies among organizations, as does the scope of this authority. In large organizations, the power of the agency is created by action of the board of directors and delegated to the purchasing agent. In smaller organizations, however, quite often the scope of the purchasing agent's responsibility and authority may have developed over a period of years without ever having been recorded in a written agreement.

In many purchase transactions, the purchaser will deal with the sales representative and not the vendor. Can sales representatives be agents, then, and if so, what authority are they likely to possess? Generally, salespersons are considered to be special agents empowered to perform one specific action—to solicit business for their principal or company, and nothing else. However, the primary interest of most salespersons, quite rightfully, is to make as many sales as possible. Most companies protect themselves and their customers by specifying in sales agreements that they will not be bound by sales personnel promises unless these appear in writing in a contract approved by an authorized person in the vendor's office.

Contracts. A contract is an agreement between two or more parties. Because contracts constitute an agent's primary source of liability, purchasers should always be certain that each contract bearing their signature is legally sound. For a contract to be considered valid and enforceable, it must fulfill five basic requirements: the offer, acceptance of the offer, consideration, competent parties, and legality of subject matter. An example of a contract award form for purchasing by a school district is shown in Figure 7.14.

- *The offer.* The first step in entering into a contract is the making of an offer, usually by the purchaser. A purchase order becomes a purchaser's formal offer to do business. When the vendor agrees to terms, a contractual relationship will be in force. A contract does not exist until both parties agree.

- *The acceptance.* The acceptance of the offer by the second party in the purchase is the next step in the formation of a contractual relationship. Most organizations include a clause in the purchase order that requires the vendor to indicate acceptance of the terms stated in the purchase order. Two copies of the order are sent to the vendor, one for the vendor to keep and the other to be signed and returned to the purchaser.

- *The consideration.* Consideration is the value, in money and in materials, that each party pays in return for fulfillment of the other party's contract promise. Failure to establish this mutuality of obligation usually means that the contract will prove legally unenforceable. Agreement must be made on quantity, price, and time of delivery between the buyer and the vendor.

Contract Award

Board of Education or School _____   Contract Award No. _____

_____   Date Awarded _____
Address

_____   Date Bid Opened _____

This is a notice of the acceptance of Bid # _____ for the period of _____ , 19 ____
to _____ , 19 ____ .

Delivery
Delivery is to be made in two shipments: Week of _____ and _____
between _____ a.m. and _____ p.m.

Notice to Contractors:
This notice of award is an order to ship. Orders against contract are listed by _____ and invoices shall be
rendered direct to the _____ . The price basis, unless otherwise noted, _____ includes delivery and
transportation charges fully prepaid F.O.B. agency. No extra charge to be made for packing or packages.

Names and Addresses of Successful Bidders

Offer
In compliance with the above award, and subject to all terms and conditions listed on the Bid Request, the
undersigned offers and agrees to sell to _____ the items listed on the attached
schedule.

Bidder _____

_____
Address

By _____
      Signature of person authorized to sign this contract

Title _____

Accepted as to items numbered _____   Accepted by _____

By _____   Date _____

Title _____

Figure 7.14. *Example of a contract award form.* **Source:** *Food and Nutrition Service, USDA:* **Food Purchasing Pointers for School Food Service.** *Program aid no. 1160, August, 1970, p. 17.*

Consideration difficulties caused by the quantity factor often arise because of a failure by the contracting parties to define precisely the exact quantity to be purchased. The responsibilities of the contract require the vendor to deliver the quantity of materials specified in the agreement, and the buyer is bound to purchase that amount.

A price is usually stipulated, but occasionally a statement may be included that the price should not be higher than that of the last shipment. This procedure would only be followed when time does not permit the vendor to provide an exact cost. Generally, any procedure other than a stipulated price would not be used except with a vendor with whom relations have been satisfactory.

Time of delivery should be specified for contract orders. The vendor has an obligation to meet the delivery date and failure to do so leaves the vendor liable for damages.

• *Competent parties and Legality.*   The final two requirements of a valid contract are competency and legality. Competency means that the agreement was reached by persons having full capacity and authority to enter into a contract. Legality means that a valid contract cannot conflict with any existing federal, state, or local regulations or laws.

Independent and Organizational Buying

Buying methods and purchasing legal concerns are just as applicable to an independent unit as they are to a central and a group purchasing arrangement. As mentioned previously, buyers must be legally authorized to act as agents of those for whom they buy.

Independent Purchasing

An independent unit is one whose management is not responsible to any larger organization or a department within a large organization that has been authorized to purchase independently. In the simplest situation, the owner might be the purchaser and, as such, could have full legal authority to execute binding contracts, as would be the case in a single-owner restaurant not using a hired manager.

In some hospitals, the head of the dietetics department may have the authority to do the purchasing for the department and thus becomes an agent for the principal, or the hospital. A similar situation may exist in some schools with purchasing responsibilities for food and supplies delegated to the foodservice manager.

Central Purchasing

In central purchasing, personnel in one specific office do all purchasing for all units in an organization. An exception to the "all purchasing" rule might be the delegation of purchasing authority to a department for specific items. For example, in foodservice, purchasing of fresh produce is generally delegated to that particular unit.

Hospitals exemplify one of the clearest applications of central purchasing. One in-house department buys for all departments; other departments signify their needs to this purchasing office and do not deal directly with vendors on a regular basis. The purchasing staff may at times, however, arrange for direct contact between a department and a vendor when a new product is being presented for possible purchase. Receiving and storage of purchased items are usually the responsibility of the purchasing department, although in some operations the receiving clerk reports directly to the comptroller. Other departments requisition their supplies from storage.

Such an in-house purchasing department in a self-contained organization is the clearest example of central purchasing. Widely dispersed units under one central management may also utilize central purchasing by the designation of one purchasing office for all. A classic example is the school foodservice for a consolidated school district, in which a central purchasing office, usually with warehouse facilities, meets the requirements for all schools in a district. Warehousing and delivery costs add to the operating budget. The cost of storage and delivery may be somewhat offset by lower prices from the vendor, who does not have to make individual deliveries to the schools.

Another example is the use of central purchasing by national commercial foodservice organizations with units in numerous cities, such as contract foodservices. The home office of the organization generally includes the purchasing department. Beyond this point, however, many modifications of this central purchasing concept exist. Storage and issue of purchased items may vary, depending on the number of units in the organization and their geographical distribution. A major management decision, then, is whether to have central storage or vendor delivery directly to the individual units.

Group Purchasing

Group purchasing, often erroneously called central purchasing, involves the union of separate units, not related to a single management, for joint purchasing. The purchasing personnel, selected by the group and paid from group funds, are usually housed in a separate building. The participating foodservice managers must agree on specifications for each item to be purchased. Obviously, wide variations in specifications defeat the purpose of group purchasing.

The economic advantage of group purchasing is that the volume of purchases is large enough to warrant good pricing by the vendors. An example of cooperation in purchasing among the group's units is the joint decisions of the unit dietitians in the selection of canned products at can cutting time, discussed previously with specifications. A similar panel could serve in the selection of other items in quantity use among group members.

Richards (1982) states that more than 100 purchasing groups are currently operating among hospitals. Movement toward group purchasing has been stimulated by pressures for cost containment in healthcare. He cited, as probably the earliest group purchasing venture, the joint purchasing program initiated in 1918 under the auspices of the Greater Cleveland Hospital Association. This program, like many others, does not include warehousing because the large number of member institutions induces enough volume that vendors readily agree to delivery direct to units. The purchasing service is supported, generally, by a fee paid by each institution as determined by the percentage of its ordered costs. This system of payment permits the small hospitals to profit from the service, as well as the larger ones. This purchasing program quite naturally assures the same item prices to all member institutions regardless of size. In smaller communities, a group of dissimilar units with foodservices, such as a hospital, a nursing home, and a school, could join in a group purchasing agreement.

An indication of the size of some of the group purchasing programs is the service operated by the Hospital Council of Western Pennsylvania, which has 330 vendor contracts covering thousands of items for 150 hospitals. Of course, not all the contracting vendors are related to foodservice.

VENDOR SELECTION AND EVALUATION

Regardless of how long a purchasing department has been in existence, the problem of vendor selection is always present. Traditionally, the seller seeks out the buyer, but for the purchasing professional this traditional approach leaves entirely too much to chance. The probability of the right salesperson entering the purchasing office with just the right product at precisely the right time it is needed is remote. Finding out which vendors can supply particular products and then determining which of them can do the job most satisfactorily are crucial elements of the purchaser's task. Vendor selection consists of two stages: survey and inquiry.

The Survey Stage

The purpose of a vendor survey is to explore all possible sources for a product. The sources of information fall into two groups: those based on experience and personal contacts, and those in printed form available in the purchasing office.

The previous experience of the purchasing organization with vendors is usually the most valuable and most reliable source of information. The usefulness of past experience is dependent upon the existence of a complete and up-to-date vendor file. Normally, such a file should contain the name and address of every vendor with whom the organization has transacted business, plus information on the types of goods purchased from this vendor. Additional helpful information would be reliability in meeting commitment dates, willingness to handle emergency and rush orders, and defect or reject ratios on shipments received. For greatest value, the vendor file should be supplemented by a cross-referenced file of items listing the sources from which they were purchased, the prices paid, and the points of shipment.

Salespersons constitute a good source of information and, although of necessity biased in favor of their own company products, if properly interviewed, can often give information about other vendors as well as their own employer. Few persons have the opportunities of salespersons to find out what is occurring in the industry.

Members of professional organizations with similar interests can also be of considerable value in the vendor selection process. The National Restaurant Association, The American Dietetic Association, the American School Food Service Association, the American Society of Hospital Food Service Administrators, and the National Association of College and University Food Services are all examples of useful organizations. On the same scale, state and national trade shows and exhibitions provide up-to-the-minute information on new products, as well as vendors associated with these products.

Finally, the classified section of the local telephone directory should not be ignored as a source of information. And the local Chamber of Commerce may be able to give some assistance. But for new products, developments, methods, and suppliers, trade publications are without question an excellent source of general information. A conscientious purchasing agent will read and keep a file of the appropriate publications.

The Inquiry Stage

In the inquiry stage of the vendor selection process, the field must be narrowed from possible sources to acceptable sources. In general, this process involves comparing potential vendors in terms of their abilities to provide the right quality and the needed quantity at the right time, all at the right price with the desired degree of service. The three points of comparison on quality, quantity, and price must be balanced against each other. The common factor of service is applicable to all purchases and, although it cannot be quantified, is an important subjective consideration.

Geographic location is a major concern in evaluating a vendor's service, in combination with transportation capabilities. Certainly, shorter delivery distances offer better opportunities for satisfactory service. The reserve facilities— or, in other terms, the inventory of the vendor—are an important consideration in selecting a vendor capable of meeting the operation's requirements. The chosen vendor should be one who keeps current with technological development and is capable of providing new and improved products as they become available and one whose quality control standards ensure that inspection and storage methods adhere to FDA and USDA standards.

The form of warranty and service offered by a vendor is a vital concern for the purchasing agent, and such information generally has to come from inquiries to other customers. A telephone call is frequently adequate, although some purchasers prefer a confidential questionnaire to be completed and returned by a former customer. For minimum time consumed and inconvenience to another purchasing agent, the following brief list of points of inquiry and suggested rating scales might be used:

- *Performance rating of vendor.*
  Excellent _____, very good _____, satisfactory _____, fair _____, poor _____.

- *Timing of deliveries.*
  Excellent _____, good _____, just meets promises _____, occasionally late, but not their fault _____, frequently late _____.

- *Complaint and reject handling.*
  Cooperative and responsible _____, slow but fair _____, hard to deal with _____, don't know _____.

- *Quotes and prices.*
  Very low _____, competitive _____, sometimes low _____, sometimes high _____, higher than competitors, but worth it _____.

- *Length of experience with vendor.*
  Minimum orders in past year _____, few orders for past three years _____, many orders for several years _____.

- *Other comments.*

The purchaser making the inquiry should assure the respondent that replies will be kept in confidence.

Another factor to consider is that the financial condition of a vendor is vital for maintaining a satisfactory business relationship. In general, the comptroller or credit manager of the purchaser's organization can provide a credit report. And, when feasible, a visit to the prospective vendor's warehouse facilities will give an indication of the efficiency and general housekeeping quality that are associated with a good business. The visit yields an opportunity to observe workers, including union relations, and also order handling procedures.

Vendor Performance Evaluation

At the conclusion of the survey and inquiry stages of the vendor selection process, the purchaser should have a relatively small number of vendors from which to choose one or more. This process is largely subjective; more objective evaluations can be made after an order has been placed with a vendor.

The true test of the purchaser's choice of the vendor is evaluation after orders have been received. The first order used in evaluation is hardly fair to the vendor and the evaluation should not be considered completely until several orders have been processed. Figure 7.15 is a simple evaluation form that might be used; such evaluations should be conducted periodically to keep the vendor's record file up to date.

Vendors who maintain a good record on the evaluations will appreciate knowing the results. Vendors who do not rate well should be told why; such disclosure might accompany the notice of severance of the business relationship.

VENDOR PERFORMANCE EVALUATION

Vendor: _____   Date: _____

Company	Excellent	Good	Fair	Poor
Size and/or capacity				
Financial strength				
Technical service				
Geographical locations				
Management				
Labor relations				
Trade relations				
Products				
Quality				
Price				
Packaging				
Uniformity				
Service				
Delivers on time				
Condition on arrival				
Follows instructions				
Number of rejections				
Handling of complaints				
Technical assistance				
Emergency deliveries				
Supplies price changes promptly				
Sales Personnel				
• Knowledge:				
Of company				
Of products				
Of foodservice industry				
• Sales calls:				
Properly spaced				
By appointment				
Planned and prepared				
Mutually productive				
• Sales service:				
Obtains information				
Furnishes quotations promptly . .				
Follows through				
Expedites delivery				
Handles complaints				
Accounting				
Invoices correctly				
Issues credit promptly				

Figure 7.15. *Example of a vendor evaluation form*

PURCHASING PROCESS

The overall procurement functional subsystem of any foodservice operates through a set of procedures intended to accomplish the routine purchasing transaction as quickly and as accurately as possible. Undoubtedly, each individual foodservice has procedures unique to its individual needs, but very likely these procedures conform to the basic pattern followed by many other foodservices. The adoption of definite purchasing procedures implies utilization of appropriate records for each phase in the purchasing process.

Purchasing Procedures

Several fundamental procedures appear in some form in virtually every purchasing unit (Figure 7.16). These procedures are not complex and should be adapted to the particular needs of the various departments of an organization. Any purchaser could think of additions to or deletions from this list that would make it more like his or her own purchasing experience. However, for clarity in presenting an image of the elementary purchasing procedures carried on by most organizations, this list is limited to the eight essential steps listed.

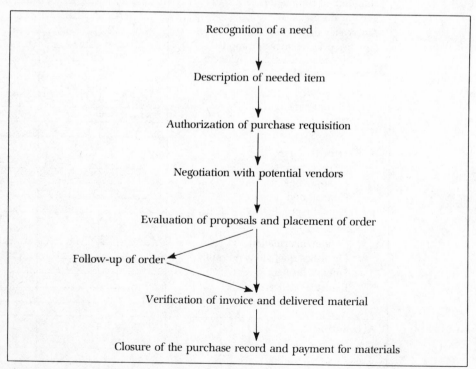

Figure 7.16. *Fundamental steps in purchasing*

Recognition of a Need

Purchasing may originate in any one of three general locations in a foodservice operation. The most obvious place of origin is the production unit. A second initiating point is the storage area, in which the concern is maintaining a proper inventory level. In the larger organizations wherein purchasing has inventory responsibility, a need for ordering a particular item may be recognized when the inventory reorder level is reached. Recognition of a need should be followed by initiation of action to remedy the deficiency, namely, preparing a requisition.

Description of the Needed Item

In all except the very smallest organizations, the production unit cooks, having recognized a need for a particular item, initiate a requisition to the storeroom for the required amount of the item. If the storeroom has an adequate inventory of the item, the requisition can be honored. If, however, honoring this requisition brings the inventory stock below the acceptable minimum, the storeroom personnel will initiate another requisition to purchasing for replenishment of the item to the desired inventory level. In any case, the requisition must contain an accurate description of the desired item and the needed quantity.

Correction or alteration of the requisition by other than initiating personnel is inappropriate unless approved by supervisory personnel. The necessity for accuracy in requisitions cannot be overemphasized.

Authorization of the Purchase Requisition

The third phase in the purchasing process is authorizing the purchasing requisition. In every organization, as a matter of policy, a clear delineation of who has the power to requisition material, supplies, and equipment is essential. With this policy in effect, no requisitions should be acted upon unless they have been submitted by an individual authorized to do so. Furthermore, the institution's vendors should be made aware of the names of persons who are authorized to issue final purchase requisitions.

Negotiation with Potential Vendors

Negotiation in purchasing is the process of working out a procurement and sales agreement, mutually satisfactory to both buyer and seller, and the process of reaching a common understanding of the essential elements of a contract. It is one of the most, if not the most, important parts of the procurement function.

Negotiation usually concerns such vital details as establishing the qualifications of a particular vendor, determining fair and reasonable prices to be paid for needed materials, setting delivery dates agreeable to both the buyer and the vendor, as well as renegotiating contract terms when conditions change. All of these details lead to the final determination of the contract terms.

Evaluation of Proposals and Placement of the Order

All vendor proposals are evaluated for compliance with the preceding four fundamental steps in purchasing (Figure 7.16). The sequel to evaluation of proposals is
the actual placement of an order. Ideally, all orders should be in writing, but if an
order is placed by telephone, confirmation in writing should be made promptly.
A written record of every purchase should always be on file.

Follow-up of the Order

Theoretically, a follow-up after the order has been placed and accepted by the
vendor should not be necessary. A follow-up in a foodservice is justified, however,
when a specific delivery time of certain items is critical to an occasion, such as a
major banquet. Most companies maintain a purchase follow-up system, usually
involving color-coded copies of the purchase order. Forms for this purpose will be
discussed later in this chapter.

Verification of the Invoice and Delivered Material

The invoice is the vendor's statement of what is being shipped to the buyer and
the expected payment. The invoice should be checked against the purchase order
for quality, quantity, and price. Without question, the delivery of materials and
their condition on delivery should be in agreement with the purchase order and
the invoice. Any differences require immediate action by the buyer. For example,
the condition of frozen food should be verified, and any indication of exposure to
higher temperatures would be a cause for rejection and immediate communication with the vendor.

Closure of the Purchase Record

Closing the purchase record consists of the clerical process of assembling the
written records of the purchase process, filing them in appropriate places, and
authorizing payment for the goods delivered. The filing system need not be
complex; its only purpose is to provide an adequate historical record of these
business transactions.

Purchasing Records

The essential records for the purchasing process are the requisition and purchase
order, originating with the buyer, and the invoice, prepared by the vendor. Because their formats vary among organizations, we will describe these records in
general terms only.

The Purchase Requisition

The initiating document in a purchase situation is the requisition, which may
have originated in any one of a number of units of an organization, as indicated

```
┌──────────────────────────────────────────────────────────────────────┐
│                      COMMUNITY HOSPITAL                                │
│                      PURCHASE REQUISITION                              │
│                                                                        │
│  To:  Purchasing Office          Requisition No.:      FS 1201         │
│  Date:      August 16, 1984      Purchase Order No.:     1842          │
│  From:        Foodservice        Date Required:   Sept. 15, 1984       │
│  Budget Account No.:   FS 1101                                         │
└──────────────────────────────────────────────────────────────────────┘
```

Total quantity	Unit	Description	Vendor	Unit cost	Total cost
20	cases	Tomatoes, whole or in pieces, #10 cans, 6/case	J.& M. Wholesale Grocers	$16.60	$332.00

Requested by _____   Approved by _____   Date Ordered   8/23/84

Figure 7.17. *Example of a purchase requisition*

previously. An example is shown in Figure 7.17. Basic information on requisitions has become fairly well standardized and includes the following.

- *Requisition number.* This number is necessary for identification and control purposes and is generally accompanied by a code designation of the originating department.

- *Quantity needed.* In foodservice, quantities should be expressed in a common shipping unit, such as cases, and the number of items in a unit should be stipulated. For example, the entry on the requisition calls for 20 cases of tomatoes, with six No. 10 cans to a case.

- *Description of the desired item.* The description and quantity needed are the two most important items on the requisition form and, therefore, occupy the central space. The information included may be such items as applicable specifications, brands, or catalog numbers.

- *Delivery date.* Obviously, this date—on which the item must be available for use—should always allow sufficient time to secure competitive bids and completion of the full purchase transaction, if at all possible.

- *Budget account number.* This number indicates the account to which the purchase cost will be charged.

In addition to the above information, which is provided by the requisitioner, the purchasing agent adds the name and address of the vendor and the details of the purchase, including number of the purchase order, date of placement of order, and price.

The Purchase Order

A <u>purchase order</u> is the means by which the purchasing agent initiates the procurement of materials to satisfy the needs expressed by a requisition. It states in specific terms the purchase and sales agreement between the buyer and the vendor. Before acceptance, it represents an offer to do business under certain terms and, once accepted by a vendor, becomes a legal contract. An example is shown in Figure 7.18.

Format of Purchase Order. The purchase order, just as the requisition, exists in a wide variety of formats that have been developed to meet the needs of individual organizations. The principal reason for this variety is that the purchase order is a legal document; the terms it presents are intended to protect the purchaser's interests, which differ from one organization to another. Almost every purchase order, however, includes the following.

- *Name and address of the organization.* In order to prevent vendor confusions, this information should be clearly and boldly printed at the top of the purchase order.

- *Name and address of the vendor.* This information is usually typed in a box in the top third of the form.

- *Identification numbers.* These include both the numbers of the purchase order and the purchase requisition. Since these numbers are used to identify the order and to reconcile shipments with the purchase requisition, they are often shown in a box in the upper right hand corner of the form. Frequently, these numbers are accompanied by instructions to the vendor to use them on all invoices and correspondence with the buyer.

- *General instructions to the vendor.* These include information on the marking of shipments, the number of invoices to be sent, the delivery date required, and shipping instructions.

- *Complete description of the purchase item.* This is a description in terms of quantity and quality. All references to the quantity being purchased should be in a separate column and should be stated in specific pricing units, such as dollars per case or dollars per unit weight. Quality descriptions should be kept as brief as is consistent with the nature of the purchase. In bid or contract buying, for example, the description can be brief since the specifications have been previously agreed upon.

Purchase Order No.: _____1842_____

To: J. & M. Wholesale Grocers

200 South Street

Sunnyvale, OK

Please refer to the above number on all invoices, two copies required

Date: _____August 23, 1984_____

Requisition No.: _____FS 1201_____

Dept.: _____Dietetics_____

Date Required: September 15, 1984

Ship to: _____ F.O.B.: _____ Via: _____ Terms: _____

Total quantity	Unit	Description	Price per unit	Total cost
20	cases	Tomatoes, whole or in pieces, U.S. Grade B (Extra-Standard) #10 cans, 6/cs.	$16.60	$332.00

Approved by _____

Title: Director of Purchasing
Community Hospital

Figure 7.18. *Example of a purchase order form*

- *Price data.* This section of the order includes the prices to be paid for the item, as well as all applicable discounts.
- *Buyer's signature.* The signature generally consists of three parts: the organization name, the signature of the buyer, and the title of the buyer. The essential reason for this complex signature is to assure the vendor that the order has been placed by a legal agent of the purchasing organization and that the requirements of purchasing law have been satisfied.

Required Number of Copies. Three copies of the purchase order are satisfactory in simplified order systems: the original, which is sent to the vendor; an acknowledgment copy, which is actually a formal acceptance that the vendor returns to the buyer; and a file copy for the purchasing agent's own records. This simplified plan offers only a minimum of control and would probably be inadequate for the procurement operations of most large organizations; however, it is the basis for other, more complex distributions of purchase order copies.

Larger organizations require an order system that offers greater control and coordination than does the basic system. The average system in such an organization uses six copies of the purchase order; rarely do any organizations require more than six. The additional three copies are customarily distributed to the following individuals or departments.

- *Receiving copy.* This copy informs receiving personnel that a delivery is scheduled on or before a certain date and is intended to alert them to be prepared to count and inspect the shipment on arrival.

- *Accounting copy.* This copy is sent to the accounting office as notification of the commitment to purchase and to allow accounting to reconcile the purchase order with the original requisition and the receiving report. If all the essential documents are in order, the purchase will be approved for payment.

- *Requisitioner's copy.* Quite often purchasing sends a copy of the order to the requisitioner as notification that the requisition has been honored and the order placed.

The Invoice

The invoice prepared by the vendor contains the same essential information as the purchase order; that is, quantities, description of items, and price. Upon arrival of the ordered material, the vendor's invoice must be compared with the purchase order and the quantity received. Any discrepancies or rejections at the receiving point should be noted on the invoice by the receiving clerk and initialed by the vendor's delivery person.

If the invoice and the purchase order are in agreement, the invoice will be forwarded to the accounting office for payment. In small operations using only three copies of the purchase order, the receiving clerk only verifies the arrival of the delivered items and sends the invoice to the accounting office for comparison with the purchase order and subsequent payment.

ETHICAL CONSIDERATIONS

Ethics has been defined as the principles of conduct governing an individual or a profession. Personal ethics should be distinguished from business ethics as expressed in the codes adopted by many professional organizations. The source of personal ethics lies in a person's religion and/or philosophy of life and is derived from definite moral standards. Business ethics may be defined as a self-generating system of moral standards to which a substantial majority of business executives give voluntary assent. It is a system or force within business that leads to industry-wide acceptance of certain standards of practical conduct (Zenz, 1981b).

Many business and professional organizations have adopted a formal code of ethics to which the members subscribe. These codes evidence the effect of personal codes, but the major emphasis is on the relationships within business and professional organizations. The observance of these codes devolves upon the responsible individuals within the organizations.

Purchasers are quite commonly advised to buy objectively, which would be ideal; that is, the buyer would always purchase on a logical basis of price, quality, and delivery from the vendor offering the best possible combination. This practice is not always an easy task, however, because of the blandishments of salespersons and prejudicial emotions toward vendors. The difficulties of buying objectively have led the National Association of Purchasing Managers to develop a code of ethics to serve as a guide (Zenz, 1981b). Paraphrased, this code states that each purchasing agent or buyer should:

- Consider first the interest of his or her company.
- Buy without prejudice.
- Obtain the maximum ultimate value for each dollar of expenditure.
- Work for honesty in buying and selling.
- Denounce all forms and manifestations of commercial bribery.
- Respect his or her obligations.
- Avoid collusion with vendors.
- Enhance the development and standing of purchasing.

The principles enunciated in this code generally touch on many of the areas in which the buyer might err ethically. Rudelius and Buchholz (1979) surveyed experienced purchasing managers and buyers, who all said that what they want most from higher levels of management are more stated policies covering purchasing practices that have ethical overtones.

Visualization of every situation in which ethical considerations might arise, however, is virtually impossible. The following are some obvious situations of which buyers should be aware of ethics, with due consideration of their primary responsibility to their employers.

- Disclosure of confidential information.
- Misuse of the organization's buying power.
- Unfair or uneconomical buying decisions.
- Conflicts of interest.
- Misuse of the concept of reciprocity, or "You scratch my back, I'll scratch yours."
- Large or frequent gifts from vendors.
- Lavish entertainment or trips at the vendor's expense.

The recently adopted code of ethics for the Foodservice Purchasing Managers of the National Restaurant Association is shown in Figure 7.19. This code was developed to promote and encourage ethical practices in the industry. To give further credence to the code, the purchasing group agreed that each member should indicate support for the principles by signing the code of ethics document.

Finally, talking about ethics is no substitute for practicing them. A possible exception to this rule is the early and positive statement by the buyer about ethical policies usually best made in the initial relationships with the vendor. The purpose of this discussion, when conducted with proper skill, should not offend a vendor and indeed should contribute to rapport between the buyer and the seller.

MATERIALS MANAGEMENT

The concept of materials management has been well expressed by Dillon (1973) as the unifying force that gives interrelated functional subsystems a sense of common direction. Its goal is to transform materials or physical resources that enter the system into an output meeting definite standards for quantity and quality.

Zenz (1981b) gave another definition, derived from the basic concept but expressed in operational terms. According to this definition, materials management is an organizational concept of centralizing responsibility for those activities involved in moving materials into, and in some cases through, the organization. While the functions vary, they usually include purchasing, inventory control, and traffic, with production control, stores, and related activities sometimes included, depending on the type of product or process involved.

Some confusion has resulted from the erroneous idea that the terms "materials management" and "procurement" are interchangeable. Procurement is an important part of the materials management concept because it includes the purchasing, storage, inventory control, and transportation of food and supplies throughout the foodservice system. Materials management, however, also includes the subsystems of prepreparation, production, and service.

The trend toward the inclusion of materials management in organizational structure has been motivated, primarily, by the need to control the overall cost of materials and to minimize those areas of conflict that have traditionally resulted in excessive inventories. The utilization of the materials management concept, although initiated in industrial manufacturing, has spread to foodservice-related industries, such as major frozen food processors and commercial bakeries. Moreover, a number of larger hospitals now have a materials manager in a staff position with advisory responsibilities for all functions.

Fundamentally, a materials manager is a consultant to all departments or units on the movement of materials through the organization. In smaller organizations that cannot justify an additional staff person, the materials management function could be performed by top level management.

FOODSERVICE PURCHASING MANAGER'S
CODE OF ETHICS

I, _____, recognized as a
Foodservice Purchasing Professional, hereby subscribe and agree to abide by the following
Principles and Standards of Foodservice Purchasing Practice. To wit my signature of agreement
appears below.

I. I will consider the interest of my company in all transactions. Acting as its
representative, I will carry out and believe in its established policies.

II. I recognize good business practices can be maintained only on the basis of honest
and fair relationships.

III. I agree to make commitments for only that which I can reasonably expect to
fulfill.

IV. I will provide a prompt and courteous reception to all who request a legitimate
business appointment.

V. I will avoid comments which may discredit or otherwise harm legitimate
competition. Likewise, information received in confidence will not be used by me
to obtain an unfair advantage in competitive transactions.

VI. I will strive to develop specifications and standards which will enable all qualified
sources to compete for the business without prejudice.

VII. I will not accept, nor encourage, the giving of gifts or entertainment where the
intent is to sway my decision in favor of the donor versus other qualified
competitors.

VIII. I abhor all forms of bribery and will act to expose same whenever encountered.

IX. I will always strive to be up to date on products, materials, supplies,
and manufacturing processes which will ensure my company receives the proper
quality at the most beneficial cost when it is required by the operator.

X. Recognizing the National Restaurant Association and its Foodservice Purchasing
Managers are engaged in activities designed to enhance the development and
standing of Foodservice Purchasing, I hereby agree to support and participate in
its programs.

I, the undersigned, hereby subscribe,

Witness:
    Chairman, NRA Foodservice Purchasing Managers

Developed by the Foodservice Purchasing Managers

Figure 7.19. *Foodservice Purchasing Managers Code of Ethics (permission of NRA Foodservice Purchasing Managers)*

Zenz (1981a) redefined materials management with the concept that it centralizes responsibility for all materials decisions and functions in one managerial position, resulting in several benefits to the organization.

- A reduction in "buck passing" between unit heads.
- A minimization of conflicting objectives and self-interest among units.
- Better utilization of on-line computer facilities, resulting in more effective information flow.
- Improved vendor relations, resulting from smoother scheduling of requirements and purchases.
- A reduction of inventory levels as less safety stock must be maintained by each unit.

Utilization of the materials management concept has been slow in spreading into the foodservice industry but, as has been predicted, is now gaining strength as a unifying force.

SUMMARY

Procurement, the first functional subsystem in the transformation element of the foodservice system, can be defined as the managerial function of acquiring material for production. Purchasing is a procurement procedure concerned with the acquisition of food and supplies and is described as obtaining the right product, in the right amount, at the right time, and at the right price.

Effective purchasing requires knowledge of the food market and the marketing channels through which commodities move. Market regulations make the food industry one of the most controlled industries in the United States. Notable strict regulations are those imposed by the Food, Drug and Cosmetic Act of 1938, which seeks to ensure that foods are pure and wholesome, safe to eat, and produced under sanitary conditions and that the packaging and labeling are truthful. The United States Department of Agriculture (USDA) also has an important role in the food regulatory process, particularly in the grading, inspection, and certification of agricultural products.

Forecasting in a foodservice is necessary to plan for the quantity of food to be produced at some future date and the amount of raw products needed for production. Numerous forecasting models have been developed but, in general, historical records provide their base.

Product selection is a vital concern for the purchaser, whose primary function is to procure the required products at the minimum cost for the desired use. Two techniques for product selection, among those most recently adapted from industry, are value analysis and make-or-buy decisions. Value analysis is the methodical investigation of all components of an existing product or service, with the goal of discovering and eliminating unnecessary cost without interfering with the effectiveness of the product or service. The decision to make or buy a menu item recurs frequently in a foodservice. A value analysis study of a purchased product may lead to a make-or-buy evaluation.

A critical element in producing quality food is the development of rigorous specifications and adherence to them. A specification is a statement, readily understood by both buyers and sellers, of the required qualities of a product. The buyer equipped with well-written specifications must next decide how to make the purchase, informally or formally. Informal purchasing should be used only in small operations or when time considerations are vital and telephone ordering is justified. Formal purchasing through bid buying is the more common method and is required for buying by an institution under federal, state, or local jurisdiction. This method consists of competition among vendors by price quotes on a buyer's specifications, culminating in a purchase/sale interchange, which is a legal and binding commitment or contract.

Purchasing may be categorized as independent, central, or group. Independent purchasing is done by an organization that is not responsible to any larger one. In central purchasing, personnel in one specific office are designated to do all purchasing for all units in an organization. Group purchasing, however, consists of the union of separate units, not related to a single management, for joint purchasing.

Vendor selection is one of the most important and critical aspects of the purchaser's task. The most reliable selection information comes from vendor performance evaluation.

A well-organized process should be followed for effective purchasing. The fundamental phases of a purchasing procedure begin with the recognition of a need and end with closure of a purchase record. The various phases of the purchasing procedure require written records, including the requisition, the purchase order, and the invoice.

Ethical considerations are involved in all business and professional activities and are extremely important in the buyer/vendor relationships.

Materials management is a concept vital to the application of the systems approach to foodservice. Materials management is an organizational concept of centralizing responsibility for all activities involved in moving materials into and through the organization, a major component of such movement being procurement.

REFERENCES

Aardsma, A. H.: Survey points to need for more efficient inventory management. *Hospitals* 56:95 (Jan. 16), 1982.

Adam, E. E., and Ebert, E. J.: *Production and Operations Management.* Englewood Cliffs, NJ: Prentice-Hall, 1978.

Aljian, G. W.: *Purchasing Handbook.* 3rd ed. New York: McGraw-Hill Book Co., 1973.

Ammer, D. S.: *Materials Management and Purchasing.* 4th ed. Homewood, IL: Richard D. Irwin, 1980.

Avery, A. C.: Secrets of food purchasing. *Food Mgmt.* 11:59 (Sept.), 1976.

Avery, A. C.: The art of writing specs. *Food Mgmt.* 13:40 (Mar.), 1978.

Axler, B. H.: *Foodservice: A Managerial Approach.* Lexington, MA: D.C. Heath and Co. in cooperation with The National Institute for the Foodservice Industry, 1979.

Baker, R. J., Kuehne, R. S., McCoy, D., and Witter, D. M.: *Purchasing Factomatic: A Portfolio of Successful Forms, Reports, Records, and Procedures.* Englewood Cliffs, NJ: Prentice-Hall, 1977.

Barath, R. M., and Hagstad, P. S.: The effects of professionalism on purchasing managers. *J. Purchasing and Materials Mgmt.* 15:25 (Spring), 1979.

Bauer, F. L.: Managerial planning in procurement. *J. Purchasing and Materials Mgmt.* 13:3 (Fall), 1977.

Berkman, J.: Foodservice needs controls to contain costs. *Hospitals* 54:79 (Mar. 16), 1980.

Boffey, L. F.: The future of scientific purchasing. *J. Purchasing and Materials Mgmt.* 11:3 (Summer), 1975.

Boss, D.: What will Jacques Bloch pay for quality? *Food Mgmt.* 14:52 (Jul.), 1979.

Brokaw, A. J., and Barstow, W. E.: Purchasing and the antitrust laws. *J. Purchasing and Materials Mgmt.* 15:27 (Winter), 1979.

Browning, J. M., and Zabriskie, N. B.: Professionalism in purchasing: A status report. *J. Purchasing and Materials Mgmt.* 16:2 (Fall), 1980.

Buchanan, R. D.: The procurement system. *NACUFS J.* 1976:10, 1976.

Bureau of Business Practice, eds.: *Purchasing Agent's Desk Manual.* Waterford, CT: Bureau of Business Practice, Inc., 1978.

Chai, J. C.: School food procurement: Procurement models and guides. *School Food Serv. Res. Rev.* 3:33 (Winter), 1979.

Corey, E. R.: *Procurement Management: Strategy, Organization, and Decision-making.* Boston: CBI Publishing Co., Inc., 1978.

Cullen, K. O., Hoover, L. W., and Moore, A. N.: Menu item forecasting systems in hospital foodservice. *J. Am. Dietet. A.* 73:640, 1978.

David, B. D.: A model for decision making. *Hospitals* 46:50 (Aug. 1), 1972.

Dickerson, J. F.: What to buy and how to get it: The cash flow factor. *Hospitals* 56:95 (Jan. 16), 1982.

Dillon, T. F., ed.: Materials management: A convert tells why. *Purchasing* 74:43 (Feb.), 1973.

Farmer, D. H.: Developing purchasing strategies. *J. Purchasing and Materials Mgmt.* 14:6 (Fall), 1978.

Fisk, J. C.: Procurement planning and control. *J. Purchasing and Materials Mgmt.* 15:16 (Spring), 1979.

Fitzsimmons, J. A., and Sullivan, R. S.: Service Operations Management. New York: McGraw-Hill Book Co., 1982.

Food and Nutrition Service, USDA: *Food Purchasing Pointers for School Food Service.* Program Aid No. 1160, Aug., 1977.

Food Safety and Quality Service, USDA: *FSQS Facts—Federal Food Standards.* FSQS—19. Rev. Oct., 1979.

Food Safety and Quality Service, USDA: *FSQS Facts—Food Acceptance Service.* May, 1978.

Foodservice Purchasing Managers: *Code of Ethics.* Chicago, IL: National Restaurant Association.

Franzese, R.: Food service systems of 79 hospitals studied. *Hospitals* 55:64 (Feb. 1), 1981.

Fulbright, J. E.: Advantages and disadvantages of the EOQ model. *J. Purchasing and Materials Mgmt.* 15:8 (Spring), 1979.

Haimann, T., Scott, W. G., and Conner, P. E.: *Managing the Modern Organization.* 4th ed. Boston: Houghton Mifflin Co., 1982.

Hancock, D. A.: Planning the change to convenience foods for a hospital. *J. Am. Dietet. A.* 63:419, 1973.

The hassles and happiness of buying. *Food Mgmt.* 14:35 (Jun.), 1979.

Haywood, B. G.: Administrators must understand and support the purchasing function. *Hospitals* 56:95 (Jan. 16), 1982.

Jacobs, J. A.: Codes of ethics and the courts. *Food Mgmt.* 16:16 (Apr.), 1982.

Janke, T. A.: Cost accounting: The vital link to cost effectiveness. *J. Am. Dietet. A.* 77:167, 1980.

Koogler, G. H., and Nicholanco, S.: Analysis of a decision framework for prepared food systems. *Hospitals* 51:95 (Feb. 16), 1977.

Kotschevar, L. H.: *Quantity Food Purchasing.* 2nd ed. New York: John Wiley & Sons, 1975.

Lee, L., and Dobler, D. W.: *Purchasing and Materials Management: Text and Cases.* 3rd ed. New York: McGraw-Hill Book Co., 1977.

Lehmann, D. R., and O'Shaughnessy, J.: Decisions criteria used in buying different categories of products. *J. Purchasing and Materials Mgmt.* 18:9 (Spring), 1982.

Lewis, H. T.: This business of procurement. *J. Purchasing and Materials Mgmt.* 11:7 (Summer), 1975.

Livestock Division, Agricultural Marketing Service, USDA: *Institutional Meat Purchase Specifications for Fresh Beef.* Washington, DC, Jan., 1975.

Livingston, G. E.: Prepared food. Part 2: Make or buy? *Hospitals* 46:95 (Sept. 16), 1972.

Loecker, K. A., Spears, M. C., and Vaden, A. G.: Purchasing managers in commercial foodservice organizations: Clarifying the role. *The Professional* 1(2):9 (Spring), 1983.

Mahaffey, M. J., Mennes, M. E., and Miller, B. B.: *Food Service Manual for Health Care Institutions.* Chicago: Am. Hosp. Assn., 1981.

Mayfield, B. K.: Line-item versus prime vendor purchasing. *J. Am. Dietet. A.* 84:685, 1984.

McLaren, A.: Containing the costs of foodservice. *Hospitals* 54:75 (Mar. 16), 1980.

McProud, L. M., and David, B. D.: Applying value analysis to food purchasing. *Hospitals* 50:109 (Sept. 16), 1976.

Messersmith, A. M., Moore, A. N., and Hoover, L. W.: A multi-echelon menu item forecasting system for hospitals. *J. Am. Dietet. A.* 75:509, 1978.

Miles, L. D.: *Techniques of Value Analysis and Engineering.* New York: McGraw-Hill Book Co., 1972.

Miller, J. G., and Gilmour, P.: Materials managers: Who needs them? *Harvard Bus. Rev.* 57:154 (Jul./Aug.), 1979.

Montag, G. M.: Obtaining meaningful cost information in dietary departments. I. Food cost information. *J. Am. Dietet. A.* 67:50, 1975.

Montag, G. M., and Hullander, E. L.: Quantitative inventory management. *J. Am. Dietet. A.* 59:356, 1971.

Morrison, L. P., and Vaden, A. G.: Foodservice purchasing practices in small hospitals. *Hospitals* 52:94 (Feb. 1), 1978.

Mutkoski, S. A., and Schurer, M. L.: *Meat and Fish Management.* North Scituate, MA: Breton Publishers, 1981.

National Association of Meat Purveyors: The Meat Buyers Guide. McLean, VA: National Association of Meat Purveyors, 1984.

Nix, M.: Purchasing, purchasing, purchasing! *School Food Serv. J.* 37:161 (Jun./Jul.), 1983.

Olsen, M. D.: Obtaining meaningful cost information in dietary departments. II. Labor cost information. *J. Am. Dietet. A.* 67:55, 1975.

Peddersen, R.: Foodservice and Hotel Purchasing. Boston: CBI Publishing Co., 1981.

Profitable Purchasing. Proceedings from NRA's 2nd Annual National Conference on Purchasing. Chicago: Educational Materials Center at Natl. Restaur. Assoc., Oct., 1982.

Purchasing. *Restaurants & Institutions* 88:21 (Feb. 1), 1981.

Reck, R., and Long, B.: Organizing Purchasing as a Profit Center. *J. Purch. Mat. Mgmt.* 19:2 (Winter), 1983.

Richards, G.: From light bulbs to CT scanners, group purchasing is filling the bill at a lower price. *Hospitals* 56:81 (Jan. 16), 1982.

Rose, J. C.: Containing the labor costs of food service. *Hospitals* 54:93 (Mar. 16), 1980.

Rudelius, W., and Buchholz, R. A.: What industrial purchasers see as key ethical dilemmas. *J. Purchasing and Materials Mgmt.* 15:2 (Winter), 1979.

Schultz, H. W.: *Food Law Handbook.* Westport, CT: AVI Publishing Co., 1981.

Spears, M. C.: Concepts of cost effectiveness: Accountability for nutrition, productivity. *J. Am. Dietet. A.* 68:341, 1976.

Stefanelli, J. M.: *Purchasing Selection and Procurement for the Hospitality Industry.* New York: John Wiley & Sons, 1981.

Strenk, T.: Inside a buying decision. *Restaurants & Institutions* 92:71 (Feb. 1), 1983.

United States Department of Agriculture: *Public Participation in Government Rulemaking.* Food Safety and Quality Service. Washington, DC: U.S. Dept. of Agric., 1978.

Unklesbay, N. F., and David, B. D.: Decision-making in hospital food procurement. *J. Purchasing and Materials Mgmt.* 12:25, 1976.

Van Dyke, J. E., Roering, K. J., and Paul, R. J.: Guidelines for competitive bidding. *J. Purchasing and Materials Mgmt.* 11:27 (Fall), 1975.

VanEgmond-Pannell, D.: *School Foodservice.* 2nd ed. Westport, CT: AVI Publishing Co., 1981.

Von Elbe, J. H.: United States food laws and regulations: An overview. *Dairy and Food Sanitation* 2:321 (Aug.), 1982.

Weston, F. C.: The multiple product make-or-buy decision. *J. Purchasing and Materials Mgmt.* 17:17 (Winter), 1981.

Zenz, G. J.: Materials management and purchasing: Projections for the 1980s. *J. Purchasing and Materials Mgmt.* 17:17 (Spring), 1981a.

Zenz, G. J.: *Purchasing and the Management of Materials.* 5th ed. New York: John Wiley & Sons, 1981b.

Ziolkowski, D. J.: Purchasing, Part One: What you should do before you place the order. *NRA News* 3:30 (Apr.), 1983.

8

Receiving, Storage, and Inventory Control

As stated previously, procurement is the managerial function of acquiring material for production. Food is the material resource that is transformed into quality meals to satisfy the clientele of a given operation. Now that purchasing procedures and principles have been discussed, this chapter will examine the remaining functions within the procurement subsystem: receiving, storage, and inventory control.

Because the entire procurement process is a profit generator, these other aspects of procurement are as critical to cost control and profit generating as purchasing is. Without proper controls in the receipt and storage of food and supplies, the careful planning in menu design and purchasing is partially nullified. Planning and control, therefore, are the management functions with direct relevance to the receiving, storage, and inventory functions.

Purchasing was defined in Chapter 7 as a procedure concerned with the acquisition of goods. Receiving can be defined as a process for ensuring that the products delivered by vendors are those that were ordered in the purchasing process. After food and supplies have been received properly, they must be placed in appropriate storage and held under proper conditions to ensure quality until time of use. Inventory is the stores of goods and products, and inventory control is the technique of maintaining items at desired quantity levels. The major objectives of this control are to maintain quality of goods and supplies, to minimize inventory costs, and to ensure adequate quantity on hand for production and service needs.

RECEIVING

The receiving process involves more than just acceptance of and signing for delivered merchandise. It also includes verifying that the quality, size, and quantity meet specifications, that the price on the invoice reflects the purchase order, and that perishable goods are tagged and marked with the date received. Furthermore, the items received should be recorded accurately on a daily receiving record, then transferred promptly to the appropriate storage or production areas to prevent loss or deterioration. Consistent and routine procedures are essential to the receiving process, along with adequate controls to preserve quality of products and prevent loss during the delivery and receipt of merchandise.

In a foodservice establishment, between 30 and 50 percent of the revenues are spent on food purchases. In far too many operations, however, the receiving of these valuable purchases is entrusted to any employee who happens to be near the unloading or storage area when shipments from vendors arrive. When responsibility for receiving is not fixed, and procedures are not systematized, a number of problems may arise, such as careless losses, failure to assure quality and quantity of goods delivered, and pilferage. These potential losses can cost a foodservice operation more than its net profit each year.

The economic advantages gained by competitive purchasing, based on complete and thorough specifications, can therefore be easily diminished by poor receiving practices. Properly designed and enforced controls in the receiving function will ensure management that a dollar's worth of quantity and quality are received for every dollar spent.

Elements of the Receiving Process

Elements of good receiving practices include competent personnel with specified responsibilities, proper facilities and equipment, well-written specifications, good sanitary practices, adequate supervision, scheduled receiving hours, and procedures to ensure security. Because receiving is initiated in the purchasing process through the procedures of specification development and issuance of purchase orders, its underlying concept is the fixing of responsibility with management of the foodservice facility.

Competent Personnel

Responsibility for the receiving function should be assigned to a specific member of the foodservice staff. In a small operation, this individual may have additional duties but, if possible, the person responsible for the receiving should not be involved in food purchasing or production. Splitting the duties of purchasing and receiving is basic to a check and balance system for ensuring adequate control. If there are insufficient personnel in the facility for this split in responsibility, then the owner or manager should assume the responsibility for one of these tasks.

As indicated above, receiving should not be done by any employee who happens to be close by and not busy at the time a delivery arrives. Ninemeier (1983) delineated the following skills and abilities for employees responsible for receiving duties.

- Know the quality specifications for each product.
- Know how to evaluate quality of products.
- Understand all steps in the receiving process.
- Know procedures to follow when problems occur with an incoming shipment of food or supplies.
- Know procedures for completing required receiving forms and maintaining adequate records.

As Keiser and Kallio (1974) point out, the receiving personnel must be able to detect old merchandise, excess shrinkage, short weight, and foods not meeting specifications. Accepting poor quality and paying for short measure is tantamount to losing money from the cash register. The receiving clerk should be provided with the same specifications sent to the vendor, with the purchase order and bid request as a basis for checking all products delivered.

Because of the specialized skills and knowledge needed to perform these tasks competently, the training of personnel assigned to receiving functions is essential. Many of the receiving tasks can be explained and demonstrated through on-the-job training; however, learning product specifications and how to evaluate products using these specifications is more difficult and may require specific training sessions.

Facilities and Equipment

Adequate space and equipment are necessary to perform receiving tasks properly. In many foodservice operations, the receiving area may serve as an entrance for employees and salespersons, a place for general storage, and an exit to the trash storage area, all of which suggest a need for monitoring and good security procedures.

Ideally, the receiving room should be located near the delivery door, storeroom, refrigerators, and freezers to minimize the time and effort in movement of food into appropriate storage. In small operations, a wide hallway may be used as the receiving area; in larger operations, additional space is needed. In either case, the receiving area should be located near the delivery door for two primary reasons: (1) union contracts of delivery persons may prevent them from transporting food any considerable distance within a facility, and (2) security and sanitary concerns arise when persons who are not employees of the foodservice facility are allowed access to production areas.

The material flow from receiving to storage and to processing should be as short as possible and cause a minimum of interruptions in production areas. For this reason, the receiving area and the entrance to storage should be located for easy supervision by the person in charge. In large facilities, a receiving office is generally located near the delivery entrance. In smaller facilities, a desk at the receiving entrance facilitates the receiving process. The receiving area is often located in view of the manager's office to permit monitoring of deliveries.

The space allocated for receiving should be ample enough to allow all products in a delivery to be inspected at one time. Many items require minimal inspection and merely call for checking package and label and counting the quantity of goods received. Other deliveries, such as meat, may call for opening packages to inspect quality, size of cuts, count, and weight. Food and supplies should be removed from receiving to storage after the delivery person has left. Time and money can be saved by providing facilities that require a minimum of rehandling of delivered products and permit direct transfer to storage and points of use.

The size of the receiving area for a specific food facility is influenced by the nature and volume of materials received or being transferred out at any one time. For example, a hand truck may be sufficient in some operations, but a fork-lift truck may be required for handling pallet deliveries (Figure 8.1) in larger ones. In commissary operations, the space must be sufficient for the various types of carts used for transporting foods to satellite service centers. A typical cart for transporting food from a commissary or base kitchen to a satellite school foodservice operation is shown in Figure 8.2. The receiving area in the satellite service center must also be designed to accommodate the delivery carts.

The receiving department requires certain equipment, including scales in good working order. Both platform and counter scales should be available (Figures 8.3 and 8.4), and portion scales are useful for checking portion cuts of meat. In large operations, the scales used print the weight of the merchandise on the reverse side of the invoice or packing slip or print a tape that can be attached to it. This system eliminates any doubt in the weighing-in process. Accuracy of all scales should be checked periodically.

An unloading platform of a convenient height for delivery trucks is needed, as well as a ramp to facilitate unloading of other delivery vehicles. Proper dollies and hand trucks are important to expedite the movement of merchandise to storage with the least amount of effort.

Other equipment in the receiving area should include a table for inspection of deliveries and tools, such as a can opener, crow bar, claw hammer, and short-bladed knife for opening containers and packages. A thermometer to check whether chilled or frozen products are delivered at the appropriate temperature according to specification, and clip boards, pencils, and marking and tagging

Figure 8.1. *Motorized vehicles for storeroom work (courtesy: Clark Material Systems Technology Co., 1984. All rights reserved.*

Figure 8.2. *Bulk food transporter insulated to keep food hot or cold (courtesy of Crescent Metal Products, Inc., Cleveland, Ohio)*

equipment are also necessary. Finally, in addition to the desk, a file cabinet should be available for storing records and reports, as well as a calculator for verifying the computations on the invoice.

Specifications

The person who receives orders should know the standards the vendors must meet and should have a notebook or file box of specifications available for reference. All deliveries should be checked against these specifications and nothing below the standard should be accepted.

As discussed in Chapter 7, a copy of all purchase orders is provided to the receiving personnel in large operations. The purchase order includes a brief specification, data on quantity ordered, and pricing information, as well as general instructions to vendors, such as delivery date and shipping instructions. With this information, receiving personnel are alerted that a delivery is scheduled on or before a certain date and that they must be prepared to count and inspect anticipated shipments.

Sanitation

Because proper sanitation is a prerequisite in this area, as in all other areas of a foodservice facility, receiving facilities should be arranged for ease in cleaning. The floor should be a surface that can be easily scrubbed and rinsed, with adequate drains and a water connection nearby to permit hosing down of the area. Storage for cleaning supplies is also needed near this area.

Since insects tend to congregate near the loading dock, adequate screening must be provided, as well as insect protection. Electrical or chemical devices for destroying insects are often mounted near the outside doors in the delivery area.

Adequate Supervision

The management of a foodservice operation should monitor the receiving area periodically, although at irregular intervals, to check security in the area and to ensure that established receiving procedures are being followed. A member of the management staff should recheck weights, quantities, and quality of merchandise received at various intervals as part of the control system for the foodservice system.

Scheduled Hours

Vendors should be directed to make deliveries at specified times. This policy makes it easier to avoid the confusion of too many deliveries arriving at the same time and ensures that deliveries will not arrive at inopportune times, such as during meals or after qualified receiving personnel are off duty.

In small operations, receiving personnel are frequently assigned other responsibilities, especially during periods around the meal service time. In many hospitals, for example, a porter may have responsibility for receiving, for transporting meal carts to patient floors, and for some maintenance duties after meal serving times. When deliveries arrive at inappropriate times, the receiving clerk may be pressured and the goods may not be checked properly. Therefore, midmorning and midafternoon deliveries are best in such operations. Another consideration in scheduling deliveries is the nature of the shipment. The receiving schedule in some operations requires that perishable foods be delivered during the morning hours and staple goods during the afternoon.

Security

Several practices should be followed to guard against theft at the time products are received. One of these was discussed with the comments on competent receiv-

Figure 8.3. *Platform scales (courtesy of Hobart Corporation, Troy, Ohio.)*

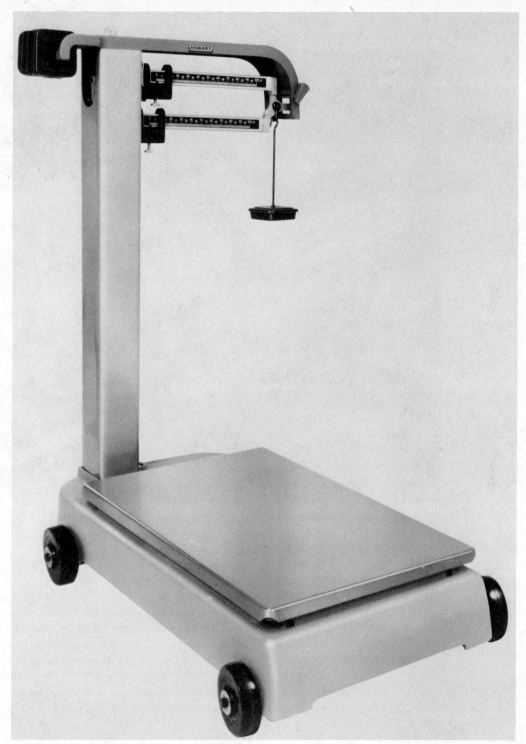

Figure 8.3. *(cont.)*

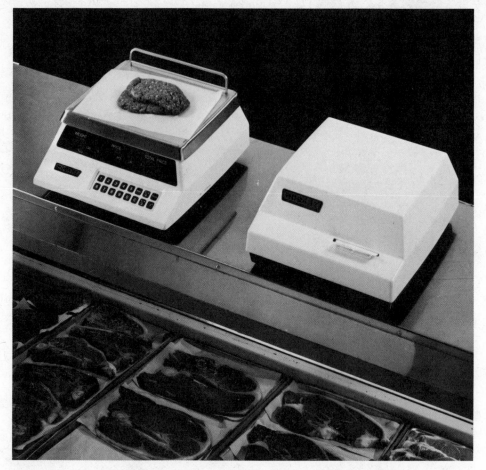

Figure 8.4. *Counter scale (courtesy of Hobart Corporation, Troy, Ohio.)*

ing personnel; that is, receiving tasks should not be performed by the person responsible for purchasing.

The other elements of a good receiving system discussed in the foregoing paragraphs also act as components of a receiving security system; scheduled hours for receiving and adequate facilities and equipment for performing receiving tasks will prevent many problems. Another important practice is to move products immediately from receiving to storage. In addition, salespersons and delivery or route persons should generally not be permitted in storage areas; if these persons are allowed into a storage area, however, they should be accompanied by the foodservice manager or another responsible employee of the foodservice facility.

An additional important security measure is to keep the outside door locked if at all possible. A doorbell can be installed to permit salespersons, delivery personnel, and others to signal that they have arrived. This practice limits access to the foodservice facility to those authorized to enter.

The Receiving Process

Detailed procedures are important to assure that incoming merchandise is received properly. The steps in the receiving process are outlined in Figure 8.5.

Inspection against Purchase Orders

Regardless of the different types of purchasing procedures used in an operation, a written record must be maintained of all orders placed to provide a basis for checking deliveries. This record can then act as the first control in the receiving process by including at least a brief description, the quantity, the price, and the vendor. In small operations that use informal purchasing procedures, this record may be as simple as a notebook for listing this basic ordering information. In large operations with more formal procedures, however, as discussed in Chapter 7, purchase orders are issued, one copy of which is generally transmitted to the receiving department as a record of scheduled deliveries.

As part of the receiving process, incoming shipments should be compared with the purchase record or purchase order to ensure that the items accepted were in fact ordered. The purchase record will also permit the receiving personnel to determine partial deliveries or omission of ordered items. If a comparison of the incoming deliveries with purchase orders indicates that the appropriate products have been delivered, quality assurance then becomes essential.

As stated previously, specialized training of receiving personnel is important to ensure that quality determinants are known and can be recognized. All products should be compared with the characteristics in the established specifications. Without exception, the quantity and quality of all items must be verified before the delivery invoice is signed. If items are purchased by the count, they should be

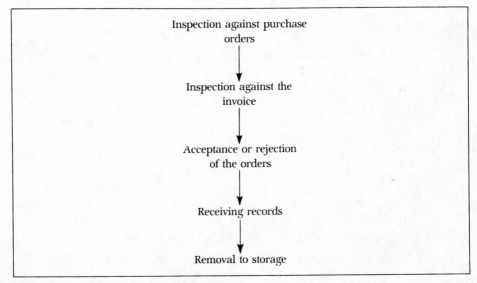

Figure 8.5. *Steps in the receiving process*

counted. If items are purchased by weight, they should be weighed. Frozen products should be checked for any thawing and portion cuts of meat should be spot-checked for appropriate weight.

Acceptable deviations from specifications should be established and, in fact, should be stated in written specifications. For example, a weight between 7.5 and 8.5 ounces may be acceptable for an 8-ounce steak. Eggs and products packaged in glass containers should be checked to assure that no breakage has occurred.

Delivery personnel sometimes exert pressure on receiving personnel to speed up the inspection. The receiving personnel, however, must be assertive and insist on performing a proper and thorough inspection while delivery personnel are still on the premises.

For some items, a foodservice operation may have a standing order and, therefore, do not maintain a specific purchase order or other record for each delivery. Instead, a predetermined amount may be delivered daily or at some other regular interval or a predetermined inventory may have been established. Such products are bread, dairy products, coffee, and eggs frequently fall into this category. In some foodservice operations, delivery personnel employed by the vendor are permitted to check the quantity on hand and suggest a delivery quantity. The foodservice manager or receiving clerk must monitor these delivery persons, however, and products should not be placed in storage until they have been checked by the receiving clerk and stored under his or her supervision.

Inspection against the Invoice

After products have been checked against the purchase order and the specifications, a delivery should be compared against the invoice prepared by the vendor. The invoice is the vendor's statement of what is being shipped to the foodservice operation and the expected payment.

Obviously, checking the quantities and prices recorded on the invoice is a critical step in the receiving process. Two receiving methods are used in foodservice operations, invoice receiving and blind receiving.

- *Invoice receiving.* This method involves having the receiving clerk check the items delivered against the purchase order or purchase record. Any discrepancies should be noted on both the purchase order and the invoice. This method is quick and economical but can be unreliable if the receiving clerk fails to make the comparison between the two records and simply uses the delivery invoice.

- *Blind receiving.* In blind receiving, the receiving clerk uses an invoice or purchase order with the quantity column blanked out. The person checking the order then must record the quantity received for each item. This method requires that each item be checked since the amount ordered is unknown. While this method takes more time, it is more reliable in ensuring that the goods charged are actually received.

In invoice receiving, if the quantities and prices are correct and the receiving employee has attested to the quality, the invoice should then be signed. Generally, two copies of the invoice are required, one for foodservice records and the other for the accounting office. In small operations, however, only one copy may be required. If errors have been made in the delivery or in the pricing, corrections must be reported on the invoice before it is signed. The delivery person should also initial the change.

Acceptance or Rejection of the Orders

The delivered products become the property of the foodservice operation when their comparison with the purchase order or other purchase record, the specifications, and the vendor's invoice reveals no problems or when problems have been corrected or noted on the invoice. Payment then will be due at the agreed upon time for items charged on the invoice.

At times, however, problems will occur during the receiving process. If at all possible, products should be rejected at the time of delivery if they are not what was ordered or if they do not meet quality specifications. Ninemeier (1983) lists several reasons why products should be refused.

- Items were not ordered.
- Products are not of required quality.
- Price is not that quoted.
- Products are not delivered on a timely basis.

Rejection at the point of delivery is much easier than returning items after they are accepted. When problems are noted after a delivery has been accepted, however, the supplier should be contacted immediately. Reputable suppliers are generally willing to correct problems. The foodservice manager, however, should use these occasions to learn why problems were not detected at the time of delivery and should make changes in receiving procedures to prevent them from recurring. Whether deliveries are returned after acceptance or rejected at the time of delivery, accounting personnel must ensure that credit is given by the vendor.

Errors during the receiving process can be handled in a number of ways and the person responsible for purchasing should always be notified when problems occur. On occasion, a product not meeting the quality standard may be accepted because it is needed for service and time does not permit exchanging the substandard product or finding an alternate source. In this instance, the purchasing manager might attempt to negotiate a price reduction with the vendor. If a required item is not available or only a partial amount is delivered, the purchasing manager must be alerted to make necessary decisions about the "back order."

Receiving Records

The receiving record, maintained by the receiving clerk, serves several purposes. It provides an accurate record of all deliveries of food and supplies, the date of delivery, the vendor, and quantity and price data. This information is helpful in checking and paying invoices and provides an important record for cost control of the unit cost of all foods delivered to the kitchen and storeroom.

COMMUNITY HOSPITAL

RECEIVING RECORD

Date: July 29, 1984

Quantity	Unit	Description of item	Name of vendor	Inspected and quantity verified by	Unit price	Total cost	Distribution	
							To kitchen	To storage
3	lugs	Tomatoes	Jones	JH	$ 6.75	$20.25		X
3	crates	Lettuce	Jones	JH	6.95	20.85		X
4	boxes	Bakers	Jones	JH	7.25	28.75	X	
1	sack	Onions	Jones	JH	6.50	6.50		X
1	lug	Avocadoes	Jones	JH	15.00	15.00		X
400	lbs.	Watermelon	Jones	JH	.05/#	20.00	X	

Figure 8.6. *Example of a receiving record*

An example of a receiving record developed by the USDA for use in school foodservice operations is shown in Figure 8.6. The columns on the form showing distribution of items are useful in some food cost control systems. Items delivered directly to the kitchen will be included in that day's food cost, whereas items sent to the storeroom will be charged by requisition when they are removed from stores as needed for production and service.

Such a receiving record documents product transfer to storage in facilities where receiving and storage tasks are performed by different employees and thus provides a check point in a control system. It is usually prepared in duplicate, one copy to be sent with the invoices to the accounting department and the other retained in the receiving department for reference.

If the receiving clerk is responsible for verifying price extensions on invoices, this should be done before the invoice is forwarded to the accounting office. Accounting personnel, however, should also check the arithmetic extensions on invoices. To facilitate the process of handling and checking invoices, in some

```
Date Received   _____
Quantity        _____
Price OK        _____
Extension OK    _____
Entered         _____
Paid            _____
```

Figure 8.7. *Invoice stamp*

operations the delivery slip or invoice is stamped using a rubber stamp, and the person performing each function initials the appropriate line (Figure 8.7). This procedure provides a simple control system, ensuring that all steps have been performed and fixing responsibility for any errors.

Removal to Storage

After products have been received, they should be removed immediately from receiving to the proper secure storage area; personnel should not be permitted to "wait until they have time" to move food and supplies to proper storage. Since the products are now the property of the foodservice facility, security measures are important to prevent theft and pilferage. Moreover, spoilage and deterioration may occur if refrigerated and frozen products are held at room temperature for any period of time.

Foodservice operations may have various procedures for tagging or marking products for delivery to the storage indicated on the receiving record. Tagging merchandise also facilitates stock rotation to ensure that older merchandise is used first, particularly important with perishable food products. The following data may be put on a tag or marked on the outside of a case or package.

- Date of receipt.
- Name of vendor.
- Brief description of merchandise.
- Weight or count when received.
- Place of storage.

Some operations follow the practice of marking every can or carton with its price, as supermarkets do. According to Keiser and Kallio (1974), proponents of this practice claim it facilitates determination of food cost and makes employees more cost-conscious.

STORAGE

Control over merchandise in storage is established by assigning responsibility to specific personnel, by effective physical security, and by sound material handling

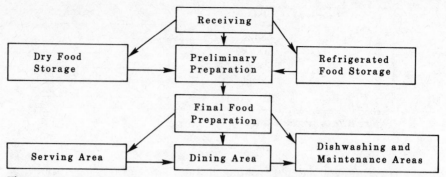

Figure 8.8. *Food flow chart.* **Source:** *Food and Nutrition Service, USDA:* **Food Storage Guide for Schools and Institutions.** *Washington, DC: U.S. Govt. Prtg. Ofc., 1975, p. 2.*

procedures. A limited number of staff should have access to storage facilities, including only those authorized personnel in the process of placing goods in storage, issuing foods, checking inventory levels, or cleaning storage areas.

Preventions of theft is a major concern in storage facilities and procedures. In some foodservice operations, locks for storage areas are replaced periodically to prevent access with unauthorized duplicate keys. Whether or not this is done, keys to the storage areas should be in the custody of designated personnel at all times.

Storage facilities and practices are critical components in a quality assurance program. Proper storage maintenance, temperature control, cleaning and sanitation, and stability are major considerations in ensuring quality of stored foods. Storage is also important to the overall operation of the foodservice system because it links receiving and preparation (Figure 8.8). Dry and low temperature storage facilities should be accessible to both receiving and food production areas to reduce transport time and corresponding labor costs.

Ideally, storage facilities should be located on the same floor as the production area. In large facilities, however, the main storage areas are often located on a lower level or in another area of the building. In institutions such as a large hospital, the dry storage for food may be a segment of the central storeroom for the entire hospital. In multiunit facilities, a central warehouse is usually maintained for major storage. In these instances, a limited storeroom and smaller low temperature storage units, adequate for a few days' supply, will be provided in the individual foodservice operations.

The type of storage facilities needed will vary greatly, depending on the type of foodservice system (refer to Chapter 5 for discussion of types of systems). In an assembly/serve system, for example, in which many fully processed frozen food products are used, the need for frozen storage would probably be much greater than in a conventional facility. In a commissary system, the magnitude of the central production facility would demand large storage capability.

Regardless of the type or location of facilities, all foods should be placed in storage as soon as possible after delivery, unless they are to be processed immediately. Dry groceries, canned foods, and staples should be placed in dry stores. Perishable foods must be placed in refrigerated or frozen storage promptly. In addition, storage facilities must be available for paper supplies, cleaning products, and other nonfood products.

Dry Storage

The dry food storage area provides orderly storage for foods not requiring refrigeration or freezing. This area should provide protection of foods from the elements, insects, rodents, and spoilage organisms as well as safeguard them from theft. Soaps, detergents and other cleaning supplies, insect powders, and rat and other poisons should not be kept in the food storeroom. Instead, a separate locked room should be provided for them, to prevent them from being mistaken for food products or contaminating the food.

Facilities for Dry Storage

The floors in the dry storage area should be slip resistant and easily cleaned. The external walls and subfloors should be well constructed, rodent and insect free, and insulated. Walls and ceiling should be painted light colors, have a smooth surface that is impervious to moisture and easy to wash and repair.

To aid in control, the number of doors allowing access to the storeroom should be limited. The main door should be heavy-duty and of sufficient width for passage of the equipment used to transport foods from receiving to dry storage or from dry storage to production areas. This door should lock from the outside; however, a turn-bolt lock or crash bar should be provided on the inside of the door to permit opening from the inside without a key in case people are inadvertently locked in. This main entrance to the storeroom is sometimes a Dutch door, with the lower half locked at all times except when large shipments are being placed in storage. With the upper door open during storeroom hours, all employees can be excluded from the storeroom except storeroom personnel, who can be observed through this door.

In large operations, a recording time lock may be used on the door to the storeroom. When the storeroom is opened at an unscheduled time, it is recorded by this type of locking system; the tape from the time lock should go to the comptroller each day for review.

A small locked area is often provided in the storeroom to accommodate small valuable food items, such as anchovy fillets, caviar, costly spices, smoked oysters, and truffles. Coffee may also be kept in a special locked storage area because it is an easily pilfered product.

If the storeroom has windows, they should be opaque to protect foods from direct sunlight. For security, most storerooms are designed without windows or have windows protected with grates or security bars. Lighting, however, should be adequate to locate and put away food. Adequate lighting will also contribute to better housekeeping by storeroom employees.

Good ventilation in the dry stores area is essential to assist in controlling temperature and humidity and prevent musty odors. A thermometer should be mounted in an area where it can be easily seen for monitoring temperatures periodically.

Humidity is an often overlooked but important factor in storeroom conditions. For most food products, a relative humidity of 50 to 60 percent is considered satisfactory, with 70 percent the maximum allowable for best storage conditions. Humidity over this level may result in rusting cans, caking of dry and dehydrated products, growth of bacteria and mold, and infestation of insects in the storeroom.

Shelving is required whenever less-than-case lots must be stored or when management prefers that canned goods be removed from cases for storage. Adjustable metal shelving is desirable because it allows for various shelf heights and is vermin proof (Figure 8.9). Shelving must be sturdy to support heavy loads without sagging or collapsing and should be located at least two inches from walls to provide ventilation. If the size and shape of the room permit, shelving should be arranged for accessibility from both sides.

A new high-density shelving (Figure 8.10) has been designed that permits maximum use of storeroom space. In this system, shelf units are installed in floor runners, with shelves that can be moved electrically or mechanically when access to products on them is needed.

Sectional slatted platforms, or pallets, or wheeled metal platforms provide a useful type of storage for case lots of canned goods or for products in bags. Their distance from the floor must be in accordance with local health department requirements.

Metal or plastic containers with tight-fitting covers should be used for storing cereal products, flour, sugar, dried foods, and broken lots of bulk foods. These containers should either be placed on dollies or have built-in wheels for ease of movement from one place to another (Figure 8.11).

Aisles between shelves and platforms should be wide enough for the use of mobile equipment. In large storerooms in which fork-lift trucks are used for moving pallets, obviously, more aisle space is needed than in smaller facilities in which hand carts are used.

Dry Storage Procedures

Foods should be arranged systematically in the storeroom and every item assigned a definite place. A great deal of time thus is saved by not having to hunt for randomly stored items. In addition, if forms for checking inventory are designed to match the physical arrangement of goods on the shelves, even more time can be saved.

In some storage systems, faster-moving items are placed near the entrance and slower-moving items are stored in less accessible locations. In other arrangements, foods are categorized into groups, then arranged either alphabetically or according to frequency of use within the groups. Foods that give off odors should be stored separately. New stock in such a system should be placed in back of older

Figure 8.9. *Metal shelving for storage area (courtesy Cresent Metal Products, Inc., Cleveland, Ohio)*

stock to prevent loss from deterioration. Foods should be checked periodically for evidence of spoilage, such as bulging or leaking cans. Ideally, canned foods should not be kept more than six months even when stored under proper conditions (Thorner and Manning, 1976), since determining the length of time foods have been canned prior to delivery is difficult.

The advantage of purchasing large quantities to save money must be weighed against the possibility of storage loss and the costs of maintaining inventories. Inventory costs will be discussed in more detail later in this chapter.

Figure 8.10. *High-density storage shelves (courtesy Market Forge, Everett, Massachusetts)*

Low Temperature Storage

Perishable foods should be placed under refrigeration or in frozen storage immediately after delivery and should be kept under these conditions until ready to use to preserve nutritive value and quality. The type and amount of low temperature storage space required in a foodservice operation will vary with the type of foodservice system and menu and purchasing policies. An excessive amount of refrigeration and frozen storage increases capital costs and operating expenses. It also encourages a tendency to allow leftovers to accumulate and spoil. Some foodservice operators have found that, by limiting the amount of refrigeration, overproduction and overordering are curtailed.

Low Temperature Storage Facilities

Low temperature storage can be categorized into four functional types (Thorner and Manning, 1976).

- *Coolers.* Medium temperature range storage units designed to hold the temperature between a minimum of 32° and a maximum of 48°F, used for thawing frozen food, storing meat at 32–38°F, storing dairy products at 36–40°F, and storing vegetables and fruits at 44–48°F.

- *Thawers or tempering boxes.* Units for thawing frozen foods, specially designed to maintain a steady temperature of 40°F regardless of room temperature or product load.

- *Storage freezers.* Low temperature units that maintain a constant temperature in the range of −10° to 0°F, used for storing frozen foods.

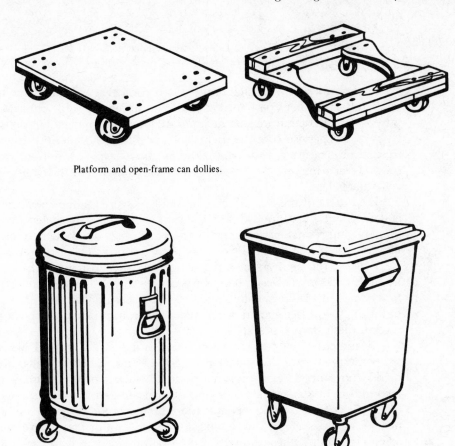

Platform and open-frame can dollies.

Container on dolly.

Container equipped with casters.

Metal and plastic food containers.

Figure 8.11. *Dollies and containers for use in storage facilities.* **Source:** *Food and Nutrition Service, USDA:* **Food Storage Guide for Schools and Institutions.** *Washington, DC: U.S. Govt. Prtg. Ofc., 1975, p. 11.*

- *Processing freezers.* Units designed to perform the actual freezing of food at temperatures of −20°F or below, generally not used for storage.

In some foodservice operations, separate refrigerated units are available for meats and poultry, fish and shellfish, dairy products, and vegetables and fruits. Separate freezers may also be available for ice cream and for other frozen foods. Having these separate facilities enhances the storage of these various products since ideal storage temperatures vary among commodity groups. Satisfactory storage of various products can be maintained with fewer units kept at the following temperatures.

- Fresh fruits and vegetables at 40 to 45°F.
- Dairy products, eggs, meat, and poultry at 32 to 40°F.
- Frozen foods at −10 to 0°F.

Low temperature storage units may be designed as walk-in units, reach-in units, roll-in cabinets, pass-through units, or upright movable units. Many special purpose low temperature storage units are available to meet the needs of varying types of foodservice operations. In large institutions, walk-in refrigerators and freezers are common; in small operations, the trend is away from walk-ins and toward reach-ins because less floor space is required and the capital investment generally is less.

Regardless of the type of units available, location is the key for saving labor and avoiding unproductive work. Reach-ins or pass-throughs are commonly available in production areas for short-term storage of products prior to production and for holding partially or fully prepared products prior to service.

Walk-in refrigerators and freezers should be flush with the floor so that movable racks or shelves or hand carts can be wheeled in and out of them easily. In very large operations, pallets and fork-lift trucks may be used in frozen storage facilities. Aisle space should be adequate to accommodate the type of equipment used in these storage areas.

Cleanability that promotes sanitation is a significant need in walk-in low temperature storage. Hard-surface, easily cleanable floors, walls, and fixtures, made from smooth, nonabsorbent material, should be used. Drains are needed for removal of scrubbing water and condensate and may be located in or immediately outside the door opening to the compartment. Finally, uniform ventilation in all areas of the low temperature storage unit and proper lighting that adequately illuminates all areas should be provided to help maintain sanitary conditions.

All low temperature storage units should be cleaned on a regularly scheduled basis according to manufacturers' instructions. Most refrigerators and freezers used in foodservices today are the self-defrosting type; if not, however, sanitation and maintenance schedules should also include periodic defrosting of these units.

Humidity control is also important for maintaining food quality in low temperature storage. Perishable foods contain a great deal of moisture; if humidity is not sufficient, evaporation will cause deterioration, such as wilting and discoloration and excess shrinkage. A humidity range between 75 and 95 percent is recommended for most foods.

For security purposes, all low temperature storage should be equipped with locks. In walk-ins, an inside lock release and alarm system are needed to prevent someone from being locked inside.

All refrigerators and freezers should be provided with one or more thermometers, which may be a remote reading thermometer, a recording thermometer, or a bulb thermometer. The remote reading thermometer is placed outside the low temperature storage unit and permits reading the temperature without opening the door. The recording thermometer is also mounted outside the unit and has the added feature of continuously recording temperatures in the storage unit. The <u>bulb thermometer</u> is mounted or hung on a shelf inside the unit. It should be placed in the warmest area of the unit and the thermostat adjusted as necessary to obtain the recommended storage temperature. Some operations have an alarm or buzzer that is activated when temperatures rise beyond a certain level in low temperature storage.

Storage shelves for use in walk-in refrigerators should be metal and may be stationary or portable. Portable shelving with casters is preferable, though, because it is easier to move for cleaning. In some new facilities, high-density shelving, such as that discussed in the section on dry storage facilities, is being used in low temperature storage also. Portable tray racks are useful for transporting food from the low temperature storage to production areas and then back to storage if needed prior to service. As in dry stores, food should not be stored on the floor of low temperature walk-ins but should be stored on metal platforms or shelves.

Low Temperature Storage Procedures

In discussing types of low temperature storage, general temperature ranges for storing various types of food were given. Figure 8.12 provides a more detailed list of recommended storage temperatures according to type of food, most of which have relatively little processing, along with maximum storage times. As in dry stores, foods should be rotated in refrigerated and frozen storage units to avoid spoilage and unnecessary loss.

Because of their high moisture content, fruits and vegetables are susceptible to freezing and should be held at a somewhat higher temperature than meats or dairy products. A temperature range between 40 and 45°F and a relative humidity of 85 to 95 percent is desirable. Fresh produce should be examined for ripeness before, and periodically during, storing. Any decaying pieces should be removed to inhibit further spoilage. Such vegetables as potatoes, squash, and eggplant can be kept at temperatures up to 60°F. In some operations, potatoes and onions are stored in dry storage.

Temperatures in all low temperature storage should be checked at least twice a day. In many foodservice operations, as part of the quality assurance program, designated personnel are assigned the responsibility for checking temperatures at specified times and a written record is maintained as a control measure. An important practice in maintaining proper storage temperatures is to train employees to open refrigerator doors as infrequently as possible by obtaining all foods needed at one time. This practice is also important for energy conservation in the foodservice system.

If temporary power failures occur, refrigerators or freezers should not be opened. Depending on the insulation and construction of the units and the ambient temperature, an acceptable temperature range can be held for 18 to 24 hours.

In both low temperature and in dry storage, foods that absorb odors must be stored away from those that give off odors. Typical foods that give off and/or absorb odors are listed in Figure 8.13.

Frozen food should be wrapped in moisture-proof or vapor-proof material to

Food	Refrigerator storage 32–40°F (0–4°C)	Freezer storage 0°F (−18°C) or below
Meat		
Roast, Steaks, Chops	3–5 days	Beef and lamb: 9–12 months
		Pork: 6–9 months
		Veal: 4–6 months
		Sausage, ham, and slab bacon: 1–3 months
		Beef liver: 3–4 months
		Pork liver: 1–2 months
Ground meat, Stew meat	1–2 days	6–8 months
Ham, not canned	1–3 weeks	1–3 months
Ham, canned	1 year	Not recommended
Poultry		
Chicken, Turkey, and so forth	2–3 days	Chicken, 6–8 months
		Turkey, 4–5 months
		Giblets, 2–3 months
Fish or Shellfish	30–32°F (−1–0°C) on ice, 2–3 days	3–6 months
Eggs		
Shell	1–2 weeks	Not recommended
Frozen	1–2 days after thawing	9 months
Dried	6 months	Not recommended
Fruits & Vegetables 40–45°F (4–7°C)		
Fresh	5–7 days	Not recommended
Frozen	—	10–12 months
Canned	—	Not recommended
Dried	Preferred	Not recommended
Cereal Products		
Regular cornmeal, whole wheat flour	Required over 60 days	Not recommended
Degermed cornmeal, all-purpose and bread flour, rice, and so forth	Preferred	Not recommended

Figure 8.12. *Recommended storage temperature and times.* **Source: Food Service Manual for Health Care Institutions,** *1981 edition, by Mahaffey, Mennes, and Miller. Reprinted with permission of American Hospital Publishing, Inc., copyright © 1981.*

Food	Gives off Odors	Absorbs odors
Apples, Fresh	Yes	Yes
Butter	No	Yes
Cabbage	Yes	No
Cheese	Yes	Yes
Cornmeal	No	Yes
Eggs, Dried	No	Yes
Eggs, Fresh Shell	No	Yes
Flour	No	Yes
Milk, Nonfat Dry	No	Yes
Onions	Yes	No
Peaches, Fresh	Yes	No
Potatoes	Yes	No
Rice	No	Yes

Figure 8.13. *Foods that give off and/or absorb odors.* **Source:** *Food and Nutrition Service, USDA:* **Food Storage Guide for Schools and Institutions.** *Washington, DC: U.S. Govt. Prtg. Ofc., 1975, p. 27.*

prevent freezer burn and loss of moisture. The original packages of most frozen food are designed with this in mind. For fresh foods that are to be held in storage, specifications may include special instructions for frozen storage wrapping.

Most frozen foods can be cooked or reconstituted directly from the frozen stage, although thawing or partial thawing is needed for some products. Foods that have been allowed to thaw should not be refrozen because of potential spoilage and loss of quality. Thawing or tempering boxes, therefore, are used for temporary storage of products scheduled for production in from one to three days.

As discussed earlier in this book, precooked frozen foods are being used more frequently in foodservice operations. Because their shelf life varies widely, quality assurance and stability of these foods require special attention. The listing in Figure 8.14 should be useful as a general guideline for storage of precooked frozen foods.

INVENTORY CONTROL

Inventory held in storage represents a significant investment of the organization's assets. Although the monetary value of food and supplies in storage will be clear to management, employees may not view this merchandise in the same light. Foodservice employees who would not steal money from the cash register may see nothing wrong in taking items from storage now and then. Nor may they see losses because of failure to store foods promptly or failure to rotate foods in storage as "money down the drain."

Foods, beverages, and supplies in storage areas must be considered as valu-

Foods with Short Storage Life (2 weeks to 2 months)

Product	Maximum storage life at 0°F (−17.8°C)
Bacon, Canadian	2 weeks
Batter, gingerbread	3–4 months
Batter, muffin	2 weeks
Batter, spice	1–2 months
Biscuit, baking powder	1–2 months
Bologna, sliced	2 weeks
Cake, sponge, egg yolk	2 months
Cake, spice	2 months
Dough, roll	1–2 months
Frankfurters	2 weeks
Gravy	2 weeks
Ham, sliced	2 weeks
Poultry giblets	2 months
Poultry livers	2 months
Sauce, white (wheat flour base)	2 weeks
Sausage	2 months

Foods with Medium Storage Life (6 to 8 months)

Chicken, fried	Meat loaf
Crab	Pies, chicken
Fish, fatty	Pies, fruit, unbaked
Fruit, purees	Pies, meat
Ham, baked, whole	Potatoes, French-fried
Lobster	Soups
Meals on a tray	Shrimp
Meat balls	Turkey

Foods with Long Storage Life (12 months or longer)

Applesauce	Candies	Peanuts
Apples, baked	Cherries	Pecans
Bread	Chicken, creamed	Plums
Bread (rolls)	(waxy rice flour-based)	Stew, beef
Blackberries	Chicken à la king	Stew, veal
Blueberries	Cookies	Waffles
Cake, fruit	Fish, lean	

Figure 8.14. *Stability of foods under frozen storage.* **Source:** *Adapted from pages 84, 85, 86,* **Quality Control in Food Service,** *Revised Ed. Thorner/Manning, The AVI Publishing Company, Inc., Westport, Connecticut, 1983.*

able resources of the operation and treated accordingly. For inventory control to be effective, access to storage areas should be controlled carefully, authorized requisitions required for removing goods from storage, and inventory levels monitored carefully. The inventory control system also requires maintenance of accurate records.

Issuing

Issuing is the process used to supply food to the production units after it has been received. Products may be issued directly from the receiving area, especially if planned for that day's menu, but, more often, food and supplies are issued from dry or low temperature storage. The issuing process entails control of food and supplies removed from storage and provides information for food cost accounting and, in some cases, information for a perpetual inventory system.

Direct Purchases

Issues sent directly from receiving to prepreparation or production without going through storage are usually referred to as direct purchases or direct issues. They are presumably used on the day they are purchased, and their cost is therefore charged to the food cost for that day. In many operations, milk, bread, and fresh produce are handled as direct issues. Requisition forms are generally used only in very large operations.

Maintaining accurate food cost records and controlling inventories requires that direct issues be processed this way. If not, the recorded food cost will be unrealistically high on the day of delivery, and the food cost on the day of actual use of the product will be understated.

Issues from Storage

All foods that are received but not used the day they are purchased are storeroom purchases; these products are issued from a storage area when needed for production or service.

Control of issuing from storage has two important aspects. First, goods should not be removed from the storeroom without proper authorization and, second, only the required quantity for production and service should be obtained. A requisition procedure is needed to provide these two controls.

In such a procedure, the cook, or other employee responsible for assembling ingredients, will prepare a list of items or complete a storeroom requisition form like the one shown in Figure 8.15. The list will be submitted to the storekeeper or other employee with responsibility for storage. The storekeeper is the person responsible for completing the requisition, using the list provided by the person requesting the food and supplies. In small operations in which a full-time storekeeper is not feasible, the manager or foodservice supervisor may have this responsibility.

| Storeroom: Dry Stores #1 | | | | | | | Date 9/20/84 | |

Req. no.	Quan- tity	Unit	Description of item	Issued to:	Unit price	Total cost	Issued by
823	10	#10 cans	Tomatoes, whole or pieces	Cook's unit	$2.77	$27.70	AV
	1	1½# box	Oregano, dried leaf		8.10	8.10	
	1	3# box	Dried, minced onion		6.27	6.27	
	1	1# box	Dried, diced green pepper		6.62	6.62	
	2	10# box	Spaghetti, long thin		3.53	7.06	
	1	#10 cans	Catsup		2.69	2.69	
	1	1# box	Bay leaves		6.30	6.30	
	1	12 oz. can	Thyme, grd.		4.85	4.85	
	1	1 gal.	Worcestershire sauce		2.50	2.50	
	1	26 oz. box	Salt, iodized		0.25/box	.25	
	3	#10 can	Tomato puree		2.50/cn	7.50	

Figure 8.15. *Daily issue record*

The requisition forms should be prenumbered to permit tracing any duplicate and missing requisitions. The name of the unit to which the items are being issued should be indicated on the form—kitchen, cafeteria, bake shop—along with the date. As shown in Figure 8.15, columns should be provided for the quantity of each item, the issue unit, and the name of the item.

If a manual cost accounting system is used, space should be provided on the form for entering the unit cost and the total cost of each issue. A line should be included for the person authorized to request the item to sign or initial. This authorizing signature must be required before items can be removed from storage. The storekeeper or other person issuing the food should also sign the form. If an employee other than the storekeeper is responsible for entering the cost data, a space should be provided for the signature or initials of this person.

If a computer-assisted inventory system is utilized, an inventory number for each item is required. The requisition form for a computer-assisted system, however, does not require that costs be entered, since these data would be available from the stored information in the computer.

Some operations use only one copy of a requisition; in others, duplicate or multiple copies may be needed, depending on the size of the operation. One copy may be returned with the order, one retained in the storeroom, and one sent to the bookkeeper or, in a computer-assisted system, to the person responsible for data entry.

In operations with an inventory control computer system, the storeroom requisition may be generated by the computer. The person responsible for ordering food and supplies would only need to review the computer-generated listing of issues and make any needed adjustments. An example of a computer-generated storeroom order form is shown in Figure 8.16.

Finally, we will briefly discuss the ingredient room, a concept that has been introduced in many foodservice operations during the last decade. This concept will be discussed in detail in Chapter 10 in the section on production but is mentioned here because of its link to issuing and control of food inventories.

If an ingredient control room has been established in a foodservice system, the personnel in this unit are responsible for requisitioning supplies from various storage areas, prepreparation and weighing and measuring ingredients for various products on the menu, and providing the needed items to the production personnel on a scheduled basis. A limited inventory may be maintained in the ingredient room, usually the balance of an issue item not needed that day, such as the remainder of a bag of flour or sugar.

Inventory Records

Placing products in storage, taking them out when needed, and ordering more when necessary is simply not sufficient for control of valuable resources. Inventory control must include adequate record keeping procedures to permit management to have up-to-date and reliable data on costs of operation. There are four basic purposes for the inventory records.

- To provide accurate information of food and supplies on hand.
- To assist in determining purchasing needs.
- To provide data for food cost control.
- To assist management in preventing theft and pilferage.

The issuing procedures previously discussed are one component of inventory records. A periodic physical count of food and supplies in storage is another requisite element of any inventory control system. More sophisticated records, such as a perpetual inventory, are maintained in many operations to assist in achieving the objectives outlined above.

Physical Inventory

A physical inventory is the periodic actual counting of products on hand in all storage areas. Normally, inventories are counted once each month, usually at the

```
018-H00-231-01 2.00                           01021        ORDER REPORT
NOVEMBER 23, 1983 AT  6.28 PM

0771-KRAMER FOOD CENTER                    346-8

MEAT        - ORDER GROUP

12/07/83 - PITTMAN DATE    12/12/83 - DELIVERY DATE    MONDAY        USAGE PERIOD WED-THU
```

STORAGE LOCATION	CODE	ITEM NAME	BRAND	BIN QT. (IN ORDER UNITS)	ORDER AMOUNT (IN ORDER UNITS)	DELIVERED AMOUNT	NEEDED AMOUNTS LBS.	NEEDED AMOUNTS ORDER UNITS	SUGG ORDER UNITS	INVENTORY ON HAND
41000	002101010102 EGGS WHOLE FRESH			4 CS			140.63	3.9 CASE		4
43000	0012113701 GROUND BEEF BULK			315 LB			314.20	314.2 POUND		315
43000	0012113700 PATTIES GROUND BEEF 6			18 BOX			288.00	18.0 BOX		18
43000	0012116831 ROAST DINNER INSIDE ROUND			108 LB			107.50	107.5 POUND		108
46000	0012141445 PORK STEAK BNLS 4/LB			75 LB			75.00	75.0 POUND		75
47000	0012145718 HAM CUBES			16 LB			16.00	16.0 POUND		16
47000	0013146025 SAUSAGE BULK			36 LB			35.90	35.9 POUND		36
47000	0014145090 HAM PULLMAN CND			21 LB			21.00	21.0 POUND		21
47500	0013166001 WEINERS BULK			40 LB			40.00	40.0 POUND		40
48000	0022001107 AMERICAN PROCESSED CHEESE LOAF			4 LB			3.60	3.6 POUND		4
46000	0022001115 AMERICAN PROCESSED CHEESE RIBBON SLI			95 LB			94.60	94.6 POUND		95
46000	0022001166 CREAM CHEESE			3 LB			3.00	3.0 POUND		3
48000	0022001409 PARMESAN CHEESE GRATED			15 LB			14.20	14.2 POUND		15
48000	0022001506 MOZZARELLA CHEESE LOAF			22 LB			21.20	21.2 POUND		22
48000	0022001603 BLUE CHEESE WHEEL			5 LB			5.00	5.0 POUND		5

END

Figure 8.16. *Computer-generated order form (used by permission, Kramer Food Center, Kansas State University)*

Quantity on hand	Unit size	Food item	Item description	Unit cost	Total inventory value
	#10	Asparagus	All green cuts and tips, 6/#10/case		
	#10	Beans, Green	Cut, 6/#10/case		
	#10	Beans, Lima	Fresh green, small, 6/#10/case		
	#10	Beets	Whole, 6/#10/case		
	#10	Carrots	Sliced, medium, 6/#10/case		
	#10	Corn	Whole kernel, 6/#10/case		
	#10	Peas	Sweet peas, 4 sv., 6/#10/case		
	#10	Potatoes, Sweet	Whole, 6/#10/case		
	#10	Tomatoes	Whole peeled, juice packed, 6/#10/case		
	46 oz.	Tomato Juice	Fancy, 12/46 oz./case		

PHYSICAL INVENTORY

Date _____   Taken by _____   Beginning Inventory $_____

Figure 8.17. *Physical inventory form*

end of the month. In large operations, a complete inventory may not be taken at one time. Instead, inventories may be taken in one storage area or in one section of a storage area each week, with all areas covered by the end of a month's time.

The process should involve two people, at least one of whom, as a control measure, is not directly involved with storeroom operations. One person will count the food, which should be arranged systematically in the storeroom, usually categorized into groups and then arranged either alphabetically or by frequency of use. At the same time, the other person records the data on a physical inventory form, an example of which is shown in Figure 8.17. This form may be designed to match the physical arrangement of goods on the shelves, thereby greatly facilitating the actual physical count, and should include space for quantity on hand, unit size, name of food item, item description, unit cost, and total value of the inventory on hand.

As discussed in the subsection on receiving, some operations mark each issue unit with the price of the item at the time deliveries are placed in storage, as supermarkets do. If this procedure is used, the unit cost is recorded at the time the physical count is done; otherwise, the pricing of the inventory will be done at a later time, either by the bookkeeper or other clerical personnel.

A physical inventory may only be done two or three times a year in a small operation with a limited inventory that is relatively stable from month to month, although expensive or fast-moving items may be counted more frequently. This method should be employed only if experience has shown that the value of the inventory varies little from month to month and when security is not a major concern. In this instance, food cost is determined by totaling the value of the purchases for the financial period, which sacrifices some accuracy in control but eliminates the tedious job of taking the inventory.

In operations in which a monthly inventory is taken, food costs can be determined in one of two ways. The simplest method is to calculate cost of food in the following manner:

> Beginning inventory
> + Purchases
> = Cost of food available
> − Ending inventory
> = Cost of food used

Using the other method, daily food cost is determined by computing the cost of the direct issues and the cost of the storeroom issues from the requisition forms. A sample form for determining food cost is shown in Figure 8.18. The monthly food cost is then calculated by adding the daily food costs for the entire month. As a check, the food cost is also determined using the formula shown above and compared to that determined from the daily food cost records. An example is shown in Figure 8.19. This procedure provides management with food cost data on a timely basis and also permits greater control. Obviously, if the food cost determined from the physical inventory and that from the daily cost records differ significantly, the foodservice manager will need to analyze the reasons for the discrepancy and, possibly, implement tighter controls over products in storage.

Perpetual Inventory

The process of maintaining a continuous record of all purchases and food issues is called a perpetual inventory. This process provides a continuous record of the quantity on hand at any given time, as well as the value of food and supplies. An example of a perpetual inventory record is shown in Figure 8.20.

Generally, a perpetual inventory record, if used, is restricted to products in dry storage and frozen storage. Produce, milk, bread, and other fast-moving items are not usually kept on the perpetual inventory but considered to be direct issues. Also, fresh meats, fish, and poultry delivered on the day of use or one or two days in advance are not usually recorded on this record but charged to the food cost for the day on which they are used.

Perpetual inventories require considerable labor to maintain and are only used in large operations that carry large inventories. In some instances, a perpetual inventory record is maintained only for selected items, usually very expensive ones. The increasing use of electronic data processing, however, makes maintaining a perpetual inventory record much easier. After the computer-assisted inventory control system has been established, the perpetual inventory record can be kept up-to-date very simply by recording issues from the storeroom on a daily basis.

However it is done, a perpetual inventory record is not sufficient for accurate

Date _____

Direct issues					Requisition issues			Nonfood	
Dairy		Bakery							
Milk	Other	Bread	Other	Produce	Meat/fish & poultry	Frozen	Groceries	Linen	Supplies

TOTAL DIRECT ISSUES _____
TOTAL REQUISITION ISSUES _____
TOTAL FOOD TODAY _____
TOTAL FOOD TO DATE _____

TOTAL NON FOOD TODAY _____
TOTAL NON FOOD TO DATE _____

Figure 8.18. *Example of a daily expense worksheet*

	Beginning inventory		$ 2,000
+	Purchases	+	8,000
=	Cost of food available	=	$10,000
−	Ending inventory	−	1,925
=	Cost of food used	=	$ 8,075
−	Total direct and requisition issues	−	7,850
=	Difference	=	$ 225

Figure 8.19. *Reconciliation of food cost records*

accounting and control of food and supplies. A physical inventory should be conducted on a monthly basis to verify it.

Inventory Control Tools

With increased pressures for cost containment in all types of foodservice operations, the need for inventory control has become more important. The major functions of a control system are to coordinate activities, influence decisions and actions, and assure that objectives are being met by providing feedback on operations all with the goal of ensuring adequate products for production and service needs while minimizing inventory investment (Flamholtz, 1979).

In foodservice operations, the activities to be coordinated and integrated are those in the procurement, production, and service subsystems. For example, if green beens amandine is a menu item and green beans are not available in the inventory, production will be disrupted and, in turn, service will be affected.

The second major function of inventory control, decision making, can be made somewhat routine through the use of computers. The role of the manager as the one responsible for establishing policies and procedures and for monitoring operations to ensure that plans are being implemented appropriately, however, is still paramount.

Using green beans as an example again, the computer may provide information on when and how many cases to order. The established policies and procedures may detail the processes for ordering, receiving, and storing merchandise. Management, however, still must decide issues such as whether or not to take advantage of forward buying if a green bean crop failure is anticipated. An essential factor in this control system is feedback from the production and service units to procurement, as the unit responsible for inventory control.

With the increasing size and complexity of foodservice operations, inventory management and control have become more complicated and critical. A variety of tools are available to assist managers in determining quantities for purchase and recommended inventory levels and for determining costs of maintaining inventories. Several of these techniques will be discussed here.

Item: Tomatoes, whole or pieces		*Purchase unit:* 6/10 cs	*Issue unit:* #10 can	
Storeroom: Dry Stores #1				
Date	**Order no. or requisition no.**	**Quantity in (purchase unit)**	**Quantity out (issue unit)**	**Quantity on hand (issue unit)**
9/15/84	PO 1842	20 cs		120 cans
9/20/84	R 823		10 cans	110 cans

Figure 8.20. *Perpetual inventory record*

ABC Method

In most foodservice operations, a small number of purchased items account for the major portion of the inventory's purchase value; therefore, a method for classifying purchased items according to value is often advisable. This procedure is generally referred to as ABC analysis (Reuter, 1976). A typical classification of this type is illustrated in Figure 8.21.

The principle underlying the ABC method is that effort, time, and money for inventory control should be allocated among items in proportion to their value. Purchased items should be divided into three groups, as shown in the figure, with the large volume A and B items controlled with particular care.

The A-class items represent only 15 to 20 percent of the inventory items but typically account for 75 to 80 percent of the value of total inventory. These items should be reviewed continually to estimate requirements, to check stock balances, and to determine material on order. The inventory level of these important dollar components should be maintained at an absolute minimum.

The B-class consists of lesser valued items that typically vary between 10 and

ABC ANALYSIS

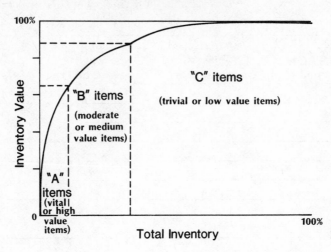

Figure 8.21. *ABC analysis*

15 percent of total inventory value while representing 20 to 25 percent of the items in inventory. C-class items are those whose dollar volume accounts for 5 to 10 percent of the inventory value but that make up 60 to 65 percent of the inventory items. Less concern, obviously, should be directed to the proportionally lower value items (Zenz, 1981).

In applying the ABC concept to a foodservice operation, an analysis of inventory items and subsequent classification into the three categories would assist the foodservice manager in deciding what time and effort priorities to assign in controlling inventory. In a commercial foodservice establishment with both food and beverage operations, liquor inventories would be categorized as A-class items and controlled very closely; whereas items like breakfast cereals or paper goods would be C-class items and monitored less closely.

Minimum-Maximum Method

One widely used method of controlling inventory involves the establishment of minimum and maximum inventory levels, commonly called the mini-max method. According to Zenz (1981), the minimum inventory level could theoretically be zero if the last unit of inventory were used up as a new shipment was received. The maximum inventory then would be the correct ordering quantity.

In reality, however, this extreme policy is not practical, since it involves planning that is much too close for safety. In the mini-max method, a safety factor is established, which becomes the minimum point below which the inventory should not fall under normal circumstances. The maximum inventory consists of the safety factor plus the correct ordering quantity. Figure 8.22 is a graphic representation of the mini-max principle.

The safety factor or safety stock is a back-up supply to ensure against contingencies, such as sudden increases in usage rate, failure to receive ordered materi-

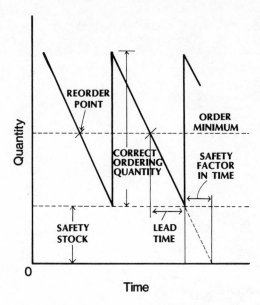

Figure 8.22. *Graphic representation of mini-max principle*

als on schedule, receipt of items that do not meet specifications, and clerical errors in inventory records. The size of the safety factor depends on the importance of the items in the operation, the value of the investment, and the availability of substitutes on short notice. It is determined by two factors: lead time and usage rate.

Lead time is the interval between the time that a requisition is initiated and receipt of merchandise, which may vary greatly depending upon source of the product. The shortest lead times occur when material is purchased from a local supplier who carries it in stock, and the longest when materials are secured from out-of-town suppliers, who often have specific delivery times. If possible, having alternate sources of supply will assist a foodservice operation in securing inventory items as needed. To prevent stockouts, however, a safety inventory to meet usage requirements during lead times is required.

Under the mini-max method, the usage rate of an item is determined by past experience and forecasts and by the length of time required to obtain delivery. An order minimum, or reorder point, is established from these data. This minimum, therefore, is the lowest stock level that can safely be maintained to avoid a stockout or emergency purchasing. The maximum inventory level is equal to estimated usage plus the safety stock.

Economic Order Quantity Method

The total annual cost of restocking an inventory item depends directly upon the number of times it is ordered in a year. To minimize these costs, orders should be placed as seldom as possible, thus generating large order quantities. The cost of holding an inventory, however, is directly opposed to the concept of large orders.

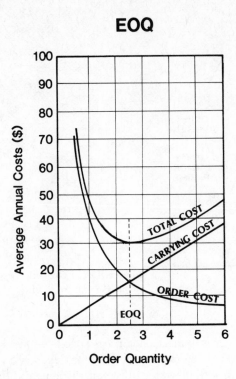

EOQ

Figure 8.23. *Graphic representation of the Economic Order Quantity concept*

The Economic Order Quantity (EOQ) concept is derived from a sensible balance of ordering costs and inventory carrying costs. The order cost diminishes rapidly as the size of the orders are increased, whereas the carrying costs of the inventory increase directly with the size of the order. In Figure 8.23, the order cost is a curve diminishing in ordinates as the abscissae, the order quantities, increase. The carrying costs of the inventory vary directly with the order quantity and, therefore, show as a straight line. The crux of the EOQ is determining the relationship between the carrying cost and the order cost that yields the minimum total cost. This occurs at the order quantity for which the carrying cost and the order cost are equal; in Figure 8.23, this is the point at which the two lines cross.

The formula for calculating the Economic Order Quantity follows:

$$EOQ = \sqrt{\frac{2 \times \text{acquisition cost} \times \text{total annual usage}}{\text{unit cost} \times \text{carrying charges}}}$$

In this formula, the acquisition cost consists of the total operating expenses of the purchasing and receiving departments, expenses of invoice payment, and data processing costs pertinent to purchasing and inventory. The cost per order (unit cost) is determined by dividing the number of orders placed per year into yearly ordering costs. Carrying charges are the total of all expenses involved in maintaining an inventory and include the cost of capital tied up in inventory, obsolescence of items, storage, insurance, handling, taxes, depreciation, deterioration, and breakage. The EOQ procedure may be utilized by the solution of a mathematical formula or by the use of tables that are the result of formula calculations.

In the development of the basic EOQ formula, several assumptions were made, as follows.

- Item demand known and constant.
- Withdrawals continuous at a constant rate.
- Quantity purchases available instantly.
- Shortages not tolerated.
- Unit cost constant.
- Order placement cost constant.
- Unit cost of inventory items constant.

The following conditions were not included in the basic EOQ development.

- Demand variations.
- Seasonal changes.
- Quantity discounts.
- Freight costs.
- Obsolescence risk.
- Stock-out costs.

Among the disadvantages of the EOQ method are its unreliability when the demand rate is highly variable, the required forecasting for all items, and the necessity of past demand data. In foodservice operations, use of the EOQ concept is contraindicated when the following conditions exist (Montag, 1971).

- Item demand uncertain.
- Withdrawals discontinuous or variable.
- Unit cost dependent on price breaks.
- Lead time not constant.
- Order placement cost variable.
- Stock holding cost variable.

The general opinion is that the EOQ procedure should not be used unless data processing equipment is available. Furthermore, the expenditure of large amounts of time and money required by this procedure is not justified on inventory analysis of items that account for very little of the total inventory costs. Whether it is used or not, however, the EOQ principle should not be considered a panacea for all inventory problems. The quantitative approach to inventory problems must be augmented by the knowledge, skills, and judgment of the foodservice manager.

Inventory Valuation Methods

In most organizations, inventories represent a significant portion of current assets. They are also an active asset, in that usage and replacement are continual. In accounting for them, the four principal methods are: specific identification method, average cost method, FIFO (first-in, first-out), and LIFO (last-in, first-out).

The specific identification method involves pricing the inventory at the exact cost of the item. This method could be used in foodservice operations if the "grocery market" pricing of each individual item is used when goods are received and placed in storage. Detailed record keeping is necessary with this method.

The second method is the average cost method in which a simple average, a weighted average, or a moving average unit cost may be employed (Cooper and Chamey, 1981). The simple average uses a straight average of the individual unit prices to cost the final inventory. The weighted average is based on both the unit purchase price and the number of units involved in each purchase. The moving average, which involves the calculation of a new unit cost after each purchase, can be used when a perpetual inventory is maintained.

Another widely used method of inventory valuation is FIFO, or first-in, first-out. Using this method for establishing cost of inventory units, inventory pricing closely approximates the physical flow of goods through an organization. The ending inventory reflects the current cost of goods, since inventory is valued at the dollar amounts for the most recent purchases.

The last major method of inventory valuation is LIFO, or last-in, first-out. According to Halperin (1981), LIFO is based on the assumption that current purchases are largely, if not completely, made for the purpose of meeting current demands of production. The latest cost of purchases, therefore, should be charged out first. The units remaining in inventory will then have the oldest purchase costs associated with them. Generally, the value of the inventory will be lowest using LIFO and highest using FIFO.

The method chosen for valuing inventory is important because it will affect the determination of cost of goods sold, which in turn will affect the profit or loss figure. The balance sheet or statement of financial condition of an organization will also be affected, since inventories are a current asset. These concepts are discussed in more detail in Chapter 21 (Section VI), Management of Financial Resources.

SUMMARY

Receiving, storage, and inventory control are important functions within the procurement subsystem of a foodservice operation. Without proper controls in receiving and storing of food and supplies, the careful planning in menu design and purchasing is partially nullified.

Receiving is a process for ensuring that the products delivered by vendors are those ordered in the purchasing process. After goods have been received, placement in appropriate storage and holding under proper conditions are necessary to ensure quality until time of use. Control of inventories is important to maintain quality of goods and supplies, to minimize inventory cost, and to ensure adequate quantity on hand for production and service needs.

Elements of good receiving include competent personnel with specific responsibilities, proper facilities and equipment, well-written specifications, good sanitary practices, adequate supervision, scheduled hours for receiving, and procedures to ensure security. As part of the receiving process, incoming shipments should be compared with the purchase order to ensure that the items accepted were, in fact, ordered. Checking of quantities and prices on the vendor's invoice is another critical step in the receiving process. A receiving record should be maintained by the receiving clerk as a control mechanism.

After products have been received, they should be removed immediately from receiving to the proper secured storage area, unless they are scheduled for use in production within a short period of time. Control over merchandise in storage is established by assigning responsibility to specific personnel, by effective physical security, and by sound material handling procedures. Proper storage maintenance, temperature control, cleaning and sanitation, and stability are major considerations in ensuring quality of stored goods. The type of storage facilities needed will vary with the type of foodservice system. The major types of storage are dry and low temperature: canned goods and staples are held in dry stores; highly perishable foods are placed in refrigerated or frozen storage.

Issuing is the process of supplying food to the production unit after it has been received and stored. The issuing process entails control of food and supplies removed from storage and provides information for food cost accounting. A requisition procedure is needed to provide adequate control in issuing goods.

A periodic physical count of food and supplies in storage is a requirement of any inventory control system. In some operations, a continuous record of all purchases and food issues, or a perpetual inventory, is maintained.

With the increasing size and complexity of foodservice operations, inventory management and control have become more complicated and critical. A variety of tools are available to assist managers in determining purchase quantities, inventory levels, and cost of maintaining inventories. These tools include the ABC method, the mini-max method, and Economic Order Quantity method.

Several techniques have been developed for valuation of inventories. These methods include the specific identification method, average cost method, FIFO, and LIFO. The choice of method to use for inventory valuation is important because of the potential effect on determination of profit and the value of current assets.

REFERENCES

Avery, A. C.: *A Modern Guide to Foodservice Equipment.* Boston: CBI Publishing Co., 1980.

Bock, M. A.: The development and comparative evaluation of a self-instructional module for quantity food storage. M.S. thesis, Kansas State University, 1979.

Bolhuis, J. L., Wolff, R. K., and Editors of NIFI: *The Financial Ingredient in Foodservice Management.* Lexington, MA: D.C. Heath and Co., 1976.

Cooper, R. S., and Chamey, L. N.: Inventory insight. *Credit & Financial Mgmt.* 83:14 (Sept.), 1981.

Fay, C. T., Rhoads, R. C., and Rosenblatt, R. L.: *Managerial Accounting for the Hospitality Service Industries.* 2nd ed. Dubuque, IA: Wm. C. Brown Co., 1976.

Flamholtz, E.: Organizational control systems as a managerial tool. *Calif. Mgmt. Rev.* 22:50 (Winter), 1979.

Food and Nutrition Service: *Food Purchasing Pointers for School Food Service.* Program Aid No. 1160. U.S. Department of Agriculture: August, 1977.

Halperin, R. M.: Effects of LIFO inventory. *Accounting Rev.* 56:977, 1981.

Hurb, S.: Watching dollars in food service. *Contemporary Administrator* 6:34 (Apr.), 1983.

Keiser, J. R., and Kallio, E.: *Controlling and Analyzing Costs in Food Service Operations.* New York: John Wiley & Sons, 1974.

Kotschevar, L. H., and Terrell, M. E.: *Food Service Planning: Layout and Equipment.* 2nd ed. New York: John Wiley & Sons, 1977.

Krupp, J. A. G.: Deterministic EOQ in a production environment. *J. Purchasing Materials Mgmt.* 19:24 (Summer), 1983.

Living with distributors. *Food Mgmt.* 17:40 (Feb.), 1982.

Longree, K.: *Quantity Food Sanitation.* 3rd ed. New York: Wiley-Interscience, 1980.

Mahaffey, M. J., Mennes, M. E., and Miller, B. B.: *Food Service Manual for Health Care Institutions.* Chicago: American Hospital Association, 1981.

Montag, G.: Obtaining meaningful cost information in dietary departments. Part 1. Food cost information. *J. Am. Dietet. A.* 67:55, 1975.

Ninemeier, J. D.: *Purchasing, Receiving, Storage: A Systems Manual for Restaurants, Hotels, and Clubs.* Boston: CBI Publishing Co., 1983.

Nix, M.: Purchasing, purchasing, purchasing! *School Food Serv. J.* 37:161 (Jun./Jul.), 1983.

Reuter, V. G.: ABC method to inventory control. *J. Systems Mgmt.* 27:27 (Nov.), 1976.

Stokes, J. W.: *How to Manage a Restaurant.* Dubuque, IA: Wm. C. Brown Co., 1982.

Thorner, M. E., and Manning, P. B.: *Quality Control in Food Service.* Westport, CT: AVI Publishing Co., 1976.

Tougas, J. G.: Refrigerated storage: Cool and collected. *Restaurants & Institutions* 90:115 (Apr. 1), 1982.

VanEgmond-Pannell, D.: *School Foodservice.* 2nd ed. Westport, CT: AVI Publishing Co., 1981.

Warfel, M. C., and Waskey, F. H.: *The Professional Food Buyer: Standards, Principles, and Procedures.* Berkeley: McCutchan Publishing Corp., 1979.

Zenz, G. J.: *Purchasing and the Management of Materials.* 5th ed. New York: John Wiley & Sons, 1981.

IV
Production

9
Production Planning

In the simplest possible terms, the objective of food production is the preparation of menu items in the needed quantity with the desired quality and at a cost appropriate to the particular service. Quantity is the element that distinguishes production in foodservices from home or family food preparation. Quality, while an essential concomitant of all food preparation, becomes an extremely vital consideration in mass food production because of the number of consumers of the product and the number of employees involved in preparation. It includes not only the aesthetic aspects of a food product but also the nutritional factors and the microbiological safety of the product. Cost, of course, determines whether or not a product should be produced for a specific clientele. An example in contrast would be serving filet mignon as a school lunch item—obviously too costly a choice. In the 1980s, foodservice operators are being challenged by increasing labor costs, rising food costs, and spiraling energy costs. The key to success is flexibility and an effort by managers to change strategies and management styles (Cichy, 1983).

After procurement, production is the next major subsystem in the transformation element of the foodservice system needed to accomplish this objective, and its place is highlighted in Figure 9.1. Because of the increased use of foods in the pre-processed state, the pre-processing subsystem will be included in the production section even though it precedes production in the foodservice systems model (Chapter 2). Production in the generic sense is the process by which goods and services are created. In the context of foodservice, production is the man-

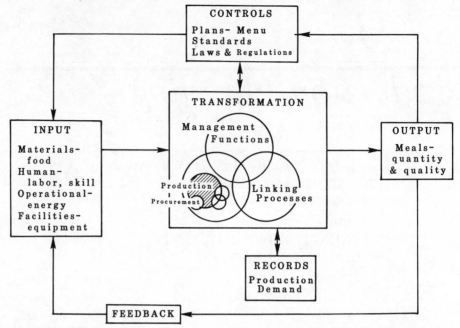

Figure 9.1. *Foodservice systems model with the production function highlighted*

agerial function of converting food items purchased in various states into menu items that are served as a meal to a customer, client, or patient.

In foodservice operations today, production is no longer considered as merely "cooking in the kitchen" but has evolved into planning, control of ingredients, production methods, quality of food, labor productivity, and energy consumption. Each of these controls will be discussed in separate chapters of the production section.

In essence, foodservice managers responsible for production are resource managers and in some organizations may be so designated. Those who rely on past experience to make decisions could have difficulty surviving in today's competitive market. Innovative approaches to decision making are required for allocation and control of these resources (Lambert and Beach, 1980). For example analytical and computer techniques used in production industries could be adapted by the foodservice manager for determining resource requirements for production.

Planning for production is the establishment of a program of action for resource transformation into goods and services. The manager identifies the necessary resources and determines how the transformation process should be designed to produce the desired goods and services. Once this process has been developed, the managerial function of planning must be integrated with the other managerial functions of organizing and controlling.

Planning, organizing, and controlling are overlapping managerial functions, however, and cannot be considered separately. For example, the foodservice manager and the production supervisor might have established a schedule of preparation times to prevent vegetables from being overcooked (controlling), but then suddenly must revise the production schedule (planning) because one essential employee went home sick and a critical task had to be reassigned. The content of jobs has to be analyzed to be sure all tasks are covered (organizing).

PLANNING DECISIONS AND OBJECTIVES

As discussed in Chapter 4, planning encompasses the setting of goals and objectives by top management and the development of policies and procedures by middle management. Eventually, decisions must be made concerning the necessary quantities to produce and the standards of quality that must be maintained within the limitations of costs. In foodservice operations, as in industry, managers must estimate future events. Thus, forecasting, planning for aggregate or total output, and production scheduling are important elements for decision making.

All of these planning decisions must be made within the constraints of the existing facility. Much too often, in a hospital or nursing home, the number of patients or residents is increased, but the capacity of the equipment in the kitchen is not. If the anticipated future demand exceeds the present capacity, then the facility must be expanded, future production curtailed, or more ready prepared foods purchased to handle the increased demand.

The prime objective of production planning is the effective synthesis of the production objectives of quantity, quality, and cost. Investigations of the tasks of industrial production managers indicate that most frequently their time is spent on labor relations, cost control, production control (quantity scheduling), and quality. Based on these observations, the secondary production objectives are to (Adam and Ebert, 1978):

- Determine characteristics of the product.
- Determine characteristics of the production process.
- Predict quantities to meet the expected demand.
- Define the desired quality level.
- Correlate the cost elements of labor, material, and facility utilization.

These industrial production planning objectives are equally applicable to foodservice operations. The characteristics of the product or menu items depend upon the type of operation: short orders in a fast food restaurant or hotel coffee shop, individual item selections in a full-service restaurant, or a fixed menu in a school. For example, a ground meat pattie would be served as a grilled hamburger on a bun for a fast food restaurant, a charbroiled ground steak for a full-service restaurant, or an oven-baked hamburger for school foodservice.

Production process characteristics include the method of food preparation, ranging from grilling to broiling to baking. The process and product characteristics are closely related because the process is actually determined by the product.

The process may have a greater bearing on the cost element in planning, though, because of labor, equipment, and energy expenditures.

Obviously, effective planning cannot be done without reasonably accurate forecasting of future demand quantities. Finally, standards of quality must be established for all products that will be produced. Maintenance of quality is a cost factor because of employee training, inventory control of both raw and prepared food items, and sanitation programs.

The cost element in planning is the result of the correlation of initial food item cost, storage, issue and utilization with the attendant items of labor cost, investment cost in facilities, and utilization of energy. These characteristics must be considered in all planning. Whenever planning goes beyond a day-to-day basis, forecasting becomes absolutely necessary.

PRODUCTION FORECASTING

As stated in Chapter 7, forecasting is the art and science of estimating events in the future and provides the data base for decision making and planning. In that chapter, forecasting was considered as it applies to procurement of materials. The specific concern of this chapter, however, is forecasting as applied to food production.

Production Demand

In line with the primary objective of food production—satisfying a quantity and quality demand, at a particular time and cost—the necessity of forecasting food production demand devolves from the facts that food preparation requires a definite length of time, that future demand must be forecast, and that specific costs are incurred with either over- or underproduction (Konnersman, 1969).

The length of time for food preparation is much shorter than it was a few years ago, generally because of the increased use of partially prepared food items, such as cake and bread mixes, portioned meats, frozen vegetables, and ready-to-serve salad greens. Preparation time may be further reduced by using more efficient equipment, including high-speed steamers and powerful mixers. Food production time, however, cannot be drastically reduced by the use of convenience foods unless a total assembly/serve system is adopted (Chapter 5).

Production demand for a hospital foodservice probably has the highest degree of uncertainty because of the unpredictable variation in special dietary requirements for patients, food preferences when selective menus are used, and the number of patients, staff, and visitors to be served. A restaurant differs in its production demand because special dietary requirements are generally not considered and because it may have a particular food specialty tending to stabilize the demand. Customers can satisfy desires for seafood or Italian cuisine by selecting a restaurant specializing in such items, rather than expecting to find those foods in all restaurants.

Overproduction generates extra costs because salvage of excess food items is not always feasible. Leftover prepared food generally spoils easily and requires extreme care in handling and storage. Even though some leftover foods might be salvageable by refrigeration, certain foods may break down and lose quality. A good example of this breakdown is a custard or cream pie that must be held under refrigeration for food safety but could develop a soggy crust and not be salable within a few hours after preparation. Policies and procedures for the storage of overproduced food items should be well-defined and rigorously enforced.

Attempts to reduce overproduction costs by using an available high-priced food item as an ingredient in a low-cost menu item can be very expensive. A typical example is using leftover rib roast in beef stew, soup stock, or beef hash, all of which could be prepared with less expensive fresh meat. In addition to the higher initial costs, planning and carrying out these salvage efforts incur higher labor costs that would have been avoided had the overrun not occurred. Customers are generally quick to suspect the use of leftovers, which certainly can be damaging to the image of a foodservice operation.

Underproduction can be just as much a cost-raiser as overproduction. A diner unable to secure a desired menu item, whether hospital patient or restaurant patron, will either suffer reduced morale or be extremely displeased. Furthermore, satisfying the customer demand in case of underproduction may involve both additional preparation costs and the frequently necessary substitution of a higher-priced item.

A wise manager will insist that a similar backup item be available when underproduction occurs. For example, in a university residence hall foodservice, if an undersupply of country fried steak occurs, an excellent replacement would be frozen minute steaks, quickly grilled. Such a substitution would certainly bolster customer morale.

Demand Forecasting

The desire for an efficient foodservice operation generates the need for production demand forecasting. Good forecasts are essential for managers in planning smooth transitions from current output to future output, regardless of size or functional type of the foodservice (i.e., schools, hospitals, or restaurants). They vary in sophistication from those based on historical records and intuition to complex models requiring large amounts of data and computer time. Care must be exercised to choose a forecasting model that is suitable for a particular situation.

Of the three types of models discussed in Chapter 7, the time series models are the most suitable for short-term forecasts in foodservice operations. They are based on the assumption that actual occurrences follow an identifiable trend over time. Actual data may indicate a trend in a general sense but not give forecast information. To make the past data useful, the variations must be reduced to a trend line that can be extended into the future. Moving average and exponential smoothing, both time series models, are used more frequently in rationalizing foodservice data than any other type, although causal models may be used as well.

Time Series Models

In all methods of forecasting, trends and seasonality in the data must be considered. For example, a major seasonal storm or interruptions of power would be indicated on the data base by wild deviations from what might seem to be a comparatively smooth time relationship. Since all food items in a service can hardly be grouped reasonably into gross demand data, the forecasts generally are developed on the most expensive and most often used items, such as meat entrees.

Moving Average. The most common and easiest of the smoothing procedures is the moving average method, which can be used only on items that are of the same kind. The process begins by taking the average of a group of five or ten data for the first point on a forecast line. The second point on the line is made by dropping the first item in the beginning group, including an additional one to make up the same number, and averaging them. The process continues for all the data with the same number of items for an average by dropping the last and moving to include a new one.

An example of the moving average method is shown in Figure 9.2. The data are for roast beef and cover a ten-day period in the past. A five-day moving average is used. The first five-day moving average is calculated by adding the demand for those days and dividing by five, giving an average of 176 pounds. The next moving average is calculated by adding the demands for days 2 through 6 and dividing by five. The procedure is repeated by dropping the earliest day and adding the next for a total of five days. The demand data values and the moving average values plotted on the graph (Figure 9.3) illustrate the smoothing effect of the method. Note that the smoothed data curve eliminates the daily variations in

MOVING AVERAGE

Day	Pounds of Beef	5-day Moving Average
1	150	
2	180	
3	185	176
4	170	186
5	195	187
6	200	182
7	185	183
8	160	180
9	175	
10	180	

Figure 9.2. *Example of moving average*

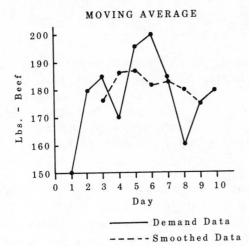

MOVING AVERAGE

———— Demand Data
– – – – Smoothed Data

Figure 9.3. *Graph illustrating moving average smoothing effect*

demand and thus indicates a trend of the past demand. This averaging process, when continued, yields data points that smooth out the data to a comparatively constant pattern for use in the forecast.

Exponential Smoothing. Exponential smoothing is a popular time series procedure. As does the moving average method, it smooths out randomness in the data. In the process, a current value and the immediate preceding value are used to compute a new smoothing one. This new value is the beginning item for the next time interval. An important feature of this method is that older data have a lesser influence on the trend curve. The mathematical expression for this smoothing method is

$$S_t = A_t + (1 - a) S_{t-1}$$

where a = a constant usually between 0.1 and 0.3

S_t = smoothed value at time t

A_t = actual observed value at time t

S_{t-1} = preceding smoothed value

This method's designation as exponential smoothing is justified by the mathematical decomposition of the equation, which results in a series wherein the expression (1 − a) acquires exponents (Adam and Ebert, 1978). Comparison of the two methods of smoothing indicates that the effect of the exponential technique is somewhat more rapid than that of the moving average.

Causal Models

Causal models are more sophisticated than the time series type and differ from them in the presumption that an identifiable relationship exists between the items being forecast and factors other than time. The most commonly used causal model is linear regression, which is treated extensively by most elementary statistics textbooks. Computer programs for regression are also readily available. These models are suitable for medium-term forecasts.

Linear Regression. The word "linear" signifies the intent of the analysis to find an equation for a straight line that closest fits the data points. In conventional statistical terminology, the item being forecast is called the dependent variable (Y) and the factors that affect it are called independent variables (X).

In the analysis, historic demand data for a single variable will result in a derived equation from a linear regression process in the form of a straight line

$$Y = a_0 + a_1X$$

in which a_0 and a_1 are numerical constants determined by the regression analysis. As shown in Figure 9.4, a_0 is the intercept of the line on the Y axis and a_1 is the slope of the line. In use, X will be a single independent variable quantity. The data points in the figure are the Y values for specific values of X. Preliminary plotting of the variables on graph paper would be advisable to ascertain if they could be represented reasonably by a straight line. The forecasting value consists of the assumption that the linear relationship between the variables will continue for a reasonable time in the future, or quite simply that the line may be extended. Use of the equation requires only substitution of an anticipated future value for X and then solution for Y as the forecasting quantity.

Examples of independent variables in hospital foodservice are total number of patient trays served, patient census, cafeteria setting capacity, number of employees, number of patients on regular diets, and the number of patients on each modified diet. For example, roast beef might be a dominant demand for a foodservice, and the relationship between the historic number of patient trays

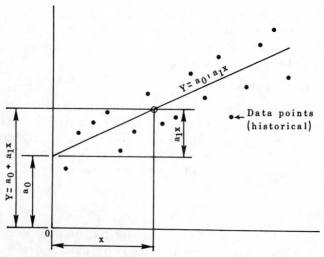

Figure 9.4. *Typical regression line*

and the pounds of roast beef could yield a regression equation. To forecast beef demand, an anticipated future count of trays served would then be inserted into the equation as X to solve for Y, the pounds of roast beef needed.

Multiple Regression. If determination of the effects of more than one independent variable $(X_1, X_2 \ldots X_n)$ on the dependent one is desired, the process is called multiple regression and the derived equation will have the following form

$$Y = a_0 + a_1 X_1 + a_2 X_2 \ldots a_n X_n$$

Multiple regression analysis is quite complex and a good computer program is needed for the solution.

PLANNING FOR TOTAL OUTPUT

Decision levels within an organization may make the separation into detailed and overall planning desirable. The forecasting models previously discussed are related to detailed planning and are generally used at the operating level. The higher levels of management are concerned with overall planning, termed aggregate planning for total output.

Aggregate planning, which is often described in the literature of industrial management, is distinguished by a reduction of planning to gross variable elements in order to enable top managers to make overall planning decisions and leave detail to the lower echelon. In the context of current literature, "aggregate" means overall or nonspecific. The process usually consists of planning in a specific time frame for the elements of product, inventory, and labor.

Foodservice operations are rarely amenable to such an aggregate planning device because of the fundamental differences in technological processes and products that exist between industrial manufacturing organizations and foodservice systems. The industrial manufacturer transforms raw materials by several distinct processes into a finished product which is stored in inventory or shipped to the customer for use at a later time. This inventory can be used to protect the manufacturer from stockouts in periods of increased demands.

By contrast, in the foodservice, the raw material transformation occurs typically in the same facility in which the product is consumed. Because the finished product is perishable, no such finished goods inventory can be maintained to meet future demand. A large hospital using cook-chill, minimal cooking, or convenience production systems could possibly utilize aggregate planning, however, if it also had extended access to a high-capacity computer, a prerequisite of this method. Connell (1981) investigated the use of aggregate planning in such large medical center foodservices. The essential element of their plans was the aggregate demand consisting of the total services, nourishments, and meals provided by the foodservice system in a production period with the accompanying labor costs.

PRODUCTION SCHEDULING

Production scheduling in foodservice operations can be defined as the time sequencing of events required by the production subsystem to produce a meal. Scheduling occurs in two distinct stages—planning and action—and is essential for production control.

In the planning stage, forecasts are converted into the quantity of each food item to be prepared and the distribution of the items to supervisors in each work center. As a very simple example, 500 servings of roast beef, scalloped potatoes, broccoli, tossed salad, dinner rolls, and cherry pie have been forecast for a special dinner. The foodservice director assigns the production of the 500 servings of beef, potatoes, and broccoli to the supervisor of the main production, the tossed salad to the salad unit, and the rolls and cherry pie to the bake shop.

The supervisors in each unit assume the responsibility for the action stage by preparing a production schedule. Each item is assigned to a specific employee and the time to start its preparation is recorded on the schedule. Careful scheduling assures that the food is prepared to serve without lengthy holding and probable deterioration in quality. The supervisors give feedback to the manager by writing comments on the schedules.

In small operations in which only one cook and perhaps a helper are on duty at a time, the foodservice manager might also need to assume the responsibility for the action stage. No operation, however small, can avoid the necessity for a production schedule.

Production Schedule

The production schedule, frequently called the production work sheet, is the major control in the production subsystem because it activates the menu. The production schedule energizes the production plan and provides a test of forecasting accuracy. The menu, of course, must be based on standardized recipes, as described in Chapter 11.

The production schedule is highly individualized in various foodservices and may vary from a single sheet for manual completion to a computer program printout. Regardless of the type of form, certain basic information must be included on each schedule: the production date, meal, and unit should be identified, as well as other pertinent information—weather, special events, and actual meal count. In addition, the following information must be included to make it a specific action plan.

- Employee.
- Menu item.
- Quantity to prepare.
- Actual yield.
- Special instructions and comments.

- Preparation time schedule.
- Overproduction and underproduction.
- Substitutions.
- Additional assignments.
- Prepreparation.

The specimen production schedule in Figure 9.5 is from a large university residence hall foodservice. Note that the general information previously mentioned is displayed at the top of the work sheet and that the production area is marked as the specific destination for this schedule. The meal count at the conclusion of production is also recorded, which validates this schedule as part of historical data. The specific headings named above constitute the column headings.

The production schedule is generally posted on a bulletin board in the unit. The name of the employee in the left-hand column readily enables the responsible personnel to find the line describing designated duties. The menu item column identifies the recipe by name. Often the unit supervisor will distribute the recipes, either in card form or as a computer printout, to the appropriate employees at the time the schedule is posted.

The quantity to prepare is the forecast amount for each menu item. The actual yield is the portion count produced by the recipe. Current practice is to include portion size and count on the recipe. If not contained on the recipe, this information should be placed on the production schedule. Note that the actual yield indicates overproduction for some items and underproduction for others. The instructions column, completed by the unit supervisor, gives special information and comments on equipment to be used and service instructions. In addition, this column should contain any specific information not included in the recipe, such as that indicated for refried beans and for broccoli: "add bean liquid as needed to maintain a moist product" and "season with melted butter."

The time schedule, completed by the unit supervisor, is intended to assure that the various menu items will be produced for service at the desired time. It also has references to preparation methods standardized in this main production unit for a particular item, such as the Country Fried Steak and the Mexican Rice.

The leftover amount column indicates over- or underproduction. Underproduction is indicated by zero leftover and a time entry in the runout time column. The substitution column is used when an item is underproduced, as in the case of the broccoli spears.

In this residence hall foodservice, cleaning assignments are additional and the name of the person responsible is recorded.

Instructions for prepreparation for the following meal, whether the same day or next, are in the same form as the production schedule, beginning with the name of the person, and followed by the menu item, quantity, and special instructions. These items listed under prepreparation will be on the schedule for the following meal.

The emphasis in this text on production scheduling is justified by its importance as an element of production control with important bearing on the cost of

Date _____ 2/27/84 _____

Meal _____ Bkf. _____ Lunch __X__ Dinner

Unit _____ Main Production _____

Meal Count 2153
Weather Fair
Comments Basketball Game

Employee	Menu item	Quantity to prepare	Actual yield	Instructions	Time schedule	Left over amount	Run out time	Substitution	Cleaning assignment
Wege Whatley	Country Fried Steak	1200	1220	Use 2 Tilting Fry Pans and oven number 3	Begin frying 2:15 See Frying Time schedule	35 servings	—	—	Whatley—Tilting fry pans
Lundin	Giant Rolled Tostados	1000	1020	Serve open face on cafeteria line and clientele will roll their own		50 tortillas 10 lbs meat mixture 1 gal cheese sce.	—	—	Lundin—slicer and attachments
McCurdy	Whipped Potatoes	1200	1150	If necessary use instant as a back up	Begin steaming potatoes at 3:00	12 lbs	—	—	
McCurdy	Cream Gravy	2000	1600	Make 4 batches 600—600—400—400 (if needed) Serve over both steak and potatoes		2 gal	—	—	

Employee	Menu item	Quantity	Instructions	Quantity	Instructions	Amount	Extra	Notes
Wege	Mexican Rice	900	Use 12 × 10 × 4 pans	900	See Baking schedule	18 lbs	—	—
Mockery	Refried Beans	850	Add bean liquid as needed to maintain a moist product	850		12 lbs	—	Mockery—Oven number 1, shelves and doors
Mockery	Broccoli Spears	1000	Season with melted margarine	850	Begin 4:00 Prepare based on demand	0	6:00 2½ lbs Asparagus Spears	
Mockery	Yogurt Cup	20	Serve whole container—blueberry, cherry, rum raisin, plain	20		8	—	—

Pre Preparation:

Employee	Menu item	Quantity	Instructions	Employee	Menu item	Quantity	Instructions
McCurdy	Roast Beef	600 lbs	Pan beef in baking pans, cover and refrigerate	Lundin	(Omelet) fresh eggs	1 case	Break into 60 qt mixer bowl
Mockery	Hard Cooked Eggs	5 doz.	For garnish on spinach	Wege	Ham	10 lbs	Dice for omelets

(used by permission of Kansas State University Residence Hall Foodservice)

Figure 9.5. *Residence hall foodservice production schedule*

materials, labor, and energy. Regardless of the perfection of the schedule and the assignment of employees to implement it, however, the production employees are the ones who make the schedule work. Realization of this simple fact implies the value of production employee meetings.

Production Meetings

Foodservice managers in small operations, or unit supervisors in large ones, should hold a meeting daily with employees in the production unit. Ordinarily, these production meetings can be rather short but, at a cycle menu change, a longer time is required to discuss new recipes and employee assignments. In foodservice operations serving breakfast, lunch, and dinner, these meetings are generally scheduled after lunch, when activity in the production unit is minimal.

During these meetings, production unit employees can be encouraged to discuss the effectiveness of the schedule just completed. Over- and underproduction, as shown on the recently completed schedule, and future corrective measures are also important topics for discussion. These production problems and suggested solutions should be recorded on the schedule for guidance when the menu appears the next time in the cycle.

The meeting should conclude with a discussion of the production schedule for the following three meals. At this time, the employees should review recipes for the various menu items, substitutions for them, and preparation for the following day. Free discussion of workloads is quite in order for such meetings and can be a morale builder for the employees who really make the schedule work.

SUMMARY

Production is the second major subsystem in the transformation element of the foodservice system and is the managerial function of converting food items purchased in various states into menu items that are served as meals to customers, clients, or patients. Planning for production establishes a program of action and encompasses the setting of goals and objectives by top management. Decisions in a foodservice concerning the quantities to produce and standards of quality should be made within the limitations of cost.

In manufacturing industries, the prime objective of production planning is the effective synthesis of the production objectives of quantity, quality, and cost. This objective is equally applicable to operations in the foodservice industry. Effective planning requires reasonably accurate forecasting of future demand quantities. Production demand in a foodservice varies widely, dependent on the type of operation. Both overproduction and underproduction are hazards of production demand planning. Overproduction generates extra costs because salvage of leftover food is not always feasible, and underproduction is a cost raiser because of customer dissatisfaction. Avoidance of these pitfalls of production requires forecasting of demand with a considerable degree of accuracy.

Forecasting varies from historical records and intuition to complex models requiring large amounts of data and computer time. Past experience is the only viable clue to the future. Historical records, thus, assume major importance as the basis for all forecasting. The time series forecasting, moving average, and exponential smoothing models are the simplest and generally most suitable for short-term forecasting in foodservice operations. Essentially, these models involve reducing the major variations in past data to produce a trend that can be extended into the future. The most useful of the causal models is linear regression. In this method, the historical data of the past are used to develop a mathematical equation involving demand causes and effects that can be extended into the future.

Management decision levels within an organization are concerned with both detailed and overall planning. Forecasting is related to detailed planning and is generally done at the operations level; overall or aggregate planning is performed at the top management level. For example, in a large medical center foodservice, the aggregate demand would involve the total meals and nourishments provided in a production period, with their accompanying labor costs.

The culmination of production planning is the production schedule, which is a time sequencing plan of events required by the production subsystem to produce a meal. Scheduling involves two distinct stages, planning and action. The production schedule activates the production plan and constitutes a test of the forecasting accuracy. Regular meetings with employees to discuss production schedules can improve functioning of the production unit.

REFERENCES

Adam, E., and Ebert, R.: *Production and Operations Management.* 7th ed. Englewood Cliffs, NJ: Prentice-Hall, 1978.

Bloetjes, M. K., Aleta, I. R., Breunig, D. J., and Schwam, E.: Production models for dietary department operations. *J. Am. Dietet. A.* 59:42, 1971.

Buchanan, P. W.: *Quantity Food Preparation: Standardizing Recipes and Controlling Ingredients.* Chicago: The American Dietetic Association, 1983.

Chandler, S., Norton, L., Hoover, L., and Moore, A.: Analysis of meal census patterns for forecasting menu item demand. *J. Am. Dietet. A.* 80:317, 1982.

Cichy, R.: Productivity pointers to promote a profitable performance. *The Consultant* 16:35 (Winter), 1983.

Connell, B. C.: An experimental investigation of aggregate planning and scheduling models within foodservice systems. Ph.D. dissertation. University of Missouri-Columbia, 1981.

Cullen, K., Hoover, L., and Moore, A.: Menu item forecasting systems in hospital foodservice. *J. Am. Dietet. A.* 73:640, 1978.

Dougherty, D. A.: Forecasting production demand. In Rose, J. C., ed.: *Handbook for Health Care Food Service Management.* Rockville, MD: Aspen Systems Corp., 1984.

Fitzsimmons, J. A., and Sullivan, R. S.: *Service Operations Management.* New York: McGraw-Hill Book Co., 1982.

Gerlach, N.: Food production controls. In Rose, J. C., ed.: *Handbook for Health Care Food Service Management.* Rockville, MD: Aspen Systems Corp., 1984.

Konnersman, P. M.: Forecasting production demand in the dietary department. *Hospitals* 43:85 (Sept. 16), 1969.

Lambert, C. U., and Beach, B. L.: Computerized scheduling for cook/freeze food production plans. *J. Am. Dietet. A.* 77:174, 1980.

Mackle, M., and David, B. D.: Developing a demand forecasting system for a foodservice operation. *J. Am. Dietet. A.* 68:457, 1976.

Matthews, M. E., Waldvogel, C. F., Mahaffey, M. J., and Zemel, P. C.: Food production relationships between entree combinations and forecasted demand. *J. Am. Dietet. A.* 72:618, 1978.

Messersmith, A.: Design of a multi-echelon menu item forecasting system. Ph.D. dissertation, University of Missouri-Columbia, 1975.

Messersmith, A. M., Moore, A. N., and Hoover, L. W.: A multi-echelon menu item forecasting system for hospitals. *J. Am. Dietet. A.* 72:509, 1978.

Rose, J. C., ed.: *Handbook for Health Care Food Service Management.* Rockville, MD: Aspen Systems Corp., 1984.

Shriwise, M.: Forecasting production demand in a residence hall foodservice system. M.S. thesis, Kansas State University, 1975.

Tienor, C., and David, B. D.: A dietary department applies procedure for developing a demand forecasting system. *J. Am. Dietet. A.* 68:460, 1976.

Urich, R. V., and Noort, A. J.: Production demand forecasting. *Hospitals* 45:106 (Feb. 1), 1971.

Wood, S. D.: A model for statistical forecasting of menu item demand. *J. Am. Dietet. A.* 70:254, 1977.

Wood, S. D.: Menu item demand forecasting for hospital food management operations. Ph.D. dissertation, University of Wisconsin-Madison, 1973.

10
Ingredient Control

Ingredient control is a major component of the quality and quantity control of the food production subsystem, as well as a critical dimension of cost control in the entire foodservice system. As discussed in Chapters 7 and 8, the process of ingredient control actually begins with the forecasting, purchasing, receiving, and storage of foods. It continues throughout prepreparation, production, and service and even after service, with the holding of food items produced in excess of the service demand.

The two major aspects of ingredient control are ingredient assembly and utilization of standardized recipes. An ingredient room, as the ingredient assembly area is often called, is an area within the storage or production area designed to send measured ingredients to the kitchen's various work centers.

The development and use of standardized recipes greatly facilitate production planning, purchasing, and actual food production. When adjusted to an accurate forecasted quantity, they provide assurance that standards of quality will be consistently maintained. As indicated by Buchanan (1983), the well-written quantity recipe is the basis for production control.

239

INGREDIENT ASSEMBLY

As discussed in Chapter 8, concepts related to receiving, storage, and inventory control are important components of ingredient control, particularly control of issuing from storage. An effective issue and assembly system can achieve the objectives of cost reduction and quality improvement in foodservice operations. Such a system controls all food and supplies from delivery to service, by requiring proper authorization for removal of goods from storage and by issuing only required quantities for production and service, as outlined in Chapter 8. The ingredient room concept was also introduced in that chapter as an aspect of issue control operational in many foodservice systems, especially those with computer-assisted management information systems.

Advantages of Centralized Assembly

Some type of issue system is operational in most foodservice organizations. Frequently, however, production personnel may have access to production areas, and materials may be issued in units larger than production demand. According to Dougherty (1984), tightening controls provides greater security, allows for more efficient scheduling of storeroom and production personnel, and improves product consistency while reducing food costs substantially. She identified the following benefits from a centralized ingredient assembly system.

- Reduced food cost.
- Reduced labor cost.
- Improved quality consistency.
- Increased production control.
- Consistent basis for planning cost and nutrient content.
- Decreased materials handling.
- Improved security.

Additional advantages identified from utilization of the ingredient room concept in state institutions in the state of New York (Division of Alcoholism, 1981) are the redirection of cooks' skills away from the simple tasks of collecting, assembling, and measuring ingredients toward production, garnishing and portioning. Other advantages identified by the state were control of production time through control of ingredient availability and decreasing of over- and underproduction by accurate measurement of menu item ingredients.

The concept of an ingredient room dates to the late 1950s (Gelepi, 1973). Flack (1959), one of the first to implement a central ingredient room, reported reduced labor cost as a major benefit. In the early 1970s, Bansal reported that ingredient control had saved $30,000 in food costs after only six months. Dougherty (1984) indicated that an approved issue control system does not require increased personnel and need not require renovation of facilities; activities being performed in other areas of the foodservice operation can be reassigned to give more emphasis to issue procedures.

Traditional vs. Central Ingredient Control

Traditionally in foodservice operations, individual cooks obtain recipe ingredients from storerooms, refrigerators, and freezers, although a procedure for requisitioning foods should be in place for inventory control, as discussed in Chapter 8. In the traditional operation, ingredients are issued by units such as cases, boxes, or bags. In the food production areas, portions of ingredients not used are generally stored on shelves or in storage bins. For example, a cook may have sugar and flour bins under the work counter and a row of spices and condiments on a shelf above a work table.

Keeping track of unused portions of issue units, particularly perishable products, provides a challenge for the cook or foodservice supervisor and represents a potential area for decreased control. For example, five pounds of frozen mixed vegetables leftover from a 30-pound case must be held and used the next time mixed vegetables are on the menu. With the many different ingredients used in foodservice operations, controlling the partially used food items can become a major problem. A cook may decide to add the extra mixed vegetables to the soup kettle rather than returning the unneeded amount to storage. Such a practice alters the recipe and adds to cost. This is only one example of the problems of the traditional method of issuing ingredients.

With central ingredient control, the cook would have been issued only the 25 pounds needed for the forecasted production demands on the day of service. The excess of five pounds would have been held in frozen storage in the ingredient room until the next time mixed vegetables were needed for a recipe or as a vegetable on a future menu. Control of the unused portions of issue units is facilitated because the storage is maintained at a central place rather than in various work units throughout the kitchen.

As Buchanan (1983) points out, food production includes basically two functions: prepreparation and production. Traditionally, both functions have been performed by cooks. As pointed out in the discussion of advantages in the central ingredient control system, focusing the cooks' efforts and attention on direct production tasks and away from the simple tasks of prepreparation, which can be assigned to less skilled workers, can lead to operational efficiencies. In addition, when prepreparation tasks are assigned to specific personnel, they can develop skill in performing these tasks, thereby reducing labor cost. Another efficiency that can result from a centralized ingredient concept is the combination of prepreparation tasks when similar ingredients are needed for two or more recipes. For example, chopped onions may be needed for meat loaf and a sauce at lunch and for soup and salad on the dinner menu. By centralizing prepreparation, all the onion could be chopped at one time and divided into separate quantities for each of the four recipes.

The ingredient room concept has become more popular with the advent of computer-assisted foodservice management systems in foodservices. Increased control of ingredients is necessary to ensure that accurate information is generated by these systems.

Functions of the Ingredient Room

The primary function of the ingredient room is to coordinate assembly, preparation, measuring, and weighing of the ingredients to meet both the daily production needs and the advance preparation needs of recipes on future menus. Buchanan (1983) indicates that specific activities vary among foodservice operations but that, in general, ingredient rooms function 24 hours in advance of production scheduling.

An ingredient room may have a very limited function in which only dry and room-temperature ingredients are premeasured, or it may be a center in which all ingredients are assembled, weighed, and measured. The availability of appropriate equipment, such as prepreparation equipment and low temperature storage, will help determine the activities to be performed in an ingredient room. A secured freezer in or near the assembly area is required, for example, if advance withdrawal and thawing of frozen products is a function of ingredient room personnel.

Canned products and staple goods should be coordinated in the ingredient room. Storeroom personnel, however, may be responsible for assembling full cases and unopened cans, which may be delivered by the same personnel or picked up in the storeroom area by production personnel. Partial amounts from cans or cartons should be weighed and measured in the central ingredient assembly area. This practice can eliminate a source of waste in a foodservice operation by avoiding partially used cans or cartons in several locations, often of the same product. For example, canned tomato sauce may be needed in both the main production and salad units with a partially used can of sauce remaining in the reach-in refrigerators in both of these areas. If a central ingredient room is operational, these needs could be coordinated and the number of partially used cans eliminated or reduced.

Meat products, which have been ordered according to production demands, may or may not be handled in the ingredient room. For example, preportioned meats that have been ordered in a quantity appropriate for the production demand may flow directly from receiving to production. Greater control is possible, however, if these products also are coordinated in the ingredient assembly area.

Prepreparation tasks, such as cleaning, slicing, or dicing produce or breading and panning meat products may be completed in a prepreparation area or may be a function in the central ingredient assembly area. The staffing for this area and the availability of appropriate equipment are the two key factors influencing whether or not these prepreparation tasks are performed in the ingredient room.

After all ingredients for each recipe have been weighed, measured, chopped, or otherwise prepared, each ingredient is packaged in a plastic bag, or other appropriate packaging, and labeled. Ingredients for each recipe are then assembled, usually with a copy of the recipe, and transported to the appropriate work unit or held until the scheduled distribution time.

In a computer-assisted operation, an adjusted recipe is an output of the computer system, with peel-off labels often printed out for each ingredient. These labels facilitate marking the ingredient packages for assembly of ingredients for each recipe.

Organization of an Ingredient Room

In the design of a new foodservice facility, an ingredient room that can be secured should be located between the storage and production areas. In an existing facility, ingredient assembly may be located in or near a storeroom, combined with the preparation area, or in a designated part of the production facilities. The chief idea, as Dougherty (1984) points out, is that the placement of a central ingredient assembly area should augment the flow of materials from storage to production.

The necessary large equipment includes refrigeration, which should be in or near the area, as well as a water supply. Trucks or carts are needed for assembly and delivery of recipe ingredients, and portable bins for storing sugar, flour, and other dry ingredients are helpful. A work table or a counter is required, with shelving over or near it essential for such products as spices. An example of an ingredient room work table, designed for use in the central ingredient area in New York state institutions (Division of Alcoholism, 1981), is shown in Figure 10.1.

Scales are the most essential pieces of equipment for a central ingredient assembly area. A countertop scale, similar to the one shown in Chapter 8, and a

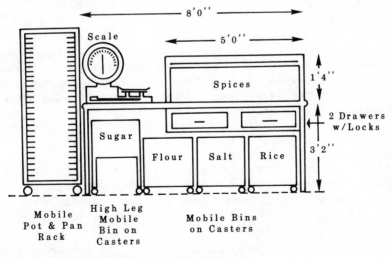

FRONT ELEVATION

Figure 10.1. *Ingredient room work table arrangement*

Measuring Utensils

Measuring spoons: 2 sets
Measuring cups
  Pint
  Quart
  2-quart
  4-quart

Utensils

Electric or table model can opener
Large punch-type can opener
Knives: french and utility
Spatula
Rubber scrapers
Cutting board
Vegetable peeler
Strainer
Spoons: slotted and solid
Dippers: various sizes
Ladles: various sizes
Scoops for storage bins

Packaging Material

Paper cups and lids: various sizes
Plastic bags
Plastic jars and containers
Sandwich bags
Paper bags
Steam table or counter pans with lids

Labeling Materials

Felt-tip pen
Grease pencil
Masking tape and dispenser
Self-adhesive labels
Scratch pad
Pencil

Assembly Equipment

Sheet pans and trays
Delivery baskets (wire racks)
Carts
Racks

Organization Equipment

Slot organizer
File box
Clipboard

Sanitation Supplies

Garbage can
Waste basket
Rags
Paper towels
Soap

Figure 10.2. *Small equipment supplies for ingredient assembly.* **Source: *Dougherty, D. A.: Issue control and ingredient assembly systems. In Rose, J. C.: Handbook for Health Care Food Service Management. Rockville, MD, Aspen Systems Corp., 1984, p. 200.***

portion scale are required for weighing the various types of recipe ingredients. Other equipment for preparation will vary, depending on the specific functions assigned to the ingredient room. This equipment may include a slicer, vertical/ cutter mixer, other chopping or dicing equipment, food waste disposal, and mixer.

A suggested list of other small equipment and supplies is shown in Figure 10.2. As was true for the larger equipment, the small equipment required in the central ingredient area varies, depending on the functions performed there.

Ingredient Room Staffing

According to Dougherty (1984), about one-third of the production staff's time in an operation without an ingredient room is spent determining supply needs, obtaining supplies, and weighing and measuring ingredients. By centralizing these activities, the production staff are free for higher-level skill tasks. This will generally allow management to reassign lower classification personnel from production to ingredient assembly. In smaller operations in which a full-time person is not needed for ingredient assembly, schedules of production staff can be arranged to permit them to weigh and assemble ingredients at the end of a shift for future preparation. As Dougherty pointed out, however, the more activities are centralized, the more benefits will be realized.

Personnel assigned to the ingredient room must be able to read and write, do simple arithmetic, and be familiar with storage facilities. They are often responsible for receiving, storage, and ingredient assembly. Qualifications and training, therefore, must be specific to both of these areas of responsibility. Training should include the following areas.

- Environmental conditions and requirements to store specific foods.
- Ventilation and humidity factors in dry storage.
- Safety precautions in handling and storage of nonfood items and toxic materials.
- Housekeeping and sanitation standards to prevent contamination of foods during storage.
- Security measures to ensure against pilferage.
- Weighing and measuring procedures.

The job description for an ingredient assembly clerk depends on the activities included in the procedures for the ingredient room. An example of a job description is shown in Figure 10.3. The following factors are among those to consider in scheduling personnel for ingredient assembly.

- Size of operation.
- Frequency and time of deliveries.
- Size of ingredient room and location of other storage areas.
- Type, number, and complexity of menu items to be assembled.
- Number of work stations to be supplied.
- Schedule for delivery of assembled ingredients to production and serving areas.
- Extent of prepreparation performed in ingredient assembly area.

Dougherty (1984) states that in a 300+ bed healthcare facility, 12-hour coverage by at least one staff member, 7 days a week, is needed. She contends, however, that the maximum number of staff needed is three, even in a large hospital, unless an extremely large quantity of prepreparation is performed.

INGREDIENT ASSEMBLY CLERK

GENERAL RESPONSIBILITIES AND DUTIES

I. Storeroom Requisition

    Pick up storeroom requisition from main kitchen office. This list is a consolidation of all ingredients needed for one day's production of menu items that would be channeled through the ingredient assembly area. Check all items against the inventory on hand in the ingredient assembly area and mark out supplies not needed with a felt pen. (For example, sugar will be issued in a 100# bag. The total amount will not be used in any one day. Annotate this requisition, give it to the storeroom clerk for filling and delivery.)

II. Production Schedule and Production Recipes

    Pick up production schedule and production recipes from the main kitchen office.

    A. Production recipes. There will be one recipe for each menu item that will be channeled through the ingredient assembly area. These recipes have been adjusted according to the forecast.

    B. Production schedule. This form will be prepared by the food production manager and will include the following information:
        1. name of employee responsible for product preparation
        2. name of recipe or menu item
        3. time that ingredients are to be delivered to specified production area

        Always check the production schedule to determine how to plan your work. Arrange production recipes according to the times listed on the production schedule so that those to be prepared first are weighed and packaged first.

III. Assembling, Weighing, and Packaging

    Accurately assemble, weigh, and measure ingredients according to the amounts on the production recipe printout. Set up ingredients on carts according to the following procedure.

    A. Choose a cart large enough to accommodate the ingredients for each recipe.

    B. Using masking tape and felt-tip pen, label trays and shelves with recipe name. All menu items set up on cart should have approximately the same delivery time.

    C. Package ingredients as follows:
        1. Paper cups and lids. Use for small amounts of liquid items, such as Worcestershire sauce, lemon juice, salad oil.
        2. Plastic bags (2 to 3 sizes). Use for all wet ingredients, such as frozen eggs, fresh vegetables. Fasten bags securely and label with felt marker. Write name of ingredient and weight on bag.
        3. Glassine sandwich bags. Use for small amounts of spices or other dry ingredients.
        4. Paper bags (assorted sizes). Use for dry ingredients.
        5. Counter pans. Use for larger quantities of ingredients, such as bread crumbs, flour, celery. Cover the pan with either a lid or plastic wrap.
        6. Original container. Always leave items in the original container whenever possible, such as no. 10 cans or wax paper around margarine.
        7. Jars (½ and 1 gal). For vinegar and salad oil.

        Put small quantities of ingredients for the same recipe on 18-inch × 26-inch sheet pan. After all items are weighed, labeled, and covered, place them on assigned cart shelves. If the cart is not to be delivered immediately, push it into a walk-in refrigerator if any items require refrigeration. Meat items, such as ground beef, should not be put on the cart until just before delivery.

        The production recipe printout should be delivered with the assembled ingredients to the production area. If necessary, inform the cook that the ingredients have been delivered. Ingredients may be transferred from the carts to a table when practical.

IV. General Responsibilities

    You are responsible for
    A. storing and refrigerating opened cans and using these opened cans first;
    B. storing items and rotating stock in the ingredient assembly area;
    C. using proper sanitation procedures;
    D. washing the equipment that you have used;
    E. keeping your work area clean and orderly at all times; and
    F. other duties as assigned.

Figure 10.3. *Job description.* **Source: *Dougherty, D. A.: Issue control and ingredient assembly systems. In Rose, J. C.: Handbook for Health Care Food Service Management. Rockville, MD, Aspen Systems Corp., 1984, pp. 203–204.***

RECIPES

A recipe is a formula by which measured ingredients are combined in a specific procedure to give predetermined results. The recipe is actually a written communication tool that passes information from the foodservice manager to the ingredient room employees and the production personnel. In addition, the recipe is an excellent quality and quantity control tool, constituting a standard for each item on the menu that meets customer and management approval. Cost controls for each recipe can be easily computed, because the ingredients and the amount of each will be the same each time the recipe is used. The well-planned menu has little value if the customer complains about the quality of the food or the manager is not satisfied with the profit.

Recipes, therefore, should be well defined by having a format understood by personnel responsible for production of menu items and for customer service. Once a recipe has been tested repeatedly and accepted by management, it becomes a standardized recipe that always gives the same results.

Recipe Format

Most recipes are written in a definite pattern or style that is identified as a format. For most effective use, all recipes in a particular foodservice should be written in the same format. This uniformity of style simplifies the recipe usage by eliminating careful reading to determine the sequence of steps.

Large quantity recipes generally differ in format from those used in households, in which the ingredients are listed in the upper portion and the procedures below, thus requiring the cook to read alternately from the top and bottom of the recipe and contributing to errors. A block format, in which the ingredients are listed on the left side of the recipe and the corresponding procedures directly opposite them on the right, is generally used for quantity recipes. In a complete block format, horizontal lines separate each group of ingredients with the pertinent procedure from those of the next, and vertical lines separate the amount, ingredient, and procedure columns. However, a modified version, in which only horizontal lines separate each procedure and the required ingredients, is often used. An example of a modified block format is the recipe for lasagne in Figure 10.4 (Shugart, Molt, and Wilson, 1984). This recipe format is applicable for both recipe cards and computer printouts.

Specific information should be included on each recipe to simplify its use by those preparing and serving the food. Generally, recipes include the following information.

- Name of food item.
- Coded identification.
- Total yield.

- Portion size and number of portions.
- Baking time, if required.
- List of ingredients.
- Amount of each ingredient by weight, measure, or count.
- Procedures.
- Panning or portioning information.
- Serving and garnishing suggestions.

The important basic information pertaining to the detailed recipe is shown in the heading of the lasagne recipe (Figure 10.4). The oven temperature and baking time are on the left and the total yield, pan size, and portion size on the right. Ingredients are listed according to procedural groups, with three ingredients in the first group, five in the second, four in the third, and three in the last. Amounts are given to the left of the ingredients. Standard U.S. weights and measures are generally used for all ingredients except small amounts of spices and oil, which are given in the common household units of teaspoons (t) and tablespoons (T).

Recipes for production greater than the 48 portions in the lasagne example could be written entirely in standard measures without the use of household units. Some foodservices, however, now use only metric measures, especially in a computerized system. The ability of the metric system to define small amounts in either weights or liquids obviates the necessity of resorting to household measures. In small foodservice operations, measures may be used primarily rather than weights; however, weighing is more accurate than measuring for determining the proper amount of an ingredient.

The procedures for preparing each group of ingredients are printed on the right side of the recipe, opposite the ingredients required. The layering combination of the ingredients in lasagne is very important and is detailed in the last procedure. The temperature, baking time, and portioning instructions are repeated for the convenience of the cook. Procedures should be checked for clarity and explicitness, permitting a cook to prepare a perfect product without asking supervisors for an explanation. In recipes requiring use of mechanical devices, such as mixers, time and speed should be specified. For example, the procedure for combining the first three ingredients in a cake might be "cream shortening, sugar, and vanilla on medium speed 10 minutes."

Additional information can be added to a recipe in a footnote, such as variations of a specific item. Special serving instructions, including garnishing and portioning suggestions, as well as storage instructions before and after service are often included in the footnote. If recipe cards are used, these additions can be printed at the bottom or on the back. The ingredient and procedure portion of a recipe, however, should never be printed on the back of a card. For long recipes, a second card or page should be used.

Before adopting a particular format, variations might be tried to give the cooks an opportunity to choose the one they like best. Once a format is chosen, all

LASAGNE

Oven: 350°F (175°C)
Bake: 40-45 minutes

Yield: 48 portions
2 pans 12 × 20 × 2 in.
Portion: 6 oz (170g)

Amount U.S.	Ingredient	Procedure
5 lb	Ground Beef	Cook together until meat has lost pink color. Drain off excess fat.
12 oz	Onion, finely chopped	
2 cloves	Garlic, minced	
3 qt	Tomato sauce	Add to meat. Continue cooking, about 30 minutes, stirring occasionally.
1 qt	Tomato paste	
1 t	Pepper, black	
1 t	Basil, crumbled	
1 T	Oregano, crumbled	
2 lb 8 oz	Noodles, lasagne	Cook noodles according to directions on p. 348. Store noodles in cold water to keep from sticking. Drain when ready to use.
2 gal	Water, boiling	
2 T	Salt	
2 T	Cooking oil	
2 lb 8 oz	Mozzarella cheese, shredded	Combine cheeses. Arrange in 2 greased 12 × 20 × 2 in. counter pans in layers in the following order:
6 oz	Parmesan cheese, grated	Meat sauce (1 qt) Noodles, overlapping (1 lb 12 oz) Cheeses (1 lb 4 oz)
2 lb 8 oz	Ricotta cheese or cottage cheese, dry or drained	Repeat sauce, noodles, and cheeses Spoon remainder of meat sauce on top. Bake at 350°F for 40–45 minutes.
		Cut 4 × 6 in.

Figure 10.4. *Example of the format of a typical quantity food recipe.* **Source:** *Shugart, G. S., Molt, M., and Wilson, M. F.:* **Food for 50**, *7th edition. New York: John Wiley & Sons, 1984, p. 355.*

recipes should be printed in that style. In converting to a new format, a good method is to adapt the most used recipes first and then gradually extend the conversion to the entire file. The production supervisor will need to conduct some inservice training sessions on the new format for the employees responsible for food preparation.

Recipes for use at a work station should be in large print, easily readable at a distance of 18 to 20 inches, meaning that large file cards or 8½ × 11 inch paper must be used. Recipes for the ingredient room or production unit should be in a plastic cover while in use, and in some type of holder or rack at the work stations. With the appropriate larger print, picking up recipes for a "closer look" should not be necessary.

The recipe name is generally indicated in bold letters either in the middle or to the side at the top of the recipe card. In most operations, a file coding system is established for quick access to each recipe. For example, major categories can be established for food items, such as beverages, breads, cakes, cheese, cookies, eggs, fish, meat, pies, poultry, salad, sandwiches, soups, and vegetables. Each category can be assigned an identifying letter and the individual recipes given sequential numbers, to be placed at the top of the recipe as well. Whatever system is developed, it should be easy for employees to follow. Today, many foodservices use color coding of major categories to make identification easier.

The means of maintaining a master file of recipes varies with the foodservice. A minimum of two sets of recipes should be available, one to be kept in a permanent file accessible only to the foodservice manager and the other in a file for use by the cooks. The number of sets depends upon how many persons in the organization need recipes for specific reasons. For example, persons planning menus or purchasing food might save many hours if the recipes are readily available in their office files.

The recipe file is the key data base for operations using a computer-assisted foodservice management system, which permits individual printouts on demand. Examples of computer-generated recipes are shown in Figures 10.5 and 10.6— one from a university residence hall foodservice and the other from a medical center foodservice. Because the recipe is generated each time the food item is on the menu, a protective cover is not needed. It can also be readily modified, enabling the foodservice manager to maintain an up-to-date file. Chapter 22 is devoted to further discussion of computer systems in foodservice operations.

Recipe Standardization

The ideal of every manager is to have recipes that consistently deliver the same quantity and quality product when followed precisely. But recipes assembled from numerous sources, even those from companies, cannot be used with the assurance of uniform products in every foodservice. The variations in ingredient characteristics, customer demands, personnel, and equipment may require alterations to the recipe or even preclude its successful use. Production procedures are

STIR FRY VEGETABLES

/ / -******

RECIPE CODE - 26-30-0-178-4   STATUS - DEVELOPMENTAL   2

****

EQUIPMENT-MIXING BOWL
WIRE WHIP
FRY PANS

```
***NUMBER OF PORTIONS                 200
   PORTION SIZE / COST                .170 LBS. /     $0.0524
   MEAL PATTERN ALLOWANCE             1 OR 2 PORTIONS
   SUGGESTED SERVING UTENSIL          SPOON
   PAN SIZE                           12X10X4
   NUMBER OF PANS
   WEIGHT PER PAN                     LBS.
   HANDLING LOSS                      0.00 PERCENT
   MINIMUM BATCH
   MAXIMUM BATCH
   FORECAST UNIT                      200 SERVINGS
  *TOTAL RECIPE WEIGHT / COST         34.0 LBS. /    $10.4800
   TOTAL RECIPE VOLUME
```

RECIPE SOURCE-KSU 83

06/12/84 10.20 AM   830427

CODE	PERCENT	INGREDIENT	WEIGHTS AND MEASURES	AP/EP	STEP	PROCEDURE
0041002105	5.92	OIL SALAD 5 GAL	2.0 LBS X		A	1. PEEL GARLIC CLOVES. COMBINE WITH GINGER ROOT AND VEGETABLE OIL IN STOCK POT. COVER-LET AGE AT ROOM TEMPERATURE AT LEAST ONE WEEK BEFORE USING.
0052000834	0.10	GINGER ROOT FRESH	0.04 LBS X			
0052000018	0.10	GARLIC WHOLE FRESH	0.04 LBS X			
0082021040	1.42	CORNSTARCH 1 LB	0.48 LBS		B	2. COMBINE AND SET ASIDE FOR STEP 10.
0000000001	6.40	WATER	2.2 LBS			
0052000508	21.33	CARROTS FRESH	7.3 LBS / 8.8 LBS	EP / AP	C	3. SLICE INTO THIN JULIENNE STRIPS
0052001709	21.33	SQUASH ZUCCHINI SUMMER FRESH	7.3 LBS / 7.6 LBS	EP / AP	D	4. CUT INTO THIN SLICES.
0052000605	21.33	CELERY FRESH	7.3 LBS / 9.7 LBS	EP / AP	E	5. SLICE DIAGONALLY INTO THIN PIECES.
					F	6. POUR FLAVORED OIL FROM STEP 1 INTO FRY PAN. HEAT TO 350 DEGREES F.
0072012005	7.11	WATER CHESTNUTS CND	2.4 LBS		G	7. ADD TO HOT OIL ALONG WITH CARROTS, ZUCCHINI AND CELERY. STIR WITH LONG SPATULAS IN AN OVER AND UNDER FOLDING MOTION. 8. COOK JUST UNTIL VEGETABLES ARE TENDER CRISP.
0082080208	0.47	SOUP BASE CHICKEN	0.16 LBS		H	9. COMBINE. ADD. MIX IN QUICKLY. TURN HEAT DOWN.
0000000001	17.77	WATER	6.0 LBS			
0082032009	2.84	SOY SAUCE	0.97 LBS			
					I	10. POUR CORNSTARCH MIXTURE OVER VEG. COOK AND STIR JUST UNTIL SAUCE THICKENS AND VEG. ARE GLAZED.
					J	11. NOTE-VEG. SHOULD BE A LITTLE CRISP.

Figure 10.5. Example of a computer-generated recipe from a university residence hall foodservice system using the percentage method for recipe adjustment (used by permission of Kansas State University Residence Hall Foodservice)

```
******************************
PNCF         DESCRIPTION              HOLDNG R/I          VALUE        PKT UNIT FRZ FRZ
                                      LOCATN UNIT         ON HAND      IND COST SPC TOL
P719 PANCAKES/BACON STRIP/FRUIT       FR2    PLATE        $78.233 N    .179

REC                                   PROD/FINISH         DAY PRD TOTAL DIRECT PKP
NUM          DESCRIPTION              UNIT                PRP FAC TIME  TIME   FAC
1 PANCAKES                            PROD HOT F          3

                 MAX  MIN  AMT    AMT    LST DT   BATCH
                 INV  INV  ONHND  ONORD  ENTER    SIZE
                 600  400  435    240    840829   80

                 MAX PAN  PANS DESCRIPTION
                 QTY QTY
                 99   4   4 2" FULL PANS

SIP TEMP  TIME   LARGEQ            SE ITEM                              QUANTITY ISSUE                     PROCEDURE LINE      LINE
NUM CONTRL HR/MIN EQUIPMENT         Q CODE    DESCRIPTION               USED     UNIT   PREPARATION                            NO
1         MIXER, WIRE WHIP          1 I191 FLOUR ALL PURPOSE ENRICHE    2.945    KG            MIX TOGETHER ON LOW            1
                                    3 I039 BAKING POWDER TYPE 1 10LB     .160    KG            SPEED 30 SEC. TURN OFF         2
                                    4 H689 SUGAR GRANULATED TYPE A       .105    KG            MIXER.                         3
2 X                                 4 K154 EGG PRODUCT CTN PACK FRZ THAW .490   KG            ADD.                           1
3 X                                 2 R462 MILK WHOLE .5GAL PAPR CTN CHIL 4.165 KG            MELT. ADD TO OTHER             1
                                    1 Q461 MARGARINE 1LB PRINTS CHIL     .490    KG            INGREDIENTS & MIX ON           2
                                                                                              LOW SPEED UNTIL                3
                                                                                              BLENDED. BATTER WILL           4

09/03/84   DT805VB1        FOOD PRODUCTION          UNIVERSITY OF KANSAS MEDICAL CENTER   PAGE 484
                           MASTER LIST              DEPARTMENT OF DIETETICS AND NUTRITION

                                                                                              BE LUMPY.                      5
3 X 325°F  4  TILTING FRY PAN        1 H533 OIL COOKING 100% CORN OIL    .030    KG            PREHEAT PAN. GREASE            1
                                                                                              LIGHTLY. DIP PANCAKE           2
                                                                                              W #24 DIPPER. PANCAKE          3
                                                                                              SHOULD BE 4" ACROSS.           4
                                                                                              BAKE ON 1 SIDE UTIL            5
                                                                                              FIRM AROUND EDGE &             6
                                                                                              & BROWN. PLACE IN              7
                                                                                              PANS, 40 PER PAN.              8
                                                                                              SEND TO PLATE ASSEM-           9
                                                                                              BLY.                           2
```

Figure 10.6. *Computer-generated recipe used in a university medical center foodservice. Source: Department of Dietetics and Nutrition, The University of Kansas College of Health Sciences and Hospital, Kansas City, Kansas (used by permission)*

complicated and difficult to establish because many people are involved and they each have definite ideas about how a product should be prepared. Recipe standardization, then, or the process of "tailoring" a recipe to suit a particular purpose in a specific foodservice operation (Buchanan, 1983), is one of the most important responsibilities a production supervisor encounters.

Standardization requires repeated testing to ensure that the product meets the standard of quality and quantity that has been established by management for that particular foodservice. Food cost and selling price cannot be correctly calculated unless recipes are standardized to use only specific ingredients in known amounts yielding a definite quantity. Even a standardized recipe at times must be retested when a small change is made in any ingredient. For example, substitution of frozen or dehydrated vegetables, in place of fresh, to reduce labor costs can change the quality of the product, requiring that the recipe be checked before use.

Why Standardized Recipes Are Used

Standardizing recipes is a time-consuming task and managers have to be convinced that the process is worth the time involved. Conviction can follow the realization that the most successful foodservice operations use only recipes that have been developed specifically for them. Probably the best example of the use of standardized recipes is in the multiunit fast food chains. Each batch of chili con carne, hot biscuits, pizza dough and toppings, fried chicken, and fried fish are the same in each unit of the chain every day. This essential uniformity is often assured by recipes classified for use by very few employees in the main ingredient room of the company. The packaged ingredients are sent to each unit throughout the region, the nation, or even the world. Without this stringent control, these fast food operations could not maintain national and international reputations for quality.

Among the advantages for using standardized recipes are the following.

- *Promotion of quality and quantity assurance for foods produced.* The final product should be the same quality each time the item is prepared. A standardized recipe reduces the probability of failures due to poor food handling and preparation, regardless of which cook prepares the product, and also prevents a cook from using a secret recipe. Portion sizes and number of portions are included on each standardized recipe, as well as serving instructions, assuring that the food item will always look the same on each plate regardless of who serves the food.

- *Saving of time of production and managerial personnel.* Total labor hours in the kitchen for cooks can be reduced if standardized recipes are used. Also, managers have more time for managerial functions if they do not have to answer cooks' questions or make decisions about how to prepare an item. During purchasing procedures they also have more time because the exact amount of each ingredient is recorded on the recipe, which eliminates the need to estimate quantities. Managers can spend more time being creative in developing recipes, merchandising, and serving.

• *Control of cost by reducing waste and regulating inventories.* Waste can be controlled by not overpurchasing or overproducing. Unusable leftovers are therefore minimal. Inventories can be maintained at adequate levels and storage space kept at a minimum.

• *Simplification of determination of menu item costs.* The calculation of accurate food cost and selling price cannot occur without knowledge of the amount of each ingredient and the number of portions from each recipe.

• *Facilitation of training of production employees.* Recipes with good procedures can be excellent training programs in good work methods and basic food production principles for new cooks. Cooks know exactly what to do, how to do it, and what kind of product is expected. The cook then has the responsibility of preparing products rather than deciding how to produce the product of desired quality in the amount required.

Although standardized recipes offer many advantages in a foodservice operation, the key to success is ensuring that recipes are followed carefully and consistently each time an item is produced. Because the human element can be a major variable in product quality and uniformity, employee supervision and training are critical aspects in a quality assurance program.

How to Standardize Recipes

Standardization is basically a recipe-testing process designed to adapt recipes to a specific foodservice operation. Few recipes from other operations can be used without modification and yield a completely satisfactory product. Generally, recipes are standardized for a particular operation from ones secured from another source. Appendix A includes a list of various sources of quantity recipes. Recipes may also be contributed by clients or employees; these are often home size and need to be adjusted for quantity proportions. Various methods for recipe adjustment are described later in this chapter.

Before any recipe is standardized, it should be thoroughly analyzed. One aspect to consider is the relative proportion of ingredients. For example, in a pour-type batter, as for pancakes or waffles, the ratio of flour to liquid should be 1:1. A recipe varying too much from this would produce a batter too thin or too thick. An initial check against standard proportions for products will indicate whether or not the recipe is balanced.

After analysis, the recipe should be tested. Careful weighing and measuring of all ingredients is especially important. Notations should be made at each stage of the standardization process: mixing and combining procedures, preparation and cooking time, temperatures, equipment and utensils used, and the method of serving should all be recorded. The total yield and number of portions produced should be determined, as well as portion size. Special attention should be paid to clarity of procedures in all stages of preparation of an item. Any changes in

---

EVALUATION OF PRODUCT

Name _____

Date _____

Points	Quality
7	Excellent
6	Very Good
5	Good
4	Medium
3	Fair
2	Poor
1	Very Poor

Directions:

1. Place the numerical score in the box in the upper left hand corner.
2. Comments should justify the numerical score. Comments must be brief.
3. Evaluation of the food products must be on an *individual* basis.

	Products			
Quality characteristic	*1*	*2*	*3*	*4*
Appearance				
Consistency or texture				
Tenderness				
Flavor				
Overall eating quality				

Figure 10.7. *Form for panel evaluation of recipes*

procedures must be noted to ensure that the product can be prepared the same way each time.

A form for taste panels should be developed for evaluating products from recipe standardization trials. A sample form is included in Figure 10.7. More detailed forms may be developed for specific kinds of products, and evaluation criteria may differ among products. Generally, however, appearance, flavor, texture, and color are the factors evaluated. A standard should be defined to establish the quality of a product being produced, even though it may need to be revised after the standardization process is complete. Initial standards for evaluating a recipe for vanilla cream pudding and a ham, macaroni, and cheese casserole are shown in Figure 10.8. Development of food standards will be discussed in more detail in Chapter 11.

Results from the initial evaluation may suggest changes for the next test run, which may include adjustments in ingredient quantities, cooking times, procedures, or serving methods. Generally, only one change should be made at a time, in order to determine the effect of the various changes.

Vanilla cream pudding

The vanilla cream pudding should be scored on appearance, consistency, flavor, and overall acceptability. The color should be an even pale yellow. The texture should be a light creamy consistency and a smooth texture, free from lumps. The flavor should be rich vanilla. Overall acceptability should be based on the judge's general reaction to the product.

Ham, macaroni, and cheese casserole

The casserole should be scored on appearance, texture, tenderness, flavor, and overall acceptability. Appearance should be pleasing and the texture firm but not stiff. Tenderness should be exhibited by a product that is easily chewed but not gummy. Ham and cheese flavor, slightly seasoned, should be apparent. Overall acceptability should be based on judge's general reaction to the product.

Figure 10.8. *Examples of quality standards for assessing recipes*

Repeat batches of a recipe should be produced until at least three successful trials have produced the quality and quantity desired. Evaluation of the product after the initial test may also include assessments from clientele. If those doing the testing are very knowledgeable about food production, only a small number of trials may be needed. To perfect some recipes, however, many tests are needed. If test products are acceptable, they may be served to clientele, even though the standardization process is not completed. An unacceptable product, however, would have to be considered an expense of doing business. In many college residence hall foodservices, new products being tested are added to the service line as bonus menu items and the students are asked to provide input on whether the items should be included on the menus.

According to Buchanan (1983), the last step in the standardization process involves retaining the recipes in the permanent file. Recipes added to the file should meet the following criteria.

- Yield in volume or number of portions results in desired quantity and is consistent.
- Quality and appearance of the product meets specified standards.
- Products are acceptable and suitable for the clientele of the operation.

Buchanan states that recipes still in a developmental stage may be used in an operation; however, this status should be clearly indicated on the recipe, as on the computer recipe in Figure 10.5. She summarized the steps in recipe standardization as follows.

- Secure written recipes to test either by buying a quantity recipe file or by writing down the recipes currently used by cooks.
- Determine if the base recipe amount is to be 50 or 100 portions, and adjust recipes to that amount.
- Identify which recipes will be standardized first.

- Develop an evaluation form to use in reviewing quality and appearance of tested recipes.

- Schedule the first trial batch of each recipe to be tested.

- Make changes in recipes based on the results of the first trial batch.

- Schedule a second trial batch of each recipe, being careful to document finished yields.

- Incorporate suggestions resulting from the second trial batch into each recipe.

- Schedule a third trial batch of each recipe.

- Incorporate suggestions resulting from the third trial batch into each recipe.

- Schedule a final fourth trial batch using a cook unfamiliar with the recipe.

- Incorporate the recipes into the permanent file, provided that they meet established standards.

Recipe Adjustment

Three procedures have been developed for the adjustment of recipes: the factor method, the percentage method, and direct reading measurement tables. Frequently, in many foodservice operations, home-size recipes are used to develop quantity recipes. This process involves special considerations in adjusting recipes designed for a small number of servings to a quantity appropriate for 100 portions or more. In the sections that follow, the three methods of recipe adjustment are described and a section on adjusting home-size recipes to quantity production is included.

Factor Method

To increase a recipe using the factor method, the ingredients are generally changed from measurements to weights and multiplied by the conversion factor. To simplify the adjustment process, the ingredients should be converted to whole numbers and decimal equivalents rather than being stated as fractions; that is, 2 lb 10 oz would be converted to 2.625 lb. Whenever possible, liquid measures should be stated in weights; however, liquid measurements may be converted to decimal equivalents of a quart or gallon. For example, 4½ qt may be stated as 4.5 qt. Table 10.1 provides data for converting ounces into decimals of a pound and cups and quarts into decimal parts of a gallon. Because scales may not be accurate for weighing very small amounts, recipe ingredients of 1 oz or less are often stated in tablespoons or teaspoons.

Conversion of a recipe using the factor method involves the following steps.

1 Change ingredient amounts to weight measures and state as whole numbers and decimals.

2 Divide the desired yield by the yield of the recipe selected for adjustment.

3 Multiply all recipe ingredients by the factor determined in step 2.

4 Reconvert the decimal unit into pounds and ounces (or quarts and cups).

Table 10.1. *Decimal conversions for weights and measures*

oz	lb	Decimal unit	cup	qt	gal	oz	lb	Decimal unit	cup	qt	gal
Weight measure			Volume measure			Weight measure			Volume measure		
½		.03125	½			8½		.53125	8½		
1		.0625	1	¼		9		.5625	9	2¼	
1½		.093	1½			9½		.59375	9½		
2	⅛	.125	2	½		10	⅝	.625	10	2½	
2½		.156	2½			10½		.65625	10½		
3		.1875	3	¾		11		.6875	11	2¾	
3½		.218	3½			11½		.71785	11½		
4	¼	.25	4	1	¼	12	¾	.75	12	3	¾
4½		.281	4½			12½		.78125	12½		
5		.3125	5	1¼		13		.8125	13	3¼	
5½		.343	5½			13½		.84375	13½		
6	⅜	.375	6	1½		14	⅞	.875	14	3½	
6½		.40625	6½			14½		.90625	14½	3½	
7		.4375	7	1¾		15		.9375	15	3¾	
7½		.46875	7½			15½		.96875	15½		
8	½	.5	8	2	½	16	1	1	16	4	1

Source: Buchanan, P. W.: *Quantity Food Preparation: Standardizing Recipes and Controlling Ingredients.* Chicago: Am. Dietet. A., 1983, p. 26.

5 If the adjusted amounts are in odd or unusual amounts, round off to an amount that is simple to weigh or measure and within an acceptable margin of error.

6 Check math for possible errors before providing the recipe to prepreparation and production personnel.

To illustrate use of the factor method, assume a college residence hall foodservice has ham loaf on the menu. The recipe in the file is for 50 portions; however, the forecast production demand is 250 portions. Using the procedure outlined above, the ham loaf recipe would be adjusted to the desired number of servings by first converting the ingredients, as appropriate, to decimal equivalents:

Ingredients	Amount	Decimal units
Ground Ham	4 lb	
Ground Beef	4 lb	
Ground Pork	4 lb	
Chopped Onion	2 oz	.125 lb
Black Pepper	½ t	
Bread Crumbs	1 lb	
Eggs	12	1.5 lb
Milk	1 qt	

The conversion factor to adjust the base recipe from 50 portions to 250 portions would be determined by dividing 250 by 50; the resulting factor is 5. The next step is to multiply the ingredient amounts by the factor. To assist the cooks in using the recipe, the ham loaf adjusted to 250 portions would be stated in pounds and ounces or quarts and cups, as shown in the last column in the example below.

Ingredients	*50 portions*	*50 × 5 =* *250 portions*	*Conversion* *from decimals*
Ground Ham	4 lb	20 lb	20 lb
Ground Beef	4 lb	20 lb	20 lb
Ground Pork	4 lb	20 lb	20 lb
Chopped Onion	.125 lb	.625 lb	10 oz
Black Pepper	½ t	2½ t	2½ t
Bread Crumbs	1 lb	5 lb	5 lb
Eggs	1.5 lb	7.5 lb	7 lb 8 oz
Milk	1 qt	5 qt	5 qt

Percentage Method

The second method of adjustment of formulas is the percentage method. Using this method, the measurements for ingredients are converted to weights and then the percentage of each ingredient of the total weight is computed. The number of portions is forecast, which provides the basis for determining the ingredient weights from the ingredient percentages. Formulas that have been converted to percentages need not be recalculated. This method allows adjustment to the portion size or forecast and permits a shift of ingredients to be done easily.

Using a desk calculator, the percentages can be readily determined. With a computer-assisted system, calculations are made even easier. Torrence and Vaden (1976) developed a recipe data base for a computer-assisted foodservice management system in the Kansas State University residence halls in which the percentage method was used for recipe adjustment.

McManis and Molt (1978) describe the following step-by-step method for recipe adjustment via the percentage method.

Step 1 Convert all ingredients from measure or pounds and ounces to tenths of a pound. Make desired equivalent ingredient substitutions, such as frozen whole eggs for fresh eggs, powdered milk for liquid milk.

Step 2 Total the weight of ingredients in a recipe after each ingredient has been converted to weight in the edible portion (EP). For example, the weight of carrots or celery should be the weight after cleaning, peeling, and ready for use. The recipe may show both AP (as purchased) and EP weights, but the edible portion is used in determining the total portion weight.

Step 3 Calculate the percentage of each ingredient in relation to the total weight. Repeat for each ingredient.

Formula:

$$\frac{\substack{\text{Individual} \\ \text{ingredient weight}}}{\text{Total weight}} \times 100 = \substack{\text{Percent of} \\ \text{each ingredient}}$$

(sum of percentage totals = 100%)

Step 4   Check the ratio of ingredients. Standards of ingredient proportions have been established for many items. The ingredients should be in proper balance before going further.

Step 5   Establish the weight needed to give the desired number of servings. It will be in relation to pan size, portion weight or equipment capacity.

Example: Total weight must be divisible by the weight per pan.

Example: A cookie portion may weigh 0.14 lbs. per serving; therefore, 0.14 times the number of servings desired equals the weight needed.

Example: Mixing bowl capacities vary, thus becoming a factor in writing recipes.

Use the established portions, modular pan charts, or known capacity equipment guides to determine batch sizes to be written. The constant number used in calculating a recipe is the weight of each individual serving.

Step 6   Cooking or handling loss must be added to the weight needed, and it may vary from 1 to 30 percent, depending on the product being served. Like items produce predictable losses which with some experimentation can be accurately assigned. The formula for adding handling loss to a recipe is as follows:

(100% − Assigned Handling Loss %) X = Desired Yield

$$X = \frac{\text{Desired Yield}}{100\% - \text{Handling Loss }\%}$$

Example: Yellow Cake has a 1% handling loss. Desired yield is 80 lb. (or 600 servings).

(100% − 1%) X = 80 lb.
.99X = 80
X = 80/.99
X = 80.80 Total lb. of ingredients to end up with 80 lb. of batter

Step 7   Multiply each percentage number by the total weight to give the exact amount of each ingredient needed. Once the percentages of a recipe have been established, any number of servings can be calculated and the ratio of ingredients to the total will be the same. One decimal place on a recipe is shown (e.g., 8.3 lb.) unless it is less than one pound, when two places are shown (e.g., 0.15 lb.).

Going through the process of expanding a recipe will help illustrate recipe adjustment by this method. Tables 10.2 to 10.4 demonstrate how to expand a

Table 10.3. *Calculate percent, Brownies*

Percent*	Ingredients	Measure	pounds
20.34	Eggs	12	1.32 lb.
30.82	Sugar	2 lb.	2.00 lb.
15.41	Fat, Melted	1 lb.	1.00 lb.
1.70	Vanilla	¼ C.	0.11 lb.
11.56	Cake Flour	12 oz.	0.75 lb.
7.71	Cocoa	8 oz.	0.50 lb.
0.49	Baking Powder	4 t.	0.0316 lb.
00.41	Salt	2 t.	0.127 lb.
11.56	Nuts, Chopped	12 oz.	0.75 lb.
100%			6.4886 lb.

Table 10.2. *Original recipe, Brownies*

Ingredients	Amount
Eggs	12
Sugar	2 lb.
Fat, Melted	1 lb.
Vanilla	¼ C.
Cake Flour	12 oz.
Cocoa	8 oz.
Baking Powder	4 t.
Salt	2 t.
Nuts, Chopped	12 oz.

Source: McManis, H., Molt, M.: Recipe standardization and percentage method of adjustment. *NACUFS J.*, 1978, p. 40.

*Individual ingredients weights = Ingredient percents total weight

Table 10.4. *Recipe for 60 Servings, 0.12 lb. each, 3% handling loss*

Percent	Ingredient	Pounds
20.34	Eggs	1.51 lb.
30.82	Sugar	2.29 lb.
15.41	Fat, Melted	1.14 lb.
1.70	Vanilla	0.13 lb.
11.56	Cake Flour	0.86 lb.
7.71	Cocoa	0.57 lb.
0.49	Baking Powder	0.04 lb.
0.41	Salt	0.03 lb.
11.56	Nuts, Chopped	0.86 lb.
100%		7.42 lb.*

Source: McManis, H. Molt, M.: Recipe standardization and percentage method of adjustment. *NACUFS J.*, 1978, pp. 40–41.

*Calculations:
60 times 0.12 lbs. each serving = Batter Needed (7.2 lbs.)
3% Handling Loss = 7.2/0.97 = 7.42 lbs.
7.42 lbs. times each individual ingredient percent = Amount of each ingredient.

recipe using the percentage method. The end result is a brownie recipe for 60 portions at 0.12 lb. each.

Direct Reading Measurement Tables

The third method of recipe adjustment uses direct reading measurement tables. These tables have the advantage of being simple and quick to use, requiring no mathematical calculations. Tables have been developed for both measured and weighed ingredients.

Buchanan (1983) developed tables for adjusting weight and volume ingredients of recipes that are divisible by 25. Beginning with weights and measures

Table 10.5. *Excerpt from a direct reading table for adjusting weight ingredients of recipes divisible by 25*

25	50	75	100	200	300	400	500
5#	10#	15#	20#	40#	60#	80#	100#
5# 4 oz	10# 8 oz	15# 12 oz	21#	42#	63#	84#	105#
5# 8 oz	11#	16# 8 oz	22#	44#	66#	88#	110#
5# 12 oz	11# 8 oz	17# 4 oz	23#	46#	69#	92#	115#
6#	12#	18#	24#	48#	72#	96#	120#

Source: Buchanan, P. W.: *Quantity Food Preparation: Standardizing Recipes and Controlling Ingredients.* Chicago: Am. Dietet. A., 1983, p. 29.

for 25, incremental values are given in these tables for various magnitudes up to 500. Use of these tables will allow adjustment of recipes with a known yield in one of the amounts indicated at the top of the columns to desired yields that can be divided by 25. An excerpt from a direct reading table for adjusting weight ingredients of recipes is shown in Table 10.5 to illustrate the following example. The amount of ground beef needed for 225 portions, using a recipe designed to produce 100 portions, can be determined easily using the table. If the 100 portion recipe requires 21 pounds of beef, by following down the column for 100 portions to the point where 21 lb. is shown, then reading to the right for the amount for 200 portions and to the left for 25 portions, the total of 47 lb. 4 oz can be determined quickly.

Adapting Home-Size Recipes

Although good quantity recipes are more readily available today than was true previously, foodservice managers often prefer to develop their own formulations, rely on expertise of cooks who may prepare an item without a written recipe, or adjust a home-size recipe to quantity production. In a residence hall or school foodservice, students may bring recipes from home and request that items be prepared in the institution foodservice. A nursing home resident might have a favorite item and share the recipe with the cook as a possible selection for the menu.

Special considerations are necessary in adjusting a recipe designed for six to eight servings to an appropriate quantity for 100 servings or more. When expanding recipes from home to quantity size, the following suggestions are given.

• Know exactly what ingredients are used and in what quantity.

• Make the recipe in the original home-size quantity following procedures exactly, noting any unclear procedures or ingredient amounts.

• Evaluate the resulting product to determine if the recipe has potential for expansion if an acceptable product is produced.

Cinnamon Biscuits

COOKING TIME: 10-15 minutes   TEMPERATURE: 450°F

PORTION 2.50 oz	8 SERVINGS	50 SERVINGS	120 SERVINGS	150 SERVINGS
PAN SIZE:				
INGREDIENTS:				
flour white	1 1/2c 2T	2qt 2c	1gal 2qt	1gal 3 1/2qt
baking powder	1T 1/4t	1/3c 2T	1c	1 1/4c
salt	1/2t	2 1/2t	2T	2T 1 1/2t
cream of tartar	1/2t	2 1/2t	2T	2T 1 1/2t
sugar granulated	1 1/2t	3T 1t	1/2c	1/2c 2T
milk nf inst dry	3T 1/2t	1 1/4c	3c	3 3/4c
shortening veg	1/2c	3c	1qt 3 1/4c	2qt 1c
water	1/2c 1T	3 1/2c	2qt 1/3c	2qt 2 1/2c
sugar granulated	1/2c 2T	3 3/4c	2qt 1c	2qt 3 1/4c
cinnamon	2 1/2t	1/4c 1T	3/4c	3/4c 3T
margarine regular	1T 1 3/4t	1/2c 2T	1 1/2c	1 3/4c 2T
milk fl 2% fat	1T 1/2t	1/3c 2T	1c 1T	1 1/3c

(HANDLING LOSS   8.0%)

1. Mix flour baking powder, salt, cream of tartar, sugar and nonfat dry milk with mixer (low speed).
2. Add shortening. Mix until crumbly and coarse crumbs (low speed).
3. Add water all at once. Mix (low speed) to form soft dough. DO NOT OVERMIX. Dough should be as soft as can be handled.
4. Place dough on lightly floured board or table. (For larger quantities, divide dough in smaller portions). Knead lightly 15 - 20 times.
5. Roll dough to approximately 1/4 inch thickness in shape of rectangle.
6. Combine sugar, cinnamon, melted margarine and milk. Spread on dough-rectangle, going close to edges.
7. With french knife, cut dough into approximately 3" x 3 " squares.
8. Bring four corners to center and pinch together. Place in 2 inch deep baking pan, having biscuits close together and touching.
9. Biscuits may be held several hours in refrigerator until time to bake.
10. Bake just before serving until light brown (DO NOT OVERBAKE).
11. Serve warm.
ABBREVIATIONS:
nf = nonfat inst = instant veg = vegetable fl =fluid

Source: "Mom", Evelyn Larson, from Great-Grandma Larson

Micro Foodcare System
(700 -5) 06-14-84

Figure 10.9. *Example of a home style recipe adjusted using a microcomputer foodservice management system (used by permission of Noaleen Ingalsbe, R.D., consultant dietitian)*

• Proceed in incremental stages in expanding the recipe, keeping in mind the quality and appearance of the original product. Evaluate the quality at each stage and decide if modifications are necessary as the recipe is adjusted.

• Determine handling or cooking losses after increasing the recipe to an amount close to 100 servings; usually 5 to 8 percent loss is typical. The actual yield of the recipe should be checked carefully. Mixing, cooking, and preparation times should be noted, especially for producing the item in quantity, since these items often increase substantially for quantity production.

• Check the proportion of ingredients against a standard large quantity recipe for a product of similar type to assist in assessing balance of ingredients.

• Evaluate products using taste panels and clientele acceptance assessments before recipes are added to the permanent file, as discussed with standardized recipes.

Consultant dietitians have often found that cooks in small nursing homes and hospitals prefer to work with recipes adjusted from home-size recipes, rather than using recipes initially designed for quantity. As mentioned previously in this chapter, cooks in these small operations also tend to prefer recipes with measures stated in volume rather than in weights. An example of a home-size recipe for cinnamon biscuits, which was adapted to various yield quantities from an original recipe for eight servings, is shown in Figure 10.9. This recipe was generated from a data base compiled for a microcomputer-assisted foodservice management system that was developed by a consultant dietitian in Kansas.

Careful evaluation is important in adjusting home-size recipes to quantity production. Some recipes that are suitable for service at home are simply not practical to make in quantity because of the time constraints of large-scale operations. A common problem may be the extensive labor time required, which may make a product too costly for institutional or commercial foodservice operations.

SUMMARY

In the food production subsystem of a foodservice operation, ingredient control is a critical aspect of quality assurance. Control of ingredient assembly and utilization of standardized recipes adjusted to the appropriate quantity are the two key aspects of ingredient control. The process of ingredient control actually begins in the procurement subsystem and continues throughout prepreparation, production, and service. Controlling ingredient usage is a critical component of cost control in the foodservice system as well.

Centralized ingredient assembly is being implemented in many foodservice operations today as one way of controlling food and labor costs and increasing production control. By centralizing the simple tasks of collecting, assembling, and measuring ingredients, cooks' skills can be redirected to more complex production, garnishing, and portioning tasks. In computer-assisted operations, an ingredient room facilitates the necessary control of ingredients to ensure accurate information.

Location of the ingredient room is important to provide for efficient flow of food and supplies from storage to production areas. Equipment and personnel needs will vary, dependent on the functions performed in the centralized ingredient area. For example, if preparation is a function performed there, chopping, dicing, or slicing equipment will be needed and personnel assignments will be affected.

A recipe provides the basic formula for products to be prepared in the foodservice operation. As such, the recipe becomes a quantity and quality control tool constituting a standard for each menu item. A definite pattern or format should be used consistently for all recipes and each recipe should include general information such as name of food item, identification code, yield and portion size, type and amount of ingredients, and procedural information for production and service of the item. In many foodservice operations today, recipes are maintained in a data file of a computerized system.

Recipe standardization is the process of tailoring a recipe to a specific foodservice operation. Standardized recipes promote quantity and quality assurance for foods produced, save time of foodservice personnel, control costs by reducing waste and regulating inventories, simplify determination of menu item cost, and facilitate training of foodservice employees. In developing standardized recipes, careful testing and evaluation are important at each stage. Repeat batches of a recipe should be produced until at least three successful trials have consistently produced the quantity and quality desired.

Three methods have been developed for adjusting recipes: the factor method, the percentage method, and direct reading measurement tables. Often, foodservice managers may also use a home-size recipe as a basis for developing a recipe for quantity production. Special considerations are necessary in expanding recipes for six to eight servings to 100 portions or more. The recipes should be expanded in incremental stages, with evaluation of quality at each stage and modification as necessary. Some recipes suitable for home are simply not practical for quantity operations.

REFERENCES

Andrews, G. T., and Tuthill, B. H.: Computer-based management of dietary departments. *Hospitals* 42:117 (Jul. 16), 1968.

Bansal, A. K.: Ingredient control saves money. *Hospitals* 47:98 (Apr. 16), 1973.

Buchanan, P. W.: *Quantity Food Preparation.* Chicago: The American Dietetic Association, 1983.

Division of Alcoholism: *Nutrition Services Ingredient Room Manual.* New York: Office of Mental

Retardation and Developmental Disabilities, Office of Mental Health, Division of Alcoholism, 1981.

Dougherty, D. A.: Issue control and ingredient assembly systems. In Rose, J. C., ed.: *Handbook for Health Care Food Service Management.* Rockville, MD: Aspens Systems Corp., 1984.

Flack, K. E.: Central ingredient room simplifies food preparation and cuts cost. *Hospitals* 33:125 (Sept. 1), 1959.

Gelepi, M. J.: The computer and the ingredient room. *Food Mgmt.* 8:60 (Aug.), 1973.

Gisslen, W.: *Professional Cooking.* New York: John Wiley & Sons, 1983.

Knight, J. B., and Kotschevar, L. H.: *Quantity Food Production.* Boston: CBI Publishing Co., 1979.

McManis, H., and Molt, M.: Recipe standardization and percentage method of adjustment. *NACUFS J.* 35, 1978.

Mizer, D. A., and Porter, M.: *Food Preparation for the Professional.* San Francisco: Canfield Press, 1978.

Shugart, G. S., Molt, M. and Wilson, M.: *Food for 50.* 7th ed. New York: John Wiley & Sons, 1984.

Torrence, B. L., and Vaden, A. G.: EDP recipe adjustment by percentage method in college foodservice system. *J. Am. Dietet. A.* 69:407, 1976.

11

Quantity Food Production and Quality Control

Production of quality food in quantity involves a highly complex set of variables. The nature of quantity food production varies widely with type and size of operation and type of system. In Chapter 1, the wide range of foodservice operations was discussed from healthcare to schools to the many types of commercial operations. As discussed, the objectives of these organizations differ substantially, affecting every aspect of operation. The one-meal-a-day pattern of a school cafeteria, for example, presents a very different production problem from the 24-hour-a-day fast food operation. Since the menu is the basic plan for the foodservice system, planning in the food production subsystem depends on the menu item selections.

In Chapter 5, the four basic types of foodservice systems were described: conventional, commissary, ready prepared, and assembly/serve. In that chapter, we pointed out the differences in processing of foods used in these various types of systems. Obviously, those systems using completely prepared foods that require only thawing and heating prior to service have quite different production demands from the conventional systems in which foods with little or no processing are used for preparing foods from "scratch." This illustrates the relationship between the procurement and production subsystem. The type of foods brought into the system determines the type of production processes.

As stated in Chapter 9, quantity food production involves control of ingredients, production methods, quality of food, labor productivity, and energy consumption. Control of the production subsystem is critical to controlling costs in foodservice operations.

The foodservice manager must understand quantity food production and have basic skills in food preparation techniques and equipment operation. This technical expertise will enable the manager to perform competently in planning and evaluation of foodservice operations. As one expert in foodservice management stated, quantity food production is the "nuts and bolts" of the field.

The production subsystem involves the primary processes of transformation of resources into the goods and services of the operation. Chapter 9 presented the critical issues related to planning for production, which provides the basis for "putting the show on the road." The true test of the plan, however, is whether the food produced is acceptable to the clientele, is produced in the appropriate quantity, is microbiologically safe, and is within the budgetary constraints of the operation. To ensure this outcome requires development of product standards, control of all phases of operations, and evaluation at each stage.

Quantity is the element that introduces complexity to food preparation in the foodservice system. Producing food for even 100 requires much more careful planning and large scale equipment than does preparing food for a small group at home. In operations serving several thousand, the complexity is drastically increased. Large scale equipment and mechanized processes are requisites to producing the vast quantities of food to serve such an audience.

In this chapter, we will first outline the basic objectives of food production and methods of production. Development of product standards will then be discussed, as well as production controls for all phases of operation in the production subsystem.

OBJECTIVES OF FOOD PREPARATION

Basically food is cooked for three primary reasons.

- To destroy harmful microorganisms, thus making food safer for human consumption.
- To increase digestibility.
- To change and enhance the food's flavor, form, color, texture, and/or aroma, thereby increasing its aesthetic value.

First, cooking can destroy microorganisms. The amount of heat required to kill a particular microorganism depends on such factors as temperature, time, method, type of food, and type and concentration of the organism. Adequate cooking is a major factor in foodservice sanitation, but proper handling before and after cooking is another critical aspect of ensuring safe food. Quantity food sanitation will be discussed in Chapter 12 in more detail.

Many food substances become more digestible as a result of the cooking process and, thus, may also become more nutritious. For example, the protein in cooked meat is more digestible than that in raw meat. Raw starch in foods such as potatoes and flour will gelatinize during cooking or baking and become more digestible.

Although cooking makes certain foods more digestible, the nutrient value of other foods can be decreased, especially if improperly cooked. Vegetables, for example, are often handled improperly during prepreparation or production, thus causing vitamin or mineral loss. These nutrients may be leached out in the cooking water or oxidized in the cooking heat. The degree of loss is affected by the amount of water used, the length of cooking time, the cooking temperature, the length of time between prepreparation and production, and the amount of cut surface exposed. Proper attention to time and temperature control is important to preserving quality of food, especially the nutrient value. This discussion merely touches on many of the principles of food preparation. The foodservice manager should be well-grounded in concepts of food science in order to understand changes that occur in food during production and to be a "trouble shooter" when problems arise.

The aesthetic quality of food can be enhanced by cooking; however, food can also be ruined or be made less palatable by improper procedures. The quality of any cooked food depends primarily on four variables.

- Type and quality of raw ingredients.
- The recipe or formulation for the product.
- The expertise of the production personnel and techniques used in preparation.
- The method and duration of holding food items in all stages from procurement through service.

The first two variables have been discussed in Chapters 7, 8, and 10. The latter two are emphasized in this chapter.

Cookery may have the effect of enhancing and conserving the normal flavor, developing a particular flavor, or blending flavors, as in a sauce or soup. Conservation of color is another aesthetic objective in cooking food; for example, the color of overcooked vegetables can become dull and unappetizing as their texture and flavor also become less appealing.

The contrast in the acceptability of meat prepared properly or improperly provides another vivid example of the effect of cooking on the aesthetic quality of food—the juicy, flavorful quality of a properly broiled steak as compared to the dry, toughness of the overcooked one. Baked products are also affected greatly by improper preparation and cooking techniques; tenderness is affected by overmixing, and the effects of over- and under-baking are obvious.

These examples all point out the importance of adequate controls throughout the prepreparation, production, and service processes. Also, dependent upon the type of production/service system, the holding stage is another critical component affecting the aesthetic quality and acceptability of food.

METHODS OF PRODUCTION

A whole range of processes are involved in production of food for service. The preparation may be as simple as washing and displaying the food, such as fresh fruit, or as complex as the preparation of a lemon meringue pie. Production may include cooking, chilling, and freezing processes or some combination of them. The emphasis in this section will be on methods of quantity food cookery.

Cooking is a science, most closely related to the sciences of chemistry and physics. The properties of many ingredients used in food production cause reactions of various types, depending on various conditions. For example, baking powder reacts to give off carbon dioxide when exposed to moisture. An emulsion results from a combination of egg, liquid, and oil to produce mayonnaise.

Heat Transfer

Heat is the factor that causes many reactions to occur, and the type and amount of heat greatly affect the resulting product. Heat is transferred in three ways: conduction, convection, and radiation.

Conduction is the transfer of heat from one object or substance to another in direct contact with it. The medium of transfer can be solid, liquid, or gas. Metals as a group are good conductors; however, different metals conduct heat at different rates. For example, copper, iron, and aluminum are more effective conductors than is stainless steel. In cooking by conduction, the heat is first transferred from a heat source, usually gas flame or electric wire, through a secondary substance to food. Conduction is the dominant means of heat transfer in grilling, boiling, frying, and, to some degree, in baking and roasting. In pan broiling or grilling a steak, for example, the heat is transferred from the source to the pan or grill and then to the meat. In frying, the heat is transferred to the fat and then to the food.

Convection is the spreading of heat by the movement of air, steam, or liquid, and may be either natural or forced. Natural convection occurs from density or temperature differences within a mass of liquid or gas. The density differences cause hot air to rise and cool air to fall. Thus, in any oven, kettle of liquid, or deep fat fryer, a constant, natural circulation distributes heat.

Forced convection is caused by a mechanical device. In convection ovens and convection steamers, for example, fans speed the circulation of heat. Thus, heat is transferred more quickly to the food and the food cooks faster. Another means of achieving the convection effect is to circulate the food, as in a rotary oven in a bake shop, in which the shelves rotate much like a ferris wheel in an amusement park. Stirring is another form of forced convection whereby heat is redistributed, preventing concentration at the bottom of the container. For example, stirring is important in cooking a sauce, cream sauce, or pudding to speed up the cooking, but also to prevent scorching and burning.

Radiation is the transfer of energy by waves from the source to the food. The waves themselves are not actually heat energy but are changed into heat energy when they strike the food being cooked. Infrared and microwave are the two types of radiation used in food production. Broiling is the most familiar example of infrared cooking. In a broiler, an electric element, or a ceramic element heated by a gas flame, becomes so hot that it gives off infrared radiation, which cooks the food. High-intensity infrared ovens are designed to heat food even more rapidly. Infrared lamps are commonly used in foodservice operations for holding food at a temperature acceptable for service. For example, in restaurants, infrared lamps are frequently placed over the counter where cooks set the plates for pickup by the servers.

In microwave cooking, the radiation generated by the oven penetrates part of the way into the food, where it agitates water molecules. The friction resulting from this agitation creates heat, which in turn cooks the product. Since microwave radiation affects only water molecules, a waterless material will not heat up in a microwave oven. Thus, disposable plastic or paper plates can be used for heating or cooking some foods in a microwave oven. Since most microwaves penetrate only about two inches into food, heat is transferred to the center of large masses of food by conduction. Microwave cooking is not a predominant method in foodservice operations; however, microwave ovens are widely used for heating already prepared foods for service. For example, microwave units are frequently available in the galley on patients units in hospitals, and vending operations often have small microwave ovens for customers to use in heating sandwiches and soups.

Cooking Methods

Cooking methods are classified either as moist heat or dry heat. Moist heat methods are those in which the heat is conducted to the food product by water or steam. Dry heat methods are those in which the heat is conducted by dry air, hot metal, radiation, or hot fat. Different cooking methods are suitable for different kinds of food. For example, tender cuts of meat should be prepared using a dry heat method, whereas a tougher cut, such as that used for stew, should be cooked using moist heat.

In quantity food production, discussing cooking methods without discussing equipment is difficult, because of the close relationship between the two. Both are important components of cooking technology. In large measure, the type of equipment available dictates the choice of cooking methods. Almost every technical problem relating to cooking involves either the equipment or the method. The choices of equipment and cooking method are vital because of their effect on many aspects of daily operations, such as labor scheduling, productivity, product quality, speed of service, sanitation and maintenance, energy conservation, menu flexibility, and cost control.

The technology of cooking has become more complex over the last few decades, primarily because of innovations in equipment, including both increased efficiency and sophistication. Convection ovens and steamers, for example, are more efficient than their conventional counterparts. A pressure fryer is much faster than the regular open-type fryer, although it produces a somewhat different product. New cooking methodologies have been introduced by the increased sophistication of equipment, such as that in which two types of heat transfer are applied simultaneously. One example is a convection roasting oven with steam injection and another is equipment that simultaneously grills and broils.

As we discuss cooking methods, we will also discuss equipment, but only in a limited way. A glossary of equipment widely used in foodservice operations, adopted from a terminology listing of the Foodservice Consultants Society International (NRA, 1979), is included in Appendix D.

Moist Heat Methods

The most common moist heat methods of cooking are boiling, simmering, stewing, poaching, blanching, braising, and steaming. The cooking methods for several of them differ only slightly.

To boil, simmer, or poach means to cook a food in water or a seasoned liquid. The temperature of the liquid determines the method. To boil means to cook in a liquid that is boiling rapidly and is agitated greatly. Boiling is generally reserved for certain vegetables and starches. The high temperature toughens the proteins of meat, fish, and eggs, and the rapid movement breaks delicate foods.

Simmering or stewing means cooking in a liquid that is boiling gently, with the temperature at about 185 to 205°F. Most foods cooked in liquid are simmered, even though the word "boiled" may be used as a menu term, such as "Boiled Corned Beef and Cabbage." Simmering or stewing is frequently done in a steam-jacketed kettle (Figure 11.1).

To poach is to cook in a liquid, usually a small amount, that is hot but not actually bubbling. The temperature range is about 160 to 180°F. Poaching is used to cook delicate food, such as fish, eggs, or fruit.

Blanching means to cook an item partially and briefly, usually in water, although some foods, such as french fries, are blanched in hot fat. Two methods are used for blanching in water. To dissolve out blood, salt, or impurities from certain meats and bones, the item is placed in cold water, brought to a boil, simmered briefly, then cooled by plunging it in cold water. Blanching is also used to set the color of and destroy enzymes in vegetables or to loosen the skins of vegetables and fruits for easier peeling. For this latter purpose, the item is placed in rapidly boiling water and held until the water returns to a boil, then cooled in cold water.

Braising involves cooking food in a small amount of liquid, usually after preliminary browning. Braised meats are usually browned in a small amount of fat first, or sautéed, using a dry heat method, such as pan frying, which gives a desirable appearance and flavor to the product and sauce. Braising also refers to cooking at low temperature in a small amount of liquid, without first browning in fat, or with only light preliminary sautéing. Foods being braised are usually not

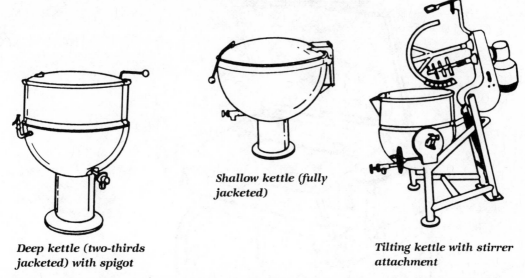

Shallow kettle (fully
jacketed)

Deep kettle (two-thirds
jacketed) with spigot

Tilting kettle with stirrer
attachment

Figure 11.1. *Three different types of steam-jacketed kettles (used by courtesy of CTX Division, Pet Inc., St. Louis, MO)*

covered by the cooking liquid. The liquid is often thickened before service by reducing the liquid over high heat rather than using a thickening agent. In some recipes for braised items, no liquid is added because the item cooks in its own moisture. Braising may be done on the range or in the oven, although today a covered tilting fry pan is frequently used, such as the one shown in Figure 11.2. Other terms describing the braising process are pot roasting, swissing, and fricasseeing.

To <u>steam</u> means to cook foods by exposing them directly to steam. In many foodservice operations, compartment and high-pressure steamers are being replaced by the convection steamer (Figure 11.3). Cooking in a steam-jacketed kettle is not steaming, because the steam does not actually touch the food. Steam-jacketed kettles are actually used for such cooking methods as stewing and simmering. In foodservice operations, steaming is most commonly used for vegetable preparation.

Dry Heat Methods

The major methods of cooking without liquid are roasting, baking, oven frying, broiling, grilling, barbecuing, and frying—including sautéing, pan frying, and deep frying.

Roasting and Baking. Cooking food by surrounding it with hot, dry air, usually in an oven, is referred to as roasting or baking. Generally, roasting is used to apply

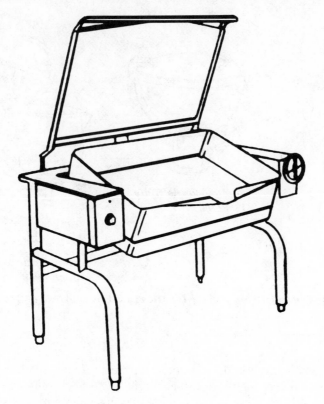

Figure 11.2. *Tilting braising pan (or tilting fry pan) (used by courtesy of CTX Division, Pet Inc., St. Louis, MO)*

to oven cooking of meat and poultry, whereas baking is frequently applied to desserts or bread. In roasting, cooking uncovered is essential. If the product is covered, the steam is held in, which changes the process from dry to moist heat cooking, such as braising or steaming.

The term "oven broiling" is sometimes used to refer to high-temperature cooking in an oven. Actually, the term "oven broiling" is a misnomer, since it is not true broiling. In this process, food such as steaks or hamburger patties is cooked on baking sheets in the oven, usually at temperatures of 400 to 450°F. Oven frying is a variation of oven broiling and involves placing food on greased pans and usually dribbling fat over it before baking in a hot oven. The resulting product is much like fried or sautéed food. These processes are frequently employed when broilers, grills, or deep fat fryers are not available or are inadequate to handle the production demand. These methods are used most often in large healthcare operations or other large institutional foodservices.

Baking or roasting uses a combination of all three modes of heat transfer: conduction, convection, and radiation. In other words, heat is transferred through the pan to the food, heat is transferred by moving currents of air, either natural or forced and heat also emanates from the hot walls of the cooking chamber.

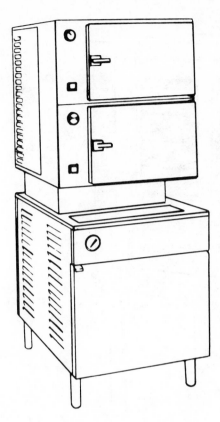

Figure 11.3. *Pressureless convection steamer (used by courtesy of CTX Division, Pet Inc., St. Louis, MO)*

A wide range of types of ovens are used in foodservice operations. The three main categories are hot air ovens, infrared broilers, and microwave ovens. Several types of hot air ovens are in use: range, deck, forced convection, conveyor, reel ovens, and low-temp roasters. Infrared broilers and microwave ovens were discussed in the heat transfer section of this chapter.

The range oven is one that is part of an institutional range and is generally seen in small operations. The deck oven has traditionally been the standby of hot air ovens in foodservice operations, so named because the oven pan is usually placed directly on the metal deck. The cooking chambers vary in size, depending on the intended use, roasting or baking. Deck ovens may be stacked on each other, up to three sections high, and are frequently called stack or sectional ovens. Most deck or stack ovens in use today have a separate heat source under each cooking chamber, although older models have only one heat source at the bottom of the stack. A major problem with deck ovens is fluctuation in temperature.

A newer type of hot air oven is the convection oven, or one in which a fan creates currents of air within the cooking chamber. This process eliminates hot and cold air zones within the chamber, thereby speeding up the rate of heat transfer. The convection oven has three major advantages over the traditional

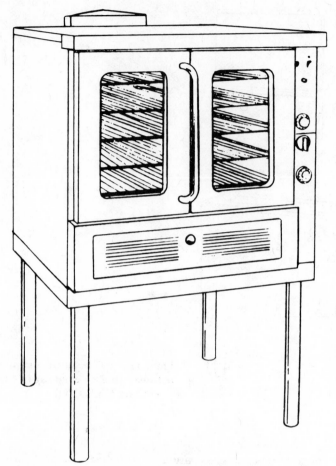

Figure 11.4. *Forced convection oven (used by courtesy of CTX Division, Pet Inc., St. Louis, MO)*

range oven. It accommodates two to three times as much food per oven space, reduces cooking time by 30 to 40 percent, and cooks at 40 to 50°F lower temperature, thus conserving energy.

The standard convection oven is the square cabinet type that holds between 6 to 11 full-size baking pans and can be double-stacked to conserve floor space. An example is shown in Figure 11.4. Another type of convection oven is the roll-in rack oven (Figure 11.5). It works on the same principle as the cabinet type convection oven, but accommodates 18 or 20 full-size baking pans. The rack can be rolled into the oven on casters.

Conveyor and reel ovens are variations of ovens with moving shelves. In a conveyor oven, pans of food are loaded onto a belt that is moved through the oven. Reel ovens contain six or more shelves that move around as a merry-go-

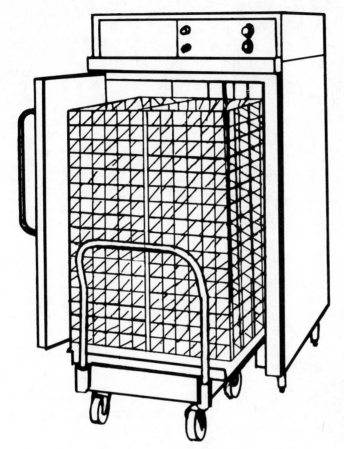

Figure 11.5. *Roll-in rack oven (used by courtesy of CTX Division, Pet Inc., St. Louis, MO)*

round or as a ferris wheel and can hold six to sixty or more bun pans 18 by 26 inches in size. These ovens are used mainly in very large operations, usually in large bake shops or commercial bakeries.

The increased product yield of meats roasted at low temperatures over longer than usual periods of time has led to the development of low-temp roasting ovens (Figure 11.6). These ovens are generally mounted on wheels and are most frequently used in catering operations.

Broiling. Cooking by radiant heat is broiling. The food is placed on a rack either below or in between the heat sources, which can be gas or electric. Generally, broilers are preheated and food is dipped in oil or another fat to prevent sticking and reduce moisture loss. Food is placed three to six inches from the heat source, depending upon the type and intensity of the heat. The temperature required depends on the fattiness, tenderness, or size of the food. Traditional broilers lack precise temperature controls and foods must be closely monitored during the cooking process. Some new types of equipment, however, such as conveyorized

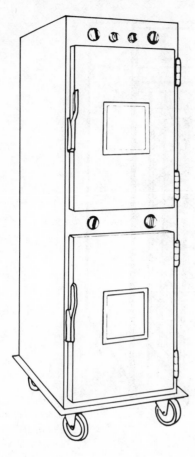

Figure 11.6. *Low-temp roaster oven (used by courtesy of CTX Division, Pet Inc., St. Louis, MO)*

infrared broilers (Figure 11.7), give more flexibility and control over the broiling process.

Charbroiling has become popular in many foodservice operations, especially in steak houses and fast food hamburger establishments. Most charbroilers (Figure 11.8) in use in foodservice operations use either gas or electricity as a heat source, with a bed of ceramic briquettes above the heat source and below the grate. A distinctive feature of charbroiling is the flavor it imparts to the food, which is caused by the fat and juice dripping onto the hot briquettes, vaporizing into smoke, and then contacting the food. Technically, since the heat source in charbroiling is from below, it is a grilling and not a broiling method.

Grilling. Grilling, griddling, and pan broiling are all dry heat cooking methods that use heat from below. Grilling is done on an open grid over a heat source, which may be an electric element, a gas-heated element, or charcoal. Griddling is done on a solid cooking surface called a griddle (Figure 11.9), with or without

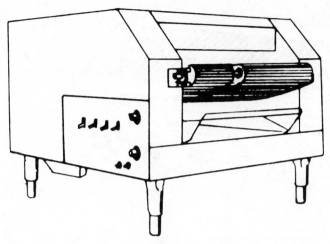

Figure 11.7. *Conveyor broiler (used by courtesy of CTX Division, Pet Inc., St. Louis, MO)*

small amounts of fat. In addition to meats, eggs and pancakes are frequently cooked on a griddle. Pan broiling is similar to griddling except that it is done in a sauté pan or skillet instead of on a griddle surface. Fat should be poured off as it accumulates, or the process becomes pan frying.

Barbecuing. Real barbecuing is roasting in a covered pit. In ovens, it is a dry heat method using broiling or grilling while basting with a special sauce. Specialized ovens have been developed to duplicate the pit process and introduce smoke that gives special flavor to the product being cooked (Figure 11.10). Temperatures are kept quite low in both oven and pit barbecuing. Charbroiling requires a higher temperature and charbroiled meats basted with a sauce are considered to be barbecued.

Frying. Frying is cooking in a fat or oil. The dry heat methods using fat include sautéing, pan frying, and deep frying. To sauté means to cook quickly in a small amount of fat. The pan should be preheated before adding food and not overcrowded. Otherwise, the food will begin to simmer in its own juices. Meats are often dusted with flour to prevent sticking and help achieve uniform browning. After a food is sautéed, wine or stock is frequently added to dissolve brown bits of food clinging to the sides or bottom of the pan, a process called deglazing. Generally, this liquid is used in a sauce served with the sautéed item. Sautéing is commonly used in restaurants featuring French and northern Italian food.

Pan frying involves cooking food in a moderate amount of fat in a pan over a moderate amount of heat. While pan frying is similar to sautéing, it uses more fat

Figure 11.8. *Electric and gas char-broilers (used by courtesy of CTX Division, Pet Inc., St. Louis, MO)*

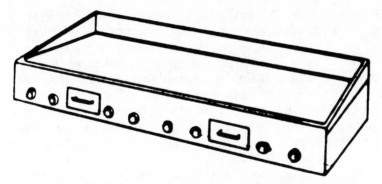

Figure 11.9. *Griddle (used by courtesy of CTX Division, Pet Inc., St. Louis, MO)*

Figure 11.10. *Example of special equipment for barbecuing (The Little Red Smokehouse, Model 250FS), used by permission of J & R Manufacturing, Mesquite, TX)*

and requires a longer cooking time. This method is used for larger pieces of food, such as chops or chicken pieces. Pan frying is not used widely in foodservice operations, except as an initial step for a braised or fricasseed product.

In deep frying, food is submerged in hot fat. A well-prepared deep fried product should have minimum fat absorption, minimum moisture loss, attractive golden color, crisp surface or coating, and no off-flavors imparted by the frying fat. Foods for deep fat frying are dipped in a breading or batter that provides a protective coating and helps give the product crispness, color, and flavor. Obviously, the type and quality of the breading and batter affect the quality of a finished product.

Tremendous improvement has been made in deep fat frying equipment for foodservice operations. Today, solid state electronics monitor the cooking cycle and control cooking temperature in modern deep fat fryers (Figure 11.11). Two of the most important new developments in frying technology are precise thermostatic control and fast recovery of fat temperature, permitting foodservice operations to produce consistent quality fried food rapidly. Fryers may be gas or electric and are much more easily cleaned than earlier models. Automatic basket lifts, fat temperature sensors, and computer-controlled cooking timers permit production of high quality food.

The most recent development in frying concepts is the pressure fryer. A pressure fryer can be described as one with an air-tight lid that fastens securely over the kettle before frying (Figure 11.12). The fryer develops steam from moisture escaping from the food. The pressurized steam creates an equilibrium of pressures between the steam within the food and the fat on the outside, thus minimizing moisture loss. The fat is pushed into closer contact with the food

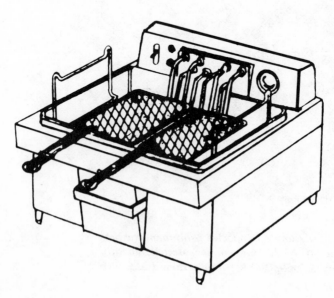

Figure 11.11. *Open-top fryer, table model (used by courtesy of CTX Division, Pet Inc., St. Louis, MO)*

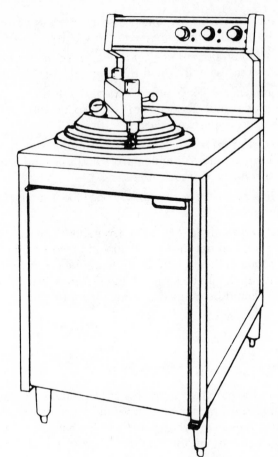

Figure 11.12. *Pressure fryer (used by courtesy of CTX Division, Pet Inc., St. Louis, MO)*

surface, which reduces cooking time. The general turbulence in the oil during frying also speeds cooking time. Pressurized fryers are used most frequently in chicken operations.

Deep fat frying equipment is an important variable in the quality of deep fried foods. The procedures, however, also are critically important to production of high quality products. The primary guidelines for deep frying are the following.

- *Fry at proper temperature.* Too low temperatures cause greasiness, while too high temperatures will result in a too brown outside and undercooked inside.

- *Don't overload the baskets.* Overloading will cause fat temperatures to fall too drastically, cause foods to stick together, and result in uneven browning.

- *Use good quality fat with high smoke point.*   Poor quality fat breaks down quickly at the high temperatures required for deep fat frying.

- *Replace about 10 to 20 percent of the fat with fresh fat before each daily use.*   Following this process will extend the frying life of the fat.

- *Change fat periodically.*   The length of time that fat can be used will vary depending on the extent and frequency of use. Old fat loses frying ability, browns excessively, and imparts off-flavors.

- *Avoid frying strongly and mildly flavored foods in the same fat.*   Strongly flavored foods will impart unacceptable flavors and make other foods unacceptable, such as fish-flavored french fries.

- *Fry as close to time of service as possible.*   Fried foods do not hold up well and become soggy quickly.

- *Take care of fat to prolong its life.*   The fryer should be turned off or the temperature lowered when not in use and should be covered between uses. Excess moisture should be removed from foods before frying and loose crumbs shaken off. Fat should be strained and skimmed frequently. Baskets and the kettle well should be cleaned thoroughly on a regular basis.

PRODUCT STANDARDS

Standards are a result of the managerial process of planning. In the discussion in Chapter 4 on the managerial function of controlling, we stated that these standards define the measurement of what we expect to happen. They therefore provide the control basis for monitoring performance of the organization and taking corrective action deemed necessary.

The word "quality" is often used in combination with standards and is central to the traditional statement of the objective of a foodservice: the production of the highest possible quality food. This leads to the difficult problem of defining quality.

As pointed out by David (1979), perhaps quality is a fancy name for whatever one likes. She contends that quality tells you where you ought to go; its physical properties are measurable in relation to standards developed for defining quality. But quality itself—excellence, worth, goodness—is difficult to measure. Improvement of any condition will be made by individuals making quality decisions.

As stated in Chapter 2, we prefer to define the objective of a foodservice somewhat differently, as the production of food to satisfy the expectations, desires, and needs of the customers, clients, or patients of a particular foodservice. The primary quality attributes of this food are nutritional, microbiologic, and sensory. Controls must be exercised throughout the procurement/production/service cycle to maintain them. Drastic changes in the preparation of food are forcing foodservice managers to use new approaches to maintain quality and standards and yet continue to meet the needs of society. As David (1979) points out, the nutritional effects of current methods of food production, processing, preparation, and distribution of varied and changing consumer preferences and demands, and of the increasing time lapse between the preparation and distribution of food to the consumer are critical and must be monitored.

Quality must also be defined with regard to the values and goals of individual situations and under varying circumstances. David (1979) defines quality food very simply as that which is satisfying to the consumer, as well as nutritious and safe. This acceptability varies widely with the type of situation and of foodservice operation. We gave an example in Chapter 2 contrasting the varying expectations of a customer when eating at a lunch counter and at a private dinner club. The quality of food that the customer expects in these two situations is quite different.

Although the consumer's interpretation of quality is certainly important in the foodservice operation, quality can also be defined from a scientific standpoint. Thorner and Manning (1983) state that the analyst or technologist refers to quality as an index or measurement obtained by grading or classifying a product's chemical and physical characteristics in accordance with explicit, predetermined specifications. The essential elements that must be evaluated in establishing the quality of a product are flavor, texture, appearance, consistency, palatability, nutritional value, safety, ease of handling, convenience, storage stability, and packaging.

Thorner and Manning (1983) conclude that there are two dominant factors in the evaluation of quality.

- The actual chemical or physical measurement of the product.
- The acceptance of the product by consumers based on whether it will fulfill their wants with complete satisfaction.

In addition, management will be concerned with the relation of quality to cost and profit, in particular to cost of the product, profits generated, and consumer acceptance in relation to selling price.

Many factors are responsible for poor quality food, among them poor sanitation, improper handling, malfunctioning equipment, incorrect prepreparation or preparation, and carelessness. Thorner and Manning (1983) compiled the following list of the prime factors responsible for significant quality changes.

- Spoilage due to microbiological, biochemical, physical, or chemical factors.
- Adverse or incompatible water conditions.
- Poor sanitation and ineffective warewashing.
- Improper and incorrect precooking, cooking, and postcooking methods.
- Incorrect temperatures.
- Incorrect timing.
- Wrong formulations, stemming from incorrect weight of the food or its components.
- Poor machine maintenance program.

- Presence of vermin and pesticides.
- Poor packaging.

Any of these factors, either singly or in combination, will contribute to poor quality and cause changes affecting food's flavor, texture, appearance, and consistency.

The management of a foodservice operation should define the quality standards appropriate to a particular operation. In Chapter 7, we gave an example of specifications for the type of steak that would be purchased for several different types of restaurants. Such an example provided an excellent illustration of the need to define quality in relation to the objectives of a specific foodservice.

In Figure 11.13, a typical menu for a university residence hall foodservice is given, along with the quality standards for evaluating each of the menu items. The presumption is made that the items will be prepared using a standardized

---

Menu:

Meat Loaf
Au Gratin Potatoes
German Carrots
Lettuce Wedge—Choice of Dressings
Oatmeal Rolls—Butter
Peach Crisp

Standards for Menu Items

Meat Loaf.   The meat should be an even brown throughout and darker brown on top. The texture should be moist and firm, but not tough or compact. There should be onion flavor with beef predominate. The product should be loaf shaped and each serving should hold its shape.

Au Gratin Potatoes.   The surface should possess a soft, light yellow sheen with areas slightly browned. Au gratin potatoes should hold its shape when served with the cheese sauce thick enough to cling to the potatoes. The potatoes should be uniform in size, tender but firm. Cheese sauce should be smooth and velvety with a light yellow color.

German Carrots.   The flavor of nutmeg should be prevalent but not strong to distinguish it from plain buttered carrots. Carrots should have a mildly sweet flavor and be in the form of uniform, bite-sized coins.

Oatmeal Rolls.   The color should be an even brown. The crust should have a slightly pebbly appearance. The crumb should be soft and moist. The roll should have been proofed sufficiently and should be light with a light yeast fragrance. The flavor should be pleasant, with a slightly sweet nut-like taste.

Fruit Crisp.   A crisp should have a crisp, crunchy top covering tender fruit filling. Topping should be a delicate brown and have a crumbly texture. Topping should be evenly distributed over fruit. The filling should be smooth in consistency and thickening should be clear. Fruit and filling may flow from underneath topping, but should not be soupy, neither should the filling be gummy or pasty. Each fruit piece should be its natural color and recognizable form. Flavor should be moderately sweet and characteristic of the fruit.

Figure 11.13. *Example of quality standards for a typical dinner menu in a university residence hall foodservice.*

recipe that defines the ingredient amounts, precise production methods, product yield, and serving directions. Too frequently, foodservice managers have failed to define standards of quality for menu items, and therefore the basis for control and evaluation is not available. In Appendix C, the product standards developed for many of the menu items for a university food service are included. These standards are good examples of the efforts of a management team to define quality for foodservice operations.

In the rest of this chapter, various types of production controls that affect the nutritional value, microbiological quality, and acceptability of foods will be discussed. Chapter 12 focuses on sanitation principles in quantity food production.

PRODUCTION CONTROLS

Control is the process of ensuring that plans have been followed. Therefore, the essence of control is comparing what we set out to do with what we did, and taking any necessary corrective action. As a review of the discussion on control in Chapter 4, the following three steps are parts of this function.

- Measuring current performance and comparing it with established standards.
- Analyzing deviations between performance and standards and determining whether or not the deviations are within acceptable limits.
- Taking action to correct unacceptable deviations.

While definition of standards is an important prerequisite for effective control, supervision of operations and personnel is critical to the action of control. Control has not been effected, though, until appropriate corrective action has been implemented if deviations are not acceptable.

In essence, then, quality control means assuring day-in, day-out consistency in each product offered for service. Quantity control, simply stated, means producing the exact amount—no more, no less. They are both directly related to control of costs and thus to profit in a commercial operation or to meeting budgetary constraints in a non-profit establishment. Under- and overproduction create managerial problems and impact on cost. Temperature and time, product yield, portion control, and product evaluation all relate directly to quality, quantity, and cost control.

Temperature and Time Controls

Time and temperature are critical elements in quantity food production and must be controlled to produce a high quality product.

Temperature is recognized as the common denominator for producing the correct degree of doneness. To assure this degree, temperature gradations vary dramatically for different food categories, depending on the physical and chemical changes that occur as food components reach certain temperatures. When foods are subjected to heat, their physical state is altered as moisture is lost. Chemical changes are complex and differ greatly among various food products. For example, heat alters the structure of meat proteins, causing a reduction in acidity.

The proper control of temperature is often dependent on thermostats, which control temperature automatically and precisely. In modern heating and refrigeration equipment, thermostats are either preset by the manufacturer or hand-operated. They should be checked periodically to determine if they are functioning properly. A well-designed thermostat should not be affected by changes in ambient temperatures, but should respond quickly to internal temperature changes, be designed to operate within a narrow range, and be constructed for easy cleaning and adjustment.

Standardized recipes should state temperatures for baking and roasting. Figure 11.14 shows the temperatures commonly used in food production, in both centigrade and fahrenheit. Charts should be developed for cooking times, and

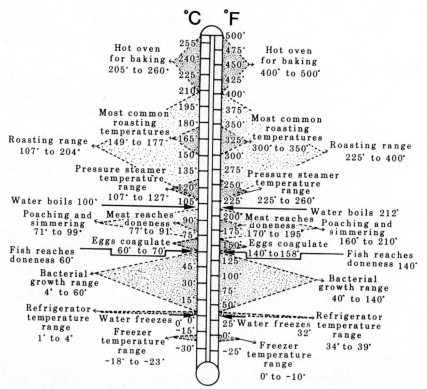

Figure 11.14. *Centigrade and Fahrenheit thermometer showing temperatures commonly used in the kitchen.* **Source: Mizer, D. A., and Porter, M.: Food Preparation for the Professional.** *San Francisco: Canfield Press, 1978, p. 88.*

Table 11.1. *Interior temperatures of cooked meats*

Meat	Rare	Medium	Well done
Beef	140°F (60°C)	160°F (71°C)	170°F (77°C)
Lamb	140–150°F (60–66°C)[a]	160°F (71°C)	170°F (77°C)
Veal	—	—	170°F (77°C)
Pork	—	—	165–175°F (74–79°C)[b]

Source: Gisslen, W.: *Professional Cooking.* New York, John Wiley & Sons, 1983, p. 191.

[a] Lamb is infrequently cooked rare. Most customers prefer lamb cooked medium.

[b] Recommended temperatures for pork have been lowered. It is no longer considered necessary to cook pork to 185°F (85°C) to eliminate the danger of trichinosis.

temperatures for cooked items on the menu and end-point cooking temperatures should be specified for various products, as appropriate. For example, the degree of doneness for meat is best stated in terms of end-point temperature.

Various types of thermometers are needed for determining end-point temperatures or for checking the temperature of foods being held. A meat thermometer, for example, should be used to determine the internal temperature of meat. The chart in Table 11.1 shows the internal temperatures of meats at three levels of doneness: rare, medium, and well done. In meat cookery, however, carry-over cooking must be taken into account, especially for large cuts of meat. Carry-over cooking means that the internal temperature of the meat will continue to rise even after the meat is removed from the oven. This phenomenon occurs because the outside of the roasting meat is hotter than the inside, and heat continues to be conducted into the meat until the heat is equalized throughout the piece.

The second most important factor in cooking is time. Timing is a critical element in all stages of food production and service. Excess moisture loss will occur in most products even if the temperature is correct, but the cooking time is extended. Various types of timing devices are available to assist in the control of time in food production processes, some of which are controlled manually, others automatically. Most food production equipment today has timing devices as an integral part of its construction.

Time and temperature are closely related elements in cooking. Some foods can be cooked at lower temperatures for a longer period of time to achieve the desired degree of doneness; others should be cooked at higher temperatures for a shorter time—for example, prime rib roast as opposed to a strip steak.

Heat transfer by any of the methods discussed previously in this chapter are also closely related to time. The integral nature of time-temperature relationships is perhaps best illustrated with baked products in which accurate timing and temperature control are critical in producing high quality products. For example, a cake baked at too high a temperature will cook too quickly on the outside before the leavening gas has developed inside the cake. As a result, the cake will crack and become too firm before the cake is done internally.

Timing becomes important in various other phases of food production. As pointed out in the discussion of deep fat frying, foods fried too long in advance of service will become soggy and unacceptable. Batch cooking, sometimes called "cooking to the line," is often used in quantity food production to avoid such problems.

In batch cookery, the estimated quantity needed is divided into smaller quantities, placed in pans ready for final cooking or heating, and then cooked as needed. The obvious advantages are that fresher food is served because it is not held as long and that fewer leftovers result because food is only cooked as needed. The example below is a time schedule worked out for steaming rice for the dinner meal in a university residence hall foodservice. It illustrates the way in which production can be scheduled to meet the demand throughout the meal service time while ensuring that a fresh product is being served.

Buttered Rice (800 servings)
Steam at 5# Pressure, 30 min uncovered

Time	Quantity[a]
3:30 pm	1 pan
3:45 pm	1 pan
4:00 pm	2 pans
4:30 pm	4 pans
4:45 pm	2 pans

[a] 4# rice/12 × 20 × 4 in. pan = 80 servings, 10 pans = 800 servings.

This type of time schedule can be attached to the master production schedule for various menu items.

The modern high-speed equipment available today, such as pressure steamers and convection ovens, has made batch cookery feasible for a broader range of menu items. Grilled, deep fried, and broiled items are obvious examples of products that should be cooked in small quantities to meet service demands. Vegetables are also frequently prepared using batch cookery because many vegetables do not hold up well in a heated serving counter. In Figure 11.15, guidelines are given for batch cookery of vegetables.

Product Yield

Yield is the amount of product resulting at the completion of the various stages of the procurement/production/service cycle and is usually expressed as a definite weight, volume, or serving size. For most foods, losses in volume or weight occur in each stage of the procurement/production/service cycle, even though a few foods, such as rice and pasta, increase in volume during production. The extent of loss from prepreparation depends on the type of food purchased. For instance, a limited amount of loss results when peeled rather than unpeeled potatoes are purchased for preparing buttered parsley potatoes.

In addition to losses during prepreparation, losses may occur during actual production, in portioning or in panning for baking. Cooking losses also account

Procedure

1 Steamers and small tilting trunnion kettles behind the service line are the most useful kind of equipment for vegetable batch cooking.

2 Divide each vegetable into batches small enough to be served within 20 to 30 minutes. Arrange in steamer pans ready to be placed in steamers, or in containers ready for pouring into the kettles.

3 Keep the prepped vegetables in the cooler until needed.

4 Cook batches as needed. In planning, allow time for loading and unloading the equipment, for cooking, for finishing the product with desired seasoning, sauce, or garnish, and for carrying to the serving line.

5 Undercook slightly if the vegetable must be held before serving.

6 Have all your seasonings, sauces, and garnishes ready for finishing the dish.

7 Do not mix batches. They will be cooked to different degrees, and colors and textures will usually not match.

Figure 11.15. *Procedure for batch cookery of vegetables.* **Source:** *Gisslen, W.:* **Professional Cooking.** *New York: John Wiley & Sons, 1983, p. 366.*

for decrease in yield of many foods, primarily because of moisture loss. As discussed previously in this chapter, the time and temperature used for cooking a menu item will affect the yield.

Handling loss occurs not only during production but also during portioning for service. McManis and Molt (1978) state that handling losses must be considered in determining desired yield. They point out that cooking and handling loss may vary from 1 to 30 percent, depending on the product being produced and served. In the brownie recipe included in Chapter 10 to illustrate the percentage method of recipe adjustment, a 3 percent handling loss was reported.

Obviously, when preparing food in quantity, these losses can have a cumulative impact on the number of portions available for service from a recipe and must be considered when estimating production demand. Total yield and number of portions should be stated in a standardized recipe, taking into account changes in yield that occur from as purchased (AP) to edible portion (EP) to serving yield.

Considerable work has been done on food yields at different stages of preparation. The most widely used resource is a USDA booklet published in 1975 (Matthews and Garrison, 1975). Work continues to be done at the USDA (Matthews, 1976), as the classic Agriculture Handbook No. 8 (Watt and Merrill, 1963) is being revised, and computerized data bases of food items are being expanded.

As Matthews (1976) points out, accurate yield data are important for estimating food costs, preparing food buying guides, requisitioning food supplies, and calculating nutrient composition of foods served. Technological developments in production on the farm and the many technological developments in all stages of processing, however, affect yield before food reaches the foodservice operation. Matthews (1976) identifies three major problems in determining and reporting accurate yield data.

- Lack of adequate description of samples.
- Lack of adequate description of preparation procedures.
- Lack of standard procedures for determining yield of foods.

Developments in foodservice equipment and cooking procedures also affect food yield, making previously published data less accurate. For example, we mentioned the moisture loss from pressurized deep fat frying earlier in this chapter. Matthews (1976) reports results of studies on shrimp, meat patties, and baked potatoes, showing the difference in yield using different cooking methods. As shown from the data in Tables 11.2, 11.3, and 11.4, cooking method can have a major impact on resultant yield. For example, a potato baked with foil resulted in 94 percent yield by weight compared to a 76 percent yield by weight for one baked without the foil wrapping.

In addition to the resources listed in the foregoing discussion, a number of other publications provide information on product yield. The <u>Food Buying Guide</u> published by the USDA for use in school foodservice programs provides data on AP amounts for 100 servings, as specified in the school lunch menu pattern, to

Table 11.2. *Percent yield by weight of shrimp cooked by two methods*

Size of shrimp	Method 1*	Method 2†
no./lb.	%	%
21–25	62	53
26–30	61	54
31–35	61	50
36–40	62	46
41–45	55	52

*Raw shrimp shelled and deveined before being boiled.

†Raw shrimp boiled before being shelled and deveined.

Table 11.4. *Percent yield by weight of potato baked by two methods*

Cultivar	Method 1*	Method 2†
	%	%
Irish Cobbler	83	97
Katahdin	77	95
Russet Burbank	76	94

*Baked in 204°C. (400°F.) oven, skin rubbed with oil.

†Baked in 204°C. (400°F.) oven, skin covered with aluminum foil.

Table 11.3. *Percent yield by weight of meat patties cooked by two methods to an internal temperature of 71°C. (160°F.)*

Type of ground beef and analyzed fat content	Method 1*	Method 2†
	%	%
regular or hamburger, 29% fat	75	72
lean or chuck, 25% fat	78	76
extra lean or round, 19–20% fat	85	80

*Cooked on grill preheated to 204°C. (400°F.).

†Baked in oven at 204°C. (400°F.).

Source: Matthews, R. H.: Guidelines for determining and reporting food yields. *J. Am. Dietet. A.* 69:398, 1976.

assist food buyers in planning amounts to purchase. Food for Fifty (Shugart et al., 1984), a widely used quantity recipe book, includes data on yield from AP amounts of food, as do a number of other quantity food production books. More limited data are available, however, on handling losses during production and service of food. Foodservice operations should perform studies to determine these data in order to have accurate information on production and service yields. In computer-assisted management information systems, data on yields from purchase to service are especially important in order for the computer to produce reliable information for ordering, recipe adjustment, production planning, cost, and nutrient composition of food items.

Portion Control

Portion control is one of the essential controls in production of food in quantity. In essence, it is the achievement of uniform serving sizes, important not only for control of cost but also for customer satisfaction. The clientele of any foodservice establishment are concerned about value received for price paid and may be dissatisfied if portions are not consistent for each patron. In a commercial cafeteria, for example, if the person in front of you is served a larger portion of spaghetti and beef, you may feel you have been treated unfairly, even though your portion may be adequate to satisfy your appetite. Not uncommonly, the customer will select the largest piece of cake or pie from a buffet service counter.

Achieving portion control results from following well-defined steps, beginning with the purchase of food according to definite specifications that are sufficiently detailed and accurate to assure that the food purchased will yield the expected number of servings. Frequently, products are ordered by count or number, with a definite size indicated. For example, for swiss steak, the food buyer may order portion cuts of round steak cut four per pound, four ounces per portion. Another specific way in which purchasing can control portion size is buying in individual serving sizes. Examples are individual boxes of cereal, butter and margarine pats, individually packaged crackers, and condiment packets.

The next step in portion control is the development and use of standardized recipes, which were discussed in Chapter 10. A standardized recipe will include information on total number of portions to be produced from the recipe and the size of portions to be served. Following recipe procedures carefully during pre-preparation, production, and service is critical, however, to ensuring that the correct number of portions will result. For example, cooking a roast at too high a temperature will result in excess moisture loss and decreased yield.

Another aspect of portion control is knowing the size and yield of all pans, ladles, and dishers and stating the specific small equipment needed in each standardized recipe during production and service. In such specifications, the terms disher, scoop, and dipper are commonly used for the same tool. Employees must use the appropriate equipment.

In Table 11.5, the approximate yield and typical uses for various sizes of dishers and ladles are given. A number is commonly used to indicate the size of a disher, which specifies the number of disher scoops per quart when leveled off.

Table 11.5. *Approximate yield for disher and ladle sizes*

Size	Use	Grams	Ounces	Teaspoons	Tablespoons	Cups
Dishers						
No. 6	Main dish salads	170	6	36	12	⅔
No. 8	Meat patties, casseroles	114	4	24	8	½
No. 10	Meat patties, cereals	92	3¼	19½	6½	⅜
No. 12	Salads, vegetables, croquettes	76	2⅔	14	4⅔	⅓
No. 16	Muffins, desserts	57	2	12	4	¼
No. 20	Sandwich fillings, desserts	42	1½	10	3⅓	
No. 24	Sandwich fillings, muffins	38	1⅓	8	2⅔	
No. 30	Large drop cookies	28.35	1	6	2	⅛
No. 40	Medium-drop cookies	23	⅖	5	1⅗	
No. 60	Small-drop cookies	15	½	3	1	1/16
Ladles						
1 oz	Sauces, relishes	28.35	1	6	2	⅛
2 oz	Sauces, gravy	57	2	12	4	¼
4 oz	Vegetables	114	4	24	8	½
6 oz	Chili, baked and creamed foods	170	6	36	12	¾
8 oz	Soups, chili, stews	227	8	48	16	1
12 oz	Large soups, goulash	340	12	72	24	1½
24 oz	Kitchen dipper	681	24	144	48	3
32 oz	Quart dipper	907	32	192	64	4
Demiliter	Kitchen dipper	500	17½	105	35	2 3/16
Liter	Liter dipper	1000	35	210	70	4⅜

Adapted from Margaret E. Terrell, *Large Quantity Recipes.* Philadelphia, PA: J. B. Lippincott Co., 1975.

For example, a level measure of a No. 6 disher yields 6 servings per quart, each portion measuring about two-thirds cup. Dishers are frequently used during production, to ensure consistent size for such menu items as meatballs, drop cookies, and muffins, and also during service to ensure correct serving size.

Ladles are used for portioning liquid or semi-liquid foods, such as gravies, soups, and cream dishes. Generally, the number of ounces a ladle will hold is marked on the handle. The one-ounce ladle dips two tablespoons, whereas a six-ounce ladle holds three-fourths cup.

A spoon is often used for serving various foods, but makes portion control much more difficult. Servers should be trained to weigh the appropriate portion of a menu item served with a spoon to establish a visual image of the correct serving size. Periodically, during the serving period, the server should weigh a typical portion as a check on accuracy. Recently, a new tool has been developed, called a spoodle, which is a spoon with a bowl (Figure 11.16). This tool permits better portion control than a regular serving spoon.

A variety of other tools are available to assist in consistent portioning of menu items. In Figure 11.16, the spoodle and some other typical pieces of small equipment for portioning are shown. One tool is the pie marker, which simplifies the cutting of pie into equal size wedges. Expandable cutters such as the ones shown are frequently used for cutting foods prepared in large pans, such as gelatin

Spoodles (used by courtesy of Vollrath Co., Sheboygan, WI)

Biscuit cutter (used by courtesy of Moline Co., Duluth, MN)

Figure 11.16. *Various tools for portion control*

salads, sheet cakes, or bar cookies. These products can be cut in exact sizes by rolling through the food with evenly-spaced wheels that have been preset to yield an exact number of portions per pan. This technique not only results in standard portion sizes but also speeds up the portioning process.

Perhaps the most elementary method of portion control is counting pieces. For example, three plums may be the specified serving, or two strips of bacon, or two pancakes dipped onto the grill with a No. 12 disher.

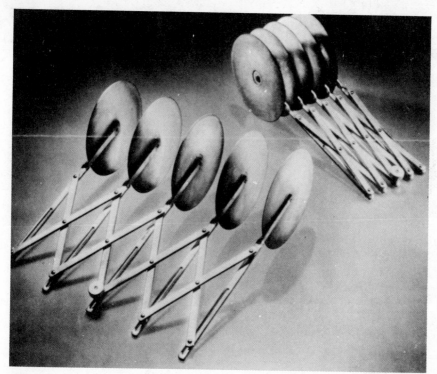

Figure 11.16. (cont.)   Bun divider (used by courtesy of Miller Bun Divider Co., Milwaukee, WI)

Figure 11.16. *(cont.)* *Pie markers*

Glass, china, or ceramic serving dishes or paper containers of various sizes may be used to control serving size. The number of ounces of beverage, for instance, can be controlled by the size of a cup.

Scales of many types are used throughout a foodservice, because weight control is essential from the time the food enters the food production facility from the purveyor until it is served. The use of scales during receiving and production has been discussed in previous chapters. Portion control scales are an important tool in quantity control in both the production and service areas. The cooks and servers should have portion scales available for checking serving sizes.

Slicers are a valuable piece of equipment to assist in ensuring portion control because they can slice foods more evenly and uniformly than can be done by hand. An example of a slicer is shown in Figure 11.17. A device on a slicer permits adjusting the blade for desired degree of thickness for a product. Portion control guides in a foodservice operation should include the correct setting on the slicer for various food items. Automatic slicers are available that do not require the operator to return the food holding device manually, which frees the worker to continue with other tasks while food is being sliced. The slicer is used most commonly for meat and meat products; however, it can also be used for vegetables, cheese, bread, and many other products. In portioning sliced foods for

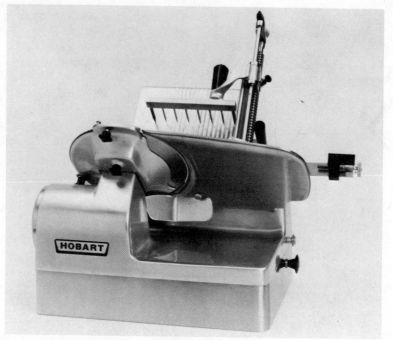

Figure 11.17. *Food slicing machine (used by courtesy of Hobart Co., Troy, OH)*

service, a portion scale should be readily available for a periodic check on portion size.

To illustrate how lack of control can create food shortages and drive up food cost, assume the server is not careful in serving beef stroganoff and serves heaping, rather than leveled-off ladles, resulting in five ladles per quart and not the intended six. The recipe calculated to serve 600 will serve only about 500; the food cost for the stroganoff should be 80 cents for the serving, but the overdipping increases the cost to 96 cents. Additional cost would also be incurred for the product that might be substituted for the 100 portion shortage; this may be a fast cook item that is more expensive than the beef stroganoff and results in further cost overruns.

Foodservice operations should develop portion control guides to be used by production and service personnel. The chart in Table 11.6 shows typical portion sizes for selected menu items served in an employee cafeteria. Training and supervision are necessary, however, to ensure that proper tools and techniques are followed.

Foodservice managers must realize that portion control is essential for operating "in the black." All food items must be purchased on the basis of weight and measure, and everything served on the basis of specified weight or portion size. Portion control is critical, not only for cost control, but also for customer satisfaction. The key steps in ensuring portion control are purchasing by exact specifica-

Table 11.6. *Portion control guide for selected menu items in an employee cafeteria*

Breakfast items	Portion Size
Bacon	2 slices
Cereal, hot	4 oz. ladle
Eggs, soft cooked or fried	2
Eggs, scrambled	#16 disher
English muffins	2 halves
Sausage link	2 links
Syrups or sauces	2 oz. ladle
Tater tots	5–6 count

Luncheon Entrees	Portion Size
Baked beans	1 #12 disher
Barbecue meat on bun	1 #16 disher
Chili	1 6 oz. ladle
Corn dogs	2
Fishwiches	4 oz. square on bun
Meat, egg, or fish salad on sandwich or cold plate	1 #12 disher or 2 #24 dishers
Soups, stews, chowders	1 6 oz. ladle
Stuffed green peppers	#8 disher stuffing in half pepper
Wiener, foot long in bun	1 (5/lb.) in 1 10″ bun

Dinner entrees	Portion size
Chicken, Country Fried	1 breast and 1 wing OR 1 thigh and 1 leg
Chicken, Curry	4 oz. ladle
Fried shrimp	4 if 16–20/lb. 5 if 18–20/lb.
Shrimp jambalaya	4 oz. ladle
Meat balls	2 meat balls, #16 disher
Stroganoff or beef strips in sauce or gravy	4 oz. ladle

Potatoes, vegetables, and substitutes	Portion size
Bread dressing	1 #12 disher
Broccoli, spears	2–3 spears
Brussel sprouts	5 sprouts
Okra, whole, french fried	5 pieces
Sweet potatoes, mashed	#12 disher
Tater tots	10–12 pieces
Refried beans	#16 disher

Table 11.6. *(Continued)*

Salads	Portion size
Cottage cheese, with fruit or vegetable on plate	#24 disher
Deviled eggs	2 halves
Egg salad	#12 disher
Potato salad	#12 disher
Stuffed celery	2 3–3 ½″ length and filling
Tomato wedge or slice	3 for salad (6 per tomato)
Wilted or creamed cucumbers	#16 disher

Desserts	Portion size
Cobblers	1 cut 7″ × 10″ (18″ × 26″ pan)
Ice Cream and Sherbets	#12 disher
Jumbo Cookie	#20 disher
Pies	9″ tin, 8 per pie

tions, using standardized recipes, and using proper tools and techniques during all aspects of production and service.

Product Evaluation

Product evaluation is an important component of a foodservice quality control program. Thorner and Manning (1983) define quality control, or quality assurance, as an activity, procedure, method, or program designed to ensure the maintenance and continuity of specifications and standards of a product. In a foodservice operation, it is all those activities focused on the production of consistent and high-quality menu items. Although quality control and quality assurance are used interchangeably in the literature, the latter term is more current and is gaining acceptance.

Food quality is evaluated by sensory, chemical, and physical methods. Sensory methods are used to determine if foods differ in such qualities as taste, odor, juiciness, tenderness, or texture and to determine the extent and direction of the differences (Palmer, 1972). These methods also are used to determine consumer preferences and acceptability. Palmer (1972) identifies two general types of sensory tests.

- *Difference test.* To determine quality differences.
- *Consumer test.* To determine preference or acceptability.

Consumer tests are generally used only after small taste panels have determined differences in one or more important qualities.

Chemical and physical methods for testing of food are often used along with sensory methods to attempt to identify the reasons for differences detected by sensory methods. These methods are usually more reproducible and less time-consuming than sensory methods. Palmer (1972) contends, however, that the use of physical and chemical methods are limited to areas in which they have been shown to measure the quality apparent to the senses.

Objective tests, the term commonly used for physical and chemical tests of food quality, have been devised for assessments of color, texture, and flavor (Jacobson, 1972). Jacobson indicates that specific characteristics within these three broad categories of attributes are often selected for measurement because color, texture, and flavor are too complex for estimation as a whole. Color, for instance, has elements of reflection, absorption, and transmission, along with a gloss effect. Texture includes such attributes as hardness, cohesiveness, viscosity, and elasticity, as well as particle size, shape, and structural detail. Flavor involves the effects of volatile and soluble compounds.

In large foodservice organizations, quality control laboratories are commonly part of the operations and routinely conduct sensory and objective testing during the initial development of new menu items. As we discussed in Chapter 5, in the large food factories, which are characteristically a part of commissary foodservice systems, food technologists and microbiologists are frequently employed as staff specialists with responsibility for regularly monitoring quality control. Large multiunit operations often have a sophisticated quality control program centralized at their corporate headquarters.

Physical and chemical testing of foods may be limited in smaller operations in which a full-scale quality control program is not justified. They are the focus of courses in food science and are beyond the scope of this text. Sensory evaluation by panels and consumer testing of new menu items, however, can be a regular part of any foodservice operation, and so we will now focus on some of their practical applications.

According to the American Society for Testing and Materials (1968), sensory testing is concerned with measuring physical properties by psychological techniques, or psychometrics. As a part of this field, sensory methods are used for tests that cannot be made directly by physical and chemical tests. That Society has developed standards for the conduct of sensory tests, including specific protocols for various types of tests.

Skelton (1984) contends that the foodservice operation should use sensory evaluation for new menu items and for maintaining quality of existing items to ensure the continuing success of an operation. As she points out, the cost of a mistaken menu innovation can be extremely high, involving such costs as reprinting menus, training staff, and loss of business from dissatisfied patrons.

Sensory panels are relatively small, ranging from 6 to 12 persons who are trained to judge quality characteristics and differences among food items. Panel members must be trained in the use of score cards and in the vocabulary of food description; they must also be able to distinguish among various levels of the basic tastes (sweet, salt, sour, and bitter) and to repeat their assessments with reasonable precision.

In contrast to the trained panel, the consumer panel usually includes 50 to 100 persons who are reasonably representative of the target market. The objective in using consumer panels is to evaluate acceptance of, or preference for, a menu item.

Skelton (1984) outlines three general purposes for sensory tests in foodservice operations: discriminating among food items, describing food items, and determining acceptability of menu items. Consumer panels are used for acceptance testing, but trained panels must be used for descriptive tests. Discrimination can be handled by either type of panel and is useful in the selection of taste panel members.

- *Discrimination.* These tests determine if a detectable difference exists among food items. For example, judges may be presented three samples and ask to choose the one that is different. If the panel has difficulty identifying the odd sample, the conclusion can be made that one recipe is not better than the other.

- *Description.* Quality control and recipe development both depend upon descriptive tests to provide information about certain sensory characteristics. Adjectives, numerical scales, and rankings are used to evaluate such attributes as taste, aroma, texture, tenderness, and consistency. Figure 11.18 gives a list of terms useful in describing food products.

---

1 Appearance: Aspect or contour

broken	scum	shriveled
cloudy	lustrous	shrunken
clear	muddy	smooth
crumbly	opaque	sparkling
curdled	plump	stringy
dull	rough	translucent
frothy	sediment	
greasy	shiny	

2 Odor: Volatile substances affecting sense of smell

acid	fragrant
acrid	strong
burnt	weak
delicate	

3 Color: Normal for substances, pleasing to the eye

bright	gray	pale
creamy	greenish	rich
discolored	golden brown	snowy white
dull	normal	
faded	off-color	

4 Consistency: Degree of firmness, density, viscosity, fluidity, plasticity, resistance to movement

brittle	gummy	soft
crisp	liquid	soggy
crumbly	rubbery	hard
curdled	runny	mealy
firm	syrupy	thin
frothy	solid	
full-bodied	stiff	

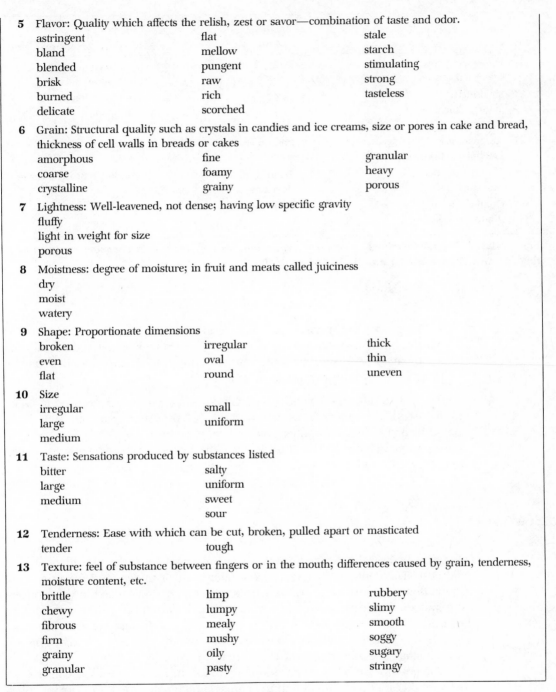

5 Flavor: Quality which affects the relish, zest or savor—combination of taste and odor.

astringent	flat	stale
bland	mellow	starch
blended	pungent	stimulating
brisk	raw	strong
burned	rich	tasteless
delicate	scorched	

6 Grain: Structural quality such as crystals in candies and ice creams, size or pores in cake and bread, thickness of cell walls in breads or cakes

amorphous	fine	granular
coarse	foamy	heavy
crystalline	grainy	porous

7 Lightness: Well-leavened, not dense; having low specific gravity
fluffy
light in weight for size
porous

8 Moistness: degree of moisture; in fruit and meats called juiciness
dry
moist
watery

9 Shape: Proportionate dimensions

broken	irregular	thick
even	oval	thin
flat	round	uneven

10 Size

irregular	small
large	uniform
medium	

11 Taste: Sensations produced by substances listed

bitter	salty
large	uniform
medium	sweet
	sour

12 Tenderness: Ease with which can be cut, broken, pulled apart or masticated

tender	tough

13 Texture: feel of substance between fingers or in the mouth; differences caused by grain, tenderness, moisture content, etc.

brittle	limp	rubbery
chewy	lumpy	slimy
fibrous	mealy	smooth
firm	mushy	soggy
grainy	oily	sugary
granular	pasty	stringy

Figure 11.18. *Terms used in judging food products*

Problem	Type of panel	Category of test
(1) Recipe development: Maximizing quality	Trained	Discrimination and Description
(2) Shelf-life: Storage time and temperature	Trained	Discrimination and Description
(3) Acceptance: Likelihood of purchase	Consumer	Acceptance or Preference
(4) Convenience food: Best substitution	Trained or Consumer	Description or Acceptance
(5) Quality control: Product consistency	Trained	Discrimination and Description

Figure 11.19. *Problems solved by sensory evaluation.* **Source:** *Skelton, M.: Sensory evaluation of food,* **Cornell Hotel Rest. Admin. Q. 24:51 (Feb.), 1984.**

- *Acceptance and preference.* The acceptance test, used with a consumer panel, is intended to answer the question of whether or not people will like the menu item. Using this test, preference for certain characteristics may be rated or an overall preference score attained.

Properly designed, executed, and analyzed sensory tests can be used to assist the foodservice manager in solving a variety of problems (Skelton, 1984) and should be an ongoing component of the quality control program in any foodservice operation. Figure 11.19 outlines typical problems and the type of sensory test appropriate to each.

SUMMARY

Quantity food production requires a variety of controls in order to control quality and cost. The competent foodservice manager must understand quantity food production techniques and equipment operation. Food produced in the foodservice system should be acceptable to the clientele, produced in the appropriate quantity, be microbiologically safe, and be within budgetary constraints of the operation. Product standards, control of all phases of production, and evaluation at each stage are dimensions of production control.

The objectives of food preparation are to destroy harmful microorganisms, to increase digestibility of food, and to change and enhance the flavor, form, color, texture, and/or aroma of food. The quality of any cooked food depends on type and quality of raw ingredients, recipe formulation, techniques used in preparation, and the method and duration of holding food items in all stages from procurement through service.

A whole range of processes are involved in quantity food production. Cooking, whether in small or large quantities, is a science closely akin to chemistry and physics, inducing chemical and physical changes in food to produce the desired product. Heat is the factor that causes many of these reactions and can be transferred in three ways: conduction, convection, and radiation.

Conduction is the transfer of heat from one object or substance to another by direct contact with it and is the dominant means of heat transfer in grilling, broiling, and frying, and, to some degree, in baking and roasting. Convection is the spreading of heat by movement of air, steam, or liquid and may be natural or forced. Today, convection ovens and steamers, which use forced air to speed cooking processes, can be seen in many foodservice operations. Radiation is the transfer of energy by waves from the source to the food. The two types of radiation used in food production are infrared and microwave.

Cooking methods are classified as either moist or dry heat. In moist heat methods, heat is conducted to the food product by water or steam; in dry heat methods, heat is conducted by dry air, hot metal, radiation, or hot fat. Selection of the appropriate cooking method for a particular type of food is critical to quality.

Equipment and methods are closely interrelated in quantity food production. The technology of cooking has become more complex, primarily because of innovations in foodservice equipment.

Boiling, simmering, stewing, poaching, blanching, braising, and steaming are moist heat methods commonly used. The major dry heat cookery methods include roasting, baking, oven frying, broiling, grilling, barbecuing, and frying.

Standards provide the basis for controlling production in the foodservice system. The primary quality attributes of food are nutritional, microbiologic, and sensory. Controls throughout the procurement/production/service cycle are critical to maintenance of quality. The complexity of today's foodservice system, in which food production is separated from service in time and/or place, makes control much more difficult.

Quality food may be defined simply as that which is nutritious and safe, as well as satisfying to the customer. From a scientific standpoint, quality refers to an index or measurement obtained by grading or classifying in accordance with explicit, predetermined specifications. The elements of quality food from this standpoint are flavor, texture, appearance, consistency, palatability, nutritional value, safety, ease of handling, convenience, storage stability, and packaging. Factors commonly responsible for poor quality food are improper handling, malfunctioning equipment, incorrect production techniques, poor sanitation, and carelessness. A foodservice operation should develop product standards to assist in controlling production.

Production control involves comparing what we set out to do with what we did and taking corrective action if needed. Quality control means assuring day-in, day-out consistency in each product; quantity control means producing the exact amount required. Time, temperature, and portion control are important for quality and quantity, as well as cost control.

Temperature is controlled or monitored with the use of thermostats and thermometers. Charts should be developed for cooking time and temperatures for all cooked items on the menu, and end-point cooking temperature should be specified for appropriate products. Time and temperature are closely related elements in cooking and must both be considered in setting up production controls. Batch cookery is a technique used to control product quality in foodservice systems and means preparing smaller amounts of food as close to service time as possible and continuing preparation throughout the service time to meet production demand. High-speed equipment available today has made batch cookery feasible for a broad range of menu items.

Product yield is related to time and temperature, and control of product yield is important to ensure the appropriate quantity is produced. Losses can occur at each stage of the procurement/production/service cycle. Handling losses occur not only during production, but also during portioning for service. These various losses must be considered in estimating quantities to purchase and produce.

Portion control is the achievement of uniform serving sizes and is basic to controlling cost and achieving customer satisfaction. It must begin with the purchase of food according to well-defined specifications and continue through production and service. Use of standardized recipes and appropriate techniques are components of portion control, as is selection and use of proper equipment for portioning and production. Portion control guides should be developed for use by production and service personnel.

Product evaluation is another component of a quality control program in a foodservice operation. Food quality is evaluated by sensory, chemical, and physical methods. Large foodservice organizations commonly have a laboratory responsible for monitoring quality control. All foodservice operations can use sensory evaluation effectively in the development of new menu items and in maintaining quality of menu items. Sensory panels, which involve use of a small group of trained panelists, are used to judge quality characteristics and differences among food items; consumer panels are useful in evaluating menu item acceptance and preference. Sensory evaluation should be an ongoing component of a quality control program.

REFERENCES

Allington, J. K., Matthews, M. E., and Johnson, N. E.: Nutritive value of food served calculated from food purchased in 14 nursing homes. *J. Am. Dietet. A.* 82:377, 1983.

American Society for Testing & Materials. *Manual on Sensory Testing Methods*, ASTM Special Technical Publication 434. Philadelphia: American Society for Testing & Materials, 1968.

Correll, J. D., and Wells, H. D.: *Applied Cooking Technology for the Food Service Operator.* Fenton, MO: Black Body Corp., 1979.

Dahl, C. A., and Matthews, M. E.: Cook/chill foodservice system with a microwave oven: Thiamin content in portions of beef loaf after microwave-heating. *J. Food Sci.* 45:608, 1980.

Dahl, C. A., and Matthews, M. E.: Forced-air convection ovens: Temperature range in oven and in beef loaf during heating. *School Food Serv. Res. Rev.* 3:11, 1979.

Dahl, C. A., and Matthews, M. E.: Hospital cook/chill foodservice systems. *J. Am. Dietet. A.* 75:34, 1979.

David, B. D.: Quality and standards—the dietitian's heritage. *J. Am. Dietet. A.* 75:408, 1979.

Dawson, E. H., Dochterman, E. F., and Vettel, R. S.: Food yields and losses in institutional food service. I. Fresh fruits and vegetables. *J. Am. Dietet. A.* 34:267, 1958.

Dawson, E. H., Dochterman, E. F., and Vettel, R. S.: Food yields in institutional food service. II. Meats and poultry. *J. Am. Dietet. A.* 34:371, 1958.

Gelepi, M. J.: The computer and the ingredient room. *Food Mgmt.* 8.60 (Aug.), 1973.

Gisslen, W.: *Professional Cooking.* New York: John Wiley & Sons, 1983.

Jacobson, M.: Physical and chemical tests of food quality. In Paul, P. C., and Palmer, H. H., eds.: *Food Theory and Application.* New York: John Wiley & Sons, 1972.

Klein, B. P., Matthews, M. E., and Setser, C. S.: Foodservice systems: Time and temperature effects on food quality. North Central Regional Research Publication No. 293. Urbana-Champagne, IL: University of Illinois, June, 1984.

Knight, J. B., and Kotschevar, L. H.: *Quantity Food Production.* Boston: CBI Publishing Co., 1979.

Kotschevar, L. H., and Terrell, M. E.: *Foodservice Planning: Layout and Equipment.* 3rd ed. New York: John Wiley & Sons, 1985.

Lee, F. A.: *Basic Food Chemistry.* 2nd ed. Westport, CT: AVI Publishing Co., 1983.

Matthews, M. E.: Quality of food in cook/chill foodservice systems: A review. *School Food Serv. Res. Rev.* 1:15, 1977.

Matthews, R. H.: Guidelines for determining and reporting food yields. *J. Am. Dietet. A.* 69: 396, 1976.

Matthews, R. H., and Garrison, Y. J.: *Food Yields Summarized by Different Stages of Preparation.* Rev. ed. USDA Agricultural Handbook No. 102. Washington, DC: U.S. Govt. Printing Office (Sept.), 1975.

McManis, H., and Molt, M.: Recipe standardization and percentage method of adjustment. *NACUFS J.* 35, 1978.

Minor, L. J.: *Nutritional Standards.* Vol. 1. Westport, CT: AVI Publishing Co., 1983.

Mizer, D. A., and Porter, M.: *Food Preparation for the Professional.* San Francisco: Canfield Press, 1978.

National Restaurant Association: *Sanitation Operations Manual.* Chicago: National Restaurant Association, 1979.

Palmer, H. H.: Sensory methods in food-quality assessment. In Paul, P. C., and Palmer, H. H., eds.: *Food Theory and Application.* New York: John Wiley & Sons, 1972.

Ross, L. N.: Food temperature control. *Hospitals* 45:67 (Jun. 16), 1975.

Sensory Evaluation Division of the Institute of Food Technologists: Sensory evaluation guide for testing food and beverage products. *Food Technol.* 35:50 (Nov.), 1981.

Shugart, G. S., Molt, M., and Wilson, M.: *Food for Fifty.* 7th ed. New York: John Wiley & Sons, 1984.

Skelton, M.: Sensory evaluation of food. *Cornell Hotel Restaur. Admin. Q.* 24:51 (Feb.), 1984.

Thorner, M. E., and Manning, P. B.: *Quality Control in Foodservice.* Rev. ed. Westport, CT: AVI Publishing Co., 1983.

U.S. Department of Agriculture and U.S. Department of Commerce. *Food Buying Guide for Type A School Lunches.* USDA and U.S. Dept. of Commerce. Washington, DC: U.S. Govt. Printing Office, 1972.

Watt, B. K., and Merrill, A. L.: *Composition of Foods—Raw, Processed, Prepared.* Rev. USDA Agriculture Handbook No. 8., 1963.

Zallen, E. M., Hitchcock, M. J., and Goertz, G. E.: Chilled food systems. *J. Am. Dietet. A.* 67: 552, 1975.

12
Quantity Food Sanitation

Food spoilage is a difficult term to define because people have different concepts about edibility and fitness to eat. Generally, however, spoilage is thought of as denoting unfitness for human consumption due to chemical or biological causes. Longree (1980) identifies the following criteria for assurance in foods of fitness to eat.

- The desired stage of development or maturity of the food.
- Freedom from pollution at any stage in the production and subsequent handling of the food.
- Freedom from objectionable chemical and physical changes resulting from action of food enzymes; activity of microbes, insects, and rodents; invasion of parasites; and damage from pressure, freezing, heating, drying, and the like.
- Freedom from microorganisms and parasites causing foodborne illnesses.

As Longree points out, enzymatic and microbial activities are undesirable when unwanted or uncontrolled.

Many opportunities exist for food contamination in a foodservice operation. As Minor (1983) points out, food must often be prepared far ahead of service, thus providing time for bacterial growth. Also, the possibility of transmission of disease or harmful substances carried by vectors (flies, cockroaches, weevils, mice, and rats) and by foodservice staff is much greater than in the home. The potential for contamination is also much greater wherever groups of people congregate. Personnel without proper training may be a hazard when they do not know safe food handling practices.

Foodborne illnesses are being recognized as a major health problem in the United States today. Recent statistics indicate that nearly 1.3 million Salmonella infections alone occur each year and more than 100 deaths are caused by salmonellosis annually (Nutrition Week, 1984). The cost of foodborne illnesses is estimated to be about $5 billion a year. The Centers for Disease Control, the Atlanta-based agency that tracks the epidemiological character of human diseases in this country, have suggested the following as among the steps to improve the food safety system.

- More training for food handlers.
- Better protocols for investigating foodborne outbreaks.
- Hazard analyses in food operations.
- Improved data on how pathogenic organisms are carried, how they spread, how food preparation contributes to proliferation, and how food handling contributes to an outbreak.

Microbial agents are not the only cause of foodborne poisonings in foodservice operations. Chemicals, herbicides, pesticides, antibiotics, metals, and hormones are among other agents that may contaminate food. In addition, certain foods can be poisonous: inedible mushrooms are an example with which we are all familiar. Over the past several years, contamination of the food supply by chemicals or other agents has been a major news topic. Although many incidents have been overdrawn, others represent serious potential health hazards.

All foods will deteriorate, some more rapidly than others. Their degrees of perishability require food handling practices that will maintain safety for consumption. The importance of avoiding food spoilage cannot be overemphasized. The clients of a foodservice establishment demand and have every reason to expect that the food served will be safe and wholesome. They can take legal action against a foodservice organization for not protecting their safety. And the adverse publicity from outbreaks of foodborne illness can be extremely detrimental to a foodservice establishment.

The foodservice organization thus has a tremendous responsibility for safeguarding its clientele. Food handling practices beginning with procurement and continuing throughout the production and service of food must be designed with this responsibility in mind.

MAJOR TYPES OF FOOD SPOILAGE

The major types of food spoilage are microbiological, biochemical, physical, and chemical. The chart in Figure 12.1 provides a classification of foodborne diseases. According to the Centers for Disease Control, about 70 percent of the outbreaks of

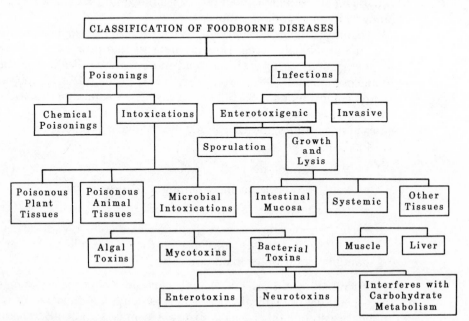

Figure 12.1. *Classification of foodborne diseases.* **Source:** *Minor, L. J.: Sanitation, Safety and Environmental Standards. Westport, CT: AVI Publishing Co., 1983, p. 13.*

foodborne illnesses were due to bacterial contamination. The causes of the other 30 percent were chemical, parasitic, or viral contamination (Minor, 1983).

The extent of contamination of some foods may be difficult to determine from their appearance, odor, and taste, as with inadequately refrigerated potato salad at a church picnic. In other foods, mold, discolored or altered appearance, off-odors, or off-flavors are obvious signs of contamination—for example, the mold on bread or odors from meat.

An in-depth discussion of food microbiology is beyond the scope of this book; most students in foodservice study this field through a course in bacteriology or microbiology. In the following pages, however, an overview will be presented from the standpoint of the importance of controlling practices to ensure production of microbiologically safe food in a foodservice operation.

Microbiological Spoilage

Thousands of species of microorganisms have been identified, the three most common forms being bacteria, molds, and yeast. They are found everywhere that temperature, moisture, and substrate allow them to live and grow—in soil, air, water, and foods. Some species are valuable and useful in preserving food, producing alcohol, or developing special flavors—as long as they are specially cultured and employed under controlled conditions. Other microbial activity, however, can be a primary cause of food spoilage.

Certain microorganisms and parasites are transmitted through food and may cause illnesses in people who ingest the contaminated items. Food may also serve as the medium in which microorganisms multiply to tremendous numbers. According to Longree (1980), microorganisms causing foodborne illnesses include bacteria, viruses, rickettsiae, protozoa, and parasites, such as trichinae. She points out, however, that although most microorganisms producing foodborne illness are bacteria, less than one percent of all bacteria can be considered "enemies of man."

Bacteria

Bacteria are microscopic, unicellular organisms of varying shape and size. The most commonly encountered shapes are spherical, rod, and spiral. In most instances, the presence of bacteria cannot be seen in food, even if the contaminants are present in sufficient number to produce foodborne illness. Sometimes, however, bacterial contamination may cause a turbid appearance or a slime on a food surface that is visible to the human eye.

Reproduction of bacterial cells takes place very rapidly, especially under the favorable conditions always present in food and food preparation areas. As temperature, moisture, time, and availability of nutrients are usually favorable in a foodservice operation, bacteria can find good growth support. And the bacteria responsible for foodborne illness thrive well in many of the foods we eat, especially in high protein food items. Bacterial food contamination is thus a continual problem in a foodservice facility.

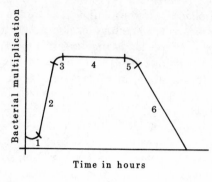

Figure 12.2. *Typical bacterial growth curve.* **Source: Longree, K., and Blaker, G. G.: Sanitary Techniques in Foodservice. 2nd ed.** *New York: John Wiley & Sons, 1982.*

The key factors affecting bacterial multiplication and death are type of organism, composition of substrate, moisture, osmotic pressure, oxygen tension, pH, temperature, and presence of inhibitors. Requirements for growth vary among different types of bacteria. As bacterial cells multiply under favorable conditions, however, they all pass through various phases. When the multiplication of bacteria is steady, the number of cells produced over a certain period of time can be plotted. Figure 12.2 shows a typical growth curve.

In general, bacteria need food of high moisture content. Their multiplication is affected by available moisture, which is expressed as water activity. Water may become less available through the presence of solutes, such as salt and sugar, through freezing, as in frozen foods, or through dehydration. Microorganisms vary in their response to oxygen, however; some bacteria require a definite minute quantity of oxygen, others do not.

The degree of a food's acidity or alkalinity, expressed as pH value, also affects bacterial growth. The pH value represents the hydrogen ion concentration and is expressed on a scale from 0 to 14, with 7 expressing neutrality. Values below 7 indicate acidity, those above, basic or alkaline materials. Bacteria vary widely in their reaction to pH. Although some are quite tolerant to acid, they generally grow best at a pH near neutral, so acid is frequently used in food preservation to suppress bacterial multiplication.

Longree (1980) points out that multiplication of the organisms causing food infections and food poisoning are supported in slightly acid, neutral, and slightly alkaline food materials. Food materials with a pH around the neutral point are mostly the animal foods, but also many vegetables. The pH of some common foods is listed in Table 12.1.

Microorganisms have specific temperature requirements for growth. At its optimum temperature, a cell multiplies and grows most rapidly. It will also grow within a range of temperatures around the optimum one, but will cease to grow both below a minimum temperature and above a maximum temperature.

Various types of bacteria respond differently to temperature. In general, spores of microorganisms are more heat resistant than vegetative mature cells. Some bacteria form spores inside the wall of their cells when they mature. These spores are more resistant to high heat, low humidity, and other adverse condi-

Table 12.1. *Hydrogen ion concentration and pH of some common foods.* Source: Handbook of Food Preparation. 7th ed. Washington, DC: American Home Economics Assn., 1975, p. 21. Reprinted by permission.

Common Indicator Changes*	Hydrogen Ion Concentration	pH	Average Values for Common Foods
R at pH 1.2	1.0×10^{-2}	2.0	Limes
	8.0×10^{-3}	2.1	
	6.3×10^{-3}	2.2	Lemons
	5.0×10^{-3}	2.3	
Thymol blue	4.0×10^{-3}	2.4	
	3.2×10^{-3}	2.5	
	2.5×10^{-3}	2.6	
	2.0×10^{-3}	2.7	
	1.6×10^{-3}	2.8	
	1.3×10^{-3}	2.9	Vinegar, plums
	1.0×10^{-3}	3.0	Gooseberries
		3.1	Prunes, apples, grapefruit (3.0 to 3.3)
		3.2	Rhubarb, dill pickles
		3.3	Apricots, blackberries
		3.4	Strawberries, lowest acidity for jelly
		3.5	Peaches
		3.6	Raspberries, sauerkraut
Bromphenol blue		3.7	Blueberries, oranges (3.1 to 4.1)
		3.8	Sweet cherries
		3.9	Pears
	1.0×10^{-4}	4.0	Acid fondant, acidophilus milk
		4.1	
		4.2	Tomatoes (4.0 to 4.6)
		4.3	
		4.4	Lowest acidity for processing at 100°C
Bromcresol green		4.5	Buttermilk
		4.6	Bananas, egg albumin, figs, isoelectric point for
		4.7	casein, pimientos
		4.8	
		4.9	
	1.0×10^{-5}	5.0	Pumpkins, carrots
		5.1	Cucumbers
Methyl red		5.2	Turnips, cabbage, squash
		5.3	Parsnips, beets
Chlorophenol red		5.4	Sweet potatoes, bread
		5.5	Spinach
		5.6	Asparagus, cauliflower
		5.7	
		5.8	Meat, ripened
		5.9	
Bromcresol purple	1.0×10^{-6}	6.0	Tuna
		6.1	Potatoes
		6.2	Peas
		6.3	Corn, oysters, dates
		6.4	Egg yolk
		6.5	
		6.6	Milk (6.5 to 6.7)
Litmus		6.7	
		6.8	
Bromthymol blue		6.9	Shrimp
	1.0×10^{-7}	7.0	Meat, unripened
		7.1	
		7.2	
		7.3	
		7.4	
		7.5	
Phenol red		7.6	
		7.7	
		7.8	
		7.9	
	1.0×10^{-8}	8.0	Egg white (7.0 to 9.0)
		8.1	
		8.2	
		8.3	
		8.4	

*Common Indicator Changes
B = Blue
P = Purple
R = Red
Y = Yellow

tions than are vegetative bacteria cells. They may remain dormant for long periods of time and germinate when conditions are favorable into new, sensitive, vegetative cells.

The heat resistance of microorganisms is their thermal death time, or the time required at a specified temperature to kill a specified number of vegetative cells or spores under specific conditions. Thermal death depends on the age of the organism, the temperature to which it is exposed, the length of time for which heat is applied, the presence of moisture, and the nature of the medium. As this discussion indicates, time and temperature are important in preserving microbiological quality of foods.

Various inhibitors have a pronounced effect on bacterial multiplication and death. As Longree (1980) points out, inhibitors may be a part of the food, developed as part of the microorganism's metabolism, developed during processing, or added purposely by the processor. The benzoic acid in cranberries and lysozyme in egg whites, for example, are natural parts of these foods. Alcohol produced in the growth and fermentation of yeast, in fruit juices, or in the production of wine is an example of an inhibitory substance that may accumulate and become toxic. And Pediococcus cerevisiae is an inhibitor added to meat in sausage-making to develop the lactic acid that will speed its fermentation.

Molds and Yeasts

Molds and yeasts are other common forms of microorganisms important in food sanitation. Molds are larger than bacteria and more complex in structure. In general, they grow on a wide range of substrates—moist or dry, acid or nonacid, high or low in salt or sugar. Molds also grow over an extremely wide range of temperature, although the optimum temperature is between 77° and 86°F. Mold growth may appear as cottony, powdery, or fuzzy tufts and patches, often highly colored and probably the most common type of spoilage that can be identified by the naked eye.

Yeasts are not known to cause foodborne illnesses, but may cause spoilage of sugar-containing foods. They are unicellular plants that play an important role in the food industry particularly in the fermentation or leavening of beer, wine, and bread. Yeasts can induce undesirable reactions, however, resulting in sour or vinegary taste.

Viruses

Capable of causing diseases in plants, animals, and humans, viruses are small pathogens that multiply in the living cells of the host but not in cooked food. Viruses can be carried in food and water, but they only multiply in the living cell. When they enter the cell, its metabolism is changed to produce more of the virus. In many respects, viruses resemble bacteria in that they need food and the right temperature, moisture, and pH in order to grow and reproduce effectively. Examples of human diseases caused by viruses are influenza, poliomyelitis, chicken pox, and hepatitis, some of which have been associated with foodborne outbreaks. Many viruses are inactivated by high temperatures (149° to 212°F) and also by refrigerated and frozen temperatures.

Other Microorganisms

Rickettsiae include such human diseases as typhus fever, Q fever, and Rocky Mountain spotted fever. Cows infected with the organism causing Q fever may transmit the disease to humans through their milk if it has not been properly heat treated. Like viruses, rickettsiae multiply in living tissues only.

Protozoa may be carried by food and cause illness when ingested. One cell animal-like forms, usually microscopic in size, protozoa are distributed widely in nature, especially in sea water, but also in lakes, streams, and soil. Amoebic dysentery is caused by one of the pathogenic protozoa that can be spread by water and food. Nearly all animals, including people, carry protozoa in their intestinal tracts, which has implications for food handling practices of foodservice personnel.

Other parasites include trichinae and tapeworms. Trichinosis occurs when persons are served a trichina-infested product, the main source being pork. This disease is preventable, however, if the food is cooked to a proper end-point temperature. Longree (1980) recommends that pork be cooked to 170°F, which provides a margin of safety for destruction of larvae in infested meat. The USDA, however, has developed processing methods for pork products that assure a safe product. Problems with trichinae can be prevented by purchasing from approved sources and by adequate cooking.

Tapeworms are parasitic intestinal worms of flattened tape-like form that may cause disease in humans when larva-infested meat, either beef or pork, is ingested. Tapeworm contamination can be prevented by appropriate sanitary measures during agricultural production and by the federally regulated inspection of cattle carcasses for evidence of tapeworms. Proper meat processing procedures—especially during boning, which involves a great deal of hand contact—are also important to prevent problems.

Biochemical Spoilage

Biochemical spoilage is caused by natural food enzymes, which are complex catalysts that initiate reactions in foods. Off-flavors, odors, or colors may develop in foods if enzymatic reactions are uncontrolled. When fruit is peeled and exposed to air, for example, the undesirable browning is due to enzyme activation by oxygen. Enzymes may have desirable effects as well, such as the natural tenderizing or aging of meat.

Enzyme formation can be controlled in much the same manner as microorganisms. As Thorner and Manning (1983) point out, heat, cold, drying, addition of inhibiting chemicals, and radiation are the principal means for controlling and inactivating natural food enzymes.

Physical Spoilage

Temperature changes, moisture, and dryness can cause physical spoilage of food. Excessive heat, for example, breaks down emulsions, dehydrates food, and destroys certain nutrients. Severe cold also causes various types of deterioration; certain starches used in preparing sauces or gravies, for instance, may break down at freezing temperatures.

Excessive moisture may lead to various types of spoilage. For example, excess moisture may support the growth of mold and bacteria, as discussed above. It may also cause physical changes, such as caking, stickiness, or crystallization, which may affect the quality of a food item. A powdered beverage product, for instance, may not be dispensed properly in a vending machine if the moisture level is too high.

Chemical Spoilage

Chemical spoilage may result from interaction of certain ingredients in a food or beverage with oxygen or light. The reaction of incompatible substances can lead to chemical spoilage, such as the effect of certain metals on foods. As an example, the zinc often used in galvanized containers may render acid food poisonous. Copper may also become poisonous when in prolonged contact with acid foods or carbonated beverages (Longree and Blaker, 1982).

A number of chemicals, many of which are used in foodservice operations, are toxic to humans. Chemical contamination may be introduced during food processing, or poisons used to protect growing plants may enter food that is later consumed. Accidental addition of chemicals in food processing—which may occur, for example, when cleaning supplies are stored adjacent to food products—has caused a number of public health problems.

Herbicides, pesticides, and fungicides are chemical products used to destroy or kill undesirable weeds, plants, pests, fungi, or bacteria and may all find their way into the food on which they are used. Various federal agencies have authority to control chemicals allowed in food, although control is somewhat difficult because of the huge volume of food moving through the market chain.

Several food additives or preservatives, when used in excessive amounts, have caused illness. Nitrites, for example, which are used for coloring and preserving meat, are toxic in large concentrations. The use of nitrites and a number of other food additives is being questioned today because of their possible carcinogenic effects.

Another foodborne illness may result from the use of too much monosodium glutamate (MSG), a salt of glutamic acid used as a flavor enhancer. Susceptible consumers may experience flushing of the face, dizziness, headache, or nausea from ingestion of high levels of MSG in food production. These symptoms have sometimes been called the "Chinese Restaurant Syndrome."

FOODBORNE PATHOGENS

The chart in Table 12.2 outlines the causes, usual sources, and effects of many of the foodborne illnesses. "Food poisoning," as outbreaks of acute gastroenteritis are popularly called, is caused by microbial pathogens that multiply profusely in food. These outbreaks are either foodborne intoxications or foodborne infections. Their symptoms, which are frequently violent, include nausea, vomiting, diarrhea, and cramps.

Foodborne intoxications are caused by toxins formed in the food prior to consumption, whereas foodborne infections are caused by the activity of large numbers of bacterial cells carried by the food into the gastrointestinal system of the victim. The symptoms from ingesting toxin-containing food may occur within a short period of time, as short as a couple of hours. The incubation period of an infection, however, is usually longer than that of an intoxication.

Staphylococcus Aureus

Staphylococcus aureus, a bacterium commonly referred to as staph or S. aureus, is one of the principal causative agents in foodborne illness. S. aureus grows in food, developing a toxin that, when ingested, causes an inflammation of the lining in the stomach and the intestinal tract, or gastroenteritis. Many strains of S. aureus are known, some of which are extremely pathogenic. Their symptoms include nausea, cramps, and diarrhea, and usually appear within two to three hours after ingestion of toxic food, but the time may vary up to six hours. The duration of the illness may be from 24 hours to two days, and mortality is low.

The distribution of S. aureus is widespread, as it is relatively resistant in injurious environmental conditions. The cells may survive for a lengthy period of time, even months, in dust, soil, or frozen foods, or on various surfaces, such as floors or walls. The human body is one of the most important sources of the organism. Even healthy people harbor S. aureus on their skin and in their mouths, throats, and nasal passages. It especially thrives in infected skin abrasions, cuts, and pimples. Although S. aureus is heat-sensitive and can be controlled and destroyed by heat, it produces a heat-stable toxin that persists long after the cells are destroyed.

Staphylococcal intoxication is a fairly frequent cause of foodborne illness, with foods high in protein the usual culprits. Cream pies, custards, meat sauces, gravies, and meat salad are among products most likely to be involved in foodborne intoxication. Not uncommonly, the appearance, flavor, or odor of the affected food items are not noticeably altered.

Temperatures must be carefully controlled to prevent multiplication of staphylococci in food. The organism multiplies even under refrigeration, if temperatures are not sufficiently low or if the cooling process does not proceed rapidly enough. Longree (1980) outlines the following for controlling foodborne illnesses caused by Staphylococcus aureus.

Table 12.2. *Foodborne illnesses: Their causes, sources, and effects*

		Illnesses of Frequent Occurrence		
Name of illness	*Causative agent*	*Foods usually involved*	*How introduced into food*	*Preventative or corrective procedures*
Staphylococcus food poisoning	Staphylococcus enterotoxin—a poison developed by *Staphylococcus* when it grows in food	Cooked ham or other meat, chopped or comminuted food, cream-filled or custard pastries, other dairy products, Hollandaise sauce, bread pudding, potato salad, chicken, fish, and other meat salads, "warmed-over" food	Usually food handlers through nasal discharges or purulent local skin infections (acne, pimples, boils, scratches, and cuts)	Refrigerate moist foods during storage periods; minimize use of hands in preparation; exclude unhealthy food handlers (having pimples, boils, and other obvious infections)
Perfringens food poisoning	*Clostridium perfringens*	Meat which has been boiled, steamed, braised, or partially roasted, allowed to cool several hours and subsequently served either cooled or reheated	Natural contaminant of meat	Rapidly refrigerate meat between cooking and use
Salmonellosis	Over 800 types of *Salmonella* bacteria, capable of producing gastrointestinal illness	Meat and poultry, comminuted foods, egg products, custards, shellfish, soups, gravies, sauces, "warmed-over" foods	Fecal contamination by food handlers; raw contaminated meat and poultry, liquid eggs, and unpasteurized milk	By good personal habits of food handlers; sufficient cooking and refrigeration of perishable foods; eliminate rodents and flies
Salmonellosis (a) typhoid fever (b) paratyphoid A	*Salmonella typhosa* *S. paratyphi* A	Moist foods, dairy products, shellfish, raw vegetables, and water	By food handlers and other carriers	Prohibit carriers from handling food; require strict personal cleanliness in food preparation; eliminate flies
Streptococcus food infection (beta-type), scarlet fever, and strep throat	Beta-hemolytic streptococci	Foods contaminated with nasal or oral discharges from case or carrier	Coughing, sneezing, or handling	Exclude food handlers with known strep infections
Streptococcus infection (alpha-type) (intestinal)	Enterococcus group; pyogenic group	Foods contaminated with excreta on unclean hands	By unsanitary food handling	Same as above; thorough cooking of food and refrigeration of moist food during storage periods
Botulism	Toxins of *Clostridium botulinum*	Improperly processed or unrefrigerated foods of low acidity	Soil and dirt; spores not killed in inadequately heated foods	Pressure cook canned foods with pH over 4.0; home-canned foods boil 20 minutes after removal from can or jars; cook foods thoroughly after removing before serving; discard all foods in swollen unopened cans

Table 12.2. *(Continued)*

Name of illness	Causative agent	Foods usually involved	How introduced into food	Preventative or corrective procedures
Bacillary dysentery (shigellosis)	*Shigella* bacteria	Foods contaminated with excreta on unclean hands	By unsanitary food handling	Strict personal cleanliness in food preparation; refrigeration of moist foods; exclude carriers
Amebic dysentery	*Endamoeba histolytica*	Foods contaminated with excreta on unclean hands	By unsanitary food handlers	Protect water supplies; ensure strict personal cleanliness with food handlers; exclude carriers
Trichinosis	Larvae of *Trichinella spiralis*	Raw or insufficiently cooked pork or pork products (also whale, seal, bear, or walrus meat)	Raw pork from hogs fed uncooked infected garbage	Thoroughly cook pork and pork products over 150°F (66°C), preferably to 160°F (71°C)
Fish tapeworm	Parasitic larvae	Raw or insufficiently cooked fish containing live larvae	Fish infested from contaminated water	Cook fish thoroughly; avoid serving raw fish
Arsenic, fluoride, lead poisoning (insecticides, rodenticides)		Any foods accidentally contaminated	Either during growing period or by accident in kitchen	Thoroughly wash all fresh fruits and vegetables when received; store insecticides and pesticides away from food; properly label containers; follow use instructions; *use carefully*; guard food from chemical contamination
Copper poisoning	Copper food contact surfaces	Acid foods and carbonated liquids	Contact between metal and acid food or carbonated beverages	Prevent acid foods or carbonated liquids from coming into contact with exposed copper
Cadmium and zinc poisoning	Metal plating on food containers	Fruit juices, fruit gelatin, and other acid foods stored in metal-plated containers	Acid foods dissolve cadmium and zinc from containers in which stored	Discontinue use of cadmium-plated utensils as food containers; prohibit use of zinc-coated utensils for preparation, storage, and serving of acid fruits and other foods or beverages
Cyanide	Silver polish		Failure to thoroughly wash and rinse polished silverware	Discontinue use of cyanide based silver polish, or wash and rinse silverware *thoroughly*

Source: National Restaurant Association: *Sanitation Operations Manual.* Chicago: National Restaurant Association, 1979.

- Sanitary precautions in connection with the food handler.
- Proper measures to preclude multiplication of the organism during preparation, service, and storage in food.
- Proper use of heat for the destruction of the organisms before toxins are formed.

Salmonella

Salmonellae have frequently been associated with foodborne illnesses and are among the bacteria causing foodborne infections. They do not release toxins into the food in which they multiply; rather, the ingested cells continue to multiply in the intestinal tract of the victim, leading to illness. The incubation period ranges from 6 to 72 hours, but is usually 12 to 36 hours. Individuals differ in susceptibility to salmonella infections; the symptoms include acute gastroenteritis, with inflammation of the small intestine, diarrhea, nausea, vomiting, and frequently a moderate fever, often preceded by headache and chills.

The primary source of Salmonella is the intestinal tract of carrier animals. A carrier is an individual who appears to be well and shows no symptoms or signs of illness but who harbors causative organisms. Various insects and pets may be reservoirs of Salmonella. Food animals are important reservoirs, especially hogs, chickens, turkeys, and ducks. Salmonellosis, the disease caused by Salmonella growth, is spread largely by contaminated food and is believed to be one of the major communicable diseases in this country.

A number of raw and processed foods have been found to carry Salmonella, especially raw meat, poultry, and shellfish, processed meats, egg products, and dried milk. Meat mixtures, dressings, gravies, puddings, and cream-filled pastries are among the menu items frequently indicted in salmonellosis. Food handlers are often associated with outbreaks, as are poor sanitation practices in the production, storage, or service of food, such as holding food for long periods at warm temperatures, slow cooling of large batches of food, and cutting on contaminated surfaces.

The organism grows best in a nonacid medium, although under certain conditions may grow at low pH levels. Multiplication of Salmonellae also occurs over a rather wide range of temperatures, although variation is characteristic of different strains. The optimum temperature for growth is the temperature of the human body, or 98.6°F. These organisms have also been shown to survive freezing and freezer storage.

Salmonellae are serious food contaminants and, therefore, control is extremely important. Since the potential for hazards is so great, precautions at each step, from purchase to storage to preparation to service and handling of leftovers, are required.

Clostridium Perfringens

Clostridium perfringens is considered the third most common cause of foodborne illness in the United States, following S. aureus and Salmonella. This bacterium is an anaerobic, Gram-positive, spore-forming rod. Several toxigenic strains that are associated with gastrointestinal illness have been differentiated. The bacterial cells and, more recently, the toxins have been implicated in the enteritis from C. perfringens. It is a common inhabitant of the intestinal tract of healthy animals and human beings and occurs in soil, sewage, water, and dust.

The incriminated food has invariably been held at room temperature or refrigerated in large mass for several hours. Outbreaks have often followed banquets or other large catered events. Symptoms usually begin between 8 to 15 hours after ingestion and continue for 6 to 12 hours. Although symptoms are similar to though milder than staph intoxication, they also include nausea, cramps, and diarrhea. Meats, meat mixtures, and gravies are foods frequently implicated. Vegetative cells succumb through cooking, but spores may survive. Overnight roasting of meat is therefore not recommended because of the low temperatures often used, and careful reheating of leftover meat is important. Prevention of C. perfringens multiplication can be achieved by refrigerating at 40°F or below or holding at 145°F or higher. In addition, rapid cooling of cooked foods is an important practice.

Clostridium Botulinum

Clostridium botulinum produces a toxin that affects the nervous system and is extremely dangerous. To illustrate this point, Minor (1983) states that the amount of C. botulinum toxin that can be placed on the point of a pin is enough to kill an individual, and a pint of the toxin could destroy almost the entire world population. The disease called botulism is the food poisoning caused by C. botulinum. Several types of the pathogen have been identified, each producing a specific toxin. The toxins are very potent and may persist in food for long periods of time, especially under low temperature storage.

The illness is treated by administering an antitoxin specific to the particular type of toxin involved. Therapy may not be satisfactory, however, because of the lag time between ingestion of the food, appearance of symptoms, diagnosis, and procurement of an antitoxin. Improved food processing techniques have led to greatly reduced incidence of botulism, although inadequately processed home canned foods are still frequently associated with botulism.

Toxin production goes hand-in-hand with growth of the organism, both of which are affected by the composition, moisture, pH, oxygen, and salt content of the food. The temperature and length of food storage are also factors influencing growth and toxin production. The toxin is stable in acid, but unstable in alkaline. Meats, fish, and low-acid vegetables have been found to support growth and toxin formation.

The temperature requirements of the strains vary. The optimum temperature for growth and toxin formation of the most common types of C. botulinum in this country is about 95°F. Freezing prevents growth in toxin formation but does not kill the organism. Destruction of the spores, however, may require several hours of boiling or a shorter heating period at higher temperatures. The toxins are less resistant to heat and are denatured readily at temperatures about 176°F; about 15 minutes at boiling temperatures should deactivate them. Precautions for avoiding botulism include procuring foods from safe sources, rejecting or destroying canned goods exhibiting such defects as swells or leaks, storing foods under recommended conditions, and using appropriate methods for thawing frozen foods.

Streptococcus

Streptococcus faecalis is an enterococci which inhabits intestinal tracts and may be discharged with feces. Transmitted by the hands of the food handler, it may contaminate food products. This bacterium is found commonly in milk, cheese, and other dairy products that are unpasteurized. It is fairly heat-resistant and can sometimes survive pasteurization. Longree (1980) stresses that clear distinction must be drawn between food poisoning attributable to this group of organisms and the Streptococcus disease transmission in which food might play a role as a simple vehicle of transmission. Comparatively few incidents have been reported in which S. faecalis has been implicated; these involved canned meats, cheeses, cream pies, prepared puddings, and canned evaporated milk.

Other Bacteria Associated with Foodborne Illness

Bacillus cereus is a large, aerobic spore-former frequently associated with grains, flours, and other cereal products. B. cereus also seems to be a common contaminant of spices. The symptoms of B. cereus-induced illness are similar to those of staph intoxication and salmonella infection, but milder. The optimal temperature range for growth is between 82 to 95°F.

Escherichia coli is another organism responsible for foodborne illness. A common inhabitant of the intestinal tract of humans and animals, E. coli frequently contaminates food via the food handler. The organism is easily killed by pasteurization and usual cooking temperatures.

SANITATION STANDARDS AND REGULATIONS

The protection of the food supply available to the consumer is the concern of governmental agencies at the federal, state, and local levels, as well as of trade associations and institutes, professional societies, and private associations and foundations, among other agencies. In Chapter 7, we discussed the key federal agencies concerned with the wholesomeness and quality of food from the agricultural producer to the purchaser. After that point, the service of food in foodservice establishments is controlled largely by state and local governmental agencies and private organizations.

Role of Governmental Agencies

The U.S. Public Health Service (PHS) and its subdivision, the Food and Drug Administration (FDA), both of which are agencies within the U.S. Department of Health and Human Services, are charged specifically with promoting the health of every American and the safety of the nation's food supply. The Public Health Service is concerned with identifying and controlling health hazards, rendering health services, conducting and supporting research, and developing training related to health.

Two agencies within the PHS specifically related to sanitation standards and regulation are the Centers for Disease Control (CDC) and the FDA. The CDC, located in Atlanta, is charged with protecting the public health by providing leadership and direction in the control of diseases and other preventable conditions. Of particular interest is its Bureau of Training, which develops programs for control of foodborne diseases in the foodservice industry. The CDC is responsible for providing assistance in identifying causes of disease outbreaks, including foodborne illnesses.

The FDA directs its efforts toward protecting the nation's health against unsafe and impure foods, unsafe drugs and cosmetics, and other potential hazards. The FDA is responsible for regulating interstate shipment of food, as discussed in Chapter 7, and for inspecting foodservice facilities on interstate carriers such as trains, planes, and ships operated under the U.S. flag. In addition, although local agencies have the primary responsibility for inspecting foodservice establishments, the FDA assists these agencies by developing model codes and ordinances and providing training and technical assistance.

Many state and local governments have adopted the U.S. Public Health Service codes in establishing standards of performance in sanitation for foodservice establishments. These codes generally require that employees have medical examinations to determine whether they are safe to handle food, and that they obtain food handler's permits. To do so, applicants must often complete a short training program on sanitation practices, as well as a medical exam.

State and local health agencies act to ensure that foodservice establishments (Longree, 1980):

- are equipped, maintained, and operated to offer minimal opportunities for food hazards to develop;
- use food products that are wholesome and safe; and
- are operated under the supervision of a person knowledgeable in sanitary food handling practices.

Periodic inspections are made by officials of the state or local agency to determine performance with standards of cleanliness and sanitation. Any deficiencies cited must be corrected prior to the next inspection. The agency generally has the authority to close an operation that has an inordinate number of deficiencies in its sanitation standards.

The Environmental Protection Agency (EPA), another agency within the U.S.

Department of Health and Human Services, also has responsibility in certain areas related to sanitation in foodservice establishments. The EPA endeavors to comply with environmental legislation and control pollution systematically by a variety of research, monitoring, standard-setting, and enforcement activities. Of particular interest to the foodservice industry are programs on water standards, air quality, pesticides, noise abatement, and solid waste management.

Role of Other Organizations

A number of other organizations are active in upgrading and maintaining the sanitary quality of various food products and establishing standards for foodservice organizations. For example, many trade and professional organizations serving various segments of the food industry have established sanitary standards for food processing operations.

The armed services have set up criteria to assure high standards of sanitation in their installations. The U.S. Army Natick Research and Development Laboratories, for example, have done a great deal of work in designing quality assurance programs concerned with maintenance of sanitation standards for military establishments (Silverman, 1982).

The National Institute for the Foodservice Industry (NIFI) has asserted aggressive leadership in developing standards and promoting training in foodservice sanitation. The National Restaurant Association (NRA) has also taken strong positions on high standards of sanitation in restaurants. For example, in Figure 12.3, the NRA's position statement on sanitation of restaurants is reproduced. Another position statement of the NRA endorsed the FDA model ordinance for foodservice establishments and pledged the NRA's support in seeking adoption of the ordinance by state and local government (NRA, 1979).

In the healthcare industry, the Joint Commission on Accreditation of Hospitals (JCAH) has encouraged high standards of sanitation by including assessment of sanitary practices in its accreditation standards and visits. The National Association of College and University Food Service (NACUFS) published a standards manual in 1982 which included standards for sanitation in college and university foodservice operations, as well as standards for other operational areas. These standards were designed to be used as a self-monitoring program for improving operations and as part of a voluntary peer review program. The American School Food Service Association (ASFSA) has provided leadership in the school foodservice segment of the industry in promoting good sanitation practices and has been active in providing personnel training.

The American Public Health Association (APHA), a professional society representing all disciplines and specialties in public health, has a standing committee on food protection that establishes policies and standards for food sanitation. Several other associations for professionals working in the area of food protection and sanitation also work to promote standards and enforcement procedures in food safety and sanitation.

The National Sanitation Foundation (NSF) is one of the most influential semiprivate agencies concerned with sanitation. The NSF, organized by a group

POSITION STATEMENT

NATIONAL RESTAURANT ASSOCIATION

Sanitation of Restaurants

1. The National Restaurant Association believes in clean restaurants.

2. We support inspections by competent, qualified health inspectors.

3. We respect and appreciate our right to have our deficiencies called to our attention and our right to take corrective action or defend alleged violations at a formal hearing.

4. We are unalterably opposed to adverse and unfair criticism based on the opinions of individuals who are not qualified in the areas of food service sanitation as it affects the public health.

5. We object to any unauthorized entry into our premises.

We are firm in our belief that the combined efforts of the proper authorities and knowledgeable restaurateurs result in clean establishments meriting the confidence of the American dining public.

The National Restaurant Association pledges to continue its program of education in the areas of public health and safety thereby continuing to recognize and fulfill its very real responsibility to protect the public.

Adopted March, 1975

One IBM Plaza/Suite 2600
Chicago, Illinois 60611
(312) 787-2525

L-5

Figure 12.3. *Position Statement of the National Restaurant Association. Chicago, IL: National Restaurant Association, 1975*

of industrial leaders and public health officials, is a non-profit, noncommercial organization that seeks solutions to problems involving cleanliness and sanitation. On the basis of research results, the NSF develops minimum sanitation standards for equipment, products, and devices. Manufacturers can request that the NSF evaluate their equipment and will receive an NSF Testing Laboratory Seal of Approval for equipment meeting the NSF standards.

Microbiological Standards

The increased number of highly processed foods now being used in some foodservice operations has caused concern about new potential hazards to the public health. In more recent years, the FDA has been concerned with the establishment of microbiological quality standards, setting acceptable microbial levels for food products to bring into account abuses at the retail or consumer level. According to a report by Wehr (1982), a number of states and municipalities have adopted microbial standards for food.

The following definitions, related to microbial contamination of foods, have been advanced by the Food Protection Committee of the Food and Nutrition Board.

- A microbiological specification is the maximum acceptable number of microorganisms or of specific types of microorganisms, as determined by prescribed methods, in a food being purchased by a firm or agency for its own use.

- A recommended microbiological limit is the suggested maximum acceptable number of microorganisms or of specific types of microorganisms, as determined by prescribed methods, in a food.

- A microbiological standard is that part of a law or administrative regulation designating the maximum acceptable number of microorganisms or of specific types of microorganisms, as determined by prescribed methods, in a food produced, packaged or stored, or imported into the area of jurisdiction of the enforcement agency.

Elliott (1970) added the following definition to supplement the preceding ones.

- A microbiological guideline is that level of bacteria in a final product or in a shipped product that requires identification and correction of causative factors in current and future production or in handling after production.

Microbiological specifications can be used as part of the procurement standards for certain food products. Large organizations, such as the U.S. Quartermaster Corps, can exert tremendous influence by using these specifications in purchasing food products. Recommended microbiological limits are useful not only in a governmental agency's official inspection program but also in a foodservice organization's internal quality control or quality assurance program. The commissary or food factory in a very large foodservice system would likely establish microbiological limits for menu items. Microbiological standards are being developed cooperatively by governmental agencies, professional societies, and industry because of concerns over the safety of the food supply.

Audits of Sanitation Standards

Evaluation of the maintenance of foodservice sanitation standards is accomplished in two ways: external and internal audits of facilities and practices. External audits may be performed by governmental or non-governmental agencies, while internal audits are the responsibility of the management of a foodservice organization and may be part of a self-inspection program for sanitation or a component of a broader quality assurance program (QA).

External Audits

Audits by Governmental Agencies. External audits are performed by federal, state, and local governmental agencies, as we indicated in our discussion of the role of these agencies in developing and monitoring sanitation in foodservice establishments. Many state and local ordinances are patterned on the Model Foodservice Sanitation Ordinance recommended by the U.S. Public Health Service (PHS, 1976). A Foodservice Establishment Inspection Report has also been developed by the PHS for use by state and local health departments (Figure 12.4).

The inspection process in a foodservice facility may begin before a facility is built, as many jurisdictions require advance review of plans and specifications for new construction or extensive remodeling. Once a facility is completed, inspection visits are usually conducted prior to issuance of permits to operate. After a foodservice operation has opened, inspections will occur periodically, depending on the work load of the responsible agency and severity of violations at previous inspections.

Using a form similar to the one in Figure 12.4, the health officer will complete a report covering such areas as those delineated on the form. Rather than being designed to penalize operations, the inspection program is concerned with correction in sanitation practices.

Emerging Concepts of Audits. The growth of the foodservice industry has not been matched by expansion of the capacity of health agencies to monitor foodservice operations. Bryan (1982), an official with the Centers for Disease Control, states that the number of sanitarians available in food protection programs is inadequate to do even two thorough inspections of each establishment annually. Therefore, he concludes that the usual type and quantity of foodservice establishment inspections must change in one or more of the following ways.

- The time must be decreased, even though it is currently too short to perform a quality job.
- The number must decrease, even though many believe too few are currently conducted for certain hazardous operations.

Based on an inspection this day, the items circled below identify the violation in operations or Facilities which must be corrected by the next routine inspection or such shorter period of time as may be specified in writing by the regulatory authority. Failure to comply with any time limits for corrections specified in this notice may result in cessation of your Food Service operations

OWNER NAME

ESTABLISHMENT NAME

ADDRESS

ZIP CODE

ESTABLISHMENT I.D.				CENSUS TRACT	SANIT CODE	DATE			INSPECT TIME (Min.)	PURPOSE		29
COUNTY	DISTRICT	TYPE	EST. NO.			YR.	MO.	DAY				
1 2 3	4 5 6	7 8 9	10 11 12	13 14 15 16	17 18 19	20 21	22 23 24	25 26 27 28		Regular . . . . 1 Complaint 3		
										Follow-up . . . . 2 Investigation 4		
										Other 5		

ITEM	WT	COL	ITEM	WT	COL	ITEM	WT	COL
FOOD			18 PRE-FLUSHED, SCRAPED, SOAKED	1	47	**GARBAGE AND REFUSE DISPOSAL**		
*01 SOURCE; SOUND CONDITION; NO SPOILAGE	5	30	19 WASH, RINSE WATER - CLEAN, PROPER TEMPERATURE	2	48	33 CONTAINERS OR RECEPTACLES, COVERED; ADEQUATE NUMBER, INSECT/RODENT PROOF, FREQUENCY, CLEAN	2	62
02 ORIGINAL CONTAINER, PROPERLY LABELED	1	31	*20 SANITIZATION RINSE - CLEAN, TEMPERATURE, CONCENTRATION, EXPOSURE TIME; EQUIPMENT, UTENSILS SANITIZED	4	49			
FOOD PROTECTION						34 OUTSIDE STORAGE AREA, ENCLOSURES PROPERLY CONSTRUCTED, CLEAN, CONTROLLED INCINERATION	1	63
*03 POTENTIALLY HAZARDOUS FOOD MEETS TEMPERATURE REQUIREMENTS DURING STORAGE, PREPARATION, DISPLAY, SERVICE, TRANSPORTATION	5	32	21 WIPING CLOTHS - CLEAN, STORED, RESTRICTED	1	50	**INSECT, RODENT, ANIMAL CONTROL**		
*04 FACILITIES TO MAINTAIN PRODUCT TEMPERATURE	4	33	22 FOOD CONTACT SURFACES OF EQUIPMENT AND UTENSILS CLEAN, FREE OF ABRASIVES, DETERGENTS	2	51	*35 PRESENCE OF INSECT/RODENTS - OUTER OPENINGS PROTECTED, NO BIRDS, TURTLES, OTHER ANIMALS	4	64
05 THERMOMETERS PROVIDED AND CONSPICUOUS	1	34	23 NON-FOOD CONTACT SURFACES OF EQUIPMENT AND UTENSILS CLEAN	1	52			
06 POTENTIALLY HAZARDOUS FOOD PROPERLY THAWED	2	35	24 STORAGE, HANDLING OF CLEAN EQUIPMENT/UTENSILS	1	53	**FLOORS, WALLS AND CEILINGS**		
*07 UNWRAPPED AND POTENTIALLY HAZARDOUS FOOD NOT RE-SERVED	4	36	25 SINGLE SERVICE ARTICLES, STORAGE, DISPENSING, USED	1	54	36 FLOORS, CONSTRUCTED, DRAINED, CLEAN, GOOD REPAIR, COVERING INSTALLATION, DUSTLESS CLEANING METHODS	1	65
08 FOOD PROTECTION DURING STORAGE, PREPARATION, DISPLAY, SERVICE, TRANSPORTATION	2	37	26 NO RE-USE OF SINGLE SERVICE ARTICLES	2	55	37 WALLS, CEILING, ATTACHED EQUIPMENT CONSTRUCTED, GOOD REPAIR, CLEAN SURFACES, DUSTLESS CLEANING METHODS	1	66
09 HANDLING OF FOOD (ICE) MINIMIZED	2	38	**WATER**					
10 IN USE, FOOD (ICE) DISPENSING UTENSILS PROPERLY STORED	1	39	*27 WATER SOURCE, SAFE, HOT AND COLD UNDER PRESSURE	5	56	**LIGHTING**		
PERSONNEL			**SEWAGE**			38 LIGHTING PROVIDED AS REQUIRED, FIXTURES SHIELDED	1	67
*11 PERSONNEL WITH INFECTIONS RESTRICTED	5	40	*28 SEWAGE AND WASTE WATER DISPOSAL	4	57	**VENTILATION**		
*12 HANDS WASHED AND CLEAN, GOOD HYGIENIC PRACTICES	5	41	**PLUMBING**			39 ROOMS AND EQUIPMENT VENTED AS REQUIRED	1	68
13 CLEAN CLOTHES, HAIR RESTRAINTS	1	42	29 INSTALLED, MAINTAINED	1	58	**DRESSING ROOMS**		
FOOD EQUIPMENT AND UTENSILS			*30 CROSS-CONNECTION, BACK SIPHONAGE, BACKFLOW	5	59	40 ROOMS CLEAN, LOCKERS PROVIDED, FACILITIES CLEAN, LOCATED, USED	1	69
14 FOOD (ICE) CONTACT SURFACES DESIGNED, CONSTRUCTED, MAINTAINED, INSTALLED, LOCATED	2	43	**TOILET AND HANDWASHING FACILITIES**			**OTHER OPERATIONS**		
15 NON-FOOD CONTACT SURFACES DESIGNED, CONSTRUCTED, MAINTAINED, INSTALLED, LOCATED	1	44	*31 NUMBER, CONVENIENT, ACCESSIBLE, DESIGNED, INSTALLED	4	60	*41 NECESSARY TOXIC ITEMS PROPERLY STORED, LABELED, USED	5	70
16 DISHWASHING FACILITIES DESIGNED, CONSTRUCTED, MAINTAINED, INSTALLED, LOCATED, OPERATED	2	45	32 TOILET ROOMS ENCLOSED, SELF-CLOSING DOORS, FIXTURES, GOOD REPAIR, CLEAN, HAND CLEANSER, SANITARY TOWELS/TISSUE/HAND-DRYING DEVICES PROVIDED, PROPER WASTE RECEPTACLES	2	61	42 PREMISES MAINTAINED, FREE OF LITTER, UNNECESSARY ARTICLES, CLEANING MAINTENANCE EQUIPMENT PROPERLY STORED, AUTHORIZED PERSONNEL	1	71
17 ACCURATE THERMOMETERS, CHEMICAL TEST KITS PROVIDED, GAUGE COCK (¼" IPS VALVE)	1	46				43 COMPLETE SEPARATION FROM LIVING/SLEEPING QUARTERS, LAUNDRY	1	72
						44 CLEAN, SOILED LINEN PROPERLY STORED	1	73

FOLLOW-UP
YES 1
NO 2   74

RATING SCORE
(100 Less Weight of Items Violated)   75 76 77

*CRITICAL ITEMS REQUIRING IMMEDIATE ACTION

RECEIVED BY (Name and Title)

INSPECTED BY (Name and Number and Title)

Figure 12.4. *Foodservice establishment inspection report. Source: Food and Drug Admin.: Food Service Sanitation Manual—1976. Washington, DC: U.S. Department of Health, Educ., and Welfare, Public Health Service, DHEW Publ. No. (FDA) 78-2081, 1978.*

- A variable inspection frequency must be developed and implemented, which will provide more emphasis on establishments with the greatest potential risk to the public.

Kaplan and El Ahraf (1979) stress that no basis exists for the traditional belief that all foodservices must undergo an arbitrary number of inspections annually. Instead, they say epidemiological data should be used to make reliable predictions of the degree and causes of risk of foodborne diseases, with attention focused on foodservice operations with high potential risk.

Bryan (1982) identifies three risk factors, which can be weighted to assign relative values, and a combined risk index that will provide measures of the potential risk that a food will be mishandled in an establishment with illness as a result. He proposes using these risk factors as a basis for designing an assessment program for foodservice establishments that would emphasize those that are high risk. His method utilizes food-property risk, food-operations risk, and average daily-patronage risk as coefficients to compute a composite risk index.

- The food-property risk is concerned with the characteristics of the food prepared in an establishment in regard to the relative frequency that these foods have been, or because of their intrinsic qualities could become, vehicles of foodborne pathogens.

- The food-operations risk is concerned with the probability that foods are or will become contaminated, that contaminants survive or are likely to survive certain processes, and that any bacterial contaminants present could multiply to quantities sufficient to cause disease.

- The average daily-patronage risk is concerned with the number of persons served. The risk that patrons become ill is somewhat proportional to the number eating at the establishment, which is intensified if the potential vehicle for contamination is eaten by a large percentage of persons who go to that establishment.

- The composite risk index is an indicator that expresses in a single score the total estimated effect of the three risk factors described above, insofar as they relate to a particular foodservice establishment. This index is a measure of the effort at foodborne disease control that should be expended in connection with that establishment to prevent food prepared there from becoming a vehicle of an outbreak.

Other External Audits. Other organizations, such as JCAH and NACUFS, perform external audits. As indicated previously in this chapter, an assessment of sanitation practices is included in evaluations by agencies, such as those listed, as part of an evaluation of the overall facility and operations. These evaluation programs are voluntary but serve to assist in upgrading practices in the institutions and to inform the public about the standards maintained in the facility.

Internal Audits

A foodservice organization should have its own program of self-evaluation as a means of maintaining standards of sanitation. In organizations with a QA program, audit of sanitation practices should be one of its major components.

Appendix E reproduces the model check list developed by the National Restaurant Association (NRA) for self-inspection as part of the sanitation program in a restaurant. The NRA recommends that foodservice organizations should design sanitation check lists meeting these criteria:

- Applicable to the facilities, policies, practices, and procedures of a specific organization.
- Compatible with the foodservice sanitation regulations that apply to an operation.
- Designed to permit separate sanitation inspection checks of specific functional areas or procedures.

Follow-up action by management is the key to the success of a self-inspection program.

A self-inspection program should not be developed primarily for the purpose of preparing for regulatory agency inspections but rather as a continual check on the adequacy of the sanitation program in a foodservice operation. Managers, supervisors, and employees should understand that the purpose of self-inspection is to promote positive sanitation practices, not to take punitive action.

CONTROLLING MICROBIOLOGICAL QUALITY OF FOOD

Goals and Objectives

The ultimate goal of the sanitation program in a foodservice operation is to protect the clientele from foodborne illness. Achievement of that goal requires a two-pronged strategy: protecting food from contamination and reducing the effect of existing contamination (NIFI, 1985).

Protecting food against contamination is difficult because pathogenic microorganisms capable of contaminating food are distributed so widely: in soil, dust, air, and water; on insects and rodents; on equipment, utensils, and facilities; and on people who come in contact with the food. Also, the food as purchased, regardless of the reliability of the source, has some degree of contamination after it arrives at the foodservice facility. Proper handling of food throughout the procurement/production/service cycle is critical to protecting food against contamination. Figures 12.5 and 12.6 illustrate the routes of food contamination. The principal offenders are:

- infected food handlers,
- contaminated food supplies,
- unsafe food handling,

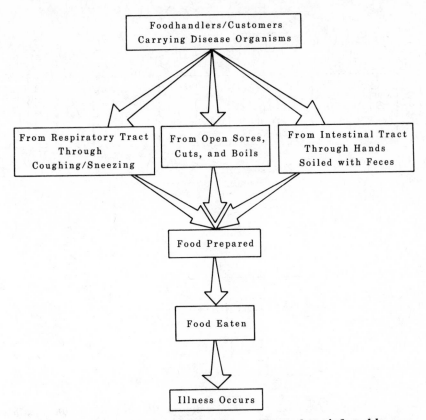

Figure 12.5. *Transmission of a foodborne illness from infected human beings to food and back to other human beings. Source: Applied Foodservice Sanitation. 3rd ed. Chicago: National Institute for the Foodservice Industry, 1985.*

- unsanitary equipment, and
- hazardous chemicals.

Time-Temperature Control

Reducing the effect of contamination is largely a matter of temperature control in the storage, production, and service of foods. As discussed in the subsection on the various types of microorganisms, the growth of harmful organisms can be slowed or prevented by refrigeration or freezing; the organisms themselves can be destroyed by sufficient heat. As we pointed out, the minimum, maximum, and optimum temperatures vary for the various pathogenic microorganisms; in general, however, they flourish at temperatures between 40 and 140°F (Figure 12.7). This temperature range is commonly called the danger or hazardous zone because the hazard of bacterial growth is greatest within that zone. The longest

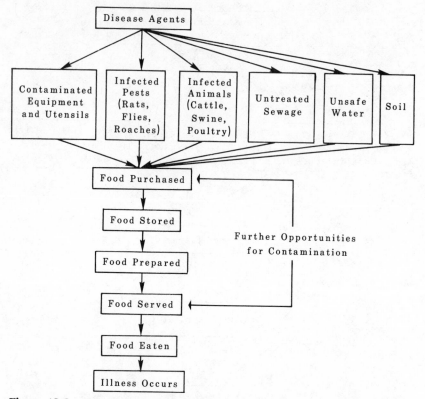

Figure 12.6. *Transmission of a foodborne illness from an intermediate source to food and on to humans.* **Source: Applied Foodservice Sanitation. 3rd ed. Chicago: National Institute for the Foodservice Industry, 1985.**

period that food may safely remain in this zone is four hours, although food should not be in the 60 to 100°F range longer than two hours. Safe temperatures, then, as applied to potentially hazardous food, are those of 40°F and below and 140°F and above. As implied by the data given above, both time and temperature are important in handling food to preserve microbiological quality.

In quantity foodservice operations, the ingredients and the partially and fully prepared menu items are subjected to a wide range of temperatures, from those in freezer storage to those in cooking of foods. In relating food handling practices to the time-temperature effects on microorganisms in foods, Longree (1980) defines the following temperature zones at which foods are handled.

- *Freezing, defrosting, and chilling zone.* Temperatures should prevent multiplication of organisms causing foodborne intoxications and infections over an extended storage period.

- *Growth or hazardous zone.* Temperatures allow bacterial multiplication.

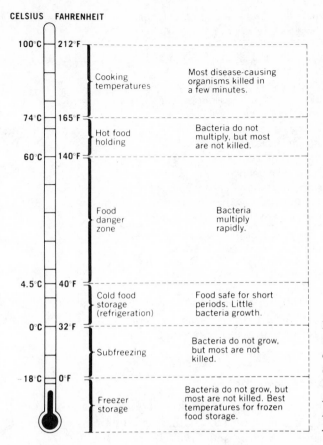

Figure 12.7. *Important temperatures in sanitation and food protection.* **Source: Adapted from** *Keeping Food Safe to Eat,* **Home and Garden Bulletin** *No. 162, U.S. Department of Agriculture, 1970.*

- *Hot holding zone.* Temperatures are aimed at preventing multiplication, but usually do not kill the organism.
- *Cooking zone.* Temperatures should be sufficiently high to destroy bacterial cells within a short period of time.

In summarizing the research literature on time-temperature relationships and microbiological quality of food, she states that, in reality, the hazardous temperature zone may extend into the refrigeration zone because of poor practices in holding and storing food in refrigerated equipment. It may also extend into the cooking zone because temperatures used in routine preparation of menu items are not always sufficiently high nor applied sufficiently long to kill pathogenic organisms present in food.

Longree (1980) points out that reports on foodborne disease episodes indicate that the implicated foods have frequently been allowed to remain at temperatures favorable to bacterial multiplication for long periods. Table 12.3 presents a summary of the factors contributing to foodborne disease outbreaks between 1973 and 1976, based on data compiled at the Centers for Disease Control (Bryan,

Table 12.3. *Microbial factors contributing to foodborne disease outbreaks (1973–1976)*

Rank	Factor
1	Inadequate refrigeration
2	Preparing food too far in advance
3	Holding food at temperatures not hot or cold enough
4	Infected personnel coming in contact with food
5	Inadequate reheating
6	Inadequate cleaning of equipment
7	Leftovers
8	Cross-contamination
9	Inadequate thermal processing
11	Contaminated raw ingredients in cooked foods
14	Obtaining foods from unsafe sources

Source: Bryan, F.: Impact of foodborne diseases and methods in evaluating control programs. *J. Environmental Health* 40:3154, 1978.

1978b). A later study reported in 1980 indicated that essentially the same factors were involved (Bryan, 1980). Obviously, lack of adequate temperature control is a critical problem area in foodservice operations.

Components of a Control System

Controlling the microbiological quality of food must focus on: the food; the people involved in handling food, either as employees or patrons; and the facilities, including both large and small equipment. Clearly, the condition of the food brought into the facilities is a critical aspect to consider, as are practices during storage, production, and service. Personal hygiene, as well as good food handling practices, are basics of a sanitation program in a foodservice facility. Control of contamination from clientele is more difficult; however, various aspects of facility design or policies and procedures can assist in this arena—for example, sneeze guards on a cafeteria service counter or salad bar or isolation procedures for a hospital patient with a highly communicable disease. The design and construction of the foodservice facilities and equipment will have a major impact on the effectiveness of the sanitation program; however, maintenance of the facilities to ensure a sanitary environment is also critical. This latter topic will be discussed in Chapter 16.

Key Principles and Practices

The National Institute for the Foodservice Industry (NIFI), a nonprofit educational foundation, has formulated ten key principles and practices that are the basis for an education and certification program in food protection for foodservice managers (NIFI, 1985). These concepts address the primary issues in controlling microbiological quality of food.

- When refrigerating potentially hazardous foods, make certain an internal product temperature of 40°F (7.2°C) or less is maintained.
- Use extreme care in storing and handling food prepared in advance of service.
- Cook or heat-process food to recommended temperatures.
- Relieve infected employees of food handling duties and require strict personal hygiene on the part of all employees.
- Make certain that hot-holding devices maintain food at temperatures of 140°F (60°C) or higher.
- Give special attention to inspection and cleaning of raw ingredients that will be used in foods that require little or no cooking.
- Heat leftovers quickly to an internal temperature of 165°F (73.9°C).
- Avoid carrying contamination from raw to cooked and ready-to-serve foods via hands, equipment, and utensils.
- Clean and sanitize food-contact surfaces of equipment after every use.
- Obtain foods from approved sources.

Critical Control Points

Nine areas or critical control points requiring monitoring for microbial quality and safety within foodservice operations have been identified (Unklesbay et al., 1977):

- Food procurement.
- Food storage.
- Food packaging.
- Preprocessing.
- Heat processing.
- Food storage following heat processing.
- Heat processing of precooked menu items.
- Food product distribution.
- Service of food.

Based on the food product flow shown in the models in Chapter 5, each type of foodservice system has between four and nine of these critical control points. The type of system adopted influences the number of areas requiring precise monitoring (Table 12.4). For example, the commissary system requires monitoring at all nine points, whereas, the assembly/serve system has only four critical control points. In the conventional foodservice system, in which food is served after heat

Table 12.4. *Location of nine critical control points applicable in four alternate foodservice systems*

Critical control points	Alternate foodservice systems			
	Com-missary	Conven-tional	Ready-prepared	Assembly-serve
Food procurement	X	X	X	X
Food storage	X	X	X	X
Food packaging	X		X	
Pre-processing	X	X	X	
Heat processing	X	X	X	
Food storage following heat processing	X		X	
Heat processing of precooked menu items	X		X	X
Food product distribution	X			
Foodservice	X	X	X	X

Source: Unklesbay, N., Maxcy, R. B., Knickrehm, M., Stevenson, K., Cremer, M., and Matthew, M. E.: *Foodservice Systems: Product Flow and Microbial Quality and Safety of Foods.* North Central Regional Research Bull. No. 245. Missouri Agricultural Experiment Station, Columbia, 1977.

processing, monitoring at control points concerned with storage following processing and the subsequent heating of precooked items is generally not applicable.

The information in Table 12.5 summarizes time-temperature relationships for potentially hazardous foods at some of the critical control points. As Unklesbay et al. (1977) indicate, further research is needed to identify time-temperature relationships for other menu items. In the following pages, each of the nine critical control points requiring monitoring within foodservice systems is discussed.

Food Procurement

With the exception of certain cultured foods, such as cheeses, only pathogen-free ingredients with low levels of microbial count should be purchased. Earlier in this chapter, we discussed the establishment of microbiological specifications applicable to food procurement.

Food Storage

Food is stored immediately after receipt in both conventional and assembly/serve foodservice systems. In commissary and ready prepared systems, foods as purchased are stored upon receipt and prepared menu items are stored after food production. The recommended storage temperatures and conditions for various types of food products were discussed in Chapter 8.

Foodservice managers should establish and monitor controls for the tempera-

Table 12.5. *Time-temperature relationships for potentially hazardous foods in different types of foodservice systems*

Stages of food production flow	Internal temperature of food product		Maximum time*
	Celsius	Fahr-enheit	
Heat-processed menu items for immediate consumption			
poultry and stuffing	73°	165°	
pork			
for safety	65°	150°	
for acceptability	76°	170°	
rare roast beef	60°	140°	
Chilled storage of processed			
menu items	7°	45°	36 hr.
	4°	40°	5 days
Storage of processed menu items			
before freezing	4°	40°	24 hr.
Tempering of frozen menu items			
refrigeration	4°	40°	
potable running water	21°	70°	
Distribution of chilled pro-cessed menu items	7°	45°	2 hr.
Distribution of hot processed menu items	60°	140°	
Reheated menu items	73°	165°	
Storage of prefried bacon	4°	40°	5 days
	−17°	0°	15 days
Storage of prefried bacon after heating	4°	40°	24 hr.

Source: Unklesbay, N., Maxcy, R. B., Knickrehm, M., Stevenson, K., Cremer, M., and Matthew, M. E.: *Foodservice Systems: Product Flow and Microbial Quality and Safety of Foods.* North Central Regional Research Bull. No. 245. Missouri Agricultural Experiment Station, Columbia, 1977.

*When applicable.

ture and length of storage for each menu item. The form in Figure 12.8 is an example of one that could be used for periodically recording refrigerator and freezer temperatures, which should be a regular practice in any foodservice operation.

Food Packaging

Proper packaging plays an important role in both the commissary and ready prepared foodservice systems by facilitating handling and protecting the food from contamination and unwanted changes in color, texture, and appearance.

Date	Time	Temperature	Initial		Date	Time	Temperature	Initial
1					17			
2					18			
3					19			
4					20			
5					21			
6					22			
7					23			
8					24			
9					25			
10					26			
11					27			
12					28			
13					29			
14					30			
15					31			
16								

MONTH: _____

UNIT: _____

Record Temperatures: 1× 2× 3× daily
(circle one)

Maintain 0°F for Freezer

Maintain 45°F for Refrigerator

Figure 12.8. *Refrigerator/freezer temperature record*

Packaging materials vary, depending on the type of foodservice system, but they must all provide an effective moisture barrier; controls are needed to ensure that they allow the food product to be sufficiently chilled in a short time.

The prepared menu items in these systems are packaged either in individual portions or in bulk quantity. The bulk quantity may vary from as few as 5 portions to as many as 100 in a single package. Some systems may utilize both bulk and individual packaging. For example, in a hospital foodservice using a cook-freeze ready prepared system, items for patient service may be packaged individually, whereas those for the employee cafeteria may be packaged in bulk.

Preprocessing

In commissary, conventional, and ready prepared systems, gross contamination of food products is eliminated during prepreparation. For example, dirt that may cling to fresh fruits or vegetables is washed off. Opportunities for cross-contamination are possible, however, between raw and processed food products; their strict separation in storage and food preparation areas is therefore necessary.

Heat Processing

The commissary, conventional, and ready prepared systems all involve heat processing of menu items. The effectiveness of heat processing in destroying microorganisms is influenced by food mass and the capacity and type of equipment used.

The data in Table 12.5 specify internal product temperatures recommended for some selected menu items. As indicated in the discussion on time-temperature relationships, appropriate heat processing is critical to maintaining microbial quality in foods. If consumed soon after preparation, as is the case in a conventional foodservice, the food should be safe if not held under inappropriate conditions or for lengthy periods of time. In a system using cook-chill or cook-freeze, in which the items are cold-stored, then reheated, the heat processing temperatures become even more important.

Food Storage Following Heat Processing

Depending on the type of foodservice system and the attributes of menu items, foods may be stored heated, chilled, or frozen. Since high temperatures and humidity cause loss of food quality, prolonged hot-holding is not recommended. In commissary and conventional foodservice systems, the hot-holding period should be as short as possible because of the adverse effects on nutritional and sensory qualities. Temperature control during this period is critical to ensure that food is not held in the hazardous zone for too lengthy a period.

In school foodservice, this concern is of particular relevance, since prepared food is frequently transported from a central production facility or a base kitchen to satellite service centers. The time between food production and end of service may be as long as four hours, which creates a potentially hazardous condition.

Chilled storage in commissary and ready prepared systems represents another critical control point. The necessity for rapid cooling after cooking, so that food does not remain in the danger zone for extended periods, has been well documented (Longree, 1980). Monitoring of temperatures during the cooling period should be part of a quality control program. Types of containers for storing foods will affect their cooling rate significantly, so specialized chilling equipment has been designed for use in cook-chill systems. For example, beef stroganoff stored in a two-inch cafeteria counter pan will chill more quickly than if stored in a stock pot.

Commissary as well as ready prepared foodservice systems utilize the cook-freeze concept. Heat processed menu items must be frozen as rapidly as possible and precautions taken to control microbial growth during both freezing and thawing processes. Specialized systems such as blast freezing have been designed for rapid freezing of food items, for storage later at usual freezer temperatures of 0°F. Periodic checks should be conducted to determine the bacterial count of menu items in these systems, however, because of the increased potential for microbial growth in prepared food items.

Heat Processing of Precooked Menu Items

Effective managerial monitoring of product temperatures and storage times is needed to ensure the sensory and microbiological quality of foods when served. The reheating process from the chilled, frozen, tempered (30°F or slightly below), or thawed stage should be fast, and an internal temperature of 165°F should be reached. Convection and microwave ovens are most often used for heat processing of prepared menu items.

Food Product Distribution

In commissary systems, chilled and/or heated menu items are transported to satellite service centers that may be widely dispersed from the central facilities. Therefore, the opportunities for contamination are dramatically increased. Menu items should be transported at temperatures either below 40°F or above 140°F. Complex managerial controls are needed for maintaining recommended time-temperature conditions in food handling and transportation.

Service of Food

During service, foods must be monitored for contamination and temperature control. Menu items should be served either at 40°F or above 140°F. Thus, the old adage, "hot foods hot and cold foods cold," is a principle important for both sensory and microbiological quality of food. Covering food aids in protecting against contamination and surface evaporation. Managerial monitoring must be effective at point of service, or as Unklesbay (1977) states, the effectiveness of all previous controls throughout the flow of food products from procurement to consumption may be nullified.

HACCP Models

The Hazard Analysis Critical Control Point (HACCP) concept refers to a system developed initially for quality control in the food processing industry, with special emphasis on microbial control. As defined by Bauman (1974), hazard analysis is concerned with identifying microbial-sensitive ingredients, critical control points during processing, and human factors that may affect the microbiological safety of the product. Critical control points are those steps in production processing where loss of control would result in an unacceptable safety risk. HACCP is a preventive approach to quality control, designed to identify potential dangers so that corrective action can be taken.

The original HACCP model was modified by Bobeng and David (1978) to include not only microbiological but also nutritive and sensory quality. They applied the model to quality control of entree production in conventional, cook-chill, and cook-freeze hospital foodservice systems. The HACCP models were developed for the three systems during three phases: identification of control points, using flow diagrams; identification of critical control points; and establishment of monitors for control.

Figure 12.9 shows the flow of entree production in hospital foodservice systems and the various control points. Twelve control points were established and four critical control points identified: ingredient control and storage, equipment sanitation, personnel sanitation, and time-temperature relationships (Table 12.6).

Silverman (1982) indicates that the difficulty in using HACCP models in some foodservice operations lies in the fact they were designed primarily for the evaluation of large production batches. In discussing the applicability to a hospital facility, he points out that the diets are varied and the items may be in a wide variety of forms. Also, production lots are not large and in fact can be quite small, such as those for modified diets.

He has developed a modified Quality Assurance Program (QAP) for military hospital feeding systems based on the HACCP model. The elements of the QAP are listed in Table 12.7 and are designed to provide reliability with a minimum of personnel and laboratory equipment. The system does not depend on analysis for each menu item, as do HACCP models, but instead classifies products into categories that are dependent on their main processing parameters. These parameters (ovens, kettles, freezers, etc.) are monitored as "stations" with the actual temperature constraint established for each product; the most critical parameters are then documented by designated personnel. Silverman reports that introduction of the QAP in a military hospital foodservice system has succeeded in eliminating the production problems associated with several highly hazardous products and reducing excessive counts of microorganisms to levels of less than 0.1 percent.

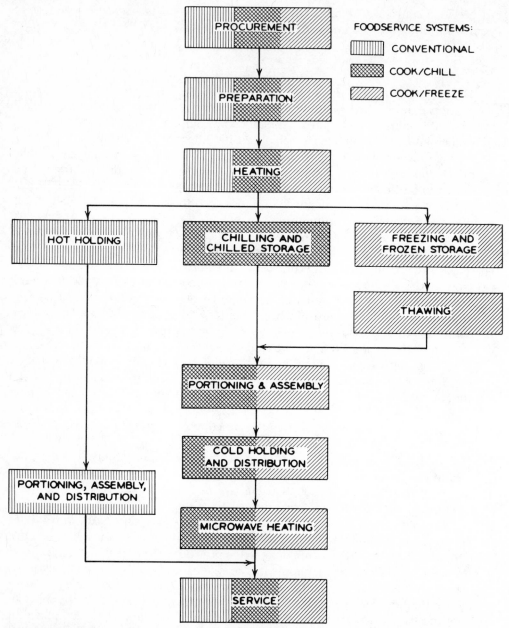

Figure 12.9. *Control points for entree production in conventional, cook-chill, and cook-freeze hospital foodservice systems.* **Source: Bobeng, B. J., and David, B. D.: HAACP models for quality control of entree production in hospital foodservice systems. J. Am. Dietet. A. 73-526, 1978.**

Table 12.6. *Critical control points during entrée production in conventional, cook-chill, and cook-freeze hospital foodservice systems*

Control points	System	Ingredient control and storage	Equipment sanitation	Personnel sanitation	Time-temperature relationship
			Critical control point		
Procurement	1,2,3*	X			
Preparation	1,2,3		X	X	X
Heating	1,2,3				X
Hot holding	1				X
Chilling and chilled storage	2		X		X
Freezing and frozen storage	3				X
Thawing	3		X		X
Portioning and assembly	2,3		X	X	X
Portioning, assembly, and distribution	1		X	X	X
Cold holding and distribution	2,3		X		X
Heating	2,3				X
Serving	1,2,3		X	X	X

Source: Bobeng, B. J., and David, B. D.: HACCP models for quality control of entree production in hospital foodservice systems. *J. Am. Dietet. A.* 73:526, 1978.

*1 = conventional; 2 = cook-chill; 3 = cook-freeze.

EMPLOYEE TRAINING IN FOOD SANITATION

As indicated throughout this chapter, trained personnel who have good personal hygiene habits and follow recommended food handling practices, as set by management, are critical to an effective sanitation program, as are strong leadership by management, provision of appropriate tools and equipment, and continual follow-up. As Longree and Blaker (1982) state, the time, money, and effort that go into a sanitation program are wasted if the foodservice staff is not aware of and knowledgeable about appropriate sanitation practices. Training principles and processes are discussed in Chapter 20, but training is mentioned here because of its critical importance in accomplishing the ultimate goal of protecting the clientele from foodborne illness.

The education of managers for the foodservice industry should include course work in microbiology and food sanitation so that they can provide leadership in design and implementation of programs that ensure high standards of sanitation. Continuing education will help them to maintain their competency.

Professional associations have played an important role in upgrading sanitation practices in the foodservice industry. As mentioned earlier in this chapter,

Table 12.7. *Elements in a quality assurance program for a military production facility*

Production

1. Known sources of raw materials
2. Classification of foods as to risk
3. Sanitation
4. Time-temperature profiles
5. Personnel training
6. End product analysis
7. Operational production guides
8. Information analysis and feedback
9. Mechanism for corrective action by management
10. Hazard analysis—critical control point (HACCP)
11. Production objectives
    —shelf-life
    —acceptability
    —uniform quality

Delivery

12. Temperature-time profile for plating, storage, delivery, and serving
13. Sanitation of delivery and serving surfaces
14. Incidence of temperature abuse

Source: Silverman, G.: Assuring the microbiological quality of hospital patient feeding systems. In *Hospital Patient Feeding Systems*, Washington, DC: National Academy Press, 1982, p. 265.

several professional associations are concerned with training standards and programs for foodservice personnel. The certification programs of several organizations include knowledge and competency in sanitation practices as a major component: for example, the certification programs of the American School Food Service Association and the Hospital, Institution and Educational Food Service Society.

A major contributor to the upgrading of sanitation practices in foodservice operations has been the National Institute for the Foodservice Industry (NIFI) through its national uniform sanitation, training, and certification plan for foodservice managers. To meet the educational needs for improved sanitation practices in foodservice operations, NIFI developed its first course in 1974, which was revised in 1978 (Clingman, 1979). Following the development of the course, NIFI developed the certification plan under a contract with the FDA. All students who complete the course and pass an examination receive an NIFI Certificate of Completion. As reported by Longree and Blaker, in 1982, 35 states had some form of foodservice manager's certification program.

Training of personnel below the managerial level is the responsibility of the foodservice manager. Initial training in safe food handling practices and personal hygiene is needed for new employees, as well as a continuing emphasis on these concepts during inservice training.

Figure 12.10. *Example of sanitation mini-posters (permission granted by National Restaurant Association)*

Many teaching aids are available to assist the manager in conducting training programs on safe food handling. Federal and state health agencies, as well as commercial and private organizations, have films, slides, posters, and manuals available for free or at low cost. In her book on quantity food sanitation, Longree (1980) includes an extensive list of available teaching aids. Many foodservice organizations have also developed comprehensive manuals for training and as a reference for their own personnel. The National Restaurant Association (1979) has published an excellent sanitation manual. It also periodically distributes brochures, mini-posters, and other aids, such as those shown in Figure 12.10, that are eye-catching and useful in assisting managers in the task of reminding personnel to use good food handling practices.

SUMMARY

Food contamination in a foodservice operation is a continual potential hazard, because food must often be prepared ahead of service and may be exposed to a variety of sources of contamination. Possible legal action and adverse publicity can be extremely detrimental to a foodservice establishment that has had an outbreak of foodborne illness.

The Centers for Disease Control have recognized foodborne illness as a major health problem in the United States. The foodservice organization has a tremendous responsibility for safeguarding its clientele through high standards of sanitation and proper food handling practices.

The major types of food spoilage are microbiological, biochemical, physical, and chemical, with most foodborne illness being the result of bacterial contamination. The two types of foodborne illness are foodborne intoxication and foodborne infections. Intoxications are caused by toxins formed in the food prior to consumption; infections are caused by the activity of large numbers of bacterial cells within the gastrointestinal system of the victim. Staphylococcus aureus, Salmonella, and Clostridium perfringens are the three most common causes of foodborne illness in the United States.

Government agencies at the federal, state, and local levels are concerned with the protection of the food supply available to the consumer. Professional and trade associations are among other agencies concerned with sanitary aspects of food.

The Food and Drug Administration (FDA) and the Centers for Disease Control (CDC) are two agencies within the U.S. Public Health Service with responsibilities specifically related to sanitation standards and regulations. Among its various functions, the CDC provides assistance in identifying causes of disease outbreaks, while the FDA directs its efforts toward protecting the public against unsafe and impure food and drugs. A model foodservice sanitation ordinance has been developed by the FDA, which has provided the basis for most state and local ordinances.

The National Sanitation Foundation (NSF) is one of the most influential semi-private agencies concerned with sanitation. Minimum standards for equipment, products, and devices have been developed through NSF research, and foodservice equipment that meets these standards receives an NSF Testing Laboratory Seal of Approval.

Microbiological quality standards are being developed by governmental and private organizations to set acceptable microbial levels for food products. Microbiological specifications and microbiological limits are being used in large foodservice organizations' quality assurance programs, especially in commissary and ready prepared systems.

External and internal audits of facilities and practices are used for evaluating maintenance of foodservice sanitation standards. Mandatory external audits are performed by governmental agencies, whereas voluntary external audits are performed by several non-governmental organizations, such as the Joint Commission on Accreditation of Hospitals (JCAH).

Internal audits are the responsibility of the management of a foodservice organization. These audits may be part of a self-inspection program focusing on sanitation, or they may be a component of a broader quality assurance program.

The ultimate goal of the sanitation program in a foodservice organization is to protect the clientele from foodborne illness, a goal requiring a two-pronged strategy: protecting food from contamination and reducing the effect of existing contamination. Controlling microbiological quality of food must focus on the food; the people involved in handling food, either as employees or patrons; and the facilities, including both large and small equipment.

Reducing the effect of contamination can be largely achieved by proper temperature and time controls in the storage, production, and service of foods. In general, pathogenic microorganisms flourish at temperatures between 40 and 140°F, a temperature range commonly called the danger or hazardous zone. Examination of the reports on outbreaks of foodborne illness indicate that the implicated foods have frequently been allowed to remain at temperatures favorable to bacterial multiplication for long periods.

Nine areas, or control points, that require monitoring for microbial quality and safety within foodservice operations are: food procurement, food storage, food packaging, preprocessing, heat processing, food storage following heat processing, heat processing of precooked menu items, food product distribution, and service of food. The type of system adopted for a foodservice operation influences the number of areas requiring monitoring.

The Hazard Analysis Critical Control Point (HACCP) system, initially developed for quality control in the food processing industry, has been adapted for use in foodservice systems. Hazard analysis is concerned with identifying microbial-sensitive ingredients, critical control points during processing, and human factors that may affect microbial safety of food products.

Trained personnel who have good personal hygiene habits and follow recommended food handling practices are a primary factor in an effective sanitation program. The time, money, and effort expended on a sanitation program are wasted if the staff is not aware of and knowledgeable about appropriate practices. Personnel training in sanitation is the responsibility of the management of a foodservice operation.

The National Institute for the Foodservice Industry has made a major contribution to upgrading sanitation practices in the foodservice industry through its training and certification plan for foodservice managers. The plan was developed under an FDA contract because of the importance for improved sanitation programs as a safeguard of the public.

REFERENCES

Avens, J. S., Poduska, P. J., Schmidt, F. P., Jansen, G. R., and Harper, J. M.: Food safety hazards associated with school food service delivery systems. *J. Food Sci.* 43:453, 1978.

Baker, K. J.: Foodservice sanitation training and reciprocity in the 80s. *J. Food Protection* 43:805 (Oct.), 1980.

Banwart, G. J.: *Basic Food Microbiology.* Westport, CT: AVI Publishing Co., 1979.

Bauman, H. E.: The HACCP concept and microbiological hazard categories. *Food Technol.* 28:30, 1974.

Bobeng, B. J., and David, B. D.: HACCP models for quality control of entree production in foodservice systems. *J. Food Protection* 40:632, 1977.

Bobeng, B. J., and David, B. D.: HACCP models for quality control of entree production in hospital foodservice systems. I. Development of Hazard Analysis Critical Control Point models. II. Quality assessment of beef loaves utilizing HACCP models. *J. Am. Dietet. A.* 73:526, 1978.

Brown, N. E., McKinley, M. M., Aryan, K. L., and Hotzler, B. B.: Conditions, procedures, and practices affecting safety of food in 10 school food service systems with satellites. *School Food Serv. Res. Rev.* 6:36, 1982.

Bryan, F. L.: Factors that contribute to outbreaks of foodborne disease. *J. Food Protection* 41:816, 1978a.

Bryan, F. L.: Food-borne diseases in the United States associated with meat and poultry. *J. Food Protection* 43:140, 1980.

Bryan, F. L.: Foodborne disease risk assessment of foodservice establishments in a community. *J. Food Protection* 45:93, 1982.

Bryan, F. L.: Hazard analysis of food service operations. *Food Technol.* 35:78, 1981.

Bryan, F. L.: Impact of food-borne diseases and methods of evaluating control programs. *J. Environ. Health* 40:3154, 1978b.

Bryan, F. L., Smith, J. D., and McKinley, T. W.: Hazard analysis of frozen dinners prepared at a catering establishment. *J. Food Protection* 43:608, 1980.

Chipley, J. R., and Cremer, M. L.: Microbiological problems in the foodservice industry. *Food Technol.* 34:59, 1980.

Clingman, C. D.: Standards for food service manager sanitation training and certification. *School Food Serv. Res. Rev.* 3:8, 1979.

Dahl, C. A., Matthews, M. E., and Marth, E. H.: Cook/chill foodservice systems: Microbiological quality of beef loaf at five process stages. *J. Food Protection* 41:788, 1978.

Dahl, C. A., Matthews, M. E., and Marth, E. H.: Cook/chill foodservice system with a microwave oven: Aerobic plate counts from beef loaf, potatoes and frozen green beans. *J. Microwave Power* 15(2):21, 1980.

Dahl, C. A., Matthews, M. E., and Marth, E. H.: Cook/chill foodservice system with a microwave oven: Injured aerobic bacteria during food product flow. *European J. Appl. Microbiol. Biotechnol.* 11:125, 1981.

Dahl, C. A., Matthews, M. E., and Marth, E. H.: Fate of *Staphylococcus aureus* in beef loaf, potatoes, and frozen and canned green beans after microwave/heating in a simulated cook-chill hospital food service system. *J. Food Protection* 43:916, 1980.

Dahl, C. A., Matthews, M. E., and Marth, E. H.: Survival of *Streptococcus faecium* in beef loaf and potatoes after microwave/heating in a simulated cook/chill foodservice system. *J. Food Protection* 44:128, 1981.

Elliott, R. P.: Microbiological criteria in USDA regulatory programs for meat and poultry. *J. Milk Food Technol.* 33:173, 1970.

Food Protection Committee, Food and Nutrition Board: *An Evaluation of Public Health Hazards from Microbiological Contamination of Foods.* Washington, DC: Natl. Acad. of Sciences, Natl. Res. Council Publ. No. 1195, 1964.

Gindin, R. L.: Sanitation and safety report: An educated staff is the best defense. *Restaur. Bus.* 81:156 (Dec. 1), 1982.

Graham, H. D.: *The Safety of Foods.* 2nd ed. Westport, CT: AVI Publishing Co., 1980.

Joint Commission on Accreditation of Hospitals: *Accreditation Manual for Hospitals and Hospital Survey Profile—1983 edition.* Chicago: Joint Commission on Accreditation of Hospitals, 1982.

Kaplan, O. B., and El-Ahraf, A.: Relative risk ratios of foodborne illness in foodservice establishments: An aid in development of environmental health manpower. *J. Food Protection* 42:446, 1979.

Kaplan, O. B., and Zalkind, D.: Improved inspection scheduling for food service establishments. *J. Food Protection* 43:408, 1980.

Longree, K.: *Quantity Food Sanitation.* 3rd ed. New York: Wiley-Interscience, 1980.

Longree, K., and Blaker, G. G.: *Sanitary Techniques in Foodservice.* 2nd ed. New York: John Wiley & Sons, 1982.

Minor, L. J.: *Sanitation, Safety & Environmental Standards.* Vol. 2 of *The L. J. Minor Foodservice Standards Series.* Westport, CT: AVI Publishing Co., 1983.

National Association of College and University Food Services: *National Association of College and University Food Services Professional Standards Manual.* East Lansing, MI: Michigan State Univ., 1982.

National Institute for the Foodservice Industry: *Applied Foodservice Sanitation.* 3rd ed. Chicago: The National Institute for the Foodservice Industry, 1985.

National Restaurant Association: *Sanitation Operations Manual.* Chicago: National Restaurant Association, 1979.

Rappole, C. L.: Sanitation in the foodservice operation: The implications of the proposed sanitation ordinance. *Cornell Hotel Restaur. Admin. Q.* 18:31, 1977.

Rivituso, C. P., and Snyder, O. P.: Bacterial growth at food service operating temperatures. *J. Food Protection* 44:770, 1981.

Rollin, J. L., Matthews, M. E., and Lund, D. B.: Cook/chill foodservice systems. *J. Am. Dietet. A.* 75:440, 1979.

Rollin, J. L., and Matthews, M. E.: Cook/chill foodservice systems: Temperature histories of a cooked ground beef product during the chilling process. *J. Food Protection* 40:782, 1977.

Silverman, G.: Assuring the microbiological quality of hospital patient feeding systems. In *Hospital Patient Feeding Systems.* Washington, DC: National Academy Press, 1982.

Tartakow, F. J., and Vorperian, J. H.: *Foodborne and Waterborne Diseases: Their Epidemiologic Characteristics.* Westport, CT: AVI Publishing Co., 1981.

Thorner, M. E., and Manning, P. B.: *Quality Control in Foodservice.* Rev. ed. Westport, CT: AVI Publishing Co., 1983.

Tucomi, S., Matthews, M. E., and Marth, E. H.: Behavior of *clostridium perfringens* in pre-cooked chilled ground beef during cooling, holding, and reheating. *J. Milk and Food Technol.* 37:494, 1974.

Tucomi, S., Matthews, M. E., and Marth, E. H.: Temperature and microbial flora of re-frigerated ground beef gravy subjected to holding and heating as might occur in a school foodservice operation. *J. Milk and Food Technol.* 37:457, 1974.

Unklesbay, N.: Monitoring for quality control in alternate foodservice systems. *J. Am. Dietet. A.* 71:423, 1977.

Unklesbay, N., Maxcy, R. B., Knickrehm, M., Stevenson, K., Cremer, M., and Matthews, M. E.: *Foodservice Systems: Product Flow and Microbial Quality and Safety of Foods.* North Central Regional Research Bull. No. 245. Columbia: Missouri Agricultural Experiment Station, 1977.

U.S. Dept. of Health, Education, and Welfare: *Food Service Sanitation Manual: 1976 Recommendations of the Food and Drug Administration.* U.S. Department of Health, Education, and Welfare, Public Health Service, Food and Drug Administration. DHEW Publication No. (FDA) 78-2081. Washington, DC: U.S. Govt. Prtg. Ofc., 1978.

U.S. food safety defense weakening; needs bolster. *CNI Nutr. Week* 14:4 (May 31), 1984.

Wehr, M. H.: Attitudes and policies of governmental agencies on microbial criteria for foods—update. *J. Food Technol.* 36:45, 1982.

Woodburn, M. J.: Educating to prevent foodborne illness. *Food Technol.* 32:56, 1978.

13

Labor Control

STAFFING AND SCHEDULING
  Variables Affecting Staffing and Scheduling
  Relief and Part-Time Personnel
  Industry Indices for Staffing
  Issues in Employee Scheduling
PRODUCTIVITY IMPROVEMENT
  Productivity Measures
  Principles of Work Design
  Work Measurement in Foodservice Operations
  Quality Circles
SUMMARY
REFERENCES

Productivity improvement is a phrase used widely today in newspapers, on television, in news magazines, in pronouncements of government and industry leaders, and in the trade and professional literature in almost all fields. The decline in productivity in this country has been a widespread concern in many organizations. Low productivity has long been considered characteristic of the foodservice industry: the popularly accepted statistic is that its productivity level is only 40 or 45 percent.

In recent years, salaries, wages, and fringe benefits have risen steadily. Fay et al. (1976) indicate that, in the hospitality service industries, the rise has outpaced that in industrial labor as a result of increased unionization, minimum wage legislation, and a realization on the part of managers that more competitive wages are necessary to attract and retain better employees. Utilizing the labor force more effectively is thus a major challenge facing managers in all types of foodservice operations.

Cost containment pressures and the new prospective payment systems in the healthcare segment of the industry, for example, have caused a major emphasis to be placed on improved productivity. All segments of the industry have been faced with inflationary pressures with a concomitant rise in costs. Since labor represents a major component of the total operational cost in a foodservice estab-

351

lishment, controlling labor cost is a key aspect of attaining financial objectives in foodservice operations.

Effective utilization of labor in the foodservice industry is especially difficult because of its unique characteristics. Among these characteristics are the following.

- Many seven-day-a-week operations, some of which may serve 24 hours a day.

- Operational schedules that may require early morning personnel for breakfast and staffing throughout the day, perhaps even for late night service.

- Peaks and valleys that create an intense demand at mealtimes or at other times, such as weekends.

- Seasonal variations in patronage of establishments.

- The highly perishable nature of the products.

- The labor intensive nature of most of the production and service operations.

- The large number of unskilled and semi-skilled personnel employed in the industry.

These and others that could be cited point out the problems facing the foodservice manager in utilizing the work force to its fullest capacity.

Many factors affect the performance of personnel. Several chapters in Section VI address such issues as job design, job analysis, job specifications and descriptions, work motivation, employee supervision, and training, all of which have an impact on employee productivity. Other factors include layout and design, equipment, the menu, the type of foods used in the operation, size and type of foodservice organization, the services provided by the organization, and the work methods used by individual employees. In this chapter, we will discuss staffing and work schedules, various considerations in scheduling, principles of work simplification, and methods of analyzing labor productivity. Lastly, we will discuss the concept of quality circles, a technique for involving personnel in the solution of quality control problems that frequently leads to improved productivity.

STAFFING AND SCHEDULING

The terms staffing and scheduling are sometimes used interchangeably; in fact, they refer to separate but interrelated functions. Staffing concerns the determination of the appropriate number of employees needed by the operation for the work that has to be accomplished. Job analyses and work production standards provide the bases for determining staffing needs.

Scheduling, however, means having the proper number of workers on duty, as determined by the staffing needs. Scheduling involves assignments of employees to specific working hours and work days. The challenge of scheduling is having sufficient staff for busy meal periods without having excess staff during slow periods between meals.

Variables Affecting Staffing and Scheduling

Operational Differences

In foodservice operations, staffing and scheduling can become extremely complex because of the highly variable nature of the business. In a commercial foodservice, for example, the weekend dinner meal is often a peak time, whereas Tuesday or Wednesday night might attract only a small number of diners. An operation catering primarily to a lunch crowd, however, may have very low volume at other meals. Hospital census generally tends to vary seasonally: patient loads are frequently at a low point during the summer vacation months and during the November and December holiday season.

In some foodservice operations, the participation of the clientele may be much more predictable; for example, in a university residence hall foodservice or in a school foodservice lunchroom. In these operations, however, a number of other factors affect participation, such as scheduled campus events at a college or university. In fact, the menu being served may itself be a major determinant of number of students who eat the meal in the university residence hall or school cafeteria. All these examples illustrate why scheduling and staffing require a great deal of time and attention from foodservice managers to ensure adequate personnel for service without overstaffing, which would drive up labor cost.

Scheduling is further complicated by absenteeism, labor turnover, vacations and holidays, days off, and differing skills of employees. In addition to all these considerations, special events and catering functions will usually have an impact on the schedule.

Determination of minimal staffing requirements is based primarily on the needed coverage for all established services and all the related tasks that must be accomplished to provide them. Fay et al. (1976) identify three distinct employee categories in the hospitality service industries.

- Employees whose work load is directly related to the number of patrons served.

- Employees, such as cashiers and supervisors, whose job requirements are determined by assigned station, which may or may not have a relationship to the number of patrons.

- Employees, such as management executives or sales representatives, whose job requirements are determined by management policy.

Type of System

The type of system used by a foodservice organization is a major determinant of its staffing needs. The most vivid example is provided by contrasting the conventional and the assembly/serve systems depicted in Chapter 5. Obviously, the staffing needs are much different in a 200-bed hospital with a conventional system, in which all or most foods are prepared from "scratch," as opposed to the institution with assembly/serve in which the foods used require little or no processing prior to service. As we pointed out in Chapter 5, only storage, assembly, heating, and service functions are performed when food products are brought into the system with a maximum degree of processing. These functions require not only less staff but also less highly skilled staff.

One of the advantages often cited for the ready prepared systems that use cook-chill or cook-freeze approaches is that the majority of the personnel, especially those in production, can be scheduled on a regular 40-hour, 5-day, Monday-through-Friday basis. This scheduling approach is possible, of course, because production is for inventory, rather than for immediate service. As a result, only a skeleton staff is needed at mealtime, during weekends, and on holidays, primarily for service, dishwashing, and cleanup; fewer people have to work the undesirable early morning, late evening, weekend, or holiday schedules.

Relief and Part-Time Personnel

Use of relief and part-time personnel is one way that foodservice operations have attempted to provide adequate personnel at peak periods without having excessive numbers of personnel during slower periods. In fact, in some types of foodservice operations, the majority of the staff are part-time employees, a practice particularly prevalent in the fast food segment of the industry.

Part-timers who are teenagers or college students often make up the bulk of the work force in fast food operations. In an attempt to reduce labor costs as much as possible, a few operations use questionable practices in dealing with these student employees. For example, a high school student may be told to report for duty at 11:00 a.m., but on arrival be told to delay clocking in because the lunch business may be slower than was anticipated. Although they may reduce cost in the short run, these practices will inevitably lead to bad will in the community in the long run.

Other types of foodservice operations that regularly utilize part-time student workers are college and university foodservices. In these operations, most of the servers and dishwashers, for example, are college students. Healthcare institutions commonly use student employees for service and cleanup during the evening meal.

Part-time personnel also make up the majority of the work force in school foodservice operations. In this instance, however, most of the workers are women who want to work outside the home for only a few hours during the day. Few school foodservice personnel work more than six hours a day, and many work as few as two hours daily, such as those who work on the serving line or in the dishroom.

In foodservice operations in which the patronage varies greatly within the week, or in establishments involved in catered events, adequate staffing is pro-

Use of staffing guide for a typical summer week in a small country club

	Tuesday–Friday Daily staff for 225 covers	Extra staff needs			Add one extra man per "covers" bracket below
		Satur-day	Sun-day	Friday night banquet	
Covers					
Average	206	325	400	250	
Excess over normal		100	175		
Kitchen					
Chef and cooks	2	1	2		70
Potwasher-vegetable cleaner	1	1	1		250
Pantry	2	1	1		160
Warewasher-porter	2	1	2		115
Dining room					
Headwaiter	1			Combined lunch and dinner covers per 4 waiters	25–28
Waiters	6	4	7		
Busboys	2	1	2		
Grill or cocktail lounge					
Waiters	2			Food and beverage covers per $175 sales	50
Bartenders	1			1	
Buffet or banquet					
Cooks				2	125
Potwasher-vegetable cleaner				1	300
Pantry				1	250
Warewashing				2	140
Waiters				10	20–25
Busboys				2	Per 7 waiters
Total staff	19	9	15	19	

Figure 13.1. *Example of staffing for a country club.* **Source: *Keiser, J., and Kallio, E.: Controlling and Analyzing Costs in Food Service Operations. New York: John Wiley & Sons, 1974, p. 49.***

vided by scheduling persons to work only on busy weekends or to assist with special events. An operation will generally have a basic staff of full-time personnel and a list of persons willing to work on an intermittent basis. This approach to staffing is often characteristic of club operations. The example in Figure 13.1 illustrates how the staffing varies from the usual weekday business in a small country club to the greater demand on weekends.

Split shift scheduling is another way in which foodservice managers have attempted to have adequate staffing during peak periods and minimal staffing during between-meal low volume times. Dining room hostesses, waiters, waitresses, and other service personnel are frequently scheduled to work during the noon meal, take a break during the afternoon when the dining room may be closed, and return for the evening meal. Split shift scheduling may be feasible when employees live within a fairly short distance from a foodservice establishment. This type of scheduling must be done carefully, however, because many states have work span laws that require the hours worked to fall within a given span of time. In the past, split shifts were a common practice in many foodservice operations, especially in hospitals and college foodservice. Today, however, many personnel are unwilling to work this type of schedule since it requires them to devote most of their day to the job, with little free time. Instead of using split shift scheduling, most operations now use part-time personnel.

Industry Indices for Staffing

Several indices have been developed for various segments of the foodservice industry to assist managers in determining staffing needs. Lundberg and Armatas (1980) propose staffing tables for commercial operations based on the number of patrons expected for a given meal on a given day, which can be used to take into account the day-to-day and meal-to-meal fluctuations in patronage. These staffing tables are shown in Tables 13.1 and 13.2, depicting staffing for a restaurant kitchen and dining room at various patronage levels.

Fairbrook (1979) indicates that industry-wide standards for staffing have not been developed to the level of sophistication of those in manufacturing industries, such as the automobile industry. He proposes a rule of thumb of approximately 10 meals per labor hour for a college and university residence hall, utilizing a combination of regular and student employees: Figure 13.2 is an example of a

Table 13.1. *Staffing table for kitchen*

Jobs to be filled	For 0–49 patrons	For 50–99 patrons	For 100–175 patrons	For 175–+ patrons
Chef	1	1	1	1
Cook	1	2	3	4
Salads—pantry	1	2	2	3
Dishwasher	1	2	3	3
Potwasher	1	1	1	1
Cleaner	0	1	1	1
Storeroom person	0	1	1	1
Baker	0	1	1	1

Source: Lundberg, D. E., and Armatas, J. P.: *The Management of People in Hotels, Restaurants, and Clubs.* Dubuque, IA: Wm. C. Brown Co. Publishers, 1980.

Table 13.2. *Staffing table for dining room, based on number of patrons*

Jobs to be filled	For 0–37 patrons	For 38–58 patrons	For 59–75 patrons	For 76–95 patrons	For 96–112 patrons	For 113–129 patrons	For 130–145 patrons	For 146–166 patrons	For 167–+ patrons
Hostess	1	1	1	1	1	1	1	1	1
Waiter/Waitress	2	3	4	5	6	7	8	9	10
Bus person	1	2	2	3	3	3	3	4	5
Bar waiter/waitress	1	1½	1½	2	2	2½	2½	2½	2½

Source: Lundberg, D. E., and Armatas, J. P.: *The Management of People in Hotels, Restaurants, and Clubs.* Dubuque, IA: Wm. C. Brown Co. Publishers, 1980.

staffing guide for a residence hall serving 750 students. As illustrated, production is the primary responsibility of regular full-time employees, and a basic full-time maintenance staff is employed. Student employees, then, are scheduled at all three meals to work on the serving line and in the dining room and dishroom.

In school foodservice, the standard of 13 to 15 meals per labor hour, including production and service personnel, has been widely used. Many of the factors affecting the number of personnel needed in an operation must be considered in evaluating school foodservice staffing, as well as that in any other foodservice operation. For example, staffing differs if breakfast is served, if multiple menu options are offered, or if the facility is a base kitchen or only a satellite service center.

Stokes (1979) states that one of the most helpful indices in determining staffing needs is the number of meals served per labor hour or the number of labor minutes per meal. Rose (1980) indicates that an index of 17 minutes per meal, or 3.5 meals per labor hour, is frequently used as a staffing standard for a conventional foodservice in an acute care facility. These standards are based on recommendations published by the U.S. Public Health Service (Coble, 1975).

Not uncommonly, however, some healthcare facilities report productivity levels as high as five to six meals per work hour. As Rose (1980) points out, this wide range of productivity levels is related to such factors as percentage of modified diets served and type of system used in both production and service. He also states that as the percentage of nonpatient meals increases, overall productivity rises. In addition, the type of services performed by dietetic personnel affects the staffing level. For example, serving patient trays may be either the responsibility of nursing or a function of the dietetic department.

Kotschevar (1973) reported that extended care facilities produce about five meals for every hour of labor. The U.S. Public Health Service prepared estimates on numbers of foodservice personnel required in hospitals and extended care facilities of 100 beds or less, which are shown in Figure 13.3.

Stokes (1979) indicates that one way to determine specific staffing needs in a healthcare facility providing seven-day-a-week, three-meal-a-day service is to establish initially the number of positions to be filled and multiply by 1.5 employees per position. Although meals must be served 365 days per year, full-time employ-

---

Staffing guide for residence hall kitchen serving 750 students

Regular Employees

A.M. Shift
*(5:00 a.m.–2:30 p.m.)**
1 Lead Cook
1 Second Cook
2 Salad and Line Workers
1 Dishwasher
1 Potwasher/Porter
1 Hostess/Cashier
(7:30 a.m.–4:00 p.m.)*

P.M. Shift
(10:00 a.m.–7:00 p.m.)
1 Lead Cook
1 Second Cook
1 Salad and Line Worker
1 Dishwasher
1 Potwasher/Porter

*Regular employees are normally scheduled for a nine-hour period, which in residence halls, allows time for two 30-minute meal periods. Those working other shifts take only one 30-minute meal period.

Student Employees

Breakfast (7:30–9:30)
Dining Room Runner 1
Serving Line 1
Serving Line Runner 1
Dishroom 1
Total Hours: 8

Lunch (11:15–1:30)
Dining Room Runner 1
Serving Lines (2) 4
Serving Line Runners 2
Dishroom 3
Total Hours: 22½

Dinner (4:15–6:30)
Dining Room Runner 1
Serving Lines (2) 4
Serving Line Runners 2
Dishroom 3
Dining Room Porters 2
Hostess/Cashier 1
Total Hours: 29¼

Please note: The above-cited staffing example gives you a productivity of approximately ten (10) meals per labor hour:

750 students × 3 meals/day = 2,250 meals paid for per day

less: 29% missed meals factor = 1,600 meals eaten per day

Total hours worked: Regular Employees   96 per day

Total hours worked: Student Employees   59¾ per day

TOTAL 155¾ per day

Meals per Labor Hours: 1,600 ÷ 155¾ = 10.3

Figure 13.2. *Example of staffing guide for residence hall foodservice. Source: Fairbrook, P.:* **College and University Food Service Manual.** *Stockton, CA: Colman Publishers, 1979, p. 125.*

ees are generally available an average of only 236 days a year because of off days and benefit days as shown below:

365 days/year

– 104 days off/year

– 10 vacation days/year

– 8 holidays

–   7 sick leave days
_____

= 236 total number actual work days/full-time employee

Suggested Levels of Personnel in Hospitals								
Number of Beds								
25	30	40	50	60	75	80	90	100
Number of Full-Time Employees								
4	4–5	5–6	6–7	7–8	9–10	9–10	10–11	11–12

Extended Care Facilities, Nursing Homes and Sheltered Care								
Number of Beds								
25	30	40	50	60	75	80	90	100
Number of Full-Time Employees								
3	3	3–4	4–5	5–6	6–7	7–8	8–9	9–10

Figure 13.3. *Suggested staffing for dietetic services in hospitals and extended care facilities.* **Source: Coble, M. C.: A Guide to Nutrition and Food Service for Nursing Homes and Homes for the Aged.** *Rev. U.S. Dept. of Health, Educ., and Welfare,* **1975.**

To determine the actual number of personnel needed, the number of full-time positions needs to be multiplied by 0.55 to find the number of relief personnel necessary in addition to the full-time staff.

Staffing needs are often stated in full-time equivalents (FTEs). The absolute FTEs indicate the actual number of employees needed to staff the facility; the adjusted FTEs take into account the benefit days and days off.

In determining staffing needs in relation to meals produced and served, a definition of a meal is sometimes needed, which is referred to as a meal equivalent. This definition is especially needed in facilities that serve many partial meals. In the healthcare industry, for example, where many nourishments are served, a meal equivalent may be determined by dividing the nourishment count by six (Ho and Matthews, 1978). Definition of a meal equivalent may be a particular concern in cafeteria operations as well.

Issues in Employee Scheduling

Types of Schedules

Three types of work schedules may need to be drawn up by the foodservice manager. One schedule will show days off, vacations, and days on duty. Another will indicate the position and hours worked and may also indicate the number of days worked per week, as well as the relief assignments for positions when regular workers are off. The third type of schedule is the production schedule, which was discussed in Chapter 9.

In most foodservice facilities, a master schedule serves as an overall plan for employee scheduling, including days off. Generally, some type of rotation is used for scheduling days off, especially in six- or seven-day-a-week operations, permitting employees to have some weekend time off on a periodic basis. A policy of every other weekend or every third weekend off is not uncommon. This master schedule provides the basis for developing the weekly, biweekly, or monthly schedule.

A paid vacation of two weeks is common in most organizations and may be extended to three weeks or longer for employees after a defined number of years of service. Holidays provided generally vary between 8 and 10 days per year. Because of the nature of the foodservice business, scheduling of vacations and holidays can present a special challenge for managers, because in many of these operations "the show must go on." In fact, in some commercial operations, holidays may be some of the highest volume days of the year and require extra staff rather than only a skeleton staff. Employees may be compensated by being paid at a double-time rate instead of being given scheduled time off.

Careful vacation planning is needed to avoid higher labor costs in the form of overtime or the excessive use of replacement workers. Managers should attempt to schedule vacations at low volume periods throughout the year, and to stagger them as well, so that only minimal relief staffing will be required. Effective scheduling of vacations can be accomplished by requesting each employee to submit preferences with alternates early in the year. A master vacation schedule can then be prepared that will permit the most effective labor utilization.

Shift scheduling may be the staffing pattern used. In the pattern shown in Figure 13.4, the staffing for a dishwashing operation for three meal periods covering 16 hours has been divided into two basic shifts. For the most part, this rigid shift scheduling is not the most effective approach to scheduling in foodservice operations. For instance, in the example in Figure 13.4, all six dishwashers arrive at 7:00 a.m., while soiled dishes in any quantity may not arrive until 7:30 or 7:45 a.m. One or two of the workers may be required to fill the dishmachine and prepare it for use for the breakfast dishes; the other workers would probably have time that would be difficult to use efficiently in some other way.

A staggered system of scheduling (Figure 13.5), on the other hand, provides for employees to begin work at various starting times, generally resulting in better utilization of the labor force. Staggered scheduling, or a combination of shift and staggered scheduling, will usually lead to reduction in idle time, and is more adaptable to the fluctuating pattern of activity in a foodservice operation.

Control of Overtime

Uncontrolled overtime is a key factor in driving up labor cost. In some instances, employees may need to work beyond their normal hours; in other cases, however, supervisors may use overtime as a substitute for proper scheduling and planning. Moreover, employees may try to create opportunities for overtime because of the time-and-a-half wage rate they may receive.

As Fairbrook (1979) indicates, if the basic staffing pattern is the first determinant of labor cost, then control of overtime is the second. He emphasizes that the key to the overtime problem is tight control: with proper staffing and realistic work schedules, overtime becomes necessary only in emergencies.

Policies regarding time cards must be formulated so that employees punch out at scheduled times, unless authorized to punch out at a later time. Controls are needed for legal reasons, as well as for control of labor cost. Labor laws define when overtime pay is due to an employee, and the recorded time from the time

Stacked or Shift Scheduling

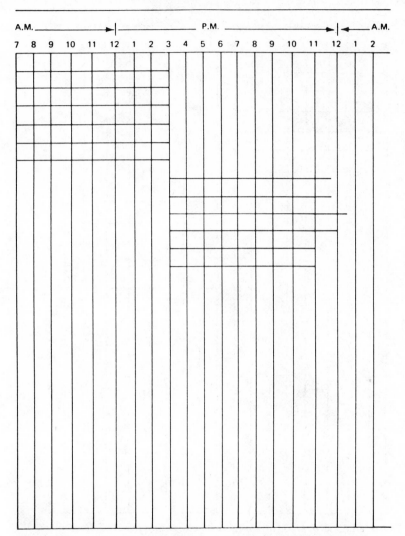

Figure 13.4. *Example of shift scheduling for a dishroom operation.* Source: *Fay, C. T., Rhoads, R. C., and Rosenblatt, K. L.: Managerial Accounting for the Hospitality Service Industries. 2nd ed. Dubuque, IA: William C. Brown Publishers, 1976, p. 338.*

clock usually provides the official record of time worked for employees covered by overtime provisions.

Only certain members of the managerial staff should be designated to authorize overtime. An overtime report form, such as the one in Figure 13.6, should be prepared within 24 hours, showing the amount of overtime worked and giving the reason for it; the report should be initialed by the manager authorizing the overtime.

Staggered Scheduling

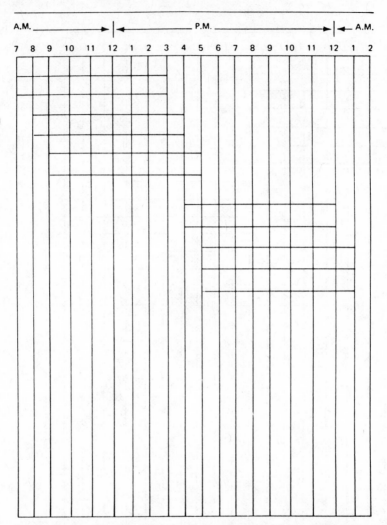

Figure 13.5. *Example of staggered scheduling for a dishroom operation.* Source: *Fay, C. T., Rhoads, R. C., and Rosenblatt, K. L.:* **Managerial Accounting for the Hospitality Service Industries. 2nd ed. Dubuque, IA: William C. Brown Publishers, 1976, p. 340.**

Alternative Work Schedules

Alternatives to the standard work week have been a topic of interest and experimentation in recent years (Newstrom and Pierce, 1979). Trends have included the introduction of several discretionary time work schedules and new forms of part-time employment. These new approaches can be grouped into three categories.

```
┌──────────────────────────────────────────────────────────────────┐
│                      Overtime authorization                        │
│                                                                    │
│                              Date _____ │
│                                                                    │
│   Name _____  Unit _____  │
│                                                                    │
│   Reason for Overtime _____│
│                                                                    │
│   _____ │
│                                                                    │
│   _____ │
│                                                                    │
│   Amount of Overtime: _____ Hrs.                             │
│                                                                    │
│                              _____  │
│                              Signature of Unit Manager             │
└──────────────────────────────────────────────────────────────────┘
```

Figure 13.6. *Example of an overtime authorization form*

- Compressed work week.
- Discretionary working time.
- Part-time employment.

Three work patterns characterize the compressed work week trend. A change in days holds the total hours constant, but reduces the number of days worked; for example, a four-day week, ten hours per day. Some foodservice operations have experimented with this approach; however, it has not gained widespread popularity in the industry. The second pattern, a change in hours worked, shortens the number of hours in the week, while the number of days worked remains the same. A seven-hour day, for instance, is characteristic of some organizational scheduling patterns. The third pattern is a change in days and hours, in which both dimensions are changed.

Discretionary working time modifications to the standard work week include the staggered start system and flexible working hours. With the staggered start system, the organization or the employee chooses, from a number of management-defined options, when they wish to start their fixed hour working day.

Flexible working hours or flexitime, as the system is sometimes called, is the second major variation of discretionary working time schedules. In the purest form of flexitime, Newstrom and Pierce (1979) indicate that individual employees exercise a daily decision with regard to the time of day they will come to work. Generally, the organization defines a period of time during the day within which employees may select their starting time. A number of variations to flexitime systems have been developed. Flexitime is impractical for many foodservice operations, however, because of the demands of production and service and scheduled mealtimes.

Task contracting is another alternative to flexible work schedules in which the employee contracts to fulfill a defined task or piece of work. This approach has been used by some foodservice caterers who may contract with an individual for preparation of particular food items or for serving a particular function.

Part-time employment is being used more widely in many different organizations today. As discussed earlier in this chapter, foodservice operations commonly use part-time employees as a way of controlling labor costs. Two new variations in part-time employment have emerged, however: job sharing and job splitting. In job sharing, a single job is divided and shared by two or more employees, each of whom must be capable of performing the entire range of tasks in the job description. In job splitting, the tasks that comprise a single job are divided, with subsets of differentiated tasks assigned to two or more employees.

Several of these alternative work schedules have been tried or are now being utilized in the foodservice industries. Others, however, are less applicable because of the unique characteristics of the industry. In their experiments with new scheduling approaches, foodservice managers should use a careful process that involves gaining employee acceptance, pilot testing the approach, and carefully evaluating outcomes of the pilot tests before adopting the new approach.

PRODUCTIVITY IMPROVEMENT

Productivity Measures

A number of methods are used to measure labor productivity in foodservice operations. These measures can be classified as operating ratios, which are discussed in more detail in the chapter on management of financial resources (Chapter 21). Because of their relevance to labor control, however, several of the frequently used measures of labor productivity are delineated here.

- Meals served per labor hour.
- Labor minutes per meal served.
- Payroll cost per day.
- Payroll cost per meal served.
- Labor cost per day.
- Labor cost per meal served.

Formulas for computing each of these measures are shown in Figure 13.7. Record keeping systems should be established to record data on a systematic basis to determine the productivity measures that the management of the foodservice organization has selected for analysis. These measures can be used to examine trends over time within a particular operation, to compare various operations within an organization, or to compare the results from a specific foodservice operation with available industry data.

$$\text{meals/labor hour} = \frac{\text{total meals served/day}}{\text{labor hours/day}}$$

$$\text{minutes/meal} = \frac{\text{labor minutes/day}}{\text{total meals served/day}}$$

$$\text{payroll cost/day} = \Sigma \text{ of hourly rate of each employee} \times \text{hours worked for all employees}$$

$$\text{payroll cost/meal served} = \frac{\text{total daily payroll cost}}{\text{meals served/day}}$$

$$\text{labor cost/day} = \text{total payroll cost/day} + \text{total of all other direct labor costs (fringe benefits, and so on)/day}$$

$$\text{labor cost/meal served} = \frac{\text{total labor cost/day}}{\text{meals served/day}}$$

Figure 13.7. *Selected productivity measures*

Principles of Work Design

Konz (1983) indicates that the objective in productivity improvement should be to assist the worker to "work smart and not hard." To work smart means to work more efficiently; to work hard means to exert more effort. He contends more potential for improvement exists in reducing excess work than through making the staff work harder.

Productivity is the ratio of output to input. Inputs and outputs in a foodservice system were described in Chapter 2, in the discussion of the systems approach in the foodservice organization. Productivity can be increased by reducing input, by increasing output, or by doing both at the same time.

As indicated in the introduction of this chapter, productivity in the foodservice industry tends to be low. High labor turnover, rising labor costs, and the relatively high percentage of the revenue dollar devoted to labor cost indicate that foodservice managers should focus efforts on increasing labor productivity.

Labor inefficiency may be the result of several factors: poor product design, manufacturing methods, management, or workers (Konz, 1983). Material waste, improper tools or methods, inadequate maintenance, poor production scheduling, absences without cause, and carelessness are examples.

Work design refers to a program of continuing effort to increase the effectiveness of work systems (Kazarian, 1979). Industrial engineers, for example, have applied work analysis and design techniques in the manufacturing indus-

(1) Minimize all material movements and storages.

(2) Use the shortest and straightest routes for the movement of materials across the workplace.

(3) Store materials as close to the point of first use as possible.

(4) Minimize handling of materials by workers unless absolutely necessary.

(5) Preposition all materials at the workplace as much as possible to reduce handling effort.

(6) Handle materials in bulk if at all possible.

(7) Provisions should be made to remove scrap, trash and other wastes at the point of creation.

(8) Take advantage of gravity to move materials when feasible.

(9) Use mechanical aids to lift heavy materials that are frequently used at workplaces.

(10) Built-in leveling devices can be used to keep materials at a convenient working height.

(11) Use mechanized conveyors to move materials that follow a fixed route across the workplace if they do not interfere with the work.

(12) Use well-designed containers and tote pans that are easy to pick up and move.

(13) Consider the use of interlocking containers for moving greater loads with ease and safety.

(14) Consider changing the design of the products involved to improve their materials-handling characteristics.

Figure 13.8. *Principles of materials handling*

tries for many years. More recently, these principles have been applied to the service industries.

Principles of work analysis and design have been developed from several different fields of study over a period of time. Among the major contributions to the study of scientific management is the classic work of Frederick Taylor and the Gilbreths. Their principles of materials handling and motion economy are the ones most directly related to labor productivity and will be discussed here.

Materials handling refers to the movement and storage of materials and products as they proceed through the foodservice system. Good design of materials movement will lead to increased efficiency and decrease activities that do not add appreciable value to the end product. The amount of materials handling is often dependent on the location and arrangement of storage areas, prepreparation and production areas, and equipment. The key principles of materials handling, outlined in Figure 13.8, should be used to develop a system for moving materials efficiently within the foodservice facility.

The principles of motion economy, primarily from the early work of the Gilbreths, relate to the design of work methods, of the workplace, and of tools and equipment. These principles, summarized in Figure 13.9, specify that movement should be simultaneous, symmetrical, natural, rhythmic, and habitual.

The principles of motion economy that pertain to the human body are aimed specifically at reducing the effort and energy required to do a job; for example, the use of both hands, coordination of hands and eyes, and continuous motion. The principles related to the design of the workplace and of tools and equipment identify situations that lead to easy body motions; for example, locating tools

A   Use of the human body

1   The number of motions required to complete a task should be minimized.

2   The length of necessary motions should be minimized.

3   Both hands should be used for work and should begin and end their activities simultaneously.

4   Motions of hands and arms should be in symmetrical and opposite directions.

5   Both hands should not be idle at the same time except for rest.

6   Motions should be confined to the lowest possible classifications needed to perform the task satisfactorily.

7   Smooth curved motions should be developed in preference to straight-line or angular motions.

8   Motion patterns should be developed for rhythmic and habitual performance.

9   The motions should be arranged to take advantage of momentum.

10   The number of eye fixations required for the task should be minimized.

11   Intermittent use of the different classifications of movements should be provided to combat fatigue.

B   Design and layout of the workplace

1   Materials, tools and controls should be located within the normal working area.

2   Materials and tools should have a fixed location.

3   Work requiring the use of eyes should be done within the normal field of vision.

4   Tools and materials should be prepositioned to facilitate picking up.

5   Gravity feed bins or containers should be used to deliver incoming materials close to the point of use.

6   Gravity should be used to deliver outgoing materials.

7   The height of the working surface should be designed to allow either a standing or sitting position.

8   The environment of the workplace should be conducive to productive motions.

C   Design of tools and equipment

1   Tools, hand equipment and controls should be designed for easy grasp.

2   Two or more tools should be combined if possible.

3   Jigs, fixtures or foot operated devices should be used to relieve the work of the hands.

4   Equipment should be designed so the inherent capabilities of the body members are fully utilized.

5   Levers and controls should be designed to make maximum contact with the body member.

Figure 13.9.   *Principles of motion economy*

within easy reach and placing objects in fixed positions. The graphics in Figure 13.10, which have been adapted from employee training materials on work simplification, illustrate several of the key principles.

Work Measurement in Foodservice Operations

Work measurement is a method of establishing an equitable relationship between the amount of work performed and the human input used to do that work. Several productivity measures were outlined previously in this chapter. In any

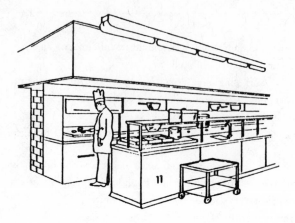

Proper equipment arrangement helps you "work smart".

**<u>Adjust</u> work heights to your elbow by:

1) changing height of work on the table. (Use different thicknesses of cutting boards or platforms to adjust the level of the work.)

2) adjusting equipment height. (Use a table to suit your height and job.)

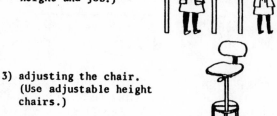

3) adjusting the chair. (Use adjustable height chairs.)

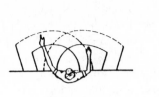
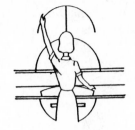
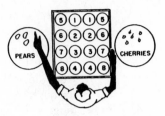

Arranging work and using both hands in rhythm and order improves your methods.

Maximum work areas, based on your reach distance, affect tiring.

Planned arrangements save time, motion, & effort.

Drop delivery using proper heights of equipment helps you "work smart".

Using continuous curved motions avoids unneeded starts and stops

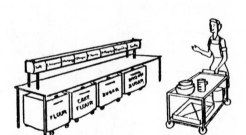

Equipment on wheels can help organize work.

Using muscles smoothly when lifting prevents strain.

Figure 13.10. *Illustrations of work designs principles in foodservice operations.* **Source:** *Konz, S., and Maxwell, J.: The Basic Four of Work. Manhattan, KS: Kansas State University, 1980.*

production operation, work measurement is necessary for effective use of human resources.

Data from work measurement studies can aid in evaluating alternative production/service systems, determining and controlling cost, staffing, scheduling work, deciding whether to make or buy, planning facilities and layout, identifying needs for changes in employee assignments, and timing or sequencing of tasks. David (1978) indicates that work measurement data are also needed for developing useful managerial aids, such as production time standards. Activity analysis, activity or occurrence sampling, elemental standard data, and predetermined motion time are the primary techniques of work measurement used for analysis in foodservice operations.

Activity analysis involves continuous observation for a chronological record of the nature of activities performed by individual workers, work performed at one work station, work units produced, or the amount of time equipment is used and for what purpose. The data are used to establish standards for short cycle work or long cycle work by persons moving about and to develop elemental standard data, discussed below. A simplified technique has been developed that involves employee recording of activities at periodic intervals, usually between 5 and 15 minutes. This technique has been referred to as an employee time log reporting

---

TIME REPORTING SHEET FOR THE LINCOLN PUBLIC SCHOOLS' FOODSERVICE STUDY

LINCOLN PUBLIC SCHOOLS

DIVISION OF BUSINESS AFFAIRS

TIME MANAGEMENT REPORTING FORM

_____

DEPARTMENT

• EMPLOYEE NAME _____   _____ WORK WEEK

Day	Unit	Function	Project	Day	Unit	Function	Project	Day	Unit	Function	Project

---

CODES FOR REPORTING FOODSERVICE ACTIVITIES: EMPLOYEES, FUNCTIONS, AND PROJECTS

Coding for Foodservices Work Analysis

Code/Function	Code/Project
1 Washing	1 Salad Fruit/Veg
2 Chopping	2 Fruit Can/Fresh
3 Dipping	3 Dessert
4 Stirring	4 Vegetables
5 Mixing	5 Entree
6 Panning	6 Juice
7 Shaping	7 Milk
8 Weighing	8 Breads
9 Buttering	9 Restroom

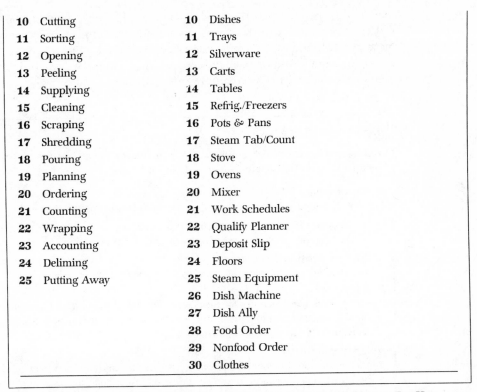

10	Cutting		**10**	Dishes
11	Sorting		**11**	Trays
12	Opening		**12**	Silverware
13	Peeling		**13**	Carts
14	Supplying		**14**	Tables
15	Cleaning		**15**	Refrig./Freezers
16	Scraping		**16**	Pots & Pans
17	Shredding		**17**	Steam Tab/Count
18	Pouring		**18**	Stove
19	Planning		**19**	Ovens
20	Ordering		**20**	Mixer
21	Counting		**21**	Work Schedules
22	Wrapping		**22**	Qualify Planner
23	Accounting		**23**	Deposit Slip
24	Deliming		**24**	Floors
25	Putting Away		**25**	Steam Equipment
			26	Dish Machine
			27	Dish Ally
			28	Food Order
			29	Nonfood Order
			30	Clothes

Figure 13.11. *Form and codes for employee time log system.* **Source:** *DenHartog, R., Carlson, H., and Romisher, J. M.: Employee logs as a basis for time analysis.* **School Food Service Research Review 2:99, 1978.**

system (DenHartog, 1978). Figure 13.11 shows a time recording sheet and the codes for reporting foodservice activities, using an employee time log from a time analysis system in a school foodservice operation. Employees are asked to enter data on the form every ten minutes during each day of a time study, according to the function and project from the code sheet. Analysis of the data permits an analysis of time devoted to various operations within the school foodservice unit.

Activity or occurrence sampling are terms used in the literature to describe a method for measuring working time and nonworking time of people employed in direct and indirect activities, and to measure operating time and down time of equipment. The term work sampling may also be used to refer to this technique. Konz (1983) states that occurrence sampling is a more accurate term than work sampling, however, since what is being sampled is the occurrence of the various types of events that may involve direct work, indirect work, and delays. By means of intermittent, randomly spaced, instantaneous observations, estimates can be made of the proportion of time spent in a given activity over a specified period of time.

Activity or occurrence sampling has been widely used for studying work in foodservice operations. Several of these studies are cited in the reference list at the end of this chapter. Much of the classic work has been done at the University of Wisconsin, where a manual was developed describing methods for conducting activity sampling studies in foodservice operations (Univ. of Wisconsin, 1967). Work functions and classifications including direct work, indirect work, and delays are defined in the manual (Figure 13.12).

Direct work functions

Any essential activity contributing directly to the production of the end product (end product is total number of meals served per day).

- *Processing*
  Act of changing the appearance of a foodstuff by physical or chemical means.

  - *Prepreparation or preliminary processing*
    Preliminary act or process of making ready for preparation, distribution, or service.

  - *Preparation or cooking*
    Final act or process of making ready for distribution or service.

- *Service*
  Act of preparing facilities for distribution and of portioning and assembling prepared food for distribution to patients and to cafeteria customers (to coffee shop also if dietary is responsible for operation of coffee shop).

- *Transportation*
  Act of transporting food, supplies, or equipment from a location in one functional area to a designated location in another area within the department or to patients' wards.

  - *Transportation of food*
    Act of moving food from a location in one functional area to a designated location in another area within the department.

  - *Transportation of equipment, supplies, and other*
    Act of moving equipment, supplies, and other items from a location in one functional area to a designated location in another area within the department.

  - *Delivery of trays to patients* (if this function is performed by dietary)
    Act of removing patients' trays from food trucks, dumbwaiter or trayveyor, and carrying to patients' bedside.

  - *Return of trays from patients* (if this function is performed by dietary)
    Act of removing trays from patients' bedside to food trucks; dumbwaiter on the ward.

  - *Transportation empty*
    Act of moving without carrying or guiding anything from a location in one functional area to a designated location in another area within the department.

- *Clerical (routine)*
  Act of receiving, compiling, distributing, and storing of routine records of data and information necessary for operation of the department.

- *Cleaning*
  Act of removing soil or dirt to provide sanitary conditions for the use of equipment, facilities, and supplies.

  - *Pot and pan washing*
    Act of scraping, washing, or rinsing quantity food containers and cooking utensils.

- *Dishwashing*
  Act of preparing for or removal of soil or dirt to provide sanitary conditions for use of tableware (china, silverware, glassware, and trays).

- *Housekeeping*
  Act of removing soil or dirt to provide sanitary conditions for the use of installed and mobile equipment and facilities.

- *Receiving*
  Act of acquiring, inspecting, and storing food and/or supplies from an area outside the department.

Indirect work functions

Any catalytic activity which contributes to production of the end product.

- *Instruction or teaching*
  Act of directing or receiving direction by oral or written communication in a training or classroom situation or on the job.

- *Appraisal*
  Act of judging or estimating the value or amount of work in order to make decisions for future planning.

- *Conference*
  Act of oral communication with one or more persons in the form of a scheduled meeting.

- *Clerical (original or non-delegable)*
  Act of compiling and formulating management control records of data and information necessary for the operation of the department.

Delays

All time when an employee is scheduled to be working and is not engaged in either a direct or an indirect work function.

- *Forced delay*
  The time an employee is not working due to an interruption beyond his control in the performance of a direct or an indirect work function.

- *Personal and idle delays*
  The time an employee is not working due to personal delays or avoidable delays.

  - *Personal delays*
    The time an employee is not working due to time permitted away from the work area.

  - *Idle time*
    Any avoidable delay (other than forced or personal delay) that occurs for which the employee is responsible.

Figure 13.12. *Work function classification and definitions.* **Adapted from Methodology Manual for Work Sampling, Productivity of Dietary Personnel.** *Univ. of Wisconsin-Madison, 1967.*

The number of observations required in occurrence sampling depends on the type of study, the type of operations, and the number of personnel. Data from an occurrence sampling study are used to calculate labor minutes per meal equivalent or labor minutes for some other specific activity. For example, Block et al. (1985) used activity sampling to study cleaning times for vegetables in a university residence hall foodservice. One advantage of occurrence sampling is that several workers in a specific area can be studied simultaneously by a single observer.

Elemental standard data are time values that have been determined for many elements and motions common to a wide variety of work (David, 1978). From these values, total times for specific tasks can be synthesized. David (1978) states that job variables significantly affecting normal time for a given type of operation must first be hypothesized, then data on times be collected on the number and variety of jobs of that type. The data are used to determine the relationship between normal time and each of the variables believed to affect normal time significantly.

Predetermined motion time includes techniques in which tasks are broken down into basic motions for which normal time values have been determined (David, 1978). The purpose of this system is to establish cycle time for a specific operation without actually performing the task. Instead, the predetermined time for the basic motions that make up the cycle are synthesized. One technique, Methods Time Measurement (MTM), is widely used in industry but it is time consuming, and David (1978) concludes that MTM is usually not applicable to long cycle work or work with limited repetition, such as that in foodservice operations. An alternative technique has been developed, called Master Standard Data (MSD), in which seven basic elements of work are combined into larger, more condensed elements.

Montag et al. (1964) were among the first to apply MSD to foodservice operations. They concluded that the method was applicable for developing coded standard elements with universal application in foodservice operations. Several studies listed in the references for this chapter cite other studies that used MSD for examining production times in foodservice facilities. One of the most recent studies (Ridley et al., 1984) used Master Standard Data to develop labor times for the assembling and microwave heating of menu items in a hospital galley. They also found that the technique could be used effectively for developing standard labor times, since data from their study indicated that total labor time under actual conditions in a hospital galley was similar to MSD predicted time.

David (1978) concludes that progress is being made in foodservice systems toward developing standards for labor time using techniques of work measurement. She asserts, however, that application of the more complex measures requires a combination of the expertise of the foodservice operator and the systems analyst. Each foodservice operation should establish its own standards of productivity because of unique differences among operations. She emphasizes that work measurement in the industry should continue, but cautions that quantitative productivity standards should not be the only index for measuring the effectiveness of a foodservice operation. At some point, increased productivity can be achieved only by sacrificing the quality of food and service or the level of employee satisfaction (Ruf and David, 1975).

Quality Circles

Quality circles (QC) began in Japan in the early 1960s, developing from the needs of Japanese industry to improve the quality of their industrial production. In the rebuilding process following World War II, the U.S. government provided assistance aimed at improving quality control methods in that country. The quality circle concept evolved from quality training initially provided to managerial personnel and first line supervisors, which was then applied to employee involvement in quality improvement. Ingle (1982) indicates that the first quality circle was registered in Japan in 1962, with the number today exceeding 100,000. By the late 1970s, the concept had spread to Korea, Taiwan, Brazil, and the United States.

Konz (1983) describes a quality circle as a small group of employees, ranging from 3 to 25 members. Since part of the concept is to get everyone to participate, a limit of about 10 members, all volunteers, seems to work best. Meetings are typically held once a month, but may be held as often as once a week, with the usual length being one hour. Normally these meetings are within working hours, but may be held outside working hours, with employees being paid extra. Projects are generally nominated by the workers and focus on quality improvement.

Four basic steps are involved in a QC team's approach to a problem.

- *Step 1.* Select the project.
- *Step 2.* Analyze present conditions.
- *Step 3.* Establish goals.
- *Step 4.* Promote control activities.

Training of team members is considered critical to the success of quality circles. It must focus not only on the quality control concept but also on brainstorming and on the various data analysis techniques used in the QC concept (fish diagrams, histograms, and check lists and other data recording devices). Managerial support is a prerequisite to success of quality circles in an organization.

In summarizing the literature on quality circles, Treadwell and Klein (1984) cite the following as among the benefits from quality circles: improved productivity, product quality, and employee satisfaction and morale; reduced tardiness, absenteeism, and work disruption; and development of the managerial ability of circle leaders. In describing their experience with implementing quality circles in a large hospital dietetics department, they indicate that the first challenge was to define objectives and a code of conduct (Table 13.3). Once these were agreed upon, the group was prepared to begin the problem solving process, illustrated in Figure 13.13.

Their initial team was established in the patient tray assembly area, and during the first 18 months, fourteen projects were completed, six concerned with workers' day-to-day frustrations, four with quality, and four with cost reduction

Table 13.3. *Patient tray assembly quality circle objectives and code of conduct*

Objectives	Code of conduct
To build better relationships among employees.	Problem solving is the focus, not personality probing.
To give employees an interest in their work through contributing ideas.	Criticize ideas, not people.
To respect each other as individuals and work together in harmony.	All questions and suggestions are accepted—the only stupid question is the one not asked.
To improve quality of work life.	Everyone enters with an open mind and is open to ideas of others.
To participate as a team member, no matter how small the input.	Everyone arrives at the meeting on time.
To participate collectively in the presentation to management.	All projects and problems are work related. Salaries, wages, and benefits are not discussed.

Source: Treadwell, B. D., and Klein, J. A. P: Quality Circles in a department of dietetics. *J. Am. Dietet. A.* 84:683, 1984.

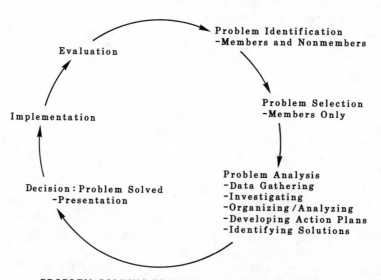

PROBLEM-SOLVING PROCESS FOR QUALITY CIRCLES

Figure 13.13. *Problem-solving process for quality circles.*
Source: *Treadwell, B. D., and Klein, J. A. P.: Quality circles in a department of dietetics. J. Am. Dietet. A. 84:683, 1984.*

and productivity improvement. Treadwell and Klein report that a savings of $10,000 was documented in this first one and a half years and that the quality of food served to patients improved, as well as the work environment for employees.

Ingle (1982) identifies three reasons behind the success of quality circles.

- Use of basic statistics.
- Group dynamics.
- Job satisfaction.

When problems are attacked in quality circles, the solutions or suggestions are not based on opinions or imagination but on data collected for analyzing a problem logically and systematically. Working together in a group helps people make better decisions and builds a cooperative spirit. Generally, communication improves, labor problems are minimized, waste is reduced, and self-inspection becomes routine. Ingle contends that job satisfaction increases as well because people feel that they are part of a company, they are listened to, and they are permitted to enjoy a greater degree of freedom and autonomy in the workplace.

As stated earlier in this chapter, the quality circle concept was not designed initially as a productivity improvement measure, but as an approach to solving quality problems in organizations. Improved productivity may be a fringe benefit, however, because reduction in waste and defects may result in an improved level of production of quality items.

SUMMARY

The low productivity in the foodservice industry has long been a concern of managers and administrators. The steady increase in salaries, wages, and fringe benefits in recent years has led to increased emphasis on utilizing the labor force more effectively, a difficult challenge because of the unique characteristics of the industry: the number of seven-day-a-week operations, the peaks and valleys of the typical operation schedule, and the labor-intensive nature of foodservice operations, among others.

Staffing means the determination of the appropriate number of employees, whereas scheduling means having the proper number of workers on duty. In foodservice operations, staffing and scheduling are extremely complex because of the highly variable nature of the business. The type of foodservice system is a major determinant of staffing needs, a key factor being the degree of processing of food products brought into the system. Some of the ready prepared systems using cook-chill or cook-freeze approaches offer the advantage of regular scheduling of many employees, since production is for inventory rather than immediate service.

Frequently, relief and part-time personnel are used as one means of providing adequate personnel during peak periods, without having excess numbers during slow periods. High school and college students are widely used as part-timers in foodservice operations, especially in the fast food segment of the industry.

Several indices have been developed for various segments of the foodservice industry to assist managers in determining staffing needs; however, these standards have not been developed to the level of sophistication of those in the manufacturing industry. Often, staffing needs are stated in full-time equivalents. A definition of a meal or meal equivalent is sometimes needed, especially in facilities that serve many partial meals.

A master schedule provides an overall plan for employee scheduling, which is used to develop the weekly or monthly schedule. Staggered scheduling, in which employees begin work at various starting times, is frequently used in foodservice operations. Because of the fluctuating pattern of activity in a foodservice operation, it allows better utilization of the labor force.

With proper staffing and realistic work schedules, employee overtime only becomes necessary in emergencies. Tight control of overtime is needed to avoid excessive labor costs.

Several alternatives to the standard work week have been introduced in recent years. The compressed work week, discretionary working time, and new variations in part-time employment are among those that have emerged.

The objective of productivity improvement is to assist the worker to "work smart and not hard." Work design refers to a program to increase the effectiveness of work systems, and principles have been developed for materials handling and motion economy that pay off in increased productivity.

Work measurement is a method of establishing an equitable relationship between the work performed and the human input used. Activity analysis, activity or occurrence sampling, elemental standard data, and predetermined motion time are the primary techniques of work measurement used in analyzing foodservice operations. Data from work measurement studies are needed for developing standards for labor time in foodservice systems. Each operation should establish its own standards because of unique differences among operations.

Although not a technique designed as a productivity measure, the quality circle concept has led to improved productivity in many operations because it results in reduced waste and defects. With quality circles, small groups of employees are involved in identifying quality problems, analyzing present conditions, establishing goals, and promoting control activities. Quality circles are considered to be an effective technique because solutions posed are based on data, because better decisions evolve from the group process, and because job satisfaction increases as people enjoy a greater degree of freedom and autonomy.

REFERENCES

Block, A. A., Roach, F. R., and Konz, S. A.: Occurrence sampling in a residence hall foodservice: Cleaning times for selected vegetables. *J. Am. Dietet. A.* 85:206, 1985.

Boss, D., and Schuster, K: The search is on: Productivity in food service. *Food Mgmt.* 16:42 (Mar.), 1981.

Campion, M. A., and Phelan, E. J.: Biomechanics and the design of industrial jobs. *Personnel J.* 60:949, 1981.

Carroll, G. H., and Montag, G. M.: Labor-time comparison of a cook-freeze and a cook-serve system of food production. *J. Canadian Dietet. A.* 40:39 (Jan.), 1979.

Cichy, R. R.: Productivity pointers to promote a profitable performance. *The Consultant* 16:35 (Winter), 1983.

Coble, M. C.: *A Guide to Nutrition and Food Service for Nursing Homes and Homes for the Aged.* Rev. U.S. Dept. Health, Educ., and Welfare, 1975.

David, B. D.: Work measurement in food service operations. *School Food Serv. Res. Rev.* 2:1, 1978.

DenHartog, R., Carlson, H., and Romisher, J. M.: Employee logs as a basis for time analysis. *School Food Serv. Res. Rev.* 2:98, 1978.

Drozda, W. J.: SUMS—A staffing methodology. *J. Canadian Dietet. A.* 39:80 (Apr.), 1978.

Ebro, L. L., ed.: Productivity measurement and improvement: Strategies and techniques for foodservice systems management. *Proceedings of the Eleventh Biennial Conference of the Foodservice Systems Management Education Council.* Norman, OK: Univ. of Oklahoma (Mar.), 1981.

Ebro, L. L., and Shaw, K. K.: Quality circles: A bibliography. *School Food Serv. Res. Rev.* 7:124, 1983.

Fairbrook, P.: *College and University Food Service Manual.* Stockton, CA: Colman Publishers, 1979.

Faulkner, E.: Will quality circles work in American foodservice operations? *Restaur. and Institutions* 93:149 (Sep-t. 15), 1981.

Fay, C. T., Rhoads, R. C., Rosenblatt, R. L.: *Managerial Accounting for the Hospitality Service Industries.* 2nd ed. Dubuque, IA: Wm. C. Brown Co. Publishers, 1976.

Ferderber, C. J.: Measuring quality and productivity in a service environment. *Industr. Eng.* 13:38 (Jul.), 1981.

Gryna, F. M.: *Quality Circles: A Team Approach to Problem Solving.* New York: AMACOM, 1981.

Harper, J. M., Shigetomi, C. T., Mackin, S. D., Iyer, P. A., and Jansen, G. R.: Alternate lunch patterns in high schools. I. Labor requirements and meal costs. *J. Am. Dietet. A.* 77:152, 1980.

Ho, A. K., and Matthews, M. E.: Activity sampling in two nursing home foodservice systems. *J. Am. Dietet. A.* 73:647, 1978.

Ingle, S.: *Quality Circle Master Guide: Increasing Productivity with People Power.* Englewood Cliffs, NJ: Prentice-Hall, 1982.

Ingle, S., and Ingle, N.: *Quality Circles in Service Industries.* Englewood Cliffs, NJ: Prentice-Hall, 1983.

Jenkins, K. M., and Shimada, J.: Quality circles in the service sector. *Supervisory Mgmt.* 26:2 (Aug.), 1983.

Kaud, F. A.: Productivity: Measures and improvement approaches. In Rose, J. C.: *Handbook for Health Care Food Service Management.* Rockville, MD: Aspen Systems Corp., 1984.

Kaud, F. A., Miller, R. P., and Underwood, R. F.: *Cafeteria Management for Hospitals.* Ch. 8. Chicago: American Hospital Association, 1982.

Kazarian, E. A.: *Foodservice Facilities Planning.* 2nd ed. Westport, CT: AVI Publishing Co., 1983.

Kazarian, E. A.: *Work Analysis and Design for Hotels, Restaurants and Institutions.* 2nd ed. Westport, CT: AVI Publishing Co., 1979.

Keiser, J., and Kallio, E.: *Controlling and Analyzing Costs in Food Service Operations.* New York: John Wiley & Sons, 1974.

Knickrehm, M. E., McConnell, R. J., Berg, C. A. T.: Labor time analysis: School lunch meal pattern versus a la carte meal service in a public school system. *School Food Serv. Res. Rev.* 5:85, 1981.

Konz, S.: *Work Design: Industrial Ergonomics.* 2nd ed. Columbus, OH: Grid Publishing, 1983.

Kotschevar, L.: *Food Service for the Extended Care Facility.* Boston: Institutions/Volume Feeding Magazine, 1973.

Lundberg, D. E., and Armatas, J. P.: *The Management of People in Hotels, Restaurants, and Clubs.* Dubuque, IA: Wm. C. Brown Co. Publishers, 1980.

Matthews, M. E.: Productivity studies reviewed, trends analyzed. *Hospitals* 49:81, 1975.

Matthews, M. E., Waldvogel, C. F., Mahaffey, M. J., and Zemel, P. C.: Master Standard Data Quantity Food Production Code: Macro elements for synthesizing production labor time. *J. Am. Dietet. A.* 72:612, 1978.

Methodology Manual for Work Sampling: Productivity of Dietary Personnel. Univ. of Wisconsin-Madison, 1967.

Montag, G. M., McKinley, M. M., and Klinschmidt, A. C.: Predetermined motion times—A tool in food production management. *J. Am. Dietet. A.* 45:206, 1964.

Newstrom, J. W., and Pierce, J. L.: Alternative work schedules: The state of the art. *Personnel Administrator* 24:19 (Oct.), 1979.

Olsen, M. D.: Obtaining meaningful cost information in dietary departments. II. Labor cost information. *J. Am. Dietet. A.* 67:55, 1975.

Patchin, R. I.: *The Management and Maintenance of Quality Circles.* New York: Dow Jones-Irwin, 1983.

Ridley, S. J., Matthews, M. E., and McProud, L. M.: Labor time code for assembling and microwave heating menu items in a hospital galley. *J. Am. Dietet. A.* 84:648, 1984.

Rose, J. C.: Containing the labor costs of foodservice. *Hospitals* 54:93 (Mar. 16), 1980.

Ruf, K. L., and David, B. D.: How to attain optimal productivity. *Hospitals* 49:77 (Dec. 16), 1975.

Ruf, K., and Matthews, M. E.: Production time standards. *Hospitals* 47:82 (May 1), 1973.

Silverstein, P., and Srb, J. H.: *Flexitime: Where, When, and How?* Ithaca, NY: Cornell Univ., 1979.

Smith, G. L.: *Work Measurement: A Systems Approach.* Columbus, OH: Grid Publishing, 1978.

Stokes, J. F.: *Cost Effective Quality Food Service: An Institutional Guide.* Germantown, MD: Aspens Systems Corp., 1979.

Stokes, J. W.: *How to Manage a Restaurant or Institutional Food Service.* 4th ed. Dubuque, IA: Wm. C. Brown Co. Publishers, 1982.

Thomas, E. C.: Scheduling of dietary personnel. In Rose, J. C., ed.: *Handbook for Health Care Food Service Management.* Rockville, Md: Aspen Systems Corp., 1984.

Treadwell, D. D., and Klein, J. A. P.: Quality circles in a department of dietetics. *J. Am. Dietet. A.* 84:682, 1984.

Yager, E. G.: The quality control explosion. *Training Dev. J.* 35:79 (Dec.), 1981.

Yung, L. S., Matthews, M. E., Johnson, V. K., and Johnson, N. E.: Productivity in foodservice systems in fourteen nursing homes. *J. Am. Dietet. A.* 77:159, 1980.

Yung, L. S., Matthews, M. E., Johnson, V. K., and Johnson, N. E.: Variables affecting productivity in food service systems of nursing homes. *J. Am. Dietet. A.* 78:342, 1981.

Zemel, P. C., and Matthews, M. E.: Determining labor production time for roast entrees in hospital food services. *J. Am. Dietet. A.* 81:709, 1982.

Zemel, P. C., and Matthews, M. E.: Master Standard Data Quantity Food Production Code: Application to production of roast entrées under actual operating conditions in a hospital food service. *J. Dietet. Am.* 81:702, 1982.

14

Energy Control

Since the early 1970s when the Organization of Oil Producing and Exporting Countries (OPEC) quadrupled the price of oil, energy conservation has become a major concern in the United States, for the individual consumer as well as business and industry. The oil crisis resulted in inflated energy prices and forced the United States to look to energy conservation and alternate sources of energy.

Prior to the 1970s, foodservice managers had little concern for energy costs, viewing them as a minor portion of overall operational costs. In most institutional foodservices, utility costs were not even that important to foodservice managers because the costs were generally absorbed by management of their overall organizations, not charged to their operations. As a result, many poor practices developed during the many years when energy costs were very low. Not uncommonly, for example, the first cook who arrived in the morning would routinely turn on all lights and ovens.

The oil crisis, however, forced managers in the foodservice industry, as in all industries, to reexamine practices and develop energy control programs. Because the foodservice industry is an energy-intensive one, the impact of rapidly increasing energy cost is especially severe. As a result, in the past few years, this industry has become increasingly conscious of the amount of energy and the kinds of energy sources needed to maintain its operation. Data indicate that the foodservice industry is responsible for approximately 4 percent of our national energy consumption (Unklesbay and Unklesbay, 1982).

The foodservice industry is as dependent on steady sources of energy as are many manufacturing industries. The final product, food ready to eat, depends greatly upon energy-consuming equipment: refrigerators, freezers, ovens, ranges, fryers, holding equipment, and water heaters. The space in which personnel work and clientele are served must be lighted, heated, cooled, and ventilated. In many foodservice systems, transportation may also be a major consumer of energy. The commissary system, for example, is highly dependent on transportation.

In the foodservice systems model in Chapter 2, we outlined the components or elements of the foodservice system, identifying utilities as an operational resource or input into the system. Obviously, heating, cooling, and lighting are important in each of the functional subsystems: procurement, preprocessing, production, distribution, service, and maintenance. The quality of the goods and services produced, or the outputs, requires energy-dependent equipment and processes. As with any resource, control measures are needed to ensure effective utilization of energy in the foodservice system (the control element). As will be discussed in this chapter, various records (the memory element) are needed to monitor energy utilization.

To illustrate the dependence of the foodservice system on energy, consider the crisis the manager faces when confronted with a power failure at a critical time during production or service. Loss of power, if prolonged, also has tremendous implications for potential losses of food stores in refrigerators or freezers.

In this chapter, we will discuss energy utilization in foodservice operations and energy conservation. In addition, an energy management system will be outlined, including methods and forms for analyzing utility consumption and cost and equipment operation.

ENERGY UTILIZATION

Thorner and Manning (1983) identify three questions relevant to the energy problem.

- Are fossil fuels running out?
- Will energy prices continue to increase?
- Why should energy be conserved?

Traditionally, an abundance of energy resources had been available in the United States. But the ever-increasing demand for energy has led to increased reliance on an imported supply, particularly for crude oil.

Oil and gas comprise almost three-fourths of the energy consumption; both are fossil fuels and, thus, nonrenewable resources. One reason for the U.S. energy problem is that the United States relies heavily on both as sources of fuel yet, as shown in Figure 14.1, has less than 12 percent of the world's oil and natural gas reserves. Future projections suggest that this reliance on oil and gas will decrease. These fuels are expected to continue to be the major sources in this country, however, still comprising almost 50 percent by the year 2000.

The cost of foodservice energy has changed drastically during the last 10 years. To illustrate this point, Borsenik (1983) states that in 1983 the foodservice industry spent more than $3 billion on new equipment, but more than $6 billion on energy, a cost projected to grow at ever-increasing rates in the future. He reports that, traditionally, only ¼ to ½ percent of total food and beverage sales was devoted to energy costs; now the range is 2½ to 8 percent.

	YEAR		
	1985	*1990*	*2000*
Domestic Oil	26%	22%	19%
Imported Oil	20%	13%	12%
Natural Gas	26%	22%	16%
Coal	20%	30%	32%
Nuclear	4%	9%	11%
Other	4%	4%	11%

Figure 14.1. *Projected consumption of energy in the U.S. for selected years.* **Source:** *Energy Research and Development Administration:* **Energy Policy: Choices for the Future.** *Washington, DC: Office of Public Affairs, 1976.*

According to Laventhol & Horwath (1981), the accounting firm that regularly tracks costs in the food and lodging industry, the cost of energy for lodging and foodservice units increased by 31 percent in 1980 alone. Rising energy costs have led all cost indicators in four of the last six years in the industry and the firm estimates that the cost of energy in the industry will increase by a factor of two every three to five years into the near future. If this trend continues, the energy bill will obviously consume increasingly greater portions of the revenue dollar.

The typical energy allocation in a foodservice operation is as follows:

49% food production and storage

30% heating, ventilation, and air conditioning

13% sanitation

8% lighting

As shown, food production and storage equipment consume almost 50 percent of the foodservice operation's energy, including electricity, natural gas, and oil.

In 1983, the National Restaurant Association (NRA) members rated the energy cost and regulations among the major issues affecting the future of the foodservice industry. After a decade in which the United States suffered two major oil shortage shocks resulting in serious recession and rapidly escalating energy prices, foodservice operators are concerned about supplies and prices for energy in the years ahead. Foodservice and the Energy Outlook for 1985 and beyond (NRA, 1984) is the third in the NRA's series of Current Issues Reports and provides an in-depth analysis of current and potential energy sources of greatest interest to NRA members.

Natural gas is by far the fuel most used in institutional and commercial foodservices for cooking and space heating. Foodservice managers should pay close attention to the supply, demand, and price for natural gas over the next several years even though the forecasts are generally optimistic. Gas demand is likely to remain soft for 1985 and will very likely continue to be soft in 1990. On an annual basis, an increase of less than two percent per year suggests that

Table 14.1. *Direct and indirect energy expenditures within foodservice operations*

Direct energy expenditures
  Food storage
    —dry, refrigerated, frozen
  Preprocessing
  Heat processing
  Food packaging
  Food storage following heat processing
    —heated, chilled, frozen
  Heat processing of precooked menu items
  Food distribution to units
  Food service

Indirect energy expenditures
  Food waste disposal
  Sanitation procedures
    —personnel, equipment
  Optimal working environment
    —light, heat, air-conditioning
    —physical facilities

Source: N. Unklesbay: Energy consumption and the school foodservice systems. School Foodservice Research Review *1*(1):6–10, 1977.

increased demands will not cause a natural gas shortage before 1990 (NRA, 1984).

Table 14.1 provides a listing of direct and indirect energy expenditures within a foodservice operation. Direct energy refers to energy expended within the foodservice operation to produce and serve menu items at safe temperatures. It is required for any storage, heating, cooling, packaging, reheating, distributing, or serving functions to be performed for any menu item prepared for service within a facility.

Indirect energy refers to that energy expended to facilitate functions that use energy directly. It supports the other necessary functions involved with the production and service of menu items: for example, waste disposal, sanitation, and maintenance of optimal work environment.

Unklesbay and Unklesbay (1982) name three vital aspects of food quality that should be assured by the effective use of direct energy.

- Appropriate sensory quality.
- Food safety.
- Appropriate nutrient retention.

Table 14.1 identifies eight categories of activities in which energy is directly used to ensure food quality. As pointed out in previous discussions, however, the activities occurring in a specific operation depend upon the type of foodservice system and the market form of foods utilized in the system.

Table 14.2. *Yearly energy use and costs for five types of foodservice operations, 1974*

Type of foodservice operation	Kilowatt-hours per year	Natural gas per year (1000 ft³)	BTUs per year (in millions)	Yearly cost of fuel and power ($)
Fast food	216,000	1500	2237	7,320
Coffee shop	249,821	1826	2679	8,648
Table service	284,000	2500	3469	10,680
Cafeteria	473,850	4754	6371	18,985
Hotel/motel	852,974	5666	8577	28,391

Source: Federal Energy Administration: Guide to Energy Conservation for Food Service. U.S. Government Printing Office, Washington, DC, 1977.

The yearly energy use and cost for five types of foodservice operations are shown in Table 14.2. These data were collected by the Midwest Research Institute, in cooperation with the National Restaurant Association and the Federal Energy Administration, as part of a national effort to examine energy usage and identify opportunities for conservation. Interestingly, the study determined that the per-meal use of energy was often lower in restaurants than in private homes. In spite of these findings, as part of the national reduction of energy usage, conservation efforts were considered a priority because of the energy-intensive nature of the industry.

From the data presented on energy supplies and energy costs, the answer to Thorner and Manning's third question, the issue of energy conservation, should be obvious. In many businesses, however, management simply has not given sufficient priority to reducing energy usage. Several reasons may be responsible: first, energy costs are currently relatively minor compared to food and labor costs; second, managers have tended to increase menu prices rather than attempt to reduce cost; and third, energy costs are of limited concern if profit margins are at projected levels. The projected trends outlined by Borsenik (1983) emphasize the fact, however, that foodservice managers can no longer be complacent about controlling energy costs.

ENERGY CONSERVATION

Data in the previous section demonstrate the need for energy conservation in foodservice operations. In the guide for energy conservation, published by the Federal Energy Administration (FEA) on the recommendation of the FEA Food Industry Advisory Committee, several suggestions were given for initiating an energy conservation program. The steps outlined include the following (Office of Industrial Programming, 1976):

- *Assign responsibility for energy conservation.* A manager and an assistant manager, or an energy committee in a large operation, should be appointed to take responsibility for formulating and executing an energy conservation strategy.

- *Conduct a survey of the facility.* A survey should be conducted in the foodservice operation to identify the major pieces of equipment that require energy. A worksheet, such as the one shown in Figure 14.2, can be used for recording the number of hours per day a piece of equipment is used, as well as the designed power and gas or electric requirements for each. This information can be found on the nameplate attached to the equipment. Equipment that requires high levels of energy and is used extensively during the day should be priority targets for conservation measures.

- *Perform an energy audit.* Energy bills from the prior year should be reviewed to determine energy use over the year's operation. Procedures for conducting such an audit are discussed in a later part of this chapter.

- *Establish energy conservation goals.* After a review of facilities and the prior year's usage, goals should be established for reducing energy that are attainable yet present a challenge.

- *Consult with representatives of utility service companies and equipment manufacturers.* These representatives can be a valuable resource for suggestions on reducing energy usage. Utility companies may assist with installation of meters on kitchen equipment that permit close monitoring and provide a measure for assessing effectiveness of conservation programs. Rates should also be reviewed with the utility company's representatives to determine costs at various usage levels.

- *Formulate an energy conservation strategy for the operation.* Data gathered from the survey, the recommendations of service representatives, and a review of literature and guidelines on energy conservation will assist in developing a strategy for energy reduction. Often, significant savings are possible by making simple changes in equipment operation. Regular preventive maintenance of energy-consuming equipment will not only reduce energy and utility bills, but may result in avoidance of breakdowns and repairs. When purchasing new equipment or remodeling, energy-saving recommendations on equipment and on layout and design should be considered.

- *Conduct an educational program for employees.* As with a sanitation program, the energy conservation program will be effective only to the degree to which employees are trained. Both initial and continuing education should be a part of the energy conservation program.

The energy conservation checklist in Figure 14.3 (Jernigan, 1981), found in the manual produced for Maryland institutions, as well as other references found at the end of the checklist, outlines measures that can be utilized within the operation to reduce energy. These measures are related to administrative policies and practices, food production techniques, and equipment utilization. Periodic use of the checklist by the individual or committee assigned responsibility for the energy conservation program will provide data for assessing its effectiveness and determining its progress.

Equipment item	Electric load or gas requirement (From nameplate data on equipment)	Hours used per day	Notes
heating unit			
air conditioner			
electrostatic precipitator			
afterburner			
exhaust fan			
oven and broiler			
range			
grill and griddle			
steam table			
refrigerator and freezer			
fryer			
dishwasher			
water heater			
indoor lighting			
exterior lighting			

Figure 14.2. *An equipment survey.* **Source: *Federal Energy Administration: Guide to Energy Conservation for Food Service. Washington, DC: U.S. Govt. Printing Office, 1977.***

ADMINISTRATION

_____ 1. Evaluate and revise cycle menus to use foods that require shorter cooking times and thus save energy.

_____ 2. Prepare a schedule distributing energy intensive operations (electric heat-producing equipment and compressors) throughout the day and night in order to limit the number of appliances used at one time, thus reducing peak demand charges.

_____ 3. Prepare a schedule of correct preheating times based on manufacturers' instructions for kitchen equipment (4).*

_____ 4. Prepare a schedule showing when backup units (such as fryers, ovens, and broilers) will be needed (i.e., during "rush" hours) (4).

_____ 5. Prepare a schedule of regular cleaning and maintenance of all equipment based on manufacturer's recommendations.

_____ 6. Keep records of equipment breakdowns, repairs, parts replacements, and maintenance.

_____ 7. Prepare a schedule of food deliveries so that cold and frozen food storage areas will not be either overloaded or underutilized.

_____ 8. Specify energy-saving models when ordering new equipment.

_____ 9. Request that the utility company check for proper gas pressure on lines coming into the building (4). Check air/gas mixture on gas appliances to ensure proper combustion.

_____ 10. Develop guidelines for overhead exhaust hood operation based on minimum health department requirements. Do not operate hoods continuously (5).

FOOD PRODUCTION

_____ 1. Prepare food in quantities for optimum utilization of equipment based on manufacturer's recommendations (4.5). This may require cooking some foods partially or completely in advance.

_____ 2. Set cooking dials to the lowest safe tem-

*See reference list on page 391.

perature which gives a satisfactory product (4,6). Dialing higher does not reduce preheating time, but a lower temperature results in lower energy consumption because less heat is lost to the surrounding air.

_____ 3. Consider using steam cookers to begin cooking some foods, to fully cook foods such as rice, pasta, and vegetables, and to maintain temperatures of all foods.

_____ 4. Use flat-bottomed pots and kettles when surface cooking for maximum transfer of heat.

_____ 5. Cover pots, pans, and kettles when cooking to keep heat in and decrease cooking time (5).

_____ 6. Do not wrap potatoes or other foods in aluminum foil before baking (4).

_____ 7. Trim food products and discard unusable parts before storing to reduce volume and quicken chilling (7).

_____ 8. Allow hot foods to cool a few minutes (but not below 140°) before refrigerating or freezing them.

_____ 9. Be sure cooking and heating units (ovens, fryers, dishwashers) are turned off when not in use (4).

_____ 10. Direct fans to cool workers, not hot food and cooking equipment (5).

_____ 11. Unpack cold or frozen food from cartons upon delivery (7).

_____ 12. Place cold or frozen food in proper storage after delivery to eliminate rechilling (7).

_____ 13. Take empty racks out of cold or frozen food storage units to eliminate the cost of cooling them (7).

_____ 14. Consolidate frozen and refrigerated foods where possible. Full units use energy more efficiently than partially full ones.

_____ 15. Thaw frozen foods in refrigerated units both to conserve energy and for proper sanitation (4,5,7). As food thaws, it cools surrounding air, placing less of a power demand on the refrigerator.

EQUIPMENT

Cold and frozen food storage units

_____ 1. Avoid frequent, lengthy openings of freezers and refrigerators (5,7).

Figure 14.3. *(Continued)*

____ 2. After entering cold and frozen food walk-ins, close the door behind you. (Be certain all walk-ins will open from the inside.)

____ 3. Install pilot lights, which light up when lights inside have been left on, on switches of walk-in units (7).

____ 4. Use calibrated thermometers to check temperatures in all refrigerated and frozen units (7).

____ 5. Set temperature controls for proper storage of particular foods in each unit (7).

____ 6. Level free-standing upright units so that doors automatically swing shut from an open position.

____ 7. Be sure that items do not jam against doors, damaging the gasket and the door. Check gaskets and seals on doors for cold air leakage (7).

____ 8. Keep an area 4 feet wide in front of compressors and coils clear. Check compressors for leakage and level of refrigerant (7).

____ 9. Maintain proper tension on compressor belts and replace when worn or damaged.

____ 10. Clean coils of ice and dust build-up (5,7).

____ 11. Check refrigerators and freezers daily for loss of temperature and short cycling times. Refrigerant level may be low.

____ 12. Check outside walls of refrigeration and freezer units for cold spots, which may indicate insulation shift or water logging.

____ 13. Defrost refrigerators and freezers on a regular basis (7).

____ 14. Check for correct cycling of automatic defrosters (7).

____ 15. Close ice-maker storage bins when they are not in use.

Ovens

____ 1. Determine the cooking capacity for each oven and select the oven with the least amount of waste space and the most energy efficient oven able to do the job (4,7).

____ 2. Schedule baking and roasting to fill ovens to capacity (4,7).

____ 3. Begin to cook foods (except for those that will overcook or dry out) while preheating the oven (4). Do not preheat ovens sooner than is necessary (4,5).

____ 4. Load and unload ovens quickly to avoid unnecessary heat loss (4).

____ 5. Avoid opening ovens to check foods. Keeping doors closed allows foods to cook faster and lose less moisture. Rely on timers to tell when a product is done.

____ 6. Calibrate oven thermostats often (7).

____ 7. Turn off oven, allowing receding heat to finish cooking (6,7).

____ 8. Level oven and oven racks often.

____ 9. Clean up spills as they occur to avoid build-ups of carbon deposits.

____ 10. Clean and repair oven doors and hinges to ensure a snug fit so that heat will not escape (6).

____ 11. Consider using a microwave for thawing (5), cooking, and reheating. A microwave may use less energy as it requires less time to cook foods.

____ 12. Contact a serviceman to check microwave timer for accuracy and to check oven for radiation leakage.

____ 13. Clean interior surfaces of convection ovens using a nonabrasive material to avoid damage.

____ 14. Check fan motors of convection ovens for proper performance.

____ 15. Clean fan blades of convection ovens following manufacturers' instructions.

____ 16. Use proper utensils and pans for convection ovens. Do not damage door seals or interior surfaces.

Deep fat fryers

____ 1. Set fryer thermostat only as high as necessary to reach optimum frying temperatures (8).

____ 2. Check temperatures of cooking oil with a reliable thermometer. Smoking fat in fryers indicates that the temperature is too high or that the fat has broken down (6).

____ 3. Load frying baskets only to stated capacity (8). Overloading increases cooking time, using more energy.

____ 4. Drain and clean fryer after each use (4).

____ 5. Filter particles from oil at least once a day and replace oil often (4,8).

____ 6. Make sure the level of oil is high enough to cover foods at all times (8).

____ 7. Clean heating elements and interiors

Figure 14.3. *(Continued)*

weekly. Remove burned foods, grease, and carbon deposits (8).

Surface cooking units

_____ 1. Group kettles and pots close together on closed top ranges to minimize heat loss (4).

_____ 2. Burners should be one inch smaller in diameter than the pots placed on them (4).

_____ 3. Reduce heat when food begins to boil, maintaining liquids at a simmer.

_____ 4. Operate gas burners only when ready to cook.

_____ 5. Clean and adjust gas burners so that flame is blue, with a distinct, white center cone.

_____ 6. Clean pilot lights, orifices, and burners often with a stiff brush (consult manufacturer's instructions) (9).

_____ 7. Remove grease and dirt build-up from range top, burner plates, and coils to allow maximum heat transfer (4,9).

_____ 8. Clean all cooking surfaces and wipe up spills as they occur.

Griddles

_____ 1. Group foods close together on griddle top to minimize heat loss (4).

_____ 2. Heat only the portion of the griddle being used (4).

_____ 3. Check thermostats against a reliable thermometer and recalibrate if necessary (9).

_____ 4. Clean griddle surfaces of food and fat particles after each use with a spatula and grill brick (4,9).

_____ 5. Clean and wipe out grease troughs daily (9).

Broilers

_____ 1. When briquets become hot, turn broiler heat to medium (4) or low.

_____ 2. Load heated broilers to maximum capacity, utilizing entire surface area.

_____ 3. Infrared broilers should be turned off when not in use as they can be reheated quickly.

_____ 4. On infrared broilers, check ceramic refactory units for cracks, blackening, or crumbling (9), and replace if units show damage.

_____ 5. Keep briquets clean (4).

_____ 6. Clean broiler drip pans. Wash grids and grease troughs after each use with a mild soap (9).

_____ 7. A clear blue flame with a distinct center cone is a sign of proper burner operation on broilers (6).

_____ 8. Clean burner orifices.

_____ 9. Check air shutters and openings to ensure that they are clear.

_____ 10. Clean and adjust pilot lights on gas broilers.

Steam cookers and tables

_____ 1. When using a steam cooker, fill cooking vessels to maximum capacity according to manufacturer's instructions.

_____ 2. Check steamer and steam table thermostats for proper calibration.

_____ 3. Clean debris from steamer and door seals so that steam will not escape when door is closed. Replace gaskets if necessary.

_____ 4. Use steam tables to keep foods hot but not allow clouds of steam to escape.

_____ 5. Check condensate traps for steam leakage.

_____ 6. Maintain proper insulation on steam lines.

_____ 7. Repair all steam leaks, no matter how small, promptly.

_____ 8. Turn off steam tables and cookers when not in use.

Hoods

_____ 1. Have an adequate air supply to the hood to make exhausted air without exhausting cooled air from public spaces.

_____ 2. Turn off hood fans when equipment underneath is not in use.

_____ 3. Adjust oversized exhaust hoods in the food preparation area so that no more air than necessary is exhausted (4,5).

_____ 4. Clean grease from exhaust hoods and filters regularly (4,8).

Dishwashing

_____ 1. Scrape and stack dishes before washing. Avoid using hot or warm water for this task (5).

Figure 14.3. *(Continued)*

_____ 2. Do not turn on booster heaters on dishwashers until they are needed.

_____ 3. Be certain that dishwashers and booster heaters are turned off when they are not in use.

_____ 4. Wash dishes only when a dishwasher is full (5).

_____ 5. Completely fill dishracks before sending them through flight-type and conveyor dishwashers.

_____ 6. Check rinse water temperature, flow controls, and pressure regularly.

_____ 7. Check power rinse for adequate but not excessive water flow and for automatic shut-off when a rack has gone through the machine.

_____ 8. Adjust power dryers to shut off when dishes are dry.

_____ 9. Clean dishwashers daily.

_____ 10. De-lime dishwashers when lime deposits are present.

_____ 11. Check for proper temperatures in dishwashers (140°F. to 160°F. for wash water, 180°F. for rinse water).

_____ 12. Consider using chemical sanitizing agents instead of excessively hot water in dishwashers.

_____ 13. Inspect pumps and feed and drain valves for leakage.

_____ 14. Lubricate the speed reducer on conveyor-type dishwashers.

_____ 15. In the pot and pan washing area, fill sinks for washing, rinsing, and sanitizing instead of using continuously running water.

Hot water

_____ 1. Do not leave faucets running.

_____ 2. Use hot water only when cold water will not do.

_____ 3. Eliminate the use of hot water for handwashing wherever possible.

_____ 4. Maintain insulation on hot water pipes. Check for missing or damaging insulation.

_____ 5. Install flow restrictors on faucets. They are particularly effective when water duration, not amount of water, is the important factor.

_____ 6. Use hot tap water for cooking when possible. A water heater uses less energy than a range top to heat the same amount of water.

_____ 7. Repair leaky faucets immediately.

References

(1) Mueller Associates, Inc.: Maryland Energy Audit Training Manual for Schools, Hospitals, Local Government, and Public Care Institutions. Baltimore: Maryland Energy Office, 1979.

(2) Department of Natural Resources: Energy Savings Workbook. Baltimore: Maryland Energy Policy Office, 1979.

(3) Moulton, C. C.: Sources to tap for energy information. Restaur. Hospitality 62:6 (Sept.), 1978.

(4) Energy Audit Workbook for Restaurants. Washington, DC: U.S. Department of Energy, 1978.

(5) Schools and Hospitals Energy Conservation Workbook. Publ. No. 2099. Milwaukee, WI: Johnson Controls, Inc., 1979.

(6) Operations/technology: Good equipment maintenance saves energy. Institutions 84:99 (April 1), 1979.

(7) West, B., Wood, L., Harger, V., and Shugart, G.: Food Service in Institutions. 5th ed. New York: John Wiley & Sons, 1977.

(8) Energy tips: Deep fat frying. Restaur. Bus. 77:2 (Dec. 1), 1978.

(9) Energy tips: Maintenance saves energy. Restaur. Bus. 77:2 (Sept. 15), 1978.

Figure 14.3. *Energy conservation checklist.* **Source:** *Jernigan, B. S.: Guidelines for Energy Conservation.* **J. Am. Dietet. A. 79:459, 1981.**

ENERGY MANAGEMENT SYSTEM

Control of energy costs requires maintaining a record keeping system for tracking utility costs and monitoring equipment utilization. Energy utilization for lighting, heating, ventilating, and air conditioning of the facilities must also be monitored and controlled. The checklist above identifies a number of control points; here, examples of some specific procedures and records useful for an energy audit are presented.

Preparing and maintaining appropriate records will facilitate identification of the amount and cost of energy use, as well as of any trends that may be developing. Energy use can then be related to the number of customers, and energy cost can be examined in relation to sales volume, which will provide indicators of the success or failure of the energy management program. Monitoring the use and cost of water can also be accomplished, thus providing an analysis of all utilities.

Dollar costs of energy are, of course, important and comparisons of current costs with those of prior years will provide one basis of comparison. Because of rising utility rates, however, those figures may not be as meaningful as utilization data. Actual utilization, therefore, should also be analyzed. An analysis of energy usage and cost is an important management function. The glossary in Figure 14.4 gives a listing of some of the key terms related to energy consumption.

The three forms in Figures 14.5, 14.6, and 14.7, developed by the National Restaurant Association, are examples of records that should be maintained regularly to track energy use and costs. Typical data for a restaurant have been

Glossary

Ampere — a unit of measure of an electric current.

British thermal unit (Btu) — a unit of heat energy. The amount of heat required to raise 1 lb. of water 1 degree Fahrenheit.

Demand charge — based on the highest electric energy use over some fixed period of time during the billing cycle, usually 15 or 30 minutes. As the peak demand determines the size of power generating plants, transmission lines and other equipment needs, it is designed to pay for the utility company's investment.

Demand charge discount — rewards a customer who has a reasonable constant monthly electrical demand. For example, a customer may earn a discount for maintaining a billing demand in excess of 75 percent of his highest maximum demand in the preceeding months.

Energy charge — determined by the electric energy used (kilowatt hours). It is designed to cover the base fuel expenses necessary in the generation of electrical energy.

High load factor discount — rewards a customer who uses his demand for many hours of operation. It is a percentage index comparing the actual kilowatt hours used, with the maximum billing demand times the total hours in a billing period.

Horsepower — a unit of power equal to 746 watts.

Kilowatt — one thousand watts. Most electrical foodservice equipment is rated in kilowatts.

Kilowatt hour — a measure of work (kilowatt x hours). The unit recorded by electric meters and utilized for billing.

Purchased energy or fuel adjustment — an incremental adjustment to rates reflecting changes in costs of purchased energy or fuel since current rates became effective. It is usually expressed as a fractional amount added to the current rate.

Therm — a unit used for measuring natural gas equal to 100,000 Btu.

Volt — the push that moves the electric current.

Watt — a unit of power. One watt equals the flow of one ampere at a pressure of one volt (watts = volts x amperes).

Figure 14.4. *Glossary of energy related terms.* **Source: Energy Management System.** *Chicago: National Restaurant Association, 1982.*

FORM A-- **MONTHLY UTILITY WORKSHEET**

Month _January_ , 19 _82_

			MBTU*	Cost

Gas _____ _____cubic feet x _____

_____ 1937 _____ therms x 100 _193,700_ _581.10_

Electricity _20,833_ kwhr x 3.412 _71,082_ _1473.18_

Fuel Oil #2 _____ gals. x 140 _____ _____

Propane _____ gals. x 91.6 _____ _____

Steam _____ lbs. x 1 _____ _____

Water _67,200_ gals. _100.80_

Total _264,782_ MBTU $ _2155.08_

Customer count for month _16,800_

MBTUs per customer $\dfrac{\text{Total MBTUs}}{\text{Customers}} = \dfrac{264,782}{16,800} =$ _15.8_

Sales for month _$ 45,360_

Utility costs as
percent of sales $\dfrac{\text{Total utility cost}}{\text{Sales}} = \dfrac{2155}{45,360} =$ _4.8 %_

*MBTU = 1000 BTU

1. Enter the month and year. In this example the information is for January, 1982.

2. From your gas bill, obtain the consumption figure. It may be expressed in therms, cubic feet or 100 and 1000 multiples of cubic feet. If gas is metered in 100 cubic feet (CCF) the multiple for conversion to MBTU is 100. If gas is metered in 1000 cubic feet (MCF) the multiple for conversion is 1000. In this example the gas is metered in therms and 1937 therms is equal to 193,700 MBTU. The cost, also obtained from the bill, is $581.10. The conversion values given are average values and satisfactory for these calculations.

3. The total number of kilowatt hours used during the month was 20,833 and the conversion to MBTU provides a value of 71,082. The total cost (including demand charges and any other miscellaneous charges) is $1473.18.

4. Water is metered in gallons or cubic feet. The total consumption during the month was 67,200 gallons at a total cost of $100.80. This includes all other charges as leak insurance and sewage.

5. These are the total figures for MBTU and dollar costs obtained by adding each of the two columns. In this example the totals are 264,782 MBTUs and $2155.08.

6. The customer count for this period is 16,800. It may be more appropriate in your operation to use number of transactions, number of parties or whatever unit is most suitable for your restaurant.

7. MBTUs per customer is obtained by dividing the total MBTUs by the customer count. In the example, dividing 264,782 by 16,800 provides a result of 15.8.

8. Sales for the month were $45,360, obtained from bookkeeping records. The total cost of utilities as determined on this form was $2155. Dividing $2155 by $45,360 results in a utility cost percentage of 4.8.

Figure 14.5. *Form for recording monthly utilities.* **Source: Energy Management System.** *Chicago: National Restaurant Association, 1982.*

entered on each form along with explanations of the data, which provides an illustration for a straightforward method of tracking utility consumption and cost. Electricity and gas utilization have been converted to MBtus to provide a standard base for comparison. As indicated in the glossary, a Btu, or British thermal unit, is a unit of heat energy equal to the amount of heat required to raise one pound of water one degree Fahrenheit; one MBtu is equal to 1,000 Btus.

FORM B-- **UTILITY CONSUMPTION AND TRACKING**

Year 1982

Month	Gas therms (1)			Electricity (2)						Water gallons (3)			(4)	
				Use KWH			Demand KW							
	1981	1982	Percent Change	1981	1982	Percent Change	1981	1982	Percent Change	1981	1982	Percent Change		Percent Change
JAN	2041	1937	-5.1	23,617	20,833	-11.8	61.2	59.5	-2.7	73,600	67,200	-8.7		
FEB														
MAR														
APR														

1. Enter your gas consumption figures in this section. In the example, consumption for January, 1981 was 2041 therms while 1937 was the figure for January, 1982. This is a 5.1 percent reduction which is indicated in the third column.

2. Electricity use is recorded in this section. Kilowatt hours were 23,617 and 20,833 for January, 1981 and January, 1982 respectively which represents a 11.8 percent reduction. Demand expressed in kilowatts decreased from 61.2 to 59.5 for a downward change of 2.7 percent. Significant increases in demand may indicate the need to stagger equipment operation or may also point to malfunctioning electrical devices and controls.

3. Water consumption information is entered in this portion. Water consumption was 73,600 gallons in January, 1981 and 67,200 gallons in January, 1982 for a 8.7 percent reduction. Increases in water consumption may indicate system leaks, improperly operating faucets and faulty valves.

4. This section is to be used for other energy sources as propane, fuel oil or steam.

Figure 14.6. *Form for analyzing utility consumption.* **Source:** *Energy Management System. Chicago: National Restaurant Association, 1982.*

As pointed out in the technical bulletin prepared by NRA on energy management (NRA, 1982), the information provided by these records will point out any "leaks" in the utility system of an operation, such as:

- development of poor operating practices,
- malfunctioning of equipment,
- structural damage to the building,
- misreading of meters, or
- improper billing by utility companies.

In recording data each month, comparable periods should be used to permit comparisons with prior years. For example, if the reading date for the electric meter is on the fifth day of the month, the consumption for a particular month should be for the period from that day to the fifth of the following month.

One factor to be taken into account in analyzing utility utilization is the extremities in the weather. Obviously, some winters are colder and some summers warmer than others; deviations in utilization may be explained by the additional demand on heating or air conditioning systems. One way of measuring these variances is the use of degree days, which are deviations of the mean daily temperatures from 65°F. In comparing the prior year's utility use with the current

FORM C -- **TOTAL UTILITY CONSUMPTION, TRACKING AND COST**

Month	Total MBTU ①			Total Utility Cost ②			MBTU per customer ③			Utility Cost as Percent of Sales ④		
	1981	1982	Percent Change	1981	1982	Percent Change	1981	1982	Percent Change	1981	1982	Percent Change
JAN	284,681	264,782	-7.0	2162.57	2155.08	no change	16.6	15.8	-4.8	5.1	4.8	-5.9
FEB												
MAR												
APR												
MAY												

1. The information for this section is obtained from the monthly utilities worksheet (Form A) where all energy used is converted to the common unit of BTUs. The 264,782 MBTU figure for January, 1982 of the example is from Form A while the 284,681 MBTU is the like figure for January, 1981. There has been a 7.0 percent reduction in the total number of BTUs from one January to the next.

2. Total utility costs, including water for January, 1982, was obtained from Form A and is $2155.08. The prior January figure was $2162.57 which indicates no significant change in utility costs.

3. This section relates energy consumption to number of customers. The 15.8 MBTU per customer figure was calculated in Form A and from historical data 16.6 was the prior year figure indicating a reduction of 4.8 percent.

4. Utility costs as a percent of sales were 4.8 for January, 1982. This figure was obtained from Form A. For January, 1981, the figure was 5.1 which indicates a change of 5.9 percent. While total utility costs remained almost constant, utility costs as a percentage of sales decreased because of larger sales volume.

Figure 14.7. *Form for computing cost and use indicators for utility consumption.* **Source: Energy Management System.** *Chicago: National Restaurant Association, 1982.*

year, a comparison in the number of degree days would perhaps explain deviations.

The form in Figure 14.5 is a worksheet designed to develop information required for the forms shown in Figures 14.6 and 14.7. After the utility bills have been received for the current month, the worksheet in Figure 14.5 should be completed. The form in Figure 14.6 will assist in monthly tracking of utility consumption, as well as in comparing the current year's consumption of gas, electricity, and water with the prior year's. The form in Figure 14.7 will enable the manager to track total energy utilization and utility cost, as well as to compute ratios that will assist in analyzing utilization and cost in relation to volume and sales. These ratios are: (1) MBtus per customer, and (2) utility cost as a percentage of sales.

Careful planning and analysis of equipment operation is an important aspect of energy control in a foodservice operation. The first planning step is to list all the equipment in an operation requiring energy as in the form shown in Figure 14.8. The data shown on this sample form are for a restaurant that serves from 11:00 A.M. to 9:00 P.M. Each piece of equipment should be listed in the appropriate column, along with its location and energy source. In some operations, the manager may wish to complete a separate form for each unit in the production area. Next, preheat times should be established for each piece of equipment; the menu

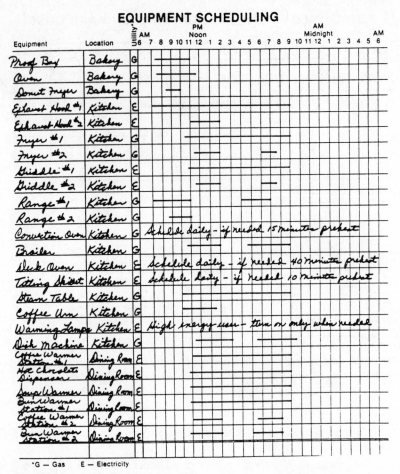

Figure 14.8. *Example of an equipment schedule for energy conservation.* **Source: Energy Management System.** *Chicago: National Restaurant Association, 1982.*

should then be examined to estimate processing and cooking times for each menu item. From this information the "on" time for each piece of equipment can be established.

In a commercial operation with a set menu, a master schedule that could be used from day to day would suffice. If operating hours or meal periods are different on certain days, a variation in the master schedule would be needed to accommodate the differences. In a foodservice operation with a menu that varies from day to day, an equipment schedule should be prepared on a daily basis.

To illustrate the use of such a schedule, based on the data in Figure 14.8, assume that the baking is done during the morning hours before the restaurant opens at 11:00 A.M. The bakers are scheduled to report to work at 6:00 A.M. With mixing and other preparation time, the proof box for yeast breads will not be needed until 7:30 A.M., and the oven will not be needed until 8:00 A.M. Therefore, with preheat time of 15 minutes for the proof box and 40 minutes for the oven, turn-on times at 7:15 A.M. and 7:20 A.M., respectively, will be sufficient for the equipment to be ready at the required times.

Prior to the days of rapidly rising energy costs, the bakers would have turned on the proof box and oven shortly after arriving at work at 6:00 A.M. This example shows how energy savings are possible by altering this type of practice with careful planning and scheduling.

As mentioned earlier in this chapter, however, employee training is one of the keys to a successful energy conservation program, and the employees are the key to the success of an equipment operation schedule. Ultimately, they are the ones responsible for turning equipment on and off at appropriate times. Prior to initiating an equipment operation schedule, employee training sessions are needed to present information on the objectives of the program and on its importance to controlling operational costs, as well as to elicit their cooperation and support.

To assist in executing the equipment scheduling aspect of the energy management program, the NRA has developed a series of labels that can be mounted on or close to various pieces of equipment to remind employees of various energy conservation issues (Figure 14.9). Data presented earlier in this chapter indicated that food production and storage equipment were responsible for approximately 50 percent of the energy use in most foodservice operations. Therefore, the importance of equipment control in these operational areas should be obvious.

Another control can result from analysis and monitoring of lighting, heating, air conditioning, and ventilation, since these represent another major component of total energy use. Lights should be turned off in areas of the facility that are not being used. For example, lighting in storerooms is needed only for short periods of time. Dining room lights can be turned off between the noon and evening meals if services are not provided during this time, or perhaps a small portion of the dining room can be used for the limited services that might be offered during between-meal periods. Thermostats should be adjusted in accordance with the utilization of various areas of the foodservice facility. The thermostat could be turned to a higher temperature after serving time in the summer, or to a lower than normal temperature during winter, for example, to conserve energy. Thermostats that permit automatic adjustment at preset times are becoming a popular method for decreasing heating and air conditioning costs. Ventilating fans in hoods over cooking and dishwashing units should be turned off when the equipment is not in use. These and other measures discussed in this chapter will assist the foodservice manager in controlling energy costs—an operational area in which rising costs are becoming a particular concern of management.

During the last decade, concern about energy costs has stimulated research in the energy utilization of foodservice operations; a number of studies are listed in the references for this chapter. Much of the work has been conducted at the University of Missouri-Columbia and at the University of Wisconsin-Madison. Research has focused on energy modification of recipes, energy utilization of various types of equipment, energy demand with differing oven loads, and energy

Figure 14.9. *Examples of energy conservation reminders (by permission of the National Restaurant Association)*

usage in the different types of foodservice systems. This research is yielding valuable data to assist foodservice managers in understanding energy utilization in foodservice operations and designing energy control programs.

SUMMARY

In the early 1970s, the oil crisis led to greatly inflated energy prices, forcing the United States to focus on energy conservation and alternate sources. The oil crisis stimulated managers in the foodservice industry, as well as those in other industries, to reexamine practices and develop energy control programs. The foodservice industry is energy-intensive, requiring steady sources of energy for all phases in the procurement/production/service cycle. Food storage equipment, production and holding equipment, dishwashers, and heating, ventilating, and air conditioning are all high energy users.

The cost of energy has increased at a greater rate than all other cost indicators in the food and lodging industry in four of the last six years. The energy bill is consuming increasingly greater portions of the revenue dollar, with production and storage equipment responsible for almost 50 percent of the energy consumption in a foodservice operation.

Energy conservation programs should be initiated in all foodservice operations. A first step is to assign responsibility for energy conservation. Other initial steps involve conducting a survey of the facilities, performing an energy audit, establishing goals, formulating an energy conservation strategy, and conducting an energy conservation program for employees. Menus should also be reviewed and revised, if needed, to take energy-saving measures into consideration. As with any program, follow-up and evaluation should be a component of an energy conservation program to provide an assessment of its effectiveness.

Regularly tracking utility costs and monitoring equipment utilization will assist in energy control. Analysis of both use and cost and comparison with similar periods in a prior year will provide the data needed to interpret current use. Since equipment consumes the major share of energy in a foodservice operation, careful planning of equipment use is an important aspect of energy control. Other reductions in utilization can occur by prudent use of lighting, heating, air conditioning, and ventilation. Current research on energy utilization in foodservice operations is yielding valuable data to assist managers in reducing energy costs.

REFERENCES

Borsenik, F. D.: Energy and foodservice equipment. *The Consultant* 16:12 (Winter), 1983.
Boss, D.: Energy and cooking. *Food Mgmt.* 12:48 (Jun.), 1977.

Claar, C. N., and Lambert, C. U.: Personnel: The key to a successful energy management program. *J. Am. Dietet. A.* 81:288, 1982.

Clark, J.: Utilities management: Part I. "Shedding Light." *Cornell Hotel Restaur. Admin. Q.* 16:19, 1975.

Dahl, C. A., Matthews, M. E., and Lund, D. B.: Effect of microwave heating in cook/chill food service system. *J. Am. Dietet. A.* 79:296, 1981.

Drew, F., and Rhee, K. S.: Fuel consumption by cooking appliances. *J. Am. Dietet. A.* 72:37, 1978.

Energy and management. *Food Mgmt.* 12:38 (Jun.), 1977.

Federal Energy Administration: *Guide to Energy Conservation for Foodservice.* Washington, DC: Food Industry Advisory Committee, Federal Energy Administration, U.S. Govt. Prtg. Ofc., 1977.

Hatsopoulos, G. N., Gyftopoulos, E. P., and Sant, R. W., and Widmer, T. F.: Capital investment to save energy. *Harvard Bus. Rev.* 56:111 (Mar./Apr.), 1978.

Jernigan, B. S.: Guidelines for energy conservation. *J. Am. Dietet. A.* 79:459, 1981.

U.S. Lodging Industry 1981. 49th Annual Report on Hotel and Motor Hotel Operations. Philadelphia, PA: Laventhol & Horwath, 1981.

McProud, L. M.: Energy use and management in foodservice systems: A bibliography. *School Food Serv. Res. Rev.* 2:110, 1978.

McProud, L. M.: Reducing energy loss in food service operations. *Food Technol.* 36:67 (Jul.), 1982.

McProud, L. M., and David, B. D.: Energy use and management in production of entrees in hospital food service systems. *J. Am. Dietet. A.* 81:145, 1982.

Michael, C.: Energy builders. *School Food Serv. J.* 32:36, 1978.

Michael, C. M.: Energy in food service operations: Use and control: A bibliography. *School Food Serv. Res. Rev.* 4:63, 1980.

National Restaurant Association: *Efficient Use of Energy: Goal of NRA.* Chicago: National Restaurant Association, 1981.

National Restaurant Association: *Energy Management System.* Chicago: National Restaurant Association, 1982.

National Restaurant Association: *Foodservice and the Energy Outlook for 1985 and Beyond.* Washington, DC: National Restaurant Association, 1984.

Odland, D., and Davis, C.: Products cooked in preheated versus nonpreheated ovens. Baking times, calculated energy consumption, and product quality compared. *J. Am. Dietet. A.* 81:135, 1982.

Office of Industrial Programming: *Energy Use in the Food System.* Washington, DC: Office of Industrial Programming, Fed. Energy Admin., 1976.

Pierce, J. E.: Refrigeration-to-water heat exchange. *The Consultant* 16:26 (Summer), 1983.

Thorner, M. E., and Manning, P. B.: *Quality Control in Foodservice.* Ch. 15. Rev. ed. Westport, CT: AVI Publishing Co., 1983.

Tinsley, E.: 1979 Equipment census: Save through smart specifying. *Institutions* 84:55 (Mar.), 1979.

Unklesbay, K., and Unklesbay, N.: Mastering basic energy concepts for effective food handling. *J. Am. Dietet. A.* 77:301, 1980.

Unklesbay, N.: Energy consumption and school foodservice systems. *School Food Serv. Res. Rev.* 1:6, 1977.

Unklesbay, N.: Integration of energy data into food industry decision making. *Food Technol.* 37:55 (Dec.), 1983.

Unklesbay, N.: Overview of foodservice energy research: Heat processing. *J. Food Protection* 45:984, 1982.

Unklesbay, N., and Unklesbay, K.: Energy expended in alternate foodservice systems for chicken menu items. *J. Am. Dietet. A.* 73:20, 1978.

Unklesbay, N., and Unklesbay, K.: *Energy Management in Foodservice.* Westport, CT: AVI Publishing Co., 1982.

Unklesbay, N., and Unklesbay, K.: Energy-modification of standardized quantity recipes. *J. Am. Dietet. A.* 76:258, 1980.

Unklesbay, N., and Unklesbay, K.: Food service equipment and energy costs. *Hospitals* 54:83 (Mar. 16), 1980.

Unklesbay, N., and Unklesbay, K.: Interrelationships of dietetics, energy resources, and menu items. *J. Am. Dietet. A.* 77:296, 1980.

Unklesbay, N., and Unklesbay, K.: Some influences of foodservice managerial policies upon direct energy consumption. *J. Can. Dietet. A.* 38:229, 1977.

Unklesbay, N., Unklesbay, K., Buergler, D., and Ellersieck, M.: Energy usage for convective heat processing of sausage patties. *School Food Serv. Res. Rev.* 6:14, 1982.

Unklesbay, N., Unklesbay, K., and Henderson, J.: Simulation of energy used by foodservice infrared heating equipment with bentonite models of menu items. *J. Food Protection* 43:789, 1980.

Watts, W. J.: Energy and foodservice equipment. *The Consultant* 16:32 (Winter), 1984.

Zimmerman, B. A.: Energy distribution systems . . . from concept to reality. *The Consultant* 16:27 (Spring), 1984.

V
Distribution, Service, and Maintenance

15

Distribution and Service in Foodservice Systems

Distribution and service will be considered as one subsystem in the transformation element of the foodservice system (Figure 15.1), although these processes may represent two distinct but interrelated functions in the final phase of the procurement/production/service cycle. Distribution/service, then, represents the third major subsystem; along with procurement and production, it meets the goal of providing quality food and services to a given clientele.

Depending on the type of foodservice system, distribution may or may not be a major function. In hospital foodservices, where patients must be served in individual rooms located on many floors and perhaps in separate buildings, distribution is a major concern. Ensuring that the appropriate food is sent to the appropriate place for service to a particular patient is a complex process, further complicated by the need to ensure that the food is at the right temperature and aesthetically appealing. In contrast, in the fast food operation, where patrons pick up the food items directly after production and either carry them off premises for consumption or to a table in the facility, distribution is relatively simple. In fact, the distribution and service becomes the responsibility primarily of the customer, not the personnel.

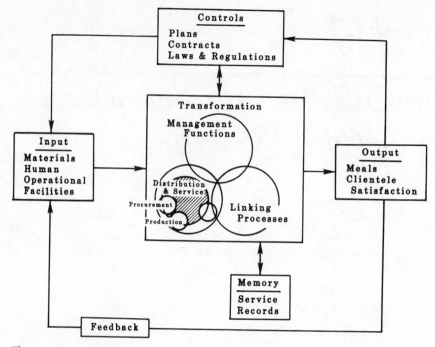

Figure 15.1. *Foodservice systems model with the distribution/service subsystem highlighted*

Service takes many forms in a foodservice establishment, from that in the upscale fine food restaurant involving several highly trained personnel to that in the many types of self-service operations—cafeteria, vending, or buffet. The method, speed, and quality of the services provided can "make or break" a foodservice establishment. The quality of food may be excellent, the sanitation of the establishment above reproach, the procurement and storage of food ideal, but if the service is lacking, the operation will be rated poor by the clientele. In some instances, clientele will repeatedly return to an establishment with only mediocre food because a favorite waiter or waitress provides high quality service, or because they can depend on being served and back to work in a short period of time.

In this chapter, the four basic types of systems (Chapter 5) will be discussed from the standpoint of distribution and service issues. Different types of service in foodservice operations will then be outlined.

DISTRIBUTION IN VARIOUS FOODSERVICE SYSTEMS

As outlined in Chapter 5, the four types of foodservice systems are conventional, commissary, ready prepared, and assembly/serve. Although some characteristics of distribution and service are common to all of them, differences in the systems lead to different demands in some aspects of the distribution function. In the following pages, then, distribution and service will be discussed for each of these systems.

Conventional Foodservice System

In the conventional system, most menu items are produced on premise and distributed for service to a serving area or areas close to the production facilities. In this system, hot and cold holding equipment is needed to maintain the proper temperature for various menu items between the time of production and service. Depending on the type of service areas, this holding equipment may be stationary or mobile. Some equipment is quite versatile and can be used for distribution, holding, and service. For example, the mobile modular serving units in Figure 15.2 could be used for transporting food for a catered function in a dining room away from the main kitchen and also for holding the food until time of service. The units then provide a service counter for self- or waiter/waitress service.

In a healthcare facility, however, patient service may take place throughout the facility, requiring more complex distribution systems than in other types of foodservice operations. Meal assembly, for example, may be centralized or decentralized. In a facility with centralized meal assembly, the time between production, assembly, distribution, and service can be minimal. The trays are first assembled for service at a central location in or close to the main production facilities. Hot menu items are held in food warming cabinets, usually in cafeteria counter pans, where they remain until placed in hot food serving units during tray assembly; cold items are held under refrigeration. The assembled trays are then distributed to the patient units using a variety of types of carts. Some institutions use heated and refrigerated tray carts, which may be motorized or pushed manually by hospital personnel. A few institutions have an automated cart transport system, which only requires setting a dial or pushing a button to move carts along specially designed corridors to designated service areas. This type of system must be a design feature of the facility during construction.

The high initial and maintenance costs of heated and heated/refrigerated carts have led to development of other methods for maintaining proper temperatures on assembled trays. One of these systems uses specially designed dishes that have been preheated in an infrared oven, then transferred to an insulated base. The hot menu items are portioned onto the plate, which is covered by a dome designed to fit the base container, thus keeping food warm until service to the patient. This unit is placed on the individual patient's tray, and other menu items that have been individually wrapped are added. The assembled trays are then transported in an unheated cart to patient units for service.

The process of meal distribution in a centralized tray system includes activities relating to the movement of assembled trays from the point of assembly to the patient area. A method for thermal retention is needed in larger operations in

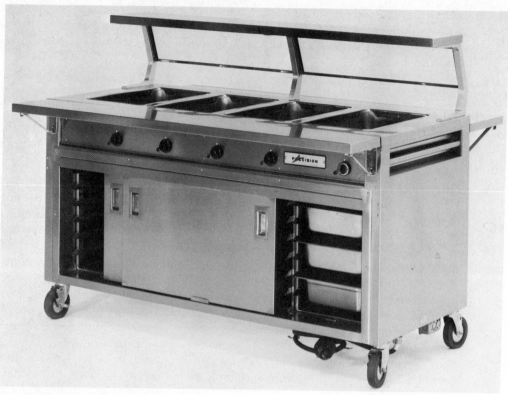

Hot serving unit

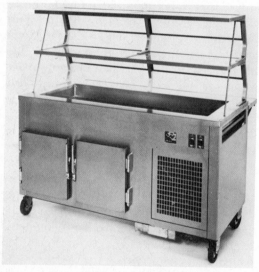

Cold serving unit

Figure 15.2. *Examples of distribution/service equipment: hot serving unit with heated storage base and cold serving unit with refrigerated storage base (used by courtesy of Precision Metal Products, Inc., Miami, FL)*

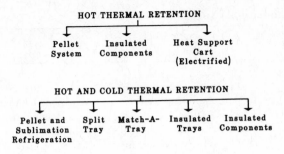

HOT THERMAL RETENTION

Pellet System | Insulated Components | Heat Support Cart (Electrified)

HOT AND COLD THERMAL RETENTION

Pellet and Sublimation Refrigeration | Split Tray | Match-A-Tray | Insulated Trays | Insulated Components

NO THERMAL SUPPORT

Figure 15.3. *Types of meal distribution systems. Source: Hysen, P. and Harrison, J.: State-of-the-art review of health care patient feeding system equipment. In* **Hospital Patient Feeding Systems. Washington, DC: National Academy Press, 1982, p. 172.**

which the time between meal assembly and service to the patient is too long to maintain proper temperatures. Refrigerated support for cold foods may also be needed. We described two types of methods that are widely used in healthcare institutions. Figure 15.3 outlines these and other methods for thermal retention/support systems used in conventional foodservice systems (Hysen and Harrison, 1982). These categories include hot thermal retention/support, hot and cold thermal retention systems, and no thermal support. Benefits and constraints of these distribution systems are described in Table 15.1.

An example of a centralized tray assembly unit is shown in Figure 15.4. The layout uses mobile equipment, which has been widely accepted because of the flexibility and the ease of facility maintenance provided. This type of set-up can be readily rearranged or moved for cleaning.

Each assembly area requires support equipment to assemble the trays, such as that shown in Figure 15.4. The size of the area and the number of trays to assemble will determine the type of conveyor system required to provide support. Hysen and Harrison (1982) outline options for tray assembly equipment (Figure 15.5), including manual conveyors, such as a trayslide; simple mechanical conveyors, such as a roller type; and motorized conveyors, which may be straight-line or circular. The straight-line layout shown in Figure 15.4 illustrates other equipment needed for holding and dispensing food and other items needed for tray assembly.

In a decentralized meal assembly, the food products are produced in one location and transported to various locations for assembly at sites near patients. Equipment to maintain proper temperatures—food warmers, hot food counters, and/or refrigerated equipment—must be provided at each location. Since some foods, such as grilled or fried menu items, do not transport or hold well, some cooking equipment may be available in the service units for these difficult-to-hold foods. Even in a centralized meal assembly system, a few menu items such as coffee and toast may be prepared on the patient units.

Since the early 1950s, healthcare institutions have moved toward centralized tray assembly systems, with the early systems patterned after airline foodservices. The centralized system has the advantages of eliminating double handling of food

Table 15.1. *Meal distribution system*

Major meal distribution system	Benefits	Constraints
Hot thermal retention systems		
Pellet system	Support equipment and system operation are conventional and uncomplicated. There is no requirement for a special plate; any standard-sized china. No special insulated delivery cart is required.	Provisions for maintenance of cold items such as milk, salads, jello, ice cream, etc., are not made. Hot food cannot be held for a long period of time (more than 45 minutes). Additional serviceware pieces need to be inventoried, stored, transported, and washed.
Insulated components	Only the dinner plate and food are heated; there are no pellet bases to heat. It is simple in operation, requiring no special pellet dispensers to purchase. There is no burn hazard to the attendant or patient because there is no hot pellet base or pellet disk. No special insulated delivery cart is required.	Additional serviceware pieces need to be inventoried, stored, transported, and washed. Attractive insulated components are often taken home by patients as useful memento of their hospital experience.
Heat support cart	Thermal energy can be controlled to plate and/or bowl as required. The cart allows for food to remain heating until tray is removed for service to the patient. Each cart has an insulated drawer for ice cream and other frozen desserts. Heat energy continues to be supplied to food during the transportation process.	Special sophisticated motorized carts and special trays with heaters are required. The potential for maintenance/repair problems is high. The cart and the trays are dependent on the use of disposable dishes. Disposable dishes could be uneconomical from an operational cost standpoint and could be considered unacceptable from an aesthetic perspective. No provisions are made for maintenance of cold food items at proper temperatures except ice cream.

Table 15.1. *(Continued)*

Major meal distribution system	Benefits	Constraints
Hot and cold thermal retention systems		
Pellet and sublimation refrigeration	A synergistic heat maintenance effect is achieved. Simplicity of cart construction and ease of sanitation. The cart is lightweight, which provides for ease of mobility.	The operational cost and complexity of the required carbon dioxide cooling system is a consideration. Patient trays are not completely assembled at a central assembly point. Final assembly occurs in patient areas.
Split tray	Centralized supervision and control of the total assembly process. No reassembly of tray components is required in the patient areas. Good temperature retention of both hot and cold items. The system accommodates late trays within a reasonable period.	The cart is heavy and bulky. A motorized version may be required if any ramps are to be negotiated. The carts are difficult to sanitize. The initial cost of the cart is high and maintenance costs can be high. Due to the relatively heavy weight and limited maneuverability, carts and wall surfaces are subject to damage.
Match-a-tray	Same as described for split tray except that consolidation is required on the patient level.	Same as described for split tray. Additional labor must be applied at the patient area to reassemble the complete patient meal.
Insulated trays	Maintains hot and cold zones well without external heat or refrigerant sources. Simplicity of transport is achieved. It does not require a heavy, enclosed delivery cart. Stacked trays protect and insulate food. There is less load on the dishwashing facility due to disposables.	The purchase of special disposable dishes results in higher operational costs. Food holding time is limited to 45 minutes. The long-range cost could be substantially higher than other systems due to disposable and lease costs. Hot foods may take on a "steamed" appearance in

Table 15.1. *(Continued)*

Major meal distribution system	Benefits	Constraints
	There are no complex components to repair, replace, or maintain.	the hot compartment due to its relatively small volume and lack of venting. Possible adverse patient reaction to eating from a compartmentalized tray. Trays can be difficult to sanitize completely due to deep cavity construction. The top and bottom tray compartments do not nest; more storage area required. Rigid presentation and placement of dishes is a limitation of the system.
Insulated components	Only the dinner plate and food are heated. There are no pellet bases to heat. It is simple in operation, requiring no special pellet dispensers to purchase. There is no burn hazard to the attendant or patient because there is no hot pellet base or pellet disk. No special insulated delivery cart is required.	Additional serviceware pieces need to be inventoried, stored, transported, and washed. Attractive insulated components are often taken home by patients as useful mementos of their hospital experience. Hot food holding time is limited to 30 minutes; cold food items can be held longer.
No thermal support Covered tray	The tray is a simple standard unit. The equipment cost of the system is low.	Requires an immediate and responsive transportation system. High labor component is required for transportation process. No thermal support is available for entree and other food items.

Source: Hysen, P., and Harrison, J.: State-of-the-art review of health care patient feeding system equipment. In *Hospital Patient Feeding Systems*. Washington, DC: National Academy Press, 1982, pp. 168–171.

280-bed hospital

Item 1 (1) Tray Make-up Conveyor 28FT. TM-10. **Item 2** (2) Tray Dispenser CM-2020-C. **Item 3** (1) Tray Starter Caddy T-560. **Item 4** (1) Temp-Lock Underplate Caddy T-545. **Item 5** (2) Cup & Saucer Dispenser CM-2620-C. **Item 6** (1) Cold Food Rack T-85. **Item 7** (1) Ice Cream Cabinet RF-302. **Item 8** (2) Soup Bowl Dispenser CM-2020-C. **Item 9** (1) Hot Soup Caddy TF-632. **Item 10** (2) Heated Plate Dispenser CM-S-302-H. **Item 11** (2) Hot Food Caddy TF-633. **Item 12** (1) Milk Cabinet RF-301. **Item 13** (1) Bread & Toast Caddy RH-790. **Item 14** (2) Toasters TR-H-60. **Item 15** (1) Bread & Butter Plate Disp. CM-T-104. **Item 16** (1) Double Overshelf ACC-6015. **Item 17** (3) Temp-Lock Dome Cover Caddy T-545. **Item 18** (1) Reject Tray Caddy T-203-B. **Item 19** (10) Patient Tray Trucks TD-630-D. **Item 20** (288) Temp-Lock Dome & Underplate TL-50. **Item 21** (288) Bowls TL-70.

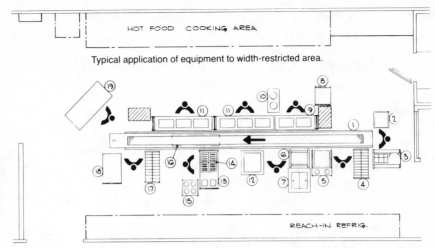

Typical application of equipment to width-restricted area.

Figure 15.4. *Centralized tray assembly unit (courtesy Caddy Corporation of America, 1984, Pitman, NJ)*

and facilitating supervision of meal assembly because the activity takes place in one location rather than in many throughout the facility. In addition, it allows for standardization of portions, uniformity in presentation, and decreased waste. Finally, less staff time is needed and the space occupied by floor kitchens can be used for other purposes. Decentralized meal assembly is still used in some institutions, however, because it offers the advantage of less time between assembly and service to patients, allowing for potentially higher quality food. Decentralized facilities also offer greater flexibility in providing for individual patient needs and in making last minute substitutions and changes.

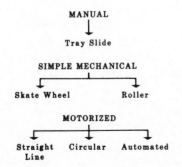

MEAL ASSEMBLY PROCESS-- CONVEYORS

Figure 15.5. *Types of conveyors for meal assembly process.* **Source: Hysen, P. and Harrison, J.: State-of-the-art review of health care patient feeding system equipment. In Hospital Patient Feeding Systems. Washington, DC: National Academy Press, 1982, p. 172.**

Depending on the layout and design of the healthcare facility, a combination of meal assembly and distribution methods may be used. Some facilities may even serve groups of patients in a dining room, while others are provided tray service in their hospital rooms. Group service is especially common in nursing homes and other types of extended care facilities, such as psychiatric hospitals.

Commissary Foodservice System

Commissary foodservice systems are characterized by centralized production, with distribution of prepared menu items to several remote areas for service and possibly final production. Service at these areas may be self-service, cafeteria service, tray service, or some other method. The centralized production facility is referred to as the commissary; in this book, we refer to the service areas as satellite service centers.

As discussed in Chapter 5, the commissary foodservice system can take many forms and may, in fact, be a combination of systems. In school foodservice operations, for example, a central kitchen may be a conventional foodservice for a secondary school but may also provide food to several satellite service centers for elementary schools in the district.

Depending on the nature of the operation, distribution and service in commissary foodservice systems can thus take many forms. The unique feature of distribution in this system is that a method must be provided for transporting food to the remote locations of the service centers. As we pointed out in Chapter 5, these facilities may be relatively close, within the same city or county, as is the case for most school foodservice operations, or they may be located great distances away from the central production unit, which is typical of many large commercial chain operations.

For this reason, a commissary system requires specialized distribution equipment, tailored to its particular needs. Food items produced in the central commissary may be transported either frozen, chilled, or hot, in bulk or in individual portions. As discussed in Chapter 8, the receiving area of the commissary and the satellite service centers must be designed to accommodate the distribution equipment. Also, as pointed out in Chapter 12, special precautions are necessary to preserve microbiological quality of foods in commissary foodservice systems because of the length of time between production and ultimate service to the customer. In evaluating commissary systems, the transportation costs must be considered, because they may add materially to the total cost of the operation, involving as they do, purchase, operation, and maintenance of the trucks for distribution.

Ready Prepared Foodservice System

In ready prepared foodservice systems, menu items are produced and held, either frozen or chilled, for service at a later time. They may be packed in bulk, in individual portions, or in combination containers. For example, in airline foodservices, two or three menu items may be portioned onto an individual serving dish.

The type of distribution equipment needed by ready prepared systems depends on whether foods are in bulk quantities or individual portions and on whether they use a cook-chill or cook-freeze approach. In systems in which foods are portioned into individual servings, an assembly system is needed. A unique characteristic of the ready prepared foodservice system is the heat processing of prepared items prior to service. Microwave, convection, and infrared ovens are commonly used in the service unit for this final heat processing step. Usually, foods are transported in the chilled or frozen state, and this final heating occurs just before service. Therefore, cold temperature support is needed during the distribution process.

Two types of carts are used predominantly for cold temperature support. One type is insulated to maintain temperature during distribution to remote pantry areas where the carts are connected to wall-mounted or floor-borne refrigeration units. Hysen and Harrison (1982) describe these carts as light-weight and thus easy to transfer; they are also easy to sanitize. In more common use is the roll-in refrigerator cart. If the cart is the enclosed type, the doors should be opened prior to placing in the refrigerated unit to permit proper circulation of chilled air.

In addition to the type of equipment used for heat processing prior to service mentioned above, two other types of equipment for patient tray service are in use in some institutions: contact plate heater carts and integral heat ovens and carts. The benefits and constraints of the various methods of heat processing for patient service are enumerated in Table 15.2 (Hysen and Harrison, 1982).

The place on the patient floors where final heat processing and meal assembly occurs is generally referred to as a galley. The equipment in a galley includes the cold temperature support equipment, the equipment needed for the final heat processing of menu items, some small equipment such as a coffee maker and toaster, a sink, a small storage area, and a desk area for the dietetic personnel.

Assembly/Serve Foodservice System

The assembly/serve foodservice system uses for the most part foods that are ready to serve or that require little or no processing prior to service. As pointed out in Chapter 5, bulk, preportioned, and preplated frozen foods are the three market forms of foods that fit into this category.

When foods are served cafeteria style, the bulk form is generally used, the primary requirement being heat processing before service. This heat processing can be done in the service unit or in an auxiliary area, using one of the methods described in the discussion of the ready prepared system. If preportioned or preplated items are purchased, heat processing similar to the methods described for ready systems can be used. Cold temperature support equipment may be needed for distributing foods to service areas and for holding prior to heat processing for service.

Table 15.2. *Meal service system*

Major meal service system	Benefits	Constraints
Microwave ovens	The food is cooked very rapidly. "On-demand" patient feeding can be achieved.	Food is easily overcooked, and some foods tend to rethermalize unevenly, leaving hot and cold spots. Food does not brown, causing some foods to have an unnatural appearance. A trained operator is required to rethermalize all food products. Employee training is essential to the success of the program. Maintenance of microwave ovens can be a significant cost factor.
Convection ovens	Oven cavities can accommodate 12 to 30 meals at a time; thus higher efficiency can be achieved in the rethermalization and reassembly process as compared to a microwave system.	The speed is increased as compared to a conventional still air oven; however, the process is not as fast as a microwave oven. Some food products experience excessive cooking losses; in others, there is a thickened surface layer on the food from the rethermalization process. Some food products do not rethermalize to a uniform temperature.
Infrared ovens	Food is rethermalized at a faster speed than conventional still air ovens. Oven cavities can accommodate 16 to 24 meals at a time; thus higher efficiency can be achieved in the rethermalization and reassembly process as compared to a microwave system.	Energy consumption for rethermalization is comparatively high. Soups are not accommodated by the infrared equipment and must be separately handled. Dishes and covers become very hot in the rethermalization process. Food products may burn to or stick to the heated dish.
Integral heat ovens and carts	Minimum intervention by employees is required to rethermalize foods. Efficiency and speed of service is enhanced due to multiplicity of meals rethermalized at the same time.	Certain food items, such as soup or hot breakfast cereals, are difficult to rethermalize. Dishes must be sprayed with a release agent to prevent sticking when using certain food items.

Table 15.2. *(Continued)*

Major meal service system	Benefits	Constraints
	Integrally heated dish acts as "pellet" system to continue to provide thermal support to hot food after service to patient	Warewashing time is increased, particularly for the breakfast service, because of the food that sticks to dishes. Ongoing operation costs are comparatively high due to replacement and lease costs. An inflexible presentation of the tray and rigid placement of items when employing the cart-borne system.
Contact plate heater carts	Reduced pantry labor due to rethermalizing and refrigerating patient trays in the delivery cart. Allows pantry to be reduced in size and lowers equipment cost by eliminating need for reheating ovens. Minimum intervention by employees after assembled tray has been dispatched from main tray assembly location.	Cart maintenance may be a problem due to complex electrical components. Special trays and dishes are required—usually disposable dishes—which can increase operating costs. Rethermalization can only be done from the chilled state, not from the frozen state. The cart is presently being field-tested; its performance has not been proven. Operating cost appears to be high, based on preliminary data available. An inflexible presentation of the tray and rigid placement of items are aesthetic limitations of the system.

Source: Hysen, P., and Harrison, J.: State-of-the-art review of health care patient feeding system equipment. In *Hospital Patient Feeding Systems.* Washington, DC: National Academy Press, 1982, pp. 178–179.

TYPES OF SERVICE

The foodservice systems model, our organizing framework for this book, defines quality meals and clientele satisfaction as its primary outputs or outcomes. As the process that provides for the culmination of these outcomes, service of food to the clientele is both a subsystem of our model and the ultimate objective of a foodservice organization.

As stated earlier, quality food poorly served will often result in complaints, whereas mediocre food well served may meet with satisfaction. Complaints about poor service rank high in the foodservice industry. People will grow frustrated and discontented if they have to stand in a long service line or wait a long time for food to arrive, or if they are served the wrong dish or an item prepared differently than was ordered.

Whether they are profit or non-profit, then, all foodservice operations must focus on service. Marketing services is the theme of the 1980s in all facets of the foodservice industry—institutional or commercial.

Service approaches can be categorized in a variety of ways and, in fact, a number of combination services exist. In this chapter, three categories of service will be discussed: table/counter service, self-service, and tray service. Catering and banquet service will also be discussed briefly, although most such service can be classified as table or self-service, depending on the function. To illustrate the combination of service approaches that have developed, consider the table service restaurant with the self-service salad bar.

Service of food and beverages is one of the most diverse activities that one can imagine, taking many forms and occurring in a wide variety of places, at all hours of the day and night. Because of today's lifestyles, it can range from fine service with tableside preparation, to coffee and doughnuts in the factory, to hot dogs at the beach.

Table and Counter Service

Table and counter service have traditionally been the most common forms of service in the commercial segment of the industry. Table service can be very simple or extremely elaborate; its distinguishing characteristic is service by a waiter or waitress. In most table service operations, a hostess, host, or maitre d'hotel is responsible for seating guests in the dining room.

The most common method of table service in the United States, often referred to as American-style service, involves plating of food in the kitchen or service kitchen, then presenting it to the guest. In more elaborate service, food is often prepared at the table—as with Bananas Foster or Steak Diane. Another type of table service is called family style, in which food is brought to the table on platters or in bowls by waiters or waitresses and then passed around the table by the guests. Restaurants featuring country-fried chicken or barbecue ribs will frequently feature family-style service, as will some institutional foodservices.

Counter service is often found in diners, coffee shops, drug store fountains, and other establishments where patrons are looking for speedy service. People eating alone can join others at a counter and enjoy the companionship. This kind of service may be combined with waiter/waitress service at booths or tables. The most common counter arrangements are shown in Figure 15.6. These arrangements provide not only fast service for a customer but also efficient operation from the labor standpoint: the counter attendant is usually responsible for taking the orders, serving the meals, bussing dishes, and cleaning the counter, and may even serve as cashier except at peak periods.

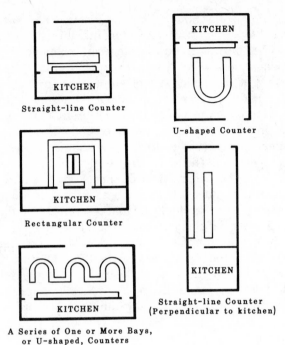

Straight-line Counter

Rectangular Counter

A Series of One or More Bays,
or U-shaped, Counters

U-shaped Counter

Straight-line Counter
(Perpendicular to kitchen)

Figure 15.6. *Various layouts for counter service.* **Source: Stokes, J. W.: How to Manage a Restaurant or Institutional Food Service.** *Dubuque, IA: William C. Brown Co., 1982, p. 105.*

Most bars and lounges use table or counter service or a combination of both. Although their emphasis is on beverage service, a great deal of innovation can be seen in these operations as their managements seek new ways to increase volume and revenues. Snack items are often available, sometimes free or at low cost to encourage beverage sales. Self-service hors d'oeuvres, courtesy of the establishment, are popular in many bars and lounges as a promotional tool to increase patronage. Some meal services are available in bars, as a way of increasing business at times that would otherwise be slack. And many hotels today offer beverage service in the lobby rather than offering this service only in a bar or in the hotel restaurants.

Well-trained and courteous waiters, waitresses, and other service personnel are the keys to successful table service operations. In upscale restaurants offering sophisticated service, the job of the waiter/waitress is highly specialized and truly an art.

Tipping is a common practice in table/counter service establishments and can be a significant component in the income of waiters, waitresses, and other service personnel. A few establishments have attempted to eliminate tipping by adding an automatic service charge that is periodically divided among the service staff. Most customers, however, seem to prefer tipping to the automatic charge because of its more direct relationship to the waiter or waitress.

The foodservice manager must be aware of federal and state legislation and regulations that have provisions covering tipping and tipped employees. After

January 1, 1980, the Fair Labor Standards Act permitted tips to be credited as wages up to a level of 40 percent of the prevailing minimum wage, providing the tipped employee receives the minimum wage in a combination of wages and tips. The foodservice manager must keep informed about current provisions for record keeping and reporting of tipped income of employees, since these do change periodically. The National Restaurant Association and the state restaurant associations work on behalf of the industry to influence legislation and maintain active programs for informing operators about proposed and current legislation.

The handling and controlling of guest checks is another concern of managers in a waiter/waitress operation. The first element of effective control is to ensure that all food items served are charged. A duplicate check system is the most widely used procedure; the waiter or waitress writes the order on a guest check, simultaneously preparing a carbon duplicate that is submitted to the preparation area to obtain food. The second element of control is to charge the proper prices. Electronic cash registers with preprogrammed prices are becoming widely used for this reason. The third element is to ensure that all checks are settled. This can be accomplished by having all guest checks sequentially numbered, keeping reserve stocks in locked storage, issuing checks to servers in numerical order, and then sorting the used guest checks periodically into numerical order to determine if any are missing.

Self-Service

Today, self-service foodservice operations cover a wide spectrum, cafeteria service being one of the most commonly used forms. Self-service is characteristic of the fast food industry, with counter pickup service, take-out, and drive-through window service the most common approaches. Other self-service operations include buffets, vending machines, refreshment stands in recreational and sports facilities, and mobile foodservice units that range from the small, hot dog cart rolled down the street by the operator to sophisticated operations in motorized vans equipped for preparing a variety of menu items. Today's round-the-clock eating in every imaginable place has created a demand, and self-service approaches have satisfied it.

Cafeteria service is characterized by advance preparation of most food and a maximum of self-service. It is the predominant form of service used in institutional foodservice and employee feeding operations. In most industrial and institutional cafeterias, self-bussing of trays and dishes is also common practice as a means of reducing labor costs.

Traditionally, the commercial cafeteria has placed a great deal of emphasis on food display, merchandising, and marketing of menu items. Managers of institutions and other organizations providing foodservice as an auxiliary function to their major objectives have come to recognize that foodservice can be a profit center for them as well and are beginning to apply these same principles of marketing in these organizations to enhance sales volume.

The straight-line counter, which may vary greatly in length depending on the number of sections it contains, is the most common cafeteria counter arrangement, for self-service as well as service. Generally, the length varies with the quantity and variety of menu items offered, rather than being dependent on the number of persons to be served.

An alternative arrangement to the straight-line counter is the hollow square, sometimes called the "scramble system." In this layout, the various stations or food counters are positioned to form three or four sides of a square, with space between the counters and perhaps a center island. This layout allows customers to move from one station to another without being held up by the entire line. They can go to those stations offering the menu items they wish to select, rather than having to go down the entire counter, as is true with the straight-line cafeteria. The hollow square layout not only decreases lines but permits more people to be served in a smaller space.

Buffet service has enjoyed increasing popularity in recent years in commercial and institutional foodservice. Periodic scheduling of buffets in a college residence hall foodservice, an employee cafeteria in a hospital, or an industrial foodservice operation can serve as a monotony breaker and a means of creating good will.

Buffet service enables a facility to serve more people in a given time with less personnel. The usual procedure in commercial operations is for guests to serve their plates with the entree, vegetables, and salad and then go to the table where servers provide flatware, napkins, and water and beverages. Salad bars and dessert bars are variations of buffet service in which selected menu items are offered using self-service, while table service may be used for the main course and beverages.

Vending machines have been around a long time for such products as candy, soft drinks, and cigarettes; however, in recent years vending has become a sophisticated operation in which a wide range of food items are offered for sale. Vending offers the advantage of automatic dispensing to customers at any hour with limited personnel—only those needed to replenish and maintain the machines on a scheduled basis.

Refrigerated machines permit a wide range of cold food items to be offered— sandwiches, fruit, salads, yogurt, and a whole array of other items. In full-service vending operations, a small microwave unit is often available, enabling patrons to heat food items; as a result, a much wider variety of food items can be offered for sale. Soups, chili, sandwiches that are normally served hot, and even omelets and other breakfast items are held in refrigerated vending machines until purchased, then heated in the microwave oven by the customer.

Both the machines and food items may be provided by a commercial vending operator on a contract basis, although many organizations such as hospitals and universities are now finding that self-operated vending can be an important revenue source. Tight controls for food items and cash are needed in any vending operation. A form such as the one in Figure 15.7 should be used for maintaining appropriate records for control. The example form is for a snack machine; each type of machine used would have a similar form with items listed appropriate to each type. The control sheet provides space for recording beginning inventory, additions, removal, ending inventory, number of items sold, price of each item, and total sales of each item. Space is also provided for recording readings on the

Date Beginning _____ Ending _____

Initials _____

Date _____

Cash audit _____

SNACK

Item	Beginning inventory	Add	Add	Add	Add	Add	Add	Add	Add	Add	Add	Add	Add	Total in	Removed	Removed	Ending inventory	Total out	Number sold	Price	Sales
Candy																					
Gum																					
Lifesavers																					
Snacks																					
Chips																					
Cakes																					

Tests

Meter ending _____

Meter beginning _____

Meter sales _____

Meter sales _____

Tests _____

Net meter _____

Total sales $ _____

Cash deposit $ _____

Over/short $ _____

Figure 15.7. *Vending control sheet. Source: Kaud, F. A., Miller, R. P., and Underwood, R. F.: Cafeteria Management for Hospitals. Chicago: American Hospital Assn., 1982, p. 94.*

transaction meter that counts the number of times the machine vends an item and for reconciliation with sales for cash collected.

Vending in the foodservice business appears to be here to stay and will probably continue to expand as a self-service alternative that has tremendous versatility and flexibility. Servicing of vending operations fits well into the operation of the traditional services of a foodservice organization. With minimal training, foodservice employees can be trained to serve and maintain vending machines on a full-time or part-time basis, depending on the size of the operation. Many managers are thus finding that vending is merely an extension of services and can be an important revenue generator. They are also beginning to find that if vending services are to be offered, the ongoing foodservice operation can often provide these services best and more profitably.

Tray Service

Tray service, in which food is carried to a person by a foodservice employee, is used primarily in healthcare institutions and for in-flight meal service in the airline industry. Room service, in which food is served on a tray or on a cart in a customer's hotel or motel room, is a variation of tray service. Because we have discussed patient service in hospitals in the first part of this chapter, we will move to in-flight service. In this kind of service, food is produced in a commissary foodservice system; a food contractor contracts with the airline company to provide meals or snacks, according to the specifications of the airline. Tray assembly systems and specialized distribution equipment are needed, tailored to the needs of the operation. On the airplane itself, thermal support is needed for heat processing of menu items to be served hot, and cold support for chilled menu items. Sophisticated control systems are required to ensure that the proper number of meals are provided and to monitor and control a wide variety of items, ranging from dishes and flatware to individual tea bags. As an illustration of the complexity, the food may be loaded onto a plane at a location around the world from the place where the soiled trays are unloaded.

Catering and Banquets

Commercial and institutional foodservices are finding that their sales can be augmented by catering and banquet services. Functions of this kind can be quite profitable because the number of guests is known in advance and the menu is fixed; most overproduction can therefore be avoided. In addition, a guarantee on the number of meals that will be paid for is generally required, within a range of 5 to 10 percent above or below the number given by the sponsor of the event.

As mentioned in an earlier part of this chapter, catering service can take many forms, depending on the nature of the event. Buffet service has become the most widely used form, although table service is still used frequently. These events may include any meal or many other functions, such as receptions, coffees, cocktail parties, or afternoon teas and may take place on or off the premises of a facility.

In off-premises catering, the food may be transported to a wide variety of places, many of which are not ideal for service of food. Temperature support equipment, both hot and cold, is needed, as well as equipment for final heat processing of prepared food items, which may have to be transported by the foodservice operation to the place of service. Even a mobile generator may be required if adequate electrical outlets are not available wherever the catered event is being held. A variety of special serving utensils and equipment must also be available—for example, a fountain for punch service, or a mobile bar unit.

As catered services become more important to hospitals and other institutions, they sometimes require assignment of service personnel on a full-time basis to cover catered events. In large catering operations, however, many part-time personnel are used, both in order to have sufficient staff when needed to serve scheduled events and to control labor costs.

SUMMARY

The third major subsystem of the foodservice system is distribution and service. By way of this and the other functional subsystems, the goal of providing quality food and services to a given clientele is achieved. High quality distribution and service are critical to the achievement of clientele satisfaction, because patrons will often judge an establishment more on the quality of its service than on the quality of its food. Even the best prepared meal can lead to dissatisfaction if it is served too slowly or in a discourteous manner.

Distribution and service differ somewhat among the four types of foodservice systems. In the conventional system, holding equipment is needed to maintain the proper temperature between production and service, which normally occurs in a dining area located adjacent, or in close proximity, to the production facility. In conventional systems with tray service, such as in a healthcare institution, distribution and service become more complex, as food must be transported to the many areas where patients are located. Assembly of trays may be centralized or decentralized, with centralized assembly being more common. In order to maintain proper temperatures, a method of thermal retention is needed between meal assembly and service to the patient. A variety of methods have been developed to provide the necessary hot and cold retention/support.

Depending on the nature of the operation, distribution and service in commissary foodservice systems can take many forms. The unique feature in the commissary system is that a method must be provided for transporting food to remote locations of the satellite service centers. Specialized distribution equipment is needed, tailored to the needs of the operation, such as trucks for transportation to the service centers.

In ready prepared foodservice systems, the type of distribution equipment needed will depend on whether a cook-chill or cook-freeze approach is used. Another factor influencing distribution and service is whether foods are distributed in bulk quantity or individual portions. A unique characteristic of these ready prepared systems is the need for heat processing equipment for final heating of prepared items prior to service. Microwave, convection, and infrared ovens are commonly used in the service area for this final heat processing step. In patient tray service in ready systems, integral heat ovens and carts or contact plate heater carts may also be used.

In the assembly/serve foodservice system, equipment for heat processing prior to service is needed for the purchased, prepared menu items used in the system. Thermal support equipment may also be needed for distributing foods to service areas and for holding prior to heat processing for service.

Service approaches can be categorized as table/counter, cafeteria/buffet, and tray. Catering and banquet service, which may use table or self-service approaches, is becoming an expanded operational area in both commercial and institutional foodservice. Table service has traditionally been a predominant form of service in the commercial segment of the industry; however, many forms of self-service have become popular over the last several decades. Self-service is the predominant form of service in many institutional foodservices. Its options cover a wide spectrum, from cafeterias and buffets to vending machines and refreshment stands. With the round-the-clock eating characteristic of U.S. lifestyles, self-service approaches permit the flexibility and versatility needed. Tray service occurs predominantly in healthcare institutions to provide for patient meal service, but is also important for in-flight meals in the airline industry.

REFERENCES

Brenner, A. M., Hitchcock, M. J., Lane, R. H., Goertz, G. E., Campbell, A. M., and Collins, J. E.: Quality control standards for cooked frozen green beans held on a steam table for varying holding times. *J. Food Sci.* 43:1066, 1978.

Dahl, C. A., and Matthews, M. E.: Cook/chill foodservice systems: Microwave heating precooked portions of beef loaf. *J. Microwave Power* 13(1):81, 1978.

Fairbrook, P.: *College and University Food Service Manual*. Stockton, CA: Colman Publishers, 1979.

Faulkner, E.: Vending foodservice's stepchild comes into its own. *Restaurants & Institutions* 94:147 (Jun. 10), 1984.

Hysen, P., and Harrison, J.: State-of-the-art review of health care patient feeding system equipment. In *Hospital Patient Feeding Systems*, Washington, DC: National Academy Press, 1982.

Kahrl, W. L.: *Advanced Modern Food and Beverage Service*. Englewood Cliffs, NJ: Prentice-Hall, 1977.

Kaud, F. A., Miller, R. P., and Underwood, R. F.: *Cafeteria Management for Hospitals*. Chicago: American Hospital Assn., 1982.

Leung, C., Koehler, H. H., and Hard, M. M.: Mineral contents of selected pre-prepared foods sampled in a hospital food service line. *J. Am. Dietet. A.* 80:530, 1982.

Miller, R. P.: Vending: Contract or self-operated. In Rose, J. C., ed.: *Handbook for Health Care Food Service Management*. Rockville, MD: Aspen Systems Corp., 1984.

Prusa, K. J., Bowers, J. A., Craig, J., and Greig, S.: Ascorbic acid, thiamin, and vitamin B_6

contents of selected menu items in different school food service approaches. *School Food Serv. Res. Rev.* 5:94, 1981.

Ridley, S. J., and Matthews, M. E.: Temperature histories of menu items during meal assembly, distribution and service in a hospital foodservice. *J. Food Protection* 46:100, 1983.

Stokes, J. W.: *How to Manage a Restaurant or Institutional Food Service.* Ch. 5. Styles of service. 4th ed. Dubuque, IA: William C. Brown Co., 1982.

Thorner, M. E., and Manning, P. B.: *Quality Control in Foodservice.* Rev. ed. Ch. 14. Quality control of vending equipment. Westport, CT: AVI Publishing Co., 1983.

Underwood, R. F.: Merchandising for satisfaction and profit. In Rose, J. C., ed.: *Handbook for Health Care Food Service Management.* Rockville, MD: Aspen Systems Corp., 1984.

Vannucci, M. R.: Between-meal feeding systems. In Rose, J. C., ed.: *Handbook for Health Care Food Service Management.* Rockville, MD: Aspen Systems Corp., 1984.

Will, B.: Hospital tray delivery carts. *The Consultant* 16:28 (Spring), 1983.

16

Maintenance of Equipment and Facilities

Maintenance is the last major functional subsystem in the foodservice system, yet it permeates all other subsystems (Figure 16.1). The receiving area needs to be checked after each delivery and thoroughly cleaned daily. Storage areas should also be put on a regular cleaning schedule to prevent vermin and rodent infestation. Foodservice utensils, dishes, equipment, and facilities require continuous cleaning. Every time a meal is produced and served, the cleaning and sanitizing previously done must often be done again. Quite literally, a foodservice's cleaning and maintenance tasks are never completed.

Facility maintenance is one of the three major components of a sanitation program, along with safe food handling practices and sanitary conditions of the physical plant and equipment, both discussed in Chapter 12. In addition to sanitation, maintenance of equipment and facilities is important for other reasons. Cleanliness of facilities, for example, ranks high among the concerns of foodservice clientele and often influences their decision to return. The safety of the surroundings is often related to cleaning and maintenance practices; spills, if not cleaned up properly, represent a serious safety hazard. Finally, grease build-up in the hoods over the production equipment is extremely dangerous and is a major cause of fires in foodservice operations.

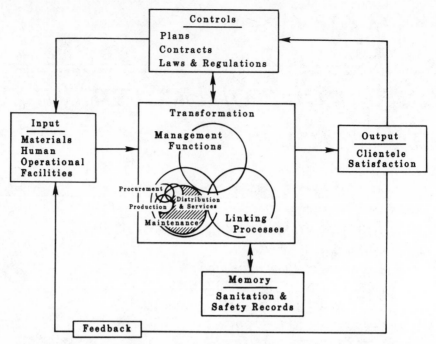

Figure 16.1. *Foodservice systems model with the maintenance subsystem highlighted*

A properly designed foodservice facility is basic to maintaining a high standard of sanitation, and the first requirement for sanitary design is cleanability. Equipment and fixtures should be arranged and designed to comply with sanitation standards, and trash and garbage properly disposed to avoid contaminating food and attracting pests.

For a facility to be clean, however, is not enough; it must also be sanitary. Although the two words are often used synonymously, clean means free of physical soil and with an outwardly pleasing appearance—a glass that sparkles, silver that shines, and a floor free from dust and grime. These objects, though clean on the surface, can in fact harbor disease agents or harmful chemicals. Sanitary means free of disease-causing organisms and other harmful contaminants. Cleaning and sanitizing, then, are both issues of concern in the maintenance of foodservice equipment and facilities; together they form the basis for good housekeeping in foodservice operations. As stated cogently in the NIFI sanitation manual (1978), the foodservice manager should operate an establishment by this rule: "Look clean—Be sanitary."

This chapter will discuss warewashing sanitation, including types of machines used in these processes. Maintenance of equipment and facilities will be outlined, along with pertinent issues regarding trash and garbage disposal and rodent and insect control. The final section will delineate safety principles in foodservice operations.

SANITIZATION

Sanitization is critical for any surface that comes in contact with food, which includes, of course, all dishes, utensils, and pots and pans. Sanitization can be accomplished in one of two ways: by heat or by chemical sanitizing compound. In either case, the object must be thoroughly clean and completely rinsed in order for the sanitizing process to work. Caked-on soils not removed by cleaning, for example, may harbor bacteria even after the use of a sanitizing solution.

Exposing a clean object to sufficiently high heat for a sufficiently long period of time will sanitize it. In general, the higher the heat, the shorter the time required. The most common method for heat sanitizing is immersion of an object in water at 170°F for no less than 30 seconds. The temperature must be increased if the time is decreased; the final sanitizing rinse in dish machines, for example, is 180° for 10 seconds. Another means of heat sanitization is through the use of live, additive-free steam, from water at a temperature of 212°F. The temperature at the surface of the object being sanitized is the critical one, not the temperature as the water or steam leaves its source.

Sanitizing can also be achieved through the use of chemical compounds capable of destroying disease-causing bacteria. Chemical sanitizers are widely used in the foodservice industry; these chemicals are rigorously regulated by the Environmental Protection Agency (EPA) to assure public safety. Chemical sanitizing is accomplished either by immersing an object in the correct concentration of sanitizer for one minute or by rinsing, swabbing, or spraying double the usual recommended concentration of sanitizer on its surface. Sanitizers are often blended with detergent so the same product can be used for cleaning and sanitizing. A wide range of detergents and sanitizers is available, specifically designed for various cleaning and sanitizing tasks within a foodservice operation. Excellent resource materials are available from the chemical companies, the major suppliers of these detergents and cleaning agents.

Some sanitizing agents are toxic to humans as well as to bacteria and are therefore acceptable for use only on nonfood contact surfaces. Other agents may not be toxic but may have undesirable flavors or odors and are thus unacceptable for use in foodservice operations. The three most common chemicals used in sanitizing are chlorine, iodine, and quaternary ammonia. Figure 16.2 summarizes the properties of these sanitizers and outlines procedures for their use.

MANUAL AND MECHANICAL WAREWASHING

Warewashing is extremely important in foodservice facilities because of its significance in protecting sanitation; utilizing labor time; saving on operational costs for power, hot water, and detergent; and preventing loss and breakage of tableware. Warewashing may be accomplished by manual or mechanical methods, although manual washing is usually limited to pots, pans, and cookware that is too large to be washed in a machine, or that is designed to require hand brushing. In most foodservice operations, dishes and other table utensils are

	Chlorine	Iodine	Quaternary ammonia
Minimum concentration			
—for immersion	50 parts per million (ppm)	12.5 ppm	200 ppm
—for power spray or cleaning in place	100 ppm	25 ppm	
Temperature of solution	75°F/24°C+	75–120°F 24–49°C Iodine will leave solution at 120°F.	75°F/24°C+
Time for sanitizing			
—for immersion	1 minute	1 minute	1 minute; however, some products require longer contact time; read label
—for power spray or cleaning in place	Follow manufacturer's instructions	Follow manufacturer's instructions	Follow manufacturer's instructions
pH (detergent residue raises pH of solution)	Must be below pH 10	Must be below pH 5.5	Most effective around pH 7 but varies with compound
Corrosiveness	Corrosive to some substances	Noncorrosive	Noncorrosive
Response to organic contaminants in water	Quickly inactivated	Made less effective	Not easily affected
Response to hard water	Not affected	Not affected	Some compounds inactivated but varies with formulation; read label. Hardness over 500 ppm is undesirable for some quats
Indication of strength of solution	Test kit required	Amber color indicates effective solution, but test kits must also be used	Test kit required. Follow label instructions closely

Figure 16.2. *Chemical sanitizing agents.* **Source:** *National Institute for the Foodservice Industry: Applied Foodservice Sanitation. 3rd ed. National Institute for the Foodservice Industry, 1985.*

430

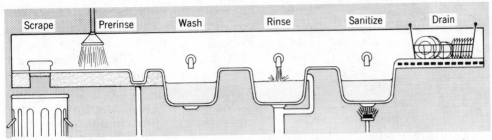

Figure 16.3. *Setup of three-compartment sink for manual dishwashing.* **Source: Gisslen, W.:** *Professional Cooking.* ***New York, John Wiley & Sons, 1983, p. 17.***

washed by machine, although manual dishwashing is still a frequent practice in small operations. Mechanical potwashing machines sometimes are used in very large facilities.

Manual Warewashing

Manual warewashing is used primarily for pots and pans, but may be used for dishes in small facilities such as day care centers or nursing homes. Figure 16.3 illustrates a typical set-up of a manual dishwashing operation. A scraping and prerinse area and three sinks are needed, one for washing, the second for rinsing, and the third for sanitizing. Counter space must be provided next to the sanitizing sink to permit air drying of dishes and utensils, since health regulations prohibit towel drying because of the potential sanitation hazard. In most operations, a garbage disposal unit is installed in the scraping and prerinsing counter.

The procedure outlined in Figure 16.4 delineates the five steps involved in manual dishwashing. Although heat sanitizing is specified in both the illustration and the procedure, a chemical sanitizer may also be used. The dishes and utensils

1 **Scrape and prerinse.** The purpose of this step is to keep the wash water cleaner longer.

2 **Wash.** Use warm water at 110 to 120°F (43 to 49°C) and a good detergent. Scrub well with a brush to remove all traces of soil and grease.

3 **Rinse.** Use clean, warm water to rinse off detergent residues. Change the water frequently, or use running water with an overflow, as in Figure 16.3.

4 **Sanitize.** Place utensils in a rack and immerse in hot water at *170°F (77°C) for 30 seconds.* (A gas or electric heating element is needed to hold water at this temperature.)

5 **Drain and air dry.** Do not towel dry. This may recontaminate utensils. Do not touch food contact surfaces of sanitized dishes, glasses, and silverware.

Figure 16.4. *Procedure for manual dishwashing.* **Source: Gisslen, W.:** *Professional Cooking.* ***New York, John Wiley & Sons, 1983, p. 17.***

must stand in a chemical sanitizer for at least one minute; generally, the sanitizing solution is mixed to twice the recommended strength so the dilution from water carried over from the rinse tank will not reduce effectiveness too quickly.

The facilities and procedure for washing pots and pans manually are similar to those for manual dishwashing. In most operations, these two processes are carried out in different areas of the foodservice operation. Separate sink set-ups are therefore provided in each area, with the pot and pan area usually located adjacent to production areas, and the dishwashing facilities in close proximity to the dining room.

Mechanical Warewashing

The dishwashing operation must include areas for accumulating soiled tableware from dining areas, or in a hospital, space must be sufficient for carts holding soiled trays from patient floors. Space is also needed for scraping, prerinsing, and stacking prior to washing; for the actual dishwashing machines; for removal of dishes and flatware from baskets or a conveyor; and finally, for stacking and storing dishes and utensils. Ideally, dishes should be routed from the dining area in a manner that creates the least noise, confusion, and unsightliness.

Dishwashing machines are generally classified by the number of tanks. A single-tank machine is the smallest capacity and is used widely in small institutions. Three styles of single-tank machines are shown in Figure 16.5. The first of

Floor mounted

Figure 16.5. *Three types of single-tank dishwashing machines: floor-mounted, under counter, and countertop (permission of Hobart Corp., Troy, OH)*

Under counter   *Counter top*

Figure 16.5. *(Continued)*

these models is floor-mounted and is used primarily in small institutions. Under-counter machines, similar to those found in the home, may be seen in small operations with limited counter space. These machines, however, operate much faster and have greater capacity than the home-style dishwashers. The third is a countertop model and is commonly used in counter service operations, such as drugstore lunch counters or coffeeshops, where it can be mounted easily in a small amount of space.

Rack conveyor machines with two or three tanks, such as the one in Figure 16.6, are used in larger operations that have greater loads of dishes to be washed. After dishes are scraped and sorted, they are placed in racks designed for various types of dishes, such as plates, cups, and glasses. An overhead hand-operated sprayer is generally used to preflush dishes with warm water. Racks are then pushed onto the conveyor, and the conveyor moves the racks through the machine at a uniform preset speed. These machines usually have a power wash cycle, a power rinse cycle, and a final rinse cycle. Large machines may have a prewash tank, while the two-tank model usually has only a power wash and a power rinse tank. The final sanitizing rinse must be 10 seconds in duration and not less than

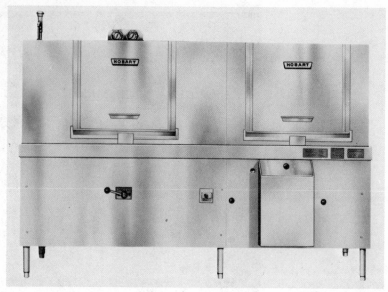

Figure 16.6. *Rack conveyor dishwashing machine (permission of Hobart Corp., Troy, OH)*

180°F. The primary purposes for the final rinse are to heat-sanitize the eating utensils and to ensure that detergent is completely rinsed off. Figure 16.7 is a diagram of the interior of a typical three-tank machine.

The rackless machines, or flight-type, as they are generally called (Figure 16.8), have become especially popular in very high-volume operations. With these machines, plates and trays are placed directly on a continuous peg or pin conveyor; smaller items are racked and sent through the machine. Detailed procedures are needed for this and all other dishwashing operations, such as the ones outlined in Figure 16.9 for dishwashing in a flight-type machine.

Specialized machines are available for washing glass and silverware because of special problems in ensuring their cleanliness and sanitization. Glass washers are common where large numbers of glasses are washed daily; in bars and lounges, for example, small counter unit glasswashers are frequently seen.

Ensuring that the final rinse reaches the required 180°F is critical for sanitizing dishes and utensils. General purpose hot water heaters, as a rule, bring the temperature to no higher than 140°F. A booster water heater with sufficient capacity to supply the final rinse water to the required temperature will usually be needed, although some dish machines are equipped with booster heaters.

Although dishwashing machines are the most reliable way to clean and sanitize dishes and utensils, many problems can occur if machines are not installed or operated correctly. Figure 16.10 enumerates some of the typical problems that occur, along with possible causes and suggested solutions to the problems.

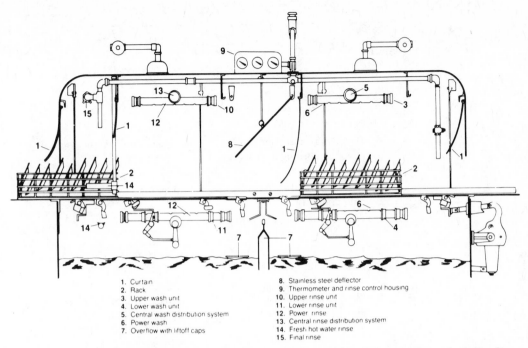

1. Curtain	8. Stainless steel deflector
2. Rack	9. Thermometer and rinse control housing
3. Upper wash unit	10. Upper rinse unit
4. Lower wash unit	11. Lower rinse unit
5. Central wash distribution system	12. Power rinse
6. Power wash	13. Central rinse distribution system
7. Overflow with liftoff caps	14. Fresh hot water rinse
	15. Final rinse

Figure 16.7. *Diagram of rack conveyor dishwashing machine. Source: Minor, L.J.: Sanitation, Safety & Environmental Standards. Westport, CT: AVI Publishing Co. 1983, p. 133, figure 1.*

Figure 16.8. *Flight type dishwashing machine (permission of Hobart Corp., Troy, OH)*

When[a]	How	Use
Soiled Dish Station		
After each use	1 Fill dish machine	Hot water
	2 Turn on steam	
	3 Fill detergent dispenser and rinse dry dispenser	
	4 Scrape, prerinse, and stack dishes according to size and type	Prerinse unit, garbage disposal
	5 Rack cups and glasses open side down	Cup and glass racks
	6 Separate flatware according to type	
	7 Place flatware into perforated baskets with business side up; soak	Perforated flatware baskets Flatware soaking sink
	8 Check temperature on wash-and-rinse tank	Prerinse 120°F (49°C) Wash 150°F (65.6°C) Pumped rinse 160°F (71°C) Final rinse 180°F (82°C)
	9 Push start button on machine	Automatic wash and rinse
	10 Place glass racks on conveyor belt	
	11 Place cup racks on conveyor belt	
	12 Rack dishes on belt according to size and type	
	13 Place filled flatware baskets in cup rack	
	(a) Place rack on conveyor belt	
Clean Dish Station		
	14 Inspect glasses for cleanliness (set aside soiled glassware and return to soiled-dish table)	
	15 Remove glass racks from belt	To a clean dolly
	16 Inspect cups for cleanliness; remove any soiled cups	
	17 Remove cup rack from belt	To a clean dolly

18	Remove dishes from belt, inspect for cleanliness, and stack according to size and type	Clean dish table or appropriate dish cart
19	Remove flatware	
	(a) Inspect for cleanliness	
20	Transfer clean flatware to clean perforated basket, business side down	Perforated flatware basket
21	Send flatware through dish machine a second time	
22	Remove flatware basket from belt	Clean dish table or appropriate flatware cart
23	Transport dishes, glasses, and flatware to point of use	Cart

[a] Dish washer could check water temperature, detergent, and rinse-dry dispensers frequently to be sure machine is being operated properly.

Figure 16.9. *Procedure for mechanical dishwashing using flight-type machine.* **Source:** *Longree, K., and Blaker, G. G.:* **Sanitary Techniques in Foodservice.** *2nd ed. New York, John Wiley & Sons, 1982, pp. 116–117.*

Machines should be equipped with dispensers for detergents and chemical rinse aids to ensure that the proper amounts are being used during the dishwashing cycle. Rinse aids are recommended to speed drying time and permit dishes to be stored more quickly and without moisture.

In some foodservices, high temperature dishwashing machines have been replaced with low temperature models that operate at 120°F. In these machines, sanitizing is accomplished by chemicals, not heat, with chlorine, for example, used commonly in their detergent formulas (Minor, 1983). The resulting energy and water savings have led to reduced operational costs using these low temperature machines. Among their disadvantages, however, are their lower capacity, problems with long drying time of dishes, and the possible blackening of some flatware by the chlorine detergent, although stainless steel is not affected. In addition, chemical costs may offset a portion of energy savings if the water hardness is excessive.

Many smaller pots and pans can be washed in the dishwashing machine. The scraping and soaking required for burned-on food particles are usually done at the pot and pan sink close to the production areas. A common procedure is to cart pots and pans that have been prerinsed to the dishroom for washing, after the bulk of the dishwashing has been completed.

In large-volume operations, specialized pot and pan washing machines, such as the one shown in Figure 16.11, are being used more frequently to assist in this unpleasant task. The potwashing machines that are being designed today for use in foodservice operations are heavy duty machines, capable of dealing with the

Symptom	Possible cause	Suggested cure
Soiled Dishes	Insufficient detergent.	Use enough detergent in wash water to ensure complete soil removal and suspension.
	Wash water temperature too low.	Keep water temperature within recommended ranges to dissolve food residues and to facilitate heat accumulation (for sanitation).
	Inadequate wash and rinse times.	Allow sufficient time for wash and rinse operations to be effective. (Time should be automatically controlled by timer or by conveyor speed.)
	Improperly cleaned equipment.	Unclog rinse and wash nozzles to maintain proper pressure-spray pattern and flow conditions. Overflow must be open. Keep wash water as clean as possible by prescraping dishes, etc. *Change water in tanks at proper intervals.*
	Racking.	Check to make sure racking or placement is done according to size and type. Silverware should always be presoaked, placed in silver holders without sorting. Avoid masking or shielding.
Films	Water hardness.	Use an external softening process. Use proper detergent to provide internal conditioning. Check temperature of wash and rinse water. Water maintained above recommended temperature ranges may precipitate film.
	Detergent carryover.	Maintain adequate pressure and volume of rinse water, or worn wash jets or improper angle of wash spray might cause wash solution to splash over into final rinse spray.
	Improperly cleaned or rinsed equipment.	Prevent scale buildup in equipment by adopting frequent and adequate cleaning practices. Maintain adequate pressure and volume of water.
Greasy Films	Low pH. Insufficient detergent. Low water temperature. Improperly cleaned equipment.	Maintain adequate alkalinity to saponify greases; check detergent, water temperature. Unclog all wash and rinse nozzles to provide proper spray action. Clogged rinse nozzles may also interfere with wash tank overflow. Change water in tanks at proper intervals.

Streaking	Alkalinity in the water. Highly dissolved solids in water.	Use an external treatment method to reduce alkalinity. Within reason (up to 300–400 ppm), selection of proper rinse additive will eliminate streaking. Above this range external treatment is required to reduce solids.
	Improperly cleaned or rinsed equipment.	Maintain adequate pressure and volume of rinse water. Alkaline cleaners used for washing must be thoroughly rinsed from dishes.
Spotting	Rinse water hardness.	Provide external or internal softening. Use additional rinse additive.
	Rinse water temperature too high or too low.	Check rinse water temperature. Dishes may be flash drying, or water may be drying on dishes rather than draining off.
	Inadequate time between rinsing and storage.	Allow sufficient time for air drying.
Foaming	Detergent. Dissolved or suspended solids in water.	Change to a low sudsing product. Use an appropriate treatment method to reduce the solid content of the water.
	Food soil.	Adequately remove gross soil before washing. The decomposition of carbohydrates, protein or fats may cause foaming during the wash cycle. Change water in tanks at proper intervals.
Coffee, tea, metal staining	Improper detergent.	Food dye or metal stains, particularly where plastic dishware is used, normally requires a chlorinated machine washing detergent for proper destaining.
	Improperly cleaned equipment.	Keep all wash sprays and rinse nozzles open. Keep equipment free from deposits of films or materials which could cause foam build-up in future wash cycles.

Figure 16.10. *Dishwashing problems and cures (reprinted by permission of the National Sanitation Foundation from "Recommended Field Evaluation Procedures for Spray-Type Dishwashing Machines")*

Figure 16.11. *Pot, pan, and utensil washer (permission of Alvey Washing Equipment, Division of AF Industries, Cincinnati, OH)*

problems of cooked- and baked-on foods. As Sadwith (1983) indicates, potwashing is quite different from dishwashing because it requires pressurized hot water sprayed directly on the soiled surface. Commissary foodservice operations are installing conveyor type washers to handle the large volume of pots and pans required in these very large operations. Sadwith indicates that, as a rule of thumb, an operation serving 1000 meals per day or more can justify the investment in a potwashing machine.

Handling and storage of clean dishes are other important aspects of a sanitation program in a foodservice operation. All dishes and utensils must be stored dry and in clean, dust-free areas. This storage should be above the floor and protected from dust, mop splashes, and other forms of contamination. Mobile equipment designed for storage of various types of dishes and glassware is ideal. Dishes and glasses can be placed directly into the storage dolly and moved readily to an area where service or tray set-up occurs. Some examples of mobile storage dollies are shown in Figure 16.12.

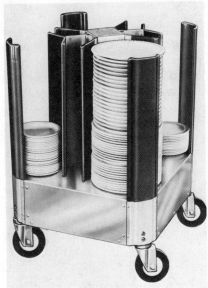

Dish dolly

Tray dolly

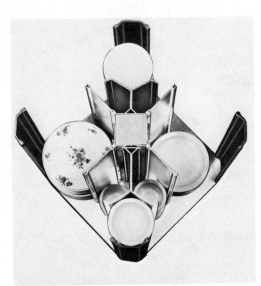

Top view of dish dolly

Cup and glass dolly

Figure 16.12. *Mobile storage dollies (used by permission of Cres-Cor Crown-X)*

MAINTENANCE OF EQUIPMENT AND FACILITIES

The physical plant of a foodservice operation includes all areas where food is received, stored, prepared, and served; areas where dishes, utensils, and equipment are washed and stored; dressing and locker rooms for employees; restrooms for employees and guests; and the area for garbage and trash disposal. Maintenance of all these facilities and equipment requires continual diligence on the part of the foodservice staff and management. Since cleaning and maintenance tasks are generally considered unpleasant but are so important to maintaining standards of sanitation, the management of a foodservice operation must exercise continual supervision to ensure that cleaning schedules are adhered to regularly. Specific procedures and schedules for cleaning all equipment and facilities must be established by management, as well as regularly scheduled training programs that focus on proper cleaning procedures.

Sanitary Facilities and Equipment

Design for sanitation must begin when the facility is being planned. As outlined in Chapter 8, floors, walls, and ceilings must be constructed for easy maintenance, and the arrangement and design of the equipment and fixtures should facilitate cleaning. Facilities for proper disposal of trash and garbage are necessary to avoid contaminating food and attracting pests.

Longree and Blaker (1982) enumerated the following issues involved in sanitation of the physical plant.

- Cleanability of walls, ceilings, and floors as a result of good construction, smooth materials, and good state of repair.
- Proper sewage disposal and plumbing and adequate drains for cleaning floors and equipment.
- Good ventilation.
- Adequate lighting.
- Conveniently located handwashing facilities.
- Sanitary dressing rooms and restrooms.
- Sanitary trash and garbage disposal.
- Control of rodents and insects.
- Storage area for cleaning materials and equipment separate from food storage.
- Regular and adequate cleaning of facilities.

Materials for floors, walls, and ceilings should be selected for ease of cleaning and maintenance, as well as for appearance. In "back of the house" areas, covering materials are generally very sturdy and are selected primarily on the basis of cleanability and durability. For the "front of the house" appearance will generally have greater priority and, as a result, dining areas may present some unique cleaning problems. Customers are very sensitive to dusty drapes, streaked or grimy windows, smudged or cracked walls, cobwebbed ceilings, loose floor tiles, or a heavily soiled carpet (NIFI, 1985). Dining room floors need continuous care and in many establishments need to be swept, vacuumed, or mopped when customers have departed after the meal. Once-a-day cleaning by the night porter is generally not adequate for heavy-use dining areas.

A variety of flooring materials are used in construction of foodservice facilities; each type presents a different cleaning challenge. The advantages, disadvantages, and suggested cleaning materials for common types of flooring are outlined in Figure 16.13. As indicated in the table, the care floors require depends on the material of which they are made. In addition to those listed, wood floors and carpeting are often used in dining rooms. Neither are acceptable in preparation areas, however, because of special problems with cleaning and sanitation. In general, the following procedures should be followed regularly in maintenance of floors.

- Spills should be wiped up promptly to avoid tracking and to eliminate a safety hazard.
- Regular schedules for cleaning floors should be established, which will depend on the extent of traffic, the area in the facility, and type of flooring. Floors subjected to heavy traffic and food spills, such as in the production areas, must be scrubbed daily and hosed and steamed down periodically for more thorough cleaning.
- Floor care equipment, including brooms, mops, etc., should be cleaned regularly.

Garbage and trash must be handled carefully in a foodservice operation because of its potential for contaminating food, equipment, and utensils and for attracting insects and other pests. The following general rules apply to trash and garbage handling.

- Garbage and trash containers must be leak-proof, easily cleanable, pest-proof, and durable and have tight-fitting lids. Today, plastic bags are frequently used for lining containers to keep cans clean and facilitate removal of discarded materials from the can.
- Garbage and trash should not be allowed to accumulate anywhere but in containers for that purpose.
- Garbage and trash should be removed from production areas on a frequent basis and should be regularly disposed of, away from the foodservice facility.
- Garbage storage areas should be easily cleanable and pest-proof. Sometimes these areas are refrigerated to assist in controlling the potential problems; if long holding times for garbage are required, this is especially useful.
- A can washing area equipped with hot water and a floor drain must be provided, located away from food production and storage areas.

Type of flooring	Hardness	Where used	Advantages	Disadvantages	Cleaner
Terrazo	Hard marble chips in cement	Kitchen; dining rooms	Durable	Damaged by alkalies; stained by grease unless well sealed	Use mild cleaners; scrub; rinse; mop dry
Ceramic tile	Hard		Resists grease stains if glazed; durable	Unglazed tile easily stained by grease; spaces between tile difficult to clean; slippery when wet	Alkaline cleaners are safe; scrub to clean between tiles; rinse; mop dry
Concrete	Hard		Durable	Gives off dust; becomes stained by grease unless well sealed	Alkaline cleaners are safe; scrub, rinse (sealing concrete will make it more cleanable)
Asphalt tile	Soft	Dining rooms	Durable; nonslippery even when wet	Poor resistance to grease	Mildly alkaline to neutral cleaners; mop; rinse; mop dry
Rubber tile	Soft		Durable	Damaged by grease	Mild cleaners; mop; rinse; mop dry; *Never use strong Cleaners*
Vinyl	Soft		Nonslippery even when wet; durable; resistant to grease		Mildly alkaline to neutral cleaner; mop; rinse; mop dry
Vinyl asbestos	Soft		Durable; resistant to grease		Alkaline cleaners safe; mop; rinse; mop dry
Cork tile	Soft			Easily damaged by sharp objects; grease will penetrate unless well sealed	Use special cleaners for cork floors (sealing cork tile makes floors more cleanable)

Figure 16.13. Suggestions for type of cleaner for various floors. Source: Longree, K. and Blaker, G. G.: Sanitary Techniques in Foodservice. 2nd ed. New York, John Wiley & Sons, 1982, p. 89.

Figure 16.14. *Hydraulic Trash Compactor (permission of Precision Metal Products Inc., Miami, FL)*

Mechanical devices are used in most foodservice facilities to assist in garbage and trash disposal. As a minimum, garbage disposal units should be available in prepreparation, pot and pan washing, and dishwashing areas. Trash compactors (Figure 16.14) have become popular to reduce the volume of trash and garbage. Can washing machines, such as the one shown in Figure 16.15, are available to facilitate the task of cleaning garbage cans.

Preventive Maintenance

Preventive maintenance has two aspects: (1) standard procedures and regular cleaning schedules, and (2) the preventive and corrective maintenance of foodservice equipment and facilities.

Some cleaning should be performed daily on a routine basis and included in the daily tasks of specific employees. Other cleaning tasks may be scheduled on a weekly, monthly, or less frequent basis, as appropriate to the operation, but must

Figure 16.15. *Can Washer (permission of Vacuum Can Company, Chicago, IL)*

be done regularly for proper maintenance of the facilities. In some instances, specific scheduling of additional employees or perhaps specialized cleaning crews may be required. Whatever the schedules, though, the proper tools, equipment, and cleaning materials are basic to an effective facility maintenance program and must be on hand as required.

All of the cleaning tasks should be combined in a master schedule, summarizing the cleaning operations in the foodservice facility. This schedule should include a list of what is to be cleaned, when each task should be done, how the task should be performed, and who has the assigned responsibility. Figure 16.16 illustrates a partial master cleaning schedule for a food production area.

Specific cleaning procedures should be developed to supplement the master schedule. Employees should be instructed on the cleaning procedures, use of cleaning equipment, and the proper use of cleaning materials. Equipment clean-

Item	When	What	Use	Who
Floors	As soon as possible	Wipe up spills	Cloth, mop and bucket, broom and dustpan	
	Once per shift, between rushes	Damp mop	Mop, bucket	
	Weekly, Thur. evening	Scrub	Brushes, bucket, detergent (brand)	
	January, June	Strip, reseal	See procedure	
Walls and ceilings	As soon as possible	Wipe up splashes	Clean cloth, detergent (brand)	
	February, August	Wash walls		Contracted specialists
Work tables	Between uses & at end of day	Clean & sanitize tops	See cleaning procedure for each table	
	Weekly, Sat. p.m.	Empty, clean & sanitize drawers, clean frame, shelf	See cleaning procedure for each table	
Hoods and filters	When necessary	Empty grease traps	Container for grease	
	Daily, closing	Clean inside & out	See cleaning procedure	
	Weekly, Wed. evening	Clean filters	Dishwashing machine	
Broiler	When necessary	Empty drip pan Wipe down	Container for grease Clean cloth	
	After each use	Clean grid tray, inside, outside, top	See cleaning procedure for each broiler	

Figure 16.16. *Sample cleaning schedule (partial), food preparation area.* **Source: Applied Foodservice Sanitation. 3rd ed. National Institute for the Foodservice Industry, 1985.**

ing procedures should be sufficiently detailed and presented in a step-by-step procedure to ensure that the correct process is followed and that any special precautions are heeded. Figure 16.17 presents the procedure for cleaning a food slicer, along with important safety precautions. Similar procedures need to be developed for all pieces of equipment. Manufacturer's instructions can be useful in developing these procedures.

Bacteriological counts on dishes, utensils, and equipment should be performed on a regular basis as a check on sanitization. In some localities, health inspectors may perform these tests. In most institutional foodservices, these tests are performed by personnel in the facility. In a healthcare facility, for example,

When	How	Use
After each use	**1** Turn off machine	
	2 Remove electric cord from socket	
	3 Set blade control to zero	
	4 Remove meat carriage	
	(a) Turn knob at bottom of carriage	
	5 Remove the back blade guard	
	(a) Loosen knob on the guard	
	6 Remove the top blade guard	
	(a) Loosen knob at center of blade	
	7 Take parts to pot-and-pan sink, scrub	Hot machine detergent solution, gong brush
	8 Rinse	Clean hot water, 170°F (76.6°C) for 1 minute. Use double S hook to remove parts from hot water
	9 Allow parts to air dry on clean surface	
	10 Wash blade and machine shell	Use damp bunched cloth[a] dipped in hot machine detergent solution
	Caution: PROCEED WITH CARE WHILE BLADE IS EXPOSED	
	11 Rinse	Clean hot water, clean bunched cloth
	12 Sanitize blade and machine shell, allow to air dry	Clean water, chemical sanitizer, clean bunched cloth
	13 Replace front blade guard immediately after cleaning shell	
	(a) Tighten knob	
	14 Replace back blade guard	
	(a) Tighten knob	
	15 Replace meat carriage	
	(a) Tighten knob	
	16 Leave blade control at zero	
	17 Replace electric cord into socket	

[a]Fold cloth to several thicknesses.

Figure 16.17. *Procedure for cleaning a food slicer.* **Source: Longree, K. and Blaker, G. G.: Sanitary Techniques in Foodservice. 2nd ed. New York, John Wiley & Sons, 1982, pp. 102–103.**

laboratory personnel usually have responsibility for bacteriological examinations in the dietetic services department on a regular basis, but without advance notice.

Maintaining facilities and equipment in a good state of repair is important for both sanitation and efficiency in the foodservice facility. To initiate a preventive and corrective maintenance plan, a listing of all foodservice equipment should be compiled. Data should include information on type of equipment, date of purchase and installation, and maintenance information. A record of repairs and service should also be maintained for each piece of equipment, and a file of equipment manuals and warranties set up and the service representative identified for the various pieces of equipment. In some foodservice operations, a computer data base has been compiled and a program developed that produces maintenance print-out reports to assist managers in scheduling needed equipment service and maintenance. Corrective maintenance should be scheduled promptly and not put off until a more serious problem occurs that might be much more expensive.

Pest Control

Controlling pests in a foodservice operation is of critical importance. The presence of rodents, such as rats and mice, and insects, such as flies and cockroaches, can be a serious problem. They are both sources of contamination of food, equipment, and utensils. Many pests carry disease-causing organisms and cause considerable spoilage and waste. Also, nothing will "turn off" patrons more than the sight of a mouse or cockroach running across the floor in the dining room. Pests can be controlled by following three basic rules (NIFI, 1985).

- Keep pests out of the facility by pest-proofing the building.
- Deprive pests of food and shelter by following good housekeeping practices.
- Work with licensed pest control operator to rid the operation of pests that do enter.

Although roaches, flies, rats, and mice are the most common pests in a foodservice facility, beetles, moths, and ants may be a problem as well. To control cockroaches, openings in ceilings, walls, and floors should be sealed and damp areas eliminated. All incoming shipments of foodstuffs should be inspected for presence of roaches, and any roach-infested goods refused. Production, storage, and garbage rooms should be inspected frequently for the presence of roaches, and facilities cleaned nightly to ensure that crumbs or other food particles are not left as food for pests.

Flies enter the facility primarily through outside doors or other external openings. Control can be facilitated by having tight-fitting and self-closing doors, closed windows, and good screening. Screened or closed storage for garbage is also important. Dispensers for insecticide sprays, fans, or lamps designed to kill insects are sometimes installed at outside entrances to control flies and other flying pests. Because insecticide sprays can be a source of food contamination, however, this form of pesticide must be used carefully in foodservice facilities.

All openings to the outside must be protected against the entrance of rats and mice. Again, constant surveillance for signs of rodents' presence and activities is needed. Regular services of a professional exterminator should be used in a food-service facility for effective control of roaches, flies, and rodents. In institutions, pest control is frequently the responsibility of the housekeeping or the maintenance department rather than the foodservice department.

Pesticides can be toxic and some may cause fire or explosions if not handled properly. They must be used with extreme care and labeled and stored properly, away from food storage areas. In the long run, good sanitation practices are the best form of pest control.

SAFETY IN FOODSERVICE OPERATIONS

In comparison with many industrial jobs, foodservice jobs are relatively safe occupations. According to the National Safety Council, however, the number of accidents in 1983 for food-related industries was slightly higher than the average for all industries but it is still not considered a high-accident industry (National Safety Council, 1984). A foodservice facility has many potential hazards. Minor injuries from cuts and burns are common, and more serious injuries occur all too frequently. The quantity of hot substances that are handled, the type of equipment used, and the often hectic pace of a foodservice operation make safety consciousness a high priority.

An accident is frequently defined as an event that is unexpected or the cause of which was unforeseen, resulting in injury, loss, or damage. An accident is also an unplanned event that interrupts an activity or function. Although they may or may not be the result of negligence, most accidents can be prevented.

Such accident prevention must be a priority for the management of foodservice operations because of the potential trauma and problems that may result when accidents occur. Many accidents involve personal injury and, as a result, cause personal problems or even death of employees or customers who have been injured. But a foodservice operation should have an accident prevention program that seeks to eliminate all accidents, not just those resulting in personal injury. Accidents can be very costly because of increased insurance premiums, loss of work, possible damage to facilities or equipment, and uninsured costs. In addition to the loss of income that will result if an operation has to close for a period of time, regaining volume may be difficult because patrons may shy away from a facility that has a reputation for unsafe conditions. Accidents can also result in fines or imprisonment, for example, if provisions of the Occupational Safety and Health Act (OSHA) are violated.

Many aspects of safety are related to the construction and maintenance of the structure and equipment. For example, floors and wiring should be in good repair, and adequate lighting should be provided in work areas, in corridors, and in areas around a facility. Exits should be clearly marked, nonslip flooring materials used, and all equipment supplied with necessary safety devices. Also, fire extinguishers of the appropriate type should be readily available in various areas of the foodservice facility. The basic traffic flow should be designed to avoid collisions.

Most accidents are the result of human error. Employees may lift heavy loads incorrectly, leave spills on the floor, fail to use safety devices on foodservice equipment, walk across freshly mopped floors, block passageways, or fail to clean greasy filters regularly. Many other unsafe practices can be added to this list. Obviously, then, training is an important part of a safety program. Employees should be taught to prevent accidents by learning to recognize and correct or avoid hazardous conditions.

Safe and healthful working conditions were mandated by the Williams-Steiger Occupational Safety and Health Act of 1970, enacted by the U.S. Congress in April, 1971. This legislation created the Occupational Safety and Health Administration as an agency to administer the act within the U.S. Department of Labor. The purpose of the act is "to assure, so far as possible, every working man and woman in the Nation, safe and healthful working conditions, and to preserve our human resources." Major provisions of the act gave OSHA authority to:

- Encourage employers and employees to reduce hazards in the workplace and to initiate or improve existing safety and health programs.
- Establish employer and employee responsibility for safety.
- Set mandatory job safety and health standards.
- Provide an effective enforcement program.
- Encourage states to assume responsibility for programs that are at least as effective as the federal program.
- Provide for reporting procedures of on-the-job injuries, illnesses, and fatalities.

The act covers every employee in a business affecting commerce that has one or more employees; however, certain workplaces covered under other federal laws are not affected by the OSHA legislation, which applies only to private firms, not to government agencies.

OSHA allows a compliance officer to enter a facility to determine adherence to standards and to examine if the workplace is free of recognized hazards. A foodservice operation may be inspected under one of the following circumstances.

- A catastrophe or fatal accident has occurred in the facility.
- A valid employee complaint has been received by OSHA.
- An apparent imminent danger exists.
- The operation has been randomly selected for inspection.

During an OSHA inspection, some of the specific conditions for which the compliance officer will be searching are as follows.

- Accessibility of fire extinguishers and their readiness for use.
- Guards on floor openings, balcony storage areas, and receiving docks.
- Adequate handrailings on stairs.
- Properly maintained ladders.
- Proper guards and electrical grounding for foodservice equipment.
- Lighted passageways, clear of obstructions.
- Readily available first-aid supplies and instructions.
- Proper use of extension cords.
- Compliance with OSHA posting and record keeping requirements.

Citations are issued by an OSHA Area Director upon a review of the Compliance Officer's inspection report if standards or rules have been violated. Several types of violations are possible, which may involve fines or legal action if the violation is sufficiently serious. For example, absence of operational guards on food choppers or grinders is considered a serious violation, or one in which substantial probability exists (1) that death or serious physical harm could result, and (2) that the employer knew, or should have known, of the hazard. Fines are generally levied for violations classified as serious.

Fire is a particular hazard in the foodservice industry because of the nature of the business. In 1982, the National Fire Protection Association (NFPA) reported nearly 27,000 fires within the foodservice industry alone (Primavera, 1983), which is an average of more than 70 fires per day. These data do not include fires extinguished without the aid of the fire department, most of which go unreported. The NFPA estimates the average loss in restaurant fires to be about $2500; however, this figure can rise dramatically when fire damages force temporary closure. For example, a recent fire in a large convention hotel, caused by greasy build-up in the hood over the production areas, resulted in closure of all foodservice operations in the hotel during a busy convention season. Not only did this incident cause a great deal of inconvenience to the hotel and its patrons and result in major revenue loss, it also created a serious potential for loss of many lives.

The NFPA has defined four classifications of fire, three of which may occur in a foodservice operation.

- *Class A fires.* Caused by ordinary combustible materials, such as wood, paper, or cloth.
- *Class B fires.* Caused by flammable liquid, gases, and greases.
- *Class C fires.* Caused by live electrical fires.

Different types of fire extinguishers are needed for the different classes of fire, and the foodservice manager should purchase and have available the proper kind of extinguishers in various areas of the operation. Figure 16.18 identifies the type of extinguishers to use for Classes A, B, and C fires, along with some operational tips. In addition to having proper fire extinguishers, heat and smoke detection devices and sprinkler systems should be installed as well. All three should be checked periodically to ensure proper operation. Also, regular fire drills should be

KIND OF FIRE

DECIDE THE CLASS OF FIRE YOU ARE FIGHTING...

...THEN CHECK THE COLUMNS TO THE RIGHT OF THAT CLASS

CLASS A FIRES
USE THESE EXTINGUISHERS

ORDINARY COMBUSTIBLES
• WOOD
• PAPER
• CLOTH
ETC.

CLASS B FIRES
USE THESE EXTINGUISHERS

FLAMMABLE LIQUIDS, GREASE
• GASOLINE
• PAINTS
• OILS, ETC.

CLASS C FIRES
USE THESE EXTINGUISHERS

ELECTRICAL EQUIPMENT
• MOTORS
• SWITCHES
ETC.

APPROVED TYPE OF EXTINGUISHER

MATCH UP PROPER EXTINGUISHER WITH CLASS OF FIRE SHOWN AT LEFT

	FOAM — Solution of Aluminum Sulphate and Bicarbonate of Soda	CARBON DIOXIDE — Carbon Dioxide Gas Under Pressure	SODA ACID — Bicarbonate of Soda Solution and Sulphuric Acid	PUMP TANK — Plain Water	GAS CART. RIDGE — Water Expelled by Carbon Dioxide Gas	MULTI-PURPOSE DRY CHEMICAL	ORDINARY DRY CHEMICAL
Class A	A B	X	A	A	A	A B C	X
Class B	A B	B C	X	X	X	A B C	B C
Class C	X	B C	X	X	X	A B C	B C

HOW TO OPERATE

FOAM - Don't Play Stream into the Burning Liquid. Allow Foam to Fall Lightly on Fire.

CARBON DIOXIDE - Direct Discharge as Close to Fire as Possible. First at Edge of Flames and Gradually Forward and Upward.

SODA-ACID, GAS CARTRIDGE - Direct Stream at Base of Flame.

PUMP TANK - Place Foot on Footrest and Direct Stream at Base of Flames.

DRY CHEMICAL - Direct at the Base of the Flames. In the Case of Class A Fires, Follow Up by Directing the Dry Chemicals at Remaining Material That is Burning.

IMPORTANT! USING THE WRONG TYPE EXTINGUISHER FOR THE CLASS OF FIRE MAYBE DANGEROUS!

Figure 16.18. *Proper use of fire extinguishers. Source: Applied Foodservice Sanitation. 3rd ed. National Institute for the Foodservice Industry, 1985.*

held so employees know evacuation procedures for guests and staff in the event of a fire.

In the discussion of the sanitation program in a foodservice operation, we discussed external and internal inspections. Both of these types of audits also apply to the safety program in a facility. In many states, a state fire marshal has responsibility for approving design and construction of buildings from a safety and fire protection standpoint. Also, we discussed OSHA inspections that are designed to assure safe and healthful working conditions. The voluntary external audits discussed in Chapter 2, such as those of the Joint Commission on Accreditation of Hospitals, will generally include an assessment of the safety conditions and practices in the facility. The foodservice manager should augment any external inspections with a periodic internal review, or self-inspection, of safety conditions and practices, followed by any necessary in-service training.

Figure 16.19. *Examples of mini-posters on safe practices in foodservice operations (permission of National Restaurant Association)*

Although many aspects of safety are concerned with construction and design of facilities, safe practices of employees are also a critical element in a safety program. Obviously, safety training must have major emphasis in both initial and in-service employee training. Many resource materials on safety and accident prevention are available, such as those of the National Safety Council and the American Red Cross. Also, personnel from state and local fire prevention agencies are often available as speakers. The National Restaurant Association has published an excellent safety operations manual (NRA, 1981) and miniposters to serve as employee reminders of safe practices (Figure 16.19).

SUMMARY

Maintenance of equipment and facilities is of critical importance in a foodservice operation. Cleanliness of facilities and safety must be high priorities of the foodservice manager. A properly designed facility is basic to maintaining high standards of sanitation and safety. Facilities must be both clean and sanitary; in other words, facilities and equipment must be clean of physical soil and free of disease-causing organisms and other contaminants.

Warewashing is extremely important in foodservice facilities because of its significance in maintaining sanitation and because of the magnitude of the warewashing operation. Manual or mechanical methods may be used, although manual washing is usually limited to pots and pans. Dishes and table utensils are generally washed by machine. Heat or chemical sanitizing must be used in manual warewashing.

Several types of dishwashing machines are available. The volume of the operation is the primary determinant in selecting a single- or multiple-tank dishwashing machine. A booster heater is needed to ensure that the temperature of the final rinse is sufficiently high to sanitize dishes and utensils. In an attempt to conserve energy costs, however, low temperature models that use chemical sanitizers are in use in some operations. In large volume foodservices, pot and pan washing machines are being installed to assist with this operation, whereas, traditionally, pots and pans have been washed manually.

Sanitation of facilities and equipment begins with proper design and construction. Floors, walls, and ceilings should be constructed for easy maintenance, and the arrangement and design of equipment and fixtures should facilitate cleanliness. Also, garbage and trash must be disposed of properly to prevent contamination of food, equipment, and utensils, and infestation by insects and other pests.

Preventive maintenance involves development of standard procedures and regular cleaning schedules, as well as preventive and corrective maintenance of foodservice equipment and facilities. A master schedule should be devised for cleaning operations in a foodservice facility and supplemented by specific cleaning procedures.

Controlling pests in the foodservice operation is critically important, and the regular services of a professional exterminator should be used. Good sanitation practices, however, are the basis of pest control.

High standards for safety and concern for accident prevention must be priorities of foodservice managers. An accident prevention program should have as an objective the elimination of all accidents, not just those resulting in personal injury.

Training is an important component of a safety program, since poor employee practices are frequent causes of accidents. Foodservice managers should be aware of the requirements of OSHA, the Occupational and Safety Health Act. This legislation, enacted in 1971, established an agency to assure safe and healthful working conditions for every working man and woman in the United States. Noncompliance with OSHA standards can result in fines or legal action.

In the foodservice industry, fires can be a particular hazard; in fact, an average of more than 70 fires a day are reported in foodservice operations. Proper extinguishers must be available, as well as smoke or heat detection devices and sprinkler systems. Foodservice operations may be subject to several types of external safety inspections. Self-inspections should also be conducted to ensure safe working conditions in the foodservice operation.

REFERENCES

American Hospital Association: *Safety Guide for Health Care Institutions.* 3rd ed. Chicago: American Hospital Association, 1983.

Fairbrook, P.: *College and University Food Service Manual.* Ch. 13. Zero in on safety. Stockton, CA: Colman Publishers, 1979.

Gisslen, W.: *Professional Cooking.* New York: John Wiley & Sons, 1983.

Kotschevar, L. H., and Terrell, M. E.: *Foodservice Planning: Layout and Equipment.* 2nd ed. New York: John Wiley & Sons, 1977.

Longree, K., and Blaker, G. G.: *Sanitary Techniques in Foodservice.* 2nd ed. New York: John Wiley & Sons, 1982.

Minor, L. J.: *Sanitation, Safety & Environmental Standards.* Westport, CT: AVI Publishing Co., 1983.

National Institute for the Foodservice Industry: *Applied Foodservice Sanitation.* 3rd ed. Chicago: National Institute for the Foodservice Industry, 1985.

National Restaurant Association: *Safety Operations Manual.* Chicago: National Restaurant Association, 1981.

National Safety Council: *Work, Injury, and Illness Rates.* Chicago: National Safety Council, 1984.

Primavera, W. J.: Fire safety planning: An ounce of prevention . . . *Cooking for Profit* 394:16 (Nov. 15), 1983.

Sadwith, G.: A potwashing potpourri. *The Consultant* 15:38 (Spring), 1983.

Stokes, J. W.: *How to Manage a Restaurant or Institutional Food Service.* Sanitation, safety, security, and fire protection. 4th ed. Dubuque, IA: Wm. C. Brown Co., 1982.

VI

Management of Foodservice Systems

17

Designing the Organization

The organization is the product of the organizing function of management, which provides the mechanism for coordinating and integrating all activity toward accomplishment of objectives. Organizing is based on the goals and objectives of the organization, formulated through the planning process.

Managers design their organization to facilitate goal accomplishment; in turn, this design establishes relationships among the various parts of the organization. Therefore, the roots of organizing lie in planning. The designs that emerge from the planning effort reflect the social, economic, and technological influences on the organization. In the organizing process, the activities are formed into subsystems that are synchronized into a larger system, often referred to as the formal organization.

Management functions have been defined as planning, organizing, staffing, leading, and controlling. In presenting the foodservice systems model in Chapter 2, these management functions were shown as an integral component of the transformation element that provide for coordination of the subsystems. In this chapter, the organizing function of management will be discussed in depth, as will the characteristics of organizations, drawing examples where applicable to foodservice.

THE ORGANIZING FUNCTION

In Chapter 4, organizing was defined as the establishment of a structure of roles by determining and enumerating the activities required to achieve organization goals. This function involves grouping activities, delegating authority, and providing for coordination among activities.

Organization is defined as a group of people working together in some type of coordinated effort to attain objectives. An appropriate organization results in the most efficient use of resources. The framework that defines the boundaries of the organization and within which the organization operates is the formal organization, depicted by the organization chart. The organization chart for the Department of Dietetics in Boston's New England Deaconess Hospital is an example (Figure 17.1).

Another element of the organization, one not shown in the organization chart, is the informal organization: the network resulting from various personal contacts, interactions, and associated groupings of people within the formal organization. Although the structure of the informal organization is not formally and consciously designed, it can be a powerful force within the formal organization that is the emphasis of this chapter.

THE ORGANIZATION STRUCTURE

General Considerations

The organization structure is designed based on the objectives that management has established and on the plans and programs developed to achieve these objectives. As indicated previously, different types of structures will be required for organizations with different objectives. Kast and Rosenzweig (1979) state that the formal structure is frequently defined in terms of:

- *Organization chart and job descriptions or position guides*. The pattern of formal relationships and duties.
- *Differentiation or departmentalization*. The way in which the various activities or tasks are assigned to different units or people of the organization.
- *Integration*. The way in which these separate activities or tasks are coordinated.
- *Delegation of authority*. The power, status, and hierarchical relationships within the organization.

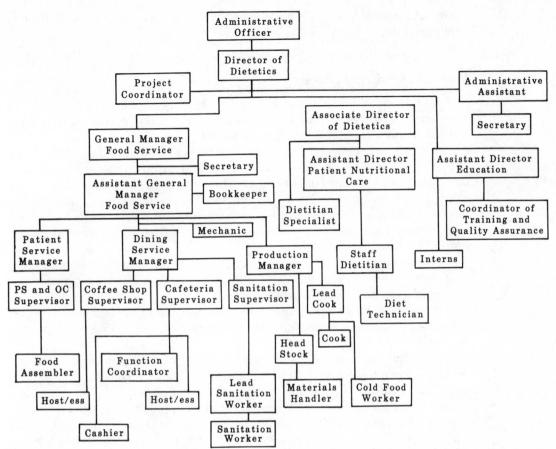

Figure 17.1. *Organization chart, Department of Dietetics, New England Deaconess Hospital, Boston, MA (used by permission)*

- *Administrative systems.* The planned and formalized policies, procedures, and controls that guide the activities and relationships of people in the organization.

One of the primary reasons for organizing is to establish lines of authority, which create order within the organization. Without delineation of authority, the chaos of everyone telling everyone else what to do may result.

Organizing also improves the efficiency and quality of work, as the coordinated efforts of people working together begin to produce a synergistic effect. As defined in the systems chapter (Chapter 2), synergistic effect means that the units or parts of an organization acting in concert can produce more impact than by operating separately. Synergism can result from division of labor and from increased coordination, both of which are products of organization.

Improved communications can also be a product of organization and its structurally defined channels of communication among members of the organization. Organizing is basically a process of division of labor, which can be divided either vertically or horizontally.

Vertical Division of Labor

Vertical division of labor is based on the establishment of lines of authority. In addition to establishing authority at various levels of the organization, vertical division of labor facilitates communication flow.

The scalar principle, which is related to vertical growth of the organization, states that authority flows through the organization from highest to lowest ranks and establishes the chain of command. This principle is based on the need for communication and the unity of command concept, which states that an employee should have only one immediate supervisor. In theory, this concept is a basis for organization design; however, employees frequently receive direction from more than one person.

For example, the dietetic technician at the New England Deaconess Hospital may receive direction from the staff dietitian, the dietitian specialist, and perhaps even nurses on the unit. This technician, however, is directly responsible to the staff dietitian as shown in the organization chart (Figure 17.1) and would consult with this individual in establishing job priorities when conflicting directions are received.

Authority, the right of a manager to direct others and to take action, is delegated down the hierarchy of the organization. The tapered concept of authority (Figure 17.2) holds that the breadth and scope of authority become more limited at the lower levels of an organization. To apply this concept to the New England Deaconess Hospital organization depicted in Figure 17.1, the manager with the broadest scope of authority, as shown in the organization chart, is the Administrative Officer; each succeeding level has a narrower and narrower scope.

Through the process of delegation, the authority and responsibility of organization members are established. Delegation is defined as the process of assigning job activities and authority to a specific individual within the organization.

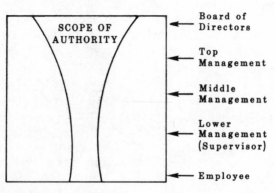

Figure 17.2. *Tapered Concept of Authority*

Responsibility is the obligation to perform an assigned activity. Since responsibility is an obligation a person accepts, it cannot be delegated or passed to a subordinate. Managers can delegate responsibilities to subordinates in the sense of making subordinates responsible to them; however, this delegation does not make managers any less responsible to their superiors. Delegation of responsibility does not mean abdication by the delegating manager. Joe, the head cook, for example, cannot say to the production supervisor "it's all his fault," regarding a product failure of one of the assistant cooks, and not bear responsibility himself.

Authority once delegated, however, is given up by the person who delegated it. According to a principle of organization called the parity principle, authority and responsibility must coincide; that is, management must delegate sufficient authority so subordinates can do their jobs. At the same time, subordinates can be expected to accept responsibility only for those areas within their authority.

One of the major considerations affecting delegation of authority is decentralization. The key question is: How much of what authority should be granted to whom and for what purpose? The degree to which an organization is centralized or decentralized is basic to this question. These concepts are at opposite ends of a continuum.

In a centralized organization, most decisions are made at the top, and lower level managers have limited discretion in decision making. The degree of centralization/decentralization is related to the number of decisions made at lower levels of the organization, the importance of those decisions, and the amount of checking required for decision making by lower level managers.

Highly centralized authority is common in small organizations in which the top manager is in close contact with all aspects of the operation. For example, in a small nursing home or restaurant, the foodservice supervisor or manager may be responsible for most decisions about the operations.

The degree of decentralization varies widely in large organizations. In some organizations, a high degree of decentralization may exist in major functions, but the auxiliary functions of purchasing, accounting, or personnel may be centralized. In a large hospital, for example, the director of dietetics may have authority over production and service functions but limited authority for purchasing, since a purchasing department has procurement responsibility for the entire hospital.

Horizontal Division of Labor

Horizontal division of labor is based on specialization of work. Its underlying premise is that, by making workers' tasks specialized, more can be produced with the same effort and with greater efficiency and improved quality. Rue and Byars (1983) define the following advantages of horizontal division of labor.

- Each worker is required to have fewer skills.
- Skills can be specified more easily for purposes of selection and training.
- Repetition or practice of the same job develops proficiency.
- Concurrent operations are possible.

- More conformity results if the product is always produced by the same person.

Job boredom is a potential hazard with horizontal division of labor; therefore, the scope and depth of jobs must be considered. Job scope refers to the number of activities or operations that make up a job. If narrow, it may result in repetitive jobs that may be boring to many workers. Job depth refers to the freedom of workers to plan and organize their jobs. A job is made up of three components: planning, doing, and controlling. Jobs that focus primarily on the "doing" component may lead to worker dissatisfaction.

Underlying Concepts of Organization

Span of management and authority are the two primary concepts underlying organization. Introduced in Chapter 4, these concepts will be discussed further here.

Establishing departments and creating different levels within management are not ends in themselves. As pointed out by Haimann et al. (1982), departments each require a manager and a staff, thereby increasing overall administrative costs. Furthermore, the creation of departments and levels increases coordination and control problems. Why, then, should organizations be departmentalized, and how can they function? The answers can be found in the two underlying concepts of organization: span of management and authority.

Because managers cannot supervise an unlimited number of subordinates, different areas of organizational activity must be defined, with someone placed in charge of each area. The span of management refers to the number of subordinates who can be supervised effectively by one manager. This concept, also called the "span of control," is the basis for the departmentalization process.

The second concept underlying organization, authority, provides the basis through which managers command work. Where it comes from and how it is used are fundamental to the effectiveness of the organization in accomplishing its goals.

Span of Management

The problem of managers being able to manage only a limited number of workers is not unique to any type of organization or to any industry. What is the appropriate span? As indicated in Chapter 4, a number of factors must be considered when answering this question. One response could be, "it depends on the situation." This situational approach, also called the contingency approach, is applicable in answering many questions about organizations. Organizational policies, availability of staff experts, competency of workers, existence of objective work standards, technology, and nature of the work are among the factors affecting the span of management in specific situations.

The narrower the span of management, the more levels needed in the organization. Because each level must be supervised by managers, the more levels that

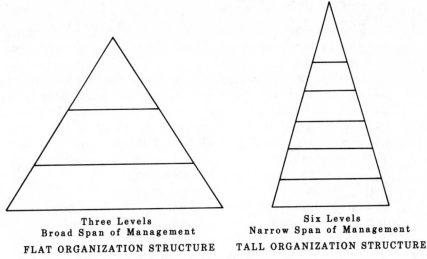

Three Levels
Broad Span of Management

FLAT ORGANIZATION STRUCTURE

Six Levels
Narrow Span of Management

TALL ORGANIZATION STRUCTURE

Figure 17.3. *Flat and Tall Organization Structures*

are created, the more managers are needed. Conversely, with a wider span, fewer levels and fewer managers are required. Thus, the resulting organizational shape is a tall, narrow pyramid or a shallow, flat, broad pyramid, as illustrated in Figure 17.3.

Early management theorists attempted to define the appropriate number of superior-subordinate relationships in terms of a mathematical formula. In 1933, Graicunas published a classic paper presenting a formula for analyzing the potential number of these relationships. Based on the work of Graicunas and others, Urwick (1938) first stated the concept of span of management as follows: "No superior can supervise directly the work of more than five, or at most six subordinates whose work interlocks."

During the years since those early publications, researchers have found that a variety of factors influence the appropriate span of management and that this span is not strictly a function of the number of relationships. In addition to those listed previously, the complexity, variety, and proximity of jobs and the abilities of the manager are other factors related to span of management.

The more complex the jobs being managed, the lower, or narrower, the appropriate span of management, and the more variety that is present, the lower the span should be. The physical dispersion of the workers is an influence; if subordinates are working in close proximity, the span of management will be greater, or wider, than if workers are divided over a large area. The leadership style and personality of the manager are other influences on span of management.

In a foodservice organization in which many of the workers have low educational levels and limited training, a narrower span of management may be appropriate. If workers are well trained and staff assistants are available, a wider span is possible and fewer supervisors are needed.

Formal vs. Acceptance Authority

Up to this point in the book, authority has been defined as the right of the manager to direct others and to take action. Actually, this definition deals only with one view of authority, that is, formal authority. This view of authority has its roots in the writings of Weber, a German sociologist, whose writing in the 1800s and early 1900s influenced the development of management thought. He viewed authority as "legitimate power," which involves the willing and unconditional compliance of subordinates based on their belief that it is legitimate for the manager to give commands and illegitimate for them to refuse to obey.

Today, two views of authority are generally recognized in the management literature, formal authority and acceptance authority. Formal authority is considered a "top-down" theory because it traces the flow of authority from the top to the bottom of the organization (Figure 17.4). As Haimann et al. (1982) point out, society is the ultimate source of formal authority in the United States because of the constitutional guarantee of private property. Obviously, this statement is directly applicable to public sector institutions, such as public schools, state universities, and hospitals operated by city, county, state, or federal government, but applies to organizations in the private sector as well.

Formal authority is also referred to as "positional authority," meaning that authority is derived from the position or office. For example, cooks and other production workers recognize the production manager as having certain authority because of the position he or she holds in the organization.

Acceptance authority is based on the concept that managers have no effective authority unless and until subordinates confer it. Although they may have formal authority, this authority is effective only if subordinates accept it. The accept-

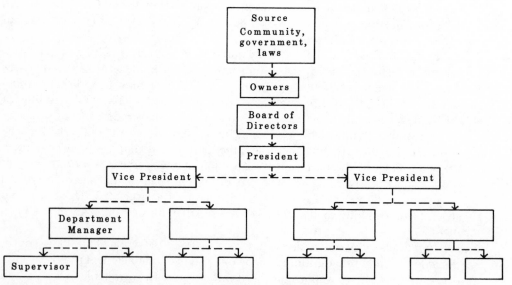

Figure 17.4. *Flow of Formal Authority in Organizations*

comply process is related to a subordinate's "zone of acceptance." In other words, an order of a manager will be accepted without conscious question if it falls within the range of job duties anticipated when the subordinate accepted employment. The employee, however, may refuse to perform a task he or she considers to be outside this range. For example, a cook would willingly prepare any item on the menu, even items that are added at the last minute; however, this same cook may be unwilling to help out in the dishroom, feeling that dishwashing is not part of the job.

Acceptance authority is also related to a manager's expertise and personal attributes. Authority of competence or expertise is based on technical knowledge and experience. A command may be accepted, not because of organizational title, but because the employee believes the person giving the command is knowledgeable.

This concept underscores the importance of foodservice managers possessing technical skills. If the foodservice manager understands technical operations, such as production methods and equipment operation, for example, the foodservice workers view the manager as knowledgeable and are generally more willing to accept direction.

Subordinates may also accept the authority of the manager because they want to please or help the person giving the command. The charismatic leadership of many well-known historical figures is the epitome of this personal authority.

Departmentalization

One of the first things that happens when people create an organization is that they divide up their work to allow specialization. As the organization grows and tasks become more numerous and varied, this division of labor is formalized into jobs and departments.

Departmentalization, which involves grouping activities into related work units, is the most frequently used method for implementing division of labor. Although these work units can be structured in a number of ways, they all divide the work and thus establish a pattern of task and authority relationships. This pattern becomes the organizational structure.

In a small delicatessen, for example, a husband and wife may informally share the tasks of preparing sandwiches, salads, and drinks, serving customers, collecting money, wiping tables, washing dishes and utensils, and performing other maintenance duties. They will probably find that each of them will take on principal responsibility for certain tasks; however, as the business grows, they may need to hire part-time workers to assist at peak periods. These workers will probably be assigned specific duties rather than being responsible for the wide range of duties performed by the husband-wife team. Thus, jobs are created around specialized tasks.

This small business could eventually be the basis for development of a large multiunit national chain of delicatessens throughout the United States. Additional levels of management would be needed, highly specialized jobs created, and formalized relationships required. At the corporate level, departments focusing on specific functions, such as marketing, procurement, and finance, would be created. This illustration is an example of the development of an organization into jobs, levels of management, divisions, and departments.

Departments are commonly organized by function, product, territory, type of customer, process, equipment, or time. As indicated earlier, the type and size of the organization are key factors influencing the form an organization structure will take.

Functional Departmentalization

Functional departmentalization occurs when organization units are defined by the nature of the work. All organizations create some product or service, market these products or services, and finance their adventures. Therefore, most organizations have three basic functions: production, sales, and finance. In the non-profit foodservice operation, the sales function may be one of clientele service and creation of goodwill, and the finance function may be considered business affairs. Even in these organizations, however, the need to apply marketing concepts is becoming widely recognized.

Each of these basic organizational functions may be further subdivided as necessary. For example, the production department may be divided into the main dish and vegetable, salad, and bakery units.

The primary advantage of this type of departmentalization is that it allows specialization within function and provides for efficient use of equipment and other resources. It provides a logical way of arranging activities, because functions are grouped that naturally seem to belong together. Each department and its manager are concerned with one type of work.

Product Departmentalization

Under departmentalization by a product or a service, all the activities necessary to produce and market a product or service are usually under the direction of a single manager. Product departmentalization allows workers to identify with the particular product. The emphasis on products encourages expansion, improvement, and diversification. Duplication of functions may be a problem, however, since each division or department may be involved in marketing, production, and so forth. This pattern of departmentalization is not common in the foodservice industry, except perhaps in large conglomerate corporations.

Geographic Departmentalization

Departmentalization by territory is most likely to occur in organizations that maintain physically dispersed and autonomous operations or offices. Geographic departmentalization permits the use of local personnel and may help create customer goodwill and a responsiveness to local customs.

National restaurant chains are often divided into regional areas, with a regional manager and staff responsible for all the operations in a particular area.

For example, several of the large contract foodservice companies are divided into several geographic regions, such as East, Midwest, Northeast, Northwest, and South.

Another example of geographic departmentalization could be drawn from school foodservices. In large metropolitan areas, the school district may be subdivided into several geographic regions, each with a supervisor responsible for overseeing the foodservice operations of the schools in a region.

Customer Departmentalization

Another type of departmentalization is based on division by type of customers served. A contract foodservice company, for example, that has divisions for schools, colleges, and healthcare is departmentalized by type of customer. Or a wholesaler who distributes products to grocery stores and to hotels, restaurants, and institutions may be subdivided into two corresponding divisions. This approach to departmentalization permits the wholesaler to serve the specialized needs of both the grocer and the foodservice operator.

Other Types of Departmentalization

Equipment, processes, and time are other bases for departmentalization. Process and equipment are closely related to functional departmentalization. In large foodservice operations, a deep fat frying section within the production unit would be an example of process/equipment departmentalization. A food factory, such as that in a commissary foodservice system, might be divided into units based on process or equipment because of the specialization needed for the large volume produced in the operation.

Time or shift is also a common way of departmentalizing in some organizations. Organizations such as hospitals that function around the clock often organize activities on this basis. Usually, activities grouped this way are first departmentalized on some other basis, perhaps by product or function. Then within that category, they are organized into shifts. For example, a hospital is departmentalized by functions, such as dietetic services and nursing services; the various departments may then have shifts with a supervisor in charge of each, such as the late shift or early shift.

Departmentalization is practiced as a means not only of implementing division of labor but also of improving control and communications. Typically, as the organization grows, it adds levels and departments. Coordination is another key objective in departmentalization. The type of departmentalization that is best depends on the specific needs of the organization.

Most complex organizations may be departmentalized according to several of the methods discussed in the foregoing paragraphs. For example, in a large, multiunit chain organization, the company may be departmentalized by function at the top level and by territory or type of customer at the next level. At the individual unit level, process, equipment, and/or time may be the method used. Referring again to the contract foodservice company for an example, it may be divided into several regions which may, in turn, be further divided by type of customer (school, healthcare, etc.).

Line and Staff

Up to this point in the chapter, we have discussed vertical division of labor through delegation and horizontal division of labor through departmentalization. A third way labor is divided is into line and staff. When the importance, scope, or sheer volume of managerial tasks becomes so great that an individual manager has difficulty handling them, a logical step is to divide the work into specialized components.

In Chapter 4, we indicated that line personnel are responsible for production of goods and services in the organization, whereas staff personnel may function in assisting or advising roles. Staff work revolves around the performance of staff activities, the utilization of technical knowledge, and the creation and distribution of technical information to line managers. In contemporary organizations, the number of people involved in staff activities and the types of staff work have increased.

Line and Staff Authority

Line authority is derived from the chain of command and is positional authority. Staff authority, however, is based on expertise in specialized activities. Generally, staff personnel provide expert advice and counsel to line managers but lack the right to command them, with two exceptions. First, staff managers exercise line authority over workers in their own departments; second, staff may have functional authority over the line in restricted areas of activity. This functional authority is delegated to an activity and gives members performing the activity the right to command. Authority granted in this manner, however, is confined to the specialized area to which it was delegated.

The quality control manager, for example, may have functional authority over the work of supervisors in other departments. If inspectors find a product quality problem, they may require the supervisor to suspend production until the problem is corrected.

This example applies directly to a commissary foodservice system. The microbiologist on the quality control staff may identify a problem with microbial count in a product being produced in a food factory and require that production be curtailed until the source of contamination is identified.

Types of Staff

Staff work may be differentiated into five functions: service, advice, control, initiation, and innovation. In addition, service staff render some specialized functions, such as maintenance.

A staff group, such as market research, may supply information and suggestions. For example, the market research staff in a large foodservice chain may provide data on prospective locations for new units.

Staff may assist the line in implementing a control function, such as the quality control example discussed earlier. Some staff assist in setting actions in motion and in initiating activities, as a planning staff does.

Finally, some staff may create new ideas, such as a research and development group. Large foodservice departments often have a recipe development staff, for example.

Other staff positions may fall into an "assistant to" or liaison category. The assistant to has no line authority but assists a manager by gathering information, performing special duties, representing the manager, and generally relieving the manager of details. The administrative assistant shown on the organization chart for New England Deaconess Hospital in Figure 17.1 is an example of this type of staff position.

Liaison staff act as representatives for their organization in dealing with other organizations. A regional dietitian in the hospital division of a food contract company might function both in a liaison and functional staff capacity, acting as a liaison between the hospital and company while also providing staff expertise to personnel in the contract company's dietetics department.

Line and Staff Problems

Line-staff relationships involve both structural and human aspects, which are related to levels of staff participation in the organization and to human interaction problems. Staff groups may provide organization-wide service or service within a division or department. Personnel or purchasing departments in a university or hospital are examples of the first; the quality control staff in the food factory mentioned earlier is an example of the latter.

Although relationships between line and staff may be specified clearly, conflict is not uncommon. Frequently, of course, line and staff work together as a team, approaching problem solving with a spirit of cooperativeness. The overlapping nature of line and staff jobs, however, provides a potential source of conflict.

Line managers may see staff as usurping their authority or providing unrealistic advice. They may also view staff specialists as working in a vacuum, concentrating on a narrow range of activities, rather than understanding problems from the perspective of the overall organization. Line managers often feel they get the blame for failures, while staff receive the credit for successes.

On the other side of the coin, staff may see line managers as resistant to new ideas and unwilling to try progressive approaches. Another common complaint is that line managers do not make use of available data. Some line managers seem to think that asking staff for advice is admitting ignorance. Staff may also complain that line managers merely go through the motions of asking for advice with no intentions of utilizing their recommendations. Staff personnel often believe they should have a greater degree of functional authority than has been delegated to them.

As mentioned in Chapter 4, the line and staff concept is often not clear-cut in

organizations. For example, managers may have both line and staff responsibilities. The nature of line and staff relationships varies widely among organizations and must be designed to meet the specific needs of a particular organization.

Organization Charts

The organization chart graphically portrays the organization structure. It depicts
the basic relationships of positions and functions while specifying the formal
authority and communication network of the organization. The title of a position
on the chart broadly identifies its activities; distance from the top indicates the
position's relative status. The lines between positions are used to indicate the
prescribed formal interaction.

The organization chart is a simplified or abstract model of the structure. It is
not an exact representation of reality and therefore has limitations. As Kast and
Rosenzweig (1979) point out, the organization chart shows few of the relationships even in the formal organization and none of those in the informal organization. For example, the degree of authority a superior has over a subordinate is not
indicated. The chart does, however, assist members of the organization in understanding and visualizing the structure. Charts should be revised periodically,
because organizations are dynamic and undergo many changes over a period of
time.

Responsibility and authority for the preparation, review, and final approval of
the organization chart generally lie with top management, although approval
may be the responsibility of the board of directors. At the departmental level, the
chart may be the responsibility of the department head, although approval may
be required from the next level up in the organization.

Vertical organization charts are the most conventional type, although occasionally a horizontal or circular chart may be used. In the vertical chart, the levels
of the organization are depicted in a pyramid form, with lines showing the chain
of command. Special relationships may be indicated by the positioning of functions and lines on the chart. Dotted lines are often used to indicate communication links in an organization. Staff functions may be depicted by horizontal
placement from a line position.

Referring again to the New England Deaconess organization chart (Figure
17.1), the Director of Dietetics, the Associate Director of Dietetics, and the General Manager-Foodservice comprise the top two levels of the department. The
elevated position on the chart for the Associate Director indicates this is a higher
level position in the department than the General Manager-Foodservice. The staff
positions of Project Coordinator and Administrative Assistant are shown separate
from the line organization by the horizontal placement on the chart.

Coordination

Not shown on the organization chart are the horizontal and diagonal relationships. The necessary coordination in complex organizations is impossible to
achieve through the vertical hierarchy.

In a large medical center, for example, horizontal interaction is required among departments. Nursing service and dietetic service staff often communicate directly rather than through the vertical organization. A staff dietitian may talk directly to the head nurse about a patient problem rather than channel the communication through the head clinical dietitian. Such lateral relationships facilitate communication in an organization.

In small organizations, coordination occurs informally. The larger the organization, the greater the need for formalized coordination mechanisms.

To illustrate these concepts, in a small residence hall foodservice, in which the manager can see the operation from the office and workers are in close proximity to each other, coordination of production and service can occur through informal communication. By contrast, a large facility on the same campus, with prepreparation on one floor and production and service on another, is a more complex operation to coordinate.

Managers establish policies, procedures, and rules to ensure consistency in operations. For example, the large commercial fast food operations usually have specific standards regarding production and service of products. One doughnut chain, for instance, requires that all products not sold within four hours after frying must be discarded. Specific formulations and frying procedures must also be followed.

The establishment of standards and procedures is an important method of coordination. Managers may also establish schedules and other plans to coordinate action. Events are often unpredictable, however, and must be coordinated by managers using their judgment. Overreliance on rules and regulations can create problems in organizations. You may recall that in Chapter 3 we identified the manager who always "goes by the book" as an ineffective manager.

Another way in which managers act to coordinate activities in an organization is in a "linking role." In other words, managers are responsible for communicating or "linking" with managers at higher levels in the organization and with other managers at their own level. This concept was derived from Likert's work (1961) in which he describes managers as linking pins (Figure 17.5).

Appointment of committees and task forces is a mechanism used in organizations for coordination. These groups serve an important role when problem solving must involve several departments. Problems involving half a dozen departments, for example, can be dealt with efficiently by such groups; otherwise, problems have to be referred upward through the chain of command.

Committees are usually organized formally, with a designated chairperson, specified membership, and regularly scheduled meetings. They are generally appointed to deal with ongoing concerns in the organization, whereas task forces are formed to deal with special problems. The organizational units or departments appoint the task force members, who may not necessarily be managers. Once a solution is reached, the task force is disbanded.

Committees and task forces are common in all types of institutions. For example, most college and university foodservices have a menu planning committee and a student advisory committee, as well as task forces to plan various special events. Healthcare institutions typically have many committees to facilitate interdepartmental coordination.

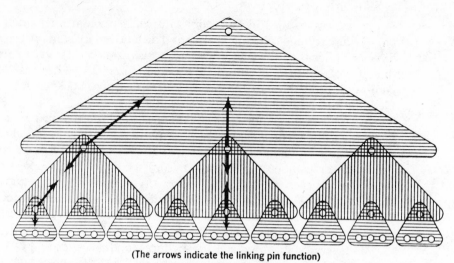

(The arrows indicate the linking pin function)

Figure 17.5. *The linking pin.* **Source:** *Likert, R.,* **New Patterns of Management.** *New York: McGraw-Hill Book Co., 1961, p. 113.*

DESIGN OF JOBS

Work design is defined as the function of specifying the work activities of an individual or group for developing assignments that meet the requirements of the organization and the technology, and that satisfy the personal and individual requirements of the job holder. Work design is a complex function because of the variety of factors determining the ultimate job structure. Several decisions must be made: Who is to perform the job? What tasks are to be performed? How are these tasks to be performed? Figure 17.6 outlines the primary factors in work design (Chase and Aquilano, 1981).

Translating the organizational structure into jobs is a process referred to as job design. A job is the set of tasks that must be performed by a given worker; tasks are the individual activities that comprise a job. Peeling vegetables and measuring or weighing ingredients, for example, are two tasks that are part of an ingredient room worker's job.

Job Analysis

Job analysis is the process of determining, through observation and study, the pertinent information relating to the nature of a specific job. In job analysis, the purpose and nature of job tasks and the skills needed to perform those tasks are identified. In addition, the mental and physical effort required, equipment used, time needed, and working conditions are evaluated. The manager asks the who, what, why, where, when, and how questions for each job. Job analysis provides the basis for staffing decisions, job descriptions, performance standards, and

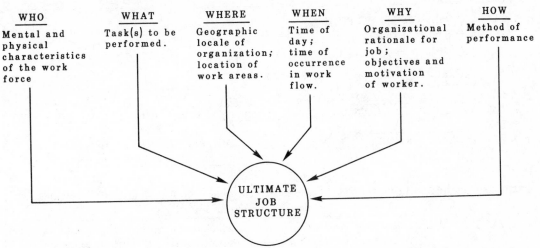

WHO	WHAT	WHERE	WHEN	WHY	HOW
Mental and physical characteristics of the work force	Task(s) to be performed.	Geographic locale of organization; location of work areas.	Time of day; time of occurrence in work flow.	Organizational rationale for job; objectives and motivation of worker.	Method of performance

ULTIMATE JOB STRUCTURE

Figure 17.6. *Factors in job design.* **Source: *Richard Chase and Nicholas Aquilano,* Production and Operations Management, *Third edition. Copyright © 1981. Richard D. Irwin, Inc. (Reprinted by permission)**

performance evaluations. Detailed job analyses involve use of some of the industrial engineering techniques described in Chapter 13.

Job Descriptions

The end products of a job analysis are a job description and a job specification. A job description is a written statement identifying the tasks, duties, activities, and expected performance results in a particular job. A job specification identifies the ability, skills, or traits necessary for successful performance of a job. In other words, a job description identifies the work to be performed in a job, while a job specification identifies the qualifications of an individual who could perform the job.

Written job descriptions should be available for all jobs in the organization. Each description should include the following information.

- Job title and classification.
- Summary of major responsibilities.
- Listing of duties and responsibilities of the job, usually in order of importance.
- Job relationships; i.e., supervision received and employees supervised.

Job descriptions should be updated periodically to reflect changes in job content. An example of a job description is shown in Figure 17.7.

The job specification, popularly referred to as the "job spec," includes a statement of the job conditions relating to the health, safety, and comfort of the employee, including equipment used and any potential job hazard in addition to the personal qualifications needed. Frequently, the written job descriptions in

NEW ENGLAND DEACONESS HOSPITAL
DEPARTMENT OF DIETETICS

JOB DESCRIPTION

JOB TITLE: _____Cook_____ DEPARTMENT: _____Dietary_____ DATE: _____AUGUST, 1984_____
JOB TITLE OF PERSON TO WHOM REPORTING: _____Production Mgr._____ JOB CODE #: _____116_____
JOB PAY: _____
REVISED: _____
NO. OF PERSONS SUPERVISED: _____N/A_____ EDUCATION REQUIREMENTS: High School or
Equivalent. Education in Food Service or Cooking
Desired.

PRIOR EXPERIENCE REQUIREMENTS: One year experience or equivalent in institutional cooking,
preferably in a health care setting.

OTHER COMMENTS: Exposed to heat, humidity, steam, cooking odors, refrigerator temperatures and
wet floors. Possible job related injuries include serious cuts from knives or
power equipment, burns from cooking equipment and strains, sprains, or falls.
Work is performed while standing or walking. Occasionally exerts considerable
physical effort in moving or lifting of supplies and/or hot food items.

JOB SUMMARY: Works as a team member with one or more cooks in the daily production requirements for patient and/or employee food services. Prepares meats, fish, fowl, vegetables, gravies, sauces, soups, salad ingredients and baked goods according to
standardized recipes. Assures freshness, proper serving temperatures, and the minimization of food waste.

Responsibilities	*Performance standards*
1 Prepares all meats, fish, fowl, vegetables, gravies, soups, sauces, salad ingredients, breads and desserts in accordance with the standardized recipes for patient and employee feeding. Assists in the preparation of hot and/or cold foods for special functions and catering activity as required.	**A** All foods will be prepared according to standardized recipes. Exceptions to the standardized recipe may be specified by the Production Manager, with appropriate recipe substitution, for special events. **B** All preparation shall be done in sufficient quantities to meet the par levels as specified on the production sheets.
2 Provides back-up services and short order support to the patient tray line and the cafeteria throughout the meal period.	**A** All foods to be served in the hot state will be prepared and held at an established serving temperature for not longer than a specified time period. Communicates closely with the designated supervisors or serving staff to establish and maintain appropriate product timing.
3 Maintains standards of quality as specified by the Department of Dietetics and all basic food handling guidelines as specified by local, state and federal health agencies. Assists in the development and testing of standardized recipes for therapeutic diets and employee feeding as required.	**A** All foods are to be stored at proper temperatures. Cold foods at or below 45°F, hot foods at 140°F or above. Holding and processing temperatures between these ranges should not exceed 4 hours. **B** All foods are to be covered, labeled and dated when stored. **C** All foods are to be rotated on a first in first out basis in accordance with the department's standards for holding and storing foods.

		D	All foods are to be presented in a wholesome and eye appealing manner. Appropriate garnishes are to be utilized where specified.
		E	All foods are to be served at the appropriate serving temperature as specified on the steam-table layout diagrams.
4	Maintains a cost awareness in the preparation and storage of all products with an emphasis on minimizing waste.	**A**	Records data utilized in the forecasting of production levels (and adjusts accordingly) in order to maintain a predetermined par.
		B	With the Production Manager or Lead Cook he/she determines the use of leftovers or their proper dating, labeling and storage.
5	Maintains standards of safety and sanitation as established by the Department of Dietetics and/or local, state and federal health agencies.	**A**	Maintains standards of cleanliness in personal appearance, personal hygiene, food handling and food storage.
		B	Maintains equipment and work area in a sanitary condition in accordance with established procedures and department standards.
		C	Reports unsafe working conditions or equipment to the lead cook or appropriate manager.

Figure 17.7. *Job description for Lead Cook, New England Deaconess Hospital, Boston, MA (used by permission)*

a particular organization may include both the job description and the job specification.

Traditionally, job descriptions and job specifications have relied heavily on personal judgment, which at times has been somewhat arbitrary. In many jobs, for example, a high school education is set forth as a requirement for performing them successfully, yet nothing employees do on those jobs may require this level of education.

Court decisions and equal opportunity legislation now require employers to demonstrate that the criteria upon which employees for each job are selected have proven validity. Employers must also be able to show that these criteria do not serve to discriminate against applicants on the basis of race, sex, age, religion, or national origin.

Job Titles

The titles assigned to jobs are primarily designed to distinguish among various jobs. The job title, however, may serve to indicate level in the organization. For example, the title "head cook" indicates that the job is higher in the organization than "cook" or "assistant cook."

The title may be used to indicate, to a limited extent, the degree of authority the job possesses. The title "sanitation supervisor" indicates the job involves more authority than "sanitation worker."

Until recently, the titles of some jobs indicated that the job was for a male or female employee. Recently, however, the trend has been to "desex" the job title by eliminating the suffixes "man" or "men" in occupational titles; e.g., flight attendant is now commonly used instead of steward and stewardess.

The Dictionary of Occupational Titles (1977), commonly referred to as the DOT and compiled by the U.S. Department of Labor, includes job titles and brief descriptions for about 20,000 jobs. Examples of foodservice jobs are shown in Figure 17.8. These descriptions have helped to bring about a greater degree of uniformity in the job titles and descriptions used by employers in different sections of the nation.

Emerging Trends in Job Analysis

Current legal requirements have stimulated development of new approaches to job analysis. Tests used in selecting employees, performance evaluations, and other decision making tools must now be more accurate and quantifiable than was previously true. The newer approaches provide for a greater functional breakdown of the tasks performed and are more worker-oriented.

According to Chruden and Sherman (1980), accurate information about job requirements has several advantages.

- It enables an organization to recruit and select personnel whose qualifications match more closely the requirements of the job.
- It provides a more objective basis for determining training needs.
- It provides a more objective and equitable basis for employee compensation and performance evaluation.

The pressures being placed on many organizations for greater affirmative action make formalized job requirements a necessity.

Job Standards

Development of job standards is becoming an issue in many organizations as they seek objective bases for performance evaluation. These systems require delineation of major responsibilities and of specific tasks related to them, which in turn provide the basis for employee evaluations.

Systems based on job standards are becoming common in public institutions. In the late 1970s, for example, job standards were required for all classified personnel in the state of Kansas, including foodservice personnel at state universities, hospitals, and other institutions.

Pesci et al. (1982) developed a methodology for devising job standards for foodservice employees. Their work involved defining major responsibilities for two job classifications, developing performance standards for these jobs, and assigning weights to measure responsibilities as a basis for performance review. The method involved securing input from the professional staff and also from personnel currently employed in the two positions. In Figure 17.9, the responsibilities and related standards for the position of Cook II are shown, as an illustration of the type of job description that emerges from this approach. Table

311.477-038 WAITER/WAITRESS, TAKE OUT (hotel & rest.)

Serves customers of a take out counter of a restaurant or lunchroom with food to be consumed elsewhere. Receives order from customer. Wraps sandwiches, hot entrees, desserts, and other menu items, and fills containers with coffee, tea, and other beverages. May accept payment for orders. May prepare fountain drinks, such as sodas and milkshakes.

313.361-014 COOK (hotel & rest.) cook, restaurant.

Prepares, seasons, and cooks soups, meats, vegetables, desserts, and other foodstuffs for consumption in hotels and restaurants: Reads menu to estimate food requirements and orders food from supplier or procures it from storage. Adjusts thermostat controls to regulate temperature of ovens, broilers, grills, roasters, and steam kettles. Measures and mixes ingredients according to recipe, using variety of kitchen utensils and equipment, such as blenders, mixers, grinders, slicers, and tenderizers, to prepare soups, salads, gravies, desserts, sauces, and casseroles. Bakes, roasts, broils, and steams meats, fish, vegetables, and other foods. Adds seasoning to foods during mixing or cooking, according to personal judgment and experience. Observes and tests food being cooked by tasting, smelling, and piercing with fork to determine that it is cooked. Carves meats, portions food on serving plates, adds gravies, sauces, and garnishes servings to fill orders. May supervise other cooks and kitchen employees. May wash, peel, cut, and shred vegetables and fruits to prepare them for use. May butcher chickens, fish, and shellfish. May cut, trim, and bone meat prior to cooking. May bake bread, rolls, cakes, and pastry [BAKER (hotel & rest.)]. May price items on menu. Usually found in establishments having only a few employees. May be designated according to meal cooked or shift worked as COOK, DINNER (hotel & rest.); COOK, MORNING (hotel & rest.); or according to food item prepared as COOK, ROAST (hotel & rest.); or according to method of cooking as COOK, BROILER (hotel & rest.). May substitute for and relieve or assist other cooks during emergencies or rush periods and be designated COOK, RELIEF (hotel & rest.). May prepare and cook meals for institutionalized patients requiring special diets and be designated as FOOD-SERVICE WORKER (hotel & rest.). Additional titles: COOK, DESSERT (hotel & rest.); COOK, FRY (hotel & rest.); COOK, NIGHT (hotel & rest.); COOK, SAUCE (hotel & rest.); COOK, SOUP (hotel & rest.); COOK, SPECIAL DIET (hotel & rest.); COOK, VEGETABLE (hotel & rest.).

319.137-010 FOOD-SERVICE SUPERVISOR (hotel & rest.; medical ser.)

Supervises employees engaged in serving food in hospital, nursing home, school, or college food service department and similar institutions, and in maintaining cleanliness of food service areas and equipment. Gives training to workers in methods of performing duties and assigns and coordinates work of employees to promote efficiency of operations. Supervises serving of meals in dining room. Oversees cleaning of kitchen and dining areas and washing of kitchen utensils and equipment, according to sanitary methods. Keeps records, such as amount and cost of meals served and hours worked by employees. Requisitions supplies and equipment to maintain stock levels. May direct preparation of foods and beverages. May assist DIETITIAN, CLINICAL (profess. & kin.) in planning menus. May interview and select new employees. May supervise FOOD-SERVICE WORKER, HOSPITAL (medical ser.) and be designated as TRAY-LINE SUPERVISOR (medical ser.).

Figure 17.8. *Job Descriptions from the* **Dictionary of Occupational Titles. Source:** *U.S. Department of Labor, Employment and Training Administration:* **Dictionary of Occupational Titles,** *4th ed. Washington, DC, Govt. Prtg. Ofc., 1977, pp. 225, 227, and 230.*

Responsibility	*Standards*
1 Produce quality food by using appropriate methods and coordinating with service.	Follow preparation instructions as stated on production sheet and/or on standardized recipes (95% of the time).
	Taste and evaluate products; correct if not meeting established standard.
	Meet food preparation deadlines by using batch cooking techniques (100% of the time).
	Assist supervisor by suggesting proper utilization of leftovers (95% of the time).
	Make production assignments in absence of supervisor.
	Assist in checking raw food supplies one to two days before preparation.
	Assist the supervisor to direct work to flow smoothly between personnel and equipment (95% of the time).
2 Maintain equipment and work areas in a safe and sanitary manner by using established procedures.	Follow operating directions as instructed in equipment manuals for each piece of equipment. Report all malfunctions of equipment to supervisor.
	Clean area and equipment promptly and properly after use.
3 Store and handle food in a safe and sanitary manner using established procedures.	See that all perishable food is properly covered and stored while away from production area more than 5 minutes.
	Label and refrigerate, freeze or place in dry storage all leftover food in proper containers within 30 minutes after service.
	Hot food is held at 140°F. or above; cold food is held at 45°F. or below (100% of the time).
4 Assist in training employees using formal and informal instruction to use food production principles.	Attend all scheduled classes to learn instructional methods.
	Assist students in clinical experience willingly.
	Assist supervisor in updating job descriptions and evaluating other classified employees.
	Assist supervisor in training lower classified employees to:
	1 Operate all equipment within 8 weeks after employment.
	2 Use and apply methods and techniques of batch cookery 12–16 weeks after employment within minimum supervision.
	3 Know and use established procedures of food storage and handling within 6–8 weeks after employment.

5 Use good grooming practices by adhering to policies in order to maintain high standards of personal hygiene.	Follow uniform and grooming regulations 7.8 through 7.9 as outlined in Kansas State University Residence Hall Foodservice policy book. No offensive body odor (95% of the time). Confine hair in a net; do not have a beard or long sideburns. Keep mustache trimmed so it does not extend below the upper lip (100% of the time).
6 Exhibit good work habits.	Maintain a productive pace. Proceed with routine work assignments with speed and accuracy, and with a minimum of supervision (90% of the time). Follow established procedures for requesting sick leave, annual leave, emergency leave, discretionary leave, or any other change in scheduled work hours. Follow absent and/or tardy regulations in Chapter 13, paragraphs 8–16, as outlined in Business Procedures Manual of Kansas State University. Is a team worker; willingly help others as need arises (90% of the time). Do not bicker, complain chronically, make petty remarks, or use foul language (95% of the time). Clock in and out as scheduled, ready for work. Report illness or tardiness before scheduled work time (95% of the time). Report all on-the-job injuries or illnesses to supervisors (100% of the time). Have no major accidents/loss of work or 3 minor accidents during a rating period. Know organization chart and follow the chain of command.

Figure 17.9. *Major Responsibilities and Job Standards for Cook II.*[1] *Source: **Pesci, P. H., Spears, M. C., and Vaden, A. G.: A method for developing major responsibilities and performance standards for foodservice personnel. NACUFS J. IV:17, 1982.***

[1] Kansas State University Residence Halls.

17.1 shows the resulting weights for the various areas of responsibility, as based on the priority ratings provided by the cooks themselves.

Job Enrichment

Critics of traditional job analysis methods have contended that workers' reactions to jobs have been given limited attention. Earlier in this chapter, we briefly discussed concepts of job scope and job depth.

Concern over "blue collar blues" and its effect on productivity, morale, absenteeism, and turnover has led many organizations to look again at the design of

Table 17.1. *Weights for each major responsibility for Cook II*

	Foodservice Unit				Final
Area of responsibility	1	2	3	Overall	weights
	←		% priority[1]	→	%
1. Food Production	48	47	43	47	45[2]
2. Equipment Care	5	5	6	5	5
3. Storage and Handling of Food	3	3	4	3	5
4. Employee Training	15	16	17	16	15
5. Personal Hygiene	3	2	3	3	5
6. Work Habits	26	27	27	26	25

Source: Pesci, P. H., Spears, M. C., and Vaden, A. G.: A method for developing major responsibilities and performance standards for foodservice personnel. *NACUFS J.* IV:17, 1982.

[1] Based on priority ratings of tasks within each area of responsibility provided by cooks in each of the food centers.

[2] Weights proposed after review of reliability data and % priority from each food center. Overall % priority data were adjusted to reflect 5% increments for each major responsibility as suggested by Kansas State University, Personnel Services.

jobs. Several researchers have developed approaches for redesigning jobs with the intent of increasing employee motivation and satisfaction.

Some of the classical work has been done by Hackman and his colleagues. His work (Hackman, 1977) resulted in the definition of five job dimensions or task characteristics: skill variety, task identity, task significance, autonomy, and feedback. If these are present to a high degree, Hackman observed that experienced meaningfulness of the work, responsibility for work outcomes, and knowledge of work results contribute to work performance and job satisfaction. The model developed from that work is shown in Figure 17.10. Growth need strength of individual workers affects these relationships, as shown in the model. Hackman concluded that the greater the extent of all five task characteristics in a job, the more likely it is that the job holder will be highly motivated and experience job satisfaction.

Hackman et al. (1975) developed an instrument called the Job Diagnostic Survey or JDS for diagnosing jobs as a basis for enriching them. The JDS provides measures of the task characteristics of jobs, as shown in the model in Figure 17.10.

Data from the JDS are used to compute a motivating potential score (MPS), which is an overall measure of the degree to which a job is enriched. Hackman et al. propose that jobs with low MPS can be enriched by the following five implementing concepts.

- Forming natural work units.
- Combining tasks.
- Establishing client relationships.
- Loading jobs vertically.
- Opening feedback channels.

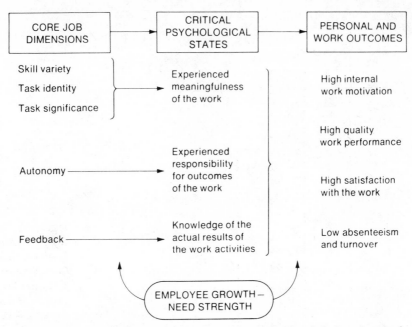

Figure 17.10. *Task characteristics and work motivation.* **Source: Hackman, J. R.: Work Design. *In Hackman and Suttle, eds.,* Improving Life at Work. *Santa Monica, CA: Goodyear, 1977, p. 129.***

Shaffer (1979) used the JDS to analyze jobs in hospital foodservice departments. He found that the jobs of cashier, cook, dietetic clerk, and storeroom worker were jobs with higher motivating potential than all other nonprofessional foodservice jobs (Figure 17.11). He also found that those workers in high MPS jobs had higher job performance and lower absenteeism.

Job enlargement and job rotation are both approaches that have been used to restructure jobs. Job enlargement means giving workers several different operations at the same skill level. For example, the dishroom worker might be assigned responsibility for vegetable peeling and chopping as well as for washing dishes.

Job rotation is a system in which workers move from one job to another on some type of scheduled basis. Going back to the example above, a foodservice worker might be assigned to the dishroom one week and vegetable preparation the next.

Job enrichment, however, is an attempt to increase the task dimensions of a job to give greater autonomy, feedback, and so forth. An example of job enrichment might be the involvement of a cook in production forecasting and scheduling or, in other words, planning of the work rather than only being responsible for food preparation.

Whatever possibilities are tried, managers in all types of foodservice operations should be concerned about the design of jobs from the standpoint of workers' reactions. The potential positive impact on job performance, morale, absenteeism, and turnover offers a substantive payoff to the foodservice organization.

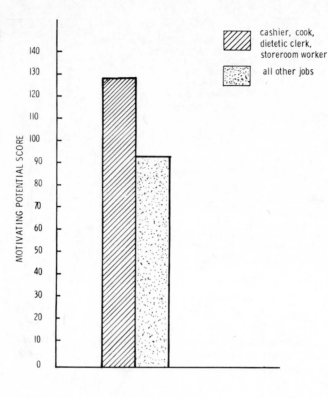

Figure 17.11. *Motivating potential of various hospital foodservice jobs.* **Source:** *Shaffer, J. G.:* **Job Design in Conventional and Highly Technical Hospital Foodservice System.** *Master's thesis, Kansas State University, 1979, p. 97.*

SUMMARY

Designing an appropriate organizational structure and then developing jobs to fit the structure are two extremely important aspects of the managerial task. Before a structure can be designed, the manager of the foodservice system must first develop the organizational goals and objectives.

Foodservice organizations are structured in many different ways, depending on such factors as the objectives, size, and technology. Function, product, territory, type of customer, process, equipment, or time may be the foundation for forming units or departments in the organization.

Line and staff relationships are established through the organizing process, with line personnel having responsibility for production of goods and services and staff having responsibility for providing assistance or advice. In many organizations, managers may have both line and staff responsibilities as part of their job.

Organization charts are the graphic portrayal of the structure and should be revised periodically because of the dynamic nature of organizations. Responsibility for developing these charts generally lies with top management.

Coordination among departments and levels in the organization is critical to its effectiveness. For example, proper coordination of production and service is necessary to serve quality food to the customer at the right time and place, regardless of whether the operation is a fast food establishment, industrial cafeteria, nursing home, or school lunchroom.

Policies, procedures, and standards are methods for achieving coordination. In addition, managers play an important role in linking their units with other units in the organization.

Designing jobs for the organizational structure is a complex process, concerned with identifying tasks to be performed, who will perform them, and how they will be performed. Job descriptions and job specifications are the results of this job analysis process.

Current legal requirements have stimulated development of new approaches to job analysis. Job standards that define performance expectations and provide a method for objective performance evaluation are being developed in some organizations.

Workers' reactions to jobs were given limited attention in traditional approaches to job analysis and design. Problems with low productivity and morale and high absenteeism and turnover rates have led many organizations to reexamine job design. Studies have shown that jobs with higher motivating potential can lead to higher job performance. Meaningful work, employee responsibility for work outcomes, and increased feedback are current issues in work design.

REFERENCES

Bobeng, B. J.: Job enrichment in job design. *J. Am. Dietet. A.* 70:251, 1977.

Burack, E. H., and Nicholas, J. M.: *Introduction to Management: A Career Perspective.* New York: John Wiley & Sons, 1983.

Campion, M. A., and Phelan, E. J.: Biomechanics and the design of industrial jobs. *Personnel J.* 60:949 (Dec.), 1981.

Chase, R. B., and Aquilano, N. J.: *Production and Operations Management: A Life-Cycle Approach.* Homewood, IL: Richard D. Irwin, 1981.

Chruden, H. J., and Sherman, A. W.: *Personnel Management: The Utilization of Human Resources.* 6th ed. Cincinnati: South-Western Publishing Co., 1980.

Drucker, P. F.: New templates for today's organizations. *Harvard Bus. Rev.* 52:45 (Jan./Feb.), 1974.

Ghorpade, J., and Atchison, T. J.: The concept of job analysis: A review and some suggestions. *Public Personnel Mgmt. J.* 9:134, 1980.

Graicunas, V. A.: Relationship in organization. Bulletin of the International Management Institute. Geneva: International Labour Office, 1933, reprinted in Papers on the Science of Administration (ed., L. Gulick and F. L. Urwick). New York: Institute of Public Administration, 1973.

Hackman, J. R.: Work design. In Hackman, J. R. and Suttles, J. L., eds.: *Improving Life at Work.* Glenview, IL: Scott, Foresman & Co., 1977.

Hackman, J. R., Oldham, G. R., Janson, R., and Purdy, K.: A new strategy for job enrichment. *Calif. Mgmt. Rev.* 17:57 (Summer), 1975.

Haimann, T., Scott, W. G., and Conner, P. E.: *Managing the Modern Organization.* 4th ed. Boston: Houghton Mifflin Co., 1982.

Hall, J., and Leidecker, J. K.: A review of vertical and lateral relations: A new perspective for managers. In Connor, P. E., ed.: *Dimensions in Management*. Boston: Houghton Mifflin Co., 1982.

Hoffman, R. R.: MJS: Management by job standards. *Personnel J.* 58:536, 1979.

Jons, J. A.: A skills audit. *Training and Dev. J.* 34:79, 1980.

Kast, F. E., and Rosenzweig, J. E.: *Organization and Management: A Systems and Contingency Approach*. 3rd ed. New York: McGraw-Hill Book Co., 1979.

Knight, K.: Matrix organization: A review. *J. Mgmt. Studies* 13:111 (May), 1976.

Likert, R.: *New Patterns of Management*. New York: McGraw-Hill Book Co., 1961.

Middlemist, R. D., and Hitt, M. A.: *Organizational Behavior: Applied Concepts*. Chicago: Science Research Assoc., 1981.

Mintzberg, H.: Organization design: Fashion or fit? *Harvard Bus. Rev.* 59:103 (Jan./Feb.), 1981.

Pesci, P. H., Spears, M. C., and Vaden, A. G.: A method for developing major responsibilities and performance standards for foodservice personnel. *NACUFS J.* 4:17, 1982.

Randolph, W. A.: Matching technology and the design of organization units. *Calif. Mgmt. Rev.* 23:39 (Summer), 1981.

Rue, L. W., and Byars, L. L.: *Management: Theory and Application*. Homewood, IL: Richard D. Irwin, 1983.

Shaffer, J. G.: Job design in conventional and highly technical hospital foodservice systems. M. S. thesis, Kansas State University, 1979.

Smith, H. R.: The uphill struggle for job enrichment. *Calif. Mgmt. Rev.* 23:33 (Summer), 1981.

Stoner, J. A. F.: *Management*. 2nd ed. Englewood Cliffs, NJ: Prentice-Hall, 1982.

U.S. Department of Labor, Employment and Training Administration: *Dictionary of Occupational Titles*. 4th ed. Washington, DC: Govt. Prtg. Ofc., 1977.

Urwick, L. F.: Scientific Principles and Organizations. Institute of Management Series, No. 19. New York: American Management Assoc., 1938.

Webber, R. A.: Staying organized. In Connor, P. E., ed.: *Dimensions in Management*. Boston: Houghton Mifflin Co., 1982.

Weber, M.: *The Theory of Social and Economic Organizations*. New York: Free Press, 1947.

18

Linking Processes

Linking processes are needed to coordinate the activities of the system toward the accomplishment of goals and objectives. These processes are decision making, communication, and balance (Figure 18.1). In Chapter 2, the critical role of these processes in the transformation element of the foodservice system was illustrated.

Decision making is the selection of a course of action from a variety of alternatives, whereas communication is the vehicle whereby decisions and other information are transmitted. Balance concerns management's ability to maintain organizational stability, which is related to effective decision making and communication.

Linking processes are integral to management's effectiveness in performing the functions of planning, organizing, staffing, leading, and controlling. In fact, decision making is sometimes described as the essence of management, since managers are making decisions in almost every aspect of their job. Decisions concerning the organizational objectives and structure, which applicant fits the job best, whether or not close supervision is needed, and whether or not deviations from plans require managerial action are examples illustrating decision making as part of each of the management functions. As stated above, all of these decisions must then be communicated to initiate action in the organization.

487

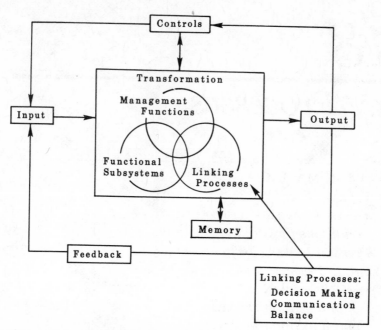

Figure 18.1. *Foodservice Systems Model with the Linking Processes Highlighted*

The decision network and the communication network overlay and connect the managerial functions. For example, decisions about standards of control are made during planning and must be communicated to those responsible for controlling activities. To illustrate this point, consider the standards for portion sizes developed in the production planning process and used as a basis for service. If periodic checks of the roast beef, for instance, indicate portions are too large, the service supervisor would communicate the need for corrective action to the cafeteria server.

The linking processes govern the flow of resources or system inputs. Through the networks of decision making and communicating, the movement of people, money, and machines through the system is accounted for and regulated. These networks also focus resources on the organization's purpose.

In Chapter 3, we described decisional roles of the manager as initiator, disturbance handler, resource allocator, and negotiator. Within each of these roles, the manager may be responsible for a range of decisions. The authority delegated to a manager will permit him or her to commit the organization to new courses of action or determine the organization's strategy. As Mintzberg (1975) indicates in describing managerial roles, communication and information come into play by providing input for decision making. In this chapter, we will discuss key elements of decision making and communication.

DECISION MAKING

Managers make decisions for the purpose of achieving individual and organizational objectives. Effective managers must be good decision makers. Decision making involves three primary stages—first, definition of the problem; second, identification and analysis of possible courses of action; and third, actual selection of a particular course of action.

Analyzing the decision processes by these stages illustrates the difference between management and nonmanagement decisions. Managerial decisions encompass all three stages; nonmanagerial decisions are concentrated in the last, or choice, stage. For example, a foodservice worker sorting fruits or vegetables in the prepreparation area is required to make decisions but is not a manager. The worker has only to make a choice as to the size or quality of the fruit or vegetable. Management, however, must place great emphasis on the problem identification and design stages of decision making.

Types of Decisions

Programmed vs. Nonprogrammed Decisions

Decisions are often classified as programmed or nonprogrammed. Programmed decisions are reached by following established policies and procedures. Normally, the decision maker is familiar with the situation surrounding a programmed decision. These decisions also are referred to as routine or repetitive decisions. Limited judgment is called for in making programmed decisions. These decisions are made primarily by lower level managers in an organization. Going back to a situation cited in Chapter 17, the doughnut chain, which had the policy of discarding products four hours after frying, provides an example in which a programmed decision would be made. The supervisor is faced with a relatively simple routine decision regarding whether to retain or discard products.

Nonprogrammed decisions are unique and have little or no precedent. These decisions are relatively unstructured and generally require a more creative approach on the part of the decision maker than programmed decisions. Often when dealing with nonprogrammed decisions, the decision maker must develop the procedure to be used. Naturally, these decisions tend to be more difficult to make than programmed decisions. Deciding on a location for a new unit for the doughnut chain or selecting a new frying process and equipment are examples of nonprogrammed decisions.

Because programmed decisions are concerned mostly with concrete problems that require immediate solutions and are frequently quantitative in nature, they tend to be reached in a short time. Nonprogrammed decisions, however, usually involve a longer time horizon because they tend to focus on qualitative problems and require a much greater degree of judgment. When making such judgmental decisions, managers must frequently rely on wisdom, experience, and philosophic insight rather than on established policies and procedures.

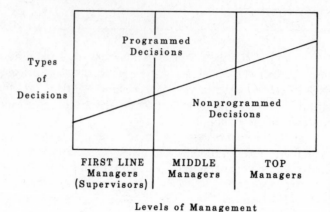

Figure 18.2. *Types of Decisions According to Levels of Management*

The type of decisions that are made is also related to level of management in the organization. If you recall the discussion in Chapter 3 in which we talked about lower level and upper level managers, the tasks of higher level managers were described as having a longer time frame and involving more judgment. Conversely, the time perspective of the lower level manager is shorter, with less judgment needed. Therefore, higher level managers tend to make mostly non-programmed and lower level managers mostly programmed decisions (Figure 18.2). The foodservice supervisor, for example, is concerned with day-to-day operational decisions, whereas the director of foodservice is responsible for decisions concerned with the overall organization's future.

Organizational vs. Personal Decisions

Organizational and personal decisions of managing should also be distinguished. Organizational decisions relate to the purposes, objectives, and activities of the organization, whereas personal decisions are concerned with the manager's individual goals. These personal decisions, however, may affect the organization, and vice versa.

A manager may decide to resign from a position in a university foodservice, for example, to take a job in a large commercial foodservice organization. After the move from the university, the commercial company may decide to transfer the manager from one regional office to another. The first decision is a personal decision affecting two organizations and the second, an organizational decision affecting the individual. Personal decisions are made primarily from the standpoint of the individual, organizational decisions primarily from the standpoint of the organization.

The Decision Making Process

Defining Objectives

Decisions are choices; however, decision making is more than making a choice. Above, we described three stages in decision making. The complete decision

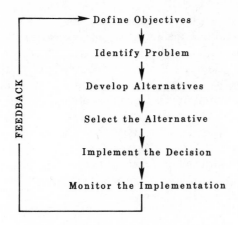

Figure 18.3. *Steps in the Decision Making Process*

making process can be expanded into several steps, as shown in Figure 18.3, starting with definition of objectives. Managers cannot make effective decisions unless they know what objectives they hope to achieve. In most situations, the manager will know what the objectives are prior to being called upon to make a decision. Effective managers set objectives and constantly monitor performance to ensure that they are reached.

Identifying the Problem

The next step in the decision making process involves an identification of the problem, which requires the manager to diagnose the situation. Gathering sufficient information in this process will help avoid the pitfall of focusing on symptoms rather than on the "real" problem. For example, too few portions of roast beef is only symptomatic of several possible problems—the product received might not meet specifications, overcooking may cause excess shrinkage, or portion controls are not adequate.

Developing Alternatives

In the third step, a list of possible alternatives is developed. The manager should not constrain or evaluate the alternatives at this point; all possible alternatives should be considered. Creative approaches may be eliminated if constraints and evaluation are introduced too soon in the decision making process. Managers must gather all possible information related to the problem area to develop these alternatives. Brainstorming offers an effective technique for developing a broad range of alternatives.

Search is costly, however, in terms of time, effort, and money. The amount of search, therefore, is usually dependent on the importance of the problem and whether it is a new one or a recurrence of an old problem.

In dealing with recurring problems, managers are likely to try solutions that have worked successfully in the past. Since conditions and people both change, solutions that worked some time ago may not apply today; therefore, managers should be cautious in using "tried and true" solutions. Obviously, problems that are considered to be very important to an organization should involve an intensive search for information that will help define issues and generate alternatives.

Even under the best of conditions, all feasible alternatives cannot be developed because of human or situational limitations. Rarely can managers make decisions that maximize objectives, because complete information about all possible alternatives and their potential results is not available. Complete knowledge of alternatives and consequences would allow the "best possible alternative" to be chosen. However, managers often have to make "satisficing" or compromise decisions because information is lacking. Also, managers may tend to choose the first satisfactory alternative discovered and discontinue search for additional alternatives. Another pitfall is to continue the search for alternatives when, in fact, the manager may be avoiding making a decision.

Selecting an Alternative

Selection of the alternative is the fourth step in the decision making process, culminating in the choice of the most effective decision alternative that allows the manager to solve the problem and accomplish the objectives. To make this choice, each alternative must be analyzed to determine the expected result.

To conduct this analysis, criteria for evaluating decisions must be delineated. For example, in selecting a vendor, a foodservice manager might consider such criteria as dependability, price, delivery time, location of various vendors, and variety of products offered. After identifying the possible choices and collecting data concerning these vendors, each would be evaluated on each criterion. Depending on the situation, these various criteria may be given different priorities. For example, if additional steaks are needed for today's dinner menu, the manager would probably be less concerned about price than about receiving them in the early afternoon.

In effective decision making, the importance of defining criteria carefully and applying them appropriately should be obvious. Once the criteria for choosing an alternative have been determined, the selection itself appears to be rather routine. The best alternative, however, is limited by information available at the time of analysis. The need to remain open-minded and allow for sufficient discussion of issues is particularly important when dealing with decisions that have considerable impact on the organization. Eventually, however, a decision has to be made and, more likely than not, it will be a compromise or "satisficing" decision (March and Simon, 1958).

Figure 18.4 represents the satisficing approach to decision making. As shown in the model, if the decision maker is satisfied that an acceptable alternative has been found, that alternative is selected. Otherwise, the decision maker searches for an additional alternative. If required, the value of this alternative to the decision maker is evaluated, which is influenced by the value of the previous best alternative and the current level of aspiration.

In the vendor selection example just discussed, the foodservice manager would select the first satisfactory supplier rather than looking at all possibilities. Both the last vendor used and the last one considered for use would influence the manager's evaluation of a new vendor.

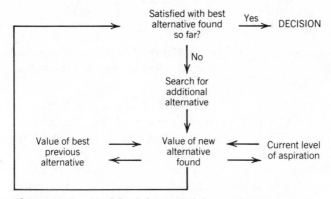

Figure 18.4. *Model of the satisficing approach.*
Source: Adapted from *March, James G. and Simon, A:*
Organizations. ***New York: John Wiley & Sons. 1958, P.***
49 (Reprinted by permission)

The double arrows in the model in Figure 18.4 indicate a two-way relationship between value and aspirations. The net result of the evaluation processes determines whether or not the decision maker is satisfied with the alternative. Thus, the manager selects the first alternative that meets the minimum satisfaction criteria and makes no real attempt to optimize; that is, the manager makes a "satisficing" or satisfactory decision, rather than making the best possible one.

Implementing and Monitoring Decisions

The decision making process does not end when the decision is made. The decision must then be implemented and the manager must follow up and monitor its results to be sure that the alternative selected leads to problem solution and achievement of objectives.

Monitoring the outcomes results in feedback that should be considered in future determination of objectives and in decision making. An effective decision is one that is timely and acceptable to those affected by it and that achieves the desired objectives. Many good decisions fail because of poor implementation. The decision must be communicated properly and support among staff must be organized. In addition, the necessary resources must be assigned to implement it. Managers often unrealistically assume that once they have made a decision, their role is over—this is far from true. Proper implementation of the decision is a critical component in decision making.

Conditions for Making Decisions

Regardless of the approach used, decisions are not always made under the same conditions with regard to the amount of information available. The "best" decision is often dependent on what happens at a later time. Take for instance the decision to produce sufficient entrees for the usual 2000 students who come to lunch on Wednesday in a university residence hall foodservice. If an unexpected

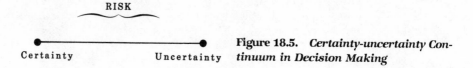

RISK

Certainty   Uncertainty

Figure 18.5. *Certainty-uncertainty Continuum in Decision Making*

downpour occurs between 11:30 A.M. and 12:30 P.M., the decision may result in a large amount of overproduction because many students choose not to dash across campus for lunch. This state of nature is obviously not under the control of the decision maker, yet it affects the outcome of the decision.

The environment within which the decision maker operates, therefore, affects the decision making process. Conditions in the environment change and predictions are difficult; yet managers must make decisions based on the information available, even though it may be incomplete or involve factors outside their control. These conditions under which decisions are made are referred to as certainty, risk, and uncertainty (Figure 18.5). They tend to vary with the time frame that encompasses the decision. The longer the future time period involved in the decision, the less certain we are concerning environmental conditions. The various degrees of certainty in relation to the time frame are illustrated in Figure 18.6. As shown, we tend to move on the certainty-uncertainty continuum into conditions of risk and uncertainty as the time frame becomes longer.

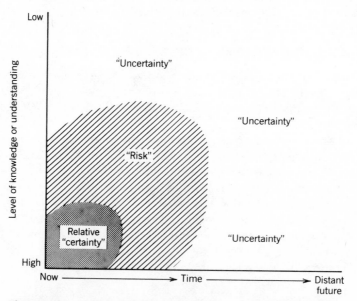

Figure 18.6. *Effect of Time and Level of Knowledge on Decision Making Situations.* **Source: Burack, E. H., and Mathys, N.J.: Introduction to Management: A Career Perspective. New York: John Wiley & Sons, 1983, p. 170. (Reprinted by permission)**

Conditions of Certainty

Under conditions of certainty, a decision maker has enough information to know what the results of a decision will be. A decision under conditions of certainty consists simply of choosing the alternative that will maximize the objective. For example, in school foodservice, the number of children scheduled to eat lunch in an elementary school is usually determined by teachers soon after school convenes each morning. These data are transmitted to the school lunch manager, who can then determine production needs based on a known number of lunch participants. No guesswork is involved in estimating the number of students who will eat.

This condition corresponds to classical economic theory, traditionally known as the rational model of decision making. According to this view, the decision maker makes optimal choices in completely specified, narrowly defined situations. Rational people maximize the objectives they seek by selecting alternatives that have optimal outcomes for the goals they want to achieve. The consequences of each alternative are known; therefore, the decision maker simply compares each outcome against the criteria and selects the best alternative. Under conditions of certainty, management science techniques, such as linear programming, break-even analysis, and inventory control models, have been used effectively.

Conditions of Risk

Since conditions of certainty are becoming less common in today's complex and rapidly changing world, estimating the likelihood or probability of various events occurring in the future is often the only possibility. This condition is called risk. Under risk conditions, various probability techniques are helpful in making decisions. In decision making under risk, managers are faced with the possibility of the occurrence of several states of nature. The assumption is that the probabilities are known regarding these various states, based on the manager's research, experience, and other available information.

Going back to the example cited earlier of the university foodservice and the effect of rain on lunch participation, at the time of production forecasting the manager might have information about the potential for rain from a weather forecast. The manager can also review past records to determine the predicted effect on weekday meal attendance when rain occurs over the lunch hour. Therefore, while the outcome is not known with certainty and the manager is taking a risk in terms of possible over- or underproduction, the weather forecast and prior records will assist in making more accurate projections than are possible if an unexpected downpour occurs.

Probabilities enable the calculation of an expected value of given alternatives. The expected value of a particular decision is nothing more than an average return in the long run. In other words, it is the average of the returns that would be obtained if the same decision were made in the same situation over and over again.

Conditions of Uncertainty

When we are not able to predict the probabilities of various future events occurring, a condition of uncertainty exists. Many changes or unknown facts can emerge when decision time frames are long. To predict what is likely to occur with any degree of certainty, therefore, is quite difficult. In these situations, managers frequently apply past experience, judgment, and intuition so that the range of choices can be narrowed. Input from others may help reduce some of the uncertainty. Therefore, involvement of knowledgeable people in the decision process may be beneficial.

Under conditions of uncertainty, some managers will delay decisions until conditions stabilize or will take a path of least risk. Burack and Mathys (1983) describe these managers as "risk avoiders."

If a decision must be made, however, even though the decision maker has little or no knowledge about the occurrence of various states of nature, one of three basic approaches may be taken. The first is to choose the alternative that is the best of all possible outcomes for all alternatives. This is an optimistic approach and is sometimes called the "maximax" approach. A second approach in dealing with uncertainty is to compare the worst possible outcome of each of the alternatives and select the alternative with the least possible negative outcomes. This is the pessimistic approach, sometimes called the "maximin" approach. The final approach is to choose the alternative that has the least variation among its possible outcomes. It is a risk-averting approach and may make for effective planning; however, the payoff potential is less than with the optimistic approach.

Decision Making Techniques

A wide variety of techniques have been developed to assist managers in making decisions. Some of these techniques are highly complex and quantitative in nature. In this section, we will describe selected techniques briefly; however, the mathematics and computations are beyond the scope of this book. In instances where these techniques have specific applications to procurement or production, they are discussed in the appropriate chapters.

Decision Trees

Decision trees allow management to assess the consequences of a sequence of decisions with reference to a particular problem. The approach involves linking a number of event "branches" graphically, which results in a schematic resembling a tree. The process starts with a primary decision that has at least two alternatives to be evaluated. The probability of each outcome is ascertained, as well as its monetary value.

A simplified example of a decision tree is shown in Figure 18.7. The decision in this example concerns the expansion of a restaurant's services to include take-out food. The two alternatives are to expand or not to expand. The restaurateur is faced with the probability of the competitor on the next block also introducing

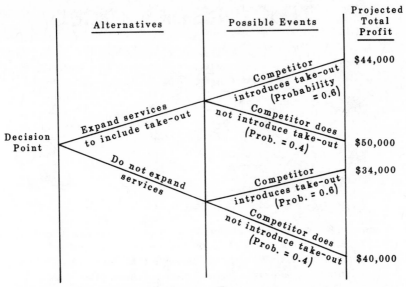

Figure 18.7. *Example of a Decision Tree for Making a Decision on Expansion of Restaurant Services*

take-out service. To assess the decision in question, the probabilities for all these occurrences should be determined, as well as the effect on net income if each were to occur. This determination will permit the restaurant owner to make the decision with the best potential payoff.

Cost Effectiveness

Cost effectiveness is a technique that provides a comparison of alternative courses of action in terms of their cost and effectiveness in attaining a specific objective. It is customarily used in an attempt to minimize dollar cost, subject to some goal requirement that may not be measurable in dollars, or in a converse attempt, to maximize some measure of output subject to a budgetary constraint.

Cost effectiveness has been given a great deal of emphasis in recent years in public programs and in public institutions. Concern over increasing costs in tax-supported services has led to the use of this type of analysis.

In Figure 18.8, the structure of choice model in cost effectiveness analysis is shown. The progress from the desired objective to the final choice of one of the alternatives for obtaining the goal is shown. After the objective has been stated, the alternatives are proposed and then ranked in order of desirability by comparison with defined criteria. The alternative selected may not be the least costly, because potential effectiveness is a major consideration.

A simplified comparison of alternatives is illustrated in Figure 18.9. The cost effectiveness curves for Alternatives A and B intersect at a point where, for the same cost, the effectiveness is identical. At a cost less than that at the point of

STRUCTURE OF CHOICE

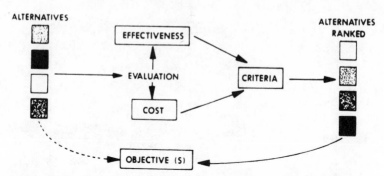

Figure 18.8. *Structure of choice: Progress from the desired objective to the choice of one of the alternate means of obtaining it.* **Source: *Spears, M. C.: Concepts of cost effectiveness: Accountability for nutrition. Copyright © The American Dietetic Association. Reprinted by permission of the American Dietetic Association, Vol. 68:341, 1976.***

intersection, Alternative B gives greater effectiveness; if costs higher than that at the point of intersection can be tolerated, Alternative A is preferable. The judgment of the decision maker comes into play in answering the question of whether or not the gain in effectiveness of A over B at a higher cost is worthwhile.

Spears (1976) provides an example of the application of cost effectiveness to a decision of whether to use foods in a foodservice facility that have been partially or fully prepared off premise. The stated goal is to prepare quality food at minimum cost. Three alternatives to meet this objective were ranked as follows.

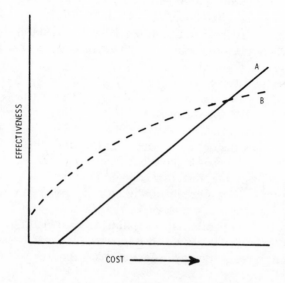

Figure 18.9. *Comparison of alternatives. At the point where cost-effectiveness curves of Alternatives A and B intersect, cost and effectiveness are identical. One question to be answered in choosing between Alternatives A and B is whether the increased effectiveness possible with Alternative A at a higher cost is worthwhile.* **Source: *Spears, M. C.: Concepts of cost effectiveness: Accountability for nutrition, productivity. J. Am. Dietet. A. 68:343, 1976.***

- Do all preparation except bakery items.
- Do all preparation.
- Use only convenience foods.

In evaluating the alternatives, the criteria include food acceptability, food and labor cost, nutritional adequacy, and availability of convenience items. The decision from this analysis is to select the highest ranked alternative: do all preparation except bakery items. As Spears concludes, cost effectivness provides a tool for minimizing costs while achieving the most effective use of funds and attaining high standards. This technique is especially appropriate in evaluating need for major change.

Network Methods

PERT (Program Evaluation and Review Technique) and CPM (Critical Path Method) are network models for decision making. A network is a graphic representation of a project, depicting the flow as well as the sequence of defined activities and events. An activity defines the work to be performed; an event marks the beginning or end of an activity.

PERT and CPM are useful techniques for assisting managers in planning, analyzing, scheduling, and controlling the progress and completion of complex projects. According to Loomba (1978), the primary use of these models is for one-time projects. Although network methods are primarily planning and control techniques, they provide the manager a basis for making decisions throughout the progress of a project.

In using a network technique, a project is first subdivided into well-defined activities with identified start and completion points. The order or sequence of activities is then specified and decisions are made on who will perform the activities and what is needed to complete them. Specification of time estimates for performing activities is the next step. In CPM, single-time estimates are used; in PERT, three-time estimates are specified:

- Most optimistic time or shortest time, assuming most favorable conditions.
- Most likely time, which implies the most realistic time.
- Most pessimistic time or the longest time, assuming the most unfavorable conditions.

The activities, events, and times are plotted on a diagram and the critical path is determined using either PERT or CPM. The critical path is the longest path through the network, which specifies the shortest time in which a project can be completed.

The manager can evaluate progress by determining if events are occurring during the time frame predicted. If behind schedule, the manager has the information to make decisions concerning the need to allocate additional resources to complete the project in the planned time. A primary use of network techniques is

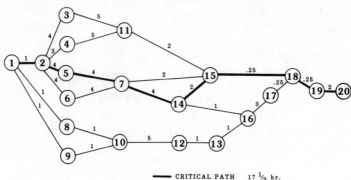

Figure 18.10. *Example of a PERT Network Chart*

in design and construction of facilities. Although network techniques focus primarily on planning and control of time, cost estimates may also be provided, which can then be monitored as a project progresses.

An example of a network model is shown in Figure 18.10, which is a simplified application of the CPM technique to the project of planning a special breakfast for a group of 50 graduating seniors. The initial activity is to decide on a date and a place for the breakfast. As shown in the diagram, two activities can be initiated after this initial decision is made, the development of the guest list and the planning of the menu. A sequence of activities must follow these initial ones. This simple example illustrates how a special project can be planned and controlled using a network model.

Linear Programming

Linear programming is a technique useful in determining an optimal combination of resources to obtain a desired objective. Loomba (1978) contends that linear programming is one of the most versatile, powerful, and useful techniques for making managerial decisions, which has been used in solving a broad range of problems in industry, government, healthcare, and education. Determination of optimal product mix, transportation schedule, plant location, and assignment of personnel and machines are a few examples of the type of problems that can be solved by linear programming.

The objective may be the lowest cost or highest profit possible from given resources. Linear programming must be considered in light of the limitations on its use, however. A general prerequisite is that a linear or straight line relationship exists among the factors involved. In any linear programming problem, the manager must identify a measurable objective or criterion of effectiveness. The constraints must also be specified.

Balintfy et al. (1980) used linear programming techniques to plan preference-maximized menus for school lunch. Balintfy is the pioneer in computer menu planning based on linear programming. In his work, nutrient constraints are specified and aesthetic factors quantified in a model designed to plan least-cost menus. His later work includes food preferences in the menu planning model.

Other Techniques

A variety of other quantitative decision making techniques have been developed, including game theory, queuing, and simulation models. In the foodservice field, many of these applications have been used in research rather than in operational decision making, and most require complex computer models. As the field develops, however, managers will probably be applying these techniques, as have managers in other industries, to improve decision making effectiveness.

Game theory introduces a competitive note in decision making by bringing into a simulated decision situation the actions of an opponent. Competition for market share is an example of a problem in which game theory might be used. The assumption is made that all involved competitors have the objective of winning the game and that the competitors or players are capable of making independent and rational decisions. The competitors are presumed to be interested in maximizing gains and minimizing losses. Game theory will show the highest gain with the smallest amount of losses, regardless of what the competitor does.

Queuing theory develops the relationships that are involved in waiting in line. Customers awaiting service or work awaiting inspection in a production line are typical of the problem that may be approached by the methods of queuing theory. The theory, in effect, balances the cost of waiting lines against the cost of preventing them by expanding facilities. The problem is figuring out the cost of total waiting—that is, the cost of tolerating the queue—and weighing it against expense of constructing enough facilities to decrease the need for the queue. Sometimes, eliminating all delay is more costly than keeping some. The basic framework of a queuing system is shown in Figure 18.11. Queuing problems can be solved by analytical procedures or simulation.

Lopez-Soriano et al. (1981) used a queuing simulation model for designing a system to improve the flow of customers in a hospital cafeteria. The nine service facilities were analyzed (Table 18.1) and a schematic representation of the physical flow of customers was developed (Figure 18.12). The computer queuing simulation permitted the analysis of several alternatives to decrease cafeteria waiting lines without disrupting the operation.

The concept of simulation is to utilize some device for imitating a real-life system and studying its properties, behavior, and operating characteristics. The device can be physical, mathematical, or some other type of model for describing the behavior of a system that a manager wishes to design, improve, or operate. For example, we can learn about the operating characteristics of a new piece of equipment by simulating conditions in a laboatory. Likewise, we can simulate behavior of a system by experimenting on a mathematical model that represents the system, as in the queuing simulation described above.

In any simulation model, the idea is to understand the behavior of a system by testing the model under a variety of operating conditions without having to

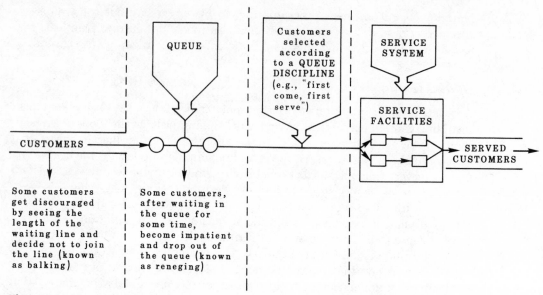

Figure 18.11. *Basic Framework of a Queuing System.* **Source:** *Loomba, N. P.,* **Management—A Quantitative Perspective.** *New York: Macmillan Publishing Co., 1978, p. 429.* **Copyright © 1978.** *(Reprinted by permission)*

Table 18.1. *Input data for the cafeteria model*

Facility	Maximum no. of customers allowed in queue	Percent of persons selecting a menu item	Time for service* (min.)
tray and serviceware†	4	100	0.25
main entrée	8	52	0.15
vegetable	3	38	0.15
soup	2	27	0.15
salad†	5	39	0.12
bread and butter†	2	6	0.12
dessert†	7	35	0.12
hot beverage†	5	18	0.15
salad bar†	8	10	0.75

Source: Lopez-Soriano, E. M., Matthews, M. E., and Norback, J. P.: Improving the flow of customers in a hospital cafeteria. *J. Am. Dietet. A.* 79:683, 1981.

*Service time at food facilities is assumed to be constant for all customers.

†Self-service facilities.

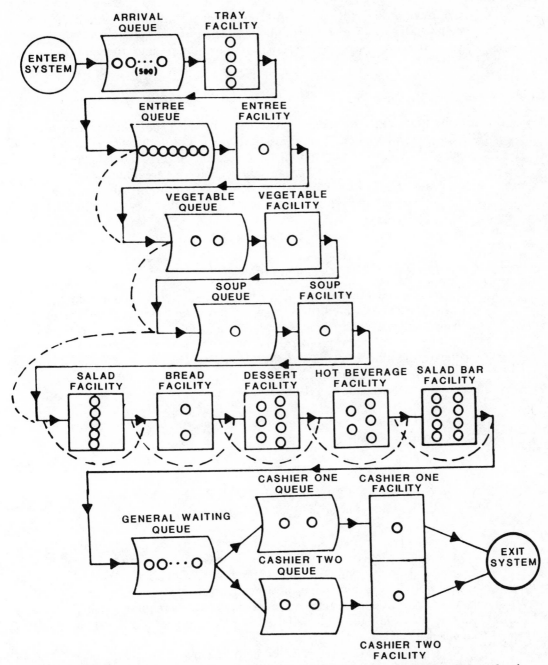

Dotted lines indicate a customer may bypass one or more facilities while moving through the cafeteria. Maximum number of customers allowed in the queue is shown by the circles within the symbols.

Figure 18.12. *Schematic Representation of the Physical Flow of Customers in the Cafeteria Studied. Source: Lopez-Soriano, E. M., Matthews, M. E., Norback, J. P.: Improving the flow of customers in a hospital cafeteria. J. Am. Dietet. Assoc. 79:683, 1981.*

experiment on the real-life system. Sophisticated computer programs have been developed for mathematical simulations. These models require careful delineation of the components of the system and translation into mathematical terms.

Group Decision Making

In the foregoing discussion we mentioned the idea that the manager may get input from others in making decisions or may wish to involve them in decision making. We have focused on individual decision makers up to this point. A great number of decisions in most organizations, however, are made by groups. These groups may be existing or specially designated committees, teams, task forces, or project groups. Often, informal groups may be called together to assist with a particular decision.

Individual vs. Group Decision Making

When should a decision be made by a group rather than an individual? This issue has been greatly debated. According to Burack and Mathys (1983), individual versus group decision making is largely dependent on factors such as complexity and importance of the problem, the time available, the degree of acceptance required, the amount of information needed to make a decision, and the usual manner in which decisions are made in an organization. They describe three possibilities for managerial decision making.

- *Individual decision.* Managers can make decisions themselves using information available to them.
- *Combination decision.* Managers can make decisions after consulting with others.
- *Group decision.* Managers can allow decisions to be made by the group, of which the manager is usually a member.

Group decision making, then, is utilized because managers frequently confront situations in which they must seek information and elicit judgment of other people—this is especially true for nonprogrammed decisions. In most organizations, rarely does an individual consistently make this type of decision alone. The problems involved are usually complex and solutions require specialized knowledge from several fields. Usually, no one manager possesses all the kinds of knowledge needed.

Group decision making may also be used when two or more organizational units are affected by the decisions reached. Since most decisions must eventually be accepted and implemented by several units, involving the groups affected in the decision making may be helpful.

In Figure 18.13, conditions for individual and group decisions are listed. As

	Factor	(1) Individual	(2) Compromise (some amount of participation)	(3) Group
			Decision styles	
1	Complexity and importance of problem	Simple, straightforward	←——→	Very complex
2	Degree of acceptance required for success	Little or none	←——→	Crucial to success
3	Time constraint	Extreme time pressure	←——→	Sufficient time to obtain needed information
4	Amount of information required	Little information is required for effective decision	←——→	Much information is needed from a variety of sources for proper interpretation
5	Accessibility of information	Decision maker has all information necessary	←——→	Information needed for decision is held by people other than decision maker
6	Organizational climate	Autocratic, centralized structure	←——→	Participative, decentralized structure

Figure 18.13. *Some Conditions for Individual Versus Group Decisions.* **Source: Burack, E. H., and Mathys, N. J.:** Introduction to Management: A Career Perspective. *New York: John Wiley & Sons, 1983, p. 174 (reprinted by permission).*

shown in the figure, the appropriate style will depend on the factors operating in a particular situation.

Strengths and Limitations of Group Decision Making

Although group decision making is used to improve individual decisions, group processes sometimes prevent full discussion of facts and alternatives. Group norms, member roles, established communication patterns, and cohesiveness may deter the group and lead to ineffective decisions. Two phenomena often occurring in decision making groups that may interfere with good decisions are groupthink and risky shift (Middlemist and Hitt, 1981).

Groupthink occurs when reaching agreement becomes more important to group members than arriving at a sound decision. In cohesive groups, members often want to avoid being too harsh in judging fellow members. They dislike bickering and conflict, perceiving them as threats to "team spirit." Janis (1977), who popularized the concept of groupthink, suggests that faulty decision making may occur because group members do not want to "rock the boat."

Risky shift is the tendency of individuals to accept or take more risk in groups than they would individually. Riskier decisions may result from group decision making because group members share the risk with others rather than having to bear responsibility individually.

Vroom (1975), who has done major work on group decision making, concludes that involvement of subordinates in group decision making may be costly in terms of time. Autocratic decision making is typically faster and thus valuable in emergency or crisis situations. Participation by subordinates, however, creates greater acceptance of decisions, which in turn is reflected in better implementation. As an additional benefit, involvement in decision making leads to the growth and development of subordinates. Vroom also contends that the effects of increased participation by subordinates on the quality of decisions tends to be positive, although these effects are likely to depend on several factors: group decisions tend to be higher in quality when the relevant information is widely distributed among group members, when the problem is unstructured, and when group members share a common goal.

COMMUNICATION

Communications play a major role in determining how effectively people work together and coordinate their efforts to achieve an organization's objectives. All types of organizations have recognized the importance of communications and have made major expenditures to improve them. Scanlon and Keys (1983) state, however, that in the view of most managers communication continues to be a major problem in organizations.

In introducing this chapter, we indicated that communication is one of the linking processes in organizations that is critical to managerial effectiveness and to the effective functioning of the foodservice system. Mintzberg (1975) found that managers spend a majority of their time communicating, much of which involves verbal communication. He described the informational roles of managers as monitor, disseminator, and spokesman (refer to Chapter 3).

Because of the importance of communication to organizations and to the personal effectiveness of managers, persons in leadership positions must be well versed on the basics of communication and apply good communication techniques in all their activities. Breakdowns in the communication process may lead to employee dissatisfaction, customer dissatisfaction, misunderstanding, misinterpretation, and a whole range of other problems in organizations.

Poor communication is often named the culprit when any organizational problem arises, even though it may simply be a symptom of a more complex problem. Good communication is not a panacea for all organizational problems. It will not, for example, make up for poor planning or poor decisions, although plans and decisions must be communicated in some manner—usually to a variety of individuals in an organization—for them to be implemented. Thus, communicating is an extremely important skill for managers; its significance cannot be overstated.

Communication Defined

Communication is the transfer of information that is meaningful to those involved. It is also defined as the transmittal of understanding. It occurs in many forms, ranging from face-to-face communication to written messages, and involves verbal, nonverbal, and implied messages. Communication in organizations is often viewed from two perspectives: communication between individuals (interpersonal communication) and communication within the formal organization structure (organizational communication). These two basic forms of communication, however, are obviously interdependent and interrelated.

The simplest model of communication is as follows

$$\text{SENDER} \longrightarrow \text{MESSAGE} \longrightarrow \text{RECEIVER}$$

Regardless of the type of communication, it includes these three elements. Before discussing interpersonal and organizational communication, we will first discuss the communication process more fully.

Communication Process

The simple model presented above does not show the complexity of the communication process. A more sophisticated model of the communication process is shown in Figure 18.14. The first element in the model is the source or sender, where the communication is initiated. The sender is the person with a purpose

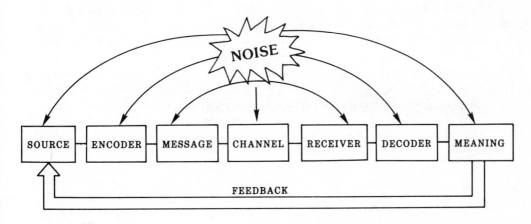

THE COMMUNICATION PROCESS

These basic ingredients of a communication model can be applied to any system, from a television network to a two person conversation.

Figure 18.14. *The Communication Process.* **Source: Vaden, R., and Vaden, A.: "Come, let us get closer to the fire so we see what it is we are saying." A dialogue on communication. In Vaden, A. G., Innovative Approaches to Nutrition Education and Related Management Processes. Manhattan, KS: Kansas State University, 1971.**

for communicating information to one or more individuals. Communicators may be managers, nonmanagers, departments, or the organization itself. In Chapter 17, we pointed out the importance of communication to effective coordination in organizations. Also, transmitting information outside the organization is becoming more and more important today. The sender or communicator has a message, an idea, or some other information to transmit to someone or some group.

The sender must <u>encode</u> the information to be transmitted into a series of symbols or gestures. Encoding is necessary because information can only be transmitted from one person to another through representations or symbols. In other words, the sender's message must be translated into a language that reflects the idea. The encoding action produces the message.

The <u>message</u> is the physical form into which the information is encoded and may be in any form that can be experienced and understood by the receiver. For example, speech may be heard, written words reads, and gestures seen or felt. Obviously, then, nonverbal messages may be as important in communication as verbal or written messages.

The <u>channel</u> is the mode of transmission and is often inseparable from the message. For communication to be effective, the channel must be appropriate for the message, and the receiver. Organizations provide information using a variety of means: face-to-face communications, telephone, meetings, letters and memos, policy statements, and computers. Unintended messages may be transmitted by silence or inaction on a particular issue.

The <u>receiver</u> is the person or group whose senses perceive the sender's message. The receiver may be a single individual or an entire organization. If the message does not reach a receiver, however, the communication has not taken place.

<u>Decoding</u> is the process by which receivers translate the message into terms meaningful to them. Decoding is affected by the receiver's past experience, personal interpretations, expectations, and mutuality of meaning with the sender. The closer the match between the receiver's decoding and the sender's intended message, the more effective the communication. <u>Meaning</u> is an abstract concept that is highly personal. No direct relationship exists between the symbols and gestures used in communication and meaning, as shown in Figure 18.15. A common problem in communication is the misinterpretation that may result from the receiver not understanding the message in the way the sender intends.

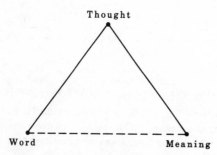

Figure 18.15. *Triangle of Meaning*

At the top of Figure 18.14, a "cloud" of <u>noise</u> is shown, which refers to all the types of interference that may distort or compete with the message at every stage of the communication process. The sender may speak too softly, the message may be distorted or not heard because of other sounds in the environment, the receiver may not be paying attention—all are examples of noise. A typical situation in a foodservice is when a manager is attempting to give instructions to the cook with interference from banging pots and pans, other employees talking, and telephones ringing.

<u>Feedback</u>, shown at the bottom of Figure 18.14, is the process by which the sender is aware that the message has been received. Feedback may take many forms, from the nod of a person's head to a written letter or memo or a telecommunications message. Feedback may also be indirect; for example, communication breakdowns may be indicated by conflict, lack of coordination, or poor quality work.

Communication may be one-way or two-way. In <u>one-way communication</u>, the sender communicates without expecting or getting feedback from the receiver. <u>Two-way communication</u> exists when feedback is provided by the receiver. Feedback enhances the effectiveness of the communication process and helps to ensure that the intended message is received by allowing the receiver to clarify the message and permitting the sender to refine the communication. One-way communication takes considerably less time but is less accurate. If communication must be fast and accuracy is easy to achieve, one-way communication may be both economical and efficient. If accuracy is important, however, and the message is complex, two-way communication is almost essential.

The communication skills, attitudes, knowledge, and the social system or culture of both the sender and receiver affect the communication. Differences in these elements between the sender and receiver may lead to communication problems. An obvious example is when the language is different for the sender and receiver. The foodservice manager responsible for supervising employees who speak little or no English would certainly understand this concept. The concept also has applicability to other types of communication. For example, when electronic communication systems are incompatible, communication breakdown also occurs.

Interpersonal Communication

A common and often incorrect assumption that we make in communicating with other people is that a message is transmitted and received accurately. We frequently operate on the assumption that a message was conveyed effectively and completely and then, that the person receiving the message was paying attention and understood completely. This assumption is far from correct and is the source of many communication problems between individuals.

Communication that flows from individual to individual in face-to-face and group settings is referred to as <u>interpersonal communication</u>. The objective in interpersonal communication should be to increase the <u>area of understanding</u> (Figure 18.16). In other words, we are attempting the overlap of "what was

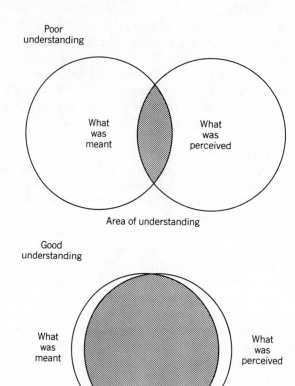

Poor
understanding

What
was
meant

What
was
perceived

Area of understanding

Good
understanding

What
was
meant

What
was
perceived

Area of understanding

Figure 18.16. *Areas of understanding.* **Source: Burack, E. H., and Mathys, N. J.: Introduction to Management: A Career Perspective. New York, John Wiley & Sons, 1983, p. 379. (Reprinted by permission)**

meant" and "what was perceived." In the following pages, we will discuss some of the common barriers to effective interpersonal communications and review techniques for improving them.

Barriers to Communication

"I didn't understand" is a common reply supervisors hear from employees when discussing why results were different from those expected. The dining room may be set up incorrectly, the wrong number of portions may be prepared, or the dietary aide may come to work at the wrong time. All of these problems may be the result of communication breakdown between the supervisor and the foodservice employee.

Sayles and Strauss (1966) identified a number of <u>common barriers</u> in interpersonal communication.

• *Hearing what we expect to hear.* Past experience leads us to expect to hear certain messages that may not be correct in some situations.

- *Ignoring conflicting information.* When we hear a message that disagrees with our preconceptions, we are likely to ignore the information. For example, the foodservice manager who believes the operation has good food and service may ignore clientele complaints.

- *Differing perceptions.* Words, actions, and situations are perceived in light of the receiver's values and experiences. Different people react differently to the same message.

- *Evaluating the source.* The meaning applied to any message is influenced by our evaluation of the source. For example, if we view the sender as knowledgeable, we interpret the message differently than if we question the sender's knowledge on a particular topic.

- *Interpreting words differently.* Because of the complexity of language, words have many different meanings.

- *Ignoring nonverbal cues.* Tone of voice, facial expressions, and gestures may affect communication. The sender, for example, may ignore the fact that the receiver seems preoccupied in an attempt to convey a message that is not heard.

- *Becoming emotional.* Emotion will affect transmission and interpretation of messages. For example, if we perceive a person we are talking to as hostile, we may respond defensively or aggressively, which may have a negative effect on the communication. A "pendulum effect" may occur, whereby emotion increases and affects the communication by causing stronger reactions and responses than would otherwise be true.

Inference may be a barrier or facilitator in communication. As Haney (1979) discusses, we are constantly drawing inferences in our communication with other people; that is, we draw conclusions based on incomplete information and take action as a result. If these inferences are incorrect, we may run into problems; but if correct, the inference may lead to efficiency in communication because needless information is avoided. A risk is involved, however, because of the potential of an inference leading to an incorrect conclusion. For example, a customer's smile may be interpreted as satisfaction with the food or service when, in fact, the customer may be reacting to seeing an employee snacking in the waiter's pantry—in this case, an incorrect inference.

Haney identified another barrier in communication that he refers to as allness. It occurs when one unconsciously assumes that it is possible to know or say everything about something. Arrogance, intolerance of other viewpoints, and close-mindedness are consequences of allness. Everyone can identify an individual whom we might call a "know it all." This person is the epitome of the allness concept.

Ability to interact effectively with other individuals is affected negatively by allness. Professionals, in particular, need to be sensitive to developing "allness" in dealing with people. A common tendency is to become prescriptive because of highly specialized knowledge and a feeling that might result of "knowing what's best" for the other person.

All of these barriers impede interpersonal communication and may lead to more serious problems in relationships. Sensitivity to and awareness of these barriers may assist in improving communication; a number of techniques can also be used to enhance interpersonal communication.

Techniques for Improving Communication

Techniques for improving communication are summarized in Figure 18.17. Using feedback can result in more effective communication because it allows the sender to search for verbal and nonverbal cues from the receiver. Questions can be encouraged and areas of confusion clarified as a result of two-way communication in which effective feedback is involved. Also, face-to-face communication may encourage feedback. People generally express themselves more freely in face-to-face situations or in other two-way communications, such as telephone conversations.

Using several channels will improve the chances that a proper message is communicated. For example, following up a verbal message with a written note will serve as a reinforcement.

Sensitivity to the receiver will enable the communicator to adapt the message to the situation. Individuals differ in their values, needs, attitudes, and expectations. Empathy with these differences will facilitate interpersonal communication.

Awareness of symbolic meanings can be particularly important in communication. For example, sensitivity to negative connotations and thus avoiding "red flag" words is a way to improve interpersonal communication.

"It's not what you say, but what you do" is another tenet for improving communication. This concept, of course, is concerned with timing of the message and reinforcing words with action.

TECHNIQUES for IMPROVED COMMUNICATION

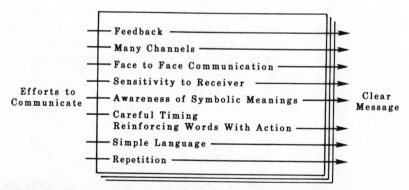

Figure 18.17. *Techniques for Improved Communication.* **Source:** *Vaden, R., and Vaden, A.: "Come, let us get closer to the fire so we see what it is we are saying." A dialogue on communication. In Vaden, A. G., Innovative Approaches to Nutrition Education and Related Management Processes. Manhatten, KS: Kansas State University, 1971.*

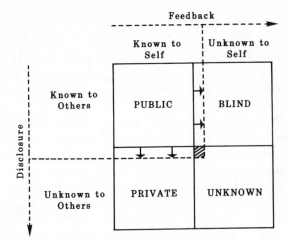

Figure 18.18. *The Johari Window.* Source: *Luft, J.: Group Processes: An Introduction to Group Dynamics. 2nd ed., Palo Alto, CA: National Press Book Co., 1970. Copyright © 1963, 1970. (Reprinted by permission of Mayfield Publishing Company)*

Using direct, simple language and avoiding jargon is another rule for improving communications. Especially important is the need to level the message to the knowledge of the receiver. This concept becomes vividly apparent in communication with children; however, it may also be important in communicating with adults who may be less willing than children to say "I don't understand." Using the correct amount of repetition can serve as a reinforcement to the receiver's understanding of the message. Unnecessary redundancy or the overuse of clichés, however, may dull the receiver's attention.

Listening is basic to effective communication, since receiving messages is as much a part of the process as sending them. Daydreaming and preoccupation with other matters or mentally arguing with points made by the speaker before the talk is finished may preclude individuals from listening. Impatience and lack of interest in the message are other impediments to listening.

Rue and Byars (1983) contend that effective listening habits can be developed. As Lesikar (1976) points out, effective listening involves putting a person at ease, removing distractions, asking questions, empathizing, and avoiding criticism. In his list of effective guides to listening, Lesikar started and ended the list with the repeated caution to "stop talking."

A framework developed by Luft and Ingham (Luft, 1970) called the Johari Window (taken from the authors' first names, Joseph and Harry) has application to improving communication (Figure 18.18). According to this framework, the "known to self" area or public arena includes individuals' knowledge of the way they are coming across. At the same time, people are unaware of how they are coming across in some areas, which is the "unknown to self" or blind arena. The arena that represents "known to self but unknown to others" is referred to as the private arena. The fourth is called the unknown arena and is that part of an individual's personality that is referred to as the subconscious or unconscious in Freudian psychology (Hersey and Blanchard, 1981). Through the processes of feedback and disclosure, an individual can expand the public arena into both the private and blind arenas, which in turn can lead to more effective interpersonal communication.

Organizational Communication

The factors discussed in relation to interpersonal communication apply to communication within organizations as well. Effective organizational communication involves getting an accurate message from one person to another. The effectiveness of organizational communication, however, is also influenced by several characteristics unique to organizations.

Lesikar (1977) identifies four factors influencing the effectiveness of organizational communication: the formal channels of communication, the authority structure, job specialization, and a factor he calls "information ownership." The formal channels influence communication effectiveness in two ways. First, as organizations grow, the channels cover a greater and greater distance. You will recall the small deli discussed in Chapter 17 that developed into a large national chain of delicatessens. In that chapter we discussed how levels of management, divisions, and departments developed as the organization grew. With this development, effective communication is more difficult to achieve because of the much greater complexity of the organization.

Second, the formal channels of communication may inhibit the flow of information between levels in the organization. The cook, for example, will almost always communicate problems to the foodservice supervisor rather than to the unit manager. While this accepted channel of communication has advantages, such as keeping higher level managers from being overloaded with too much information, it also has disadvantages. Higher level managers may not always receive all the information they need for staying "on top of operations." With additional levels in an organization, the accuracy of messages up and down the organization will also be affected.

The structure affects communication because of status and power differences among organizational members. The content and accuracy of communication will be affected by authority differences. For example, conversation between the director of foodservice and a foodservice worker may tend to be strained politeness or somewhat formal. Neither one is likely to say much of importance.

Job specialization can be both a help and hindrance in communication. It facilitates communication within a work group because members share the same jargon and frequently develop a group cohesiveness. Communication between work groups, however, may be inhibited. The cafeteria workers may have free flowing communication, as may also be true of the production workers. Communication between these two groups may not be as effective as that within each group.

The term information ownership means that individuals possess unique information and knowledge about their jobs. Such information is a form of power for those who possess it, making them unwilling to share the information with others.

Overcrowded work areas, too many individuals competing for the attention of a manager, the improper choice of a communication channel, and time pressures are other factors that impede organizational communication. For example, a typed letter rather than face-to-face conversation for handling a touchy matter may lead to hurt feelings.

Within the organization, managers must provide for communication in four distinct directions: downward, upward, horizontal, and diagonal. Understanding and effective use of the informal networks, or the grapevine, is also important in managing organizations. Although discussed only briefly in this chapter, managers must communicate effectively with individuals and groups outside the organization. Another dimension of organizational communication is knowing when and how to use written and oral communications. The complexities of organizations have led to the design of sophisticated management information systems to facilitate communication. These issues related to organizational communication are discussed in the remainder of the chapter.

Downward Communication

Downward communication flows from individuals at higher levels of the organization to those at lower levels. The most common forms of communication used are job instructions, policy statements, procedure manuals, and official publications of the organization. In addition, middle and lower level managers are usually contacted by written memos or with some other official directive. A summary of various channels available to carry information downward are listed in Figure 18.19.

External means, such as radio, television, and newspaper press releases, may be used to communicate not only with employees but also with the general public. For example, a school district closing because of snow is usually announced over the radio and television as a way of communicating to the school district staff, parents, and students.

Upward Communication

An effective organization needs open channels of upward communication as much as it needs downward communication. In large organizations, good upward communication is especially difficult. Suggestion boxes, group meetings, and appeal procedures are devices used for upward communication. Some channels for upward flow of information are summarized in Figure 18.20.

Effective upward communication is important because it provides employees with an opportunity to "have a say." Equally important, however, is the need for management to receive vital information from lower levels in the organization.

Horizontal Communication

Provision for horizontal flow of communication will enhance organizational effectiveness. This issue was touched on in Chapter 17 in the discussion of coordination. We described, for example, communication between nursing service and dietetic service personnel concerning problems with patients. Within the foodservice unit, effective horizontal communication between production and service is critical to ensure that quality food is available at the right time in the right place.

The chain of command	Orders and information can be given face-to-face or in written fashion and transmitted from one level to another. This is the most frequently used channel and is appropriate on either an individual or a group basis.
Posters and bulletin boards	Many employees refuse to read such boards, and thus this channel is useful only as a supplementary device.
Company periodicals	A great deal of information about the company, its products, and policies can be disseminated in this manner. To attract readership, a certain percentage of space must be devoted to personal items about employees, and thus the periodical plays a part in developing the social life of the organization.
Letters and pay inserts	This is a form of direct mail contact and is ordinarily used when the president of the organization wishes to present something of special interest. Letters are usually directed to the employee's home address. The use of pay inserts ensures exposure to every employee.
Employee handbooks and pamphlets	Handbooks are frequently used during the hiring and orientation process as an introduction to the organization. Too often, however, they are unread even when the firm demands a signed statement that the employee is acquainted with their contents. When special systems are being introduced, such as a pension plan or a job evaluation system, concise, highly illustrated pamphlets are often prepared to facilitate understanding and stimulate acceptance.
Information racks	In a relatively small number of organizations, racks containing free paperback literature of all types are provided. Mixed in with books on hobbies and sports are pamphlets on the profit system, the company, management techniques, and the like.
Loudspeaker system	The loudspeaker system is used not only for paging purposes, but also to make announcements while they are "hot." Such systems can also be misused, as in the case where the president of a company sent his greetings from his cool vacation place in the mountains to the hot, sweaty workers on the production floor.
Grapevine	Though the grapevine is an informal means of communication, it has been suggested that management should "feed, water, and cultivate" its growth by providing factual information to combat rumors.

| Annual reports | A review of typical annual reports would indicate that they are increasingly being written for the benefit of the employee and the union as well as for the stockholder. It is a channel that appears to be designed for one group, the owners, to which others "tap in," hoping to obtain information not intended for them. |
| The labor union | The union can be very helpful in communicating certain philosophies to company employees. The union voice, added to the management voice, can be highly persuasive. |

Figure 18.19. *Downward Channels of Communication.* **Source:** *Monday, R. W., Holmes, R. E., and Flippo, E. B.:* **Management: Concepts and Practices, 2nd ed.,** *Boston: Allyn and Bacon, 1983, pp. 388–389. Copyright © 1983 (reprinted by permission).*

Department head meetings are one way to facilitate interdepartmental communication. The more interdependent the work of organizational units or departments, the greater the need for horizontal communication.

Diagonal Communication

The use of diagonal channels of communication is a way of minimizing time and effort expended in organizations. Having reports and other information flow directly between departments or units that have a diagonal placement in the organization may result in more effective flow of information.

For example, the ordering clerk in a foodservice department may send requests directly to the purchasing department rather than through the channels of the foodservice department. As long as procedures for this practice exist, the function of ordering and receiving goods is facilitated by this direct communication.

Informal Networks

Informal communication networks develop in organizations to supplement formal communication channels. The grapevine, as the informal channels are usually called, may facilitate organizational communication and also meet the social needs of the individuals within the organization. Although the grapevine may filter or distort messages and occasionally transmit rumors and gossip, its speed and accuracy in getting messages through an organization are often very useful.

The effective manager is one who has learned to use the grapevine to advantage and recognizes its importance in fulfilling the communication needs of members of the organization. The grapevine can and should work for the manager. Informal communication systems can help to speed the work-related flow of information by making use of the natural interaction among people in organizations. Ignoring the grapevine and rumors is a dangerous alternative, according

The chain of command	Theoretically, the flow of communications is two-way between superior and subordinate. The superior should have an open-door attitude as well as some of the skills of a counselor. If one has more courage, group meetings can be held in which expression of gripes and attitudes is encouraged.
The grievance procedure	A systematic grievance procedure is one of the most fundamental devices for upward communication. The subordinate knows that there is a mechanism for appeal beyond the authority of the immediate supervisor. If this grievance procedure is backed up by the presence of a labor union, one is even more encouraged to voice true feelings.
The complaint system	In addition to grievance procedures, some firms encourage all types of upward communication by establishing means of preserving the identity of the complainant. "Gripe boxes" may be established, into which an employee can place a written complaint or rumor, which management will investigate. In one firm, a blackboard was divided into halves, one side being for employee complaints or rumors, the other for management's replies. An answer of some sort was guaranteed within a twenty-four hour period.
Counseling	Though all supervisors have a counseling obligation, the authority barrier makes true communication difficult. For this reason, special staff counselors may be provided to allow employees to discuss matters with them in privacy and confidence.
Morale questionnaires	This channel also preserves the identity of the employee when answering specific questions about the firm and its management.
An open-door policy	An open-door attitude on the part of each supervisor toward immediate subordinates is to be highly commended. With regard to higher management it is seldom used, because the employee is usually reluctant to bypass his or her immediate supervisor.
Exit interview	If the employee leaves the organization, there is one last chance in the exit interview to discover feelings and views about the firm in general and reasons for quitting in particular. Follow-up questionnaires are also used at times, because employees are reluctant to give full and truthful information at the time of departure.

Grapevine	Though management may be reluctant to feed and cultivate the grapevine, it should always listen to it. The grapevine is a spontaneous and natural phenomenon that serves as a means of emotional release and provides management with significant clues concerning the attitudes and feelings of organization members. If the grapevine should ever become silent, that is the time to worry. Management should remember that although the grapevine is usually quite accurate, "it is nearly always uncharitable."
Labor union	A prime purpose of the labor union is to convey to management the feelings and demands of employees. Collective bargaining sessions constitute a legal channel of communication for any aspect of employer-employee relations.
Special meetings	Special employee meetings to discuss particular company policies or procedures are sometimes scheduled by management to obtain employee feedback. The keystone of teamwork in one company is monthly meetings in all departments involving all employees. In addition, a central employee council of 13 employee representatives meets with top executives on a monthly basis. Employees on this main council are elected for two-year terms and devote full time to investigating company problems and improving communication processes.
The ombudsman	Though little used in this country, it has been suggested that corporate justice in nonunionized firms requires a special person to act as the president's eyes and ears. In essence, the ombudsman acts as a complaint officer to whom employees may go when they feel they have exhausted the typical avenues of receiving an acceptable hearing. An ombudsman has only the rights of acceptance or rejection of complaints, investigation, and recommendation of action to the top organizational official. Most complaints center around salary, performance appraisal, layoff, and fringe benefits. In many instances, low-level managers make voluntary adjustments precluding specific recommendations from the ombudsman. Though the position has existed for about 150 years, only recently have some American business firms adopted the concept. Xerox Corporation inaugurated the position in 1972 and reports that 40 percent of the final decisions clearly favored the employee, 30 percent were against the employee, and 30 percent represented some type of compromise.

Figure 18.20. *Upward Channels of Communication.* **Source:** *Monday, R. W., Holmes, R. E., and Flippo, E. B.:* **Management: Concepts and Practices, 2nd ed.,** *Boston: Allyn and Bacon, 1983, pp. 389–390. Copyright © 1983 (reprinted by permission).*

to Burack and Mathys (1983). A rumor usually has some element of truth and may be a symptom of a larger problem.

Written vs. Oral Communication

Written communication usually gives the appearance of being more formal and authoritative than oral communication. It tends to be interpreted more accurately, since the same words are communicated to all who receive these messages, and is often used when consistent action is required and a record of the communication is necessary.

A common problem with written communication, however, is proliferation of paperwork that is of questionable importance. Excessive "red tape" in organizations is often the result of excessive requirements for written communication.

Oral communication is usually viewed as more personal and fosters two-way communication. Its major drawback, however, is the distortion that can result. When transmitting factual information in organizations, written communication is generally more effective than oral communication. If information needs to be communicated quickly, oral communication is frequently followed by a confirming written memorandum.

Management Information Systems

The complexities of today's organizations have led to the development of management information systems (MIS) to ensure that the right information is available at the right time. MIS refers to the techniques used to select, store, process, and retrieve information required by management for decision making and control. Computer technology has enabled managers in complex organizations to obtain this information. These systems are designed to fulfill the need for information by identifying *what* information is required *by whom* and at *what time* within the organization.

Telecommunications and word processing capabilities have significantly changed how communication takes place in organizations. Much paperwork and time are saved with the new electronic technology.

An important issue concerning these new systems is the protection of privacy for individuals and organizations. Who can access information and for what purposes are considerations that must be thought through carefully in their design.

SUMMARY

Decision making and communication are the organizational linking processes critical to coordination of activities toward accomplishment of goals. Decision making is the selection of a course of action and communication is the vehicle for transmitting decisions and other information in organizations. The effective manager must be competent in both.

Managers make programmed or routine decisions, which are based on established policies or procedures, and nonprogrammed decisions, which are unstructured decisions having little or no precedent. Lower level managers are involved most frequently in making programmed decisions, whereas upper level managers tend to make primarily nonprogrammed decisions.

The decision making process involves defining objectives, identifying the problem, developing alternatives, selecting alternatives, implementing the alternative selected, and then monitoring implementation. Decisions often are made based on incomplete information or involve factors outside the control of the decision maker. Conditions under which decisions are made are referred to as certainty, risk, and uncertainty. Managers frequently make satisfactory decisions rather than always selecting the optimal alternative because of incomplete information or other factors.

A wide variety of techniques have been developed to assist managers in making decisions. These techniques include decision trees, cost effectiveness analysis, network models, linear programming, game theory, and queuing theory and other types of simulation.

Many decisions in organizations are made by groups rather than by individuals. Group decision making may be appropriate when problems are complex, when adequate time is available, when group acceptance is required, and when group members have information that will assist in decision making. Group decisions tend to be higher in quality in many instances; however, some pitfalls do exist, such as groupthink and risky shift.

Communication plays a role in determining how effectively people work together and coordinate efforts to achieve objectives. Defined as the transmittal of understanding, communication occurs in many forms in organizations and has two dimensions: interpersonal communication and organizational communication. Breakdown in communication may be related to a number of barriers, such as hearing what we expect to hear, ignoring conflicting information, differing perceptions, evaluating the source, interpreting words differently, ignoring nonverbal cues, and becoming emotional. A number of techniques can be used to improve communication; feedback and listening are among the most important.

The effectiveness of organizational communication is influenced by a number of factors, two key ones being the size and complexity of organizations. Downward, upward, horizontal and diagonal communications are aspects of managing communication within organizations. The informal network or grapevine also should be used by the manager to enhance communication within the organization. The complexities of organizations have led to the design of sophisticated communication systems to provide information for decision making and control.

REFERENCES

Balintfy, J. L., Jarret, K., Paige, F., and Sinha, P.: Comparison of Type A-constrained and RDA-constrained school lunch planning computer models. *School Food Serv. Res. Rev.* 4:54, 1980.

Balintfy, J. L., Rumpf, D., and Sinha, P.: The effect of preference-maximized menu on consumption of school lunches. *School Food Serv. Res. Rev.* 4:48, 1980.

Bass, D., and Moore, D.: The body speaks. *Food Mgmt.* 16:39 (Apr.), 1981.

Burack, E. H., and Mathys, N. J.: *Introduction to Management: A Career Perspective*. New York: John Wiley & Sons, 1983.

Chase, R. B., and Aquilano, N. J.: *Production and Operations Management: A Life-Cycle Approach*. Homewood, IL: Richard D. Irwin, 1981.

Driver, M. J.: Individual decision making and creativity. In Kerr, S., ed.: *Organizational Behavior*. Columbus, OH: Grid Publishing, 1979.

Driver, R. W.: Opening the channels of upward communication. *Supervisory Mgmt.* 25:24 (Mar.), 1980.

Fielden, J. S.: "What do you mean you don't like my style?" *Harvard Bus. Rev.* 60:128 (May/Jun.), 1982.

Haimann, T., Scott, W. G., and Conner, P. E.: *Management*. 4th ed. Boston: Houghton Mifflin Co., 1982.

Haney, W. V.: *Communication and Interpersonal Relations*. 4th ed. Homewood, IL: Richard D. Irwin, 1979.

Hanson, P.: The Johari Window: A model for soliciting and giving feedback. *The 1973 Annual Handbook for Group Facilitators*. San Diego, CA: University Associates, 1973.

Hersey, P., and Blanchard, K.: *Management of Organizational Behavior: Utilizing Human Resources*. 4th ed. Englewood Cliffs, NJ: Prentice-Hall, 1982.

Hines, W. W.: Vertical slice: A problem-solving technique. *Training and Dev. J.* 35:96 (Feb.), 1981.

Hughes, R. Y.: A realistic look at decision making. *Supervisory Mgmt.* 25:2 (Jan.), 1980.

Indian, H. D.: Impact of crisis situations on organizational decision-making. *J. Ind. Relations* 16:181, 1980.

Ivancevich, J. M., Donnelly, J. H., and Gibson, J. L.: *Managing for Performance*. 2nd ed. Plano, TX: Business Publications, 1983.

Janis, I. L.: Groupthink. In Staw, B. M., ed.: *Psychological Foundations of Organizational Behavior*. 2nd ed. Glenview, IL: Scott, Foresman & Co., 1983.

Kast, F. E., and Rosenzweig, J. E.: *Organization and Management: A Systems and Contingency Approach*. 3rd ed. New York: McGraw-Hill Book Co., 1979.

Keeney, R. L.: Decision analysis: How to cope with increasing complexity. *Mgmt. Rev.* 68:24 (Sept.), 1979.

Kikoski, J. F.: Communication: Understanding it, improving it. *Personnel J.* 59:126 (Feb.), 1980.

Lesikar, R. V.: A general semantics approach to communication barriers in organization. In Davis, K., ed.: *Organizational Behavior: A Book of Readings*. 5th ed. New York: McGraw-Hill Book Co., 1977.

Lesikar, R. V.: *Communication Theory and Application*. Homewood, IL: Richard D. Irwin, 1976.

Levine, E.: Let's talk: Communicating with the new worker. *Supervisory Mgmt.* 25:12 (Aug.), 1980.

Levine, E. L.: Let's talk: Tools for spotting and correcting communication problems. *Supervisory Mgmt.* 25:25 (Jul.), 1980.

Levine, E. L.: Let's talk: Understanding one-to-one communication. *Supervisory Mgmt.* 25:6 (May), 1980.

Loomba, N. P.: *Management—A Quantitative Perspective*. New York: Macmillan Publishing Co., 1978.

Lopez-Soriano, E. M., Matthews, M. E., and Norback, J. P.: Improving the flow of customers in a hospital cafeteria. *J. Am. Dietet. A.* 79:683, 1981.

Luft, J.: *Group Processes: An Introduction to Group Dynamics.* 2nd ed. Palo Alto, CA: National Press Book Co., 1970.

Magee, J. F.: Decision trees for decision making. *Harvard Bus. Rev.* 42:126 (Jul./Aug.), 1964.

March, J. G., and Simon, H. A.: *Organizations.* New York: John Wiley & Sons, 1958.

Mason, R. O., and Swanson, E. B.: Measurement for management decision: A perspective. *Calif. Mgmt. Rev.* 21:70 (Spring), 1979.

McCaskey, M. B.: The hidden messages managers send. *Harvard Bus. Rev.* 57:135 (Nov./Dec.), 1979.

Middlemist, R. D., and Hitt, M. A.: *Organizational Behavior: Applied Concepts.* Chicago: Science Research Assoc., 1981.

Mintzberg, H.: The manager's job: Folklore and fact. *Harvard Bus. Rev.* 53:49 (Jul./Aug.), 1975.

Monday, R. W., Holmes, R. E., and Flippo, E. B.: *Management: Concepts and Practices.* 2nd ed. Boston: Allyn and Bacon, 1983.

Munter, M.: Beyond words. *The Stanford Magazine* 10:46 (Summer), 1982.

Norback, J. P.: Potential applications of optimization in the food service. *Food Technol.* 36:110, 1982.

Norback, J. P., and Matthews, M. E.: Data structure for integrating quality and cost factors in a food service operation. *J. Food Protection* 44:364, 1981.

O'Reilly, C. A., and Pondy, L. R.: Organizational communication. In Kerr, S., ed.: *Organizational Behavior.* Columbus, OH: Grid Publishing, 1979.

Potter, B. A.: Speaking with authority: How to give directions. *Supervisory Mgmt.* 25:2 (Mar.), 1980.

Raudsepp, E.: Can you trust your hunches? *Admin. Mgmt.* 42:34 (Oct.), 1981.

Rue, L. W., and Byars, L. L.: *Management: Theory and Application.* 3rd ed. Homewood, IL: Richard D. Irwin, 1983.

Samaras, J. T.: Two-way communication practices for managers. *Personnel J.* 59:645 (Aug.), 1980.

Sanders, B. D.: Less talk, better meeting decisions. *Supervisory Mgmt.* 25:34 (Sept.), 1980.

Sayles, L. R., and Strauss, G.: *Human Behavior in Organizations.* Englewood Cliffs, NJ: Prentice-Hall, 1966.

Scanlon, B., and Keys, B.: *Management & Organizational Behavior.* New York, John Wiley & Sons, 1983.

Silverman, B. R. S.: The optimum legibility formula: A written communication system. *Personnel J.* 59:581 (Jul.), 1980.

Spears, M. C.: Concepts of cost effectiveness: Accountability for nutrition, productivity. *J. Am. Dietet. A.* 68:341, 1976.

Stoner, J. A. F.: *Management.* 2nd ed. Englewood Cliffs, NJ: Prentice-Hall, 1982.

Vaden, R., and Vaden, A.: "Come, let us get closer to the fire so we see what it is we are saying." A dialogue on communication. In Vaden, A. G., *Innovative Approaches to Nutrition Education and Related Management Processes.* Manhattan, KS: Kansas State University, 1971.

von Bergen, C. W., and Kirk, R. J.: Groupthink: When too many heads spoil the decision. *Mgmt. Rev.* 67:44 (Mar.), 1978.

Vroom, V. H.: Leadership revisited. In Cass, E. L., and Zimmer, F. G., eds.: *Man and Work in Society.* New York: Van Nostrand Reinhold Co., 1975.

Wycoff, E. B.: Canons of communication. *Personnel J.* 60:208, 1981.

19

Organizational Leadership

What makes a leader effective? This question has been asked numerous times over the years in attempts to understand the concept of leadership. In spite of intensive research, knowledge of what it takes to be an effective leader is still limited. We do know, however, that leaders play a critical role in helping groups, organizations, and even societies achieve their goals. Also, a number of factors affecting managers' effectiveness in attempts to lead organizations have been identified. Leadership is important in all types of organizations; in this chapter, however, we will focus on leadership within the work organization.

In Chapter 3, the leader role was identified as a key aspect of the interpersonal role of managers in organizations. Also, human skill, or the ability to work effectively with others, was identified as critical for managers at all levels of the organization. Human skill includes an understanding of motivation and the application of effective leadership in working with and through people to achieve organizational goals. Human skill was described as effectiveness in working not only within one's own work group but also with other groups in the organization.

Leading was described as one of the functions that managers perform in the process of coordinating activities of the foodservice system. The leading function involves directing and channeling human effort for the accomplishment of objectives. Therefore, leading is concerned with creating an environment in which members of the organizations are motivated to contribute to organizational goals. In other words, leadership is the process of creating a work environment in which people can do their best work.

In this chapter, motivation at work and factors affecting leadership effectiveness will be discussed. Several other issues related to organizational behavior will be examined, such as job satisfaction, power, and philosophies of human behavior.

MOTIVATION AND WORK PERFORMANCE

Motivation is concerned with the causes of human behavior. Understanding of human behavior is important to managers as they attempt to influence this behavior in the work environment. The study of motivation and behavior is a search for answers to perplexing questions about human nature.

Because of the importance of the human element in organizations, managers must have an understanding of human behavior, not only to understand past behavior but also to predict or change future behavior. Highly motivated employees in a foodservice or any other organization can bring about substantial increases in performance and decreases in such problems as absenteeism, turnover, grievances, low morale, and tardiness.

The Meaning of Motivation

Numerous definitions are given for motivation. Usually included are such words as aim, desire, intention, objective, goal, and purpose. A definition commonly quoted is that of Berelson and Steiner (1964): "all those inner striving conditions described as wishes, desires, drives, etc. . . . . It is an inner state that activates or moves."

The process of motivation can be viewed as a causative sequence:

Needs ⟶ Drives or motives ⟶ Achievement of goals

In the motivation process, needs produce motives that lead to the accomplishment of goals or objectives. Needs are caused by deficiencies that may be physical or psychological. Physical needs, also called innate or primary needs, include needs for food, water, and shelter.

Psychological needs, also referred to as acquired needs, are those we learn in response to our culture or environment. They include needs for esteem, affection, or power.

Motives are the "whys" of behavior. They arouse and maintain activity and determine the general direction of an individual's behavior. Hersey and Blanchard

(1982) explain a motive as something within an individual that prompts that person to action.

Achievement of the goal in the motivation process satisfies the need and reduces the motive. When the goal is reached, balance is restored; however, other needs arise, which are then satisfied by the same sequence of events.

A distinction should be made between positive and negative motivation. Motivation can be either a driving force toward some object or condition (positive motivation) or a driving force away from some object or condition (negative motivation).

Goals can be either positive or negative. A positive goal is one toward which behavior is directed—a worker's desire to do the best job possible; a negative goal is one away from which behavior is directed—a worker doesn't want to lose his or her job. Goals depend on an individual's subjective experiences, physical capacity, prevailing norms and values, and the potential accessibility of the goal. Furthermore, an individual's self-perception also serves to influence goals.

Both needs and goals are interdependent, and individuals are not always aware of their needs. In addition, needs and goals are constantly changing. As individuals attain goals, they develop new ones or substitutes if certain goals are not attained. Failure to achieve a goal may lead to feelings of frustration, which in turn may lead to various types of dysfunctional behavior. Some individuals are adaptive and manage to cope; others are less adaptive and regard inability to achieve goals as a personal failure.

Individuals who are blocked in attempts to satisfy their needs or achieve goals may exhibit dysfunctional or defensive behavior. On occasion, all of us employ defensive behavior as a protective function in our attempts to cope with frustration. Some types of defensive behavior have limited negative consequences in the organization, although others may become quite destructive.

Withdrawal, which may be exhibited by apathy, excess absences, lateness, or turnover, is one mechanism used to avoid frustrating situations. Aggression is a common reaction to frustration that involves a direct attack on the source of frustration or on another object or party. For example, a foodservice worker who is upset with his or her supervisor may "slam and bang" the pots and pans as a way of venting frustration.

Substitution occurs when an individual puts something in the place of the original object. For example, a foodservice employee who is bypassed by promotion may seek leadership positions in organizations outside the workplace.

When a person goes overboard in one area or activity to make up for deficiencies in another, the defense mechanism is compensation. Other individuals may revert or regress to childlike behavior as a way of dealing with an unpleasant situation. For example, "horseplay" in the dishroom is an example of regression.

Some individuals repress frustrating situations and problems; in repression, an individual loses awareness of or forgets incidents that cause anxiety or frustration. Projection is another coping behavior in which an individual attributes his or her own feelings to someone else. For example, a foodservice employee who is displeased about a rule or policy may tell the supervisor about how upset another employee is, rather than admit personal dissatisfaction.

Rationalization is probably one of the most common reactions to frustration. This behavior enables an individual to present a reason that is less ego-deflating or more socially acceptable than the true reason. An example of this defense mechanism is a baker blaming the oven for the poor bakery products.

Everyone relies to some extent on defense mechanisms; however, a worker's overreliance on defensive behavior can be minimized if supervisors provide conditions that encourage constructive behavior. Also, managers who understand defensive behavior should have greater empathy and realize that such behaviors are methods of coping with frustration.

Theories of Motivation

A number of theories of motivation have been developed: need hierarchy theory, achievement-power-affiliation theory, two-factor theory, expectancy theory, and reinforcement theory. These theories, described briefly in the following pages, are all different constructs that may prove useful in understanding behavior.

Need Hierarchy Theory

One of the most popular theories of motivation was proposed by Maslow in the 1940s. This theory, frequently referred to as the need hierarchy theory, states that people are motivated by their desire to satisfy specific needs, which are arranged in the following ascending hierarchical order (Figure 19.1).

- *Physiological.* Needs of the human body that must be satisfied to sustain life.
- *Safety.* Needs concerned with the protection of individuals from physical or psychological harm.
- *Social.* Needs for love, affection, belonging.
- *Esteem.* Needs relating to feelings of self-respect and self-worth, along with respect and esteem from one's peers.
- *Self-actualization.* Needs related to one's potential or to the desire to fulfill one's potential.

According to this theory, each need is prepotent or dominant over all higher level needs until it has been partially or completely satisfied. A prepotent need is one that has greater influence over other needs. Also, according to this theory, a satisfied need is no longer a motivator. A prepotent lower order need, however, might not have to be completely satisfied before the next higher one becomes potent or dominant. For example, the safety need may not have to be completely satisfied before social needs become motivators.

In our society, the physiological and safety needs are more easily and generally more satisfied than other needs. Many of the tangible rewards (pay, fringe benefits, etc.) offered by organizations are primarily directed to physiological and safety needs.

The strengths of an individual's needs may shift in different situations. For example, during bad economic times, providing for physiological and safety

MASLOW'S HIERARCHY	EXAMPLES OF METHODS FOR SATISFYING NEEDS
Self-Actualization Needs (Realizing one's potential growth using creative talents)	Challenging work allowing creativity, opportunities for personal growth, and advancement
Esteem Needs (Achievement recognition and status)	Title and responsibility of job, praise and rewards as recognition for accomplishments, promotions, competent management, prestigious facilities
Social Needs (Love, belonging, affiliation, acceptance)	Friendly associates, organized employee activities such as bowling or softball leagues, picnics, parties
Safety Needs (Protection against danger, freedom from fear, security)	Benefit programs such as insurance and retirement plans, job security, safe and healthy working conditions, competent, consistent, and fair leadership
Physiological Needs (Survival needs, air, water, food, clothing, shelter and sex)	Pay, benefits, working conditions

Figure 19.1. ***Maslow's need hierarchy and methods for satisfying needs in organizations.*** **Based on *Hierarchy of Needs in "A Theory of Human Motivation" in* Motivation and Personality, *2nd Edition by Abraham H. Maslow. Copyright © 1970 by Abraham H. Maslow. By permission of Harper & Row, Publishers, Inc.***

needs may dominate an individual's behavior; in good economic times, higher level needs might dominate. Also, different methods may be used by different individuals to satisfy particular needs.

Interesting work and opportunities for advancement are means used by organizations to appeal to higher order needs. Obviously, determining the need level of each individual foodservice worker can be a difficult process; however, managers may find this theory useful in attempting to understand the individual motivations of their employees.

Achievement-Power-Affiliation Theory

In his writing on motivation, McClelland (1961) emphasizes needs that are learned and socially acquired as the individual interacts with the environment. This theory holds that all people have three needs:

- A need to achieve.
- A need for power.
- A need for affiliation.

Achievement Motive. The need for achievement is a desire to do something better or more efficiently than it has been done before. An individual with a high need for achievement tends to be characterized as follows:

- Is goal oriented.
- Seeks a challenge but establishes attainable goals with only a moderate degree of risk.
- Has greater concern for personal achievement than rewards of success.
- Desires concrete feedback on performance.
- Wants to take personal responsibility for finding solutions to problems.
- Has a high energy level and is willing to work hard.

Persons high in the need for achievement tend to gravitate toward managerial and sales positions. In these occupations, individuals are often able to manage themselves and thus satisfy the basic drive for achievement. Individuals with high achievement needs tend to get ahead in organizations because they are producers—they get things done. These individuals are task-oriented and work to their capacity, and they expect others to do the same. As a result, the foodservice manager who has a high need for achievement may sometimes lack the human skills and patience necessary in managing employees with lower achievement motivation.

Power Motive. The need for power is basically a concern for influencing people. An individual with a high power need tends to exhibit the following types of behavior:

- Likes to compete with others in situations that allow him or her to be dominant.
- Is concerned with acquiring and exercising power or influence over others.
- Enjoys confrontation with others.

McClelland and Burnham (1976) identify two aspects of power: positive and negative. Positive use of power is essential for a manager to accomplish results through the efforts of others in an organization. The negative aspect of power is when an individual seeks power for personal benefits, which may be detrimental to the organization.

Affiliation Motive. The need for affiliation is the need to be liked by others and the need to establish or maintain friendly relationships. A person with a high need for affiliation tends to be one who:

- Wants to be liked by others.
- Seeks to establish and maintain friendships.
- Enjoys social activities.
- Is a joiner.

McClelland maintains that most people have a degree of each of these needs but the level of intensity varies. For example, an individual may be high in the need for achievement, moderate in the need for power, and low in the need for affiliation. Managers should recognize these differing needs in dealing with employees. A foodservice employee with a high need for affiliation, for instance, would probably respond positively to warmth and support, whereas an employee with a high need for achievement would tend to respond to increased responsibility or feedback.

Two-Factor Theory

Herzberg (1966) developed a theory of work motivation that has been widely quoted in management literature. This theory is referred to by several names: two-factor theory, dual-factor theory, motivation-hygiene theory, and motivation-maintenance theory. This concept focuses on the rewards or outcomes of performance that satisfy needs.

Two sets of rewards or outcomes are identified—those related to job satisfaction and those related to job dissatisfaction. Those factors related to satisfaction, called motivators, include achievement, recognition, responsibility, advancement, the work itself, and the potential for growth. All of these factors are related to the content of a job.

Those factors related to dissatisfaction, called hygiene or maintenance factors, include pay, supervision, job security, working conditions, organizational policies, and interpersonal relationships on the job. These factors are related to the environment or context of the job.

Based on his research, Herzberg concluded that although employees are dissatisfied by the absence of some job conditions, the presence of those conditions does not cause motivation. These conditions are the hygiene or maintenance factors, since they are necessary to maintain a minimum level of need satisfaction.

In addition, some job factors cause high levels of motivation and job satisfaction when present; however, the absence of these factors may not be highly dissatisfying. This second group of factors, which are internal to the job, are a major source of motivation.

Although Herzberg's research has been considerably criticized, most authorities believe his work has made a major contribution to understanding work motivation. The theory is considered to be most applicable to managerial and professional personnel but may have less application to lower level or manual workers.

An examination of Herzberg's and Maslow's theories of motivation reveals some similarities. Maslow's theory is helpful in identifying the needs or motives; Herzberg's theory provides insights into the goals and incentives that tend to satisfy these needs. The two theories are compared in Figure 19.2. Maslow's physiological, safety, and social needs are hygiene factors. The esteem needs, however, involve both status and recognition. Because status tends to be a function of the position one occupies, and recognition is gained through competence

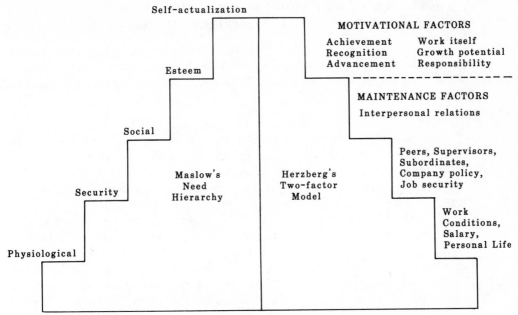

Figure 19.2. *A comparison of Maslow's and Herzberg's models of motivation*

and achievement, esteem needs are related to both hygiene and motivation factors. Self-actualization needs in Maslow's conceptualization are related to Herzberg's motivational factors.

In Chapter 17, we discussed the redesign or enrichment of jobs as a way of increasing employee motivation and satisfaction. Job enrichment, which involves giving workers greater autonomy, more feedback, and more responsibility for work outcomes, has roots in Herzberg's two-factory theory.

Expectancy Theory

Managers should develop an understanding of human needs and the variety of organizational means available to satisfy the needs of employees. The needs approach to motivation, however, does not account adequately for differences among individual employees or explain why people behave in many different ways when accomplishing the same or similar goals.

To explain these differences, several expectancy approaches to motivation have been advanced in the last several years. Two of the most prominent ones were developed by Vroom (1964) and Porter and Lawler (1968). Expectancy theory attempts to explain behavior in terms of an individual's goals, choices, and expectations of achieving these goals. This theory assumes people can determine the outcomes they prefer and make realistic estimates of their chances of attaining them.

Expectancy theory is based on the belief that people act in such a manner as to increase pleasure and decrease displeasure. According to this theory, people are motivated to work if (1) they believe their efforts will be rewarded, and (2) they value the rewards that are being offered. The first requirement can be broken down into two components:

- The expectancy that increased effort will lead to increased performance.
- The expectancy that increased performance will lead to increased rewards.

These expectancies are developed largely from an individual's past experiences.

The second part of expectancy theory is concerned with the value the employee places on the rewards offered by the organization, also referred to as valence. Organizations have tended to assume that all rewards will be valued by employees. Obviously, however, some rewards are more valued than others and certain rewards may be viewed negatively by some employees.

According to this theory, these factors—expectancy and valence—determine motivation, and both must be present for a high level of motivation. In other words, high expectancy or high valence alone will not ensure motivation. For example, if a foodservice employee places a high value on money (high valence) but believes there is little chance of receiving a pay increase (low expectancy), the employee will probably not be highly motivated to work hard because of the low probability of receiving the pay increase.

All employees in an organization do not share the same goals or values regarding pay, promotions, benefits, or working conditions. Therefore, managers must consider an employee's goals and values in attempting to create a motivational climate. A key factor in expectancy theory is what the employee perceives as important or of value—or, "what's in it for me"—not what the manager believes the employee should value.

A major contribution of expectancy theory is that it explains how the goals of employees influence behavior at work. Employee behavior is influenced by assessments of the probability that certain behavior will lead to goal attainment.

Reinforcement Theory

Reinforcement theory, which is associated with Skinner (1971), is often called "operant conditioning" or "behavior modification." Rather than emphasizing the concept of a motive or a process of motivation, these theories deal with how the consequences of a past action influence future actions in a cyclical learning process.

According to Skinner, people behave in a certain way because they have learned at some previous time that certain behaviors are associated with positive outcomes and that others are associated with negative outcomes. Further, because people prefer pleasant outcomes, they are likely to avoid behaviors with unpleasant consequences. For example, foodservice workers may be likely to follow the rules and policies of the organization because they have learned during previous experiences—at home, at school, or elsewhere—that disobedience leads to punishment.

The general concept behind reinforcement theory is that reinforced behavior will be repeated, and behavior that is not reinforced is less likely to be repeated. Reinforcers are not always rewards and do not necessarily have to be positive in nature. The example cited above of the foodservice employee wishing to avoid disciplinary action is an avoidance reinforcer. The current emphasis in management practices is on the use of positive reinforcers, including both tangible and intangible rewards, such as pay increases, promotions, or recognition for good performance.

JOB SATISFACTION

Closely related to motivation is the concept of job satisfaction. In fact, many managers view motivated employees as being synonymous with satisfied employees; however, important differences should be noted. Job satisfaction is concerned with an individual's general attitude about his or her job.

Smith et al. (1969) identify five components of job satisfaction: satisfaction with opportunities for promotion, pay, supervision, the work itself, and coworkers. Other factors, such as attitudes toward life in general, health, age, level of aspiration, social status, self-concept, and other activities, also affect job satisfaction.

Job satisfaction refers to the individual's mental set about the job, which may be positive or negative. It is not synonymous with organizational morale; while morale is related to group attitudes, job satisfaction is concerned with individual attitudes.

Traditionally, managers have believed that satisfied workers will be good workers; the goal, then, was to keep workers "happy." The satisfaction-performance relationship is much more complex, however. Schwab and Cummings (1970) delineate the three dominant points of view:

- Satisfaction $\longrightarrow$ Performance
- Performance $\longrightarrow$ Satisfaction
- Satisfaction $\underline{\quad\quad}?\underline{\quad}\longrightarrow$ Performance

In other words, some theories hold that satisfaction leads to performance, while others contend that performance leads to satisfaction. The third view is that the relationship between satisfaction and performance is moderated or influenced by a number of variables.

Research generally rejects the more popular view that satisfaction causes performance. According to Greene (1972), some evidence provides support for the view that performance causes satisfaction and that the satisfaction-performance relationship is affected by a number of factors. Further, rewards constitute a more direct cause of satisfaction than does performance; also, rewards that are clearly related to current performance influence subsequent performance.

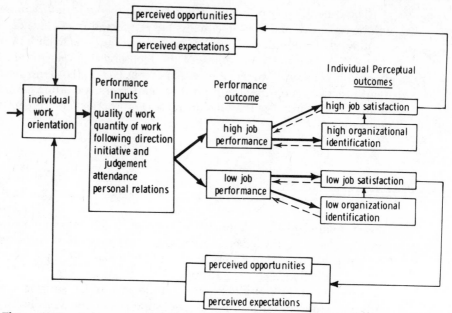

Figure 19.3. *A conceptual model for analyzing work performance in foodservice organizations.* **Source: Hopkins, D. E., Vaden, A. G., and Vaden, R. E.: Some aspects of organization identification among school food service employees. School Food Serv. Res. Rev. 4:40, 1980.**

The complexity of the job satisfaction performance relationship is illustrated in the model in Figure 19.3, which was developed from research on job satisfaction and job performance of foodservice employees (Hopkins et al., 1979). Results of the study on which the model was based showed that higher performers had higher job satisfaction and higher organizational identification, which in turn may affect future job performance. They also showed that expectations and opportunities arise from the job situation that may affect job performance and satisfaction.

Hopkins et al. (1979) found that foodservice workers with high performance ratings on several dimensions (quality of work, initiative, judgment, etc.) were more satisfied with all aspects of their job except pay and promotion (Figure 19.4). The high performing group had longer tenure on the job and were mostly full-time, rather than part-time, workers.

Job satisfaction does have a positive impact on turnover, absenteeism, tardiness, accidents, and grievances (Schwab and Cummings, 1970). Research among foodservice employees indicates job satisfaction should be a concern of managers, even though the relationship to job performance may not be clear. Martin and Vaden (1978) found that satisfaction was lower for workers employed from six months to three years and higher for those employed less than six months or more than three years (Figure 19.5).

Figure 19.4. *Job satisfaction of high- and low-performance foodservice employees.* **Source: Hopkins, D. E., Vaden, A. G., and Vaden, R. E.:** *Some determinants of work performance in foodservice systems.* **Copyright** © **The American Dietetic Association.** *Reprinted by permission from* **Journal of the American Dietetic Association, Vol. 75:640, 1979.**

*Mean job satisfaction scores different at $P \leq .05$.

In general, though, low job satisfaction and high employee turnover have characterized the foodservice industry. Poor working conditions, boredom, limited job opportunities, no recognition for performance, low wages, and poor fringe benefits are among factors believed to contribute to the problems of low job satisfaction and low productivity in the industry.

As Rue and Byars (1983) point out, satisfied employees are preferred if for no other reason than that they make the work situation more pleasant. Also, individual satisfaction tends to lead to organizational commitment. Foodservice employ-

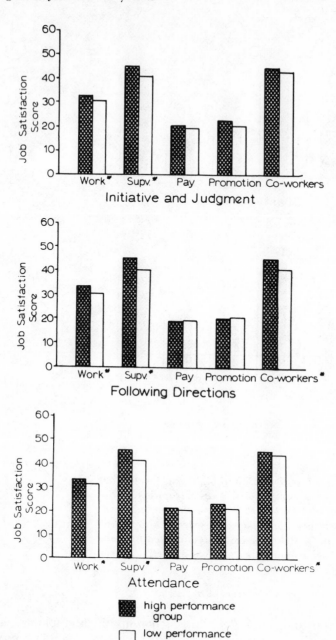

Figure 19.4. *(cont.)*

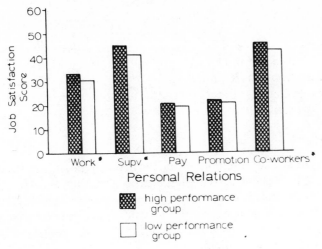

Figure 19.4. (cont.)

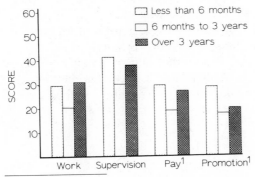

Figure 19.5. *Job satisfaction of foodservice workers according to length of employment.* **Source:** *Martin, P. J. and Vaden, A. G.: Behavioral science research in hospital foodservice. II. Job satisfaction and work values of foodservice employees in large hospitals.* **Copyright © The American Dietetic Association. Reprinted by permission from** Journal of the American Dietetic Association, *Vol. 73:127, 1978.*

ees who like their jobs, supervisors, and other job-related factors, for example, will probably be more loyal employees; those who dislike their jobs will probably be disgruntled by being late or absent, behaving in a disruptive way, or quitting.

Before leaving this topic, an important point must be reiterated—satisfaction and motivation are different concepts. Motivation is a drive to perform, but satisfaction reflects an individual's attitude in a situation. Factors that determine satisfaction with a job differ from those that determine an individual's motivation. Satisfaction is largely determined by conditions in the environment and in the situation; motivation is determined by needs and goals that may be related to expectations and rewards. The result of motivation is increased effort, which in turn increases performance if the individual has the ability and directs effort appropriately. As we pointed out in Chapter 17, foodservice workers in jobs with higher motivating potential tend to be high performers (Shaffer, 1979). The result of satisfaction is increased commitment to the organization, which may or may not result in increased performance.

LEADERSHIP

Leadership is the process of influencing the activities of an individual or group in efforts toward goal achievement in a given situation. As Hersey and Blanchard (1982) point out, from this definition, the leadership process (L) is identified as a function of the leader (1), the follower (f), and other situational (s) variables. This relationship can be expressed as follows:

$$L = f (1, f, s)$$

This definition makes no mention of any particular type of organization. In any situation in which someone is trying to influence the behavior of another individual or group, leadership is occurring; thus, everyone attempts leadership at one time or another in his or her activities at work, in social settings, at home, or elsewhere. As stated previously, our emphasis in this chapter, however, is on leadership in the work organization.

Dynamic and effective leadership is one major attribute that distinguishes successful from unsuccessful organizations. Leaders are those who are willing to assume significant leadership roles and who have the ability to get the job done effectively. The effective organizational leader is one who has the ability to influence people to strive willingly for group objectives.

In Chapter 17, we discussed formal and acceptance authority. From that discussion, leadership is obviously related to acceptance authority. Managers are increasingly finding that subordinates are less willing to follow without question; therefore, a leader today must depend on the acceptance of that leadership by those being led.

Leadership and Power

Leaders possess power and this power has various dimensions. The concept of power is closely related to the concepts of leadership and authority, because power is one of the means by which a leader influences the behavior of followers.

While leadership can be viewed as any attempt to influence, power can be described as a leader's influence potential (Hersey and Blanchard, 1982). Power is the resource that enables a leader to induce compliance or influence others. Some authors distinguish between position power and personal power. Position power relates to that derived from one's official position in an organization, whereas personal power is derived from personal attributes and expertise.

Several other authors have developed more specific power base classifications; the one devised by French and Raven (1959) is probably the most widely accepted. They proposed five bases of power: legitimate, reward, coercive, expert, and referent power. Information power and connection power are two additional bases identified by other authorities (Raven and Kruglanski, 1975; Hersey and Blanchard, 1982). These seven bases of power, or potential means of influencing the behavior of others, are defined as follows.

- *Legitimate power.* This power comes from the formal position held by an individual in an organization; generally, the higher the position, the higher legitimate power tends to be. A leader high in legitimate power induces compliance from others because the followers believe this person has the right to give directions by virtue of his or her position.
- *Reward power.* This power comes from a leader's ability to reward others. Examples of formal rewards are increases in pay, promotions, or favorable job assignments.
- *Coercive power.* This power comes from the authority of the leader to punish those who do not comply. A leader with coercive power can fire, demote, threaten, or give undesirable work assignments to induce compliance from others.
- *Expert power.* This power is held by those leaders who are viewed as being competent in their job. Knowledge gained through education or experience and a demonstration of ability to perform are sources of expert power. A leader high in expert power can influence others because of their respect for his or her abilities.
- *Referent power.* Sometimes called charisma, referent power is based on identification of followers with a leader. A leader high in referent power is generally well liked and admired by others; thus, the leader can influence others because of this identification and admiration.
- *Information power.* This power is based on the leader's possession of or access to information that is perceived as valuable by others. This power influences others either because they need the information or want to be "in on things."
- *Connection power.* This power is based on the leader's "connections" with influential or important persons both inside or outside the organization. A leader high in connection power induces compliance from others who aim at gaining the favor or avoiding the disfavor of the influential connection.

These concepts have application to understanding the power of leaders in any organization, including those in the foodservice industry. We can describe, for example, a hypothetical but typical situation in a country club operation. David Lott, the chef at Stoneyville Country Club, is a highly skilled chef who has responsibility for directing the foodservice operations at the club. Mr. Lott is considered to be fair and consistent but an "all-business" type of supervisor. He is responsible for hiring and firing all foodservice staff and for recommending pay increments and promotions to the club manager.

Mr. Lott's potential means for influencing the foodservice staff, or in other words his power, is derived from the position he holds in the organization. He has legitimate, coercive, and reward power; that is, he is in charge of the foodservice and has authority for punishment and rewards. Also, from the description, we infer that he has expert power because he is described as a "highly skilled" chef; however, describing him as "all-business" implies that his referent power might be limited.

Although all these dimensions of power are important to leaders, expert and referent power tend to be related to subordinates' satisfaction and performance, while coercive is the most negative. Expert and legitimate power appear to be the most important for compliance. In general, depending on the situation, any one of these dimensions is of value to the leader.

Philosophies of Human Nature

The assumptions that managers have regarding other people are major factors determining the climate for motivation. In order to learn how to create an environment conducive to a high level of employee motivation, managers should develop an understanding and philosophy of human nature and an understanding of how this philosophy might influence leadership style. A review of the work of McGregor (1960) and Argyris (1957) is useful in gaining this understanding.

McGregor's Theory X and Theory Y

McGregor stressed the importance of understanding the relationship between motivation and philosophies of human nature. In observing the practices and approaches of managers, McGregor concluded that two views of human nature were predominant. He referred to these views as Theory X and Theory Y. These two distinct views of human nature, one basically negative—Theory X, and the other basically positive—Theory Y, relate to basic philosophies or assumptions that managers hold regarding the way employees view work and how they can be motivated. These philosophies are summarized in Figure 19.6.

Theory X suggests that motivation will be primarily through fear and that the supervisor will be required to maintain close surveillance of subordinates if the organizational objectives are to be attained. Further, the manager must protect the employees from their own shortcomings and weaknesses and, if necessary, goad them into action. While by no means without its supporters, Theory X is not in keeping with more current concepts of behavioral science. Theory Y, in contrast, emphasizes managerial leadership by permitting subordinates to experience personal satisfaction and to be self-directed. These contrasting sets of assumptions lead to different leadership styles among managers and different behaviors among employees.

Managers who hold to the Theory X view tend to be autocratic; managers with a Theory Y philosophy tend to be more participative. In practice, many managers control subordinates closely, not giving them much free reign; in other words, many managers are oriented to Theory X. Burack and Mathys (1983) point out that, correspondingly, current research suggests that many workers carry out the role that they believe represents the manager's view—thus, a Theory X worker. In an analysis and review of McGregor's work, Schein (1975) points out that when workers fail to exhibit behavior consistent with Theory Y assumptions, past management practices and organizational traditions likely have conditioned them to seek their involvement elsewhere.

If one accepts the Theory Y philosophy of human nature, Mondy et al. (1983)

Theory X

1   The average human being has an inherent dislike of work and will avoid it if he/she can.

2   Because of this human characteristic of dislike of work, most people must be coerced, controlled, directed, and threatened with punishment to get them to put forth adequate effort toward the achievement of organizational objectives.

3   The average human being prefers to be directed, wishes to avoid responsibility, has relatively little ambition, and wants security above all.

Theory Y

1   The expenditure of physical and mental effort in work is as natural as play or rest. Depending upon controllable conditions, work may be a source of satisfaction (and will be voluntarily performed) or a source of punishment (and will be avoided if possible).

2   External control and the threat of punishment are not the only means for bringing about effort toward organizational objectives. Man will exercise self-direction and self-control in the service of objectives to which he/she is committed.

3   Commitment to objectives is a function of the rewards associated with their achievement. The most significant of such rewards, e.g., the satisfaction of ego and self-actualization needs, can be direct products of effort directed toward organizational objectives.

4   The average human being learns, under proper conditions, not only to accept but to seek responsibility.

5   The capacity to exercise a relatively high degree of imagination, ingenuity, and creativity in the solution of organizational problems is widely, not narrowly, distributed in the population.

6   Under the conditions of modern industrial life, the intellectual potentialities of the average human being are only partially utilized.

Figure 19.6. *McGregor's Theory X and Theory Y*

suggest that the following managerial practices might be considered seriously: flexible working hours, job enrichment, participative decision making, and abandonment of time clocks. One should not conclude, however, that McGregor advocated Theory Y as the panacea for all management problems. While Theory Y is no utopia, McGregor argued that it provided a basis for improved management and organizational performance.

Argyris's Maturity Theory

Review of the work of Argyris will also assist managers in developing an understanding of human behavior. According to Argyris, a number of changes take place in the personality of individuals as they develop into mature adults over the years (Figure 19.7). Further, these changes reside on a continuum and the "healthy" personality develops along the continuum from immaturity to maturity.

Immaturity	Maturity
Passive	Increased activity
Dependence	Independence
Behave in a few ways	Capable of behaving in many ways
Erratic shallow interests	Deeper and stronger interests
Short time perspective	Long time perspective (past and future)
Subordinate position	Equal or superordinate position
Lack of awareness of self	Awareness and control over self

Figure 19.7. *Argyris's maturity theory*

Argyris questioned the assumption that widespread problems of worker apathy and lack of effort in organizations are simply the result of individual laziness. He suggested that this may not be the case. When people join the work force, he contended that many jobs and management practices are not designed to support the mature personality. Workers may have minimal control over their environment and, thus, are encouraged to be passive, dependent, and subordinate; therefore, they may behave immaturely.

According to Argyris, treating people immaturely is built into traditional organizational principles such as task specialization, chain of command, unity of direction, and span of control. He contended that these concepts of formal organization lead to assumptions about human nature that are incompatible with the proper development of maturity in human personality. In colloquial terms, the Argyris theory can be summarized as follows: management creates "Mickey Mouse" jobs and then is surprised with "Mickey Mouse" behavior.

Argyris challenged management to provide a work climate in which individuals have a chance to grow and mature as individuals while working for the success of the organization. He contended that giving people the opportunity to grow and mature on the job allows employees to use more of their potential. Further, although all workers do not want to accept more responsibility or deal with the problems responsibility brings, the number of employees whose motivation can be improved is much larger than many managers suspect.

The Argyris theory has application to understanding jobs and work behavior in the foodservice industry. Although essential to operations, the industry has many jobs that are routine, repetitive, unchallenging, dirty, and boring. The foodservice manager should not be surprised to find that workers are not "turned on" to such jobs as potwasher, dishwasher, or general kitchen worker. As we pointed out in Chapter 17, some jobs in foodservice organizations have more motivating potential than do others. The challenge to the foodservice manager is to attempt to enrich jobs to the degree possible. We must acknowledge, however, that the potential is limited for making some jobs in the foodservice operation highly motivating and exciting.

Leadership Effectiveness

For many years, the study of leadership concentrated on traits or characteristics essential for effective leadership, particularly focusing on physical attributes and personal qualities. According to Hersey and Blanchard (1982), a review of the research using this trait approach to leadership reveals few significant or consistent findings. The best that can be said is that intelligence, self-confidence, empathy, emotional stability, motivational drive, and the ability to solve problems tend to be associated with effective leaders more often than with those led.

As suggested by the empirical studies already cited in this chapter, effective leadership is now viewed as a dynamic process, varying from situation to situation with changes in leaders, followers, and conditions, rather than being a function of certain traits or characteristics of leaders. These leader behavior or situational approaches are concerned with the behavior of leaders and their group members in various situations.

With this emphasis on behavior and environment, the possibility exists for training individuals in adapting styles of leader behavior to varying situations. Most people can generally increase their effectiveness in leadership roles through education, training, and development.

We have defined leadership as the process of influencing the activities of an individual or a group in efforts toward achievement of objectives in a given situation. In essence, then, leadership involves accomplishing goals with and through people; therefore, a leader must be concerned with both tasks and human relationships. This two-dimensional view of leadership is the basis of current leadership theories. Also, the situational dimension is a third aspect of leadership models.

Basic Leadership Styles

Early studies on leadership identified three basic styles: autocratic, laissez-faire, and democratic (Rue and Byars, 1983). Responsibility for decision making is the key factor differentiating these leadership styles. Generally, the autocratic leader makes most decisions, while the laissez-faire leader allows the group to make the decisions. The democratic leader, however, guides and encourages the group to make decisions.

In the early work on leadership styles, democratic leadership was considered to be the most desirable and productive. Current research does not necessarily support this conclusion; rather, various styles of leadership have been found to be effective in different situations, which will be discussed in more detail later in this chapter. The primary contribution of this early research was the identification of the three basic styles of leadership.

Behavioral Concepts of Leadership

When research shifted from emphasis on personality and physical traits to an examination of leader behavior, the focus was on determining the most effective leadership style, with several concepts proposed. Many of the studies on leader behavior were conducted at the University of Michigan and Ohio State University. Building on the work at Michigan and Ohio State and results from their own research, Blake and Mouton (1964) proposed another leader behavior model, the Managerial Grid.

University of Michigan Leadership Studies. The leadership studies conducted at the Institute for Social Research at the University of Michigan were designed to characterize leadership effectiveness. These studies isolated two major concepts of leadership: employee orientation and production orientation (Kahn and Katz, 1960).

Employee-centered leaders were identified by their special emphasis on the human relations part of their job; whereas production-oriented leaders emphasized performance and the more technical characteristics of work. Results of the Michigan studies showed that supervisors of high producing sections were more likely to:

- Receive general rather than close supervision from their superiors.
- Spend more time in supervision.
- Give general rather than close supervision to their employees.
- Be employee-oriented rather than production-oriented.

Likert (1967), former director of the Institute of Social Research at the University of Michigan, summarized the results of years of leadership research and developed a continuum of leadership styles ranging from autocratic to participative. The four basic systems of management he proposed are as follows:

- *System 1.* Exploitive autocratic.
- *System 2.* Benevolent autocratic.
- *System 3.* Consultative.
- *System 4.* Participative.

Likert examined the characteristics of communication flow, decision making processes, goal setting, control mechanisms, and other operational characteristics of organizations and assessed managerial and leadership styles. The results of these studies indicated that System 4 was the most effective style of management. The emphasis in this management system was on a group participative role with full involvement of the employees in the process of establishing goals and making job-related decisions.

Ohio State Leadership Studies. Beginning in the 1940s, researchers at Ohio State University began a series of in-depth studies on the behavior of leaders in a wide variety of organizations. These studies were conducted about the same time as those at the University of Michigan and used similar concepts. Two dimensions of leader behavior emerged from those studies (Stogdill, 1974): consideration and initiating structure.

<u>Consideration</u> indicates behavior that expresses friendship, develops mutual trust and respect, and develops strong interpersonal relationships with subordi-

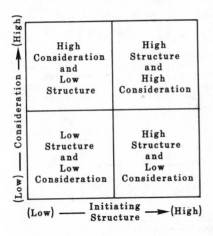

Figure 19.8. *The Ohio State leadership quadrants*

nates. Leaders who exhibit consideration are supportive of their employees, use employee ideas, and allow them to participate frequently in decisions.

Initiating structure indicates behavior that defines work and establishes well-defined communication patterns and clear relationships between the leader and subordinate. Leaders who initiate structure emphasize goals and deadlines, give employees detailed task assignments, and define performance expectations in specific terms.

In studying leader behavior, the Ohio State researchers found that initiating structure and consideration were separate and distinct dimensions; a high score on one dimension does not necessitate a low score on the other. In other words, the behavior of a leader can be described as a mix of both dimensions. In depicting various patterns of leader behavior, the two dimensions were plotted on two axes, which resulted in four quadrants describing four leadership styles (Figure 19.8).

In general, they found that leaders high in initiating structure and consideration for people tended to have higher performing and more satisfied subordinates than did others. They also concluded that the relationship between these dimensions and leader effectiveness is dependent on the group.

Managerial Grid. The two-dimensional view of leadership is the basis for the Managerial Grid developed by Blake and Mouton (1964 and 1978). The two dimensions of the grid are concern for people and concern for production, which are similar to the dimensions of the Ohio State model.

The grid, shown in Figure 19.9, has nine possible positions along the vertical and horizontal axes for a total of 81 possible leadership styles, although five basic styles are generally discussed. The grid has been used widely in organization development and has become so popular among some managers that they refer to the styles by number. For example, 9,9, rather than team manager, is often used to refer to the leader who has high concern for both people and work.

The Managerial Grid was designed to serve as a framework for enabling managers to identify their own management styles and to develop a plan for moving toward a team management style of leadership. The problem with this

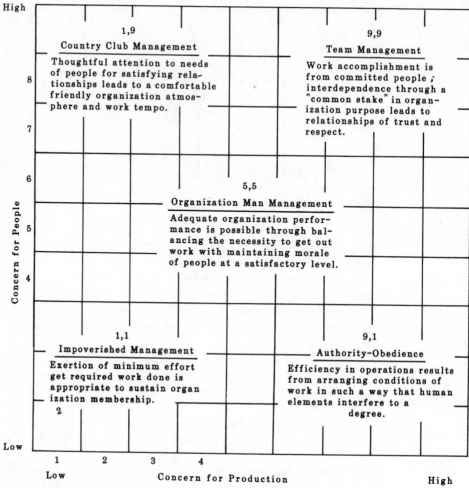

Figure 19.9. *The Managerial Grid®. Source: Blake, R. R., and Mouton, J. S.: The New Managerial Grid®. Houston: Gulf Publishing Co., 1978, p. 11. (Copyright © 1978 by Gulf Publishing Company. Reproduced by permission.)*

model, and the other two-dimensional models of leadership, is that situational factors have been underemphasized.

Situational or Contingency Approaches to Leadership

Situational or contingency approaches emphasize leadership skills, behavior, and roles that are thought to be dependent on the situation. These approaches are based on the hypothesis that behavior of effective leaders in one setting may be substantially different from that in another. The current emphasis in leadership research, which is largely focused on the leadership situation, has shifted because previous attempts to determine characteristics and behaviors that are not effective were inconclusive.

One of the first situational approaches to leadership was developed by Tannenbaum and Schmidt (1958). Fiedler (1967) has also made significant contributions to understanding contingency or situational approaches to leadership. Reddin (1967), and more recently Hersey and Blanchard (1982), have developed situational models of leadership. The path-goal leadership model is another contingency approach.

Leadership Continuum. Tannenbaum and Schmidt (1958) developed a continuum or range of possible leadership behaviors. Each type of behavior is related to the degree of authority used by the manager and the amount of freedom available to subordinates in reaching decisions. The actions range from those in which a high degree of control is exercised to those in which a manager releases a high degree of control.

This continuum was revised and published again in 1973. The revised model, shown in Figure 19.10, reflects two major changes. The interdependencies between the organization and its environment were acknowledged, as shown by the circular addition to the diagram depicting the organizational and societal environment. Also, originally, the terms "boss centered" and "subordinate centered" were used. In revising the model, the terms "manager" and "nonmanager" were substituted to denote functional rather than hierarchical differences. They concluded that power sharing, cooperation, and collaboration needed in organizations today are reflected more clearly in the terms "manager" and "nonmanager" than in "boss" and "subordinate."

Three forces were identified as affecting the leadership appropriate in a given situation:

- Forces in the manager.
- Forces in the subordinates or nonmanagers.
- Forces in the situation.

In Figure 19.11, the factors within each of these forces are listed. These forces differ in strength and interaction in different situations; therefore, one style of leadership is not effective in all situations. In fact, the underlying concept of the continuum is that the manager may employ a variety of approaches, which are dependent on the forces operating in a particular situation.

For example, the foodservice manager who is generally democratic and involves employees in decision making has to take charge in a crisis situation, such as a fire in the kitchen. The manager needs to be directive and authoritarian because of the emergency, even though this is not the style usually preferred by this manager.

Successful leaders are keenly aware of the forces most relevant to their behavior at a given time and are able to act appropriately in relation to other individuals involved in a situation and to the organizational and social environmental forces. In general, however, Tannenbaum and Schmidt encouraged managers to shift toward more participative approaches to decision making. Several benefits identified from more participative styles are that they:

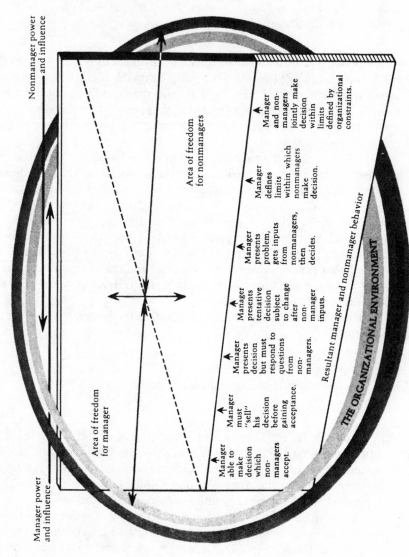

Figure 19.10. *Continuum of manager-nonmanager behavior. Reprinted by permission of the Harvard Business Review. Source: Tannenbaum, R., and Schmidt, W. H.: How to choose a leadership pattern. Harvard Business Review 51:162 (May/June 1973). Copyright © 1973 by the President and Fellows of Harvard College; all rights reserved.*

Forces in the manager	*Forces in nonmanagers*	*Forces in the situation*

Value system:
  How the manager personally feels about delegating
  Degree of confidence in staff
Personal leadership inclinations:
  Authoritarian versus participative
Feelings of security in uncertain situations
	Need for independence:
	  Some people need and want direction while others do not
	Readiness to assume responsibility:
	  Different people need different degrees of responsibility
	Tolerance for ambiguity:
	  Specific versus general directions
	Interest and perceived importance of the problem.
	  People generally have more interest in and work harder on important problems
	Degree of understanding and identification with organizational goals:
	  A manager is more likely to delegate authority to an individual who seems to have a positive attitude about the organization.
	Degree of expectation in sharing in decision making:
	  People who have worked under subordinate-centered leadership tend to resent boss-centered leadership
		Type of organization:
		  Centralized versus decentralized
		Work group effectiveness:
		  How effectively the group works together
		The problem itself:
		  The work group's knowledge and experience relevant to the problem
		Time pressure:
		  It is difficult to delegate to subordinates in crisis situations
		Demands from upper levels of management
		Demands from government, unions, and society in general

Figure 19.11. *Forces in the leadership situation.* **Source: *Tannenbaum, R., and Schmidt, W. H.: How to choose a leadership pattern. Harvard Bus. Rev. 36:95 (Mar./Apr.), 1958.***

- Raise employees' motivational level.
- Increase willingness to change.
- Improve quality of decisions.
- Develop teamwork and morale.
- Further the individual development of employees.

A criticism of the continuum is that managers will be viewed as inconsistent or "wishy-washy" if they react differently in every situation. The key to effective leadership using the continuum, however, is that the leader will behave consistently in situations in which similar forces are operating.

Contingency Approach to Leadership. Fiedler (1967) developed a leadership contingency model in which he defined three major situational variables. In his theory, Fiedler proposed that these three variables seem to determine if a given situation is favorable to leaders:

1 Their personal relations with the members of their group (leader-member relations).

2 The degree of structure in the task assigned to the group (task structure).

3 The power and authority that the leader's position provides (position power).

Fiedler defines the favorableness of a situation as the degree to which the situation enables the leader to exert influence over the group. The most favorable situation for leaders is one in which they are well liked by the members (good leader-member relations), have a powerful position (high position power), and are directing a well-defined job (high task structure). He examined task-oriented and relationship-oriented leadership to determine the most effective style.

In both highly favorable and highly unfavorable situations, a task-oriented leader seems to be more effective. In highly favorable situations, the group is ready to be directed and is willing to be told what to do. In highly unfavorable situations, however, the group welcomes the opportunity of having the leader take the responsibility for making decisions and give directions. In moderately favorable situations, however, a relationship-oriented leader tends to be more effective. Fiedler's work has been important in demonstrating particular styles of leadership that are most effective in given situations.

The Leader Effectiveness Model. Hersey and Blanchard (1982) developed a leadership model that has gained considerable acceptance. In their model, task behavior and relationship behavior are used to describe concepts similar to consideration and initiating structure in the Ohio State studies:

• *Task behavior.* The extent to which leaders are likely to organize and define the roles of group members and to define when, where, and how tasks are to be accomplished.

• *Relationship behavior.* The extent to which leaders are likely to maintain personal relationships between themselves and members of their group by such actions as opening up channels of communication and providing emotional support.

Recognizing that the effectiveness of leaders depends on how their style interrelates with the situation in which they operate, an effectiveness dimension was added to the two-dimensional model based on the Ohio State studies (Figure 19.12). The effectiveness dimension was drawn from the work of Reddin (1967), who contends that a variety of leadership styles may be either effective or ineffective.

By adding the effectiveness dimension to the task and relationship behavior dimensions, Hersey and Blanchard (1982) are attempting to integrate the con-

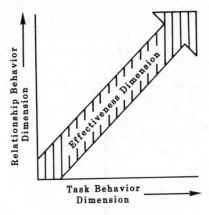

Figure 19.12. *The effectiveness dimension of leadership*

cepts of leader style with situational demands of a specific environment. When the leader's style is appropriate to a given situation, it is termed <u>effective</u>; when the style is inappropriate, it is termed <u>ineffective</u>. The difference between effective and ineffective styles is often not the actual behavior of the leader but the appropriateness of the behavior to the environment in which it is used.

As illustrated in their model (Figure 19.13), leadership style in a particular situation can fall somewhere between extremely effective to extremely ineffective; effectiveness, therefore, is a matter of degree. As summarized in Figure 19.14, the appropriateness of a leader's style in a given situation is related to the reactions of followers, superiors, and associates. The issue of consistency pointed out with the Tannenbaum and Schmidt leadership continuum might also be raised with the effectiveness model. Hersey and Blanchard conclude that consistency is not using the same style all the time; instead, consistency is using the same style for all similar situations and varying the style appropriately as the situation changes.

Not reflected in the discussion thus far is the complexity of the situational variables affecting leadership style. Hersey and Blanchard (1982) summarized the variables that affect leadership styles as follows.

- Leader's style and expectations.
- Followers' styles and expectations.
- Superiors' styles and expectations.
- Associates' styles and expectations.
- Characteristics of the organization.
- Job demands.
- Other situational variables.

The Hersey and Blanchard leadership model is also based on the notion that the most effective style varies according to the level of maturity of the followers, as well as the demands of the situation. <u>Maturity</u> in the work situation is defined as a desire for achievement based on challenging but attainable goals, willingness and ability to accept responsibility, and education or experience and skills rele-

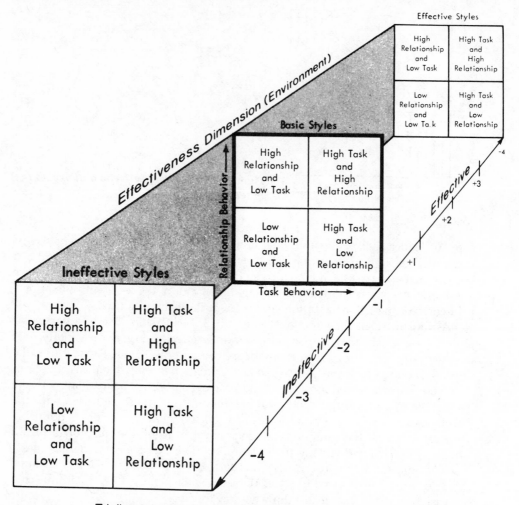

Tri-dimensional leader effectiveness model

Figure 19.13. *Leader effectiveness model.* **Source: Hersey, P., and Blanchard, K. H.: Management of Organizational Behavior: Utilizing Human Resources. 4th ed. Englewood Cliffs, NJ: Prentice-Hall, 1982, p. 98.**

vant to the particular task. They defined four leadership styles appropriate to various maturity levels of followers (Figure 19.15).

Leadership Styles		Maturity Level of Followers	
S1	*Telling*	M1	*Low maturity*
	High task		Unable and unwilling
	and		or
	low relationship		insecure

Basic styles	Effective	Ineffective
High Task and Low Relationship Behavior	Seen as having well-defined methods for accomplishing goals that are helpful to the followers.	Seen as imposing methods on others; sometimes seen as unpleasant and interested only in short-run output.
High Task and High Relationship Behavior	Seen as satisfying the needs of the group for setting goals and organizing work, but also providing high levels of socioemotional support.	Seen as initiating more structure than is needed by the group and often appears not to be genuine in interpersonal relationships.
High Relationship and Low Task Behavior	Seen as having implicit trust in people and as being primarily concerned with facilitating their goal accomplishment.	Seen as primarily interested in harmony; sometimes seen as unwilling to accomplish a task if it risks disrupting a relationship or losing "good person" image.
Low Relationship and Low Task Behavior	Seen as appropriately delegating to subordinates decisions about how the work should be done and providing little socioemotional support where little is needed by the group.	Seen as providing little structure or socioemotional support when needed by members of the group.

Figure 19.14. *Effective and ineffective leadership styles.* **Adapted from** *Reddin, W. J.,* **The 3-D Management Style Theory,** *Theory Paper #2—Managerial Styles. Fredericton, N.B., Canada: Social Sciences Systems, 1967.*

Leadership Styles	Maturity Level of Followers
S2 *Selling* High task and high relationship	M2 *Low to moderate maturity* Unable but willing or confident
S3 *Participating* Low task and high relationship	M3 *Moderate to high maturity* Able but unwilling or insecure
S4 *Delegating* Low task and low relationship	M4 *High maturity* Able/competent and willing/confident

STYLE OF LEADER

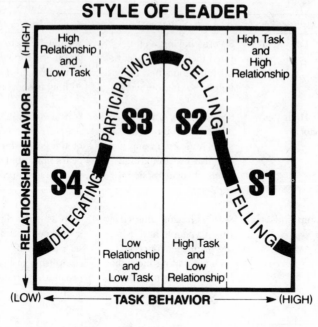

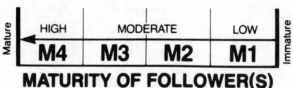

MATURITY OF FOLLOWER(S)

Situational leadership

Figure 19.15. *Relationship of leadership style and maturity of followers.* **Source:** *Hersey, P. and Blanchard, K. H.:* **Management of Organizational Behavior: Utilizing Human Resources.** *4th ed. Englewood Cliffs, NJ: Prentice-Hall, 1982, p. 152.*

In summary, Hersey and Blanchard's leadership effectiveness model provides a useful framework for leadership. Their model suggests that no one best leadership style is appropriate to meet the needs of all situations. Rather, leadership style must be adaptable and flexible enough to meet the changing needs of employees and situations. The effective leader is one who can modify styles as employees develop and change or as required by the situation.

This leadership model has direct application to leadership in foodservice organizations. Situational leadership contends that strong direction with immature followers is appropriate if they are to become productive. As followers reach high levels of maturity, however, the leader should respond not only by decreasing control but also decreasing relationship behavior as well. To apply these concepts, if a foodservice manager is responsible for opening a new unit with a new group of employees who are unaccustomed to working together, the manager, appropriately, should exhibit a directing or telling style of leadership.

After the unit has been in operation several years, and the work group has become accustomed to working as a team, assuming turnover is low and each employee knows his or her job well, a change in leadership style is indicated. A participative or delegating style would probably be more appropriate. The food-service manager, as with any other person in a leadership role, must be flexible in adapting his or her leadership style to changing situations and conditions.

Path-Goal Leadership Model. Another important contingency leadership concept, which focuses on the leader's effect on the subordinate's motivation to perform, was developed by Evans (1970) and House (1971). The model is based on the expectancy concept of motivation, which emphasizes expectancies and valences, previously discussed in this chapter. The path-goal concept focuses on the leader's impact on the subordinate's goals and the paths to achieve those goals.

As you will recall, expectancies are beliefs that efforts will be rewarded and valences are the value or attractiveness of those rewards. Basically, the path-goal theory assumes that individuals react rationally in pursuing certain goals, because those goals ultimately result in highly valued payoffs to the individual.

Leaders may affect employees' expectancies and valences in several ways:

- Assigning individuals to tasks for which they have high valences.

- Supporting employee efforts to achieve goals.

- Tying extrinsic rewards (pay increases, recognition, promotion) to accomplishment of goals.

- Providing specific extrinsic rewards that employees value.

These actions on the part of the leader can increase effectiveness because employees reach higher levels of performance through increased motivation on the job. Additionally, the path-goal theory implies that the degree to which the leader can be effective in eliciting work-goal directed behavior depends on the situation.

The path-goal leadership concept focuses on four types of leader behavior and two situational factors (House and Mitchell, 1974):

- *Directive.* Leadership behavior characterized by providing guidelines, letting subordinates know what is expected from them, setting definite performance standards, and controlling behavior to ensure adherence to rules.

- *Supportive.* Leadership behavior characterized by being friendly and showing concern for subordinates' well-being and needs.

- *Achievement-oriented.* Leadership behavior characterized by setting challenging goals and seeking to improve performance.

- *Participative.* Leadership behavior characterized by sharing information, consulting with employees, and emphasizing group decision making.

The situational factors include subordinates' characteristics, such as locus of control, and characteristics of the work environment, such as structure and complexity of the task. Locus of control refers to the tendency of people to rely on internal or external sources. Internal locus of control is operational with people who attribute task success or failure to their own strengths and weaknesses,

	Situational factors		
Subordinate characteristics	*Characteristics of the work environment*		*Effective leader behaviors*
High need for affiliation			Supportive
High need for security			Directive
Internal locus of control			Participative
External locus of control			Directive
	Structured task		Directive
	Unstructured task		Supportive
High growth need strength	Complex task		Participative and achievement oriented
Low growth need strength	Complex task		Directive
High growth need strength	Simple task		Supportive
Low growth need strength	Simple task		Supportive and directive

Figure 19.16. *Interaction of leader behavior and situational factors.* **Source: Middlemist, R. D., and Hitt, M. A.: Organizational Behavior: Applied Concepts. Chicago: Science Research Associates, 1981, p. 362 (reprinted by permission of the publisher).**

whereas external locus of control is characteristic of people with a tendency to attribute success or failure to the nature of the situation around them.

In Figure 19.16, effective leader behaviors in relation to various situational factors are summarized. As an application of the path-goal concepts, foodservice employees with a high need for affiliation will be more satisfied with a supportive leader; those with a high need for security will be more satisfied with a directive leader. As indicated in the chart, the nature of the task also influences the leadership behavior appropriate to a given situation.

Implications of Leadership Theories

From this discussion of leadership theories, one might believe that being a truly effective leader is almost impossible. Although effective leadership is difficult to achieve, it is possible. Managers must exercise effective leadership to be effective, and many managers have been able to do so.

A common thread emerges from observations of effective leaders in all types of organizations. Successful leaders have either analyzed situational factors and adapted their leadership style to them, or changed the factors so an effective style-situation match resulted.

This overview of the leadership literature should make one major conclusion obvious—there is no one best style of leadership. The notion that a most effective style is possible should be seen as unrealistic and overly simplistic. Instead, leadership should be seen as a function of forces in the leader, in the followers, and in the situation. A range of leader behaviors can be effective or ineffective, depending on styles and expectations of superiors, followers, and associates, as well as on job demands and organizational characteristics.

The successful leader must have a concern for both tasks and people in the work situation, since leadership is defined as a process of influencing activities of individuals in efforts toward goal achievement. Thus, flexibility and adaptability to changing conditions and situations is an underlying concept of effective leadership in all types of organizations.

EMERGING CONCEPTS IN ORGANIZATIONAL LEADERSHIP

Is it possible to enhance employee motivation, increase job satisfaction, and improve productivity all at the same time? This question poses a significant challenge for foodservice managers and for managers in all types of organizations.

Increasingly, America's more highly educated work force has expectations for jobs that not only provide for basic needs but also allow for satisfaction of needs for achievement, growth, recognition, and self-fulfillment. Another important challenge is increasing the productivity of the American worker by finding ways to "unlock potential that exists in the overwhelming majority of the work force" (Guest, 1981).

During the past decade, the decline in the productivity growth rate in the United States compared to most other industrialized nations has been a concern. In the foodservice industry, low productivity has been a long-standing problem. Job satisfaction of workers in all types of organizations has declined over the past couple of decades. As a result, managers are searching for approaches to deal with these problems.

Japanese Management

Since World War II, Japan has experienced increased prosperity, job security, and growing, successful, and stable business organizations. Seeking to discover the secrets of Japan's high productivity has become almost an obsession in U.S. organizations. New books and articles on Japanese management are appearing almost daily.

Among those looking to the Japanese model for answers to problems of American organizations have been Ouchi and Pascale and Athos (1981). Ouchi's studies of Japanese organizations led him to infer a style he calls Theory Z.

The Theory Z approach to management suggests that involved workers are the keys to increased productivity. Ouchi describes Type Z organizations as having a general pattern of long-term employment, frequent and explicit performance reviews, a balance between quantitative techniques and subjective judgments based on experience, and a "family-type" environment.

In contrasting Japanese and American organizations, Ouchi found many

Japanese organizations	vs.	American organizations
Lifetime employment		Short-term employment
Slow evaluation and promotion		Rapid evaluation and promotion
Non-specialized career paths		Specialized career paths
Implicit control mechanisms		Explicit control mechanisms
Collective decision making		Individual decision making
Collective responsibility		Individual responsibility
Wholistic concern		Segmented concern

Figure 19.17. *Comparison of Japanese and American companies.* **Source: Ouchi, W. G.: Theory Z: How American Business Can Meet the Japanese Challenge.** *Reading, MA: Addison-Wesley, 1981, pp. 48–49. Reprinted with permission.*

differences (Figure 19.17). He proposes that American organizations seeking to improve productivity and quality of output would do well to incorporate some of the Theory Z characteristics. The most important change would be the involvement of employees at all levels of the organization. Another intriguing lesson from the art of Japanese management, and one that is close in spirit to Theory Z, according to Ouchi, is the quality control circle we discussed in Chapter 13.

In their discussion of lessons from the Japanese, Pascale and Athos describe well-managed companies as having superordinant goals expressed in terms of the firm's responsibility to its employees, to its customers, and to the surrounding community. The most effective firms link their purposes and ways of realizing them to human values as well as to economic measures.

Attributes of Successful Organizations

In their analysis of management excellence, Peters and Waterman (1982) identified several characteristics of continuously innovative and successful large American corporations. Eight attributes emerged to characterize these organizations:

- *A bias for action.* Even though the excellent companies examined are analytical in their approach to decision making, they are not paralyzed by that fact. The standard operating policy appears to be "do it, fix it, try it."

- *Close to the customer.* These companies learn from the people they serve and provide unparalleled quality, service, and reliability.

- *Autonomy and entrepreneurship.* The innovative companies foster many leaders and innovators throughout the organization, encourage practical risk-taking, and support "good tries."

- *Productivity through people.* The excellent companies treat the "rank and file" as the source of gains in quality and productivity.

- *Hands-on, value driven.* The philosophy of these organizations has more to do with values and achievements than technological and economic resources and organization structure. Personal attention, persistence, and direct intervention are characteristic behaviors of managers at all levels.
- *Stick to the knitting.* With a few exceptions, the excellent performing companies seem to stay reasonably close to operations and products they know.
- *Simple form, lean staff.* The underlying structural forms and systems in the excellent companies are relatively simple and corporate staffs tend to be small in relation to the size of the company.
- *Simultaneous loose-tight properties.* The excellent companies are both centralized and decentralized. These organizations are, on the one hand, rigidly controlled yet at the same time allow autonomy and innovation among the rank and file. Painstaking attention to detail is characteristic.

Interestingly, several companies in the food industry and the service industry are among the 62 companies identified as America's best-run companies. In the consumer goods category, Frito-Lay (Pepsico) and General Foods are included. McDonald's and Marriott are among those in the service classification.

Peters and Waterman indicate that although all eight attributes were not present or conspicuous to the same degree in all the excellent companies, in every case these attributes were clearly visible and quite distinctive. One of their primary conclusions can be applied to all types of organizations in the foodservice industry, not only to those in the profit sector. They contend that too many managers have lost sight of the basics: quick action, service to customers, practical innovation, and the need for widespread commitment in organizations.

Current Organizational Concepts

Common threads that seem to emerge from the discussion of current approaches to leadership, Japanese management, and characteristics of excellently run companies is the need for innovation and for dynamic, flexible leadership in organizations. As stated by Zalenik (1977) in contrasting leaders and managers, leaders develop "fresh" approaches to long-standing problems and open issues for new options. Leaders create excitement and work from high-risk positions, especially when opportunity and reward appear high. He contends that leaders search out opportunities for change.

Maccoby (1981) proposes some similar ideas of leadership for today's organizations. In his view, leadership is needed to develop consensus and revitalize organizations in democratic ways. He describes successful leaders as intelligent, ambitious, optimistic, and persuasive communicators who tend to have critical views of traditional authority. But, Maccoby says, they are also caring and flexible and use participative approaches, willing to share power, and concerned about self-development and development of others.

Another characteristic that appears to be emerging in successful organizations is the trend away from rigid hierarchical structures. A management system based on the networking model appears to be evolving (Naisbitt, 1982). As defined by Naisbitt, <u>networks</u> are people talking to each other, sharing ideas, information, and resources. Lateral, diagonal, and bottom-up communications are characteristic. Organizations are being restructured into smaller, more participatory units. The organizations examined by Ouchi and Peters and Waterman appear to be based somewhat on a network model.

Open communication, participation in decision making, and receptivity to change and innovation appear to be characteristics of successful organizations. Concern for employees and customers and a strong feeling of social responsibility are attributes of effective managers. Further, a commitment to quality and a penchant for action in all aspects of operations appear to be components of a successful managerial style.

SUMMARY

Leadership is a key aspect of the interpersonal role of managers in organizations. Human skill, an important skill for effective management, includes an understanding of motivation and human behavior and the application of effective leadership in working with and through people to achieve organizational objectives.

Motivation is concerned with the causes of human behavior. In the motivation process, needs produce motives that lead to the accomplishment of goals or objectives. Needs and goals are constantly changing and individuals blocked in an attempt to satisfy needs may exhibit dysfunctional behavior in a workplace.

A number of theories of motivation have been developed, which include need hierarchy theory, achievement-power-affiliation theory, two-factor or motivation-hygiene theory, expectancy theory, and reinforcement theory. Understanding of these theories will assist the foodservice manager in understanding human motivation.

Closely related to motivation is the concept of job satisfaction; however, these concepts are different. While motivation is a drive to perform, satisfaction reflects an individual's attitude in a situation. Job satisfaction is affected by a number of factors such as poor working conditions, limited job opportunities, and ineffective leadership. Even though the relationship of satisfaction and job performance may not be clear, job satisfaction does have a positive impact on turnover, absenteeism, tardiness, accidents, and grievances. Therefore, foodservice managers should be concerned about job satisfaction of employees, if for no other reason than because the work situation is more pleasant with satisfied employees.

Leadership is the process of influencing the activities of an individual or group in efforts to achieve goals in a given situation. Dynamic leadership is a key to the success of organizations.

Power is a concept related to leadership and is one means by which a leader influences the behavior of followers. Power, described as a leader's influence potential, has several dimensions: legitimate, reward, coercive, expert, referent, information, and connection power. Depending on the situation, any one of these dimensions is of value to a leader.

The assumptions that managers have regarding other people are factors determining the climate of motivation. Managers should develop an understanding and philosophy of human nature and an understanding of how this philosophy will influence leadership style.

Earlier leadership studies concentrated on traits or characteristics essential for effective leadership; however, few significant or consistent findings emerged. The current emphasis is on the behavior of leaders and their group members in various situations. Effective leadership is viewed as a dynamic process varying from situation to situation with changes in leaders, followers, and conditions.

Decreasing productivity and declining job satisfaction have led managers to seek new approaches to managing organizations. Japanese management is among those being examined. Also, identification of attributes of successful corporations in this country has been a thrust of authorities in the management field.

REFERENCES

Argyris, C.: *Personality and Organization*. New York: Harper & Row Publishers, 1957.

Berelson, B., and Steiner, G. A.: *Human Behavior*. New York: Harcourt Brace Jovanovich, 1964.

Blake, R. R., and Mouton, J. S.: *The Managerial Grid*. Houston: Gulf Publishing Co., 1964.

Blake, R. R., and Mouton, J. S.: *The New Managerial Grid*. Houston: Gulf Publishing Co., 1978.

Burack, E. H., and Mathys, N. J.: *Introduction to Management: A Career Perspective*. New York: John Wiley & Sons, 1983.

Evans, M. G.: The effects of supervisory behavior on the path-goal relationship. *Organ. Behav. and Human Perf.* 5:277, 1970.

Fiedler, F. E.: *A Theory of Leadership Effectiveness*. New York: McGraw-Hill Book Co., 1967.

Flowers, V. S., and Hughes, C. L.: Choosing a leadership style. *Personnel* 13:48, 1978.

French, J. R. P., and Raven, B.: The bases of social power. In Cartwright, D., ed.: *Studies in Social Power*. Ann Arbor: Univ. of Michigan, Institute for Social Research, 1959.

Greene, C. N.: The satisfaction-performance controversy. *Bus. Horizons* 15:31 (Oct.), 1972.

Guest, R. H.: Review of work redesign. *Harvard Bus. Rev.* 59:46 (Jan./Feb.), 1981.

Hersey, P., and Blanchard, K. H.: *Management of Organizational Behavior: Utilizing Human Resources*. 4th ed. Englewood Cliffs, NJ: Prentice-Hall, 1982.

Herzberg, F.: One more time, how do you motivate employees? *Harvard Bus. Rev.* 46:53 (Jan./Feb.), 1968.

Herzberg, F.: The wise old Turk. *Harvard Bus. Rev.* 52:70 (Sept./Oct.), 1974.

Herzberg, F.: *Work and the Nature of Man*. Cleveland: World Publishing, 1966.

Hopkins, D. E., Vaden, A. G., and Vaden, R. E.: Some aspects of organization identification among school food service employees. *School Food Serv. Res. Rev.* 4:34, 1980.

Hopkins, D. E., Vaden, A. G., and Vaden, R. E.: Some determinants of work performance in foodservice systems: Job satisfaction and work values of school foodservice personnel. *J. Am. Dietet. A.* 75:640, 1979.

House, R. J.: A path-goal theory of leader effectiveness. *Admin. Science Q.* 16:324 (Sept.), 1971.

House, R. J., and Mitchell, T. R.: Path-goal theory of leadership. *J. Contemporary Bus.* 3:81, 1974.

Kahn, R., and Katz, D.: Leadership practices in relation to productivity and morale. In Cartwright, D., and Zander, A., eds.: *Group Dynamics: Research and Theory.* Elmsford, NY: Row Peterson, 1960.

Karlins, M.: *The Human Use of Human Resources.* New York: McGraw-Hill Book Co., 1981.

Lester, R.: Leadership: Some principles and concepts. *Personnel J.* 60:868 (Nov.), 1981.

Likert, R.: *The Human Organization.* New York: McGraw-Hill Book Co., 1967.

Maccoby, M.: *The Leader. A New Face for American Management.* New York: Simon & Schuster, 1981.

Martin, P. J., and Vaden, A. G.: Behavioral science research in hospital foodservice. II. Job satisfaction and work values of foodservice employees in large hospitals. *J. Am. Dietet. A.* 73:127, 1978.

Maslow, A. H. *Motivation and Personality.* 2nd ed. New York: Harper & Row, 1970.

Maslow, A. H.: A theory of human motivation. *Psychol. Rev.* 50:370, 1943.

McClelland, D. C.: *The Achieving Society.* New York: The Free Press, 1961.

McClelland, D. C., and Burnham, D. H.: Power is a great motivator. *Harvard Bus. Rev.* 54:100 (Mar./Apr.), 1976.

McGregor, D.: *The Human Side of Enterprise.* New York: McGraw-Hill Book Co., 1960.

Meyer, M. C.: Demotivation—Its cause and cure. *Personnel J.* 57:260, 1978.

Middlemist, R. D., and Hitt, M. A.: *Organizational Behavior: Applied Concepts.* Chicago: Science Research Assoc., 1981.

Mondy, R. W., Holmes, R. E., and Flippo, E. B.: *Management: Concepts and Practices.* 2nd ed. Boston: Allyn and Bacon, 1983.

Naisbitt, J.: *Megatrends: Ten New Directions Transforming Our Lives.* New York: Warner Books, 1982.

Nebel, E. C.: Motivation, leadership and employee performance: A review. *Cornell Hotel Restaur. Admin. Q.* 19:62, 1978.

Ouchi, W. G.: *Theory Z: How American Business Can Meet the Japanese Challenge.* Reading, MA: Addison-Wesley, 1981.

Pascale, R., and Athos, A.: *The Art of Japanese Management: Applications for American Executives.* New York: Simon & Schuster, 1981.

Pascale, R. T.: Zen and the art of management. *Harvard Bus. Rev.* 56:153 (Mar./Apr.), 1978.

Peters, T. J.: Leadership: Sad facts and silver linings. *Harvard Bus. Rev.* 57:164 (Nov./Dec.), 1979.

Peters, T. J., and Waterman, R. H.: *In Search of Excellence: Lessons from America's Best-Run Companies.* New York: Harper & Row, 1982.

Porter, L. W., and Lawler, E. E.: *Managerial Attitudes and Performance.* Homewood, IL: Irwin-Dorsey, 1968.

Raven, B. H., and Kluganski, W.: Conflict and power. In Swingle, P. G., ed.: *The Structure of Conflict.* New York: Academic Press, 1975.

Reddin, W. J.: The 3-D management style theory. *Training Dev. J.* 21:8 (Apr.), 1967.

Rue, L. W., and Byars, L. L.: *Management: Theory and Application.* 3rd ed. Homewood, IL: Richard D. Irwin, 1983.

Schein, E. H.: In defense of Theory Y. *Organizational Dynamics* 4:17 (Summer), 1975.

Schwab, D. P., and Cummings, L. L.: Theories of performance and satisfaction: A review. *Ind. Relations* 9:408, 1970.

Shaffer, J. G.: Job design in conventional and highly technical hospital foodservice systems. M. S. thesis, Kansas State University, 1979.

Skinner, B. F.: *Beyond Freedom and Dignity*. New York: Alfred A. Knopf, 1971.

Smith, P. C., Kendall, L. M., and Hulin, C. L.: *The Measurement of Satisfaction in Work and Retirement: A Strategy for the Study of Attitudes*. Chicago: Rand McNally & Co., 1969.

Steers, R. M., and Porter, L. W.: *Motivation and Work Behavior*. 2nd ed. New York: McGraw-Hill Book Co., 1979.

Stogdill, R. M.: *Handbook of Leadership*. New York: The Free Press, 1974.

Swartz, R. L., and Vaden, A. G.: Behavioral science research in hospital foodservice. I. Work values of foodservice employees in urban and rural hospitals. *J. Am. Dietet. A.* 73:120, 1978.

Tannenbaum, R., and Schmidt, W. H.: How to choose a leadership pattern. *Harvard Bus. Rev.* 36:95 (Mar./Apr.), 1958. Retrospective commentary 51:162 (May/Jun.), 1973.

Terpstra, D. E.: Theories of motivation—Borrowing the best. *Personnel J.* 58:376, 1979.

Vroom, V.: *Work and Motivation*. New York: John Wiley & Sons, 1964.

Zaleznik, A.: Managers and leaders: Are they different? *Harvard Bus. Rev.* 55:67 (May/Jun.), 1977.

20
Management of Personnel

The most important resources in an organization are its human resources. The collective efforts, talent, creativity, initiative, knowledge, and skills of people in the organization are critical to organizational effectiveness. Thus, staffing is an essential management function, and the selection, training, and development of people are among the most important tasks of a manager. Without competent people at the managerial and all other levels, organizations either have difficulty in achieving appropriate goals or pursue inappropriate goals.

As discussed in Chapter 4, staffing is a management function concerned with the recruitment, selection, placement, training, and development of organization members. In other words, staffing is concerned with bringing human resources into the system and maintaining the work force. Like other management functions, it is performed by managers continuously, sometimes in an independent way but often in collaboration with a personnel department.

HUMAN RESOURCE PLANNING

Human resource planning is the first step in the staffing process and is concerned with ensuring that the personnel needs of the organization will be met constantly and appropriately. It involves estimating the size and composition of the future work force; in other words, forecasting. The four components of a human resource planning system include:

- *Human resource inventory.* Assessing the skills, abilities, and potential of current staff in an organization.
- *Forecasting.* Predicting future personnel requirements.
- *Human resource plans.* Developing strategies for recruiting, selecting, placing, and promoting personnel.
- *Development plans.* Assuring that a continuous supply of trained managers is ready to fill vacant and new positions.

The human resource or personnel planning process attempts to define the human resources necessary to meet the organization's objectives. The integration of personnel planning with organizational planning is important because having the right people at the right time has a major impact on the overall success or failure of the organization.

Both external and internal factors affect human resource planning. A strategy for expansion will mean that additional personnel will have to be hired, but the external environment will affect the labor force. In a booming economy, fewer job candidates may be available because unemployment may be low; in a depressed economy, organizations may have to cut back on operations and consequently on the number of employees. Technological changes will affect the type of specialized personnel an organization will require. Thus, the organization's internal and external environment will define the limits within which a human resource plan must operate.

Human Resource Inventory

Through the process of job analysis, which was discussed in Chapter 17, the nature of the specific jobs in an organization are determined. As you recall, job descriptions and job specifications are the end products of job analysis. A job description identifies the tasks, duties, activities, and the performance results of a particular job. A job specification identifies the skills, abilities, and attributes necessary for performance in a job. With such an analysis, an organization can define its human resource needs on the basis of current or newly created jobs.

Combining the information from job analyses and a skills inventory—basic information on all employees in an organization—enables an organization to evaluate the present status of its human resources. In addition, anticipated changes in the work force due to retirements, promotions, and transfers can be projected. Patten (1972) outlines seven categories of information to be included in a skills inventory:

1 *Personal data history.*

2 *Skills.* Education, experience, training.

3 *Special qualifications.* Memberships in professional groups, special achievements, etc.

4 *Salary and job history.* Present and previous salaries, dates of increments, jobs held, etc.

5 *Company data.* Benefit plan data, retirement information, seniority, etc.

6 *Capacity of individual.* Test scores, health information, etc.

7 *Special preferences of individual.* Location or job preferences, etc.

Human Resource Forecasting

Human resource forecasting involves determination of the number, type, and qualifications of individuals who will be needed to perform specific duties at a certain time. Some of the many variables to be considered in forecasting human resource needs include composition of the current work force, technological changes, general economic conditions, skills required in potential new ventures, and anticipated changes in volume. For example, a fast food chain that has plans for opening 50 new units during the next year must be concerned with the human resource needs as well as the construction of the facilities and the marketing strategies.

Human Resource and Development Plans

Personnel planning involves determination of how the organization can obtain the quantity and quality of human resources to meet its objectives, as reflected by the personnel forecast. This phase of human resource planning includes activities involved with recruiting and selecting new employees, developing current and new employees, promoting or transferring employees, laying off employees, and discharging employees. In determining how forecasted human resources will be obtained, organizational policies on promotion, transfers, layoffs, and discharges must be considered. Generally, the coordination of these activities is delegated to a personnel department.

If an organization is unionized, union contracts influence personnel planning if they include clauses on regulating transfers, promotions, and discharges. Government legislation also plays a vital role in personnel planning. Four significant pieces of legislation that affect personnel planning are the Equal Pay Act of 1963, the Civil Rights Act of 1964, the Age Discrimination and Employment Act of 1967 as amended in 1978, and the Federal Rehabilitation Act of 1973.

The Equal Pay Act, which become effective in June, 1964, prohibits wage discrimination on the basis of sex; the Civil Rights Act of 1964 is designed to eliminate discrimination in employment related to race, color, religion, sex, or national origin. The 1978 Civil Rights Act Amendment prohibits discrimination because of pregnancy, childbirth, or related medical conditions. The Age Discrimination and Employment Act was initially designed to protect individuals between the ages of 40 and 65 from discrimination in hiring, retention, compensation, and other conditions of employment. The 1978 amendment extended coverage to individuals up to age 70. The Federal Rehabilitation Act prohibits discrimination in hiring of the handicapped by federal agencies and federal contractors. If a hospitality or foodservice facility is a government contractor, the Federal Rehabilitation Act applies to its employment practices as well. Also, government operated facilities, such as hospitals operated by the Veterans Administration, are covered by the provisions of this legislation. According to Stokes (1979), the legislation in many states includes protection in employment practices for those physically and mentally handicapped.

The handicapped—physically, mentally, or socially—have been rejected for employment in many instances because of the mistaken belief they might be unable to perform many jobs effectively. Physical handicaps may constitute limitations only with respect to specific job requirements. By making minor changes in layout or restructuring job duties, job openings that utilize the abilities of handicapped persons can be created.

Often, employers are reluctant to hire those who are mentally retarded or emotionally disturbed. If placed in the proper jobs and given the type of assistance and supervision needed, these individuals can be valuable members of the work force. In fact, in the foodservice industry the mentally retarded have been placed successfully in many of the routine, repetitive jobs, particularly those in prepreparation and sanitation.

Individuals with criminal records often have problems finding employment as well. Recognizing that exconvicts should have an opportunity to earn a livelihood to avoid recidivism, government agencies and other organizations are assisting these individuals to obtain jobs and become functioning members of society.

In personnel planning, foodservice managers should not overlook these groups of employees. To assist organizations in utilizing the skills of individuals with various kinds of handicaps, services are available from state rehabilitation departments. These services include helping employers to develop positions for the handicapped and also assisting and counseling on problems that may be encountered in orienting and supervising handicapped persons.

THE EMPLOYMENT PROCESS

The employment process includes the recruitment, selection, and placement, as well as the orientation and initial training for new personnel in an organization— all based on the data and other information generated in human resource planning. These employment functions involve cooperative efforts between line managers and personnel staff, although in a small organization the line manager may have total responsibility.

Recruitment

Recruitment includes the activities of seeking and attracting a supply of people from which qualified candidates for job vacancies can be selected. Recruiting is a crucial step in staffing the organization. The amount of recruitment that must be done is determined by the difference between the forecasted personnel needs and the talent available within the organization, as identified by the skills inventory.

Types of Recruiting

General recruiting takes place when the organization needs a group of workers of a certain kind—for example, cooks, or typists—and is usually most appropriate for operational or clerical employees. Comparatively simple standardized procedures are followed in general recruiting. Specialized recruiting, which is used mainly for higher level managers or staff specialists, occurs when the organization needs a particular type of individual.

An important part of the recruiting process is the job description or the position description, which is the term often used for managerial level jobs. The job specification is also important, since it includes a statement of the qualifications an individual must have for the job vacancy.

Recruitment takes place within a labor market, the pool of people available with the needed skills to fill the job vacancies in the organization. The labor market is dynamic and constantly changing.

After the decision to recruit has been made, the sources of supply must be explored. The sources will vary according to the availability of people in the labor pool and the nature of the positions to be filled.

Sources of Applicants

Promotion from Within. One of the best sources for job openings is an organization's own employees. Promotion from within, a policy in many organizations, has several advantages. Employee morale and motivation are positively affected by internal promotions, assuming such promotions are perceived as being equitable. Organizations have a sizable investment in their employees; therefore, using the abilities of present employees to their fullest extent improves the return on this investment. Recruitment or promotion from within is usually less expensive than hiring from outside the organization. And individuals recruited from within will be familiar with the organization and therefore may need less training and orientation.

Certain potential pitfalls must be acknowledged, however, with regard to a policy of promotion from within. One danger, popularized as the Peter Principle (Peter and Hall, 1969), is that managers tend to be promoted to their level of incompetence. According to this principle, successful managers are promoted until they reach a level at which they are unable to perform. This problem commonly occurs when persons are promoted on the basis of performance on one job when requirements may be very different in the higher level job. For example, a production supervisor may be promoted to unit manager because of excellent job performance in supervising production employees and operations. This same individual, however, may fail as unit manager of the foodservice operation because his or her scope of skills and knowledge may be inadequate for this higher level position.

A second danger of promoting from within is the problem of inbreeding of ideas. New ideas and innovations are sometimes stifled when most or all vacancies are filled from within. Also, complacency may be encouraged if employees believe that seniority will assure promotions.

A number of methods are used for recruiting from within. Seniority lists of persons eligible for job openings may be compiled. Vacancy notices may be posted on bulletin boards or published in newsletters and employees invited to bid on vacant positions. Qualified candidates, who might otherwise be overlooked, may be located with this method of internal recruitment.

External Sources. A wide range of external sources are available for obtaining personnel. One of the most widely used is "help wanted" advertisements in newspapers. For managerial personnel and staff specialists, recruitment on college and university campuses is a common practice.

Other sources include both public and private employment agencies, employee referrals, labor unions, high schools, vocational schools, community colleges, unsolicited applications, and management consulting firms. Specialized executive search services are sometimes used by large corporations for recruiting top level managers. Advertisements in trade and professional journals are also important sources for recruiting managerial and professional personnel.

In state and federal government agencies and in some cities and counties, the selection of individuals to fill job openings is made from lists or registers of eligible candidates. These lists contain the names of those who meet the qualifications and who received passing grades on any required examinations. Ordinarily, three to five names at the top of the register are provided to the administrator in the department or unit in which the vacancy occurs. These provisions of governmental civil service systems give administrators some latitude in making a selection and at the same time preserve the merit system.

A prerequisite for effective recruitment is that the organization must have identified requirements for the jobs it is attempting to fill. In public and in other types of nonprofit organizations, search committees are frequently appointed to clarify a job description and conduct the recruitment and screening process for professional level personnel.

In all recruitment activities, organizations must be cognizant of the legal requirements. As pointed out by Stoner (1982), organizational practices or policies that adversely affect employment opportunities for any group are prohibited unless the restriction is a justifiable job requirement.

Selection and Placement

The ultimate objective of recruitment is to select individuals who are most capable of meeting the requirements of the job. The selection process includes a comparison of applicant skills, knowledge, and education with the requirements stated in the job description and job specification. The actual selection is based on these criteria.

The selection process involves mutual decision making. In the organization, decisions are made about whether or not to offer a job to an applicant and how attractive the offer should be. The applicant decides if the organization and the offer will fit his or her needs and objectives.

The job market will affect the decision making process greatly. If several candidates are available for a job vacancy, the organization is in a more favorable position; if few candidates are available, or the organization is attempting to hire a highly qualified person who is being courted by other organizations, the job candidate is in a more favorable position.

The steps in the selection process are depicted in Figure 20.1. In practice, the

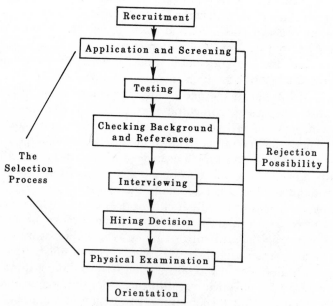

Figure 20.1. *Steps in the selection process*

actual selection process varies between organizations and between levels in the same organization. For example, the selection interview for production and service employees may be quite perfunctory. In selecting the unit manager for a foodservice operation, on the other hand, the interviewing may be extensive and a résumé may initially be submitted rather than a formal application.

Application and Screening

The application form serves three purposes. First, it indicates that the applicant is interested in a position; second, it provides the interviewer with basic information to conduct an interview; and third, it becomes a part of the personnel file if the applicant is hired. In organizations with a personnel department or personnel officer, the application and initial screening steps will be conducted in that department or by that staff member.

The application form or blank is used to obtain information that will be helpful in reaching an employment decision. The application collects objective biographical information about an applicant, such as education, work experience, special skills, and references. Questions referring to an applicant's age, sex, race, religion, national origin, or family status may violate provisions of the civil rights legislation discussed previously. Information requested on an employment application should not lead to discrimination against applicants.

In some organizations, preliminary interviews may be used to screen out unqualified applicants. Inadequate educational level or experience record or obvious disinterest may be reasons for eliminating the individual from the applicant pool at this point in the process. In effect, the initial interview determines for both the applicant and the interviewer if the selection process should proceed. The applicant may be asked questions on previous experiences, salary expectations, and other issues related to the job. In foodservice organizations, an important issue to discuss initially is the applicant's willingness to work weekends and holidays or early morning and late evening hours.

Testing

One of the most controversial areas related to staffing is employment testing. Through testing, the organization attempts to judge an applicant's capacity to learn on the job or to assess whether or not the candidate has the skills needed to perform the job.

Tests must be both reliable and valid. Reliable tests are those that consistently yield a similar score each time they are taken by the same individuals. Tests are valid when performance on a test is closely associated with performance on the job.

In the past, organizations frequently used tests without establishing their validity or reliability; as a result, testing has come under a great deal of attack. As Rue and Byars (1983) point out, civil rights legislation and decisions by the Supreme Court have had a profound impact on the use of testing by organizations. The Supreme Court rulings have specified that tests must be validated as job related.

Because they are obviously job related, tests to determine specific skills such as typing or shorthand are in wide use. In recent years, however, many organizations have curtailed or eliminated psychological and intelligence preemployment testing because of potential charges of discrimination.

Background and Reference Checks

The practice in many organizations is to conduct background and reference checks after the initial screening interview. In others, however, this checking may be done after the employment interview. The purpose of checking a person's background and references is to verify information provided by the applicant. The manager or interviewer will either telephone or write previous supervisors or persons listed as references to confirm information supplied, possibly requesting an evaluation of the applicant's skills and abilities as well. Such an investigation is useful since studies with the U.S. have shown that as many as half of the applications submitted contain false information (Goldstein, 1971).

In recent years, however, thorough and reliable reference checks have often been difficult to obtain, as pointed out by Mondy et al. (1983), because of the Privacy Act of 1974. Under this act, the former employer may be required to obtain a release from the ex-employee to provide information to prospective employers on quality of performance. The reference check has therefore tended to become a process of verifying that the prospective employee was at a certain place, doing a certain job for a specified period of time, for a given level of compensation.

Interviews

The selection interview is the most widely used and probably the most important method of assessing qualifications of job applicants. It is designed to fill in gaps on the candidate's application or résumé, find out more about the applicant as an individual, and obtain information to assess the suitability of the candidate for the job and the organization.

The employment interview is usually conducted by the manager to whom the candidate would report if employed. For managerial and professional personnel, a series of interviews may be conducted. For example, a potential director of dietetics in a large medical center hospital would probably be interviewed by several different administrators, by the professional staff in the department, and perhaps by several of the other department heads. An applicant for a cook's position in this same hospital, however, might be interviewed by only the foodservice supervisor and the production dietitian.

Types of Interviews. Three general types of interviews are used: structured, semistructured, and unstructured. In the structured interview, the interviewer asks specific questions of all interviewees. The interviewer knows in advance the questions that are to be asked and merely proceeds down the list of questions while recording the responses. This interview technique gives a common body of data on all interviewees, allows for systematic coverage of all information deemed necessary for all applicants, and provides a means for minimizing the personal biases and prejudices of the interviewer. It is frequently used in interviews for lower level jobs.

In the semistructured interview, only some questions are prepared in advance. This approach is less rigid than the structured interview and allows more flexibility for the interviewer.

The unstructured interview allows the interviewer the freedom to ask questions he or she believes are important. Broad questions, such as "tell me about your previous job," are asked. The unstructured interview may be useful in assessing characteristics of an individual, such as ability to communicate, interpersonal skills, and other factors. Comparison of answers across interviewees is difficult with unstructured interviews, however, since questions may be quite different or asked in a different context. Unstructured interviews are generally used with higher level personnel in the organization, because of the broad nature of these jobs.

Guidelines for Interviews. Regardless of the method used, the interview must be planned in advance. First, interviewers must acquaint themselves with the job description and specifications for the vacant job. Second, they must review the application file carefully, including the information from background and reference checks. Third, for structured and semistructured interviews, the questions should be formulated in advance; for the unstructured interview, a general outline should be developed.

As with other aspects of the employment process, interviews are subject to numerous legal questions. In Figure 20.2, a list of permissible questions and questions to be avoided in an interview with a job applicant is given.

In conducting an interview, the interviewer should first attempt to establish rapport with the applicant. Sufficient time should be allowed for an uninterrupted interview, which should occur in a place where privacy is possible. In addition to avoiding questions that may be discriminatory, the interviewer should try not to ask either "yes/no" questions that do not require applicants to express themselves, or leading questions where the expected response is obvious.

Other common pitfalls may be encountered in interviewing a job applicant. Personal biases play a role in the interview process. For example, a qualified male applicant may be rejected because he has long hair. Another problem is the halo effect. The halo effect occurs when a manager allows a single prominent trait to dominate judgment. A person who is verbally fluent may impress an interviewer who may then overlook the applicant's poor employment record.

Inadequate interviews can lead to poor employment decisions. Nehrbass (1977) asserts that interviews focusing on the requirements of the job and the skills and abilities of candidates will provide the most useful information about job candidates and be better predictors of performance.

	Subject	Permissible inquiries	Inquiries to be avoided
1	Name	"Have you worked for this company under a different name?" "Is any additional information relative to change of name, use of an assumed name or nickname necessary to enable a check on your work and educational record? If yes, explain."	Inquiries about name which would indicate applicant's lineage, ancestry, national origin, or descent. Inquiry into previous name of applicant where it has been changed by court order or otherwise. Inquiries about preferred courtesy title Miss, Mrs., Ms.
2	Marital and family status	Whether applicant can meet specified work schedules or has activities, commitments, or responsibilities that may hinder the meeting of work attendance requirements. Inquiries as to a duration of stay on job or anticipated absences which are made to males and females alike.	Any inquiry indicating whether an applicant is married, single, divorced, or engaged, etc. Number and age of children. Information on child-care arrangements. Any questions concerning pregnancy. Any such questions which directly or indirectly result in limitation of job opportunities.
3	Age	Requiring proof of age in the form of a work permit or a certificate of age—if a minor. Requiring proof of age by birth certificate after being hired. Inquiry as to whether or not the applicant meets the minimum age requirements as set by law, and requirements that upon hire proof of age must be submitted in the form of a birth certificate or other forms of proof of age. If age is a legal requirement, "if hired, can you furnish proof of age?," or statement that hire is subject to verification of age. Inquiry as to whether or not an applicant is younger than the employer's regular retirement age.	Requirement that applicant state age or date of birth. Requirement that applicant produce proof of age in the form of a birth certificate or baptismal record. The Age Discrimination in Employment Act of 1967 forbids discrimination against persons between the ages of 40 and 70.
4	Handicaps	For employers subject to the provisions of the Rehabilitation Act of 1973, applicants may be "invited" to indicate how and to what extent they are handicapped. The employer must indi-	An employer must be prepared to prove that any physical and mental requirements for a job are due to "business necessity" and the safe performance of the job.

Subject	*Permissible inquiries*	*Inquiries to be avoided*
	cate that: (1) compliance with the invitation is voluntary; (2) the information is being sought only to remedy discrimination or provide opportunities for the handicapped, (3) the information will be kept confidential, and (4) refusing to provide the information will not result in adverse treatment. All applicants can be asked if they are able to carry out all necessary job assignments and perform them in a safe manner.	Except in cases where undue hardship can be proven, employers must make "reasonable accommodations" for the physical and mental limitations of an employee or applicant. "Reasonable accommodation" includes alteration of duties, alteration of work schedule, alteration of physical setting, and provision of aids. The Rehabilitation Act of 1973 forbids employers from asking job applicants general questions about whether they are handicapped or asking them about the nature and severity of their handicaps.
5 Sex	Inquiry or restriction of employment is permissible only where a bona fide occupational qualification exists. (This BFOQ exception is interpreted very narrowly by the courts and the EEOC.) The burden of proof rests on the employer to prove that the BFOQ does exist and that all members of the affected class are incapable of performing the job. Sex of applicant may be requested (preferably not on the employment application) for affirmative action purposes but may not be used as an employment criterion.	Sex of applicant. Any other inquiry which would indicate sex. Sex is not a BFOQ because a job involves physical labor (such as heavy lifting) beyond the capacity of some women nor can employment be restricted just because the job is traditionally labeled "men's work" or "women's work." Applicant's sex cannot be used as a factor for determining whether or not an applicant will be satisfied in a particular job. Questions about an applicant's height or weight, unless demonstrably necessary as requirements for the job.
6 Race or color	General distinguishing physical characteristics such as scars, etc., to be used for identification purposes. Race may be requested (preferably not on the employment application) for affirmative action purposes but may not be used as an employment criterion.	Applicant's race. Color of applicant's skin, eyes, hair, etc., or other questions directly or indirectly indicating race or color.
7 Address or duration of residence	Applicant's address. Inquiry into length of stay at current and previous addresses.	Specific inquiry into foreign address which would indicate national origin.

(Continued)

Subject	Permissible inquiries	Inquiries to be avoided
	"How long a resident of this State or city?"	Names and relationship of persons with whom applicant resides. Whether applicant owns or rents home.
8 Birthplace	"Can you after employment submit a birth certificate or other proof of U.S. citizenship?"	Birthplace of applicant. Birthplace of applicant's parents, spouse, or other relatives. Requirement that applicant submit a birth certificate before employment. Any other inquiry into national origin.
9 Religion	An applicant may be advised concerning normal hours and days of work required by the job to avoid possible conflict with religious or other personal conviction. However, except in cases where undue hardship can be proven, employers and unions must make "reasonable accommodation" for religious practices of an employee or prospective employee. "Reasonable accommodation" may include voluntary substitutes, flexible scheduling, lateral transfer, change of job assignments, or the use of an alternative to payment of union dues.	Applicant's religious denomination or affiliation, church, parish, pastor, or religious holidays observed. Any inquiry to indicate or identify religious denomination or customs. Applicants may not be told that any particular religious groups are required to work on their religious holidays.
10 Military record	Type of education and experience in service as it relates to a particular job.	Type of discharge.
11 Photograph	May be required for identification after hiring.	Requirement that applicant affix a photograph to his or her application. Request that applicant, at his or her option, submit photograph. Requirement of photograph after interview but before hiring.
12 Citizenship	"Are you a citizen of the United States?" "Do you intend to remain permanently in the U.S.?" "If not a citizen, are you prevented from becoming lawfully employed because of visa or immigration status?" Statement that, if	"Of what country are you a citizen?" Whether applicant or his/her parents or spouse are naturalized or native-born U.S. citizens. Date when applicant or parents or spouse acquired U.S. citizenship. Requirement that applicant pro-

	Subject	Permissible inquiries	Inquiries to be avoided
		hired, applicant may be required to submit proof of citizenship.	duce his or her naturalization papers. Whether applicant's parents or spouse are citizens of the U.S.
13	Ancestry or national origin	Languages applicant reads, speaks, or writes fluently. (If another language is necessary to perform the job.)	Inquiries into applicant's lineage, ancestry, national origin, descent, birthplace, or native language. National origin of applicant's parents or spouse.
14	Education	Applicant's academic, vocational, or professional education; school attended. Inquiry into language skills such as reading, speaking, and writing foreign languages.	Any inquiry asking specifically the nationality, racial or religious affiliation of a school. Inquiry as to how foreign language ability was acquired.
15	Experience	Applicant's work experience, including names and addresses of previous employers, dates of employment, reasons for leaving, salary history. Other countries visited.	
16	Conviction, arrest, and court record	Inquiry into actual convictions which relate reasonably to fitness to perform a particular job. (A conviction is a court ruling where the party is found guilty as charged. An arrest is merely the apprehending or detaining of the person to answer the alleged crime.)	Any inquiry relating to arrests. Any inquiry into or request for a person's arrest, court, or conviction record if not substantially related to functions and responsibilities of the particular job in question.
17	Relatives	Names of applicant's relatives already employed by this company. Names and address of parents or guardian (if applicant is a minor).	Name or address of any relative of adult applicant.
18	Notice in case of emergency	Name and address of persons to be notified in case of accident or emergency.	Name and address of relatives to be notified in case of accident or emergency.
19	Organizations	Inquiry into any organizations which an applicant is a member of providing the name or character of the organizations does not reveal the race, religion, color, or ancestry of the membership. "List all professional organizations to which you belong. What office do you hold?"	"List all organizations, clubs, societies, and lodges to which you belong." The names of organizations to which the applicant belongs if such information would indicate through character or name the race, religion, color, or ancestry of the membership.

(Continued)

	Subject	Permissible inquiries	Inquiries to be avoided
20	References	"By whom were you referred for a position here?" Names of persons willing to provide professional and/or character references for applicant.	Requiring the submission of a religious reference. Requesting reference from applicant's pastor.
21	Credit rating	None	Any questions concerning credit rating, charge accounts, etc. Ownership of car.
22	Miscellaneous	Notice to applicants that any misstatements or omissions of material facts in the application may be cause for dismissal.	Any inquiry should be avoided which although not specifically listed among the above, is designed to elicit information concerning race, color, ancestry, age, sex, religion, handicap, or arrest and court record unless based upon a bona fide occupational qualification.

Figure 20.2. *"The Pre-Employment Inquiry Guide," by Clifford M. Koen, Jr., copyright October 1980. Reprinted with the permission of Personnel Journal, Costa Mesa, California; all rights reserved.*

The Hiring Decision

While all of the steps in the selection process are important, the most critical one is the decision to accept or reject applicants for employment. The final decision must be made very carefully because of the cost of placing new employees on the payroll, the relatively short probationary period in most organizations, and affirmative action considerations.

Many factors must therefore be considered in making hiring decisions. The factors for one class of employees may differ from those used for another class. Some of the issues are as follows:

- What effect will the decision have on meeting affirmative action goals?
- At what grade or wage level should the individual be started?
- Should individuals who are overqualified for a job be hired?
- Should the concern be to match the employee to the job or select and place applicants with the most potential for growth and advancement?

When all the information about an applicant has been assembled, a method must be developed for summarizing it. Checklists and summary forms are commonly used as a means of assuring that all the pertinent information is included in the evaluation of an applicant. Two basic approaches are used for making the hiring decision: judgmental and statistical. In the judgmental approach, the decision maker reviews all of the data and, on the basis of understanding of the job and experience in hiring personnel, makes the decision. With the statistical approach, various types of numerical rating scales are used and applicants are scored on relevant criteria. Applicants are rank ordered according to total score, which provides an objective basis for evaluating them in the decision making process. While the decision is not based solely on scores, this technique will force the decision maker to analyze the relevant factors and the candidates in a systematic fashion.

The effectiveness of a selection decision is largely dependent on the number and quality of applicants who have been recruited. If the number of applicants is small, either because of a short labor supply or ineffective recruiting effort, the degree of selectivity is reduced. The manager making the decision should recognize that none of the applicants may be satisfactory in some cases. If this occurs, the job may need to be reexamined, the compensation adjusted to attract more qualified candidates, or a more aggressive recruitment strategy needed. A pitfall in decision making is to accept the best qualified candidate who has been interviewed, even if that individual is not completely qualified for the job.

The manager or supervisor to whom the new employee would report generally makes the hiring decision. In large organizations, however, approvals by higher level managers may be required. Before a final offer is made, the selection recommendation may also need to be reviewed by affirmative action personnel.

The job offer will generally confirm the details of the job, working arrangements, and salary or wages, and specify a time limit in which the applicant must reach a decision. Individuals who are rejected should be advised of this fact in a tactful manner.

The salary offered should be competitive with those of similar jobs in other organizations in the area and should be compatible with the existing salary structure in the organization. Too low an offer may cause the new employee to feel disgruntled; on the other hand, too high an offer may cause problems with current employees.

A Physical Examination

After a prospective employee has completed the other phases in the selection process successfully, many organizations require a physical examination. According to Mondy et al. (1983), the physical exam has three primary objectives.

- To determine if the applicant can meet the physical demands of the job.
- To provide a record protecting the organization against claims for previous injuries.
- To identify communicable diseases an applicant may have.

According to Chruden and Sherman (1980), the preemployment physical is particularly valuable in the placement of handicapped persons; it also provides an opportunity through laboratory analysis to detect applicants on drugs. In the past, requirements for certain physical characteristics were often specified on the basis of unvalidated notions of what should be required. Many of these requirements have tended to discriminate against women and minorities and have thus been questioned and modified in terms of actual job demands.

Health regulations in some cities or counties specify that foodservice workers have food handler permits or cards prior to employment. The requirements for securing such a permit differ according to local regulations and may include successful completion of a sanitation training program, a test on food handling practices, and a limited physical exam. Because of the particular concern in foodservice organizations about preventing contamination of food and spreading communicable diseases, blood tests and stool cultures are sometimes required prior to employment and at periodic intervals thereafter. This practice is especially common in healthcare organizations.

Orientation

The recruitment and selection of employees are important steps in the employment process, yet the careful planning and decision making will be negated if the orientation to the organization and the job are not carried out properly. Induction and orientation are designed to provide new employees with the information they need to function comfortably and effectively in the organization. Three types of information are typically included in orientation:

- Review of the organization and how the employee's job contributes to the organization's objectives.
- Specific information on policies, work rules, and benefits.
- General information about the daily work routine.

In large organizations, the orientation tends to be more formal than in small organizations; however, it is an important process for getting employees "off to a good start" regardless of the formality of the orientation or size of the organization. If an organization has a personnel department, staff in that department generally provide information about the overall organization policies and benefits. The departmental orientation then focuses on job related orientation.

If new employees are properly oriented, several objectives can be achieved. First, start-up costs can be minimized; without proper orientation, a new employee can make costly mistakes. Second, anxieties can be reduced. Third, orientation can help create realistic job expectations.

Unfortunately, the importance of an orientation program is underestimated in many organizations. New employees are often given a policy and procedure manual and told to study it until given another assignment. At this point, policies and procedures may have little meaning to many employees, who may quickly become bored.

The first day of employment is crucial to the success or failure of a new employee. An actual incident that occurred in a hospital foodservice provides an example of how weak the orientation process may be in some situations. On the first day at work, after completing the formal two-hour group orientation session conducted by staff in the personnel department, Bill, a new dishwasher, walked

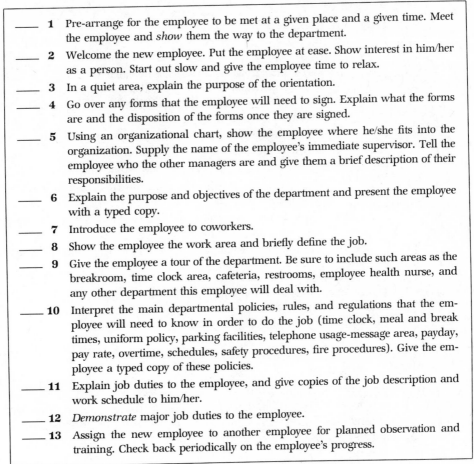

_____ 1   Pre-arrange for the employee to be met at a given place and a given time. Meet the employee and *show* them the way to the department.

_____ 2   Welcome the new employee. Put the employee at ease. Show interest in him/her as a person. Start out slow and give the employee time to relax.

_____ 3   In a quiet area, explain the purpose of the orientation.

_____ 4   Go over any forms that the employee will need to sign. Explain what the forms are and the disposition of the forms once they are signed.

_____ 5   Using an organizational chart, show the employee where he/she fits into the organization. Supply the name of the employee's immediate supervisor. Tell the employee who the other managers are and give them a brief description of their responsibilities.

_____ 6   Explain the purpose and objectives of the department and present the employee with a typed copy.

_____ 7   Introduce the employee to coworkers.

_____ 8   Show the employee the work area and briefly define the job.

_____ 9   Give the employee a tour of the department. Be sure to include such areas as the breakroom, time clock area, cafeteria, restrooms, employee health nurse, and any other department this employee will deal with.

_____ 10   Interpret the main departmental policies, rules, and regulations that the employee will need to know in order to do the job (time clock, meal and break times, uniform policy, parking facilities, telephone usage-message area, payday, pay rate, overtime, schedules, safety procedures, fire procedures). Give the employee a typed copy of these policies.

_____ 11   Explain job duties to the employee, and give copies of the job description and work schedule to him/her.

_____ 12   *Demonstrate* major job duties to the employee.

_____ 13   Assign the new employee to another employee for planned observation and training. Check back periodically on the employee's progress.

Figure 20.3.   *Orientation checklist.* **Source:** *Puckett, R. P.: Dietetics: Making or breaking the new employee.* **Contemporary Administrator 5:14 (Oct.), 1982.**

into the department of dietetics and was told by the director, "There is the dishroom. Go find Joe; he'll show you the ropes." Needless to say, the anxiety of a new employee was probably not reduced by that experience!

Planning for orientation is as important as it is with all other managerial activities. A checklist is a valuable tool to ensure that all pertinent information is included. Puckett (1982) developed the checklist in Figure 20.3 for the initial orientation of new foodservice employees. She cautioned that new employees should not be overloaded with information on the first day and stressed the need for follow-up sessions during the first week, with a review session during the first month on the job. Periodic monitoring and reinforcement during the early weeks on the job are also necessary. The checklist in Figure 20.4 outlines the follow-up orientation that Puckett suggested be held at the end of the second or third week on the job.

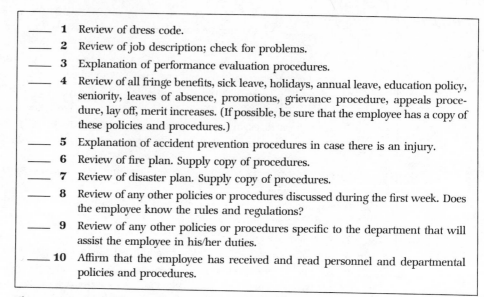

——— **1**   Review of dress code.

——— **2**   Review of job description; check for problems.

——— **3**   Explanation of performance evaluation procedures.

——— **4**   Review of all fringe benefits, sick leave, holidays, annual leave, education policy, seniority, leaves of absence, promotions, grievance procedure, appeals procedure, lay off, merit increases. (If possible, be sure that the employee has a copy of these policies and procedures.)

——— **5**   Explanation of accident prevention procedures in case there is an injury.

——— **6**   Review of fire plan. Supply copy of procedures.

——— **7**   Review of disaster plan. Supply copy of procedures.

——— **8**   Review of any other policies or procedures discussed during the first week. Does the employee know the rules and regulations?

——— **9**   Review of any other policies or procedures specific to the department that will assist the employee in his/her duties.

——— **10** Affirm that the employee has received and read personnel and departmental policies and procedures.

Figure 20.4. *Checklist for follow-up orientation session with a new employee.* Source: *Puckett, R. P.: Dietetics: Making or breaking the new employee.* **Contemporary Administrator 5:15 (Oct.), 1982.**

Proper orientation pays off in terms of decreased turnover and increased job performance. Stoner (1982) reports that early job experiences and subsequent performance are related. He also reports that turnover rates are often highest among new employees, which may be the result of unrealistic expectations leading to dissatisfaction or disillusionment.

DEVELOPING AND MAINTAINING THE WORK FORCE

The employment process includes only the initial stages in building an efficient and stable work force. Employees also require continual development if their potential is to be utilized effectively in an organization. This development process begins with orientation, but should be continued throughout employment in the organization.

Employee development has become increasingly vital to the success of organizations. Changes in technology require that employees possess the knowledge and skills to cope with new processes and techniques.

Performance evaluation is another step in the development and maintenance of the work force. Other staffing functions include promotions, transfers, demotions, and separations, as well as compensation management or the administration of salaries, wages, and fringe benefits.

Training and Development

Training is and must be the responsibility of all managers. The term "training" is frequently used to refer to the teaching of technical skills to nonmanagerial personnel, whereas "management development" refers to programs designed to improve the technical, human, and conceptual skills of managers.

The initial step in training is to determine training needs and then, based on this assessment, plan training and development programs. Evaluation of training programs is critical to their success.

The need for training new employees and employees promoted to new jobs is obvious; however, training is needed for all employees to maintain standards in a foodservice operation. In healthcare facilities, training for all employees is mandated in federal regulations and accreditation standards. In other segments of the foodservice industry, the positive benefits of training in terms of increased productivity and morale are gradually being recognized.

In large organizations, a training staff may be available to assist with various aspects of a training program. Some training is conducted on a group basis, although individual training is also necessary.

Stoner (1982) outlines four procedures for determining individuals' training needs in an organization:

- *Performance appraisal.* Measurement of employees' work against the performance standards or objectives of the job.

- *Analysis of job requirements.* Examination of skills and knowledge specified in job descriptions and determination of employees without skills and knowledge.

- *Organizational analysis.* Review of organizational effectiveness, including such measures as turnover rate and performance records and other measures that may suggest training needs.

- *Personnel surveys.* Surveys of employees to determine their assessment of problems in work performance and of their training needs.

After needs have been identified, managers should then initiate appropriate training efforts. On-the-job training methods include job rotation, internships, and apprenticeships. In job rotation, employees are assigned to work on a series of jobs over a period of time, thereby permitting them to learn a variety of skills. In an internship, job training is combined with classroom instruction. In an apprenticeship, employees are assigned to highly skilled coworkers responsible for their training.

One commonly used method for structuring on-the-job training is based on the job instruction training (JIT) system developed during World War II. The steps involved in JIT are summarized in Figure 20.5. The advantages of on-the-job training are that no special facilities are required and that the employee is engaged in productive work during the training period. A major disadvantage, however, is that the pressure of the work place can lead to haphazard or inadequate instruction.

Determining the Training Objectives and Preparing the Training Area

1 Decide what the trainee must be taught so he or she can do the job efficiently, safely, economically, and intelligently.
2 Provide the right tools, equipment, supplies, and material.
3 Have the workplace properly arranged just as the employee will be expected to keep it.

Presenting the Instruction

Step 1. Preparation of the trainee

1 Put the trainee at ease.
2 Find out what the trainee already knows about the job.
3 Get the trainee interested in and desirous of learning the job.

Step 2. Presentation of the operations and knowledge

1 Tell, show, illustrate and question to put over the new knowledge and operations.
2 Instruct slowly, clearly, completely, and patiently, one point at time.
3 Check, question, and repeat.
4 Make sure the trainee understands.

Step 3. Performance tryout

1 Test the trainee by having him or her perform the job.
2 Ask questions beginning with why, how, when or where.
3 Observe performance, correct errors, and repeat instructions if necessary.
4 Continue until the trainee is competent in the job.

Step 4. Follow-up

1 Put the trainee on his or her own.
2 Check frequently to be sure the trainee follows instructions.
3 Taper off extra supervision and close follow-up until the trainee is qualified to work with normal supervision.

Figure 20.5. *Steps in the JIT system.* **Source:** *Adapted from* **The Training within Industry Report** *(War Manpower Commission. Bureau of Training, 1945), p. 195.*

Off-the-job training takes place outside the actual workplace. Methods used in off-the-job training range from laboratory experiences that simulate actual working conditions to other types of participative experiences, such as case studies or role playing, and to classroom activities such as seminars, lectures, and films.

With proper planning and preparation, group training sessions can be effective. The schedule of in-service training meetings should be publicized well in advance, with the date, time, and subject of each session clearly stated.

Because varied work shifts and alternating days off are common practices in foodservice operations, employee work schedules and workloads need to be considered in planning in-service sessions. If the daily work routine does not allow time for training sessions, they may need to be held at the end of the work day or overlapping two work shifts. Today, employees are generally given extra compensation for attending training sessions if scheduled outside the regular work day. In-service sessions conducted during the work day are usually fairly short, varying in length from 15 minutes to no more than one hour.

Whenever possible, discussions should be supplemented with visual aids, demonstrations, or printed material. Resource persons from other departments in the organization or from outside sources who can answer questions or present information will add interest to the in-service training program. Sessions should start and end promptly and should provide for employee involvement.

Because of the difficulty in some foodservice organizations in scheduling formal training sessions, training is being integrated with employee breaks or lunch periods. Videotapes, slide-tape programs, or film strips may be made available for viewing by a single employee or a group of employees in the lunch room or coffee break area. Another alternative is to establish a small training center in an area of the foodservice facility in which printed materials are provided to encourage employees to devote idle times to reading and reviewing the training materials. Computer-assisted instruction is also becoming a widely used technique for training.

Regardless of the type of training method used, carefully formulated objectives and a well-planned outline are critical to the success of the training effort. An example of a simple form for developing a lesson plan is included in Figure 20.6.

This and Lippitt (1966) summarize several conditions for effective learning that should be taken into consideration in employee training (Figure 20.7). Managers should be aware of several common pitfalls to avoid. Lack of reinforcement is a common training error; frequently, mistakes are pointed out but praise is not given when an employee does the job correctly.

"Practice makes perfect" is a phrase that definitely applies to the training process; all too often, managers expect employees to perform a job perfectly the first time, forgetting practice and repetition are important aspects of learning. Managers also forget that people learn at different rates—some learn rapidly and some more slowly. If a person is a slow learner, he or she is not necessarily a poor performer. Training, therefore, must take into consideration the differences among individuals.

Development of managers and other professional staff may include continuing education opportunities provided by colleges and universities, professional and trade associations, or other organizations. These may include workshops, short courses, seminars, trade shows, or conventions. Some organizations have programs to assist managers in obtaining degrees either while working or during an educational leave.

Even though some of these continuing education experiences may not be directly related to a supervisor's or manager's job, they may serve to renew enthusiasm, introduce the person to new ideas, or provide new personal contacts, which may later be a resource for information. The manager's participation may

Training Session Title: Work Simplification		Date: January 10, 1985

Objective: After completing the training session, the employee will be able to apply work simplification principles to his or her job.

Content Outline	Learning Experience, Activities, Evaluation	References, Resource Material
1 What is work simplification? • Define work simplification. • Identify benefits of work simplification. 2 How do you apply work simplification? • Discuss questions for analyzing present methods—what, why, how, when, where, who. • Identify changes that can be made in present methods based on the analysis, e.g., materials used, finished appearance, steps in assembly. • Discuss types of changes that can be implemented and evaluation of effectiveness of change.	• Class discussion • Demonstration of several work simplification techniques in food production. • Written examination on principles of motion economy. • Observation of work performance.	Neil, C. A.: Working smarter not harder. *School Food Service Journal* 37:51 (Nov./Dec.), 1983.

Figure 20.6. *Form for planning in-service training session*

be fully or partially funded by the organization, and administrative leave is generally given. Funds for travel, however, are becoming limited in many organizations, especially in public institutions.

Any training and development program is not complete until evaluation is done. Employees may be asked to evaluate individual and group training in terms of satisfaction, benefit derived, and suggestions for future training. The true test of the effectiveness of any training effort, however, is improvement in employee performance.

Performance Evaluation

Performance refers to the degree of accomplishment of the tasks that make up an individual's job. Often confused with effort, performance is measured in terms of

1	Acceptance that all people can learn.
2	The individual must be motivated to learn.
3	Learning is an active, not passive, process.
4	Normally, the learner must have guidance.
5	Approximate materials for sequential learning must be provided: hands-on experiences, cases, problems, discussion, reading.
6	Time must be provided to practice the learning, to internalize, to give confidence.
7	Learning methods, if possible, should be varied to avoid boredom.
8	The learner must secure satisfaction from the learning.
9	The learner must get reinforcement of the correct behavior.
10	Standards of performance should be set for the learner.
11	A recognition that there are different levels of learning and that these take different times and methods.

Figure 20.7. *Conditions for effective learning.* **Source: *This, L., and Lippitt, G.: Learning Theories and Training.* Training and Development Journal, *April 1966, pp. 2–11. Copyright © 1966 by the American Society for Training and Development, Inc. (Reprinted with permission. All rights reserved.)**

results. In most organizations today, formal employee performance evaluation systems are operational. However, performance evaluation occurs whether or not an organization has a formal evaluation program. Supervisors are observing the manner in which employees are carrying out their assignments and forming impressions of the quality of their work on a continual basis.

The term merit rating is associated with an evaluation system whereby employees are rated on scales with assigned point values. The points are used for determining if employees merit or deserve wage increases, promotions, or other rewards. With the extension of performance evaluation to white collar and managerial personnel, the terms performance appraisal and performance evaluation are now widely used.

The success or failure of performance evaluation depends on the philosophy and attitudes of managerial and supervisory personnel and their skills in implementing an evaluation system. Collecting data or actual rating of performance is the first step in the process; however, the real benefit comes from the improvement of personnel performance.

Objectives of Performance Evaluation

The primary objectives of performance evaluation are:

- To provide employees with feedback on their performance.
- To serve as a basis for encouraging more effective work performance.
- To provide data for decision making regarding future job assignments and compensation.

Individuals want feedback about their performance, and performance appraisal can provide an opportunity to obtain such information. If performance compares favorably with that of other employees, an individual will obviously react favorably to performance review; however, feedback on poor performance is more difficult to accept.

When wages and promotion are dependent upon the performance appraisal, the individual will want as favorable an evaluation as possible and may seek to cover up deficiencies or problems. Thus, performance evaluation may present a conflict between the manager and the employee.

In actual practice, appraisal programs have often yielded disappointing results. The focus too frequently is on past performance with little attention given to future performance. According to Chruden and Sherman (1980), the following are among the reasons for failure of performance evaluation programs:

- Managers see little or no benefit from the time and energy devoted to the process.
- Managers may dislike the face-to-face confrontation that may occur in evaluating poor performance.
- Many managers may not be sufficiently skilled in conducting evaluation interviews.
- The judgmental aspect of evaluation may be in conflict with the developmental dimension.

Evaluation systems may include appraisals by superiors, peers, and subordinates, as well as self-appraisal. In all cases, the evaluator must understand the job requirements and have the opportunity to observe performance.

Criteria for measuring performance should be relevant to the job, understandable, and measurable. Job descriptions provide the basis for performance evaluation. The newer forms for job descriptions that include a specification of job standards, such as the one presented in Chapter 17, provide an objective basis for assessing employee performance in terms of job requirements. An example of this type of evaluation form is shown in Figure 20.8.

Evaluation Techniques

Commonly used performance appraisal methods include the following: checklist, rating scale, and critical incident. In the checklist method, the rater does not evaluate performance but merely records it. A list of statements or questions that are answered by "yes-no" responses are the basis for the evaluation.

A wide variety of rating scales have been developed. The traditional rating scale includes a number of dimensions on which an employee is rated on a three- to five-point scale for measuring quality of performance. These dimensions might include knowledge of work, initiative, quality of work, quantity of work, and interpersonal relationships. An example is shown in Figure 20.9. Raters may also be asked to provide comments or documentation on unsatisfactory and perhaps

DA 228, Revised 2-82
STATE OF KANSAS
Department of Administration
Division of Personnel Services

EMPLOYEE PERFORMANCE EVALUATION

Agency **Kansas State University**	Class Title **Cook II**
Major Subdivision **Housing**	Position Number **00-18-00-517**

Employee's Name (Last, First, MI)

SIMONIS, PATRICIA L.

Rating Period:
FROM: 5/18/84 TO: 5/17/85

Social Security Number

OVERALL RATING
(Adjective and points)

Above Standard
390

Check one of the following:
- [X] Annual rating
- [ ] Probationary rating
- [ ] Special rating

Evaluation Recommendation
- [ ] Recommend permanent status
- [X] Satisfactory completion of annual or special evaluation
- [ ] Unsatisfactory—Dismissal Recommended
- [ ] Recommend return to former permanent class
- [ ] Extend probation _____ months.
- [ ] Other_____

Rater's Comments

Employee is a very efficient worker and plans ahead to get work load done.

Linda K. Yarrow   4-29-85
Signature of Rater   Date

Reviewer's Comments

Employee has shown considerable improvement in her work attitude during spring semester. She needs to continue the progress in this area. She is a good supervisor and has potential for more development.

Della M. Rieley   4/30/85
Signature of Reviewer   Date

Employee's Acknowledgement and Comments

I will work on my attitude and try not to be moody.

Patricia L. Simonis
Signature of Employee
Does Not Necessarily Signify Agreement   4/29/85
Date

A permanent employee, with seven calendar days after being informed of his or her evaluation, may appeal the evaluation in writing to the appointing authority. The same applies to certain employees on probation. See personnel regulation 1-7-2.

Frances E. Jensen   5/2/85
Signature of Appointing Authority   Date

Figure 20.8. *Performance evaluation based on job standards. (Used by permission of Kansas State University Residence Hall Food Service)*

DA 228, Revised 2-82

MAJOR RESPONSI-BILITY NUMBER (From DA 229, Standards)	WT.	ACTUAL WORK PERFORMANCE (How were standards met, not met, or exceeded?)	1 UNSAT-ISFACTORY	2 BELOW STANDARD	3 STANDARD	4 ABOVE STANDARD	5 OUTSTAND-ING	(WEIGHT) X (RATINGS)

Both sides of this form are to be completed before the end of the evaluation period. Copies are to be given the employee, the supervisor, and the Division of Personnel Services, and a copy is to be retained in the agency's files. For Division of Personnel Services, attach DA 229 (Standards).

MAJOR RESP. NO.	WT.	ACTUAL WORK PERFORMANCE	1 UNSAT	2 BELOW STD	3 STD	4 ABOVE STD	5 OUTST	WEIGHT X RATINGS
1.	45	Follows recipes very closely. Asks good questions if recipes are unclear or incomplete. Checks bakery employees to insure recipes are followed. Keeps own notes on problem recipes. Leftovers are planned as soon as possible. Makes viable suggestions for incorporation of leftovers. Not always open-minded about new recipes developed at other food centers. Production sheets always completed.				X		180
2.	5	Takes proper care of equipment. Is very meticulous and operates a clean area. Very conscious of cleanliness.			X			15
3.	5	Knows quantities on hand in freezer. Follows sanitary practices in food handling.			X			15
4.	15	Plans ahead with other staff to meet demands of bakery. Has worked well in preparing bakery items as close to service time as possible. Patient in training employees in preparation of new products. Gives equal consideration to each employee without regard to race or sex.				X		60
5.	5	Always neat and clean. Wears a hair net at all times.				X		20
6.	25	Completes duties as assigned. Much improvement noted in attitude toward work. Much more cooperative. Occasionally moody but is more aware of this and is trying to control her emotions. Went above and beyond job standards in February to be at work during bad weather.				X		100
	100	OVERALL RATING	100-150 U	151-250 B	251-350 S	(351-450 A)	451-500 O	390 TOTAL POINTS

625-T

Figure 20.8. *(cont.)*

PERFORMANCE EVALUATION OF HOSPITAL PERSONNEL

		1 *Unsatis-factory*	2 *Needs Improvement*	3 *Satis-factory*	4 *Above Average*	5 *Superior*
1	**Quality of Work**					
a	Accuracy	( )	( )	( )	( )	( )
b	Neatness	( )	( )	( )	( )	( )
c	Organization of work	( )	( )	( )	( )	( )
d	Thoroughness	( )	( )	( )	( )	( )
2	**Quantity of Work**					
a	Amount of work performed	( )	( )	( )	( )	( )
b	Completion of work on schedule	( )	( )	( )	( )	( )
c	Consistency of work production	( )	( )	( )	( )	( )
3	**Following Directions**					
a	Compliance with work instructions	( )	( )	( )	( )	( )
b	Observance of rules and regulations	( )	( )	( )	( )	( )
c	Care and use of equipment	( )	( )	( )	( )	( )
d	Observance of safety rules	( )	( )	( )	( )	( )
4	**Initiative and Judgment**					
a	Use of initiative	( )	( )	( )	( )	( )
b	Use of judgment	( )	( )	( )	( )	( )
c	Adapting to new situations, unusual demands or emergencies	( )	( )	( )	( )	( )
5	**Attendance**					
a	Punctuality	( )	( )	( )	( )	( )
b	Regularity of attendance	( )	( )	( )	( )	( )
6	**Personal Relations**					
a	Getting along with other employees	( )	( )	( )	( )	( )
b	Meeting and handling the public	( )	( )	( )	( )	( )
c	Attention to personal appearnace, cleanliness, hygenic measures	( )	( )	( )	( )	( )

Figure 20.9. *An example of a rating scale for performance evaluation*

on outstanding performance. Other, more sophisticated rating scale systems have been developed but are not widely used in foodservice organizations.

The critical incident technique involves identifying and recording incidents of employee behavior. An incident is considered "critical" when it illustrates that the employee has done, or failed to do, something that results in unusual success or failure on some part of the job. Therefore, critical incidents may include both positive and negative examples of employee performance. Although this method has the advantage of providing a sampling of behavior throughout the evaluation period, it is also a time-consuming technique.

Management by objectives (MBO) is another method sometimes used for performance evaluation, primarily with managerial and professional personnel. In an MBO system, managers and their superiors agree on the objectives to be achieved, usually for a one-year period. Periodic assessment of progress on the objectives is conducted at several intervals during the year and objectives are revised if deemed appropriate. The degree to which these objectives are achieved, then, provides the basis for evaluation at the end of the period. Although MBO systems thus provide a great deal of objective feedback, many organizations have modified them or adopted other systems because of the significant amounts of time and paperwork they involve.

Common Errors in Evaluation

In addition to the reasons discussed previously for failure of performance evaluation programs, rating errors can also present problems. In some situations, raters are either extremely harsh or excessively easy in their evaluations. These rater errors are referred to as strictness or leniency. The harsh rater tends to give lower than average ratings to most subordinates, whereas the lenient rater tends to give higher than average ratings.

Another type of rater error is called the halo error, which is caused by the rater's inability to discriminate among different dimensions or the assumption that a particular dimension is extremely important. The rating on one dimension influences evaluation on all other dimensions. For example, the foodservice supervisor may consider interpersonal relations to be extremely important and may give high ratings on all performance dimensions to a cook who relates well to other employees, even though the cook is frequently tardy and fails to follow recipes.

The central tendency error occurs when the rater tends to give all employees similar ratings. Everyone is judged to be about the same—average. In this instance, the supervisor is "playing it safe." Such ratings, however, provide little guidance for decisions on promotions, compensation, training, and development.

In many instances, the most recent behaviors tend to bias ratings of employee performance. This error is referred to as the recency of events error. Employees are often aware of this tendency of raters and become interested, productive, or cooperative just before evaluation time.

These problems can be avoided when raters can observe employees on a regular basis and rating scales are understood clearly. Also, problems can be avoided if supervisors do not have to rate large numbers of employees; fatigue and difficulty in discriminating are pitfalls when a supervisor has too many employees to evaluate. Supervisory training is important to improve the quality of evaluation and raters should be trained to avoid errors such as those mentioned.

The problems identified are more frequent with the use of rating scales in performance evaluation. Critical incident, job standards, and MBO techniques are evaluation approaches designed to minimize these rater errors.

The Evaluation Interview

The evaluation interview provides the supervisor with the opportunity to discuss an employee's performance and explore areas of improvement. Also, the employee should have the opportunity to discuss his or her concerns and problems in the job situation. In some instances, employees may be asked to complete a self-evaluation prior to the interview, which is then used during the interview session for comparison with the supervisor's assessment. Evaluations should be scheduled several days in advance and conducted in a private setting because of the sensitivity involved.

Chruden and Sherman (1980) list the following as objectives to achieve in the performance evaluation interview:

- Emphasize strengths on which the individual can build rather than stress weaknesses.
- Avoid recommendations involving changing of traits; instead, suggest more acceptable behaviors.
- Concentrate on opportunities for growth within the employee's present job.
- Limit plans for change or growth to a few objectives that can be accomplished within a reasonable period of time.

They suggest that frequent evaluation sessions may be more effective than only an annual evaluation in which many criticisms are enumerated. The employee-supervisor relationship, work pressures, health, off-the-job pressures, recency of salary increase or other recognition, and length of time on the job are factors that influence employee reactions to evaluation.

Personnel Actions

The evaluation process will provide the basis for various types of personnel actions. If deficiencies in employee performance are noted, plans for improvement should be developed or disciplinary actions may be needed. Changes in job placement may be suggested during evaluation and may include promotions, demotions, transfers, or separations. Separations include dismissals, resignations, and retirements. Leaves with or without pay are other types of personnel actions for which a manager must plan in order to maintain an adequate work force.

Promotions

A promotion involves moving an employee to a job involving higher pay, status, and higher performance requirements. Advancement can serve as an incentive for improved performance for employees at all levels of the organization. In the recruitment section, we discussed promotions from within as a source of employees for job vacancies.

The two basic criteria for promotions are merit and seniority. If an organization is unionized, the union contract often requires that seniority be considered.

Promotions should be tied closely to the performance evaluation system and should be a way for recognizing good performance; however, individuals should not be promoted to positions in which their abilities are not appropriate. For example, a unit or regional manager in a large multiunit foodservice organization, who is very action-oriented and a good decision maker, might be misplaced in a staff position in the central office. Instead, this individual should probably be considered for a higher level line position.

Promotions should be fair, based on merit, and untainted by favoritism. Even when promotions are fair and appropriate, problems may occur. A major problem is resentment by employees bypassed for promotion, which may result in lowered morale or productivity. If the promotion process is handled as a "top secret" affair, this problem may be compounded because of unrealistic expectations among employees.

Another problem in promotions is discrimination. In many organizations, legal obligations to avoid discrimination in the hiring process have been understood and accepted; however, less attention has been paid to this issue in promotion decisions.

Demotions

A demotion consists of a change in job assignment to a lower organizational level in a job involving less skill, responsibility, status, and pay. Employees may be demoted because of reduction in positions of the type they are holding or because of reorganization. Demotion may also be used as a disciplinary action for unsatisfactory performance or for failure to comply with policies, rules, or standards in the organization. Acceptance and adjustment to loss of pay and status are difficult for most employees. Demoted employees may need special supervision or counseling as a result.

When the abilities or skills of a long-service employee decline, the solution may be to restructure a job rather than demote a loyal employee. In some instances the problem is solved by "kicking the person upstairs" to a job with an impressive title but little authority or responsibility.

Transfers

Transfer involves moving an employee to another job at approximately the same level in the organization with basically the same pay, performance requirements, and status. A transfer may require an employee to change work group, work place, work shift, or organizational unit or even a move to another geographic area. A transfer can result from an organizational decision or an employee request.

Transfers permit the placement of employees in jobs where the need for their services is greatest. Also, transfers permit employees to be placed in jobs they prefer or to join a more compatible work group.

Planned transfers can serve as an excellent employee development technique and can also be helpful in balancing departmental work requirements. A problem can occur, however, when a "problem employee" is unloaded on an unsuspecting manager. Training, counseling, or corrective action may be preferable to transfer. If the employee cannot be rehabilitated, discharge may be the solution.

Separations

A separation involves either voluntary or involuntary termination of an employee. In instances of voluntary terminations or employee resignations, many organizations attempt to determine why employees are leaving by asking them to complete a form or by conducting an exit interview. Data resulting from these questionnaires or interviews may provide insights into organizational problems that should be corrected.

Involuntary separation, or firing of an employee, should be considered an action of last resort because of the investment of the organization in each employee. Training and counseling should be tried before termination is considered. Also, because of legal implications, thorough and complete documentation of poor performance is necessary when firing an employee.

Another type of separation may be the result of a decision to reduce the work force. In this instance, the layoff may be the result of elimination of jobs, new technology, or depressed economic conditions. Decisions on layoffs should be made carefully and assistance in finding another job should be given to the laid-off employee, if at all possible.

Employee Discipline

Discipline is an organizational action against an employee who fails to conform to the policies or rules established by the organization. It is used to aid in obtaining effective performance and to ensure adherence to work rules. It also serves to establish minimum standards of performance and behavior. Some of the more common problems with employees that necessitate disciplinary action are listed in Figure 20.10.

Disciplinary actions must be judged on the merits of specific situations. While discipline is a punishment for past behavior, it should be used as a tool for improving behavior, productivity, and human relations at the work place. Unfortunately, discipline is often viewed strictly as a punitive measure, rather than as a learning process for guiding future behavior.

Attendance Problems	On-the-Job Behavior Problems
Unexcused absence	Intoxication at work
Chronic absenteeism	Insubordination
Unexcused/excessive tardiness	Horseplay
Leaving without permission	Smoking in unauthorized places
	Fighting
	Gambling
Dishonesty and Related Problems	Failure to use safe devices
Theft	Failure to report injuries
Falsifying employment application	Carelessness
Willful damage to company property	Sleeping on the job
Punching another employee's time	Abusive or threatening language to
card	supervisors
Falsifying work records	Possession of narcotics or alcohol
	Possession of firearms or other weapons

Figure 20.10. *Common disciplinary problems.* **Source: Chruden, H. J., and Sherman, A. W.: Personnel Management: The Utilization of Human Resources, 6th ed. Cincinnati: South-Western Publishing Co., copyright © 1980.**

Disciplinary Procedures. Usually, several steps are involved in a disciplinary procedure, which may include the following:

- Unrecorded oral warning.
- Oral warning with notation in an employee's personnel file.
- Written reprimand.
- Suspension.
- Discharge.

Exceptions do occur in the above steps, depending on the nature of the employee's offense. For example, a foodservice employee caught in the act of theft would probably be fired immediately, rather than being warned, orally or in writing, or suspended.

A key element in discipline is consistency. An employee should feel that any other employee would receive the same discipline under essentially the same circumstances. Also, disciplinary action should be the consequence of an employee's behavior, and not of a personality conflict with the supervisor. Discipline should be administered in a straightforward, calm way without anger or apology. The manager should avoid arguing with an employee and should generally administer discipline in private to avoid embarrassing the employee. In a few instances, public reprimand may be necessary to enable a manager to regain control of a situation.

In most organizations, a grievance procedure has been established to ensure that employees have due process in disciplinary situations. In other words, grievance procedures allow an employee to have a fair hearing when he or she believes a personnel action has been administered unfairly. These procedures generally involve a multistep process whereby the employee first requests a review by the next highest level supervisor. If a satisfactory solution is not found at this level, then a higher level review can be requested. Grievance committees are often appointed to review actions not settled through the chain of command. In cases where the organization is unionized, grievance procedures are specified in the union contract and include provisions for hearings by an outside arbitrator when problems cannot be solved within the organization.

Grievances and disciplinary action can be reduced in a number of ways. These methods include:

- Preparation of accurate job descriptions and specifications.
- Selection of individuals with appropriate qualifications for job requirements.
- Development of effective orientation, training, and performance evaluation systems.
- Utilization of good human skills by supervisors.

Identifying Causes. An employee's immediate supervisor has the primary responsibility for preventing or correcting disciplinary problems. In attempting to uncover reasons for unsatisfactory behavior, the supervisor must first consider if the employee is aware of certain policies and work rules before initiating disciplinary action. If the employee is aware of these policies, the supervisor must then realize that understanding the causes underlying the problem is as important as dealing with the problematic behavior; any attempt to prevent recurrence requires an understanding of these causes.

Health problems, personal crises, emotional problems, or chemical dependency may be the source of the unsatisfactory performance. Marital, family, financial, or legal problems are the predominant personal crisis situations that may affect employee performance.

Another factor affecting job performance may be stress (Heneman et al. 1980), an occupational health hazard that is now being increasingly recognized. While most employees are able to cope with stress, some employees are not and become "troubled" employees. Impaired mental health, alcoholism, and drug abuse may be symptomatic of the troubled employee.

Supervisors need to be alert to all these possible causes of problematic behavior. While the supervisor may not be prepared to assist or counsel an employee, many organizations provide supervisors with some combination of training, policy guidance, and opportunities to consult with, or refer employees to, specialized counseling or medical personnel both inside and outside the organization.

Some organizations are beginning to take a more positive approach to dealing with troubled employees by establishing employee assistance programs. The objective of these programs is to provide treatment or facilitate seeking of treatment to enable employees to function normally and remain productive members of the organization. These programs typically include supervisory training, internal staff counseling, referral services to community agencies, and involvement of the employee's dependents. Organizations are recognizing that discharging a troubled employee may not only be inhumane but also an ineffective solution, because similar problems may occur with a new employee.

Compensation Management

Employee compensation represents a substantial part of the operating costs of an organization. Along with good working conditions and sound employment practices, compensation appropriate for an individual's qualifications and the responsibilities of a job is essential for recruitment and retention of capable employees.

Compensation

Compensation includes salaries or wages and benefits. Salary is the term used to refer to earnings of managerial and professional personnel; wages refer to hourly earnings of workers covered by the Fair Labor Standards Act, sometimes called the Minimum Wage or Wage-Hour Law. Benefits refer to compensation offered other than salary or wages and include:

- Statutory benefits for payment required by law to ensure the worker and family an income in the event of unemployment, injury, or death.
- Compensatory benefits or pay for time not worked.
- Supplementary benefits, which include any other compensation, such as life and health insurance.

Lawler (1975) contends that pay can be an incentive if pay and performance are related and if employees believe that they are paid fairly compared to others. Compensation is thus considered an exchange—labor or services for money. Hersey and Blanchard (1982) contend that money is a complicated motivator that may be related to several basic needs: material acquisitions, status, and self-actualization.

Methods of Determining Compensation

An employer must choose a position on compensation by deciding where along a continuum the organization will stand: a leader, top pay for the cream of the labor force; minimum pay to keep jobs filled; or somewhere in between. According to Henderson (1979), the decision is influenced by the economy, collective bargaining, the labor market, the financial status of the organization, and other factors. Among the criteria used by organizations for rationalizing pay decisions are the following:

- *Comparable wage.* Surveys determine the "going rate" in the area for each occupation. Comparable wage has special value in a tight labor market in which competition is strong for the available labor but timely and accurate information difficult to obtain.

- *Cost of living.* This criterion ensures keeping up with inflation.
- *The employer's ability to pay.* The organization must compare the projected wage bill with the projected resources.
- *The labor market.* Some industries scan the market, especially when certain labor groups are in short supply, to draw the power they need to fill job openings.

The first step of compensation is a job evaluation to identify the work content of each job: required responsibilities, education, experience, and the skill necessary for performing the duties under the existing conditions. Compensable factors are individual parts on a job that when considered together define the job and determine its value. The functions of the variety of jobs in an organization determine the choice of factors to be used.

Quantitative and non-quantitative methods are the traditional classifications of job evaluation. Job ranking and job classification are considered non-quantitative. In job ranking, organizational job descriptions are ranked by an official from most to least complex. This method is simple and requires little time but is subjected to raters' skill and information.

In job classification, a number of classes or grades are defined and the jobs are then "fit." This method is designed to place jobs of the same general value in the same pay grade and provides a smooth progression for advancement.

The quantitative methods of job evaluation are used more widely. In the factor method, jobs are compared by determining important compensable factors; judgments are then made on the degree to which each job has these factors. The point method breaks down jobs into compensable factors, giving each factor a numerical score, then adding the scores for a job total.

Government Influences

Since the 1930s, a broad spectrum of federal laws has been enacted with significant impact on the compensation practices in organizations. Several of the laws discussed in the Human Resource Planning section of this chapter include provisions related to compensation, most of which address issues relating to nondiscrimination in compensation. A number of other laws and regulations also serve to regulate compensation of employees: the Fair Labor Standards Act, workers' compensation laws, Social Security, Unemployment Compensation, retirement protection, and garnishment of wages. In addition, in foodservice and other segments of the hospitality industry, legislation and regulations applying specifically to tipped employees have been enacted. Foodservice managers in operations in which employees frequently receive tips must stay up-to-date on the current provisions of these laws and regulations as well as other legislation related to compensation and employment practices.

Fair Labor Standards Act. The enactment of the Fair Labor Standards Act in 1938 (FLSA) established minimum wages for hourly employees and overtime wage requirements. Through the years, amendments to the Act have enlarged the number of work groups covered by the law and have steadily increased the minimum wage. Employees in the foodservice industry were not covered by the minimum wage legislation until the mid-1960s. The act requires employers to pay time-and-a-half the regular rate received by employees for all hours worked in excess of 40 hours a week. The FLSA forbids the employment of minors under the age 18 in hazardous occupations. Employment of minors under 16 is also controlled under the Act.

The Act also defines specific occupations that are exempt from the minimum wage and overtime requirements. Executive, administrative, professional, and sales personnel are included in the exempt category. Employee exemption depends on the responsibilities and duties of a job and the salary paid. Definitions and requirements for the job responsibilities and salary provisions are defined by the U.S. Department of Labor for these exempt categories.

Workers' Compensation. The first U.S. legislation providing compensation to workers disabled in industrial accidents was enacted in 1911. Today, workers' compensation legislation covers most American workers. Each of the 50 states has its own laws and agencies to administer them. In general, these laws provide for income and medical benefits to victims of work-related accidents, reduce court delays arising out of personal injury litigation, encourage employer interest in safety and rehabilitation, eliminate payment of fees to lawyers and witnesses, and promote study of accident causes.

Social Security. The Social Security Act of 1935 established a program designed to protect covered employees against loss of earnings resulting from retirement, unemployment, disability, or in the case of dependents, from the death or disability of the person supporting them. The Social Security program is supported by means of a tax levied against an employee's earnings that must be matched by the employer. Self-employed persons are required to pay a tax on their earnings, higher than that paid by employees.

In recent years, the tax rate and the maximum amount of earnings subject to the tax have periodically been adjusted upward to cover liberalization of benefits. In the mid-1960s, the Medicaid and Medicare programs, which provide health insurance benefits, were established by amendments to the Social Security Act. According to Henderson (1979), concern over the economic stability of the social security system may lead to the enactment by Congress of significant changes in the coming years.

Unemployment Compensation. Employees who have been working in employment covered by the Social Security Act and who are laid off may be eligible for compensation during their unemployment for a period up to 26 weeks. When workers become unemployed through no fault of their own, states provide them with certain weekly benefits. Each state has its own unemployment insurance law that defines the terms and benefits of its program. Employers are required to pay a tax that may be adjusted up or down, depending on the extent of terminations by an employer.

Pension. At the present time, the majority of the nonfarm work force receives some form of retirement protection through either private pension, deferred profit-sharing plans, or savings plans. In recent years, these programs increasingly have been placed under federal regulations. Various laws and court rulings over the years have restricted the right of management in the operation and control of pension programs. To protect pension plans from failures, the Employed Retirement Income Security Act of 1974, commonly known as ERISA or the Pension Reform Law, was enacted. This law establishes employer responsibilities, reporting and disclosure, employee participation and coverage, vesting, and other requirements.

Garnishment of Wages. Another government law that protects the income of the worker is the Federal Wage Garnishment Law, which limits the amount of the employee's disposable earnings that may be garnished in any one week and protects the worker from discharge because of garnishment for indebtedness. A garnishment is a legal action by which earnings of an individual are required to be withheld for the payment of a debt.

Benefits

Benefits have grown and changed in the last 40 years because of social, economic, and legislative events. During the 1930s, the need for economic recovery led to enactment of the social security program and various other aid programs. In 1935, the Wagner Act was passed, establishing the National Labor Relations Board and permitting labor to organize and bargain collectively for benefits. Many fringe benefits, such as vacations, holidays, and medical insurance, have become the norm as a result.

According to Beadle (1980), today's employee benefits continue to increase more rapidly than wages. Lindsey (1981) reported that in 1980 private employers were offering benefits accounting for 37.1 percent of payroll, while the benefits of 67 surveyed hospitals averaged only 29.6 percent of payroll.

The statutory benefits, required by law, include social security, unemployment insurance, and workers' compensation. Compensatory benefits are paid time off, such as vacation, sick leave, holidays, and personal leave. Leave time has shown a slow but steady increase over the years.

Health insurance, life insurance, retirement plans, profit-sharing or annuity plans, and continuing education payments are commonly included in supplementary benefits (Martin, 1980). Medical insurance is the most costly benefit offered. Dental insurance is a relatively new addition to the benefit package. If life insurance plans are offered, the employer usually pays the entire premium. Other supplementary benefits are being offered to employees in various organizations.

These include child care reimbursement, uniforms, discounts for products or services of the organization, and tuition reimbursement.

According to Martin (1980), a new idea in supplementary benefits is the cafeteria plan. The organization has the basic benefits of all employees, then offers a variety of other benefits from which an employee may choose, depending on personal needs.

LABOR-MANAGEMENT RELATIONS

Since the 1800s, labor unions have played an important role in American economic and political life by representing the interests of their members. In the private sector, unions have been a powerful force for many years. Approximately 25 percent of the nonagricultural work force are union members. In recent years, employees of federal, state, and local government agencies and of educational and other nonprofit organizations have become unionized in increasing numbers. Labor relations, thus, has become an important function of personnel management in many types of organizations. Labor relations, or labor-management relations, is a term referring to the interaction between management and a labor union. A closely related term is collective bargaining, which focuses on the negotiation and administration of labor unions.

Unions generally have three primary goals: (1) to organize workers, (2) to negotiate favorable terms and conditions of employment, and (3) to guard and protect the rights of workers in the day-to-day operation of the organization. As already discussed in this chapter, union agreements include provisions related to a number of aspects of personnel management, such as promotions and grievances.

Historically, unions have had their greatest success in the manufacturing, mining, transportation, and construction segments of the economy. With the decline in these sectors and the relative growth in the service industries, unions have begun to focus organizational efforts on service employees.

According to Dilts and Deitsch (1983), retailing establishments and restaurants, once believed to be immune to unionization because of their largely unskilled labor force, have yielded large numbers of new union members. Legislation in the 1970s removed the previous exemption of nonprofit healthcare institutions from unionization of employees. These developments indicate that managers of foodservice operations must be knowledgeable about labor legislation, collective bargaining, and other aspects of labor-management relations.

Reasons Workers Join Unions

Labor unions have usually developed as a reaction to the decision making power of management. The power of employees to bargain with their employer on an individual basis and to protect themselves from arbitrary and unfair treatment is limited. As a result, many employees find that bargaining collectively with their employer through a union is advantageous. Moreover, this method of bargaining is protected by legislation. When employees are unionized, personnel management is subject to negotiation with the union and to the terms of the agreement resulting from these negotiations.

Employees join unions for a variety of reasons, including real or perceived needs for greater job security, compensation, and social affiliation. Another important reason is a possible contract provision called the <u>union shop</u> clause, which requires that workers join the union within a prescribed period of time after being employed.

Bad experiences with management, such as an unjust disciplinary action, or general distrust of management may result in workers organizing or joining a union. In addition, peer group pressure, social values, appeals by union organizers, poor working conditions, and low wages are other factors.

Development of Labor Unions

Modern unionization has its roots in the guilds of artisans of the Middle Ages. For centuries, workers of similar skill backgrounds have formed organizations to govern entry to an occupation, define standards of occupation conduct, and regulate employment. In the United States, the first union activity dates to the late 1700s.

After the Civil War, the first attempts to build national unions began. According to Dilts and Deitsch (1983), the basic organizational structure and guiding philosophy of the American labor movement were determined with the formation of the American Federation of Labor (AFL) in 1886. Union membership thrived during the early 1900s.

The First World War proved a boon to organized labor, which then fell upon hard times during the Great Depression that began with the collapse of the stock market in 1929. Strife among the segments of the union movement was great in the 1930s.

As a federation of trade unions for craft workers, the AFL had ignored the unskilled and semiskilled workers in the rapidly expanding mass production industries that were developing in the early 1900s. As a result, a number of labor leaders spearheaded efforts to organize factory workers into industrial labor organizations throughout the decade of the thirties. In 1938, the Congress of Industrial Organizations (CIO) was formed as a national federation of these unions. After two decades of rivalries and conflict, the AFL and CIO were united in 1955 into a single organization. Although the majority of the national and international labor unions belong to the AFL-CIO, a number of unions are unaffiliated.

Structure of Unions

The American labor movement is comprised of three basic formalized components: the local union, the national or international union, and the federation. The <u>local union</u> is the organizational component that handles day-to-day problems arising under collective bargaining. Unionized workers are members of the local rather than the national union with which the local is affiliated. The local is typically chartered by a national union, which in turn may be affiliated with the AFL-CIO. Some independent local unions do exist; however, they are becoming relatively scarce because of the advantages of being part of a larger national union.

A primary function of the local union is to represent employees in the collective bargaining process, although contract negotiations may be done on the national level. The local is also involved in working with management on the administration of the contract. Under the terms of the contract, the union steward represents the interests of members in their relations with their immediate supervisors and other members of management.

The <u>national union</u> provides technical assistance in negotiating and administering labor contracts, financial assistance during strikes, administration of union-sponsored pension plans and other fringe benefits, training programs for local union officers, and publications. In addition, national unions are generally active in lobbying efforts in the U.S. Congress, as well as at the state level. Finally, the national union also organizes, establishing the rules and conditions under which the local unions may be chartered.

Among national unions active in the hospitality service industries are the Hotel, Motel, and Club Employees Union and the Hotel and Restaurant Employees and Bartenders International Union. Employees in the foodservice industry may be affiliated with other unions, however, and those in the healthcare and public organizations are often members of unions specifically organized for those sectors.

National unions are autonomous organizations that may opt voluntarily for affiliation with the AFL-CIO or remain independent. A primary benefit of affiliation in the AFL-CIO is some protection from membership raiding by other unions. Other advantages of affiliation include facilitation of coordinated bargaining, assistance in organizing efforts, and lobbying on behalf of organized labor.

Major Labor Legislation

In the private sector, four major federal laws regulate employer and/or union conduct in labor-management relations: the Norris-LaGuardia Act, the Wagner Act, the Taft-Hartley Act, and the Landrum-Griffin Act. In the public sector, state and local government employees are covered by state laws, while federal civil service workers are covered by the Civil Service Reform Act of 1978.

Norris-LaGuardia Act

The Norris-LaGuardia Act of 1932, or the Anti-injunction Act, severely restricted the ability of employers to obtain an injunction in a federal court forbidding a union from engaging in picketing or strike activities. The Norris-LaGuardia Act also nullified <u>yellow-dog</u> contracts, which were agreements that required workers to state they were not union members and promise not to join one.

Wagner Act

The Wagner Act of 1935, or the National Labor Relations Act, has had the most significant impact on labor-management relations of any legislation. Through its creation of the National Labor Relations Board (NLRB) to administer its provisions, the Act placed the protective power of the federal government behind employee efforts to organize and bargain collectively through representatives of their choice.

The Act established the right of a union to be the exclusive bargaining agent for all workers in a bargaining unit. A bargaining unit is a group of jobs in a firm, plant, or industry with sufficient commonality to constitute the unit represented by a particular bargaining agent.

The law declared the following to be unfair labor practices:

- Management support of a company union.
- Discharge or discipline of workers for union activities.
- Discrimination against workers making complaints to the NLRB.
- Refusal to bargain with employee representatives.
- Interference with the rights of employees to act together for mutual aid or protection.

The primary duties identified for the NLRB were to hold secret ballot elections to determine representation and to interpret and apply the law concerning unfair labor practices. The courts may review decisions on unfair labor practices but the NLRB's decisions on representation elections are final.

Taft-Hartley Act

The Taft-Hartley Act was passed in 1947 over President Truman's veto to amend the Wagner Act, although most of its major provisions were retained. The major thrust of the legislation was to balance the powers of labor and management. Before passage of the Wagner Act, employees had little power to organize and bargain and, therefore, the early labor legislation restricted only employer activity. Because the bargaining power of unions increased significantly following the passage of the Wagner Act, restraints on union practices were considered to be necessary.

The following activities were defined as unfair union practices in the Taft-Hartley Act:

- Restraining or coercing employers in the selection of parties to bargain on their behalf.
- Persuading employers to discriminate against any employees.
- Refusing to bargain collectively.
- Participating in secondary boycotts and jurisdictional disputes.
- Attempting to force recognition from an employer when another union is already the representative.
- Charging excessive initiation fees.

- Practicing "featherbedding" or requiring payment of wages for services not performed.

According to Chruden and Sherman (1980), a major effect of the Taft-Hartley Act was to relax the restrictions that the Wagner Act had placed on employers' freedom of speech. Under Taft-Hartley, employers were given some opportunity to express views regarding unions and unionizing efforts.

Also, the Act denies supervisors the legal protection of forming their own unions and denies the closed shop. The closed shop requires that an employer hire only union members. Other provisions include government authorization to seek an injunction preventing work stoppage for 80 days in a strike that imperils the nation's health and welfare and authorization for states to pass "right-to-work" laws. The right-to-work provision contained in Section 14b of Taft-Hartley allows states to enact laws prohibiting the negotiation of contracts requiring union membership as a condition of continued employment. In 1983, 20 states had "right-to-work" statutes.

In 1974, Congress extended coverage of Taft-Hartley to private nonprofit hospitals and nursing homes. Provisions require unions representing hospital employees to give 90 days' notice before terminating a labor agreement—30 days more than in other industries. Also, a labor dispute in a healthcare facility is automatically subject to mediation efforts of the Federal Mediation and Concilia-tion Service (Sloane and Witney, 1981).

Landrum-Griffin Act

The Landrum-Griffin Act, passed in 1959, is entitled the Labor-Management Reporting and Disclosure Act. According to Heneman et al. (1980), it resulted from widespread investigations into labor racketeering in the 1950s. These inves-tigations revealed that a few labor organizations and employers were denying employees' rights to representation and due process within their labor orga-nizations.

The Act requires that labor organizations hold periodic elections for officers, that members be entitled to due process both within and outside the union, that copies of labor agreements be made available to covered employees, and that financial dealings between union officials and companies be disclosed to the U.S. Department of Labor. The law tightens the Taft-Hartley Act restrictions against secondary boycotts. A secondary boycott occurs when a union asks firms or other unions to cease doing business with someone handling a "struck product." The union can only ask that the product not be used.

Civil Service Reform Act

For most federal workers, no union representation existed before the 1960s. Prior to enactment of the Civil Service Reform Act, executive orders established the right of government employees to be represented by labor organizations and to enter into agreements regarding working conditions. The Civil Service Reform Act of 1978 was designed to improve the federal civil service system and to codify the relationship between federal-employee unions and the federal government. According to the law, these unions are prohibited from striking or making demands in the staffing area. The Act established an independent body, the Federal Labor Relations Authority, to monitor labor-management relations and provide for arbitration of unresolved grievances.

Contract Negotiations

After a union wins recognition as the employees' bargaining agent, negotiations will begin on a contract with management. Bargaining is a difficult and sensitive proceeding.

In local negotiations, the union side is represented by its local negotiating committee and may include a field representative of the national union with which it is affiliated. The management team may be made up of personnel staff, financial or operations managers, and perhaps an attorney. Negotiations at the national level are led by top-level officials from the national union and by top-level corporate managers and staff.

Major bargaining issues usually fall into five areas:

- Economic issues deal with such provisions as base pay, shift differentials, overtime pay, length of service increases, and cost of living allowances, as well as with benefits such as pension plans, insurance, holidays, and vacations.

- Job security means both an entitlement to work or, in lieu of work, an entitlement to income protection. Procedures for handling layoffs, promotions, transfers, assignment to specific jobs, unemployment benefits, severance pay, and call-in pay are among the job security provisions generally included in union contracts.

- Working conditions issues include work rules, relief periods, work schedules, and safety and health.

- Management rights issues detail the rights of management to give direction and discipline employees.

- Individual rights issues concern establishment of grievance procedures for employees.

Careful preparation for negotiations is critical and should include planning the strategy and assembling data to support bargaining proposals or positions. The conditions under which negotiations take place vary widely among organizations and are dependent on the goals that each side seeks to achieve and the strength of their relative positions. First-time negotiations are usually more difficult than subsequent negotiating sessions after a union has become established. The negotiation of an agreement often takes on the characteristics of a game in which each side attempts to determine its opponent's position while not revealing its own.

Proposals or positions of each side are generally divided into those that it feels it must achieve, those on which it will compromise, and those submitted primarily for trading purposes. Throughout the negotiations, all proposals or positions submitted by both sides must be disposed of if agreement is to be reached; that is, each proposal or position must be accepted by the other side, either in its entirety or in some compromised form, or it must be withdrawn. To achieve its bargaining proposals or positions, each side presents arguments and evidence necessary to support them and exerts pressure on the other side. The outcome of this power struggle determines which side will make the greater concession to avoid a bargaining deadlock.

The power of the union may be exercised by striking, picketing, or boycotting the employer's product. An employer who is struck by a union may continue to operate or opt for a lockout, shutting down operations. If a strike or lockout occurs, both parties are affected. Therefore, both participants usually are anxious to achieve a settlement.

When the two parties are unable to resolve a deadlock, a third party, either a mediator or an arbitrator, may be called in to provide assistance. A mediator attempts to establish a channel of communication between the union and management but has no power to force a settlement. In mediation, compromise solutions are only offered by the third party. If the contract calls for binding arbitration, an arbitrator is called in, who then renders a decision that is binding on both the union and the employer. After an agreement has been reached through collective bargaining, the written document must be signed by representatives of both parties.

In recent years, union-management relations have been characterized by greater accommodation and cooperation. As Chruden and Sherman (1980) point out, employers have learned the futility of attempting to destroy a union or to be on the defensive when negotiating with a union. Also, union leaders, and even the rank-and-file members, have increasingly become aware that a company must remain competitive if it and the jobs it provides are to continue in existence. Consequently, union members are frequently exhibiting a more conciliatory attitude in making concessions during collective bargaining.

SUMMARY

The most important resources in the organization are its human resources. To be effective, an organization must have competent people at the managerial and all other levels.

Staffing is a management function concerned with bringing human resources into the system and maintaining the work force. The first step in the process, human resource planning, involves estimating the size and composition of the future work force. Personnel planning must be integrated with organization planning to ensure that the right people are available at the right time for changes in organization structure, for expansions, and for other corporate goals.

Government legislation has a critical impact on personnel planning. Laws enacted during the last two decades are designed to eliminate discrimination in employment and other personnel practices.

The employment process involves a series of activities including recruitment, selection, placement, and orientation and initial training for new personnel. Development and maintenance of the work force includes training, performance evaluation, and also changes in job placement, such as promotions, demotions, transfers, or separations.

Disciplinary actions may be necessary to establish minimum standards of performance and behavior of employees. These procedures usually involve a series of steps, beginning with oral warning and ending in discharge if corrective action does not occur. Also, grievance procedures should be established to ensure that employees have due process in disciplinary situations. Understanding the causes of problematic behavior is important and supervisors should be trained to recognize problems and assist employees in seeking help or treatment if deemed necessary.

Sound employment practices, appropriate compensation, and good working conditions are important for recruitment and retention of capable employees. Compensation includes salary or wages and various benefits that may be provided by an organization. Compensation systems should be related to performance and must be administered equitably.

Since the 1930s, a broad spectrum of legislation has been enacted that has had a significant impact on compensation practices in an organization. These laws have established minimum wages, workers' compensation for victims of work-related accidents, the social security program, unemployment compensation, and pension protection.

If an organization is unionized, union contracts influence many aspects of personnel planning and supervision. Labor relations refers to the interaction between management and a labor union; collective bargaining focuses on the negotiation and administration of labor agreements. In the private sector, labor unions have been a powerful force for many years; more recently, employees in public and other nonprofit organizations have become unionized in increasing numbers. Several federal laws have been enacted to regulate labor-management relations and union activity. The most recent legislation applies to unionization in the public sector. In the 1980s, union-management relations have been characterized by greater accommodation and cooperation, primarily because of the economic times.

Managers must be knowledgeable about the many laws affecting the employment and direction of employees and, if their organizations are unionized, must be skillful in working with unions. Foodservice managers must also be competent in all aspects of the staffing function to ensure that qualified people are employed and retained by the organization.

REFERENCES

Beadle, C. E.: Revitalizing employee benefit programs. *Compensation Rev.* 12:61 (2nd Quarter), 1980.

Chruden, H. J., and Sherman, A. W.: *Personnel Management: The Utilization of Human Resources.* 6th ed. Cincinnati: South-Western Publishing Co., 1980.

Conducting the Lawful Employment Interview: How to Avoid Charges of Discrimination When Interviewing Job Candidates. 2nd ed. New York: Executive Enterprises Publications Co., 1979.

Dalton, D. R., and Todor, W. D.: Turnover turned over: An expanded and positive perspective. *Acad. Mgmt. Rev.* 4:225, 1979.

Dilts, D. A., and Deitsch, C. R.: *Labor Relations.* New York: Macmillan Publishing Co., 1983.

Doherty, R. E.: *Industrial and Labor Relations Terms: A Glossary.* ILR Bulletin No. 44. 4th ed. Ithaca, NY: Cornell University, 1979.

Franke, A. G., Harrick, E. J., and Klein, A. J.: The role of personnel in improving productivity. *Personnel Admin.* 27:83 (Mar.), 1982.

Frantzreb, R. B.: Human resource planning: Forecasting manpower needs. *Personnel J.* 60:850 (Nov.), 1981.

Goldstein, I. L.: The application blank: How honest are the responses? *J. Appl. Psychol.* 55:491 (Oct.), 1971.

Grimes, R. M., and Rutsohn, P. D.: Collective bargaining: *Quo Vadis* for the allied health profession. *J. Allied Health* 6:52 (Fall), 1977.

Harrison, E. L.: Legal restrictions on the employer's authority to discipline. *Personnel J.* 61:135, 1982.

Haynes, M. G.: Developing an appraisal program. Part I. *Personnel J.* 57:14, 1978.

Haynes, M. G.: Developing an appraisal program. Part II. *Personnel J.* 57:66, 1978.

Henderson, R. I.: *Compensation Management: Rewarding Performance.* 2nd ed. Reston, VA: Reston Publishing Co., 1979.

Heneman, H. G., Schwab, D. P., Fossum, J. A., and Dyer, L. D.: *Personnel/Human Resource Management.* Homewood, IL: Richard D. Irwin, 1980.

Hersey, P., and Blanchard, K.: *Management of Organizational Behavior: Utilizing Human Resources.* 4th ed. Englewood Cliffs, NJ: Prentice-Hall, 1982.

Howe, W. C.: Management still must train. *Supervisory Mgmt.* 22:26 (Jul.), 1977.

Jackson, T.: *Interviewing Women: Avoiding Charges of Discrimination.* New York: Executive Enterprises Publications Co., 1976.

Keith, R. W.: The role of innovation in personnel planning. *Banking J.* 7:60 (Dec.), 1979.

Lawler, E. E.: Pay, participation, and organizational change. In Cass, E. L., and Zimmer, F. G., eds.: *Man and Work in Society.* New York: Van Nostrand Reinhold Co., 1975.

Lindsey, F. D.: Employee benefits bigger bite. *Nation's Bus. J.* 69:75 (Dec.), 1981.

Malinowski, F. A.: Job selection using task analysis. *Personnel J.* 60:288, 1981.

Martin, G. M.: Fringe around the paycheck: Employee benefits. *Occupational Outlook Q.* 24:17 (2nd Quarter), 1980.

Mier, C. S.: Methods and techniques for inservice education. *J. Am. Dietet. A.* 79:692, 1981.

Mitchell, D. J. B.: Collective bargaining and wage determination in the public sector: Is Armageddon really at hand? *Public Personnel Mgmt.* 7:80 (Mar./Apr.), 1978.

Mondy, R. W., Holmes, R. E., and Flippo, E. B.: *Management: Concepts and Practices.* 2nd ed. Boston: Allyn and Bacon, 1983.

Nehrbass, R. G.: Psychological barriers to effective employment interviewing. *Personnel J.* 56:60 (Feb.), 1977.

Neil, C. A.: Working smarter not harder. *School Food Service Journal* 37:51 (Nov./Dec.), 1983.

Pati, G. C., and Adkins, J. I.: Hire the handicapped: Compliance is good business. *Harvard Bus. Rev.* 58:14 (Jan./Feb.), 1980.

Patten, T. H.: *Manpower Planning and the Development of Human Resources.* New York: John Wiley & Sons, 1972.

Peter, L. J., and Hall, R.: *The Peter Principle.* New York: Bantam Books, 1969.

Puckett, R. P.: Dietetics: Making or breaking the new employee. *Contemporary Administrator* 5:14 (Oct.), 1982.

Reed, L. E.: Training effectiveness in school food service. *J. Am. Dietet. A.* 81:176, 1982.

Roseman, E.: *Managing Employee Turnover: A Positive Approach.* New York: AMACOM, 1981.

Rue, L. W., and Byars, L. L.: *Management: Theory and Application.* 3rd ed. Homewood, IL: Richard D. Irwin, 1983.

Schneider, H. L.: Personnel managers look to the '80s. *Personnel Admin.* 24:47 (Nov.), 1979.

Sheahan, R. E.: Labor relations. *Personnel J.* 61:114 (Jan.), 1982.

Sloane, A. A., and Witney, F.: *Labor Relations.* 4th ed. Englewood Cliffs, NJ: Prentice-Hall, 1981.

Stokes, A.: *The Equal Opportunity Handbook for Hotels, Restaurants and Institutions.* Boston: CBI Publishing Co., 1979.

Stoner, J. A. F.: *Management.* 2nd ed. Englewood Cliffs, NJ: Prentice-Hall, 1982.

Summers, C. W.: Protecting *all* employees against unjust dismissal. *Harvard Bus. Rev.* 58:132 (Jan./Feb.), 1980.

The Supervisor's EEO Handbook: A Guide to Federal Antidiscrimination Laws and Regulations. 3rd ed. New York: Executive Enterprises Publications Co., 1981.

Tauber, M. S.: New employee orientation: A comprehensive systems approach. *Personnel Admin.* 26:65, 1981.

Taylor, W. C.: Absenteeism in health care food service. *J. Am. Dietet. A.* 79:699, 1981.

War Manpower Commission.: The Training Within Industry Report. War Manpower Commission, Bureau of Training, 1945.

White, R.: Performance enhancement by reciprocal accountability. *Public Personnel Mgmt.* 8:262 (Apr.), 1979.

Witzy, H. K.: *The Labor-Management Relations Handbook for Hotels, Motels, Restaurants, and Institutions.* Boston: Cahners Books, 1975.

Yager, E.: A critique of performance appraisal systems. *Personnel J.* 60:129, 1981.

21

Management of Financial Resources

Effective management of financial resources is critical to the success of any foodservice operation. Control of costs within the framework of available revenue is important in both profit and non-profit foodservice organizations. The foodservice manager must understand key accounting and financial management concepts and procedures in order to analyze the financial performance of the foodservice operation.

KEY ACCOUNTING CONCEPTS

Accounting is often characterized as the "language of business." The accounting system is designed to provide a framework for the accumulation of financial data in such a way as to present the financial position of an organization and the results of its operation. Accounting has been defined as the process of identifying, measuring, and communicating economic information to permit informed judgment and decisions by users of the information (American Accounting Association, 1966). This information is composed principally of financial data about business transactions expressed in terms of money.

Niswonger and Fess (1981) describe the "basic raw materials" of accounting as business transactions, and its "primary end products" as various summaries, analyses, and reports. The accounting process results in the presentation of financial data to a variety of users who are interested in an organization's performance. Formal financial statements and informal management reports are generated on a regular basis for these purposes. The formal statements are the balance sheet, the income statement, and the funds flow statement.

Management reports are generally internally oriented and are designed to reflect measures of financial performance useful in making operating decisions. These reports provide managers at various levels of the organization information on progress during a specified period.

Users of Financial Statements

The users of financial statements may be classified in terms of their specific needs, which will differ depending on whether the organization has a profit or not-for-profit objective. Profit making organizations respond to a demand for a product or service with the expectation of earning net income, or an excess of revenue over the expenses incurred in earning the revenue. The resulting net income or profit is distributed to the owners of the business after taxes have been paid and funds retained for facility and operational improvements.

For the profit making organization, five groups of users can be identified: owners and potential owners, creditors and suppliers, managers, government agencies, and employees. Owners and potential owners or investors need information about the financial status of the organization and its future prospects. Creditors and suppliers are interested in the financial soundness of the organization to assess the risk involved in making loans or granting credit. Managers are concerned with assessing the financial performance of the organization, and government agencies are concerned with taxation and regulation. Employees and, if unionized, their union representatives are vitally interested in the stability and profitability of the organization that employs them.

To apply these concepts to a commercial foodservice organization, a potential franchisee of a new seafood restaurant would be interested in the profitability of the parent organization and its potential for continuing business success. The franchisee's banker, who would potentially make a loan for purchasing the land, constructing the building, and buying the equipment, would be interested not only in the financial stability of the parent organization but also in the potential credit risks of the franchisee. The suppliers would be interested in the ability of the franchisee to pay bills on time, and the manager of the unit, probably employed on a profit sharing basis, would be interested in the income potential of the business. Federal and state tax agencies would be concerned with an accurate reporting of net income after the restaurant is in operation as the basis for income and sales tax liability. The employees would be interested in the ability of the restaurant to make a profit and stay in business so their jobs will continue.

Non-profit organizations provide goods or services that fulfill a social need and do not have a conscious profit motive. Excess revenues over expenditures are not distributed to those who contributed to support through taxes or voluntary donations but are used to further the purposes of the organization. In tax-supported organizations, the public is interested in the efficiency of the organization in using public monies. A key concern in all types of non-profit organizations is the appropriate use of funds. Suppliers are concerned about the ability of the organization to pay bills and administrators about controlling expenditures in relation to available funds. Some non-profit organizations are established to provide services to a specific clientele for a fee that closely approximates the cost of providing the service. Therefore, the clientele are concerned about the efficiency of the organization to assure that costs for services are maintained as low as possible. In the foodservice industry, most healthcare, college and university, and school feeding operations, as well as many clubs, are non-profit organizations.

Key Aspects of Accounting

Selected aspects of accounting are listed in Figure 21.1. The first listed, <u>financial accounting</u>, is concerned with the reporting of transactions for an organization and the periodic preparation of various reports from the records. The "generally accepted accounting principles," or the established rules of accounting, must be followed in recording and reporting financial data.

Bookkeeping, an integral part of this process, is concerned with the recording and reporting of business data in a prescribed manner; whereas accounting is concerned with the design of the system of records and the preparation and interpretation of reports based on the reported data. Although usually not involved in the specifics of the bookkeeping and accounting functions, the manager must be able to understand the financial reports and effectively communicate with bookkeepers and accountants.

Financial accounting
Auditing
Cost accounting
Managerial accounting

Figure 21.1. *Selected aspects of accounting*

Auditing is an area of accounting concerned with an independent review of accounting records. An audit involves examining the records that support financial reports and rendering an opinion regarding the fairness and reliability of these reports.

Cost accounting involves the determination and control of cost. It focuses on assembling and interpreting cost data for use by management in controlling current operations and planning for the future. Traditionally, the cost of production processes and of production products has been its emphasis, but increasing attention is being given to distribution costs. In a foodservice organization, service costs are also of particular concern.

Managerial accounting employs historical and estimated financial data to assist management in daily operations and in planning future operations. Identifying the cost of alternative courses of actions is one important function of managerial accounting. Another is budgeting, which involves developing a plan for revenues and expenditures and using the plan in controlling operations.

Selected Accounting Principles

Users of financial statements need a basic understanding of the principles underlying the preparation of these statements if they are to interpret them properly. This subsection is concerned with the discussion of the underlying assumptions, concepts, and principles of accounting with the greatest importance and widest applicability (Figure 21.2). The Financial Accounting Standards Board (FASB), established in 1973, has the primary responsibility for formulating financial accounting standards, although several accounting organizations have contributed to the development of accounting principles. Among these organizations are the American Accounting Association (AAA), the American Institute of Certified Public Accountants (AICPA), the National Association of Accountants (NAA), and the Financial Executives Institute (FEI). A number of governmental agencies also have an interest in the development of accounting principles, the most influential being the Securities and Exchange Commission.

The business entity
The fundamental equation
Going concern concept
Money as a unit of measure
Cost
Recognition at time of exchange
Accounting period
Matching revenue and expense
Adequate disclosure
Consistency
Materiality
Conservatism

Figure 21.2. *Selected accounting principles*

The Business Entity

The business entity concept assumes that a business enterprise is separate and distinct from the person or persons who supply its assets. Without this distinction, determining the organization's true performance and current status would be impossible. For example, if an individual restaurateur makes personal or family purchases from funds available in the cash register without recording these purchases, he or she violates good business procedures but also destroys the integrity of the business as separate from the owner's personal affairs. For accounting purposes, only those resources that are set aside for the business and those debts directly related to it are properly included in the accounts of that business.

The Fundamental Equation

In accounting terminology, the resources, debts, and ownership interests of an organization are referred to as its assets, liabilities, and capital, respectively. The relationship among them, "assets equal liabilities plus capital," is an expression of the business entity known as the fundamental or accounting equation.

Assets are the resources of the organization and are defined as any object, right, or other economic resource owned by the firm that has a monetary value. Thus, assets are things of value that the organization has the right to use or control for its own benefit. Liabilities are amounts owed by the organization to any other party; in other words, they represent the claims of the creditors. Capital is the amount invested in the organization by the owners or stockholders, plus the retention of income that is reinvested in the organization. Thus, capital represents the rights of owners to the assets of the organization.

All business transactions, from the simplest to the most complex, can be stated in terms of their effect on these three basic elements of the accounting equation. For accounting records to be in balance, each increase in assets must be accompanied by a corresponding decrease in another asset or an increase in liabilities or capital.

Going Concern Concept

One of accounting's basic assumptions is that an organization will continue to operate for an indefinite period of time. This is not to imply that a given organization will exist permanently, but simply that it will continue. Only in rare instances is an organization initiated with the expectation of remaining in existence for only a specified period of time. The going concern assumption is the basis for reporting many business transactions, which in turn affect the data reported in the financial statement. This assumption provides the justification for recording fixed assets at acquisition cost rather than at current market value, because the intent is to use these assets in generating revenue for a continuing business operation.

Money as a Unit of Measure

Money is the basis for business transactions and is the unit of measure in accounting for these transactions. In other words, to lend uniformity to financial data, all business transactions are recorded in terms of the dollar amounts involved. Using money as the unit of measure, however, ignores changes in the purchasing power of the dollar. The assumption is that the dollar has the same value today as it had in earlier periods, which is referred to as the stable dollar assumption. Because of the significant changes in the purchasing power of the dollar over the last decade, however, this assumption has been challenged. For example, assets purchased 20 years ago represent a different dollar value than assets purchased today.

Cost

The cost principle is closely related to the "money as a unit of measure" concept. It involves recording transactions or valuing assets on the basis of dollar amounts. Cost is the amount measured in dollars of cash expended for goods or services. The arguments in support of the concept include the following.

- Cost is objective and easily verified.
- Profit can be determined by matching costs against related revenues.
- Market value appraisals tend to be subjective.

Recognition at Time of Exchange

The recognition at time of exchange principle states that a sale has occurred only when an exchange of assets is completed. For example, when a restaurant patron receives and pays for the food he or she has ordered, an exchange of assets has occurred.

Customarily, revenue from the sale of commodities is considered realized at the time title passes to the buyer. At this point, the sales price has been agreed upon, the buyer acquires ownership, and the seller has an enforceable claim. The realization of revenue from sale of services may be determined similarly, although a time lag between the time of agreement and the completion of service frequently occurs. The price and terms agreed upon in the contract do not constitute revenue until the work has been performed.

Accounting Period

A complete and accurate picture of the degree of success of an organization cannot be obtained until it discontinues operations, converts assets into cash, and pays off its debts. Many decisions about the organization, however, must be made by management and others throughout its existence. Periodic reports on operations, financial positions, and changes in financial position are therefore necessary as the bases for these decisions. For this reason and others, including custom and various legal requirements, the maximum interval between these periodic reports is one year. This need for definition of an accounting period has resulted in the necessity for adjustments to account for income and expenses applicable to this accounting period.

Matching Revenue and Expense

The relating of revenue with expenses, or the matching concept, involves recognition of revenue during the accounting period in which it occurs and matching it with all applicable expenses. For example, a restaurant owner may purchase food in one accounting period and sell it in the following period. If the matching concept is not used, the cost of the food would be recorded in the accounting period prior to when the sale was recorded, thereby overstating cost in the first period and profit in the succeeding one.

The matching concept is the basis for accrual accounting, which provides the tools or procedures necessary for deferring and accruing revenues and expenses to achieve the proper matching of earned revenues and applicable expired costs. Accounting for depreciation, an aspect of accrual accounting, is a systematic means by which the costs associated with the acquisition and installation of a fixed asset are allocated over the estimated useful life of the asset. A number of methods are used for depreciation, a common one being the straight-line method. Take, for example, a $12,000 dish machine that is expected to last 20 years and to have a salvage value of $2000. If the straight-line method is used, the depreciation expense each year would be $500.

Because long-lived assets frequently decline in value faster during the first few years, a number of depreciation methods are used in which the rate of depreciation is greater in earlier years and decreases during the later years. These methods are referred to as accelerated depreciation methods.

Adequate Disclosure

Financial statements and their accompanying footnotes or other explanatory materials should contain full information on all data believed essential to a reader's understanding. This accounting principle of disclosure is particularly valuable to external users of accounting information who may be making financial and investment decisions on the basis of this information.

Consistency

An organization should use consistent accounting methods from one period to another so that their financial data will be comparable. Without consistent methods, financial statements could be interpreted incorrectly. For example, a change in depreciation methods would affect the amount of depreciation expense, and net income from one period to the next would be affected. Changes in accounting practices may be warranted on occasion; however, these changes should be noted in explanatory footnotes under the principle of adequate disclosure.

Materiality

Absolute accuracy and complete full disclosure may be neither practical nor economically feasible in presenting accounting information. The relative importance or materiality of any event, accounting procedure, or change in procedure must be considered. The accountant will exercise a degree of judgment in determining the degree of precision appropriate in financial statements. Generally, an item is considered as material if its inclusion or omission would change or influence the judgment of a reasonable person.

Conservatism

Conservatism refers to the concept of moderation in recording transactions and assigning values. Historically, accountants have tended to be conservative, favoring the method or procedure that yielded the lesser amount of net income or of asset value. The principle of conservatism is often expressed as "anticipate no profits and provide for all losses." Applied to the budgeting process, for example, revenue would tend to be understated and maximum expenses projected. According to Niswonger and Fess (1981), however, current accounting thought has shifted somewhat from this philosophy of conservatism.

BASIC FINANCIAL STATEMENTS

The primary financial statements generated by the accounting system are the balance sheet, or statement of financial condition; the income statement, or statement of profit and loss (also referred to as statement of revenue and expenditures, in a non-profit organization); and the funds flow statement, or statement of changes in financial position.

The balance sheet is a statement of assets, liabilities or debts, and capital or owner's equity at a given point in time or at the end of the accounting period. The income statement is the financial report that presents the net income or profit of an organization for the accounting period. It also provides information about the revenues and expenses that resulted in the net income or loss. The funds flow statement provides information about the sources of funds and how funds are used.

The income statement and the funds flow statement are considered to be flow or dynamic statements in that they present operating results over a period of time. In contrast, the balance sheet is considered a static statement because it presents the financial position as of a specific date or time. The manager usually is interested primarily in the income statement because it is concerned with the results of operations.

Standard methods of accounting and presentation of financial statements have been established in a number of industries, including certain segments of the hospitality services industries. These uniform systems of accounts within a particular industry provide for the uniform classification, organization, and presentation of revenues, expenses, assets, liabilities, and equity. They include a standardized format for financial statements, which enhances comparability of financial data within an industry. Uniform systems have been adopted by the American Hotel and Motel Association and the National Restaurant Association, and the American Hospital Association has defined a chart of accounts for hospitals to assist in standardizing accounting procedures.

Balance Sheet

The balance sheet or statement of financial condition is a listing of the assets, liabilities, and capital of a business entity as of a specific date, usually at the close of the last day of a month, quarter, or year. An example of a balance sheet for the Oakwood Country Club is shown in Figure 21.3.

Assets

The first section of the balance sheet is a listing of assets, which are generally categorized as current or fixed. As shown in the example in Figure 21.3, two additional categories of assets are used for the Oakwood Country Club accounts, "other assets" and "funded reserves." Funded reserves are accounts that have been established for specific purposes, in this case for various improvements of the club house and other facilities. Current assets include cash and all assets that will be converted into cash in a short period of time, generally one year. Cash on hand and cash in savings and in checking accounts are the cash accounts. Other current assets include accounts receivable, marketable securities, inventories, and prepaid expenses.

Fixed assets are those assets of a permanent nature, most of which are acquired to generate revenues for the business. Fixed or long-term assets are not intended for sale and include buildings, furniture, fixtures, equipment, and land, in addition to small equipment such as linen, china, and glassware. Because fixed assets generally lose value over their expected life, their value is adjusted for accumulated depreciation.

Liabilities

Liabilities are categorized as current and long term. Current liabilities represent those that must be paid within a period of one year, including such items as

Oakwood Country Club
BALANCE SHEET
December 31, 1984

Assets		*Liabilities and members' equity*	
Current Assets		**Current Liabilities**	
Cash on hand and in checking	$ 14,721	Accounts payable	$ 28,585
Cash in savings	5,521	Accrued expenses	8,590
Accounts receivable	67,278	Mortgage payable, current	24,000
Inventory	5,330		$ 61,175
	$ 92,850		
Fixed Assets (Estimated value)		**Long-Term Liabilities**	
Capital improvements, 1978	$ 28,856	Mortgage payable	$390,047
Furniture, fixtures, and equip-		Less current portion	24,000
ment	50,000		$366,047
Club house and structures	400,000		
Land	360,000		
	$838,856		
Other Assets		**Members' Equity**	
Prepaid expenses	$ 5,688	Capital Stock	$ 47,000
Escrow account	6,083	Surplus	448,003
Entrance fees receivable	19,885	Reserves	17,950
	$ 31,656	Net income (9 mos.)	41,137
			$554,090
Funded Reserves			
Building and depreciation	$ 10,000		
Swimming pool replacement	5,000		
Cart path	2,950		
	$ 17,950		
		TOTAL LIABILITIES AND	
TOTAL ASSETS	$981,312	MEMBERS' EQUITY	$981,312

Figure 21.3. *Example of a balance sheet*

accounts payable for merchandise, taxes payable, and accrued expenses due but not paid at the end of the accounting period, such as salaries, wages, or interest. Fixed liabilities, on the other hand, are obligations that will not be paid within the current year. An example of a long-term liability is a mortgage for building and land, although payments due during the current year are considered current liabilities, as shown in Figure 21.3.

Capital or Equity

The capital or equity section of the balance sheet represents that portion of the business that is the ownership interest, as well as earnings retained in the business from operations. In profit-oriented enterprises, the ownership may be one of three kinds: a proprietorship, a business owned by a single individual; a partnership, a business owned by two or more people; or a corporation, a business incorporated under the laws of the state with ownership held by stockholders. In a non-profit corporation, the members may be the owners. As indicated in the example from the Oakwood Country Club (Figure 21.3), the equity section includes the value of the members' stock, surplus, reserves for special purposes, and the retained net income.

Income Statement

As previously indicated, the income statement is a primary managerial tool, reporting the revenues, expenses, and profit or loss as a result of operations for a period of time. In a non-profit organization, it is often called a statement of revenue and expense. The basic form for the income statement is as follows:

Sales	$XXX
Less: Cost of goods sold	− XX
Gross profit	$XXX
Less: Labor and operating expenses	− XX
Net income (or loss)	$ XX

An example of an income statement is shown in Figure 21.4.

Sales or revenues include the cash receipts or the funds allocated to the operation for the period. For example, in a college residence hall, revenues include cash sales to nonresidents who may eat in the foodservice facility and the portion of the students' room and board allocated to the foodservice.

In a foodservice establishment, the cost of goods sold—or cost of food consumed, as this section of the income statement may be called—is based on the purchases for the accounting period covered by the income statement and the opening and closing inventories. The cost of goods sold is calculated in the following manner:

Inventory at beginning of period	$XXX
Plus: Purchases during the period	+ XXX
Total value of available food	$XXX
Less: Inventory at end of period	− XXX
Cost of goods sold during period	$XXX

Gross profit or income is determined by subtracting cost of goods sold from sales or revenue.

The remaining expenses of the operation may be categorized in various ways, depending on its needs. In the uniform system of accounts for restaurants, ex-

The Corner Deli
INCOME STATEMENT
for
January 31, 1985

Food Sales		$20,000
Cost of Food Sold		
Inventory January 1, 1984	$ 7,000	
Add: Purchases for January	8,400	
	$15,400	
Less: Inventory January 31, 1984	7,400	
Total cost of food sold		8,000
Gross profit		$12,000
Labor Cost		
Salaries & wages	$ 6,000	
Fringe benefits	800	
Social security taxes	300	
Total labor cost		$ 7,100
Operating Expenses		
Office expenses	$ 350	
Laundry & uniforms	250	
Utilities	700	
Repairs & maintenance	300	
Printing & advertising	200	
General expense	500	
Depreciation	550	
Taxes	125	
Insurance	225	
Interest on notes & mortgage	300	
Total operating expense		3,500
Total labor & operating expense		10,600
Net Income		$ 1,400

Figure 21.4. *Example of an income statement*

penses are categorized as controllable or noncontrollable. In many operations, labor costs and other operating expenses are the two major categories of expenses other than cost of goods sold. The labor cost section may be categorized into supervisory expense, full-time employees, part-time employees, and may also include employee meals and social security taxes. The operating expense section would include such items as rent, utilities, laundry, repairs, office expenses, insurance, taxes, and depreciation.

The net profit or loss is determined by subtracting labor and other operating expenses from gross profit. In a non-profit organization, net profit is often referred to as excess revenue over expenditures.

TOOLS FOR COMPARISON AND ANALYSIS

The foodservice manager should use a variety of tools to analyze financial data, among them are ratio analysis, trend analysis, common-size statements, and break-even analysis. The resulting operational indicators help the manager to understand financial information and compare performance to prior periods. The manager should make several kinds of comparisons in reviewing and analyzing financial information. These comparisons can be categorized as internal and external.

Standards of Comparison

Internal comparisons include a review of current performance in relation to budgeted performance. Because the budget represents the plan for financial operations for a period of time, comparisons with the budget indicate whether or not operations are proceeding as planned. The other type of internal comparison involves analysis of current performance in relation to past performance.

External standards of comparison include a review of performance in relation to similar operations or comparisons with industry performance. For example, in multiunit operations, managers may wish to compare the food cost of unit A with that of units B and C. In using industry data, comparisons are most useful if uniform systems of accounting and financial reporting are followed.

Several external comparisons are available. Annually, the National Restaurant Association and the international accounting firm Laventhol & Horwath publish a restaurant industry operations report. This comprehensive report includes financial information on full and limited menu restaurants with table service, limited menu restaurants without table service, and cafeterias. Information is broken down by restaurant type, location, sales volume, and menu theme, as well as by years of operation.

In addition, Hospital Administrative Services (HAS) of the American Hospital Association provides a national service called MONITREND, which permits management in participating hospitals to relate their institution's activities, expenses, and staffing patterns to those of comparable institutions. HAS/MONITREND reports are based on financial, labor-hour, and statistical data submitted each month in a standardized format by the participating institutions. The computerized reports furnish the hospital with national and local comparisons to other institutions providing similar services. For internal trend analysis, departmental indicators are available for each hospital department. Statistics for a dietetics department, for example, include total dietary expense percent, direct expense per meal, and salary expense per meal.

Ratio Analysis

Most financial information is presented as a collection of totals or balances of accounts, the meaning or significance of which may not be readily apparent. For example, the total amount spent on food during a period yields limited information; however, if food cost is determined as a percentage of sales, the data become more meaningful. Analysis of financial data in terms of relationships permits interpretation and understanding. Computation of various types of financial ratios is an important tool in analysis.

A ratio is a mathematical expression of the relationship between two items and may be expressed in several ways.

- *As a common ratio.* The ratio between x and y may be stated as x:y, such as 3 to 1.
- *As a percentage.* The ratio may be expressed as a percentage, such as a percentage of sales.
- *As a turnover.* Some relationships are best expressed as a turnover, or the number of times x must be "turned over" to yield the value of y, calculated by dividing y by x.
- *On a per unit basis.* The relationship may also be expressed in dollars per unit, such as sales dollars per bar stool at a restaurant counter.

Ratios are frequently categorized as financial and operating. Financial ratios examine relationships between items on the balance sheet or between one item on the balance sheet and one on the income statement. The primary question answered by financial ratios is "What is the financial health of the organization?" Operating ratios examine relationships among items on the profit and loss statement.

Ratios are also categorized according to primary use. The major categories include the following:

- Liquidity.
- Solvency.
- Activity.
- Profitability.
- Operating.

Examples for each of these major types are listed in Figure 21.5.

Liquidity Ratios

Liquidity ratios indicate the organization's ability to meet current obligations—in other words, its ability to pay bills when they are due. An organization may be making a profit but have insufficient cash to pay current bills. Several ratios are used to analyze the liquidity of a business, two of the most common being the current ratio and the acid-test ratio. The current ratio is the relationship between current assets to current liabilities and is computed as follows:

Types	*Examples*
Liquidity Ratios	Current Ratio
	Acid-Test Ratio
Solvency Ratios	Solvency Ratio
	Debt-Equity Ratio
	Debt-Assets Ratio
Activity Ratios	Inventory Turnover
	Occupany Percentage
Profitability Ratios	Profit Margin
	Return on Equity
	Return on Assets
Operating Ratios	Percentage of Total Sales from Various Sources
	Food Cost Percentage
	Labor Cost Percentage
	Average Customer Check

Figure 21.5. *Ratios categorized by primary use*

- Current ratio $= \dfrac{\text{Current assets}}{\text{Current liabilities}}$

Traditionally, a current ratio of $2:1$ has been considered ideal for all types of businesses. Time and experience, however, have shown that there is no ideal ratio. Much depends on the nature of the business and types of current assets. According to Fay et al. (1976), a current ratio of approximately $1:1$ is considered reasonable in the hospitality services industry. Creditors may consider a high current ratio as assurance they will receive payment for goods and services, but managers may wish to maintain a lower current ratio by avoiding excess build-up of cash or inventories.

The acid-test ratio, also called the quick ratio, is another comparison of current assets and current liabilities, but yields a more accurate measure of bill-paying capability. Current liabilities are measured against cash and other assets quickly convertible to cash, such as accounts receivable and marketable securities. The acid-test ratio is calculated as follows:

- Acid-test ratio $= \dfrac{\text{Cash + Accounts receivable + Marketable securities}}{\text{Current liabilities}}$

Solvency Ratios

Solvency ratios are used to examine an establishment's ability to meet its long-term financial obligations. The basic solvency ratio is the relationship between total assets and total liabilities, calculated as follows:

- Solvency ratio $= \dfrac{\text{Total assets}}{\text{Total liabilities}}$

Other solvency ratios examine the relationship between debts and assets and between debts and equity. Creditors see the equity ratio as an indicator of the risk involved in extending credit to an organization.

Activity Ratios

Activity ratios are designed to examine how effectively an organization is utilizing its assets. These ratios are usually expressed as either percentages or turnovers. The inventory turnover ratio, one of the most widely used activity ratios, shows the number of times the inventory is used up and replenished during a period. Inventory turnovers are calculated by dividing the cost of goods sold by the average inventory for an accounting period:

- Inventory turnover $= \dfrac{\text{Cost of goods sold}}{\text{Average inventory}}$

A high ratio indicates a limited inventory is being maintained by a foodservice organization, whereas a low ratio indicates larger amounts of money are tied up in inventories.

Percentage of occupancy is another activity ratio important in many segments of the industry. Hotels, hospitals, college or university residence halls, and nursing homes compute occupany percentages regularly. These percentages indicate the relationship between the number of beds or rooms available and the number being used by the clientele of the operation:

- Percentage of occupancy $= \dfrac{\text{No. of beds/rooms available}}{\text{No. of beds/rooms occupied}}$

Profitability Ratios

Profitability ratios measure the ability of an organization to generate profit in relation to sales or the investment in assets. Whereas profit or net income is an absolute term expressed as a monetary amount of income remaining after all expenses have been deducted from income or revenue, profitability is a relative measure of the profit making ability of an organization. Most foodservice operations, whether profit or not-for-profit, must generate some level of net income, as discussed earlier in this chapter; the disposition of the profit is a primary difference between these two types of operation. Also, the not-for-profit organization may have a lower expectation with regard to level of profit. Three major profitability ratios are utilized:

- Profit margin $= \dfrac{\text{Net profit}}{\text{Sales}}$

- Return on equity $= \dfrac{\text{Net profit}}{\text{Equity}}$

- Return on assets $= \dfrac{\text{Net profit}}{\text{Total assets}}$

The profit margin is the most commonly used measure of operating profitability as an assessment of overall financial efficiency. The return on equity measures the adequacy of profits in providing a return on owners' investments; the return on assets, however, is a measure of management's ability to generate a return on the assets employed in generating revenue.

Operating Ratios

Operating ratios are primarily concerned with analysis of the success of the operation in generating revenues and in controlling expenses. Analysis of the revenue mix of the operation is one type of sales analysis. For example, a restaurant may analyze its food and beverage sales to determine the relative proportion of revenues generated by these two aspects of the operation; in a student union, the relative percentage of sales from catering, vending, and cafeteria operations may be of interest.

The average customer check is another measurement of generation of sales dollars. Sales per seat in a restaurant, per meal, per waitress, and per menu item are other sales ratios that may be utilized in a foodservice establishment.

As stated initially in this chapter, control of costs is a primary responsibility of foodservice managers: their organizations' profitability is strongly related to their effectiveness in such control. In foodservice organizations, one of the main control areas is the level of various categories of expenses in relation to sales. For example, the food cost percentage and the percentage of dollars devoted to labor in relation to sales are performance indicators commonly scrutinized by foodservice managers. Also, a percentage breakdown of the food dollar spent on various food categories may reveal possible cost problems. If an analysis of expenditures indicates that dollars spent on meat have increased for two successive months, for example, the manager may need to examine menu offerings, purchase prices, inventory control procedures, production methods, portion controls, or selling prices.

Another performance indicator is food cost per patient or food cost per student, used commonly for analyzing food cost in healthcare or university foodservices. Also, various types of ratios are computed to analyze labor cost: meals per labor-hour, labor minutes per meal, and the percentage of payroll of various categories of workers, such as regular or part-time.

The percentage of the sales dollar expended for various types of other operating expenses has attracted increased attention from foodservice managers as the cost of some of these expenses has increased. For example, foodservice managers are monitoring energy costs and paper supply costs more carefully today than previously.

Using Ratio Analysis

Ratio analysis constitutes an effective tool for evaluating financial stability and operating effectiveness, providing managers with the information they need to make decisions and control operations. The ratios selected for analysis of financial results must be appropriate to the operation, however, and the relationships measured must be understood by the foodservice manager.

Managers should use a variety of ratios in analyzing operations because a single ratio is insufficient for sound decision making. They should be used in combination with trend analysis to compare changes over a period of time. Although, consistency in accounting methods is required to yield comparable data for comparisons over a period of time.

Trend Analysis

Trend analysis is a comparison of results over several periods of time; changes may be noted in either absolute amounts or percentages. It is also used to forecast future revenues or levels of activity. Trend analysis may utilize several of the various types of ratios discussed in the preceding section.

Often a graphic analysis of the financial data over a period of time will help managers detect and understand changes. For example, many foodservice managers regularly plot the percentage of sales spent on food, labor, and other operating expenses on a graph. The one shown in Figure 21.6 plots a hospital cafeteria's food cost percentage on a weekly basis to monitor food costs.

Common-Size Statements

Comparison among financial statements for various periods or from different units or departments within an organization may be difficult because of the different levels of volume, especially when these differences in size of operation are very great. If the financial data are expressed as percentages, however, meaningful comparisons can be made because data are presented on a common base. Financial statements in which data are expressed as percentages are called common-size statements.

Common-size statements are especially useful in comparing results of the income statement of an operation from one accounting period to another or for comparing results among units of a multiunit operation, such as a chain restau-

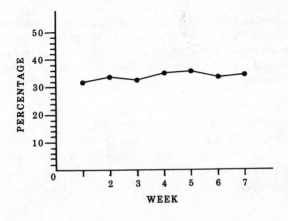

Figure 21.6. *Trend chart for weekly food cost, hospital cafeteria*

Income	
Food sales	72.1%
Beverage sales	27.1
Other income	0.8
Total income	100.0%
Expenses	
Cost of sales	
Food costs	27.1%
Beverage costs	7.1
Total cost of sales	34.2%
Controllable expenses	
Payroll expenses	29.0%
Employee benefit expenses	4.5
Direct operating expenses	5.7
Music and entertainment expenses	0.7
Advertising and promotion expenses	2.4
Utility expenses	2.9
Administrative and general expenses	5.3
Repair and maintenance costs	1.9
Total controllable expenses	52.4%
Occupation costs	
Rent, property taxes, insurance cost	5.2%
Interest	1.2
Depreciation	2.9
Total occupation costs	9.3%
Net income	
Net income before income tax and other deductions	4.5%
Other deductions	(0.4%)
Net income before income tax	4.1%

Figure 21.7. *The restaurant industry dollar: 1981 food and beverage restaurants.* **Source: Restaurant Industry Operations Report '82, published by the National Restaurant Association and Laventhol & Horwath, November 1982. Reprinted with permission of the NRA News, the monthly magazine of the National Restaurant Association.**

rant or foodservice centers in a residence hall. Comparisons with industry performance are facilitated by expressing the income statement in percentages. For example, in Figure 21.7, the breakdown of the restaurant industry dollar is shown as a common-size statement for the industry. Restaurateurs could use data, such as those depicted, to analyze and compare their operating ratios and profit margins.

Break-Even Analysis

Break-even analysis is another tool for analyzing financial data. The technique gets its name from the term "break-even point," or the point at which an operation is just breaking even financially—making no profit but incurring no loss. In other words, total revenues equal total expenses.

Break-even analysis requires classification of costs into fixed and variable components. Fixed costs are those costs required for an operation to exist, even if it produces nothing. These costs do not vary with changes in the volume of sales and stay fixed or constant within a range of sales volume. The size of the existing physical plant and the equipment capacity define this volume. If either is expanded, however, fixed costs will increase. Depreciation, insurance, rent, and property taxes are examples of fixed costs.

Variable costs are those costs that change in direct proportion to the volume of sales. As the volume of sales increases, a proportionately higher amount of these costs is incurred, as with direct materials or food cost. A complication in defining fixed and variable costs is the fact some costs cannot be clearly classified as either variable or fixed costs and are referred to as semivariable costs.

Semivariable costs change as the volume of production or sales changes, but not in the direct proportion that variable costs do. An example is labor cost in a foodservice operation. A staff of five may be able to produce between 100 and 150 meals but an additional staff member may be required to serve more than 150 meals. These semivariable costs must be divided into their fixed and variable components for purposes of break-even analysis.

The formula for calculating the break-even point is expressed as follows:

$$\bullet \quad \text{Break-even point} = \frac{\text{Fixed cost}}{1 - \dfrac{\text{Variable cost}}{\text{Sales}}}$$

To illustrate, the following data are available for XYZ cafeteria:

Fixed cost = $28,000
Variable cost = $60,000
Sales = $100,000

Substituting the figures in the formula, the break-even point for XYZ cafeteria is calculated as shown below:

$$\text{Break-even point} = \frac{\$28,000}{1 - \dfrac{\$60,000}{\$100,000}}$$

$$= \frac{28,000}{1 - .60}$$

$$= \frac{28,000}{.40}$$

$$= \$70,000$$

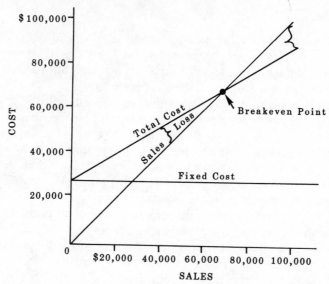

Figure 21.8.   *Break-even chart for XYZ cafeteria*

The denominator in this formula, or the ratio of variable cost to sales sub-tracted from 1, is referred to as the contribution margin or the profit-volume ratio. It represents the proportion of sales that can contribute to fixed costs and profit after variable costs have been covered. In the illustration, the contribution margin is .40 or 40 percent. The break-even point for XYZ cafeteria is shown graphically in Figure 21.8.

Break-even analysis is a tool for projecting income and expense and profit under several assumed conditions. It can assist the foodservice manager in under-standing the interrelationships among volume, cost, and profits but requires that operational costs of an organization are known and can be segmented into fixed and variable classifications. This tool is thus more effective for short-range than for long-range planning and may be useful in helping a manager determine the volume required for a given level of profit. In many institutions, for example, break-even analysis is used to define the occupancy level needed to cover all costs—in other words, to break even.

Other Analysis Tools

Other types of analysis tools include comparative financial statements, determi-nation of standard costs, and variance analysis used in combination with tech-niques previously discussed in this chapter. Also, variance analysis is an impor-tant tool in analyzing differences between the budget and actual performance.

Comparative financial statements may present data on more than one period for the same operation or for two or more units within the same operation. In addition, data on cumulative operations to date may be presented along with results of current operations. Budgeted figures may be shown for comparisons with actual revenues and expenditures for an accounting period. Also, trend

Oakwood Country Club
COMPARATIVE FINANCIAL STATEMENT[1]

	Prior year 1983	Current year 1984 (Projected)	Proposed budget 1985
Revenue	$306,461	$323,300	$376,100
Expenses			
House	$ 59,251	$ 67,000	$ 76,250
Golf committee	8,298	9,500	8,000
Grounds and greens	64,797	82,000	104,000
Swimming pool	6,929	12,300	12,000
Tennis	1,658	3,000	3,000
Entertainment	6,025	6,000	6,850
General	93,683	97,300	100,000
Capital expenditures	36,489	28,856	42,000
Debt retirement	21,011	22,500	24,000
TOTAL	$298,141	$328,456	$376,100

[1] Prepared for budget planning meeting of Finance Committee, November 10, 1984.

Figure 21.9. *Example of a comparative financial statement*

analysis utilizes comparative financial statements. In Figure 21.9, a comparative financial statement from the Oakwood Country Club is shown. In this case, the comparative statement was compiled for budget planning purposes and shows actual revenue and expenditures for a prior period (1983), the projected year-end data for the current year (1984), and the proposed budget for the ensuing year (1985).

Standard cost is defined as the expected average cost of producing a product or service at a given level of sales or volume of business. Once determined— through technical methods, such as those developed in industrial engineering— standard costs provide standards of comparison for analyzing actual costs. The manager must determine an acceptable deviation from standard cost and the deviation at which control actions are indicated. For example, Mandigo (1982a) indicates that a variance of 1.5 to 2.0 percentage points is generally acceptable for actual menu item cost compared to expected or standard cost.

BUDGETING

A budget is a plan for operating a business expressed in financial terms or a plan to control expenses and profit in relation to sales. Budgeting is the process of budget planning, preparation, control, reporting, utilization, and related procedures. Budget control involves the use of budgets and performance reports throughout the planned period to coordinate, evaluate, and control operations in accordance with the goals specified in the budget plan.

In a governmental operation, however, the budget represents something different: a schedule of authorizations for a given period or purpose and the proposed means of financing it. Funds are established, representing a sum of money or other resources segregated for carrying on specific activities or attaining certain objectives in accordance with specific regulations, restrictions, and limitations. These funds constitute an independent fiscal entity.

Planning, coordination, and control are the three primary objectives of budgeting. Budgeting provides an organized procedure for planning and for development of standards of performance in numerical terms. A well-constructed operating budget gives a picture of the overall structure of the operation and enables staff in all areas to see where they fit into it.

Budgets provide a basis for control, yet they do not control in and of themselves; they must be implemented by operational personnel up and down the organization. They provide a tool for periodic examination, restatement, and establishment of guidelines. However, a budget is merely a yardstick and should be fairly constructed and capable of being attained. To be effective, all relevant staff members should have input.

Steps in Budget Planning

The *first step* in the budgeting process is the development of the sales budget or revenue estimates. Various internal and external influences must be considered in constructing the sales budget. Past experience should be examined, including both past performance and past budgets, and any unusual aspects clarified.

Changes in pricing must also be considered. For example, if board rates are increasing for a college residence hall, the effect on the allowance per student for the foodservice operation should be determined. National and local indicators should also be considered, such as new competitors, other new businesses in the area, industry trends, and changes in the national economy.

The profit objective of the organization must be taken into account. The projected profit from a given volume of sales should be estimated and the capacity to attain the profit objective determined. Seasonal variations in sales should also be projected, and segmentation of sales in various units of the organization forecast. For example, in a hotel, the sales forecast for room service, catering, coffee shop, and the dining room may be appropriate.

The *second step* in the budgeting process is development of the expenditure budget. Expenditures in relation to the projected level of revenue should be estimated for food, labor, and other operational expenses. In estimating food costs, anticipated changes in food prices should be taken into account.

Increments in salaries and wages and in payroll taxes are key aspects to consider in estimating the labor budget. Also, the foodservice manager must project the impact of menu changes or other operational changes that may affect

Purple Pride Inn
PROJECTED CASH BUDGET
1st Qtr, 1985

	Jan.	*Feb.*	*Mar.*	*Apr.*
Cash				
Beginning bank balance	$10,000	$15,000	$ 3,000	$17,000
Sales	40,000	60,000	80,000	
Cash available	$50,000	$75,000	$83,000	
Payments				
Food & beverage	$10,000	$15,000	$20,000	
Labor	15,000	20,000	22,000	
Operating expense	5,000	7,000	9,000	
Lease	5,000	5,000	5,000	
Insurance		20,000		
Interest		5,000		
Property tax		10,000		
Total	$35,000	$82,000	$56,000	
Ending balance	$15,000	($ 7,000)	$27,000	
Borrowed funds		$10,000		
Repayment of funds			$10,000	

Figure 21.10. *Example of a cash budget*

the labor needed in the operations. Similar factors should be considered in projecting expenditures for other operating expenses.

The *third step* in the budget process involves development of the cash budget, which is a detailed estimate of anticipated cash receipts and disbursements throughout the budget period. The cash budget will assist management in coordinating cash inflow and outflow and in synchronizing cash resources with need. Seasonal effects on cash position thus become apparent, and the availability of cash for taking advantage of discounts is identified. Also, the cash budget assists management in planning financial requirements for large payments, such as tax installments or insurance premiums, and also points out availability of funds for short-term investments. A simplified hypothetical example of a cash budget for an operation called the Purple Pride Inn is shown in Figure 21.10.

The development of the capital expenditure budget is the *fourth step* in the budget planning process. Improvements, expansions, and replacements in building, equipment, and land are the major types of capital expenditures. These major capital investments may be for purposes of expanding or improving income-producing or nonincome-producing facilities. Nonincome-producing capital expenditures include those required to improve facilities for safety, health, and welfare of employees, to protect facilities, or to meet legal requirements.

Careful planning is particularly important in capital budgeting because of the magnitude of funds and the long-term commitments involved. Capital expenditures may be prorated over several budget periods and, therefore, may affect budgets for a five- or ten-year period. A number of sophisticated techniques are available for evaluating capital budgeting alternatives, beyond the scope of this book. Careful decision making is critical, however, to ensure appropriate decision making.

The last or *fifth step* in the budget planning process is the compilation of a forecast or a proforma income statement, which is a composite of the sales and expenditure budgets and includes a projection of profit. The budget planner should compute various ratios to determine if the appropriate relationship of expenditures to sales or to revenues have been projected.

The basic steps of the budget process outlined in the foregoing paragraphs may vary in different organizations, and the foodservice manager may be involved in only certain aspects of budget planning. For example, in a very large organization, the cash budget and compilation of the total budget is often the responsibility of the comptroller and other top management staff. Rather than compiling the capital budget, the foodservice manager may only develop capital budget requests, which are rank-ordered according to departmental priorities. In a small operation, however, the manager in consultation with the accountant is usually involved in the total process.

After the budget planning process has been completed, various types of review and approval are needed before the budget document is finalized; these vary widely, depending on the size and type of the organization. The approved budget then becomes the standard against which operations are evaluated. Periodic reports are issued comparing operating results with budget estimates. The manager's job becomes one of using these comparative reports to bring about operational changes so that actual costs conform to budget plans—unless, however, data suggest that budget amendments are in order. An example of the budget for a non-profit club, approved by the Board of Directors, is shown in Figure 21.11. In this example, a net loss is anticipated because of some planned renovations and improvements to the club's facilities. By projecting this deficit in advance, however, the Board of Directors can be prepared to make financial decisions with this in mind.

Budgeting Approaches

Several budgeting approaches are used, the most common being the fixed or forecast budget. In this approach, a budget is prepared at one level of sales or revenue, as was the case with the sample budget shown in Figure 21.11. Incremental budgeting involves using the existing budget as a base and projecting changes for the ensuing year in relation to the current budget.

The flexible budget is a budget adjusted to various levels of operation or sales useful for operations with varying sales or revenues throughout the year. A foodservice organization may develop budgets at two or three possible levels of sales to assist in adjusting expenditures to actual sales volume. For example, resort hotels and hospitals have wide variations in occupancy rates. A flexible budget

City Club
PROPOSED BUDGET
1984–85

Estimated Receipts

Participating club dues	$ 23,000	
Annual member dues	244,000	
Profit from food service	35,000	
Donations	4,000	
Special events	5,000	
Interest income	3,000	
Miscellaneous income	7,000	
Total Estimated Receipts		$321,000

Estimated Expenditures

Salaries	$ 48,000	
FICA taxes	3,000	
Note and interest payments	87,000	
Utilities	32,000	
Repairs and maintenance	2,700	
Office supplies and postage	3,500	
Insurance	21,000	
Lease on lights	1,080	
Dishes	4,000	
Newsletter	5,750	
Special events	7,900	
Accounting fee	1,750	
Christmas bonus	1,850	
Flowers and decorating	7,000	
Upholstering furniture	3,500	
Remodel kitchen	40,000	
Carpets	36,000	
Miscellaneous expenses	8,670	
Total Estimated Expenses		325,000
Estimated Net Loss		($ 4,500)

Figure 21.11. *Example of a budget*

will enable the management of these organizations to adjust expenditures in relation to occupancy levels. An example of a flexible budget for the Country Kitchen Cafe in a resort hotel is shown in Figure 21.12. Budgets have been prepared for three potential volume levels for this operation.

Zero base budgeting (ZBB) gained popularity in the late 1970s as an alternative to incremental budgeting. ZBB is a concept that implies periodic or an-

Country Kitchen Cafe PROPOSED BUDGET Year—1985			
	Level of Sales		
	90%	*100%*	*110%*
Sales			
Food	$53,275	$59,195	$65,115
Beverage	17,775	19,730	21,705
Total	$71,030	$78,925	$86,820
Cost of Sales			
Food	$20,245	$22,495	$24,745
Beverage	5,325	5,920	6,510
Total Cost of Sales	$25,570	$28,415	$31,265
Total Gross Profit	$45,460	$50,510	$55,555
Operating Expenses			
Salaries & wages	$21,700	$22,100	$22,800
Employees' meals	1,530	1,580	1,650
Other operating expenses	13,500	14,365	15,100
Occupancy costs	3,940	3,940	3,940
Total Operating Expenses	$40,670	$41,985	$43,490
Net Profit	$ 4,790	$ 8,525	$12,065

Figure 21.12. *Example of a flexible budget*

nual reevaluation of all programs or activities of the organization. In theory, the concept encompasses the total budget request; existing activities are to be scrutinized as closely as proposed new activities. Alternative ways of providing services are to be considered as well as alternative funding levels. According to Letzkus (1980–81), ZBB in theory requires managers to document their entire budget request in detail, shifting the burden of proof to the manager to justify why funds should be allocated to various activities.

In ZBB, the initial step involves the development of various planning assumptions, sometimes called an environmental assessment. In this assessment, the organization attempts to identify changes and environmental influences anticipated to have impact on the organization's operations. The four basic elements of ZBB are as follows (Letzkus, 1980–81).

1 Identification of decision units (programs or organizational units).

2 Analysis of decision units and the formulation of decision packages. This analysis requires identification of the:

- Purpose of the decision unit.
- Measure of performance.
- Alternative courses of action or levels of activity.
- Costs and benefits.

3 Formal ranking of decision packages.

4 Allocation of resources based on the ranking process.

A hypothetical example of a decision package for a foodservice operation is shown in Figure 21.13.

DECISION PACKAGE

Department: Foodservice

Program or activity name: Prepare and serve food for Title VII feeding program participants.

Purpose: To assume responsibilities for this program to meet the needs of feeding the elderly. This program is not possible without this department's involvement.

Legal implications: Is this program legally required? _____ Yes __X__ No

Feasibility: The addition of this program is feasible with present equipment and storage space. Sources of supply are the same as the present. Production scheduling would allow more efficient use of equipment capacity. Production of extra items would permit more even production schedules, eliminating peaks and valleys. Increase overall productivity by 5 meals per manhour. Cost increases would occur in serving and packaging of meals. At minimum level of service, 8 additional manhours are required; at average service level of 250 patrons, 12 hr. are needed; and at maximum level (250 patrons plus 50 Meals on Wheels), 15 additional manhours are necessary.

Cost/Benefit Analysis[a]

	Minimum	*Average*	*Maximum*
Revenues (no. of patrons)	200	250	300
Costs			
Labor	$ 24	$ 37	$ 45
Food	120	150	180
Utilities[b]	—	—	—
Disposables	20	25	30
Administrative	10	12	15
Total marginal costs	$174	$224	$270
Probable net benefits	$ 26	$ 26	$ 30

(Continued)

Intangible Benefits

1 Improve nutritional care of elderly in the community.
2 Improve community image.

Net Economic Risk: _____ high _____ medium __X__ low

Consequences of Not Approving Package

1 No elderly feeding will be available in the area—a serious community problem.
2 Failure to capitalize on the opportunity to improve productivity.

Alternative Methods

1 The only alternatives are the levels of production and the selection of products themselves. The minimum level of production should be tried first, using the present menu mix. If successful, then upper levels of production should be sought.
2 Instead of paying for the additional labor hours, volunteers could be sought.
3 The project could not be undertaken.

Priority Ranking 1

[a]This is only a hypothetical situation meant to illustrate a concept and not designed to approximate any situation.

[b]Equipment would be using utilities regardless of this program.

Figure 21.13. *Example of a decision package for a zero-base budgeting system.* Source: *Michael Olson: The figure "Decision Package" in "Zero-based budgeting in foodservice departments of health care facilities." Copyright © The American Dietetic Association. Reprinted by permission from* Journal of the American Dietetic Association, *Vol. 74:146, 1979.*

The advantages of zero base budgeting have been identified as follows:

• Establishment of minimum service level.
• Provision of blueprint for high and low priorities.
• Allowance for evaluation of alternatives.
• Facilitation of communication among units of the organization.
• Provision of documentation of decision making.

Critics of ZBB believe, however, that it consumes an inordinate amount of managerial time, involves tremendous amounts of paperwork, and contributes to "game playing" among managers of the various units in an organization.

SUMMARY

The foodservice manager must be skillful in managing financial resources in order to perform efficiently and effectively. In today's economy, control of costs in all types of organizations has been accorded top priority by boards of directors, high level administrators, and policy makers.

The increased cost of living is affecting the choices that consumers make in their eating-away-from-home behaviors. As pointed out in the first chapter, in many instances consumers are opting for lower and moderately priced restaurants rather than full service gourmet establishments. In the daily newspapers, on television, and in news magazines, as well as in the healthcare literature, cost containment is a pervasive topic with regard to healthcare costs.

All of these concerns underscore the importance of managerial proficiency in controlling costs and managing financial resources. While managers do not perform the bookkeeping and accounting functions, they must understand basic accounting concepts and be able to read financial statements. They must also know how to use and understand a variety of techniques for analyzing and interpreting financial data.

To achieve the objectives of the organization, planning for the utilization of financial resources is critical. The manager, therefore, must be competent in all aspects of budget planning and control.

REFERENCES

Abdelsamad, M. H.: The cash budget: An indispensable tool for small businesses. *Mgmt. World* 8:22 (Jul.), 1979.

Ameiss, A. P.: Application of zero-base budgeting. *Managerial Planning* 30:28 (Mar./Apr.), 1982.

American Accounting Association: *A Statement of Basic Accounting Theory.* Evanston, IL: American Accounting Assoc., 1966.

Anthony, R. N., and Herzlinger, R. E.: *Management Control in Nonprofit Organizations.* Homewood, IL: Richard D. Irwin, 1975.

Anton, H. R., Firmin, P. A., and Grove, H. D.: *Contemporary Issues in Cost and Managerial Accounting.* 3rd ed. Dallas: Houghton Mifflin Co., 1978.

Barrett, M. E., and Fraser, L. B.: Conflicting roles in budgeting for operations. *Harvard Bus. Rev.* 55:137 (Nov./Dec.), 1977.

Berkman, J.: Food service needs controls to contain costs. *Hospitals* 54:79 (Mar. 16), 1980.

Bolhuis, J. L., Wolff, R. K., and Editors of NIFI: *The Financial Ingredient in Foodservice Management.* Lexington, MA: D.C. Heath and Co., 1976.

Chou, C. W., and Waller, W. S.: Management accounting and organizational control. *Mgmt. Accounting* 63:36 (Apr.), 1982.

Coltman, M. M.: *Hospitality Management Accounting.* Boston: CBI Publishing Co., 1978.

Criddle, R. L.: Managing cost constraint program. *J. Can. Dietet. A.* 39:300, 1978.

Dearden, J.: Cost accounting comes to service industries. *Harvard Bus. Rev.* 56:132 (Sept./Oct.), 1978.

Doering, R. D.: Break-even analysis for restaurant decision making. *Cornell Hotel Restaur. Admin. Q.* 19:7 (Feb.), 1979.

Eiler, R. G., Goletz, W. K., and Keegan, D. P.: Is your cost accounting up to date? *Harvard Bus. Rev.* 60:133 (Jul./Aug.), 1982.

Fay, C. T., Rhoads, R. C., and Rosenblatt, R. L.: *Managerial Accounting for the Hospitality Service Industry.* 2nd ed. Dubuque, IA: Wm. C. Brown Co., 1976.

Foodservice trends. *NRA News* 2:30 (Oct.), 1982.

Freimuth, R. C.: Cash management for small business: A new technique. *Mgmt. Accounting* 63:58 (Jun.), 1982.

Geller, A. N.: Inflation: Its effects on financial statements. *Cornell Hotel Restaur. Admin. Q.* 19:28 (May), 1978.

Geller, A. N.: Inflation's effects on financial statements revisited: FASB 33. *Cornell Hotel Restaur. Admin. Q.* 21:4 (May), 1980.

Geller, A. N., and Heath, L. C.: Solvency, financial statements, and importance of cash-flow information. *Cornell Hotel Restaur. Admin. Q.* 22:45 (Nov.), 1981.

Gotcher, J. W., and Raihall, D. T.: Establish priorities, price guidelines, and responsibilities to make an efficient capital budget. *Mod. Hospital* 121:62 (Dec.), 1973.

Herzlinger, R.: Can we control health care costs? *Harvard Bus. Rev.* 56:102 (Mar./Apr.), 1978.

Janke, T. A.: Cost accounting: The vital link to cost effectiveness. *J. Am. Dietet. A.* 77:167, 1980.

Kaud, F.: The numbers game. Part II. Budgets that work. *Food Mgmt.* 15:39 (Feb.), 1980.

Keiser, J., and Kallio, E.: *Controlling and Analyzing Costs in Food Service Operations.* New York: John Wiley & Sons, 1974.

Kim, S. H., and Farragher, E. J.: Current capital budgeting practices. *Mgmt. Accounting* 63:26 (Jun.), 1981.

Lesure, J. D.: The breakeven point. *Restaur. Hospitality* 67:134 (Jan.), 1983.

Lesure, J. D.: Strategic business planning. *Restaur. Hospitality* 66:88 (Nov.), 1982.

Letzkus, W. C.: Zero base budgeting and planning-programming-budgeting: What are the conceptual differences? *Govt. Accountant J.* 29:47 (Winter), 1980–81.

Lin, W. T.: Corporate planning and budgeting: An integrated approach. *Managerial Planning* 27:29 (May/Jun.), 1978.

Lukowski, R. F., and Eshbach, C. E.: Using break-even analysis in food service establishments. Food Management Program Leaflet 13, Cooperative Extension, College of Agriculture, University of Massachusetts.

Lukowski, R. F., and Eshbach, C. E.: Using financial statements in food service establishments. Food Management Program Leaflet 11, Cooperative Extension, University of Massachusetts.

MacIntosh, N. B.: Differing attitudes to budgetary controls: Organizational implications. *Cost & Mgmt.* 57:19 (Jan./Feb.), 1983.

Mackle M., and David, B. D.: Developing a demand forecasting system for a foodservice operation. *J. Am. Dietet. A.* 68:457 (May), 1976.

Mandigo, T. R.: How to determine your "ideal" food cost. *Foodserv. Marketing* 44:19 (Jun.), 1982a.

Mandigo, T. R.: How you can control payroll costs. *Foodserv. Marketing* 44:22 (Mar.), 1982b.

Mandigo, T. R.: Your accounting format: Consistency counts! *Foodserv. Marketing* 44:30 (Sept.), 1982c.

Matthews, M. E.: Serving meals with fiscal responsibility. *Hospitals* 54:77 (Apr. 1), 1980.

Menu census. *Restaurants & Institutions* 92:37 (Mar. 1), 1983.

Montag, G. M., and Olsen, M. D.: Obtaining meaningful cost information in dietary departments. *J. Am. Dietet. A.* 67:50 (Jul.), 1975.

Mullet, M. J.: Benefits from standard costing in the restaurant industry. *Mgmt. Accounting* 18:47 (Sept.), 1978.

Nickerson, C. B.: *Accounting Handbook for Nonaccountants.* Boston: Cahners Books, 1975.

Niswonger, C. R., and Fess, P. E.: *Accounting Principles.* 13th ed. Cincinnati: South-Western Publishing Co., 1981.

Olson, M.: Zero-based budgeting in foodservice departments of health care facilities. *J. Am. Dietet. A.* 74:146, 1979.

Phare, G. R.: Beyond zero-base budgeting. *Managerial Planning* 27:18 (Jul./Aug.), 1979.

Rodewig, T.: The 1981 composite performance index. *Restaurant Hospitality* 66:37 (Dec.), 1982.

Sasser, W. E., Olsen, R. P., and Wyckoff, D. D.: *Management of Service Operations.* Boston: Allyn and Bacon, 1978.

Seawell, L. U.: *Introduction to Hospital Accounting.* Chicago: Hospital Financial Mgmt. Assoc., 1977.

Selby, C. C.: Better performance from "nonprofits." *Harvard Bus. Rev.* 56:92 (Sept./Oct.), 1978.

Spears, M. C.: Concepts of cost effectiveness: Accountability for nutrition, productivity. *J. Am. Dietet. A.* 68:341, 1976.

Suver, J. D., and Brown, R. L.: Where does zero-base budgeting work? *Harvard Bus. Rev.* 55:76 (Nov./Dec.), 1977.

Sweeny, A.: Accounting fundamentals for nonfinancial managers, Part 1: The basic concepts. *Supervisory Mgmt.* 19:8 (Jun.), 1974.

Sweeny, A.: Accounting fundamentals for nonfinancial managers, Part 2: A closer look at balance sheets and income statements. *Supervisory Mgmt.* 19:9 (Jul.), 1974.

Sweeny, A.: Accounting fundamentals for nonfinancial managers, Part 3: The basic accounting process. *Supervisory Mgmt.* 19:10 (Aug.), 1974.

Sweeny, A.: Accounting fundamentals for nonfinancial managers, Part 4: Manufacturing cost essentials. *Supervisory Mgmt.* 19:6 (Sept.), 1974.

Sweeny, A.: Accounting fundamentals for nonfinancial managers, Part 5: Basic financial analysis. *Supervisory Mgmt.* 19:23 (Oct.), 1974.

Sweeny, A., and Wisner, J. N.: Budgeting basics: A how-to guide for managers, Part 1: The purposes and uses of a budget. *Supervisory Mgmt.* 20:2 (Jan.), 1975.

Sweeny, A., and Wisner, J. N.: Budgeting basics: A how-to guide for managers, Part 2: Budget control through responsibility centers. *Supervisory Mgmt.* 20:11 (Feb.), 1975.

Sweeny, A., and Wisner, J. N.: Budgeting basics: A how-to guide for managers, Part 3: Responsibility accounting. *Supervisory Mgmt.* 20:18 (Mar.), 1975.

Sweeny, A., and Wisner, J. N.: Budgeting basics: A how-to guide for managers, Part 4: Types of costs and their behavior. *Supervisory Mgmt.* 20:20 (Apr.), 1975.

Sweeny, A., and Wisner, J. N.: Budgeting basics: A how-to guide for managers, Part 5: Manufacturing cost systems and the contribution concept. *Supervisory Mgmt.* 20:16 (May), 1975.

Sweeny, A., and Wisner, J. N.: Budgeting basics: A how-to guide for managers, Part 6: Preparing and presenting a budget plan. *Supervisory Mgmt.* 20:7 (June), 1975.

Sweeny, A., and Wisner, J. N.: Budgeting basics: A how-to guide for managers, Part 7: Carving monthly targets out of the annual budget. *Supervisory Mgmt.* 20:23 (Jul.), 1975.

Sweeny, A., and Wisner, J. N.: Budgeting basics: A how-to guide for managers, Part 8: Hitting budget targets and protecting profits. *Supervisory Mgmt.* 20:15 (Aug.), 1975.

Tipgos, M. H., and Crum, R. P.: Applying management accounting concepts to the health care industry. *Mgmt. Accounting* 64:37 (Jul.), 1982.

Tolpin, H. G.: Economics of health care. *J. Am. Dietet. A.* 76:217, 1980.

Tuthill, B. H.: Dietitians use computer assistance to contain costs. *J. Am. Dietet. A.* 76:479, 1980.

Williams, J. J.: Designing a budgeting system with planned confusion. *Calif. Mgmt. Rev.* 24:75 (Winter), 1981.

Wrisley, A. L.: Operating budgets for food service establishments. Food Management Program Leaflet 12, Cooperative Extension, College of Agriculture, University of Massachusetts.

22

Computer-Assisted Management

Over the past several decades, electronic data processing has increased in foodservice operations because of the need for information to achieve effective planning and control in foodservice systems. Before the widespread use of electronic computers, managers often could not use large amounts of valuable information about an organization's activities because it either reached them too late or was too expensive to gather in usable form. Today, a wide range of data processing and information tools are available.

According to Davis (1971), the modern computer represents a fundamental advance in computation on a par with the development of the zero or the discovery of calculus. The computer is both the result of and a major contributor to the current technological explosion.

Over the past ten years, the computer has found its way into every aspect of organizations. It has simplified, standardized, and systematized our world to a degree never dreamed possible. The rate of technological advances has made highly detailed systems available, cost effectively, even in small organizations.

In the foodservice systems model in Chapter 2, information was identified as one of the primary resources in the system. The computer has revolutionized the information capability in all types of organizations, including those in the foodservice industry. The incredible speed, memory capacity, and accuracy of the computer have made information available for planning, decision making, and control. If utilized effectively, the computer can enhance the effectiveness of all aspects of the system. Information is available for decisions on allocation of resources and functions of the subsystems.

The computer is an important tool in decision making and communication. As discussed in Chapter 18, many of the decision making techniques available to managers utilize computer technology. Communication in organizations is enhanced by the rapid transferral of information made possible by the technology. The computer plays an important role in the control, memory, and feedback elements of the system.

While the computer has been a boon to management in all types of operations, it is not a panacea. A foodservice operation must be well organized and well managed regardless of whether the computer is available or not. The quality of the information available from the computer is dependent on the quality of the data fed into the computer system. The computer cannot manage operations; it can only assist managers in a wide variety of ways in managing operations— hence the term computer-assisted management. As an example, a computer can expand a recipe, cost it, generate a list of food items needed to prepare the product, and produce an analysis of the nutrient composition of the menu item. If the recipe is not accurate when entered into the recipe data base, however, the resulting food product will be of poor quality. Also, if cost information or nutrient information is not accurate, the computer output is useless, thus the term "garbage in, garbage out."

HISTORICAL DEVELOPMENT

In 1954, an important news item was the first installation of a computer by an industrial concern (Davis, 1971). Ten years later, the number of nonmilitary computers was over 13,000, and the number has increased geometrically since those early days.

Modern computers were not developed until the late 1940s, but some important prior developments were the algebra of logic, the punched card, and the calculator. Although not a direct influence on the design of modern computers, the work in the 1800s of Babbage was also a major contribution. He devised a machine called a "difference engine" to perform simple computations automatically.

The computers of the 1950s, often referred to as "first generation" computers, used vacuum tubes, were very large, required much air conditioning, and were relatively slow (Figure 22.1). The computers of the period 1959 to 1965 were referred to as "second generation" and used transistors rather than tubes. "Third generation" computers were characterized by the use of hybrid or integrated circuits, by the integration of hardware with software, and by an orientation to data communications and the handling of multiple operations simultaneously.

Vacuum Tube
(First Generation)

Transistor
(Second Generation)

Integrated Circuitry
(Third Generation)

Miniaturization
(Fourth Generation)   **Figure 22.1.** *Evolution of computers*

The "fourth generation" computers use tiny "chips" that can hold hundreds of integrated circuits.

Improved and enhanced systems have been developed continuously since the introduction of those first computers. The field of computer technology is changing so rapidly that speaking authoritatively of future developments is difficult because these are being translated into current use so quickly. What can be said, however, is that a clear and continuous trend has emerged in computer hardware toward reduced size, reduced cost, increased speed, and an improved cost/performance ratio.

A new generation of computers small enough to sit on a desktop have made computer technology more widely available. Mini- and microcomputers became available in the late 1970s and are contributing to the development of a computer-literate society. Many of these new small computers are referred to as "user-friendly" because a person does not have to be a programmer to use them. They are programmed in English-like languages and virtually carry on a dialogue through print on a screen or cathode ray tube with a user at a keyboard terminal. Increasingly, managers have these computers readily available to access information for monitoring operations.

Computer applications in the foodservice industry date to the early 1960s (Youngwirth, 1983). In 1962, pioneering research under the direction of Balintfy at Tulane University was designed to plan lowest cost menus that met criteria for nutritive values, menu pattern, and frequency of offering food items. This research demonstrated that computer utilization for dietary management was feasible. His CAMP program, or Computer Assisted Menu Planning, was donated to IBM to foster computer research in other institutions. Under a U.S. Public Health Service grant, four hospitals tested the program. One of these institutions was the University of Missouri Medical Center, where development has continued on computer applications to foodservice management. The developmental work at the University of Missouri-Columbia involved development of four systems: an inventory system for automatically producing purchase orders, maintaining a perpetual inventory, and costing food purchases and issues; a food cost accounting system; a menu planning system; and a production control system designed to coordinate flow of materials from the storeroom to production areas and to provide assistance in control over quality and quantity in food production.

Following those early developments, computer-assisted management systems have been developed in many hospital dietetic service departments. Inventory, production, and cost control systems have been the major applications for computer technology, as well as nutrient analysis of menus and of individual patient food intake.

Computer-assisted foodservice management systems have been designed through the years for school and for college and university foodservice operations. Inventory and production control have been primary applications.

In the commercial field, some of the early applications were in the hotel/motel segment of the industry. According to Fay et al. (1976), the hospitality service industries were relatively slow in adopting electronic data processing techniques, with one notable exception. The airline sector has embraced EDP as a necessary technique to an extent paralleled in few other industries. Early applications of the computer in the hospitality industry were in airline and hotel/motel reservation systems. During the 1970s and 1980s, however, widespread use of the computer has become prevalent in all aspects of operations.

ELEMENTS OF INFORMATION PROCESSING SYSTEM

The basic elements in an information system that uses a computer for processing data and performing computations and other functions are hardware and software. Hardware is the equipment used in data processing. Software includes the programs and routines with the instructions for processing information.

Hardware

Computer hardware is the equipment that performs in the major functional units of data processing (Figure 22.2). In the computer, information is presented to the processor in one form and returned in a different form. The former is the input information or data, which is the raw material of the process, and the latter is the output information.

The modern computer consists of a central processing unit with peripheral equipment, such as input/output devices and auxiliary storage. Input can be provided in a variety of ways. Punched card readers were one of the first devices

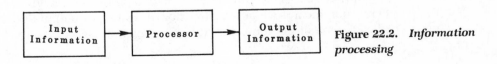

Figure 22.2. *Information processing*

used for this purpose. The positions of the punched holes on the cards are a coded form of information, and these positions are sensed electrically by reading brushes in the card reader. Cards can be read at the rate of several hundred per minute. Magnetic tape units allow much faster transmission of information—in fact, hundreds of times faster than card reading. Typewriter-like terminals can be used to enter data into the computer or to produce diskettes, commonly known as floppy disks, which are later read into the computer by disk drives. Magnetic ink readers are a specialized input device.

Upon entry, information is stored. Computer storage, or memory, usually consists of two parts: main storage and auxiliary storage. Main storage can be thought of as part of the "brain" of the system. Depending on the size of the computer, it may have capacity to hold several thousands or several millions of characters. The instructions and data needed for work in progress will be stored in the main memory. The hardware used for this unit are silicon chips containing integrated circuits and magnetic cores, which allow stored information to be accessed independently without the need to work through a file of information. For this reason, they are called Random Access Memory (RAM) units. The operational requirements of main storage make it expensive and, therefore, auxiliary or secondary capacity is usually necessary. Cheaper units can hold information not immediately needed in processing. Types of auxiliary storage include magnetic disks, which offer random access to data items, and magnetic tape, which are sequential in nature and must, therefore, be read from the beginning to locate a particular piece of information.

With information stored in the computer, processing can be initiated. The central processing unit, or CPU, which controls and supervises all operations, consists of the main storage, a control system, and the arithmetic/logic unit. The CPU is connected to the input/output devices and to the auxiliary storage. The control section contains circuitry capable of activating peripheral equipment, analyzing instructions, and authorizing computations and all other processing steps. It coordinates and directs all activity, following the expressed intentions of the users. Basically, then, the CPU is the computer's brain.

The arithmetic/logic unit contains circuits that perform computations and compare data items. The results of such comparisons are used to determine the possible course of action to be followed. This unit then is the computer's decision making capability. A key CPU function is the continual shifting of information back and forth between main and secondary storage.

The type of output devices parallels that of input. Cards may be punched, magnetic tapes or disks written, or video displays made. Printed output, sometimes called hard copy, is a major type of output medium. Serial printers, such as the ordinary typewriter, print one character at a time, but at impressive speed. Line printers do an entire line at a time and page printers an entire page. Graphs and charts may be the output, in addition to tabular presentations of data.

To summarize, the computer consists of a simple processing unit with peripheral equipment, such as auxiliary storage and input/output devices. A more detailed version of the computer system is shown in Figure 22.3.

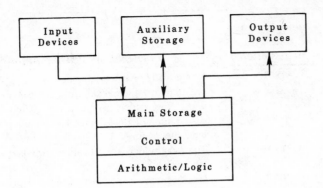

Figure 22.3. *The computer system*

Software

Computer software consists of the program, which is the set of instructions and routines for processing the data. Computer language uses only two numbers, 0 and 1, and is referred to as the binary system. These numbers correspond to the electrical current in the computer.

Programming languages have been developed for communicating with the computer. A wide variety of programming languages is available. A user provides detailed instructions to the computer in a programming language specifying in step-by-step fashion just what is to be done. Translating these instructions into machine language is then done by the machine itself, using procedures developed by a manufacturer. These translation programs are called compilers or interpreters. Procedures sometimes called the operating system are designed for efficient machine use, such as identifying users, reading input, following instructions, keeping records of time used, and pointing out user errors. In spite of their impressive capabilities, computers still have to be told exactly what to do in a step-by-step fashion.

Computer programming is defined as the entire series of steps involved in solving a problem on a computer. Schneider et al. (1982) describe the following eight steps involved in computer programming.

1 *Defining the problem.* A clear understanding of exactly what is needed is necessary for creating a workable solution.

2 *Outlining the solution.* A program generally is composed of many interrelated tasks that must be outlined initially to ensure the pieces are designed in the context of the whole.

3 *Selecting and representing algorithms.* An algorithm is the specific method used to solve a problem, which may be one already developed or one designed by the programmer. An algorithmic representation should be used for describing the details for the proposed solution prior to coding the algorithm into a programming language.

4 *Coding.* After defining the problem, organizing a solution, and sketching out the step-by-step details of the algorithm, the next step is coding into a

Language	Approximate date of introduction	General application areas
FORTRAN	1957	Numerically oriented language. Most applicable to scientific, mathematical, and statistical problem areas. Very widely used and very widely available.
ALGOL	1960	Also a numerically oriented language but with new language features. Widely used in Europe.
COBOL	1960	The most widely used business oriented computer language.
LISP	1961	Special-purpose language developed primarily for list processing and symbolic manipulation. Widely used in the area of artificial intelligence.
SNOBOL	1962	Special-purpose language used primarily for character string processing. This includes applications such as text editors, language processors, and bibliographic work.
BASIC	1965	A simple interactive programming language widely used to teach programming in high schools and colleges.
PL/1	1965	An extremely complex, general-purpose language designed to incorporate the numeric capabilities of FORTRAN, the business capabilities of COBOL, and many other features into a single language.
APL	1967	An interactive language that introduced a wide range of new operations and language features.
PASCAL	1971	A general-purpose language designed specifically to teach the concepts of computer programming and allow the efficient implementation of large programs.

Figure 22.4. *Widely used computer languages.* **Source:** *Schneider, G. M., Weingart, S. W., and Perlman, D. M.:* **An Introduction to Programming and Problem Solving with Pascal.** *New York: John Wiley & Sons, 1982 (reprinted by permission).*

computer language. Three considerations will dictate the language to be used: the nature of the problem, the language available on the computer, and the limitations of a particular computer installation. Some languages are general purpose; others have been designed for certain classes of problems. Some of the widely used computer languages are listed in Figure 22.4.

5 *Debugging.* After the program has been coded, the inevitable errors must be located and corrected, often a time-consuming and agonizing task.

6 *Testing and validation.* To ensure that correct results are produced by the program, explicit testing is necessary.

7 *Documenting.* This step includes both technical documentation by the programmer who will be working with and modifying the program and user-level documentation for users of the program.

8 *Program maintenance.* Programs should not be considered static entities. They frequently become outdated as new problems need to be solved, errors are discovered, or new equipment becomes available.

Many programs are commercially available and are commonly referred to as "canned programs." These programs are designed for generalized use for given types of problems. Users need only provide the data and some other specific information for using the program for their particular problem or situation. A number of these programs are available for applications in the foodservice field.

An important component for using a computer program, whether or not it is a specifically written or a canned program, is the compilation of data bases. Depending on the type of problem, the data needed varies. For inventory control, for example, information should include type of products, usage levels, purchase quantities, cost, and issue units. For foodservice applications, the food item file and the recipe file are the basic data bases. In healthcare and in other types of organizations where nutritional considerations are especially important, a nutrient file is maintained to facilitate computer-assisted nutrient analysis.

COMPUTER APPLICATIONS IN FOODSERVICE SYSTEMS

Computer-assisted foodservice systems have provided management with updated, timely information for cost control and labor utilization, improving the effectiveness and efficiency of the total operation by facilitating better management decisions. Dietitians and foodservice managers have been relieved of repetitive, routine tasks, enabling them to utilize their specialized skills and knowledge for planning and evaluation. Computers have not replaced foodservice managers and dietitians; instead, the computer has proven to be a powerful tool for assisting in complex decision making and systems development.

The foodservice manager assumes an important role during the planning and development of computerized management systems and, thus, should have a basic understanding of computer functions and terminology to work effectively with systems analysts and other computer personnel. The foodservice manager contributes technical expertise in foodservice systems, whereas the computer personnel provide the technical expertise in computer technology.

Implementing a Computer System

The uniqueness of each organization must be considered in designing a computer-assisted management system. The following factors must be considered.

- Clarifying goals and objectives of the foodservice system.
- Ensuring that the current operation is well organized and functioning effectively.

- Identifying functions most appropriate for computer assistance in a given organization.

- Evaluating the personnel, time, and money for developing a computer-assisted system.

- Considering the availability and cost of hardware and software.

- Identifying training needs for personnel in the organization.

The goals and objectives of the foodservice system provide the foundation for development and implementation of computer-assisted management systems. As indicated earlier, a well-organized operation is a prerequisite to initiating a computer-assisted system. For example, established purchasing and ordering procedures and perpetual inventory records, standardized recipes, and specified portion sizes are necessary for initiating computer assistance in inventory and production control. All data must be accurate and precise for the computer-assisted system to provide valid and reliable data for management decisions.

Computer-assisted management information systems have been designed for inventory control, production control, and cost control. Computer information systems are practical in these areas because many routine, repetitive elements are involved. Also, these operations are frequently sources of problems for management. In addition, accurate and updated information is needed for management control and effective decision making in these areas. Computers also have been used in menu planning, nutritional analysis, and in a variety of other aspects of foodservice operations. Major applications of computer-assisted foodservice management will be discussed in subsequent sections.

The personnel, time, and money needed to develop computer-assisted systems must be evaluated carefully because the developmental process is costly. The output generated by the computer must be justified in relation to the cost of development and use of the computer programs. If reports generated are not timely and meaningful for assisting in controlling and increasing the effectiveness of the operation, then the functions should not be computerized. The feasibility of adapting computer programs developed by other organizations or the possibility of using one of the commercially available packages should be considered.

An organization need not have a computer center with a large computer for initiating electronic data processing. A computer system may be shared by a group of institutions, or computer time may be purchased from another institution or from a commercial company, thus eliminating the need for costly computer installations within each organization. Also, the relatively low cost of micro- and minicomputers has brought computer assistance within the reach of most organizations. Even if an organization has a large computer, or "main frame," as they are sometimes called, microcomputers may be available in individual departments for specialized needs.

As Youngwirth (1983) points out, the impact of computerization on employees and the possible resistance to change emphasizes that employees should be involved in the planning process for computer-assisted management systems. In addition, after a system has been implemented, a well-planned training program is needed to ensure that the system is utilized effectively.

Inventory and Purchasing Applications

Computer-assisted management in inventory control was one of the earliest applications of computer technology in foodservice systems. The initial step in designing a management information system (MIS) for inventory control involves development of an item file of all food and supplies required for use in food production and service. Master item files include the following types of data: code number, description, purchase unit, unit cost, issue unit, and storage location for each item. In addition, minimum and maximum stock levels and reorder points may be included. This data base is used in other aspects of the computer-assisted system and, thus, may include additional information needed for those components. For example, the item file information is used in constructing the recipe file, and therefore information needed to identify food ingredients for recipes may also be included.

Several types of transactions are needed for the inventory control MIS with the item file as the data base. Inventory transactions include the following.

- Place on order.
- Cancel on order.
- Item received.
- Return to vendor.
- Issue.
- Return to inventory.

An inventory control MIS is usually designed to produce daily and monthly usage level and cost reports as well as purchasing reports. An updated inventory listing is generated daily in most systems.

Although a perpetual inventory record can be maintained using a computer-assisted information system, periodic physical inventories are required to reconcile discrepancies and ensure the accuracy of the inventory information. Computer-assisted systems are often designed to produce a form periodically to be used in the physical count of the food and supplies on hand in the various storage areas.

Wilcox et al. (1978), in describing enhancements of the inventory control system used in the Department of Nutrition and Dietetics at the University of Missouri, indicated the purpose was to optimize inventory levels of food items, while minimizing stock outages. The model in Figure 22.5 provides the design of the computer-assisted system for integrating production with inventory control. Improvement was achieved by calculating an order quantity based on a menu item forecast and current stock levels. Computer-printing of purchase requisitions was another enhancement accomplished. As shown in Figure 22.5, a number of reports are generated from the system to assist in purchasing and inventory control, typical of other computer-assisted inventory systems.

Production Control Applications

Quality control and ingredient control can be facilitated with a management information system for production. The recipe file is the key data base for com-

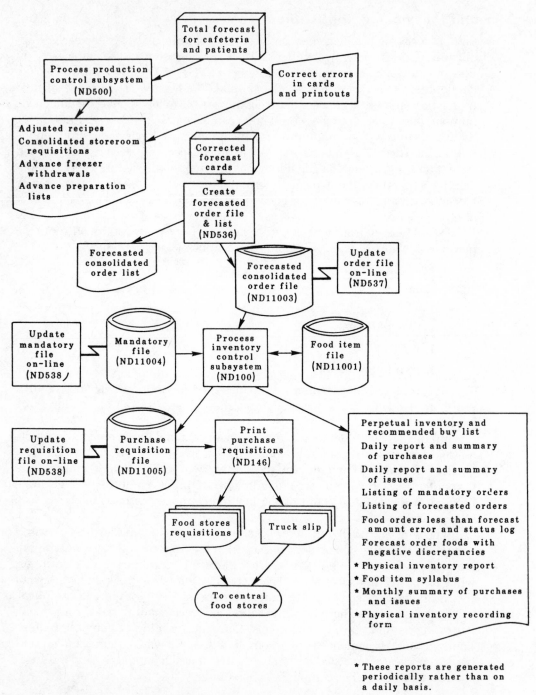

Figure 22.5. *Integration of production control and inventory control subsystems to generate food stores requisitions.* Source: *Wilcox, M. M., Moore, A. N., Hoover, L. W.: Automated purchasing: Forecasts to determine stock levels and print orders. J. Am. Dietet. Assoc. 73:401, 1978.*

puter-assisted production control. Three types of information for each recipe are contained in the recipe file: general, ingredient, and production. The general recipe information includes the recipe number, name, portion yield, portion size, and serving information. Other information might include maximum and minimum batch size, recipe source, equipment needed for production, and selling price information.

The ingredient information includes the individual food item codes corresponding to those in the food item file, in addition to descriptive information and data on the quantity of each ingredient required by the recipe. The production information includes procedures and instruction for prepreparation, production, and service. Obviously, carefully standardized recipes are needed prior to embarking on a computer-assisted production control system.

Adjusted recipes, storeroom requisitions, and advanced preparation reports are reports commonly generated from computer-assisted production control systems. In most operations in which computer-assisted systems have been implemented, an ingredient control room has been incorporated as part of the system to assist with control of food items.

Computer applications also have been developed for work schedules and determination of production times. Many of these applications, however, are experimental and not widely used in foodservice operations at this time.

In many hospitals, computer menu tallying systems are used to provide data for production planning. In many types of operations, both institutional and commercial, in which foods are sold to customers, cash register or point of sale (POS) systems are designed to compile data on all items purchased, which can then be used in estimating production demand for future periods.

OTHER APPLICATIONS

Computer-assisted menu planning has been the focus of much of the earlier work in the application of electronic data processing in dietetics and foodservice management. As indicated in Chapter 6, because of difficulties in quantifying esthetic factors in menu planning, computer menu planning has not been used widely. According to Youngwirth (1983), benefits of planning or printing menus by computer in healthcare institutions include allowing dietitians to spend more time in patient care, providing greater control of foodservice operations, and controlling costs.

Rather than using the computer for menu planning, in many hospital foodservices the computer has been used in menu management in a number of other ways. Anderson et al. (1977) developed a system to generate the master menu, production forecast and usage forms, production work sheets, food order report, and a master copy of selective menus for various diets. Further development led to an on-line menu management system (Hoover et al., 1982), which uses a master recipe file and recipe nutrient and cost file in addition to three new data bases created for the system: the master menu file, menu transaction file, and production forecast file. The major benefits of the system are flexibility and

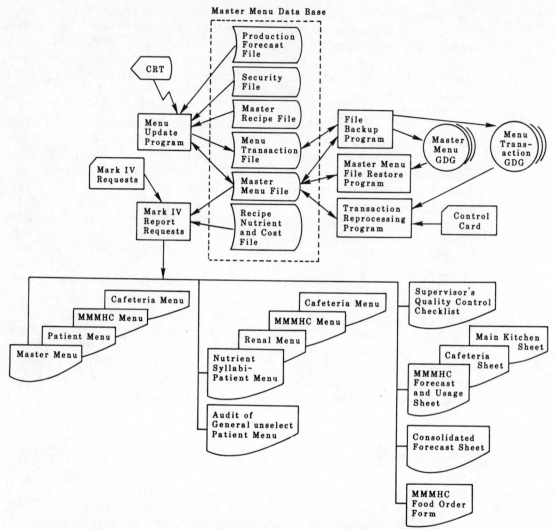

Figure 22.6. *System flowchart for menu management system.* **Source: Hoover, L. W., Waller, A. L., Rastkar, A. R., Johnson, V. A.: Development of on-line real-time menu management system. J. Am. Dietet. Assoc. 80:46, 1982.**

elimination of typing worksheets because forms are generated by computer. Also, with the master menu stored in the computer, updates and changes in menus are facilitated. Figure 22.6 provides an illustration of this menu management system.

Other hospitals have used the computer to produce personalized selective menus for patients. Ford and Wesley (1979) indicate that savings have resulted from using a computerized selective menu system, primarily because of the printing costs that are eliminated. Computer-assisted tallying of patients' selections of menus has been widely used in hospitals and has eliminated the time-consuming manual task.

Computers have also been used in hospitals for developing patient information systems. Information on new admissions, patients' diagnoses, diet orders, and even a list of patients' birthdays can be readily provided. As indicated earlier, nutrient analysis of menus for planning and monitoring diets is another frequent use of the computer in dietetic services. Also, a technique for patient interviewing using the computer has been developed (Youngwirth, 1983).

A widespread use of the computer in all types of foodservice operations has been in assisting with financial management. Because of the need for up-to-date information on costs, the computer can be particularly useful in providing information for controlling costs in foodservice operations. Tuthill (1980) contends that the computer can assist the foodservice manager in containing costs by providing accurate and current reports on food costs as well as providing cumulative cost information on foodservice operations. At the University of Missouri Medical Center, a personnel data system was developed to provide information for controlling labor costs. Reports generated by the computer include number of hours and dollars used for full- and part-time employees and time and money spent for overtime, sick leave, holidays, and vacation.

Computer applications in foodservice management continue to be developed. Production scheduling and employee scheduling are among other applications. The increasing availability of software packages has enabled foodservice managers to implement management information systems without the time-consuming and costly developmental processes necessary in designing a system specifically for a particular operation. Decreasing cost and increasing sophistication of microcomputers are permitting managers even in small operations to enjoy the benefits of computer-assisted information systems.

SUMMARY

The computer has revolutionized organizations and their management. The computer is the result of, and a major contributor to the current technological age. Computers make information available to managers in a timely fashion and with an accuracy impossible to achieve otherwise. This increased information capability is assisting managers in making better decisions and in controlling operations.

Nonmilitary use of computers dates to the 1950s. Although the early computers were large and relatively slow, a continuous trend in computer technology has been characterized by reduced size, reduced cost, and increased speed. New, small "user-friendly" computers are making computer technology accessible even to small organizations.

Applications in foodservice operations date to the work of Balintfy at Tulane University in computer-assisted menu planning. Development of computer applications to foodservice management has also been pioneered at the University of Missouri Medical Center where inventory control, production control, and food cost control systems have been designed.

The basic elements of a computer system are the hardware, or equipment, and the software, or the programs and routines for processing information. The major functional units are the input devices, central processing unit, output devices, and auxiliary storage.

Computer software, or the instructions and routines for processing data, provides a method for communicating with the computer. Programs are commercially available, often called canned programs, or may be designed specifically for an organization.

Computer-assisted foodservice systems have been developed to relieve managers of repetitive, routine tasks and to assist in complex decision making. Design of a computer-assisted management systems must include clarification of goals and objectives. Also, current operations must be well organized and functioning effectively before computer applications are feasible.

Inventory and production control have been the two areas in which computer assistance has been applied most frequently in foodservice operations. Also, a widespread use of computers in foodservice has been in assisting with financial management and cost control.

The increasing availability of software packages has enabled foodservice managers to implement management information systems in all types of foodservice operations. Improved and advanced systems are being developed continuously. Computer technology is changing so rapidly that future developments are difficult to predict. To function in this computer age, foodservice managers must become computer literate and be able to utilize the computer as a tool to increase effectiveness.

REFERENCES

Anderson, A. L., Moore, A. N., and Hoover, L. W.: Development of automated form generating system for menu item data. *J. Am. Dietet. A.* 71:124, 1977.

Andrews, J. T., and Tuthill, B. H.: Computer-based management of dietary departments. *Hospitals* 42:117 (Jul. 16), 1968.

Brisbane, H. N.: Computing menu nutrients by data processing. *J. Am. Dietet. A.* 44:453, 1964.

Clithero, W. A.: The computer as a dietetic tool. *J. Am. Dietet. A.* 44:451, 1964.

Davis, G. B.: *Introduction to Electronic Computers.* 2nd ed. New York: McGraw-Hill Book Co., 1971.

DeMarco, M. R., Mann, S. L., and Mason, H. A.: Computer recipes in quantity food production. *Hospitals* 41:88 (Apr. 16), 1967.

Fay, C. T., Rhoads, R. C., and Rosenblatt, R. L.: *Managerial Accounting for the Hospitality Service Industries.* 2nd ed. Dubuque, IA: Wm. C. Brown Co., Publishers, 1976.

Ford, M. G., and Wesley, N. W.: Dietitians improve patient care with computerized selective menu. *Hospitals* 53:76 (Mar. 1), 1979.

Fromm, B., Moore, A. N., and Hoover, L. W.: Computer-generated fiscal reports for food cost accounting. *J. Am. Dietet. A.* 77:170, 1980.

Guley, H. M., and Stinson, J. P.: Computer simulation for production scheduling in a ready foods system. *J. Am. Dietet. A.* 76:482, 1980.

Hart, P. E.: Computerized systems cut dietary department's costs. *Hospitals* 51:123 (Dec. 16), 1978.

Hoover, L. W.: Computers in dietetics: State-of-the-art, 1976. *J. Am. Dietet. A.* 68:39, 1976.

Hoover, L. W., and Leonard, M. S.: Automated hospital information system functions for dietetics. *J. Am. Dietet. A.* 80:312, 1982.

Hoover, L. W., and Moore, A. N.: "Dietetic Com-Pak": An educational model simulating computer-assisted dietetics. *J. Am. Dietet. A.* 64:500, 1974.

Hoover, L. W., and Moore, A. N.: *Dietetic Com-Pak Student Guide.* Columbia, MO: Lucas Brothers, 1973.

Hoover, L. W., Waller, A. L., Rastkar, A., and Johnson, V. A.: Development of on-line real-time menu management system. *J. Am. Dietet. A.* 80:46, 1982.

Johnson, R. A., and Moore, A. N.: Inventory and cost control by computer. *J. Am. Dietet. A.* 49:5, 1966.

Lambert, C. U., and Beach, B. L.: Computerized scheduling for cook/freeze food production plans. *J. Am. Dietet. A.* 77:174, 1980.

Lambert, C. U., and Beach, B. L.: Computerized scheduling for cooks. *J. Am. Dietet. A.* 77:174, 1980.

Lawson, B. A.: Hospital food service management with computer assistance. *J. Can. Dietet. A.* 40:27, 1979.

Marko, J. A., and Moore, R. G.: How to select a computing system, Part I. *Cornell Hotel Restaur. Admin. Q.* 21:60 (May), 1980.

Moore, A. N., and Tuthill, B. H., eds.: *Computer Assisted Food Management Systems.* 2nd ed. Columbia, MO: Technical Education Services, Univ. of Missouri-Columbia, 1974.

Orsner, J., and Mutschler, M.: A computer-tallied menu system. *J. Am. Dietet. A.* 67:570, 1975.

Rochford, C. C.: Inquiry into computer applications in dietetics. *J. Am. Dietet. A.* 66:374, 1975.

Sager, J. F., and Ostenso, G. L.: Computerized recipe adjustment and food ordering. *J. Am. Dietet. A.* 52:498, 1968.

Scheid, F.: *Computers and Programming.* New York: McGraw-Hill Book Co., 1982.

Schill, T. G., Norback, J. P., and Matthews, M. E.: Integrating labor data into a computer model for a foodservice system. *Food Technol.* 36:72 (Jul.), 1982.

Schneider, G. M., Weingart, S. W., and Perlman, D. M.: *An Introduction to Programming and Problem Solving with Pascal.* 2nd ed. New York: John Wiley & Sons, 1982.

Seliger, N.: Computers in University of Kansas Medical Center. *Food Mgmt.* 16:48 (Aug.), 1981.

Shick, G. L., Hoover, L. W., and Moore, A. N.: A computer-assisted personnel data system for a hospital department of dietetics. *J. Am. Dietet. A.* 74:448, 1979.

Torrence, B. L., and Vaden, A. G.: EDP recipe adjustment by percentage in a college foodservice system. *J. Am. Dietet. A.* 69:407, 1976.

Tuthill, B. H.: Dietitians use computer assistance to contain costs. *J. Am. Dietet. A.* 76:479, 1980.

Unklesbay, N., and Unklesbay, K.: An automated system for planning menus for the elderly in Title VII nutrition program. *Food Technol.* 32:80 (Aug.), 1978.

Wheeler, M. L., and Wheeler, L. A.: Nutrient menu planning for clinical research centers. *J. Am. Dietet. A.* 67:346, 1975.

Wilcox, M. M., Moore, A. N., and Hoover, L. W.: Automated purchasing: Forecasts to determine stock levels and print orders. *J. Am. Dietet. A.* 73:400, 1978.

Willard, R. S.: Computers in dietetics. *Dietetic Currents* 9:7 (May/Jun.), 1982.

Youngwirth, J.: The evolution of computers in dietetics: A review. *J. Am. Dietet. A.* 82:62, 1983.

APPENDIX A

Sources of Quantity Recipes

BOOKS

Burchfield, J. C., et al.: *Contemporary Quantity Recipe File*. Boston: Cahner Publishing Co., 1975.

Caviani, M., and Urbashich, M.: *Simplified Quantity Recipes for Nursing, Convalescent Homes and Hospitals*. Chicago: National Restaurant Association, 1974.

Gisslen, W.: *Professional Baking*. New York: John Wiley & Sons, 1985.

Gisslen, W.: *Professional Cooking*. New York: John Wiley & Sons, 1983.

Johnson, H.: *Quality, Quantity Cuisine*. Boston: Cahner Publishing Co., 1976.

Kraft Kitchens: *Travel Your Taste with Kraft Foodservice: International Recipes from the World of Foodservice*. Boston: CBI Publ. Co., no date.

National Association of College and University Food Services: Recipes from the Heartland '80. Cleveland, OH: L. J. Minor Corp., 1980.

National Frozen Food Association and Restaurants and Institutions: *Frozen Food Cookbook*. Boston: Cahner Publishing Co., 1981.

Sultan, W. J.: *Practical Baking*. 3rd ed. Westport, CT: Air Publishing Co., 1981.

Terrell, M. E.: *Large Quantity Recipes*, 3rd ed. Philadelphia: J. B. Lippincott, 1975.

Wallace, J.: *The American Quantity Cookbook: Tracing our Food Traditions*. Boston: Cahner Publishing Co., 1976.

Shugart, G., Molt, M., and Wilson, M.: *Food for Fifty*, 7th ed. New York: John Wiley & Sons, 1984.

RECIPE CARD FILES

Hotel, Restaurant, and Institution Management Department, Iowa State University: *Standardized Quantity Recipe File for Quality and Cost Control*. Ames, IA: Iowa State University Press, 1972.

Hotel, Restaurant, and Institution Management Department, Iowa State University: Quantity Recipes: Supplement to Standardized Quantity Recipe File for Quality and Cost Control. Ames, IA: Iowa State University Press, 1984.

U.S.D.A. *Quantity Recipes for School Lunches*. Washington, DC: Supt. of Documents, PA 631, 1965.

PERIODICALS

These publications contain quantity recipes and sources of recipe information each month:

Food Management, Harcourt Brace Jovanovich Publishers, 1 E. First St., Duluth, MN 55806. ($15 per year)

Restaurants and Institutions, 270 St. Paul St., Denver, CO 80206. ($40 per year)

School Food Service Journal, 4104 Iliff Avenue, Denver, CO 80222. ($30 per year)

ADDITIONAL SOURCES

Food companies, such as

Campbell Soup

General Foods

Kellogg

Pillsbury

Rich's

Sunkist

Educational divisions of food industry organizations, such as

American Dry Milk Institute

California Raisin Advisory Board

Cling Peach Advisory Board

Florida Citrus Commission

Idaho Potato Commission

National Live Stock and Meat Board

Wheat Flour Institute

Government publications obtained from Superintendent of Documents, Washington, DC.

ELECTRONICALLY FORMATTED PRECODED STANDARD QUANTITY RECIPE FILES

Available from The CBORD Group, Inc., Ithaca, New York.

Gisslen, W.: *Professional Baking.* New York: John Wiley & Sons, 1985.

Gisslen, W.: *Professional Cooking.* New York: John Wiley & Sons, 1983.

Shugart, G. S., Molt, M. K., and Wilson, M. F.: *Food for Fifty*. 7th ed. New York: John Wiley & Sons, 1984.

The Culinary Institute of America and the Editors of Institutions Magazine: *The Professional Chef*. A CBI Book published by Van Nostrand Reinhold Co., 1974.

Wenzel, G. L.: *Wenzel's Menu Maker*. 2nd ed. A CBI Book published by Van Nostrand Reinhold Co., 1979.

Hotel, Restaurant, and Institution Management Department, Iowa State University: *Standardized Quantity Recipe File for Quality and Cost Control*. Ames, IA: Iowa State University Press, 1984.

U.S. Army Food Service Center, U.S. Army Natick Laboratories: *Arm Forces Recipes Service*. Washington, DC: U.S. Govt. Prtg. Ofc., Feb. 1969.

APPENDIX B

Resources for Writing Specifications

Food and Nutrition Service, USDA: *Food Purchasing Pointers for School Food Service*. Program Aid No. 1160, August, 1977.

Kotschevar, L. H.: *Quantity Food Purchasing*. 2nd ed. New York: John Wiley & Sons, 1975.

Livestock Division, Agricultural Marketing Service, USDA: Institutional Meat Purchase Specifications. Washington, DC.

- General Requirements, August 1971.
- Cured, Cured and Smoked, and Full-cooked Pork Products, Jan. 1979.
- Cured, Dried, and Smoked Beef Products, Nov. 1976.
- Edible By-Products—Series 700, Jan. 1971.
- Fresh Beef, Jan. 1975.
- Fresh Lamb and Mutton, Jan. 1975.
- Fresh Pork, Jan. 1975.
- Fresh Veal and Calf, July 1975.
- Sausage Products, July 1976.

Morin, T. H., Bloom, T., and Zaccarelli, H.: *The Nifda Canned Goods Specifications Manual*. West Lafayette, IN: Purdue University Restaurant, Hotel, and Institution Management Institute, 1984.

Ninemeier, J. D.: *Purchasing, Receiving, and Storage: A Systems Manual for Restaurants, Hotels, and Clubs*. Boston: CBI Publishing Co., 1983.

Oakley, H., ed.: *The Buying Guide*. 7th ed. Hagerstown, MD: Blue Goose, 1980.

Peddersen, R. B.: *Foodservice and Hotel Purchasing*. Boston: CBI Publishing Co., 1981.

Peddersen, R. B.: *SPECS: The Comprehensive Foodservice Purchasing and Specification Manual*. Boston: CBI Publishing Co., 1977.

The Almanac of the Canning, Freezing, Preserving Industries. Westminister, MD: Edward E. Judge & Sons (Published annually).

The Meat Buyers Guide. 5th ed. McLean, VA: Natl. Assoc. of Meat Purveyors, May, 1983.

Warfel, M. C., and Waskey, F. H.: *The Professional Food Buyer: Standards, Principles, and Procedures*. Berkeley, CA: McCutchen Publishing Corp., 1979.

APPENDIX C

Standards on Food Products

BREADS, QUICK

Banana Bread The crust should be even, medium brown, and moist. It will typically have a crack down the middle section. The bread should have a medium coarse grain free from tunnels, a light texture with a moist, beige colored crumb with dark brown banana flecks. The flavor should be sweet and mild.

Biscuits The appearance should be a golden brown top, with lighter sides, symmetrical shape, uniform size; fairly smooth, level top; 2–3 times size of unbaked biscuit; free from excess flour; creamy white inside; flaky, free from yellow or brown spots. Tenderness: crisp and tender crust, moist and tender on the inside. Texture: light and flaky, peeling off in thin sheets; medium fine grain; slightly moist. Flavor: pleasing, well-blended, without any taste of bitterness.

Biscuits, Angel The biscuits should be of good volume with a lightly golden brown crust. The biscuits should be uniform in size and shape. The inside texture should be fine, even-grained, moist, and fluffy. The crumb should pull away in thin flakes or layers. The flavor should be delicate, not bready or too sweet.

Corn Bread The crust is crisp, shiny, pebbly and golden brown. The top should be well rounded and free from knobs. The interior crumb should be moist, light and tender with no tunneling. Flavor should have a well-balanced corn taste.

Coffee Cake Should have an uneven, but slightly peaked surface. The golden brown crust has the appearance of being sugary and shiny and is slightly crusty. The texture of the coffee cake is coarse and the cells are large. The odor and flavor should be pleasing, but characteristic of the ingredients. The cake should be served warm as it loses its freshness rapidly.

Muffins Crust is crisp, shiny, pebbly, and golden brown. The top should be well-rounded and free from knobs. The muffin should be large in volume compared to weight. The interior crumb should be moist, light, and tender with coarse even grain and no tunneling. Flavor should be delicate and natural, not bready or too sweet. Muffin may vary with addition of nuts, fruit, spices, and other flavorings.

Source: Used by permission, Kansas State University Residence Hall Foodservice.

BREADS, YEAST

Bread Sticks The crust should be of a golden brown color. The sticks are to be crisp and remain crisp. The grain of the bread should be fine and the texture uniform. The flavor is pleasant, without traces of soured or yeasty odor. The sticks should be approximately 5″ in length and 1″ in circumference.

French Bread The crust should be crisp, tender, and relatively thin with an even, golden-brown color. The loaf should be uniformly shaped. The grain should have uniformly-thin cell walls. The crumb color is a creamy white and the crumb texture should be moist, soft, elastic, and resilient with a nutty, wheaty flavor.

Rolls Desired characteristics are: Even brown top crust, even shape, with smooth round top, and light-brown bottom. Inside texture should be soft, velvety, light, and tender with uniform cell structure. The grain should have uniformly thin cell walls. The crumb color should have a creamy white interior with some luster. The crumb should be resilient to touch. The aroma of the roll should have a light yeast fragrance. The flavor should be pleasant, not too sweet or too salty. The lightness will vary depending on what kind of flavor used: rye, wheat, or white.

Rolls, Herb Refer to "Rolls" standard except that the interior should be white with flecks of herbs apparent with the cells even in size and evenly shaped. Flavor is judged by aroma and taste and should be characteristic of the spices used (dill weed, caraway seed, and nutmeg).

Rolls, Hofman The crust should be richly browned, tender, and thin with fine specks of cinnamon-sugar evenly distributed on all the outside surfaces. The twisted oblong shape is about 2½–3″ long and 1–1½″ in diameter. Texture should be tender with a fine satiny, slightly elastic crumb. Inside color should be creamy white and free from streaks with evenly shaped thin-walled cells. Flavor is pleasantly mild and wheaty with a sweet cinnamon flavor. Aroma is predominantly cinnamon.

Rolls, Oatmeal The color should be an even brown. The crust should have a slightly pebbly appearance. The crumb should be soft and moist. The roll should have been proofed sufficiently and should be light with a light yeast fragrance. The flavor should be pleasant, with a slightly sweet nut-like taste.

Rolls, Popcorn Refer to "Rolls" standard except that the top of the roll should have four uniform peaks.

DESSERTS

Cake

Brown Sugar The crust should be thin, soft, and lightly browned, free from cracks or peaks. The crumb color is a light brown with no evidence of dark streaks. Small uniform cells free from tunnels are desired. Flavor should be mild and sweet with no after-taste of maple.

German Chocolate   The cake should have a flat or slightly rounded top, with a uniform color of light to medium brown and a fine grain of small uniform cells. The crumb should be soft and moist, resulting in a light tender cake. The flavor should be mildly sweet chocolate, with no evidence of a soapy taste caused by excess alkalinity.

Orange Chiffon   The lightly browned top crust should look rough, be flat or slightly rounded, and be an even, delicate brown. Texture should be delicate, springy, and light. Small, fine, uniform cells with thin cell walls are desired. Crumb should be moist, soft with a definite but delicate orange flavor and color.

White or Silver   The crust should be fine grained and a uniform golden brown. The slightly rounded top should be free of cracks. The grain should be small and uniform in size, the cell walls thin, and the crumb resilient, soft, and velvety. The cake should be light, tender, and slightly moist. It should taste mildly sweet with a pleasing flavor.

Cookies

Butterscotch Chip   This cookie should be 3–3½" in diameter, symmetrically round, with tawny to light walnut-brown color. It should have a crisp outer texture and slightly tender interior with small, slightly round crumb. The pecans and chips should be readily discernible and evenly distributed. Flavor should be a delicately rich blend of butterscotch and pecans.

Gingersnaps   This cookie should be symmetrically round, 3" in diameter. The exterior top should be crinkled or creviced with light sugar coating. Both exterior and interior should be a rich brown color. Interior should be slightly more moist than the exterior with small, compact air cells. The flavor should be a pleasing blend of all spices—ginger, cinnamon, and nutmeg—with no overpowering molasses flavor. The cookie should be crisp and mildly sweet.

Cookies, Bar

Butterscotch Brownie   The bar should be about 3" × 2½". Exterior should be medium brown, evenly browned on top and bottom. Cut edges should be even. Texture should be chewy, free of crumbling. The nuts should be fresh, coarsely chopped, and evenly distributed. Flavor should be rich and sweet, with a hint of butterscotch and a secondary nutty flavor.

Cereal Nougat Squares   This candy-like bar should have a smooth marshmallow-margarine coating on crisp golden-brown corn flakes. The walnut pieces and shredded coconut should be evenly distributed between the flakes and be visible on cut edge. Each square should be light in weight in relation to volume and should hold its shape when cut. The top should be thinly coated with glossy smooth semi-sweet chocolate. The flavor should be a blend of the ingredients. The texture should be firm and crisp.

Mince Squares   The bar should be approximately 3″ × 2½″ with a medium to light brown exterior and a light brown interior. Cut edges should be even. The mince should be distributed evenly throughout the bar and the flavor should be of a slightly spiced fruit taste with a sweet overtone of brown sugar. The cookie should be thick and chewy.

Custard

Blue Ribbon   The custard mixture should be clear, creamy, and shiny. The surface should be shiny and clear and should be a light delicate tan. The texture should be smooth, not stiff, tough, rubbery, curdled, or uneven. The tender gel should be uniformly coagulated and with no signs of porosity. The product should possess a delicate, egg-like flavor.

Pumpkin   The color should be golden brown. The custard should glisten and have a smooth appearance. When cut, the texture should be porous with a creamy yet slightly coarse appearance. The gel should be tender, hold its suspension, and be easily cut. The flavor should possess a mild blend of pumpkin with the spices ginger, nutmeg, and cinnamon. The custard should be served chilled, at approximately 40°F.

Frosting

Brown Sugar   The base of the frosting should be of a smooth, spreadable consistency. The brown sugar flavor should be moderate in relation to the flavor of the cake and complement it.

Coconut-Pecan (for German Chocolate Cake)   The base of the frosting should be of a smooth consistency, adhering to the surface of the cake and avoiding excessive viscosity and stickiness. The coconut and nuts should be evenly dispersed.

Pumpkin Cream   Consistency should be smooth with ability to spread. Color should be a pumpkin shade. Flavor should be sweet with mild pumpkin taste to complement flavor of cake.

Pie

Cherry (Filling)   Appearance should have a rich, red color with whole berries in a transparent syrup. Fruit should roll out gently from beneath crust when served. Fruit should retain shine and luster. Texture should be smooth. Consistency of juice should be like thick syrup, not a thick gelatin-like mass. The pie should have a sweet-tart flavor, characteristic of red sour-pitted cherries.

Chocolate Cream (Filling)   The filling should be a dark brown color and the flavor should be sweet chocolate. The texture is creamy smooth, free of lumps. The filling should fill the pastry shell and be viscous enough to hold its shape when cut. A chocolate cream pie should be topped with whipped topping.

Meringue Topping   Meringue has a pale golden brown exterior and is white inside. It should be tender, light, fluffy, moist, and have a sweet flavor. It should completely cover the pie, meeting the crust at the edge. It should hold its shape when cut.

Pastry   Texture of both top and bottom crusts should be crisp, flaky, and fork tender, but not crumbly; both crusts should be rolled thin. Appearance of the crust surface is a little blistery or irregular, and the top has a soft luster rather than a dull look. The color of the center of the top crust should be light and golden, with brown deepening slightly toward edges. The flavor is bland, with a characteristic flavor depending on proportion of salt and kind of fat used.

Pudding

Butterscotch   The color is a soft brown, the surface free from heavy film with a slightly molded, uneven appearance. This pudding should be smooth and feel light to the tongue, not gummy or sticky. When poured from the spoon, it should form mounds that fade away. The flavor should have a delicate, brown sugar taste.

Chocolate Marshmallow   Appearance should be a smooth, creamy brown. It should have a slightly molded surface and hold its shape when portioned into a serving dish. It should be smooth and be free of any burnt or scorched taste. It should have a semi-sweet chocolate and delicately sweet marshmallow taste with an accompanying delicately sweet aroma, and no visible flecks of unmelted chocolate.

Other

Bavarian   This product is a whipped topping folded into sweetened gelatin mixture. The best Bavarian contains milk instead of water. Bavarians should be smooth and tender, not tough, and should mound when spooned into dish. Flavor should be creamy-smooth, sweet, and characteristic of the fruit ingredients used.

Cobbler, Fruit   This rich biscuit topping is set over sweetened fruit. The topping has a crisp, tender, golden brown crust with a fine even-grained, moist, light and tender interior crumb. The flavor should be delicate, not bready or too sweet. The fruit should be slightly thickened and sweetened, should have recognizable form and be a clear fruit color, with natural fruit flavor.

Crisp, Fruit   A crisp should have a crisp, crunchy top covering tender fruit filling. Topping should be a delicate brown and have a crumbly texture.

Topping should be evenly distributed over fruit. The filling should be smooth in consistency and thickening should be clear. Fruit and filling may flow from underneath topping, but should not be soupy, neither should the filling be gummy or pasty. Each fruit piece should be its natural color and recognizable form. Flavor should be moderately sweet and characteristic of the fruit.

English Toffee Dessert This refrigerator dessert should have an evenly distributed crumb-nut base and topping. The rich chocolate creamy filling should be smooth in texture, chocolate flavored, and of a firm consistency, not stiff or runny, to hold its shape when cut. Flavor is rich, sweet, and richly chocolate with secondary nutty taste.

Gelatin Gelatin should be firm enough to hold its shape yet tender, quivery, and transparent. Enough gelatin must be used so that the gelatin resists melting at normal serving temperature. A gelatin must have clear-cut edges, firm and delicate but not rubbery texture, and a definite but not rigid form. Flavor should have a slightly sweet, natural fruit taste.

Sour Cream Cheesecake Color of filling is off-white. The surface should be even and have full volume. The graham cracker crumbs should be spread lightly and evenly across the top and on the bottom. Cheesecake should be smooth, light, and creamy to tongue, firm and evenly coagulated. It should hold its shape when cut. The flavor should be mild, sweet, and pleasant.

ENTREES, BREAKFAST

Omelet The appearance should be shiny, slightly moist and good volume. Texture and consistency should be completely coagulated and fairly light. Omelet should be well-seasoned, hot, carefully served, and tender.

Omelet with Ham The omelet should be a light yellow in color, fluffy, shiny, and slightly moist. The omelet should have a good volume and be light and tender. The ham should be in small cubes.

Pancakes Appearance should be an even brown color, with uniform round shape and no pitting. The texture may be slightly moist, light, even-grained, open, and about ¼" thick. They should be well cooked and tender with firm, slightly crisp exterior. They should be hot. Flavor should be pleasing and only slightly bready.

ENTREES, LUNCH AND DINNER

Cheese

Broccoli Cheese Strata The entree should stand with layers sandwiched evenly together. The bread should be golden brown. Broccoli pieces should be about ¼″ in size, spread evenly through each layer and remaining between layers. The cheese should be melted. Each layer of the entree should remain distinct from the others. The top layer should be slightly crisp, the broccoli very tender, and the melted cheese smooth and tender. The bottom layer should be firm and free of excess moisture. The inside layers should be moist and light in texture. The flavor should be a mild blending of broccoli with a slightly salty mellow cheese flavor and nut-like bread flavor.

Cheese Rarebit   The sauce should be smooth and of medium consistency with a mild cheese flavor. It should spread when dipped and served over toast. Toast should be crisp and cut into uniform triangles. The Rarebit should be garnished with a crisp bacon slice and tomato wedge.

Cheese Souffle   The souffle should be light, have a good volume, and have a golden brown color. The top should be slightly rounded, well-puffed, and only slightly cracked, with a surface that is smooth, shiny, and unsunken. Its color should be an even delicate brown. No unmixed egg whites should be apparent. The souffle should have an even cheese flavor throughout and the texture should be slightly spongy.

Meat

Beef Biscuit Roll   Biscuit roll should be oval in shape and of consistent height. Biscuit crust should be tender, moist, and flaky. Color of the crust should be a light golden brown. The texture should be fine, even-grained, and fluffy with a creamy color. Biscuit should break with little resistance. Meat filling is a moist, slightly thickened blend of coarsely chopped flakes of meat, gravy, and a hint of pepper. There should be an absence of starchy flavor and no indication of starch granules in the filling. The meat filling should hold its shape within the biscuit roll. Flavor should be characteristic of the meat. The entree should be served with gravy on top.

Beef Pot Pie   The pastry top crust should be golden brown, crisp, and flaky. The casserole should contain the colors characteristic of peas, potatoes, carrots, and meat. The vegetables and meat should be in a smooth, medium-thick, beef-flavored sauce. The beef and vegetables should be tender yet hold their shape and be in bite-size pieces. The casserole should have the characteristic flavor of the beef and vegetables.

Beef Stew   The bite-size beef chunks should be well done, tender, and free from gristle. The vegetables should be bite-size and tender while still maintaining their shape. The sauce should be a mild, beef-flavored sauce of a smooth, thin consistency. When combined, the sauce should enhance the flavor of the beef and vegetables with the flavor of beef being mildly predominant.

Braised Beef Strips   The beef should be tender, with no large amounts of gristle or fat, juicy, dark brown, and not stringy. The sauce will have a smooth medium consistency, light brown color, with the taste of beef, lightly seasoned, and an even flavor. The mixture should flow slightly when dipped to serve.

Chili Con Carne   The color of the meat and beans should be a deep reddish-brown tomato color, with the meat and beans mixed evenly through the mixture. The meat should be moist, not dry or crumbly. The ground meat pieces should be the size of the beans or slightly smaller. The beans should be tender yet firm. The flavor should be distinct with meat, tomatoes, chili powder, and seasonings but well blended. The chili should be of a thick sauce consistency, not soupy. The chili con carne should be served hot: 170°F or hotter.

Chipped Beef, Creamed   The bite-size pieces of dried beef should be tender and fresh tasting. The medium white sauce should have a smooth and creamy texture. The consistency should be such that it spreads slightly when dipped and served. The flavor should be predominantly of dried beef.

Chop Suey and Chow Mein   The entree should be a combination of tender bite-size pieces of beef, pork, and vegetables in a thin translucent smooth sauce. The fresh vegetables should retain some of their original crispness and bright colors. The sauce should enhance the flavors of the other ingredients and be mildly flavored.

Hamburger Bean Bake   The meat should be a light brown color in small uniform pieces. It should not be greasy. The beans should be in a distinct and clear form, tender but not mushy. The beans should be distributed evenly with the hamburger. The spices should be blended throughout the product but should have a subtle flavor.

Hamburger Goulash   The appearance should be of the noddles occupying the majority of the casserole with meat and vegetables added. The beef should be in tender, bite-size pieces. The cooked noodles should be tender but not pasty. Having a characteristic flavor, the corn needs to be tender. The goulash should have a slightly spicy tomato taste and should flow slightly when spooned onto a plate.

Hamburger Stroganoff   The meat should be in small pieces. The sauce should be of smooth, medium-thick consistency, lightly seasoned, a light brown color and free of grease. The mixture should spread slightly when dipped to serve.

Ham Turnovers   The pastry should be light golden brown and flaky. The ham mixture should be tender and juicy. The ham flavor should be predominant and not masked by other flavors.

Kraut Hamburger Bake   The ground beef should be in small uniform pieces and be free of excess grease. The sauce should be mixed into the meat, and the topping should be bright red in color. The casserole should have blended flavors of sauerkraut, beef, tomato, and seasonings.

Meat Loaf   The meat should be an even brown throughout and darker brown on top. The texture should be moist and firm, but not tough or compact. There should be onion flavor with beef predominant. The product should be loaf shaped and each serving should hold its shape.

Pizza Appearance should be orange-red with small uniform meat pieces, melted cheese, and basil sprinkled evenly on top. Portions should be uniform. The crust should be tender and easily cut but not doughy. Its flavor should have a mild bready taste. The sauce should be spicy, juicy, but not greasy and should be evenly distributed over crust. Cheeses should be evenly distributed over sauce.

Salisbury Steak This entree should have a round patty or oval shape, be uniform in size, and evenly brown. The product should be moist and tender, easily cut by a fork, yet hold its shape. The beef flavor and odor should predominate; however, the onion should be evident.

Shepherd's Pie The potatoes on top should be firm, evenly spread, and an even golden brown color. The filling should consist of tender bite-size pieces of beef and vegetables, which hold their shape and are evenly distributed. The casserole should have a beef flavor with a blend of vegetable flavors. The gravy should be of smooth, medium-thick consistency and the casserole should hold its shape on a plate.

Six Layer Dinner The casserole should have a red tomato sauce top with layers of meat, vegetables, and potatoes. The vegetables should be firm but tender and cut in large enough pieces to be recognized. The meat should be in small, uniform pieces. The casserole should have a combination flavor of tomato, beef, onion, celery, and potato and should hold its shape when served.

Spanish Rice The casserole is orange-red with the flavors of tomato, green pepper, and spices predominant. Meat should be in small uniform pieces. The mixture should appear moist and should be firm enough to hold the shape of a spoon. The rice should be light, separate, and tender but not mushy.

Stuffed Green Peppers Refer to "Spanish Rice" standard for meat mixture. Mixture should be contained within the pepper and be topped with tomato sauce. The pepper should retain its moisture and its form, yet cut easily with a fork. Flavor should be distinct with meat, tomato, and seasonings blended well and enhanced by the green pepper flavor.

Swiss Steak The meat should be tender, with no large amounts of gristle and fat. The sauce should be reddish-orange, smooth and medium thick, with the flavors of tomato, green pepper, and spices enhancing the meat flavor.

Taco Meat The mixture should be reddish-brown in color with the meat in small uniform pieces. It should be spicy but not too hot. The mixture should be free of excess grease.

Texas Straw Hat The meat in the sauce should be a uniform small size. The sauce should be a deep orange-red color, moderately thick and free of grease. It should spread slightly when dipped. The sauce should have a chili powder and tabasco sauce flavor. This dish should be served over corn chips and have cheese sprinkled over it.

Pasta

Beef Noodle Casserole   The beef cubes should be tender, lightly browned. The noodles should be tender but not mushy, and should hold their shape. The gravy-type sauce should be smooth with no starch taste. The mixture should flow from the serving spoon. The flavor should be predominantly beef, with a pleasing blend of spices.

Beef, Tomato, and Macaroni Casserole   The elbow macaroni should be ivory white and tender but not pasty. The casserole should appear moist and should spread slightly when served. The casserole should have an even distribution of ingredients and should taste slightly spicy.

Chicken Tetrazzini   The sauce should contain uniform pieces of cubed chicken and tender yet firm spaghetti. The flavor of the chicken sauce should include onions, celery, pimiento, and cheese all blended to enhance the chicken. The chicken pieces should be tender. The overall color should be a creamy yellow. Casserole should flow when spooned onto plate.

Chipped Beef and Macaroni   The beef should be in bite-size pieces, evenly distributed. Macaroni should be ivory white, tender, not mushy or pasty, and still retain its shape. The white sauce should be smooth and velvety with no lumps. There should be no evidence of uncooked starch either in taste or texture. The consistency should be compact but not firm. The flavor should be a delicate blend of flavors with no one flavor predominating. Casserole should flow slightly when dipped onto a plate.

Creole Spaghetti   The casserole should be orange-red with green peppers distributed within it. The sauce should appear moist. The meat should be in small uniform pieces. The peppers in the sauce should be small and tender. The spaghetti should be tender but not pasty or gummy. The consistency should be compact but not firm. The seasoning should be spicy, and the casserole should not be obviously greasy.

Lasagne   The top should have tomato-red color. The layers of ingredients should be identifiable as cooked ribbon-edged lasagna noodles, yellow American or white mozzarella cheese, white cottage cheese, grated parmesan cheese, and meat sauce. Lasagna should hold its shape when served. The noodles should be tender but firm enough to hold shape. Cheese should have a soft smooth consistency. Lasagna should have a spicy tomato-beef flavor blended with the mild pleasant American or mozzarella cheese flavor and a hint of parmesan cheese. The product should have a blended flavor of spices and herbs. It should be served hot, at about 165°F.

Macaroni and Cheese   The sauce should be a delicate golden orange, surrounding ivory white macaroni, topped with golden brown bread crumbs. The product should have a medium-consistency, smooth white sauce with the flavor of cheddar and American cheese evenly distributed throughout the sauce. The macaroni should be tender, not mushy without the taste of starch. The casserole should spread slightly when spooned onto a plate.

Neapolitan Noodles   Uniform small pieces of ground beef should be distributed evenly throughout the casserole. Noodles should be tender yet firm and retain shape. Texture should be creamy with parmesan cheese blended with other ingredients. Casserole should spread slightly when spooned onto a plate. Ingredients should blend together to enhance the spicy-tomato flavor and aroma.

Spanish Noodles   The beef should be in tender and uniform small pieces. The orange-red sauce should be smooth. Consistency should be compact but loose enough to flow from the serving spoon. It should appear moist. The cooked noodles should be tender but not mushy. Flavor should be a spicy blend of ingredients with Mexican seasoning.

Tuna Noodle Casserole   The entree should have an overall semi-solid consistency and retain its body to flow slightly on the plate when served. The tuna is chunked, the celery chopped in ¼″ pieces, the onion finely chopped and dispersed throughout the noodles and sauce. The sauce is smooth and blends the flavors of tuna, noodles, and vegetables. The sauce holds the tuna and noodles in an even mixture giving the casserole body and a homogeneous mixture. The noodles are done "al dente." They should retain their shape and form. The tuna is the prominent flavor in this dish, with the celery and onions adding color and flavor to complement. The noodles, sauce, and vegetables complement and mellow the tuna to a smooth, flavorful dish. It is served steaming hot with the melted cheese and paprika adding a colorful touch to the surface of the casserole.

Poultry and Fish

Chicken à la King   The creamy yellow sauce should be smooth and of medium consistency. The chicken pieces should be tender, bite-size cubes. The vegetables should be finely chopped, slightly crisp, and provide the red and green color to contrast with the yellow sauce. The sauce should have an even blended flavor. Its consistency should allow it to flow slightly when served over bread or pasta.

Chicken Rice Casserole   The rice should be tender and the chicken pieces and vegetables should be tender and bite-size. The casserole should be moist but not pasty. The sauce should be smooth, holding the ingredients together. The characteristic flavor of chicken should be predominant.

Scalloped Turkey   The product should be uniformly brown in color with tender meat layered between two layers of dressing. The square form should not have a packed appearance. The flavor should be a blend of turkey and dressing, complemented by poultry spices blended evenly throughout the product.

Turkey Pot Pie   The casserole should contain the colors green from the peas, white from the potatoes, and orange from the carrots. The pastry top crust should be golden brown, crisp, and flaky. The turkey and the vegetables should be tender yet hold their shape and be in bite-size pieces in a smooth medium-thick turkey-flavored sauce. The casserole should have the characteristic flavor of turkey.

Halibut, baked   The fish should be white, translucent in appearance. The fish should be moist and flake easily with mild flavor.

SANDWICHES

Barbecue Beef   The product should look like sliced roast beef, thinly sliced, covered with a medium-thick sauce of hickory tomato flavor. The meat should be tender, free of gristle and fat. The sauce should be reddish-orange and smooth with flavors to enhance the meat.

Chicken Salad   The chicken should be tender, light in color and in bite-size pieces. The salad dressing base should bind all ingredients together. The salad should have both a soft texture from the chicken and a crisp texture from the celery.

Pizza Burger   Meat sauce should contain uniform small pieces of meat. Sauce should be moderately thick, free of obvious grease, and have an orange-red color. Flavors should be those of onions, green stuffed olives, and cheese, blended to enhance the flavor of the meat.

Tuna Fish Salad   The salad should be soft enough to spread easily but firm enough to hold a shape. The salad dressing should coat all of the ingredients and act as a binding agent. The green color of the celery and relish should be distinct but should complement the brownish beige color of the tuna which predominates. The Worcestershire sauce, lemon juice, and pickle relish should complement the mild flavor of the tuna. The salad's texture should be tender but the tuna should keep its natural flaky appearance. The crisp texture of the celery should complement the texture of the tuna. The bread should be firm with a close smooth crumb and have good flavor and moisture. The bread should be able to support the salad.

SAUCES

Creamed Pea   The medium white sauce should possess an opaque quality and cream color. The texture should be smooth and velvety, with no lumps. The sauce should be a delicate blend of flavors with no evidence of a starchy flavor. The peas should be bright green, undamaged, and crisp. The sauce should flow when dipped and served.

Italian Spaghetti   The meat sauce should be orange-red with uniform small pieces of meat and green peppers distributed within it. The sauce should be smooth, free of grease, and spread slightly when served over cooked spaghetti. The sauce should be spicy and not bland or salty.

SOUPS

Beef Rice   The transparent brown beef broth stock should possess body and may have a slight sheen due to dispersed fat globules from the meat. The browned stew meat should be tender with beefy flavor. The bite-size celery, finely chopped onions, and rice should be tender yet firm enough to hold shape, with mild and pleasant flavors. Flavor should be a blend of the distinct, mild, and characteristic flavors of each ingredient.

Canadian Cheese   This soup should be a light yellow-orange color. The soup base should be creamy and smooth—free of lumps. The vegetables should be small and uniform. The cheese soup should have a characteristic cheese flavor.

Chicken Gumbo   The form of the vegetables should be distinct and clear, not mushy or broken. The broth should be thin but have body. The flavor should be predominantly chicken.

Chowder, Clam   The chowder should be a rich, light cream color. The vegetables should be evenly cut and firm yet tender. The white sauce base should be smooth and free from lumps. It should have a distinct clam flavor.

Chowder, Manhattan Clam   The broth should be light brownish-red, without obvious grease, and have body. The vegetables and clams should be in tender, bite-size pieces. The flavors should blend with the clam flavor predominant.

Chowder, Manhattan Fish   The chowder should be reddish in color, thick, and without obvious grease. The fish and potatoes should be bite-size and the remaining vegetables in uniform finely chopped pieces. The flavor of the fish should be distinct, mild, and pleasant.

Cream of Celery   Consistency should be smooth, free of lumps and curdling, and delicately coat a spoon. The celery should be distinct and clear, firm, and hold its shape. Onions should be firm and mild. Color of the soup should be creamy with a slight sheen with bits of green celery suspended in the soup. Flavor should be distinct, mild, and pleasant, characteristic of celery blended with the cooked flavor of the white sauce and the delicate seasonings. Recommended serving temperature is 140–150°F.

Cream of Vegetable   The thin white sauce base should be an off-white opaque color, with the characteristic color of the vegetables distributed throughout. The soup should be smooth, coating a spoon lightly. The vegetables should be finely chopped, retaining a slightly crisp but tender texture and their original colors. The flavor should be mild with natural blend of ingredients.

French Onion   The broth should be a golden color and have body (not thin or watery). The onions should be thinly sliced and fully cooked. The onion flavor should be mild.

Navy Bean This soup should be beige in color. The soup base should be smooth. The ham should be in small, cubed pieces and both the ham and beans should be tender but not mushy. The flavors should blend and the seasonings should be mild.

Oriental The transparent stock should be light greenish-yellow. Each vegetable's color should be distinct and bright. The chicken should be in tender ½″ cubes. The noodles, mushrooms, and bean sprouts should be tender yet retain shape. The remaining vegetables should be in crisp, bite-size pieces, except the onions, which should be about ⅛″ size. The soup should have a mild flavor where chicken and vegetables blend together to provide a full flavor.

Pepper Pot The translucent, brownish-yellow broth should be thin but have body and be free of floating fat pools. The vegetables should maintain a distinct shape. The onions and peppers should be finely chopped with translucent quality associated with doneness while the other vegetables should be more coarsely chopped in bite-size pieces. The vegetable colors should be bright but characteristic of the particular cooked vegetable. All vegetables are tender, not crunchy or overcooked. Flavor should be mild with a hint of black pepper and herbs with no single flavor predominant. The broth is beef-flavored. Recommended serving temperature is 170°F minimum.

Plaza III Steak This soup should have a full, rich flavor. The soup base should be thick and smooth. The vegetables should be in uniform bite-size pieces and their form should be distinct and clear, not mushy. The seasoning should be delicate.

Potato The milk-base broth should be medium-thick in consistency and free from lumps. The potatoes should be in tender, bite-size pieces. The flavors of potato, onion, and seasoning should blend. The base should be a rich, cream color.

Split Pea The soup should be a mild green color and of smooth, medium-thickness in consistency. The vegetables (fresh carrots, onions, and potatoes) should be small and in uniform, finely chopped pieces. The ham pieces are chopped to half that of bite-sized. Both the vegetables and meat are cooked to tenderness. They add some contrasting texture to the product, being less than half the total volume of the soup. Flavor and odor is that of cooked, dried split peas, with some blending of the ham. Salt and pepper is just light enough to provide seasoning.

Turkey Rice This soup should be a light yellow color with a transparent stock. The turkey should be in small, cubed pieces, and both the turkey and rice should be tender. The vegetables should be finely chopped. The soup should have a mild flavor of turkey, rice, and vegetables.

Turkey Vegetable The reddish-orange broth base should be thin but have body. The vegetables should be in bite-size pieces and be firm in texture. The turkey should be in small, tender cubes. The flavors should blend and the seasoning should be delicate.

Vegetable   The broth base should be thin but have body. The vegetables should be bite-size pieces with distinct shape and firm texture. The flavors should blend and the seasoning should be delicate.

STARCHES AND VEGETABLES

Starches

Dressing, Baked   The product should be a pleasing brown color, be light in texture, and tender. It should be moist enough to hold together when spooned onto the plate. The dressing should possess an equal blend of onion and celery flavors, with the predominant seasoning being thyme. The delicate flavors of the particular bread used as well as the poultry base should be distinctive.

Potato Salad, Hot German   The potatoes should be firm and not mushy. A slight vinegar and bacon flavor should be prevalent. It should be served warm.

Potatoes, Au Gratin   The surface should possess a soft, light yellow sheen with areas slightly browned. Au gratin potatoes should hold their shape when served with the cheese sauce thick enough to cling to the potatoes. The potatoes should be uniform in size, tender but firm. Cheese sauce should be smooth and velvety with a light yellow color.

Potatoes, Scalloped   The white, slightly opaque potatoes should be distinct, of uniform size, tender yet firm, and about 2″ in diameter and ⅛″ thick. The creamy smooth, medium white sauce should contain tender, finely chopped onions that are barely noticeable. The served product should form a slightly rounded mass. The white sauce, which clings to the potatoes, should possess a soft sheen. The mild potato flavor should be pleasant and blend with the delicate mild cooked flavor of the sauce. The seasonings should enhance, not dominate.

Rice Pilaf   The brown rice should be tender but not pasty or gummy. The grains should be light, fluffy, and remain separate. The onions dispersed evenly throughout the rice should be tender and enhance the flavor of the product. The chicken soup base and other seasonings also add to the flavor of the rice.

Vegetables

Beets, Harvard   The product should possess a deep-toned red color, with the beet slices having a tender yet firm texture, round shape, and smooth surface. The sauce should be a flowing gelatinous glaze with deep, red translucence.

The beets should be evenly glazed and readily discernible. Flavor should be mildly sweet with a slight sour sensation. Flavors of ingredients should be well-blended.

Carrots, German   The flavor of nutmeg should be prevalent but not strong to distinguish it from plain buttered carrots. Carrots should have a mildly sweet flavor and be in the form of uniform, bite-sized coins.

Green Beans Supreme   The top crumb should be fine, lightly browned, and golden in color. The French style green beans should be tender, moist, and green in color. The sauce should be smooth, milky in color, a medium consistency and the flavor and appearance of mushroom soup. The cheese should be melted, smooth, tender, and of the characteristic Swiss cheese flavor. The product should hold together and be a gentle mound when served. The inside should be moist, the top lightly browned and served hot. The green beans and mushroom sauce should be topped by a layer of Swiss cheese and then golden crumbs. The overall flavor should be a mild blending of Swiss cheese, mushroom sauce, and green beans.

Vegetable Timbale   The color and flavor of the timbale varies with the type of vegetables used. A dark green product with the flavor characteristic of the vegetable and a delicate custard flavor makes the most desirable product. The timbale should not be tough or rubbery, but tender and light, and easily cut with a fork. The product should have a good volume that easily retains its shape when served. Timbales should not be watery or have any definite layerings of vegetables and custards.

APPENDIX D

Listing of Foodservice Equipment

FOOD SERVICE EQUIPMENT

This glossary is a portion of one prepared by the Foodservice Consultants Society International and is reprinted with their permission. Additional terms appear in the complete glossary.

Au Gratin Oven Enclosure with hinged door mounted on top of a broiler. Also called finishing oven.

Bainmarie Sink-like depression in a tabletop with a water bath heated by steam, gas or electricity into which containers of food are placed to keep foods heated. Often used by chefs as a double boiler.

Baker's Table Table whose top has curbing along the rear and sides to minimize spillage of flour onto floor during preparation. Often furnished with mobile or tilt-out ingredient bins under the top.

Banquet Cart Insulated or non-insulated mobile cabinet with a series of interior shelves and/or racks to hold plates and/or platters of food. Usually equipped with an electric heating unit or refrigeration device.

Barbecue Grill A live charcoal or gas fired, open hearth, horizontal grill having spits set across the top of the unit with rotisserie-type drive mechanism along the front working side.

Beef Cart Mobile unit, with or without bottled gas, alcohol or electric heating unit. Used for display and slicing of roast beef in the dining room.

Beer Cooler Cooler in which kegs, cans or bottles of beer are refrigerated. The direct draw cooler is a low counter type with self-contained tapping equipment and dispensing head(s).

Bin Semi-enclosed, rectangular or round container, open on top, with or without lift-off, sliding or hinged cover. Floor-type bins are usually mobile, of height to roll under a tabletop. Bins under a baker's table may be mobile or built-in to tilt out. An ingredient bin may be used for flour, sugar, salt, beans, dry peas, etc. A vegetable storage bin has a perforated or screened body. An ice storage bin is fully enclosed and insulated with hinged or sliding insulated

Source: Sanitation Operations Manual, Chicago: National Restaurant Assn., 1979.

door(s) at the front; it is normally stationary, and set under an ice-making machine (head). A silverware (flatware) or cutlery bin is small and mounted in a holder set on or under countertop with other bins.

Blender Vertical mixing machine with removable cup or jar, having mixing and stirring blades in the bottom and mounted on a base with a drive motor. Normally set on a table or countertop. Used in preparing special diets in hospitals, mixing cocktails in bars, as well as to whip or puree food generally at home.

Blower-Dryer Motor-driven attachment with a blower and electric or steam-heated coil, mounted on top of a dishwasher for quick drying of ware at the end of the final rinse cycle.

Board A rectangular or round board, small for easy handling, set on a hard surface or countertop, to prevent dulling the knife blade when cutting food. It can be made of laminated or solid hard rock maple, or composition of rubber or thermal plastic material. Usually furnished with a handle or grip. Sandwich and steam table boards are rectangular and narrow; they are mounted on a sandwich unit or the corresponding section of a countertop. Also called Work Board in preparation areas of a kitchen.

Bobtail A unit designed for the dispensing of carbonated beverages and milk drinks but having no ice cream storage. Components include draft arms, water coolers, syrup containers and cold storage compartments. These may be with or without integral sink section.

Bowl A round bottom container open at top for mixing food. The salad bowl is a shallow type for mixing and displaying leafy vegetables. A coffee bowl is the lower of a two-piece, siphon-type coffee maker, used as a decanter.

Bread Molder Machine with a series of rollers and conveyor belts to shape the ball of dough to pan bread, hearth bread or long rolls of varied length.

Breading Machine Horizontal rotating cylinder, set on a base with a drive motor and filled with breading mix. Food is placed in one end, carried through the cylinder by an internally mounted auger, and discharged at the other end. Food is tumbled in breading mix.

Briquette One of the coal-size pieces of permanent refractory material used in open hearth, gas-fired grills to provide radiant broiling heat.

Broiler, Backshelf Broiler with overhead gas-heated ceramic radiants or electric heating elements, having an adjustable sliding grill. The unit is normally mounted on a panel and brackets above the rear of the range. Also called Salamander Broiler.

Broiler, Char or Open Hearth 1. Horizontal type with gas-heated briquettes under a grill at the top. 2. Horizontal type with non-glowing electric strip heaters at the top. May also be equipped with an adjustable electric grill above the top grill to broil both sides at once.

Broiler, Conveyor   1. Horizontal type unit with openings at both ends using a motor driven grill-type conveyor to transport food between or under gas-fired ceramics or electric heaters. 2. Horizontal type unit, open at both ends, using a motor-driven, revolving, heated griddle to transport food under gas-fired ceramics or electric heaters.

Broiler, Upright   Vertical type with an opening at the front, and gas-heated radiant ceramics or electric heating elements at the top of the cavity. Food is placed on a sliding adjustable grill set under the radiants. May be mounted on countertop, oven or cabinet base, or stand. Often aligns with ranges. May be equipped with removable charcoal pan.

Broiler-Griddle, Combination   1. Unit with food opening with griddle plate set into top, equipped with gas-heated radiants under the griddle. Radiants heat food and griddle simultaneously. 2. Unit with front opening door(s) having gas-heated radiants at the top of the cavity and food placed on a sliding or swinging type griddle plate set below.

Buffet Unit   One or more mobile or stationary counters having flat surfaces, with cold pans or heated wells at the top, on which chafing dishes, canape trays or other food displays can be placed for self service.

Cafeteria Counter, Serving Counter   In a cafeteria, top which is usually provided with recessed cold pans, recessed pans for hot foods section, display and protector cases, and drain troughs for beverages; set on legs or masonry base with enclosure panels, semi- or fully-enclosed cabinets with refrigeration or warming units beneath; all as required to accommodate foods to be served. Unit may be equipped with tray slide.

Canopy Hood   An overhead hood which completely covers the equipment it is designed to serve.

Can Washer   1. Enclosed cabinet with spray heads for washing the interior and exterior of a can, mounted on open legs. 2. Round platform with a rotating spray head at its center for washing the interior of a can, mounted on a stand with foot-operated water valves. 3. Rinse nozzle built into a floor drain and connected to a hand-operated quick-opening mixing valve.

Carbonator   Motor-driven water pump, with tank and control valves, to combine cold water and CO^2 gas in a storage tank, producing soda water. Used for soda fountains, carbonated beverage dispensers, and dispensing systems.

Chinese Range   Range with one or more large diameter gas burners on an inclined top, and a raised edge around each burner opening. Food is cooked in shallow bowls called Woks. Range top is cooled by water flowing from a front manifold to a rear trough, with strainer basket at one end. A swing spout faucet mounted on high splashguard at rear fills the bowl when the spout is turned 90° (1.6 rad.).

Coffee Maker   1. Hand or automatically operated, electric-heated unit in which a measure of hot water at the proper temperature is poured over a measured bed of coffee grounds contained in a filtering unit. The extracted beverage is discharged into a container and/or serving unit. 2. Hand or automatically operated, electric-heated unit in which a measure of hot water at the proper temperature is combined with a measure of instant coffee mix and discharged into a container. 3. Unit consisting of one or more sets of upper and lower bowls set on gas- or electric-heated range. The measure of water boiled in the lower bowl is forced by pressure into the upper bowl containing measured coffee grounds. When the set is removed from the heat source, the cooling lower bowl creates a vacuum, causing the liquid to flow back down through a filter in the bottom of the upper bowl. The upper bowl is then removed to permit use of the lower bowl as a server or decanter.

Coffee Urn Enclosed container of water with jar (liner) set into top. Urn water is heated by gas, electric or steam. A measure of hot water at the proper temperature is poured over measured bed of coffee grounds contained in a filtering unit. Beverage collects in jar and is discharged through bottom connection to draw-off faucet. Urn water is not used for coffee making. Equipped with water inlet valve to fill urn body.

Coffee Warmer Countertop range with one or more gas, electric or canned heaters to maintain coffee at serving temperature; each with coffee bowl or decanter. Also called Coffee Server.

Cold Pan Insulated depressed pan set into a table or countertop; provided with waste outlet; may be refrigerated with crushed ice, refrigeration coil fastened to the underside of the lining, or a cold plate. A perforated false bottom is provided when ice is used.

Cold Plate Acts as a heat exchanger for cooling beverages or beverage syrup. Usually cast aluminum with stainless steel imbedded coils.

Condensate Evaporator Finned coil through which compressed refrigerant flows, absorbing the heat inside refrigerator or freezer.

Condensing Unit, Refrigeration Assembly consisting of mechanical compressor driven by electric powered motor with either air or water cooling device. 1. Open-type unit has major components separate but mounted on same base. 2. Hermetic-type has major components enclosed in same sealed housing, with no external shaft, and motor operating in refrigerant atmosphere. 3. Semi-hermetic type unit with hermetically sealed compressor whose housing is sealed and has means of access for servicing internal parts in field.

Convection Oven Gas- or electric-heated. Heat is circulated through the oven interior with fan or blower system. Interior may be equipped with racks and/ or shelves. Ovens may be stacked or set on stand. Oven bottom may be constructed as part of the platform of a mobile basket rack cart.

Convenience Food Any food item that has been processed by any method from the raw state, packaged for resale and/or further processing or use at later date.

Cooker/Mixer   Direct steam, gas, or electric steam jacketed kettle, with hinged or removable agitator mounted to supporting frame or brackets.

Cooling Coils   Elongated, spiral coils or similar devices containing soda and plain water, which are in a refrigerated area to cool the liquid in the coils.

Creamer   1. Insulated container for cream, having ice or mechanical refrigeration, and provided with adjustable draw-off faucet for each cream measure. Often anchored to counter or wall. Also called Cream Dispenser. 2. Soda fountain unit with self-contained ice cream cabinet.

Cutlery Box   Unit consisting of one or more compartments for storage and dispensing of flatware (knives, forks, spoons). Often set on a counter or tabletop, and sometimes built into the front of a cabinet under the top, or as a drawer.

Defrost System   Refrigeration system for a freezer consisting of a blower evaporator coil, heating unit and controls. Electric-type employs heating elements; hot gas type uses heat exchanger to remove frost from the coil and allow condensate to flow to the drain pan under the coil.

Dessert Cart   Cart with several shelves for display and serving of desserts. May be equipped with mechanical or ice-refrigerated cold pan or plate, and with transparent domed cover.

Detergent Dispenser   Device mounted on a dishwater or sink for storage and dispensing of liquid detergent, or mixture of powdered detergent and water, into the wash tank of the unit through the pump manifold or incoming water line. Some units are equipped with control device, electrically operated, to detect detergent strength in tank.

Detergent Meter   A device for indicating the concentration of detergent in the wash tank. It may be used with or without a detergent dispenser.

Dipper Well   A container or receptacle which is equipped with running water and a drain and is intended for the storage of frozen dessert dippers.

Dish Cart   Cart for storage and dispensing of clean or soiled dishes. Usually of height to roll under counter or tabletop.

Dishes   Multi-use eating and drinking utensils and multi-use utensils adaptable to machine washing and which are used in the preparation and serving of food.

Dish Table   Work surface with raised sides and end(s) having its surface pitched to a built-in waste outlet, adjoining a sink or warewashing machine. There may be a soiled table used for receiving, sorting and racking ware, located at load end of the sink or washing machine; and a clean table at unload end for draining of rinse water, drying, and stacking ware.

Dishwashing Machine (Commercial Spray-Type)   A machine designed, constructed and intended for use in a food service establishment and which effectively washes and sanitizes dishes by means of a sprayed wash and sanitizing rinse.

Display Case A semi- or fully-enclosed case of one or more shelves, mounted on countertop or wall, for display of desserts. Semi-enclosed type have transparent end panels and sneeze guards along customers' side to protect uncovered foods. Refrigerated type have insulated transparent panels and doors. Heated type are usually provided with sliding doors and electric heating unit, with or without humidifier.

Dolly Solid platform or open framework mounted on a set of casters, for storage and transportation of heavy items. May be equipped with handle or push bar.

Dough Divider Motor-driven, floor-type machine to divide dough (usually for bread) in equally scaled pieces. Pieces are removed from work surface by conveyor to next operation. Normally used for bread dough. Also called Bread Divider.

Dough Mixer 1. Motor-driven machine with verticle spindle to which various whips and beaters are attached. Bowl is raised to the agitator. Mixers of 5 to 20 quart (4.7 to 18.9 liter) capacity are bench-mounted. Mixers of 20 to 140 quart (18.9 to 132.3 liter) capacity are floor-type. 2. Motor-driven, floor-type horizontal machine with tilting type bowl and horizontal agitator(s) for a large dough batch. Also called Kneading Machine or Mixer.

Dough Retarder May be upright reach-in, low counter bench-type, or walk-in refrigerator with series of racks or tray slides and/or shelves, in which dough is kept cool, to retard rising.

Dough Rounder Motor-driven, floor-mounted machine into which a piece of dough is dropped and rounded to ball shape, by means of a rotating cone and fixed spiral raceway running from top to bottom. See Roll Divider and Rounder.

Dough Sheeter Motor- or hand-driven machine with a series of adjustable rollers to roll dough to sheets of even thickness. Also called Pie Crust Roller.

Dough Trough Large tub with tapered sides, usually mounted on casters, for storing and transporting large batches of dough. Some troughs have gates at the ends for pouring dough when the trough is lifted above a divider and tilted.

Doughnut Machine Unit consisting of hand- or motor-driven batter dropper and shallow fryer. Doughnuts are conveyed through heated cooking fat or oil bath, turned over, and discharged out of bath into drain pan.

Draft Arm A unit used to dispense soda, plain water or mixed beverages.

Draft Stations An assembly having a drip plate and a drip pan together with draft arms.

Drink Mixer Vertical counter-type unit with one or more spindles with motor at top. Switch is activated by drink cup when placed in correct position. Also Malted Mixer.

Drop-in Unit Any warming, cooling, cooking or storage unit that is dropped into an opening in a counter or tabletop and is fitted with accompanying mounting brackets and sized flange.

Drying Agent Injector A device which automatically injects, or otherwise adds a drying agent to the final rinse.

Dunnage Rack Mobile or stationary, solid or louvered platform used to stack cased or bagged goods in a storeroom or walk-in refrigerator or freezer.

Enclosed Food Transport Cabinet Enclosed cabinets capable of being transported and intended for the conveyance of foods. It is not intended to include mobile dish or utensil storage or dispensing equipment.

Equipment Stoves, ovens, ranges, hoods, slicers, mixers, meatblocks, tables, counters, refrigerators, sinks, dishwashing machines, steam tables, and similar items other than utensils, used in the operation of a food service establishment.

Fat Filter 1. Gravity-type has disposable paper or muslin bag strainer set in holder on top of fat container. Unit is placed under drain valve of fat fryer. 2. Siphon-type uses disposable paper or muslin bag strainer over fat container, attached to rigid siphon tube mounted on fat fryer, with other end of tube in fat tank. 3. Motor-driven, pump-type, portable or mobile, uses disposable paper strainer. Has flexible hose from fat tank of strainer. Strainer set on fat container.

Fire Extinguisher Hand operated, sealed with chemicals inside, most commonly wallmounted and provided with control and directional hose, or horn.

Fish Box 1. Ice refrigerated, insulated cabinet with counter-balanced hinged or sliding door(s) at the top, and drawer(s) at the bottom front. 2. Ice or mechanically refrigerated cabinet with tier(s) of self-closing drawers with insulated fronts. Also called Fish File.

Flash or Instantaneous Coolers Mechanically-refrigerated units for cooling soda and plain water.

Flatware Term for knife, spoon and fork used by the diner.

Floor Scale 1. Unit fixed in a pit, its platform flush with finished floor. May have dial or beam mounted on top of the housing at the rear of platform framing, plus tare beam. Used for weighing heavy objects on mobile carriers. 2. Mobile type—See Platform Scale.

Food Any raw, cooked, or processed edible substance, ice, beverage or ingredient used or intended for use or for sale in while or in part for human consumption.

Food Cutter 1. Motor-driven bench- or floor-mounted machine with a rotating shallow bowl to carry food through a set of rotating horizontal knives whose axis is perpendicular to the radii of the bowl. Knives are set under hinged-up cover. 2. Motor-driven, floor-mounted high-speed machine with vertical tilting bowl having a vertical shaft with rotating knife. Also called vertical cutter/mixer or sold under various brand names.

Food Shaper 1. Motor-driven unit with loading hopper, bench- or floor-mounted. Shapes food into rectangular or round patties of varying thickness. May be equipped with paper interleaving, removing and conveying devices. 2. Attachment to meat chopper to shape ground food into rectangles of varied thickness. Also called Food Former.

Food Warmer 1. Insulated mobile or stationary cabinet with shelves, racks or tray slides, having insulated doors or drawers. May be electric, steam or gas heated, and provided with humidity control. 2. Infra-red lamp or electric radiant heating element with or without a glass enclosure, mounted above the serving unit in a hot food section.

French Fry Cutter Hand-operated or motor-driven machine, or attachment to food machine, that pushes potato through grid of knives set in square pattern in frame.

Fry Pan, Tilting Rectangular pan with gas- or electric-heated flat bottom, pouring lip and hinged cover. Floor-mounted on a tubular stand or wall-mounted on brackets with in-wall steel carriers. A small electric pan may be table-mounted on legs. Also called Braising Pan, Tilting Griddle, or Tilting Skillet.

Fryer 1. Floor- or bench-mounted unit heated by gas or electricity with tank of oil or fat into which foods are immersed. Common type has deep tank. Special types have shallow tanks for fish, chicken, doughnuts, etc. and a basket conveyor type has a shallow tank for draining with baskets, arms, mesh-type belt, or rotating auger to move food through the bath. Pressure type has a lift or hinged cover to seal the top of the fryer tank.

Glass Washer 1. Multi-tank horizontal machine with hand-activated rinse nozzle in one tank, revolving brushes in a second tank, and final rinse nozzles in a third. 2. Single or double tank door-type or rack-conveyor-type dishwasher.

Grater 1. Bench-mounted, hand- or motor-driven machine in which food is forced against the face of a revolving grater plate by a pusher or hopper plate. 2. Part of vegetable slicing attachment to food machine.

Grease Filter or Extractor 1. Removable rectangular or round frame having several layers of wire mesh or baffles and mounted in the exhaust equipment above or behind cooking units. 2. A series of baffles mounted in exhaust equipment, from whose surfaces grease deposits are flushed with wash water into a waste outlet. 3. Manifold-mounted water nozzles in exhaust equipment producing a fine spray mist which collects grease from laden air and drains through a waste outlet.

Griddle   Extra thick steel plate with a ground and polished top surface, heated by gas or electricity. Surface edges are raised or provided with gutters and drain holes leading to catch trough or pan. May be set on countertop with legs, stand, or oven base.

Grill   Bench-mounted unit with fixed lower and hinged upper electrically heated plates. Plates have a waffle pattern for waffles, grooves for steaks, and are smooth for sandwiches.

Heat Exchanger, Steam   Device used to transfer heat from "house" steam to clean water for use in cooking, dishwashing, etc.

Heat Recovery Unit   Device or apparatus capable of transferring heat from waste air or water for reuse.

Hood   A device intended for collecting vapors, mists, particulate matter, fumes, smoke, steam, or heat before entering an exhaust duct.

Hot Dog Steamer   Counter-mounted cabinet with transparent display panels and hinged covers or doors. The unit is electrically heated with a water bath and immersion device to generate steam for heating hot dogs, and dry heat for warming rolls.

Hot Plate   Countertop and floor-mounted unit with one or more open gas or tubular electric burners arranged left to right and/or front to rear. French hot plates are round or square solid steel plates, gas or electrically heated.

Hot Water Booster   Electric-, steam-, or gas-heated insulated tank or coil used to raise the incoming hot water from house temperature to sanitizing temperature, as required by code. Booster may be mounted inside housing or at end of warewashing machine, under warewashing table, or may be remotely located.

Humidifier   Electric-, steam- or gas-heated unit used to evaporate and distribute water inside proofing equipment and hot food warmers. May be fixed or removable attachment.

Ice Cream Cabinet   1. Mechanically refrigerated low-type chest with removable, hinged, flip-flop covers, used for storage and dispensing of ice cream. 2. Mechanically refrigerated upright cabinet with hinged door(s) for storage of ice cream.

Ice Cream Display Cabinet   Ice cream cabinet with sliding or hinged transparent doors or covers. Mostly used in self-service stores.

Ice Cream Freezer   Floor- or counter-mounted machine with mechanically refrigerated cylinder, having a dasher to mix and refrigerate an air-and-ice cream mix to flowing ice cream. The product is then placed inside a hardening cabinet.

Ice Dispenser   A floor-, counter-, or wall-mounted stationary ice storage bin with motor driven agitator and conveyor mechanism, or gravity feed, that dispenses a measure of ice (cubed or crushed) through a discharge chute into a container at working level.

Ice Maker   Floor-, counter-, or wall-mounted unit containing refrigeration machinery for making cubed, flaked and crushed ice. Maker may have integral ice storage bin. Larger capacity machines generally have a separate bin in which ice is received via a connecting chute. Capacity is rated in pounds of ice per 24-hour day.

Ice Storage Bin   Insulated mobile or stationary cabinet of one or more compartments with hinged or sliding door(s) or cover(s). It is commonly mounted under an ice-making machine, with opening(s) in the top to receive product(s) and is fitted with a waste outlet in the bottom. Ice is normally scooped out of bin. Unit may be built into counter.

Infra-red Heater or Warmer   Unit consisting of one or more lamps or electric strip heaters, with or without protective covering or reflector, mounted in a bracket or housing. Usually set over hot-food-serving and display areas, or inside enclosed displays. Unit produces infra-red heat to keep food warm.

Infra-red Oven   Oven having heat generated and radiated from electric infra-red heating elements encased in a glass tube, or from an exposed quartz infra-red plate.

Kettle, Steam Jacketed   Kettle having live steam introduced between the inner and outer shell to heat the inner shell for cooking. Deep-type kettle generally is two-thirds jacketed. Shallow-type kettle generally is fully jacketed. May be mounted to the floor with tubular legs or pedestal base, or mounted to the wall with brackets and in-wall steel carriers. Tilting- or trunnion-type may be floor- or wall-mounted, having a worm gear device for hand operation. The stationary kettle has a draw-off valve. The tilting kettle has a pouring lip and may have a draw-off valve. The kettle may be equipped with lift-off or hinged cover, filling faucet, water cooling system, thermostat, etc.

Kettle, Tabletop   Two-third steam jacketed kettle, tilting type, with operating lever up to 20 qt. (18.9 liter) capacity, or tilting worm gear device for 40 qt. (37.8 liter) capacity; all direct steam, electric heated. All kettles have a pouring lip. Tilting type have 20 and 40 qt. (18.9 and 37.8 liter) capacity with a lever handle. Oyster stewing kettle is shallow tilting type kettle.

Kitchenware   All multi-use utensils other than tableware.

Kneading Machine or Mixer   See Dough Mixer.

Malted Mix Dispenser   Counter- or wall-mounted unit with a transparent, covered hopper, having a lever for dispensing a measure of malted mix powder.

Meat Chopper   Table- or floor-mounted, hand- or motor-driven horizontal machine. Food placed in top-mounted hopper is fed by a stomper into cylinder with tight fitting auger to drive food against rotating knife and perforated plate. Also called Meat Grinder.

Meat Tenderizer   Counter-mounted machine having two sets of round knives with spaced cutting edges, set apart on slow speed rollers. Meats are inserted into a slot in the top, pass through the rollers and are discharged at the bottom front through which the meats to be tenderized pass.

Menu Board   Sign with fixed or changeable letters, or removable lines listing the food items and prices.

Microwave Oven   Stand- or counter-mounted oven in which foods are heated and/or cooked when they absorb microwave energy (short electromagnetic waves) generated by magnetron(s).

Milk Cooler   1. Low-insulated chest with mechanical or ice refrigeration, for storing and dispensing half-pint to two-quart (0.2 to 1.9 liter) containers of milk. 2. Counter- or stand-mounted refrigerator with one or more 2- to 10-gallon (7.56 to 37.8 liter) containers equipped with sanitary tube connections which extend through flow control handles for dispensing loose or bulk milk.

Mixer, Food   Motor-driven machine with vertical spindle having several speeds on which various whips and beaters are mounted. Bowl is raised up to agitator. Mixers of 5 to 20 quart (4.7 to 18.9 liter) capacity are bench-type. Mixers of 20 to 140 quart (18.9 to 132.3 liter) capacity are floor-type.

Mixer, Vertical Cutter   See Vertical Cutter/Mixer.

Mixing Tank   Vertical type has center-, bottom- or side-mounted agitator assembly. Horizontal type has end agitator assembly. All are floor-mounted and provided with removable or hinged cover and draw-off valve. Tank may be provided with recirculating pump and filtering system.

Oven   Fully enclosed insulated chamber with gas, electric or oil-fired heat, provided with thermostatic control. Deck-type units have chambers or sections stacked one above the other. Bake-type decks are approximately 7″ (177.8mm) high inside. Roast-type decks are 12″ to 14″ (304.8 to 355.6mm) high inside.

Order Wheel   Metal- or wood-spoked wheel with clips or hooks on its perimeter, located between cooks' and servers' areas, on which order slips are placed to maintain rotation and visibility.

Pan and Utensil Rack   1. One or more bars and braces suspended from a ceiling, or mounted on posts or a wall, housing fixed or removable hooks for hanging pots, pans and utensils. 2. Upright mobile or stationary unit, open or semi-enclosed, with tiers of angle- or channel-shaped slides to support pans. 3. Heavy-duty rectangular wire basket to hold pans and utensils upright in a pot washer.

Pass-Thru Window or Opening Trimmed opening between kitchen and serving areas having a shelf for a sill. May be equipped with hinged or sliding door or shutter.

Peeler Floor- or bench-mounted machine having a vertical, stationary abrasive-lined cylinder open at the top, a motor-driven agitator bottom plate, and an over-the-rim water supply. Product discharged through door in cylinder side. Waste water is discharged at bottom and may be equipped with a peel trap basket that can be hung on a pipe over sink, or set inside a cabinet base under the peeler. May also be equipped with garbage disposal unit.

Pizza Oven Baking-type oven of one or more decks, gas-, electric- or oil-fired, having temperature range from 350°F to 700°F (177°C to 371.1°C). Deck(s) are of heat-retaining masonry material.

Platform Scale Mobile unit with a dial or beam, for weights up to 1500 pounds (675 kilograms). May be floor- or stand-mounted.

Pot and Utensil Washer, or Pot Washing Machine Machine of one or more tanks with hood or wash chamber above, inside which large ware is washed, using very big, high pressure pumps. Water is pumped from tanks and sprayed over ware placed in racks or set on a conveyor or platform. One or more final fresh water rinses sanitizes ware. Machine has a 34" to 36" (863.6 to 914.4mm) working height. 1. Door-type, single-tank machine has power wash and final rinse only. 2. Door-type, two-tank machine has power wash and power rinse tanks, and final rinse. 3. Belt conveyor machine is straight-through type machine having one to three tanks plus final rinse. Ware is set directly on a belt. 4. Revolving tray table-type has two to three tanks plus final rinse. Ware is set directly on turntable platform.

Pre-rinse or Pre-wash Sink Sink constructed as an integral part of a soiled dish table, located near a dishwashing machine, and furnished with removable perforated scrap basket(s) and spray hose.

Proof Box or Cabinet Fully-enclosed binet with gas, steam or electric heater and humidifier. Sometimes unit may be insulated type with thermostatic and humidity controls. Box may be mobile. Traveling-type proofer has a conveying mechanism inside the overhead cabinet, as in large commercial bread bakery.

Quartz Oven Oven which employs an electrically heated quartz plate or infra-red quartz element inside a glass tube to generate heat. Also called Infra-Red Oven.

Rack: Cup, Dish, Glass, Plate or Tray 1. Rectangular or round shaped basket of wire or plastic construction, with or without compartments or intermediate lateral supports, used for washing and/or storage of small ware. Racks are self-stacking type for cups and glassware. 2. See Tray Rack for upright unit.

Rack Washer   Machine of one or two tanks with hood or wash chamber oven, with one or two doors, using large size high-pressure pumps, and final sanitizing rinse. Steam or electric heated water is pumped from tanks and sprayed over racks wheeled onto tracks inside washer. Machine is made to recess in floor to have tracks set flush with finished floor.

Range   Unit with heated top surface or burners which heat utensils in which foods are cooked, or cook foods direct. Some ranges are equipped with an insulated oven base. Hot or even heat tops, and fry or griddle tops, are gas- or oil-fired, or electrically heated. Open or hot plate tops have electric or gas burners. Fry or griddle tops are gas- or oil-fired, or electrically heated.

Refrigerated Shelves   Shelves of wire, solid, embossed or slotted material with reinforced hemmed edges, mounted on tubular posts with adjustable sanitary brackets. May be in stationary or mobile sections.

Revolving Tray Oven   Gas-, electric- or oil-heated oven with a motor-driven ferris wheel device inside having four or more balanced trays. Bake or roast pans are loaded and unloaded from a single opening with a hinged down door. Steam may be added for humidity requirements of products.

Rinse Injector   Device mounted to top or side of washing machine for storage and automatic dispensing of liquid water softener into the final rinse manifold.

Roll Divider   Hand- or motor-operated machine that divides a ball of dough into equal pieces. Hand-operated unit is stand- or table-mounted. Motor-driven unit is floor mounted with a cabinet base and may be combined with a rounding device. Also called Bun Divider.

Rotisserie   1. Upright, enclosed cabinet with a vertical grill having gas-fired ceramics or electric heating elements. A side-mounted motor drives revolving spits set in a tier in front of the heaters. The unit has hinged or sliding glass doors. 2. Upright enclosed cabinet containing a motor-driven ferris wheel provided with food cradles or baskets passing under gas-fired ceramics or electric heating elements. 3. Enclosed, square, upright cabinet with meat suspended from top in center revolving motor-driven cradle, heated by four infra-red lamps radiating from the corners.

Salad Case   Unit consisting of a refrigerated counter with refrigerated food pans set into the top, and a refrigerated or non-refrigerated display case mounted on the countertop.

Salamander   A backshelf or cabinet mounted over the rear of a range or steam table, and absorbing the heat therefrom to keep foods on it warm.

Shake Maker   Floor- or counter-mounted machine with one or two mechanically refrigerated cylinders, having dashers to mix and refrigerate an air-and-milk mixture to a flowing frozen dessert beverage. Unit may be equipped with syrup tanks and pumps, and mixing spindle to blend various flavors in shakes.

Silver Burnisher, Holloware and Flatware   Machine with a tumbling barrel or vibrating open top tub filled with steel balls and compound, in which silver-plated utensils are placed. Tumbling or vibrating action causes steel balls to roll down plating onto base metal. Units may be bench- or floor-mounted, or made mobile to fold under a tabletop.

Single-Service Articles   Cups, containers, lids, closures, plates, knives, forks, spoons, stirrers, paddles, straws, napkins, wrapping materials, toothpicks and similar articles intended for one-time, one-person use and then discarded.

Sink   1. Preparation, Cook's or Utility: one- or two-compartment type with drainboard on one or both sides. 2. Pot and Pan or Scullery: three- or four-compartment type with drainboard on one or both sides, and possibly between compartments.

Slicer   Bench- or stand-mounted machine with a stationary motor-driven round knife and slice thickness gauge plate, and reciprocating feed trough or carriage. Flat trough may have hand and/or spring pressure type feed plate. Gravity trough may have hand or automatic feed plate. Trough may be hand-operated or motor-driven. Slicer can be equipped with automatic stacking and conveying device.

Soda Dispenser   1. Part of soda making and refrigeration system: dispensing head attachment for mounting on a soda fountain, bar, counter or at a waiter station, complete with drainer. 2. Enclosed cabinet, ice or mechanically refrigerated, to dispense pre-mixed soda or combine soda water and syrup stored in a cabinet or remote tanks. 3. Floor- or counter-mounted cabinet with a self-contained soda and refrigeration system having remote or self-contained syrup tanks.

Soda Fountain   A generic term referring to a complete unit equipped for the storing and dispensing of frozen desserts and carbonated beverages. Where food also is served, the equipment is referred to as a "Luncheonette Fountain."

Soda Maker   Unit consisting of mechanical refrigeration system, carbonator and soda storage tank.

Soda System   Assembly consisting of soda maker, syrup tanks, syrup, soda and refrigeration tubing, and soda dispensing head(s) and/or cabinet(s). Also known as Carbonated Beverage System.

Soft Ice Cream Maker   Floor- or counter-mounted machine with one or two mechanically refrigerated cylinders having dashers to mix and refrigerate air and ice cream mix to a flowing frozen dessert. Unit is equipped with hand- or foot-operated dispensing head or control.

Splash Back   The vertical facing of a unit above the working surface of the unit—designated as "rear" and "end" splash. This area is also known as "flashing" or "splash board."

Steam Cooker   Enclosed cabinet with one or more sealed compartments having individual controls into which (chemically clean) steam is introduced for cooking or heating. Cooker may be direct connected or equipped with gas-fired, electric or steam coil generator in the base. 1. A cooker with compartments in tiers cooks with low pressure steam. Each compartment has a hinged door with a floating inner panel and a sealing gasket made tight with a wheel screw. Unit is floor-mounted, or if direct connected, may be wall-mounted. 2. Cooker with high pressure has self-sealing door(s) with a gasket made tight by interior steam pressure. May be floor-, counter- or wall-mounted. Also called High Speed Cooker.

Storage Rack   Unit consisting of one or more shelves mounted on angle, channel or tubular posts, for storage of goods or ware.

Swill Trough   1. Narrow depression in dish table equipped with waste outlet, strainer basket, and perforated cover. 2. Extra sink compartment of shallow depth located between compartments of pot-washing sink, equipped with strainer basket.

Syrup Rail   A refrigerated section of a creamer or bobtail where syrup pumps and jars are stored.

Tableware   Multi-use eating and drinking utensils.

Toaster   1. Counter-mounted pop-up type having two- or four-slice capacity. Electric only. 2. Counter-mounted conveyor type with a motor-driven conveyor carrying the product between electric- or gas-fired radiants. 3. Sandwich type.

Tray Rack   Upright mobile or stationary unit, open or semi-enclosed, having angle, channel or tubular posts and one or more tiers of angle or channel-shaped slides to support trays or pans. Rack may be built-in to cabinets or suspended from under tabletops.

Tray Slide or Rail   Horizontal surface to accommodate the width of a tray, extended out from, and running the length of, cafeteria countertop. May be constructed of solid material with or without raised edges and vee beads; or of several tubular or solid rails or bars. Mounted on and fastened to brackets secured to countertop and/or counter body. Also called Tray Rest.

Tray Stand   Low height mobile or stationary four-legged stand with solid top. Top may have raised back and sides to prevent tray stacks from falling over.

Unit Cooler   Semi-enclosed cabinet open at front and rear or top and bottom, depending on air flow, with a motor-driven fan blowing air through a mechanically refrigerated finned coil. Device is normally suspended inside a refrigerator or freezer. Also called blower (evaporator) coil.

Utensil   Any implement used in the storage, preparation, transportation, or service of food.

Vegetable Slicer or Cutter   1. Hand- or motor-driven counter-mounted machine having rotating removable plates with varied knives. Product is forced against plates and knives for slicing, dicing, grating, shredding, etc. 2. Similar attachment to a food machine with rotating removable plates and knife arrangements.

Vertical Cutter/Mixer   Floor-type machine with a vertical tilting mixing bowl having a 25 to 80 quart (23.6 to 75.6 liter) capacity. The bowl is equipped with a two-speed motor and a high-speed agitator shaft at bowl bottom with cutting/mixing knife. A hand- or motor-driven stirring and mixing shaft is fixed to the bowl's cover. A strainer basket may be included.

Water Heater   Counter-mounted instant electric heating device with faucet for making tea and hot chocolate drinks.

Water Station   Section of a counter or stand with a glass and/or pitcher filling faucet and drain trough.

Wheeled Equipment   Equipment which is placed on casters or wheels and can be easily moved for auxiliary food processing or service, but shall not include licensed motor vehicles.

Wood Top   Tabletop constructed of kiln-dried, hard rock laminated maple Sstrips, hydraulically pressed together, glued and steel doweled through.

Self-Inspection Checklist

Source: *Sanitation Operations Manual*, Chicago: National Restaurant Assn., 1979.

PERSONAL SAFENESS — 1 (Infections and illness, hygiene and grooming)

Date Inspected: _____   Inspected By: _____

ITEM	YES	NO	Comments on Deficiencies Noted and Action Required	Date Corrected
Do any food handlers have infected burns, cuts, boils?				
Do any food handlers have acute respiratory illness?				
Do any food handlers have infections or contagious illness transmittable through foods?				
Are food handlers wearing clean outer garments?				
Are food handlers free of body odors?				
Are food handlers' hands clean — washed at start of work day and as frequently as necessary?				
Are food handlers wearing hats, caps or hairnets or other effective hair restraints?				
Are food handlers observed picking nose or pimples, scratching head or face?				
Are food handlers observed smoking or eating in food preparation or serving areas?				
Are fingernails of food handlers short and clean?				

PERSONAL SAFENESS — 2 (Infections and illness, hygiene and grooming)

Date Inspected: _____   Inspected By: _____

ITEM	YES	NO	Comments on Deficiencies Noted and Action Required	Date Corrected
Are instances of spitting in sinks, on floor or in disposal area observed?				
Are food servers seen to cough in hands?				
Are food handlers wearing rings (other than plain band), dangling bracelets, wristwatches, etc. while preparing or handling food?				
Are cloths used to wipe off perspiration on face used for no additional purpose?				
Have all employees been instructed on minimum sanitation and food protection requirements?				

FOOD HANDLING PRACTICES

Date Inspected: _____   Inspected By: _____

ITEM	YES	NO	Comments on Deficiencies Noted and Action Required	Date Corrected
Is food, in pans or containers, on floor?				
Are perishable or potentially hazardous foods being held at room temperature?				
Are fruits and vegetables thoroughly washed prior to preparation and serving?				
Are food warmers, steam tables and bainmaries used to reheat prepared foods?				
Are frozen foods being properly thawed under refrigeration or under cold running water or cooked directly from frozen state?				
Are raw and cooked or ready to serve foods being prepared on the same cutting board without washing and sanitizing the board between changed use?				
Are hands being used to pick up rolls, bread, butter pats, ice, or other food to be served?				
Are waitresses or busboys handling place settings and serving food without washing hands after wiping tables and bussing soiled dishes?				
Are food servers touching food contact surfaces of plates, tumblers, cups and silverware when setting table or serving customer?				

700

FOOD AND SUPPLIES RECEIVING

Date Inspected: _____   Inspected By: _____

ITEM	Y E S	N O	Comments on Deficiencies Noted and Action Required	Date Corrected
Is food inspected immediately upon receipt for spoilage or infestation?				
Is perishable food moved promptly to refrigeration?				
Are unattended perishable food deliveries on loading dock or dolly?				
Are non-food supplies checked for infestation?				
Are empty shipping containers and packing removed to disposal area promptly?				
Is receiving area free of food particles and debris?				
Is floor of receiving area clean?				
Are packages dated upon receipt to assure "first-in — first-out" use?				
Are shellfish packages identified with processor or packer's name and number?				

DRY STORES — 1

Date Inspected: _____   Inspected By: _____

ITEM	YES	NO	Comments on Deficiencies Noted and Action Required	Date Corrected
Is all food stored at least 6 inches off the floor — on shelves, racks or platforms?				
Is the floor clean and free from spilled food?				
Are shelves high enough off floor to permit cleaning underneath, or is area beneath shelf enclosed to preclude accumulation of soil?				
Are shelves away from wall to permit ventilation and discourage nesting of insects and rodents?				
Have empty cartons and trash been removed?				
Are canned goods removed from cartons to shelving to maximum extent practicable?				
Are food storage shelves clean and free of dust and debris?				
Are food supplies stored in a manner to insure "first-in — first-out" use?				
Is storeroom dry — free from dampness?				
Are non-food supplies stored separately from food stock?				

REFRIGERATOR STORAGE — 1

Date Inspected: _____   Inspected By: _____

ITEM	YES	NO	Comments on Deficiencies Noted and Action Required	Date Corrected
Are refrigerators equipped with accurate thermometers located in warmest part of cabinet?				
Are all refrigerators operating and maintaining potentially hazardous foods at temperatures of 45°F or lower?				
Are refrigerators clean and free from mold and objectionable odors?				
Is all potentially hazardous food, not in actual preparation or hot holding, stored under refrigeration?				
Is all food being stored off the floor of walk-in refrigerators?				
Are foods stored on shelves spaced to provide for adequate air circulation and is shelving free of linings that retard circulation?				
Are panned raw or cooked foods, on shelves, covered to prevent contamination?				
Are cooked foods such as ground meat, stew, dressing or gravy not stored in large quantity containers?				
Are foods stored in a manner to permit "first-in — first-out" use?				
Is proper cleaning and maintenance being conducted?				

DRY STORES — 2

Date Inspected: _____   Inspected By: _____

ITEM	Y E S	N O	Comments on Deficiencies Noted and Action Required	Date Corrected
Are all toxic materials, including pesticides, conspicuously labeled and used from original containers only?				
Are pesticides separately stored in a well marked cabinet?				
Is there evidence of insects or rodents?				
Is there evidence of misuse or spillage of insecticides or rodenticides?				
Are bulk foods (sugar, flour), if no longer stored in original package, now stored in a covered container with identifying name?				
Are food and containers stored under exposed or unprotected sewer or water lines, or close to "sweating" walls?				
Are most frequently needed items on lower shelves and near entrance?				
Are heavy packages stored on lower shelves?				

REFRIGERATOR STORAGE — 2

Date Inspected: _____   Inspected By: _____

ITEM	Y E S	N O	Comments on Deficiencies Noted and Action Required	Date Corrected
Are any spoiled foods present?				
Are raw foods stored separately from cooked foods?				
Are shelves high enough from the floor to permit cleaning underneath?				
Are shelves free from food husks, leaves, wrappings or debris?				
Are there sufficient refrigeration facilities to handle normal delivery schedules?				
Is there sufficient space in the refrigerators to permit good air circulation around the stored food?				
Is there awareness that ice used for cooling food will not be used for human consumption?				
Are solid cuts of meat (except quarters and sides) covered in storage and placed to allow circulation of cool air?				
Are cooked foods or other products removed from original containers in clean, sanitized, covered container and identified?				
Are dairy products stored separately from strong-odored foods?				

REFRIGERATOR STORAGE — 3

Date Inspected: _____   Inspected By: _____

ITEM	YES	NO	Comments on Deficiencies Noted and Action Required	Date Corrected
Are fish stored apart from other food products?				

FREEZER STORAGE

Date Inspected: _____   Inspected By: _____

ITEM	YES	NO	Comments on Deficiencies Noted and Action Required	Date Corrected
Are freezer storage units operating?				
Do all boxes or cabinets have accurate thermometers?				
Are freezer storage units maintaining an interior temperature of 0°F, or lower?				
Is there excessive traffic in and out of walk-in freezer storage boxes?				
Is food stored in a manner which permits "first-in — first-out" use?				
Is food stored in a manner to insure air circulation?				
Do cabinet walls or coils need defrosting?				
Are foods wrapped well to prevent freezer burn?				
Are all food containers covered?				
Is proper cleaning and maintenance being conducted?				

VEGETABLE PREPARATION

Date Inspected: _____   Inspected By: _____

ITEM	Y E S	N O	Comments on Deficiencies Noted and Action Required	Date Corrected
Is the vegetable preparation area clean and free from objectionable dampness and odor?				
Are non-refrigerated vegetables stored in ventilated bins or in crates on elevated platforms?				
Is area free from empty containers and debris?				
Is vegetable sink(s) used for hand washing or for warewashing?				
Is vegetable sink used for dumping mop water or pan drippings?				
Are peelers or paring knives present in vegetable sink?				
Are vegetable preparation equipment parts washed in the vegetable sink?				
Are vegetable peelers, slicers, choppers, etc. not in use, clean?				
Are vegetable peelers, slicers, choppers, etc. being cleaned between changed uses?				

MEAT CUTTING AREA

Date Inspected: _____   Inspected By: _____

ITEM	YES	NO	Comments on Deficiencies Noted and Action Required	Date Corrected
Is meat cutting area clean and free from objectionable odor, cartons and other debris?				
Are meat cutting wastes discarded into approved containers and removed to the disposal area?				
Are cutting boards in good condition — free from splits, holes or cuts?				
Are cutting boards cleaned and sanitized between changed use?				
Are all cutting boards, tables, grinders, slicers, meat saws, boning knives and other meat cutting equipment clean and sanitized if not in use?				
Is raw meat awaiting preparation or processed meat cuts, in containers, off the floor?				
Is raw meat awaiting processing or processed cuts being held for excessive periods at room temperature?				
Is frozen meat, poultry or fish being thawed out with warm water?				

BAKING AREA

Date Inspected: _____   Inspected By: _____

ITEM	Y E S	N O	Comments on Deficiencies Noted and Action Required	Date Corrected
Is bakery area clean and dry, free from empty cartons and debris?				
Are flour and other non-perishable bakery food ingredients off the floor and if in other than original containers properly marked?				
Are dough mixers, kettles and other bakery equipment and utensils which are not in use, clean?				
Are mixing bowls, pots and other bakery utensils stored in a manner to prevent splash and contamination?				
Are potentially hazardous bakery ingredients and unbaked fillings and liquid mixes not held at room temperature longer than absolutely necessary during preparation?				
Are pie fillings not being held and cooled in stock pots or other large containers and at room temperature?				
Are pesticides or cleaning supplies not stored or present in the bakery area?				

FOOD PREPARATION AND HOLDING — 1

Date Inspected: _____   Inspected By: _____

ITEM	YES	NO	Comments on Deficiencies Noted and Action Required	Date Corrected
Is food preparation area generally clean and free from accumulated debris?				
Is floor of kitchen and other food preparation and service areas clean and dry?				
Is food preparation equipment not in use, clean?				
Are utensils not in use clean, sanitized and stored in a manner which will protect them from contamination?				
Is preparation equipment cleaned and sanitized between changed use? (This especially pertains to grinders, slicers, choppers and mixers, and to knives.)				
Are cleaning supplies and pesticides present in the food preparation and service areas?				
Is cook's sink being used for employee hand washing or dumping of mop water?				
Is unused equipment or utensils stored behind ranges, ovens or in other floor spaces in the kitchen area?				
Is there evidence of rodents or insects in the kitchen or serving lines of the establishment?				
Are thermostats operating and accurate on ranges and deep fat fryers?				

FOOD PREPARATION AND HOLDING — 2

Date Inspected: _____ **Inspected By:** _____

ITEM	YES	NO	Comments on Deficiencies Noted and Action Required	Date Corrected
Is hot-holding equipment maintaining food at or above 140°F?				
Are cold foods being held at 45°F or lower and are cabinets equipped with thermometers?				

712

DINING ROOM AND SERVING AREA

Date Inspected: _____   Inspected By: _____

ITEM	YES	NO	Comments on Deficiencies Noted and Action Required	Date Corrected
Is dining area, including floor, tables and chairs, clean and dry?				
Is tableware clean and sanitized and stored in a manner to prevent splash and contamination?				
Are single-service items stored and dispensed in a sanitary manner?				
Are single-service items disposed of after single use?				
Are clean and sanitary cloths used for wiping dining tabletops and used for no other purpose? Are they stored in sanitizing solution between uses?				
Are silverware and serving utensils stored and presented in a manner to prevent contamination and to insure their being picked up by the handles?				
Are cloths or sponges used for wiping food spills on tableware being served to customers clean and dry and used for no other purpose?				

WAREWASHING AND STORAGE

Date Inspected: _____   Inspected By: _____

ITEM	YES	NO	Comments on Deficiencies Noted and Action Required	Date Corrected
Are wash and rinse temperatures proper for the type of machine and ware being washed, being maintained? (See Manufacturer's Specifications on data plate)				
Is rinse temperature of at least 170°F being maintained for tableware and utensils? (Manual dishwashing)				
Are dishes and utensils being prescraped and flushed prior to washing?				
Is detergent concentration being maintained at the necessary level for effective washing?				
Is separate personnel used for removing and storing clean tableware or do warewashing personnel wash hands between handling soiled tableware and sanitized ware?				
Is warewashing equipment cleaned after each day's use to remove chemicals, food particles, soil and debris?				
Are jets and nozzles cleaned of food particles and other obstructions and contaminants?				
Are cleaned and sanitized wares and utensils stored off the floor and in a clean, dry location?				
Is improper toweling of tableware and utensils observed?				

EMPLOYEE FACILITIES (Toilets, lavatories, locker rooms, lunchrooms)

Date Inspected: _____   Inspected By: _____

ITEM	Y E S	N O	Comments on Deficiencies Noted and Action Required	Date Corrected
Are employees' facilities clean, dry and free from odor?				
Is there sufficient soap, towels and tissue for employee needs?				
Is all sanitary equipment operational and in good repair?				
Are proper receptacles available for waste materials?				
Are these receptacles emptied frequently?				
Are soiled uniforms and other soiled clothing improperly stored in lockers or left in the facilities?				
Are containers provided for soiled employees' uniforms?				
Is unwrapped food stored in lockers or left in employee facilities?				
Is there evidence of rodents or insects in the facilities?				

715

STORAGE ROOMS FOR SUPPLIES AND EQUIPMENT

Date Inspected: _____   Inspected By: _____

ITEM	YES	NO	Comments on Deficiencies Noted and Action Required	Date Corrected
Are storage facilities for supplies and equipment clean, dry and free of trash and debris?				
Are storage facilities free of empty cartons and wrappings which might provide nesting for rodents?				
Are supplies stored in a neat and orderly manner?				
Are supplies stored off the floor and away from walls to permit access for cleaning and to prevent harborage of rodents and roaches?				
Is perishable or unpackaged food present?				
Are containers of pesticides in marked cabinet and apart from detergents and other chemicals?				
Is there evidence of rodents or insects?				
Are single-service articles stored at least 6 inches off the floor, in closed containers and not placed under exposed sewer or water lines?				
Are utensils, single-service items or food equipment stored in toilets or vestibules?				

716

GARBAGE AND TRASH STORAGE AND DISPOSAL AREAS — 1

Date Inspected: _____   Inspected By: _____

ITEM	YES	NO	Comments on Deficiencies Noted and Action Required	Date Corrected
Is area generally clean and orderly, free of spilled food and liquids?				
Is floor, platform or ground surface free from spilled particles of food and constructed of nonabsorbent material such as concrete or asphalt?				
Is area free from objectionable odor?				
Are spilled food particles and litter present in front of incinerator, dumpsters, etc.?				
Are trash and garbage containers clean on the outside?				
If can liners are not in use, are all garbage containers closed with tight-fitting covers?				
Is trash confined in orderly fashion or in suitable containers?				
Is there an accumulation of trash or garbage because of infrequent pick-up?				
Are there puddles of wash water and food particles and liquids?				
Is there any evidence of rats, ratholes or nests in the vicinity of the disposal area?				

GARBAGE AND TRASH STORAGE AND DISPOSAL AREAS — 2

Date Inspected: _____   Inspected By: _____

ITEM	YES	NO	Comments on Deficiencies Noted and Action Required	Date Corrected
Are empty garbage and refuse containers washed prior to being returned for use?				
Is mop water properly disposed of as sewage?				
Are drain plugs in place on those containers designed with drains?				
Are hot water, brushes and detergent or steam provided for washing containers?				
Is room constructed of easily cleanable nonabsorbent material?				

MECHANICAL ROOMS

Date Inspected: _____   Inspected By: _____

ITEM	YES	NO	Comments on Deficiencies Noted and Action Required	Date Corrected
Are boiler rooms, compressor rooms and other utilities rooms clean, dry and free of foods, soiled or greasy utensils and food preparation equipment?				
Are they free of soiled linen and rags, empty containers and cartons, trash and debris?				
Is there evidence of rodents and insects?				
Is adequate ventilation provided?				

ENTRYWAYS, EXITS AND EXTERIOR SURROUNDINGS (Including parking lots and drive-in service areas)

Date Inspected: _____   Inspected By: _____

ITEM	YES	NO	Comments on Deficiencies Noted and Action Required	Date Corrected
Are entryways clear of trash and debris?				
Are doors, windows and screens tight fitting to prevent entry of insects and rodents?				
Is there any evidence of ratholes or entry points near or into the building?				
Are there wet spots or pools, or long grass or weeds which could form breeding spots for insects?				
Is the parking lot or surrounding area free of litter, trash and debris?				
Do noxious birds nest or roost on ledges or eaves of the establishment?				

VEHICLES USED FOR TRANSPORTING FOOD

Date Inspected: _____ Inspected By: _____

ITEM	YES	NO	Comments on Deficiencies Noted and Action Required	Date Corrected
Is the cargo area of the vehicle thoroughly clean and free from dirt and debris?				
Has all food in containers been removed for proper disposal or storage?				
Is potentially hazardous food being carried at proper temperatures of heat or cold?				
Is food being carried in adequately insulated containers?				
Are all food spills on shelving or floor washed from the vehicle after each use?				
Is there any evidence of insect infestation of the vehicle body?				

RESTROOMS CUSTOMER CONCERNS

Date Inspected: _____   Inspected By: _____

ITEM	YES	NO	Comments on Deficiencies Noted and Action Required	Date Corrected
Are customer restrooms clean, dry, light, well ventilated and free of odor?				
Is all sanitary equipment operating satisfactorily?				
Is there a satisfactory supply of soap, tissue, towels or a hand drying device?				
Are waste containers covered, kept clean and emptied frequently?				
Is there adequate hot and cold water, tempered by means of a mixing valve or combination faucet?				
Is there any sign of rodents or insects?				
Are toilet doors solid, self-closing and in good working order?				

ENTRANCE AND FOYER OR WAITING ROOM CUSTOMER CONCERNS

Date Inspected: _____   Inspected By: _____

ITEM	YES	NO	Comments on Deficiencies Noted and Action Required	Date Corrected
Is the entryway and waiting room clean and attractive?				
Is it free from litter?				
Are chairs and benches clean and lamps and fixtures clean and free from dust?				
Are posters and printed materials clean and neatly racked or posted?				
Does the customer's first view of your establishment convey the image of cleanliness and freshness?				

GENERAL CLEANLINESS OF DINING AREA CUSTOMER CONCERNS

Date Inspected: _____   Inspected By: _____

ITEM	YES	NO	Comments on Deficiencies Noted and Action Required	Date Corrected
Is the floor dirty or littered, particularly with food particles and napkins?				
Are there crumbs, spilled liquid on chairs or benches?				
Are menus food-marked or worn and dirty, and are condiment containers unclean?				
Are table linens food-marked? Are they tattered or torn?				
Is tableware cracked, chipped, streaked or food-soiled or silverware thumb-marked or food-soiled?				
Are soiled dish trays left near customer tables?				
Are insect sprays being used when food is exposed or customers are present?				
Is floor being swept while food is exposed, being served or when customers are eating?				
Is adequate lighting available for cleaning?				

CLEANLINESS OF SERVICE PERSONNEL CUSTOMER CONCERNS

Date Inspected: _____   Inspected By: _____

ITEM	YES	NO	Comments on Deficiencies Noted and Action Required	Date Corrected
Are waitress uniforms wrinkled or soiled?				
Are service personnel using strong or offensive perfume or smelling of body odor?				
Are servers sniffing, coughing or rubbing or wiping nose?				
Do servers handle drinking glasses by their tops or silverware by their blades, tines or bowls?				
Are servers using effective hair restraints?				
Do cooks and servers smoke in view of customers?				
Do servers handle rolls, butter, ice, etc. by hand in filling dishes and water glasses?				
Do employees scratch head, face or body in view of customers?				
Does server touch food with thumb or fingers when serving plated food?				

725

INDEX